THE OXFORD HA

COMPARATIVE INSTITUTIONAL ANALYSIS

THE OXFORD HANDBOOK OF

COMPARATIVE INSTITUTIONAL ANALYSIS

Edited by

GLENN MORGAN, JOHN L. CAMPBELL,
COLIN CROUCH, OVE KAJ PEDERSEN

and

RICHARD WHITLEY

OXFORD

UNIVERSITY PRESS

OXFORD
UNIVERSITY PRESS

Great Clarendon Street, Oxford OX2 6DP

Oxford University Press is a department of the University of Oxford.
It furthers the University's objective of excellence in research, scholarship,
and education by publishing worldwide in

Oxford New York

Auckland Cape Town Dar es Salaam Hong Kong Karachi
Kuala Lumpur Madrid Melbourne Mexico City Nairobi
New Delhi Shanghai Taipei Toronto

With offices in

Argentina Austria Brazil Chile Czech Republic France Greece
Guatemala Hungary Italy Japan Poland Portugal Singapore
South Korea Switzerland Thailand Turkey Ukraine Vietnam

Oxford is a registered trade mark of Oxford University Press
in the UK and in certain other countries

Published in the United States
by Oxford University Press Inc., New York

© Oxford University Press, 2010

British Library Cataloguing in Publication Data

Data available

Library of Congress Cataloging in Publication Data

Data available

Typeset by SPI Publisher Services, Pondicherry, India
Printed in Great Britain
on acid-free paper by
Ashford Colour Press Ltd,
Gosport, Hampshire

ISBN 978–0–19–923376–2
978–0–19–969377–1 (pbk)

1 3 5 7 9 10 8 6 4 2

ACKNOWLEDGEMENTS

The original idea for this Handbook came from David Musson at Oxford University Press. David and his colleague Matthew Derbyshire have, as usual, been patient and supportive editors. Early versions of some of the chapters were presented at the Annual Conference of the Society for the Advancement of Socio-Economics (SASE) in June 2007 held at Copenhagen Business School. We want to thank participants in those sessions and in other arenas for their comments when earlier versions of the chapters have been presented.

Warwick Business School (WBS), Copenhagen Business School (CBS), and especially the International Centre for Business and Politics (CBP) have all played important roles in supporting the Handbook. Glenn Morgan would like to thank WBS and the University of Warwick for providing study leave in 2008–9, which enabled him to oversee the completion of the project. Part of that time was spent at CBP and this supportive environment greatly facilitated the completion of the project. The fact that John Campbell and Ove Kaj Pedersen were at CBP at the same time was also very helpful in coordinating the final version. Ove Kaj secured funding from CBP to employ student assistance in producing final publisher-ready versions of the chapters—thanks to CBP and Jurate Beniulyte for this work. The final manuscript was produced in WBS with the able assistance of Katy Carpenter and Jo Sheehan.

Finally thanks go to all the contributors for their patience and cooperation in the production of the Handbook.

GM, JC, CC, OKP, and RW

CONTENTS

PART II: INSTITUTIONS, STATES, AND MARKETS

PART III: THE ORGANIZATION
OF ECONOMIC ACTORS

PART IV: CHALLENGES FOR COMPARATIVE
INSTITUTIONAL ANALYSIS

EPILOGUE

List of Figures

LIST OF TABLES

ABBREVIATIONS

ACVT	Advisory Committee on Vocational Training
AEA	American Economic Association
AIAS	Amsterdam Institute for Advanced Labour Studies
APSA	American Political Science Association
ASCON	*Associazione Conciatori*
CEO	Chief Executive Officer
CME	coordinated market economy
CSR	Corporate Social Responsibility
DQP	diversified quality production
ECJ	European Court of Justice
EES	European Employment Strategy
EMCO	European Employment Committee
ESOP	employee share ownership plans
FARC	Revolutionary Armed Forces of Colombia
FCC	Federal Communications Commission
IALS	International Adult Literacy Survey
IFSL	International Financial Services, London
IMD	Institute for Management Development
IMF	International Monetary Fund
IOSCO	International Organization of Security Commissions
ISDA	International Swaps and Derivatives Association
MNC	Multinational Corporation
MIC	Ministry of Information Communications
MITI	Japanese Ministry of Trade and Industry
NAFTA	North American Free Trade Agreement
NASDAQ	The National Association of Securities Dealers Automated Quotations
NBER	National Bureau of Economic Research
OECD	Organization for Economic Coordination and Development
OMC	Open Method of Coordination

PISA   Programme for International Student Assessment
PIU   Performance and Innovation Unit
QCA   qualitative comparative analysis
SPACs   Special Purpose Acquisition Companies
SPC   European Social Protection Committee
TAN   transnational advocacy network

LIST OF CONTRIBUTORS

John L. Campbell Class of 1925 Professor, Department of Sociology, Dartmouth College and Professor of Political Economy, Department of Business and Politics, Copenhagen Business School

Steven Casper Associate Professor, Keck Graduate Institute, California

Colin Crouch Emeritus Professor, Warwick Business School, University of Warwick

Richard Deeg Associate Professor of Political Science, Temple University

Marie-Laure Djelic Professor, ESSEC, Paris

Ewald Engelen Professor, Amsterdam Metropolitan Institute for Development Studies, University of Amsterdam

Michel Goyer Associate Professor, Warwick Business School, University of Warwick

John A. Hall James McGill Professor of Sociology, McGill University

Gary Herrigel Professor, Dept. of Political Science, University of Chicago

Gregory Jackson Professor, School of Business and Economics, Freie Universität, Berlin

Lane Kenworthy Professor of Sociology and Political Science, University of Arizona

Martijn Konings Lecturer, Dept. of Political Economy, University of Sydney

Bruce Kogut Sanford C. Bernstein & Co. Professor of Leadership and Ethics Director Sanford C. Bernstein & Co. Center for Leadership and Ethics, Columbia Business School, Columbia University

Glenn Morgan Professor of International Management, Cardiff Business School, University of Cardiff

Ove Kaj Pedersen Professor of Comparative Political Economy, the Department of Business and Politics, Copenhagen Business School

Sigrid Quack Professor, Max Planck Institute for the Study of Societies, Cologne

Jill Rubery Professor, Manchester Business School, University of Manchester

Leonard Seabrooke Professor, Dept. of Politics and International Studies, Director, Centre for the Study of Globalisation and Regionalisation, University of Warwick

Ivan Szelenyi Professor, Dept. of Sociology, Yale University

Kathleen Thelen Ford Professor of Political Science, MIT

Linda Weiss Professor, Dept. of Government and International Relations, University of Sydney

Richard Whitley Professor, Manchester Business School, University of Manchester

Katarzyna Wilk Policy Adviser, Bureau of European Policy Advisers, European Commission

Jonathan Zeitlin Professor of Public Policy and Governance, Dept. of Political Science, University of Amsterdam

INTRODUCTION

GLENN MORGAN

JOHN L. CAMPBELL

COLIN CROUCH

OVE KAJ PEDERSEN

RICHARD WHITLEY

PRODUCING a handbook is in some ways an act of faith. It presumes that there exists a range of debates, concepts, and arguments that are sufficiently similar to each other (and different from other concerns) as to constitute a shared field of interest. It is therefore inevitably a boundary-drawing exercise no matter how fuzzy those boundaries may sometimes appear. A handbook also presumes that there is an audience that will recognize this as a shared field and will use the resources which it contains in order to develop their own thinking and research. Given that the construction of a handbook is, however, ultimately the responsibility of the editors, it is important that the assumptions underpinning this project are laid out in more detail. This is the purpose of our introduction. We therefore focus on three key issues. What do we understand by the term 'comparative institutional analysis'? Why did we think it was important to produce a handbook on this topic at this particular time? How did we decide on the structure of the Handbook and the nature of the contributions?

COMPARATIVE INSTITUTIONAL ANALYSIS

It is increasingly accepted that 'institutions matter' for economic organization and outcomes, but such a phrase conceals a multitude of issues and perspectives. In the chapters that follow many of these complexities are revealed and discussed; we do not attempt to repeat them here but to provide an initial account of the approach to institutions taken in this Handbook.

The field in which we are interested can be defined in terms of how the forms, outcomes, and dynamics of economic organization (firms, networks, markets) are influenced and shaped by other social institutions (e.g. training systems, legal systems, political systems, educational systems, etc.) and with what consequences for economic growth, innovation, employment, and inequality. Institutions are usually defined by our contributors as being formal and informal rules, regulations, norms, and understandings that constrain and enable behaviour (e.g. Scott 2008; Campbell 2004).

The approach taken to these questions here is comparative and the central comparisons made are those between different societies. The reason for this level of comparison (as opposed to comparisons across regions or cities, or between sectors or firms, useful and essential as these are) is theoretically driven in that the sort of institutions in focus have been fundamentally shaped by and through processes at the level of the nation-state. Nation-states vary in their degree of centralization and in the strength of regional or other local ties. Nevertheless, since at least the time of Weber's definition of the state as the collectivity monopolizing the legitimate use of physical force within specific territorial boundaries, social scientists have been interested in nation-states as being the most significant containers and producers of populations, economic organizations, and institutions (Hall, 1986, 1994; Mann, 1986, 1993). It is therefore not surprising that it is through national comparisons that much of this field has been defined (see, for example, classic contributions such as Bendix, 1956; Berger and Dore, 1996; Boyer and Drache, 1996; Boyer and Durand, 1997; Crouch, 1993; Crouch and Streeck, 1997; Hall and Soskice, 2001; Hamilton, 2006; Hollingsworth and Boyer, 1997; Hollingsworth, Schmitter, and Streeck, 1994; Lane, 1989, 1995; Maurice, Sellier, and Silvestre, 1986; Orrú, Biggart, and Hamilton, 1996; Shonfield, 1965; Sorge and Maurice, 2000; Streeck, 1992; Whitley, 1992a, b, 1999, 2007; Whitley and Kristensen, 1996, 1997).

These comparisons serve at least two purposes. The first is that through comparisons we are able to understand more clearly any particular society and its economic performance by distinguishing its particular institutional structures, how these link together, and the impact that they have on firms and their competitive abilities in local and global markets. The second is that through comparisons, our understanding of processes of diffusion, learning, and emulation between societies become more sophisticated and complex. This is not to underestimate the methodological problems associated with comparative studies and drawing conclusions about which institutions are most significant, and for what aspects of firm behaviour, and with what impact on performance outcomes. What is a simple idea can rapidly become swamped by methodological problems associated with small number samples, with contamination effects (since societies are not self-contained but intricately connected), with historically complex inter-relationships, and with a morass of specific detail that makes broader conclusions extremely difficult to draw (see Kogut in this volume).

Nevertheless, the aspiration remains to produce an academically rigorous set of comparative studies revealing how social institutions affect economic organization and performance. Indeed, the aspiration is inevitable because the public policy arena is full of comparisons between countries. There are multiple systems of ranking the competitiveness of countries against each other (see Pedersen in this volume) in which institutional features are scored and compared. Country rankings can also be performed through international private institutions such as credit rating agencies (evaluating the security of sovereign debt), through international public institutions (World Bank and IMF evaluations of economic policy and growth prospects), and through international non-governmental organizations (such as the World Economic Forum annual competitiveness reports). Such evaluations affect flows of investment, taxation levels, and employment levels inside countries. The globalization of the economy has made comparisons increasingly transparent and increasingly visible. In a world where much finance can flow across national boundaries with relative ease, governments feel that they are competing against each other in order to attract funds and in that way increase levels of employment, wages, conditions of work, and the standard of living. Increasingly governments recognize that reshaping their institutions is crucial to competing in this context. The sort of benchmarking and comparisons that occur at this level are, however, inevitably one-dimensional. They are often highly misleading, because they are based on data that are easily available rather than on full research, and on over-simplifications (e.g. the tendency of the OECD to see things in terms of states and markets only, and to be unable to deal with other institutions). They are also often based on the perspectives of dominant countries (e.g. the tendency to measure national innovation capacity by the number of patents registered in the USA). And, as the recent role of the ratings agencies in the financial crisis has shown, they are not always carefully conducted. How these institutions emerged, how they link together, and why they have particular sorts of impact are deeper questions, as is the question of how to reform institutions to improve performance (in reality and in benchmarking comparisons). We therefore live in a world of comparisons and it makes sense for academics to develop the theoretical frameworks, conceptual tools, and methodological techniques in order to conduct comparisons that go beyond static benchmarking and seek to penetrate to the heart of the relationship between institutions and economic organization.

However, as the previous discussion suggests, we also live in a world that is interconnected in multiple ways. Comparative institutional analysis has increasingly sought ways of conceptualizing that interconnectedness that does justice to the idea of institutional embeddedness and avoids the wilder flights of fancy that come from certain analyses of globalization. One way to understand this is to provide a more historical and global account of the emergence of societies and the development of institutions. This requires moving from embedding these developments in a wider international context and seeing the two as interdependent not separate. For example, up to the early modern period Europe was characterized by competing forms of political authority and efforts to create bounded states were made difficult by the existence of feudal rights, rights granted to towns and cities, and the power and authority of the clergy. At the same time, however, there were features of social life that were common across Europe and were reflected in a notion of a 'Christian civilization', particularly amongst the nobility and monarchies, the Church, and the small professional and educated class (Davies, 1996). Some of that commonality remains, for example, in the continued influence of Roman Law, and in the aspirations towards and symbols of European identity in the European Union. Institutions in different societies may have common roots; they may have co-evolved through the diffusions of ideas, individuals, and technologies of governance. Similarly European countries created empires that created certain common forms in the Americas, in Africa, in parts of Asia, and in Australasia, as well as providing models to emulate and adapt in countries like Japan.

At the level of economic activity and trade, it is becoming increasingly clear that there was considerable interaction across huge distances from early on in human history and that these patterns of trade grew and shrank for various reasons to do with the technology of warfare and communication as well as the rise and fall of empires, states, and other forms of political authority (Bayly, 2004; Bernstein, 2008; Brook, 2008; Darwin, 2007; Greif, 2006). It is not necessary to subscribe to Wallerstein's world systems theory (Wallerstein, 2004) to agree that the national and the international are intricately related. Thus if states and national institutions are our primary units of comparison, we also have to recognize that their existence has always been embedded in wider world and continental systems. Whilst the current era of globalization may be qualitatively distinct in many ways, from another perspective it is perhaps the era of the all-powerful nation-state that is the historical anomaly and the more complex multi-layering of political, social, and economic forms across different contexts is the 'normal' state of affairs viewed over the very long term.

Thus focusing our attention on how institutions are now being built at the transnational level is simply returning to something that was always there in one way or another. In sum, comparative institutional analysis does not mean 'neglecting' globalization in favour of nation-states; on the contrary it means restoring the historical interconnectedness of societies to our analysis and analysing current efforts at transnational institution building and their inter-relatedness to change in national institutions as part of our normal way of conceiving of how institutions matter.

It may be tempting to think, given all this discussion of states, empires, societies, etc. that comparative institutional analysis is inherently structural and determinist in its orientation, that it sees actors, individual and collective actors as 'cultural dopes', without agency, simply performing the structure. Clearly this takes us into the heart of one of the central debates in the social sciences, concerning the relationship between structure and agency. It would be foolish to claim that such a diverse field of study as comparative institutional analysis with researchers from so many different disciplines could even begin to agree on the terms of this debate, never mind how to resolve it. However, what we can claim is that this debate is fully present in comparative institutional analysis, that it permeates many empirical analyses and efforts at conceptual clarification as researchers seek to understand how actors can be both the products of structures and the origin of changes in structure. This debate repeatedly recurs in comparative institutional analysis as the chapters in this Handbook demonstrate.

Arguably we can go further and suggest that institutions are now less likely to be discussed as exogenous constraints on actors and more as resources, which actors can draw on to develop depending on the context. Further, it is increasingly clear that institutions in a society may offer different resources from those that seem dominant at a particular time, and it is through combining and reorganizing institutional resources that the possibility for institutional experimentation and change arises. Similarly, institutions require resources to survive and prosper and for various reasons such resources may be withdrawn or fail, leading to relative decline or possibly a new role for the institution; the relationship between religious institutions, secularization, and economic organizations would certainly be a case in point given the importance Weber placed on the elective affinity between the Protestant Ethic and the Spirit of Capitalism. In a context of flows and connectedness across national contexts, sometimes formalized into systems such as the EU or the WTO, it is clear that these issues of resources, constraints, and processes of recombination have become more intensive.

In summary, comparative institutional analysis as we define it in this book begins with an analysis of how institutions shape forms of economic organization and the consequence of this for performance outcomes. It engages in this analysis by comparing firms, institutions, and processes in different societies. It takes on board that societies are not hermetically sealed containers but rather are open systems where flows of capital, labour, ideas, technologies, etc. are to various degrees the norm. It also accepts that societies are internally diverse with regional differences, with institutions that are diverse and connected in a variety of tight and loose linkages. We therefore need to understand how these connections and flows inside and across societies are governed and managed through their embeddedness in the development of regional, national, international, and transnational institutions. These tasks require a longitudinal frame of analysis, a willingness to take history seriously (not just national histories but the newly emergent sub-discipline of 'global history'). Taking this perspective does not require a commitment to a determinist account of institutions, but on the contrary to understanding the tension between structure and agency in specific contexts where change is always a possibility and where collective and individual actors, particularly those driven by sharp survival imperatives (i.e. firms in competitive markets) look to build new practices, experiment with new frames and engage in institution-building and the process of institutionalization.

Developing this approach means committing to a view of social sciences that is holistic, interdisciplinary, historical, and international in its scope. It is holistic in the sense that the different institutions inside societies cannot be studied in isolation. They are inter-related and interdependent and, perhaps, complementary (see Crouch's chapter). It is interdisciplinary in the sense that it draws from sociology, political science, political economy, history, and other disciplines in order to provide an explanation for these complex processes. It is historical in that it searches for the roots of institutions in the interaction between social actors over time. It is international in scope because (a) it seeks to learn by comparisons across nation-states and other salient units of analysis, (b) it takes seriously patterns of diffusion of ideas, practices, and institutions, and (c) it considers the role of international actors and international institutions. This approach, therefore, inevitably eschews the search for general universal laws about institutions and pursues instead the understanding of particular configurations of actors and institutions.

The chapters in this Handbook therefore cast doubt over rationalistic models of institutional design, suggesting instead the need to take into account path dependencies, institutional complementarities, the unanticipated outcomes of action, and the susceptibility of change processes to unexpected contingent events. This is a difficult path to take. To some extent, it goes against some trends in social sciences towards increasing academic specialization, towards the advocacy of parsimonious models, towards formal hypothesis testing, towards the use of large databases of quantitative indicators generating mathematical modelling of social processes, firm behaviour, and markets. In contrast, it tends to embrace interdisciplinary dialogue, historically contextualized models, and empirical descriptions of fundamental socio-economic processes.

WHY NOW?

Why is now a good time to produce a handbook of comparative institutional analysis? A handbook implies that there is firstly a sufficient body of knowledge and research in an area to merit the sort of effort at consolidation that a handbook implies, and secondly there is an audience interested in such an effort at consolidation.

To begin with, there is an acute awareness in the world today of the important impact that institutions have for economic performance. The Asian financial crisis in 1997 as well as the 2008 crisis in international financial markets, which stemmed from a rash of dubious investment practices, has drawn attention to how important institutions really are for governing economic activity. Indeed, as this volume goes to press policymakers are grappling with how all sorts of institutions should be changed in order to avoid further crises in the future, and whether these changes should be uniform across countries or not.

In relation to the field itself, we can see that whilst comparative institutional analysis has always played a central role in the social sciences, it is in the last two decades that the focus on the inter-relationship between institutions, economic organization, and states has developed a significant distinctive trajectory in terms of empirical research, theoretical debates, and methodological rigour. As the chapters in this Handbook make clear substantial advances in our understanding have occurred during this period. Indeed, it would appear that momentum in this area has continued to build as new areas are opened up and developed. In our judgement, there are now deep and rich theoretical and empirical literatures on specific issues within the comparative institutionalist approach and it is therefore timely to ask leading scholars in these areas to take overviews of particular topics and provide a review of developments and perspectives on future issues.

This momentum reflects the growth of an international, interdisciplinary research community pursuing topics in this area and developing programmes of research and research training for younger scholars. In the European context, it is clear that from the 1980s, in particular, the growing influence of the European Union as an arena of policy, of funding for academic research, and of aspiration to nation-states outside its boundaries has contributed to more intensive collaborations and debates on issues of comparative institutionalism. North American scholars have also been intensely involved in these events on two fronts—one in terms of the debate on developments in the European context and another in terms of tackling the entry of Asian societies into the global economy, ranging from Japan through the interest in the early 1990s in the Asian tigers, through to the hugely significant influence of China in the last ten to fifteen years, and the more recent rise of India.

This research community inevitably spreads across disciplinary areas—from politics to business and management to sociology in particular—and in such a broad field, connections may be lost or overlooked. This is another reason why a handbook such as this can perform such a useful service. The selection of authors reflects these different disciplinary backgrounds as well as different geographical origins. In this respect, we hope that this Handbook will not only consolidate knowledge in the area but also contribute to a consolidation of the community of scholars working on these themes, helping people see connections, which they had not previously considered, and providing a series of common reference points for discussion, debate, and teaching purposes.

Of course, there are still gaps—perspectives on Asian countries are mainly derived from scholars educated in Europe and the US even though increasing numbers of them originate from Asia. There remains very little work on Africa beyond the analysis of failed states and development studies, and the analysis of Latin American contexts is limited in spite of the interest particularly of US political scientists in this area. Nevertheless, there is no reason why in the next decade we cannot expect to see this field become even more internationalized and the range of examples and discussions to extend beyond Europe, East Asia, and the US; a development that can only be positive.

WHY THIS STRUCTURE?

Finally, what choices lay behind the selection of chapters that now go to make up the Handbook? What became clear as the Handbook began to develop was that there were many common themes that were going to be explored from a variety of different angles and that the Handbook would be more valuable if it allowed authors to develop their chapters relatively freely once the overall topic had been agreed. As a result, we have produced something that differs in some respects from standard versions of a handbook in that rather than impose a tight word limit and a strict instruction regarding the content of the chapter, we identified broad areas of debate and research, we identified authors with expertise in the field, and we then allowed them to develop their chapter in detail through discussions with the editors. As a result, our chapters aim to offer substantially more than a simple literature review and guide to the reading. They aim to make contributions to the conceptual organization of the field and its future direction.

In terms of structure, we chose four very broad headings. The first part focuses on the nature of comparative institutional analysis, variants of institutional theory, issues of actors, institutional change and institutional complementarity, as well as methodological problems. It is primarily theoretical and conceptual in scope. It covers many of the definitional issues referred to earlier in this introduction, demonstrating the breadth and provenance of institutional theories (Djelic), the importance of historical and comparative perspectives (Thelen), the intricate relationship between institutions and actors (Jackson), the nature of institutional reproduction and change (Campbell), the problem of institutional complementarities (Crouch), and methodological issues and solutions in comparative studies (Kogut).

The second part focuses on key social institutions, understanding their emergence, and how they relate to economic organization and performance outcomes. In this section, the state is a central object of analysis and in particular its interaction with firms, markets, and other societal institutions. Weiss examines different models of the state and how states interact with the economy; a theme that is also taken up by Morgan in analysing markets and money as social institutions. In his chapter, Seabrooke examines how states and non-state actors emerge in international regimes and transnational institutions and with what effect. In their chapter on law and economic organization, Morgan and Quack seek to show how the Weberian identification of law with the state needs to be rethought in the context of multi-level fields of hard and soft law, where private actors and dynamic innovative law firms seek to establish new forms of authority and law. Deeg's discussion of financial systems also inevitably identifies how states and state regulation and reform impact on the organization of financial systems, with an impact on the financing of firms and through this on their strategy and structure. Casper's analysis of innovation shows the intricate ways in which firms, educational institutions, and states develop distinctive innovative competences and how these affect firm performance. Whitley shows that over time, distinctive competition models have emerged in particular institutional contexts and that the degree to which such models remain viable and/or capable of growth varies leaving firms, societies, and states with different problems of adjustment in the current period. Kenworthy provides an overview of the state of knowledge in terms of economic and performance outcomes between different societies and how these may be related to specific institutional features.

The third part focuses most directly on firms and the interrelationship between institutions and the structure and competences of firms. One of the key debates in this area concerns how institutions influence corporate governance and with what effect on firm strategy and structure. Goyer provides an account of this debate and draws on a wide range of empirical research to explore this issue. Whitley provides a focus on the relationship between key aspects of the internal structuring of firms and their institutional preconditions. He identifies different types of capitalism in which key institutions cohere in order to produce specific forms of economic organization with their own distinctive set of capabilities. Rubery concentrates on employment relationships and shows how these vary across contexts with impacts on how skill and production is organized. Herrigel and Zeitlin build on their recent work concerning the reorganization of firms in global supply chains. They show that the disaggregation of the firm and the reconstitution of supply chains create different sorts of networks of cooperation with an impact on innovation and competition.

The final part identifies areas in which comparative institutionalism is developing new insights. Two of these concern the analysis of societies beyond the core European, North American, and Asian examples. The first is the chapter by Szelenyi and Wilk which looks at institutional change in Eastern and Central Europe and raises questions concerning the inter-relationship of political processes, welfare systems, and economic organization. The other is the chapter by Hall which examines failed states and what this tells us about the nature of institutions. In their chapter on financialization, Engelen and Konings look at the growth of financial markets and how the global nature of these markets affects national institutional systems. Finally, Pedersen examines how the discourse of institutional competitiveness has become itself institutionalized and with what effect.

In his Epilogue contribution, Wolfgang Streeck, a distinguished long-time contributor to these debates, reflects on what he sees as the key challenges for the future for comparative institutional analysis.

Finally, it is important to note that this Handbook cannot in any way constitute the 'last word'. On the contrary, whilst it is meant to deliver to the audience a sense of the achievements of this strand of research, it is also expected to leave a sense of the unfinished nature of this process. In a way, the Handbook has not succeeded if it does not leave some sense in the audience of a belief that there is more to say, more to research, and more to think about. There are many questions about institutions and economic organization that remain open, many new questions to be considered, and many new forms of comparison to be made. Similarly, at a time when simple models of markets are in crisis due to turmoil in the financial sector and its knock-on effects elsewhere, it is more important than ever to emphasize the institutional underpinning of markets, the way they are shaped by social factors, and the role which conscious political action can play in this process. Engaging with the sort of comparative institutional analysis discussed in this Handbook offers access to such an understanding.

REFERENCES

BAYLY, C. A. (2004). *The Birth of the Modern World, 1780–1914: Global Connections and Comparisons*, (Malden, MA; Oxford: Blackwell Publisher).

BENDIX, R. (1956). *Work and Authority in Industry*, (London: Wiley).

BERGER, S. and R. P. DORE (1996). *National Diversity and Global Capitalism*, (Ithaca; London: Cornell University Press).

BERNSTEIN, W. (2008). *A Splendid Exchange: How Trade Shaped the World*, (London: Atlantic Books).

BOYER, R. and D. DRACHE (1996). *States against Markets: The Limits of Globalization*, (London: Routledge).

——and J.-P. DURAND (1997). *After Fordism*, (Basingstoke: Macmillan Business).

BROOK, T. (2008). *Vermeer's Hat: the Seventeenth Century and the Dawn of the Global World*, (London: Profile).

CAMPBELL, J. L. (2004). *Institutionalization and Globalization*, (Princeton, NJ: Princeton University Press).

CROUCH, C. (1993). *Industrial Relations and European State Traditions*, (Oxford: Clarendon Press).

——and W. STREECK (1997). *Political Economy of Modern Capitalism: Mapping Convergence and Diversity*, (London: Sage).

DARWIN, J. (2007). *After Tamerlane: The Global History of Empire since 1405*, (London: Allen Lane).

DAVIES, N. (1996). *Europe: A History*, (Oxford: Oxford University Press).

GREIF, A. (2006). *Institutions and the Path to the Modern Economy: Lessons From Medieval Trade*, (Cambridge; New York: Cambridge University Press).

HALL, J. A. (1986). *Powers and Liberties: The Causes and Consequences of the Rise of the West*, (Harmondsworth: Penguin in association with Blackwell).

——(1994). *The State: Critical Concepts*, (London: Routledge).

HALL, P. A. and D. SOSKICE (2001). *Varieties of Capitalism: The Institutional Foundations of Comparative Advantage*, (Oxford: Oxford University Press).

HAMILTON, G. G. (2006). *Commerce and Capitalism in Chinese Societies*, (London: Routledge).

HOLLINGSWORTH, J. R. and R. BOYER (1997). *Contemporary Capitalism: The Embeddedness of Institutions*, (Cambridge: Cambridge University Press).

——P. C. SCHMITTER, and W. STREECK (1994). *Governing Capitalist Economies: Performance and Control of Economic Sectors*, (New York; Oxford: Oxford University Press).

LANE, C. (1989). *Management and Labour in Europe: The Industrial Enterprise in Germany, Britain and France*, (Aldershot: Elgar).

——(1995). *Industry and Society in Europe: Stability and Change in Britain, Germany and France*, (Aldershot: Edward Elgar).

MANN, M. (1986). 'The Sources of Social Power', vol. 1, *A History of Power from the Beginning to A.D. 1760*, (Cambridge: Cambridge University Press).

——(1993). 'The Sources of Social Power', vol. 2, *The Rise of Classes and Nation-States 1760–1914*, (Cambridge: Cambridge University Press).

MAURICE, M., F. SELLIER, and J.-J. SILVESTRE (1986). *The Social Foundations of Industrial Power: A Comparison of France and Germany*, (Cambridge, MA: MIT Press).

ORRÚ, M., N. W. BIGGART, and G. G. HAMILTON (1996). *The Economic Organization of East Asian Capitalism*, (London: SAGE).

SCOTT, W. R. (2008). *Institutions and Organizations*. 3rd edn., (Thousand Oaks: Sage).

SHONFIELD, A. (1965). *Modern Capitalism: The Changing Balance of Public and Private Power*, (London: Oxford University Press).

SORGE, A. and M. MAURICE (2000). *Embedding Organizations: Societal Analysis of Actors, Organizations, and Socio-Economic Context*, (Amsterdam, Philadelphia, PA: John Benjamins Publisher).

STREECK, W. (1992). *Social Institutions and Economic Performance: Studies of Industrial Relations in Advanced Capitalist Economies*, (London: Sage).

WALLERSTEIN, I. M. (2004). *World-Systems Analysis: An Introduction*, (Durham: Duke University Press).

WHITLEY, R. (1992a). *Business Systems in East Asia: Firms, Markets and Societies*, (London: Sage).

——(1992b). *European Business Systems: Firms and Markets in their National Contexts*, (London: Sage).

——(1999.) *Divergent Capitalisms: The Social Structuring and Change of Business Systems*, (Oxford: Oxford University Press).

——(2007). *Business Systems and Organizational Capabilities: The Institutional Structuring of Competitive Competences*, (Oxford; New York: Oxford University Press).

————(1996). *The Changing European Firm: Limits to Convergence*, (London; New York: Routledge).

——and P. H. KRISTENSEN (1997). *Governance at Work: The Social Regulation of Economic Relations*, (Oxford: Oxford University Press).

PART I

THEORIES AND METHODS IN COMPARATIVE INSTITUTIONAL ANALYSIS

CHAPTER 1

....

INSTITUTIONAL PERSPECTIVES— WORKING TOWARDS COHERENCE OR IRRECONCILABLE DIVERSITY?

....

MARIE-LAURE DJELIC[1]

INTRODUCTION

....

Over the past thirty years or so, the labels 'institutional' and 'institutionalism' have spread like wildfires across most social science disciplines. The shared context to the emergence and diffusion of institutional or neo-institutional perspectives during this period has been a questioning of conventional and dominant perspectives in those different disciplines. The common thread has been a critical take on key defining

[1] I want to thank Colin Crouch, John Meyer, and Marc Schneiberg for useful comments on earlier versions of this chapter.

features of these conventional perspectives—such as context-free agency, rationality and rational choice hypotheses, efficiency and utility maximization, unrestricted and free-flowing information, naturalistic evolution or 'one-best-way' structures and solutions. The perception of a complex empirical reality rendered those simplistic and simplifying features increasingly unsatisfactory and frustrating (Meyer and Rowan 1977; March and Olsen 1984; Dobbin 1994).

The reaction, across disciplines, was to underscore the importance of the environment and, in particular, to bring institutions back in. Across disciplines, an institutionalist perspective starts from the basic recognition that human activities, including activities of an economic nature, are embedded and framed within larger institutional schemes that tend to be stable (Weber 1978; Polanyi 1944; Veblen 1904; North 1990). A core dimension of the institutionalist project has been to understand, here again across disciplinary boundaries, how embeddedness matters, how institutions constrain and structure action, create regularities and stability, limiting at the same time the range of options and opportunities.

The success of institutional or neo-institutional perspectives reflects in part their ability to integrate complexity. The different variants of institutionalism have that in common that they make it possible to take into account the contextual embeddedness of economic rules, actors, organizations, or behaviours. Still, under the broad label of 'institutionalism', there is also a fair amount of diversity and resilient differences. There are, I propose, at least three broad kinds of divides or boundaries. A first divide is disciplinary. There is an institutionalist temptation in most social science disciplines—and particularly in sociology, political science, and economics. Those disciplines build upon different intellectual foundations and they have evolved and developed through time in relative distance and autonomy from each other. A second divide is epistemological or conceptual. Naturally, there is a fair amount of parallelism between this divide and the disciplinary one but the overlap is not perfect. There are, I argue, three main categories of institutionalist perspectives, each reflecting a different epistemological orientation. I use the terms 'rational choice', 'historical', and 'cultural' to label those categories.[2] There is a third divide that translates in part in geographical terms. Even though institutionalism was originally strongly embedded in European, mainly German, institutional economics, its transfer to the United States in the early part of the twentieth century would turn out to have consequences. Today, there are partial but identifiable differences, within disciplines, between institutionalist projects on both sides of the Atlantic (Aglietta 1976; Tempel and Walgenbach 2007; Greenwood et al. 2008).

---

[2] This typology is both compatible with and slightly different from other existing typologies. Considering only politicial science, Thelen and Steinmo (1992) identify two 'institutionalisms'—rational-choice and historical. Kato (1996) identifies in political science a third category that brings institutions together with public choice theory, using Simon's concept of bounded rationality. Hall and Taylor (1996) differentiate between historical, rational-choice and sociological institutionalism. DiMaggio (1998) points to rational-action neo-institutionalism (RAN), social constructivist neo-institutionalism (SCN), and mediated-conflict neo-institutionalism (MCN).

Those different kinds of divides cannot be ignored and they generate today a double sense of vibrancy on the one hand and confusion on the other. The richness, profusion, and vitality of contributions from an institutionalist perspective cannot be denied. But this also often comes together with complexities, apparent contradictions, and stunning differences between separate strands of institutionalism. The question at the core of this chapter derives from this. If we take the category 'institutionalism' in its broadest sense, are we moving today towards increasingly acute differentiation or else towards greater coherence overall? Is institutional theory exploding further into so many strands and variants, increasingly distant from each other and only rarely in discussion with each other? Or else are we moving towards greater coherence and compatibility and, possibly, more fluid discussions and exchanges?

This chapter starts with a description in broad strokes of the intellectual heritage shaping institutionalism in different social science disciplines. Then, a number of current debates serve as points of entry to approach the question of coherence or diversity. The definition of institutions, the double issue of change and emergence, and the question of action and agency are explored in turn. Those are key questions today, with which scholars are grappling, across and beyond disciplinary boundaries. A red thread, throughout the chapter, is to ponder whether the exploration of these questions reveals enduring and tight boundaries or whether it shows instead increasing coherence and proximity within the broad institutionalist family. In our conclusion, we go back to this red thread.

Intellectual Foundations of Institutionalism

The objective here is to explore in broad strokes the intellectual lineage of the institutionalist argument in different social science disciplines.

If we go back in time, we find a common intellectual ground and a shared inspiration behind, and in spite of, contemporary differences. This shared inspiration can be traced back to a small number of sources. The German historical school had a profound impact, particularly on political science and economics (Herbst 1965; Hodgson 2001; 2004). Scholars such as Max Weber or Werner Sombart, who have sometimes been depicted as representing a later evolution of the historical school, were also profoundly influential (Veblen 1901; Hodgson 2001). More marginally, the 'early' Karl Marx or Emile Durkheim also played a role in sociology and even in parts of political science. This small pool of intellectual sources had an important shaping role for the institutionalist argument in its many 'old' and 'new' guises.

In American social science, a first generation seized upon this tradition already at the turn of the twentieth century. There was an unmistakable and direct 'genetic' transmission from the German tradition to this 'old American institutionalism' (Herbst 1965; Hodgson 2001, 2004). The mechanisms of that transmission are easy to follow. American 'old institutionalists' had often studied in Germany. Those who did not generally had a teacher who had been to Germany and/or had studied in one of the American universities or schools that had become hotbeds of institutionalism— Johns Hopkins University, Columbia University, Madison-Wisconsin or later the New School in New York City. The purpose is not to propose here an overly simplistic genealogy. American 'old institutionalists' also found inspiration for example in British historicism, evolutionary theory, pragmatism, or even classical economics. The interplay between those different components on American soil in fact generated increasing complexity and differentiation through time. Still, behind a diversity that sometimes appears overwhelming, it is important not to neglect the common historical intellectual filiation.

From the second quarter of the twentieth century, 'old institutionalism' came to lose out, in American social science, to rational action, universalizing and context-free perspectives and this across disciplines. The revival of institutionalist arguments started in the different disciplines somewhere during the 1970s. Contemporary variants of the argument have tended to adopt the qualifying prefix 'neo' (or new) to refer to—and possibly take distance from—earlier institutionalist contributions.

The German Historical School

Historicism had its roots in Germany and as an intellectual programme it was dominant there during the nineteenth century among economists, lawyers, and policymakers alike. The German Historical School rejected the idea of natural and universal economic laws as well as the possibility of universal theoretical systems (Shionoya 2001). Instead, its proponents argued that economic 'laws' were contingent upon the particular historical, social, and institutional context in which economic action happened to be embedded. There was hesitation, though, between a merely descriptive and a more normative perspective.

Descriptive historicism pointed to the embeddedness of economic arrangements and to the need for historically and sociologically grounded empirical economics (Iggers 1968). The descriptive project of the German Historical School was to show the multiplicity of economic, legal, or political arrangements and in a sense their social and historical relativism. The idea was to adopt an inductive and historical approach that could make it possible to recognize the diversity of economic, legal, or political circumstances. From that perspective, market economies had no prime of place. Markets were institutional and social objects like any other that had to be contextualized and the efficiency of which could not be presumed.

Normative historicism went one step further. It associated unique economic paths with national trajectories and recognized that the state was the main carrier of such national identity. The consequence was strong support for the status quo, which was supposed to reflect the very essence, spirit (*Geist*) of a people and nation and a preoccupation for nation-building through state-led economic policy. In Germany, this meant that normative historicism found perfectly legitimate, towards the end of the nineteenth century, a combination of highly organized capitalism and strong state intervention. Such a combination, expressing itself at the moment of German unification, marked, as it were, the culmination of the German 'spirit'. Needless to say, such combination left little room to 'free markets'. The latter were more readily associated with an earlier, 'disorganized', association of German states that predated unification (Fourcade-Gourinchas 2001: 407).

In retrospect, the fate of German historicism was closely linked to two developments. First, German historicism in time lost the *methodenstreit*—the intense and at times bitter methodological dispute that opposed it to Austrian liberal and classical economists during the 1880s (Hodgson 2001). Basically, the Austrian Carl Menger violently rejected the possibility that more historical economics could lead to better theory. He asserted instead that the prime task of economic analysis was the elaboration of theory and that theoretical knowledge did not result from empirical work. This position would progressively become uncontroversial in economics and the legitimacy of historicism was in the process considerably weakened. A second development stemmed from the association of historicism, at least in its normative form, with Prussian and later on German nationalism. This association undeniably contributed further to its loss of legitimacy. The progressive weakening of the German Historical perspective on the old continent certainly had implications for 'old institutionalism' in the United States and its fate in that country.

Old institutionalism in economics and political science

It would naturally be beyond the scope of this chapter to propose an overview of 'old institutionalism' in American economics and political science. We only sketch out here a few broad features that bear upon the questions explored in this chapter.

Firstly, some of the most prominent 'old institutionalists' played an essential role in the structuration and professionalization of social science disciplines in the United States. The experiences many of them had in Germany certainly shaped their intellectual agenda. It also framed their conception of universities, research, and higher education. Those experiences coloured, in fact, many organizational initiatives. A number of those initiatives contributed to the professionalization but also to the differentiation and separation of social science disciplines. Others tended instead to put forward and encourage transdisciplinarity. In 1885, Richard T. Ely, who held a German doctorate and had been strongly influenced by the German Historical School, founded the American Economic Association (AEA). The creation of the AEA retrospectively proved an important step for the structuration and professionalization of economics as a self-standing social science. Only a few years later, though, Ely launched another initiative that tended this time to entrench transdisciplinarity.

In 1892, he formed a new School of Economics, Political Science, and History at the University of Madison-Wisconsin. Another pioneer was Westel W. Willoughby, a PhD from Johns Hopkins University but also the founder there of the Political Science Department. He was amongst the early founding members (and the first Secretary General and Treasurer) of the American Political Science Association (APSA) in 1903. The APSA was willingly and explicitly modelled on the AEA. This type of initiative naturally contributed to the transformation of political and legal theory into political science and to the structuration and professionalization of the latter as a social scientific discipline. Thorstein Veblen, who had done graduate work at Johns Hopkins, was in his turn instrumental in bringing to life another important transdisciplinary project. While he had refused the presidency of the AEA in 1925, he became around that time one of the founders of the Faculty at the New School for Social Research in New York.

Secondly, some of the key features of the German Historical School found their way in to and shaped the agenda of 'old institutionalism'. One such feature was the refusal of a universal and universalizing perspective. The American 'old institutionalists' did not believe in the existence of natural, hence universal, laws. Instead, they searched for an explanation to the contingency of economic arrangements and behaviours. In the German Historical School, an important dimension of that contingency had been historical. In 'old institutionalism', the importance granted to history varied. Hodgson even argues that, overall, 'the problem of historical specificity received only limited attention' in American 'old institutionalism' (Hodgson 2001: 152). The way contingency was defined increasingly turned out to be a-historical, particularly in economics and political science. The core focus was the (relatively a-historical) interplay between economic arrangements and broader societal or institutional frames. This interplay was well expressed, later on, in the notion of 'embeddedness'. The conceptualization of the embedding environment also revealed similarities. In 'old institutionalism', just as in the German Historical School, the environment is concrete and localized—often taking the form of structures, organizations, rules, or laws. However, while the national dimension seemed predominant in the German Historical School, 'old institutionalism' in American social science considered more proximate local communities (DiMaggio and Powell 1991: 13).

Thirdly, and on the other hand, differences set apart 'old institutionalism' from the German Historical School. In 'old institutionalism', empirical data collection remained important. At the same time, theory and theory making progressively gained in significance. Some of the most prominent amongst 'old institutionalists' even saw the absence of theoretical ambition as a major weakness of the German Historical School. Thorstein Veblen criticized German historicism on that ground when he claimed that 'economists of what may be called the elder line of the historical school can scarcely be said to cultivate a science at all, their aim being not theoretical work at all . . .' (Veblen 1901: 71–2). Joseph Schumpeter agreed—for him German historical economics was nothing but endless history! Even though John R. Commons devoted an important part of his professional life to empirical data collection, he also attempted to come forward with a theoretical manifesto (Commons 1934). Empirical data collection made sense, not as such and per se, but mostly because it could generate theory, he argued. In parallel, the form in which the data were presented often changed. Detailed narratives and story-telling that were the mark of the German Historical School increasingly gave way to more formalized model building and data aggregation. There was naturally variability here and Thorstein Veblen, for example, remained more of a story-teller.

Another important evolution needs to be mentioned. 'Old institutionalism', in economics, political science, or sociology, distanced itself from and at times criticized the conservatism and *stasis* often associated with German historicism. In German historicism, powerful institutional framing explained and often justified a degree of determinism or even a normative defence of the status quo. The 'old institutionalism' looked instead for some of the key mechanisms generating change and adaptation in the interplay between economic actors and broader environments (Selznick 1957: 39; DiMaggio and Powell 1991: 12–14). Thorstein Veblen, for example, clearly distanced himself from what he saw as a 'Hegelian' temptation in the oldest branch of German historicism. Veblen rejected explanations that harked back to the logic of systemic wholes—whether material or spiritual. He regretted the tendency in the German Historical School to easily turn to a simple if not simplistic explanatory premiss—the *Geist* of a country, of a period, which often became the supreme criterion of historical differentiation between socio-economic systems (Veblen 1901). Veblen called instead for a focus on detailed, causal processes; he underscored the importance of a processual explanation of origins, growth, and variation of institutions. He emphasized in particular the need to problematize the *Geist* and to explore how it came about, how it stabilized and was reproduced, possibly even how it came to be contested and to change over time (Hodgson 2001: 139–51).

Let us underscore still one more difference. Where the German Historical School implied a reflection on societal issues and the consideration of conflicts of interests, power plays, questions of justice and injustice, issues of preference formation, this progressively disappeared from 'old institutionalism', in economics and in great part also in political science. Veblen was naturally a notable exception (Thelen and Steinmo 1992). In complete contrast the 'old institutionalism' in sociology, as represented by Karl Polanyi or Philip Selznick for example, seized upon those issues directly (Perrow 1986: ch.5, DiMaggio and Powell 1991: 12). In fact, this focus would weaken in sociology only later, with the neo-institutionalist revival of the 1970s (Meyer and Rowan 1977; DiMaggio and Powell 1983; 1991: 12–14).

Finally, the fate of law represents another significant—and surprising—evolution. The German Historical School put a lot of emphasis on studies of legal structures and texts—particularly with a comparative scope. The 'old institutionalism', on the other hand, seemed to forget about law. This is particularly striking of institutionalism in political science, where one would have most expected law and legal structures to retain an important role (Engel and Héritier 2003). Recently, in the more contemporary evolution of neo-institutionalism, the significance and role of law are being rediscovered. The thrust, arguably, stems even more from economics (e.g. the Law and Economics school) or from sociology than from political science. Law still remains relatively absent from the institutionalist frame in political science—whether of the rational or historical kind (Steinmo 2001).

Different readings of Max Weber and old institutionalism in sociology

In sociology, extending into organization studies, institutionalism has historically found a significant source of intellectual inspiration in the thought and work of Max Weber. We have already touched on the question of Max Weber's connection to the German Historical School. Some see him 'in'; others 'out' (Hodgson 2001; Schneider 1995). Thorstein Veblen and others (e.g. Koslowski 1997) propose a convincing compromise. They differentiate between 'early' and 'late' (or else 'old' and 'new') *Historismus*. Early historicists were mainly drawn to systematic empirical data collection. Later historicists—including Werner Sombart and Max Weber according to Veblen and others—were also out to develop theory even if of a middle range kind (Hodgson 2001: 108). According to Max Weber, the 'most general laws' are 'the least valuable' because the 'more comprehensive their scope' the 'more they lead away' from the task of explaining a given phenomenon (Weber 1949: 72–80). Max Weber also took some distance from the tendency in old *Historismus* (as described above) to search for ultimate explanations in national socio-economic systems understood as essentialist collectives, static *Geiste* (Mommsen 1965).

For those reasons, Max Weber was often identified by 'old institutionalists' as avoiding the traps in which the older German Historical School tended to fall (Hodgson 2001). In contrast to the idealist organicism and collectivism of the older German Historical School, Max Weber brought the intentional individual back in as the ultimate causal agent behind socio-economic phenomena. In the words of Max Weber, 'action in the sense of subjectively understandable orientation of behaviour exists only as the behaviour of one or more *individual* human beings' (Weber 1978: 13). This methodological individualism, though, was compatible in Weber's thought with the understanding that institutions and social frames played a structuring, constraining, but also enabling role with respect to individual belief and preference formation. Weber made this very clear:

These concepts of collective entities (states, firms, social collectives, etc . . .) which are found both in common sense and in juristic and other technical forms of thought, have a meaning in the minds of individual persons, partly as of something actually existing, partly as something with normative authority. . . . Actors thus in part orient their action to them and in this role such ideas have a powerful, often a decisive, causal influence on the course of action of real individuals.   (Weber 1978: 14)

The fate of Max Weber's thought after his death has been unique. Weber has certainly strongly influenced 'old institutionalism', particularly but not only in sociology (Hodgson 2001; Powell and DiMaggio 1991). At the same time, Max Weber's work was also a source of inspiration for an economist like Frank Knight—one of the 'ancestors' of the

Chicago School of Economics (Djelic 2006). In 1927, Frank Knight went as far as saying that 'if (he) were to start again, (he) would build upon his (Weber's) ideas' (quoted in Schweitzer 1975: 279). We are even more aware, naturally, of the influence Max Weber had on Talcott Parsons—or should we say of the influence Talcott Parsons had on our reading of Max Weber! Without exploring this discussion in detail (see e.g. Beckert 2002; Hodgson 2001), let us just emphasize that Talcott Parsons was instrumental in spreading an a-historical reading of Max Weber's work and in masking, as it were, the 'embeddedness' of Weber in the German Historical School and its debates. Parsons chose to underscore the importance of general theory and to dismiss at the same time the question of historical specificity. In so doing, he '(broke) without acknowledgement from the letter and spirit of Weber's work' (Hodgson 2001: 195; see also Zaret 1980: 1193). Parsons had early on been strongly influenced by prominent 'old institutionalists' at Amherst College. He went on to get a doctoral dissertation in Germany and was there in contact with and inspired by the German Historical School. By the early 1930s, though, when he had moved to Harvard, Parsons had evolved in a striking way. He was then violently rejecting both institutionalism and historicism (Parsons 1976). He kept Max Weber but he erased as much as possible, from his reading of Weber and from his own work, any reference and connection to historicism. There were two main objections Parsons had with regard to historicism and old institutionalism. First, he objected to the fact that 'in the name of generalized radical empiricism, (institutionalism) denied the legitimacy of analytical abstraction'. Second, he claimed that institutionalism 'neglected cultural-normative factors' (Parsons 1976: 178). The presentation, in the previous section, of 'old institutionalism' clearly shows that those objections had little ground but Parsons's fight against historicism and institutionalism was certainly consequential!

In the end, it is ironic that Max Weber's thought had such an influence both on old institutionalism and on one of its most fervent critics! If anything, it shows the breadth of Weber's thought and hence its malleability. After the Second World War, there were in any case different paths for students to access Weber's thought. And the path that was followed was obviously not without consequences for the reading of Weber that ensued. Remaining at a broad strokes level, we can see the influence of the history of ideas sketched above and of its different stages on the diversity of contemporary sociological neo-institutionalism. On the one hand, the different variants of sociological neo-institutionalism all claim to be heirs to Weberianism (Powell and DiMaggio 1991; Tempel and Walgenbach 2007). On the other hand, those different variants clearly emphasize different dimensions of Weber's thought. I only point here to two strikingly different and consequential readings of Weber—a 'West Coast' reading and an 'East Coast/European' one.

The 'West Coast' label is in reference to the role of California—particularly Stanford—as a 'hub' for this variant of neo-institutionalism (e.g. Meyer and Rowan 1977). This particular variant has combined Max Weber's insight that social activity was shrouded in webs of significance with his claim that social action and change were constrained by a system having inherent dynamics of its own and leading, in an unavoidable manner, towards increasing rationalization. This is a Durkheimian and even Parsonian reading of Weber, I propose, with a strong evacuation of action and conflict. It emphasizes the notion of order and stabilization (if not stability), the structuring power of culture and norms and the overpowering strength of a collective and in a sense 'global' *Geist*. This reading completely de-emphasizes the role of individuals (and hence Weber's particular form of methodological individualism), history and its accidents or contingencies, as well as notions of disorder, conflict, or power.

The 'East Coast' label, in turn, is in reference to a post-Parsonian 'Harvard' school (e.g. Skocpol 1979). This East Coast sociological institutionalism happens to be compatible with historical institutionalism in political science (Thelen and Steinmo 1992; Hall and Soskice 2001) and with a West European tradition of political and sociological economy (Whitley 1999; Maurice and Sorge 2000; Streeck and Yamamura 2001; Morgan et al. 2001). To put it simply, this variant of neo-institutionalism has not forgotten the embeddedness of Max Weber's thought in the German Historical School. The notion of historical specificity remains present. However, this notion is often coupled with and sometimes even diluted into a notion of geographical specificity—with the nation-state as a key unit. The state or the national polity are instrumental in shaping and reproducing institutional frames. Some contributions have underscored the role of conflict and disorder—often by pushing a little bit of Marx on Weber (e.g. Skocpol 1979; Evans et al. 1985; Steinmo et al. 1992)! Others have pointed to the possibility of reconciling the structuring power of institutions with a space for individual agency and conflictual encounters (Djelic 1998; Beckert 1999; Djelic 2004). On the whole, though, most contributions under this label have tended, until recently, to emphasize order and stability rather than change and disorder, collective determinism rather than individual action. This variant of neo-institutionalism has avoided falling into the trap of a universal/universalizing *Geist* only to claim the multiplicity, the great resilience through time but also the nearly deterministic power of different national structural (in a few cases cultural) frames (Dobbin 1994; Guillèn 1994; Whitley 1999; Hall and Soskice 2001).

EXPLORING KEY DEBATES—COHERENCE OR DIVERSITY?

After this rapid discussion of intellectual foundations, let us turn now to contemporary debates. Once again, it is impossible to be exhaustive. Hence, I focus only on certain debates—particularly lively and central today. I explore in turn discussions around the definition of institutions, the double issue of change and emergence, and the question of action and agency. The objective in what follows is simply to point to key arguments and developments. A background puzzle is whether those developments suggest a degree of coherence or else irreconcilable diversity across variants of institutionalism.

What are institutions? Exploring definitions

Douglas North and other neo-institutional economists define institutions as (rational) 'rules of the game in a society' or 'more formally the humanly devised constraints that shape human interaction' (North 1990: 3; North 2005: 48). Shepsle and other political scientists see institutions as '*ex ante* agreements about a structure of cooperation' that 'economize on transaction costs, reduce opportunism and other forms of agency "slippage" and thereby enhance the prospects of gains through cooperation' (Shepsle 1986: 74). This rational-choice variant of neo-institutionalism has a tendency to propose, in the end, that existing institutional frames are efficient and reflect rationality. This is expected to impact directly upon organizational and behavioural solutions.

In Philip Selznick's words, 'to institutionalize means to infuse with values' (Selznick 1957: 16–17). An institution is hence an organization that has moved from being an instrument to becoming a meaningful community. For Veblen, institutions referred to 'widely prevalent habits of thought in a given community such that they are analogous to cultural themes or a *Weltanschaung*' (Weed 1981: 72). For Meyer and Rowan, institutions are broad abstractions, 'wide cultural and symbolic patterns', 'rationalized and impersonal prescriptions', powerful 'rational myths' that infuse and diffuse in the organizational world (Meyer and Rowan 1977). Those cultural patterns, furthermore, are becoming increasingly homogeneous and rationalized the world over, suggesting in turn a process of organizational and behavioural isomorphism.

Historical neo-institutionalists, in sociology and in political science, conceive of institutions as essentially structural frames, organizational solutions, and formal rules or systems. They insist upon the particular significance of states and national boundaries for the structuration, stabilization, and reproduction of those institutional frames (e.g. Whitley 1999; Hall and Soskice 2001; Morgan et al. 2005; Streeck and Thelen 2005). Historical neo-institutionalism tends to underscore entrenched and path-dependent differentiation (mostly across national boundaries). National institutional environments are historical constructs, the crystallized sediments of a past national history. They generate deep-rooted systemic and behavioural inertia.

This rich diversity of definitions reveals important fault lines within the broad institutionalist family. Those fault lines have generated intense discussion through time and they help account for diversity across variants of institutionalism. Firstly, are we talking about only formal rules or do we include also informal conventions when we talk of institutions? Secondly, and relatedly, are institutions 'material' objects—laws and codes, systems of coordination, organizational arrangements, technologies and routines—or are they instead cognitive scripts and cultural patterns? Thirdly, are institutions locally and territorially bounded constraints or else are they broad and virtual patterns without boundaries? Fourthly, are institutions external to the actors, pre-existing constraints for human action or else the products of human design and action? Fifthly, are institutions rational and efficient or else do they reflect the irrationality of historical accidents? Finally, are institutions the 'rules of the game' or do the rules of the game become institutions only if and when they are acted out?

Looking at more recent contributions, it would seem that a form of compromise if not a common position is emerging, including across disciplines. For some time now, Richard Scott has proposed a definition of institutions that clearly goes well beyond some of the disagreements identified above. 'Institutions are comprised of regulative, normative and cultural-cognitive elements that, together with associated activities and resources, provide stability and meaning to social life' (Scott 1995; Scott 2008: 48).

Djelic and Quack (2003: 18) work from a definition of institutions as having 'both a structural dimension, including formal and informal rules and systems and an ideational dimension, including normative and cognitive patterns'. Recent contributions in institutional economics come very close. According to Avner Greif, 'an institution is a system of rules, beliefs, norms and organizations that together generate a regularity of (social) behaviour' (Greif 2006: 30). A coherent discourse is shaping around a definition of institutions as 'rules of the game providing stability and meaning' but with a multidimensional conception of the nature of rules of the game (Hall and Taylor 1996; Djelic and Quack 2003; Greif 2006). The latter are formal and informal, material and cognitive, organizational and cultural and the combination of these dimensions will vary through time and space. Contemporary contributions also often come to acknowledge the increasing role of broad, decontextualized and uprooted institutional patterns (Djelic and Quack 2003; Djelic and Sahlin-Andersson 2006; Scott 2008; Greenwood et al. 2008). Those, however, only become of real significance if they get anchored into localized territories, if they get appropriated by real actors and are in the process acted out, endogenized, and indigenized. In other words, floating ideas are potential institutions. They won't be real ones, though, in any concrete sense before they are acted upon and turned into 'rules of the game providing stability and meaning'. Institutions, ultimately, should be understood as the sum of (abstract and formal) rules of the game and of the ways in which those rules are concretely acted upon and played out. Finally, there is an emerging consensus around a picture of institutions as being at the very same time products of human action and powerful constraints on actors. Institutions reflect the historical aggregation of multiple human actions. Still, at any single point in time, they also frame and constrain individual agency. Institutions are the products of human action. But they are complex products built through time and through a long succession of processes that includes unanticipated developments. Institutions do not reveal nor embody efficient and rational design—at least not necessarily. At any point in time, furthermore, institutions are external 'facts', 'objects' that structure and constrain individuals and their projects. This emergent coherence undeniably echoes a complete reading of Max Weber's methodological individualism as presented above (Weber 1978: 13–14). Interestingly, it also opens the door for a theoretical reconciliation of institutional constraints and human agency.

Change and emergence

In the 1970s, the revival of the institutionalist argument initially came together with a focus on the constraining and resilient character of institutions. In the words of Clemens and Cook (1999: 441)

Institutions endure. As a reaction against methodological individualism, technological determinism and behaviorralist models . . . the resurgence of institutionalist analysis in recent years has forcefully reminded social scientists of the significance of this relative permanence of a distinctly social sort.

Across different variants of neo-institutionalism, behaviours and structures were understood to be deeply embedded and constrained if not fully determined. Institutional persistence and its structural and behavioural impact were core preoccupations, and this across disciplinary boundaries (Powell and DiMaggio 1991; Djelic and Quack 2003; Streeck and Thelen 2005; Greenwood et al. 2008).

In the 1990s, calls for a partial reorientation spread fast. Across disciplines, the problematization of institutional change and emergence was clearly missing. Talking about rational-choice neo-institutionalism, Avner Greif has argued that the 'institutions-as-rules approach is limited in analyzing institutional dynamics—that is the forces leading institutions to change and the influence of past institutions on subsequent ones' (Greif 2006: 9–10). Talking about historical institutionalism in political science, Thelen deplored the predominant emphasis on comparative statics and the relative underdevelopment of theories of institutional formation and change (Thelen 1999; see also Streeck and Thelen 2005). This was an issue in fact for all variants of historical neo-institutionalism, across disciplines (e.g. Clemens and Cook 1999; Quack and Morgan 2000; Sorge 2000; Djelic and Quack 2003; Crouch and Farell 2004). Cultural neo-institutionalism in its early form also left little room for the exploration of change and emergence. The double question of the origins and transformation of 'rational myths' or potentially global 'cultural patterns' was not at all on the agenda (Djelic 1998; Djelic and Quack 2003).

If change was considered at all, it was in one of three ways. Some contributions approached change only to de-emphasize it. Institutional systems were depicted as coherent—the subsystems being linked to each other through complementarities. This generated a picture of profound entrenchment and nearly unshakable stability, even in the face of external shocks. At most, those perspectives pointed to small, progressive, marginal and non-consequential alterations (Whitley 1999; Zeitlin and Herrigel 2000; Hall and Soskice 2001). Some of the resilience of institutional systems has been related to an inherent 'flexibility for stability'. These are mechanisms and properties which enable societal systems to adapt and readjust to changes in their environment without breaking with the overall system logic (Burns and Flam 1987; Offe 1995; Pempel 1998; Quack and Morgan 2000). Other contributions acknowledged the possibility of institutional change but essentially as a dramatic and rupture-like process, often implying a major crisis (Westney 1987; Djelic 1998). This has meant a picture of punctuated equilibria—a Kuhnian-type succession between periods of stability and moments of paradigm shift (Kuhn 1962; Krasner 1983). Finally, a third group of contributions pointed to a long-term evolutionary process and a progressive building up of a 'world-society' carrying standardized and rationalized cultural and normative patterns. Beyond the evolutionary trajectory, though, there was little specification in that approach of the concrete ways in which this global frame was building up, stabilized, or changed.

Recent contributions tend to question the simplistic alternative between no change and radical rupture. They are also wary of an understanding of change as predetermined evolution (Campbell and Pedersen 1996; Campbell 2004; Djelic and Quack 2003; Garud and Karnøe 2001; Sorge 2005; Streeck and Thelen 2005; Greif 2006; Djelic and Quack 2007; Schneiberg 2007). A form of compromise and coherence, here again, seems to emerge across disciplines. This compromise is defined by the possibility of 'incremental change with transformative results' (Streeck and Thelen 2005) or 'gradual but consequential change' (Djelic and Quack 2003). This understanding of change moves away from the model of punctuated equilibrium and points instead to the cumulative effects of ongoing and often subtle changes (Djelic and Quack 2007).

A number of mechanisms open up the possibility for change, including from within the institutional system itself. Campbell and Pedersen (1996: 207) find that 'revolutionary change' in post-communist societies often 'embodied significant evolutionary qualities'. Stark (1992) suggests that institutional transformations 'are more likely to entail processes of complex reconfigurations of institutional elements rather than their immediate replacement' (Padgett 2001 makes a parallel argument for organizational genesis). Johnson (2001) proposes the concept of 'path contingency' to reconcile the possibility of 'choice and chance' and the importance of 'past paths and institutional legacies' (Johnson 2001: 255). Both Stark (1992) and Johnson (2001) underscore the time dimension of institutional transformation and the importance of sequencing and cumulative stages. Certain studies suggest the importance of interpretation as a mechanism opening up the possibility for change. Fligstein (1990) for example, looks at the role of courts and court interpretation, Garud and Karnøe (2001) consider the 'mindful deviation' associated with entrepreneurs, and Campbell (2004) explores the role of ideas in institutional transformation. Other contributions point to the importance of the 'diffusion' of institutions and institutional elements and to associated processes of translation, adaptation, hybridization (Westney 1996; Djelic 1998; Jacoby 2000). Thelen (2003) talks of institutional conversion. Existing institutional frames are redirected to new purposes and in a sense 'revisited'. She identifies 'layering' as another mechanism where new institutional arrangements are 'layered' upon pre-existing ones. Crouch and Farrell (2004) or Schneiberg (2007) emphasize the fact that a multiplicity of institutional repertoires, including contradictory ones, can coexist in a particular institutional space. At any point in time, some may be active and others dormant but subtle external or internal pressures may lead to a rebalancing. Greif (2006: 16) also suggests going beyond (without forgetting them though) exogenous shocks to understand institutional change. He calls for a perspective treating institutional dynamics as a historical process and integrating a focus on endogenous micro-mechanisms. 'Institutions', he argues 'can remain stable in a changing environment and can change in the absence of environmental change while past institutions can influence the details of subsequent ones' (Greif 2006: 16).

Action and agency

A closely related debate is that of action and agency. The question of change also raises the question of human action and intervention. Neo-institutionalist arguments have tended to hesitate there between two perspectives. On the one hand, we find a 'post-Hegelian or Durkheimian temptation'. Institutions—as structure or culture—transcend individuals and represent pre-existing legacies that significantly constrain, if not determine, behaviours and patterns of action or organization. On the other hand, we find the 'agency temptation'. From that perspective, institutions are human constructions and the direct consequence of human agency and intervention. As such, they reveal and express the needs and interests of individuals. Those two temptations have had a different place and role across variants of neo-institutionalism.

Rational-choice variants of neo-institutionalism, whether in economics or political science have interestingly explored both temptations at the same time. The key here is a distinction between rule-takers and rule-makers. When it comes to rule-takers, rational-choice neo-institutionalists leave very little space to agency, emphasizing instead the determinant weight of institutional constraints. Rule-takers face institutions very much as external and powerful sets of constraints (North 2000: 13). In the meantime, rational-choice neo-institutionalism interprets institutions as 'humanly devised' rules of the game that reflect and reveal human agency, intentionality, and rationality (North and Thomas 1973; Williamson 1975; Levi 1989; Milgrom et al. 1990). In general, rational-choice neo-institutionalists have kept in their theoretical frameworks the assumption of actor rationality. In contrast to mainstream economics, though, rational-choice neo-institutionalists acknowledge the bounded nature of rationality and point also to the fact that, in any given situation, rationality combines with pre-existing institutional conditions thus leading to context-specific decisions and solutions. While the hypothesis of rationality is used more cautiously than in mainstream economics, it still structures the argument. This hypothesis has the marked disadvantage of significantly limiting the types of behaviours and motives that can be picked up through such theoretical frameworks. Although the actor does appear, he/she never appears in her full complexity. In turn, this has naturally reflected negatively on the explanatory power of rational-choice neo-institutionalist arguments, particularly in contexts where 'non-rational' types of behaviours and motives play a significant role. The sense that the territory for this type of behaviour may be much broader than initially thought has furthermore significantly increased in recent years. In partial reaction, some recent developments in rational-choice neo-institutionalism are today receiving considerable attention (North 2005; Greif 2006). What we see is an attempt at 're-incorporating the old institutionalism's assertions' not only 'about limited rationality' but also about 'cognition' and the role played by institutions in shaping cognition (Greif 2006: 11). According to Greif, 'institutions provide the cognitive, coordinative, informational and normative micro-foundations of behaviour', while they at the very same time 'reflect the actions of the interacting agents' (Greif 2006: 384). So agency is thinkable both with respect to rule-making and rule-taking. In both kinds of situations, though, we are talking about an embedded form of agency where 'past institutional elements provide opportunities as well as constraints in the process of institutional change that able coordinators take advantage of' (Greif 2006: 201). This undeniably resonates with the old institutionalists' attempt at reconciling a theory of institutional constraints and a theory of action. It also brings to mind, obviously, the complete reading of Max Weber's methodological individualism where the intentional individual is the ultimate causal agent behind socio-economic phenomena, but an agent highly structured and constrained by institutional frames (Weber 1978: 13–14).

Historical and cultural variants of neo-institutionalism have tended to err, at least during the first period of their development, on the side of structural constraint and determinism. Let us remember that those perspectives often emerged, in the different disciplines, in reaction to the predominance of behavioural perspectives, of actor- and rationality-centred theories (Thelen and Steinmo 1992). In contrast, they chose to focus on the constraining, if not determining, power of institutional frames. This does not necessarily imply an incompatibility with a theory of action. But as it turns out, most of those perspectives came to maturity with only limited consideration for the question of agency. Historical institutionalism has underscored the path-dependent nature of institutional frames and an 'iron cage'-like structuring impact. Cultural institutionalism points to the inescapable framing weight of institutions understood as 'wide cultural and symbolic patterns'. 'What actors do', in the words of key proponents of this theoretical perspective, 'is inherent in the social definition of the actor himself. The particular types of actors perceived by self and others and the specific forms their activity takes reflect institutionalized rules of great generality and scope' (Meyer, Boli, and Thomas 1994: 18). So actorhood and agency are not in principle unthinkable but they are necessarily of the 'soft' kind; we should never forget their deep embeddedness (Meyer 1996).

Towards the end of the 1980s, this disregard for agency was increasingly identified as a weakness—together with the lack of concern for the issue of change. Calls for the integration of a theory of agency then flourished (DiMaggio 1988; DiMaggio and Powell 1991; Scott 1995; Fligstein and Mara-Drita 1996; Beckert 1999; Clemens and Cook 1999). There were initially two main paths for this integration. A first path was to acknowledge that the institutional constraints human beings were embedded in were not simple, homogeneous, or coherent systems. Rather, the complexity, heterogeneity, and partial incoherence of institutional frames allowed individuals to use them as enabling bits and pieces, as toolkits. Individual and collective actors could creatively recombine the various institutional elements at their disposal to devise new or rather partially reinvented solutions to their problems (Sewell 1992; Campbell 1997; Beckert 1999; Clemens and Cook 1999; Djelic and Quack 2003; Streeck and Thelen 2005). They could also pick and choose alternative solutions that lay around in a complex, multi-layered, institutional landscape. Plowing through institutional sediments, they could potentially revive in the process previously discarded solutions (Schneiberg 2007). A second path went through the introduction of the concept of institutional entrepreneurship. When actors have a strong interest in a particular institutional arrangement or solution and manage to mobilize and use resources to push for this solution, then we have, according to DiMaggio, 'institutional entrepreneurs' (DiMaggio 1988). There was a danger, though, with this particular path. One could easily fall into the juxtaposition of a theory of (external) institutional constraints with a theory of (rational) action and strategic resource mobilization. So the path could lead either to something very much like the early version of rational-choice neo-institutionalism and its limits as underscored above or else to a profoundly schizophrenic construct.

The conception of institutions as deeply constitutive of actors, their expectations and their interests, is difficult to reconcile ontologically speaking with a conception of strategic, disembedded, and merely resource-based agency. Initially, this contradiction was recognized only by a small number of scholars (e.g. Beckert 1999: 781). The concept of 'institutional entrepreneurship' hence flourished in the literature and generated a fair amount of empirical and some theoretical work (Garud et al. 2002; Maguire et al. 2004; Greenwood and Suddaby 2006; Levy and Scully 2007; Garud et al. 2007, for a review see Hardy and Maguire 2008). Most of the time, it was used in a manner that is deeply incompatible with an institutionalist perspective. This has led recently to calls for reconsideration (Djelic and Sahlin-Andersson 2006; Schneiberg and Clemens 2006). In a recent contribution, Greenwood, Oliver, Sahlin, and Suddaby express this clearly:

A critical contribution of institutional analysis is its recognition that actors are not motivated solely by self-interest. Yet, at times, studies that analyze the strategies used by actors/entrepreneurs to achieve institutional change often ignore how and why institutional forces shape the strategies accepted as appropriate and the choice of strategies made by particular actors. Unless political processes are explicitly couched within an institutional context, the resultant story becomes premised upon actors behaving quasi-rationally and knowingly pursuing their interests. For us, this would be a political or resource dependence account, not an institutional one.   (Greenwood et al. 2008: 31)

There is a possible way out of this contradiction if we build upon a number of contributions. Firstly, it is important from an institutionalist perspective to reaffirm that any form of actorhood is always of the 'soft' kind (Djelic and Sahlin-Andersson 2006; Schneiberg and Clemens 2006). With this concept, Meyer (1996) emphasized a view of actors—be they organizations, states, or individuals—as culturally and institutionally embedded and hence both constrained but also enabled (see also March 1981). This conception of 'soft actor' resonates with Avner Greif's strong reminder that agency is always of the embedded kind (Greif

2006). It is also profoundly compatible with Schumpeter's understanding of entrepreneurship as difficult to recognize as such *ex ante*, as historically and institutionally bounded and located, as partly an exercise in *bricolage* and recombination
(Schumpeter 1947; 1949; Jones and Wadhwani 2006). Secondly, we have by now a
rich empirical and theoretical literature pointing to the great (and possibly increasing) heterogeneity of institutional resources (Clemens and Cook 1999; Crouch and
Farrell 2004; Thelen 2003; Streeck and Thelen 2005; Djelic and Quack 2003; Morgan
and Kubo 2005; Morgan et al. 2005; Djelic and Sahlin-Andersson 2006; Schneiberg
2007). We should naturally build upon those contributions. Actors are embedded
at the very same time in multiple layers of institutional constraints. Institutional
memories and sediments persist and can be reinvented. Actors move across multiple kinds of boundaries and cross over many different institutional spheres. This
clearly points to the possibility of *bricolage* and recombination as significant source
of institutional 'activity' (Douglas 1986; Djelic and Quack 2007; Djelic and Quack
2008). Thirdly, some of the insights from the literatures on social networks and
social movement may be useful to escape the 'hero' imagery that is both too
simplistic and inadequate when we talk about institutional emergence and change
(Padgett and Ansell 1993; Schneiberg and Lounsbury 2008). Most of the time, the
emergence of new institutional practices or their transformation 'result from
spatially dispersed, heterogeneous activity' (Lounsbury and Crumley 2007).
'Entrepreneurship' in other words is often a collective process that implies and
involves multiple actors with different kinds of resources and different patterns of
embeddedness (Kleiner 2003; Djelic 2004; Botzem and Quack 2006; Lounsbury and
Crumley 2007). Fourthly, physical and spatial dispersion and the collective and
aggregative dimension of the process combine with temporal sequencing. Institutional transformations take time; they are long-drawn-out processes with multiple
stages and sequences (Munir and Phillips 2005; Djelic and Ainamo 2005; Botzem
and Quack 2006). This suggests the possibility of a fair amount of decoupling
between the particular, locally- and temporally-bound objectives of certain actors
and longer-term developments. This takes us far away from heroic, strategic, and
interest/rational-based accounts of institutional transformations and brings us
instead much closer to institutional emergence, stories of partial lack of intentionality, 'path generation' or 'robust action' epics. In the words of Padgett and
Ansell, 'ambiguity and heterogeneity, not planning and self-interest, are the raw
materials of which powerful states and persons are constituted' (Padgett and Ansell
1993: 1259). This applies well, we suggest, to processes of institutional emergence
and transformation. Finally, the emerging contributions on and around the concept of 'institutional work'—institutionalization and deinstitutionalization as
combination and aggregation of situated practices—can provide interesting insights (e.g. Lawrence and Suddaby 2006). There is a risk, though, here again of a
'return to the rational actor model' and the main contributors to this perspective
underscore the importance of not falling into the trap (Lawrence and Suddaby
2006: 219).

Conclusions

The paths explored in this chapter point to a highly vibrant and dynamic literature indeed. The first section highlighted insights and debates that have historically been common, beyond and behind the multiplication and often the increasing estrangement of different variants of institutionalism across as well as within disciplines. The following section turned to contemporary discussions on a number of key issues. Neo-institutionalists of all kinds and stripes are today grappling with the definition of institutions, with issues of change and emergence, and with the challenge of agency. At a superficial level, we see a flurry of contributions and an apparent tower of Babel. When we enter more systematically into the debates, though, we find a fair amount of coherence. We cannot talk about convergence but we certainly can about the possible emergence of a coherent compromise that spans different variants of institutionalism. Interestingly, this emerging compromise—across disciplines—brings us closer to some of the key insights associated with an earlier 'old institutionalism' in American social science.

With respect to the definition of institutions, the emerging compromise has three main dimensions. Firstly, if institutions are understood as 'rules of the game providing stability and meaning', the associated conception of the nature of those rules is multidimensional. Rules can be formal or informal, external structures or cognitive and cultural frames and the combination will vary through time and space. Secondly, there is an increasingly widespread conception that there is no institution without some degree of appropriation, rooting, and stabilization. Institutions, ultimately, are the sum of rules of the game and of the ways in which those rules are concretely played out. Thirdly, institutions are increasingly understood as reflecting the historical aggregation of multiple human actions and at the same time, as framing, at any single point in time, an external constraint to individual agency. Institutions are the products of human action. But they are complex products built through time and aggregate processes with partly unanticipated developments.

With respect to institutional change, the emerging compromise points to processes at the same time gradual and consequential. Recent contributions move away from the simplistic alternative between rare and radical, rupture-like, change on the one hand and powerful path dependencies implying little if no change on the other. They point instead to incremental change with transformative results. The model of change that emerges across variants of neo-institutionalism moves away from the model of punctuated equilibrium and points instead to the cumulative effects of ongoing and often subtle changes. Mechanisms can be both exogenous and endogenous to the institutional system itself. There is still room, naturally, for external shocks and pressures but also for more subtle patterns of diffusion, translation, and interpretation. But endogenous mechanisms also play a significant role. *Bricolage* and recombination from and around a broad institutional repertoire can generate change endogenously. The rediscovery and reinvention of institutional sediments is also a possibility. Institutional conversion—where given institutional frames are redirected to new purposes—is another form of endogenous mechanism. So is institutional layering—where institutional elements are layered upon pre-existing institutional arrangements. Micro-mechanisms of engagement with institutional frames, if they are repeated, aggregated and combined, can ultimately bring about both *de*institutionalization and *re*institutionalization.

Finally, with respect to agency, the emerging compromise has five main dimensions. Firstly, a theory of agency is compatible with a theory of institutional constraints but the associated conception of agency should be a 'soft' one. From an institutionalist perspective, action is always embedded action. Secondly, institutions are constraints but also resources—and very often a rich and heterogeneous pool of resources. There is, undeniably, room for agency in the multiplicity and heterogeneity of this pool of resources. Thirdly, institutional entrepreneurship is rarely a case of individual 'heroism'. Most of the time, it reflects instead a spatially dispersed, multi-nodal and complex process; institutional entrepreneurship is often of a collective kind. Fourthly, this process also has an important temporal dimension and institutional transformation has, most of the time, several stages and sequences. Finally, the type of agency associated with institutional transformation is generally better described by terms like ambiguity, unexpected developments, and complex motives than by an image of self-interested and rational strategic action.

The issues discussed above remain important in contemporary debates. However, they are not the only frontiers for institutional theory. As a final note to this conclusion, I would like to just briefly mention three other important areas for exploration. A first challenge has to do with the interplay between institutions and transnationalization. Contemporary transnationalization implies processes of deinstitutionalization and reinstitutionalization that go across and beyond the level of the field, or of the industry, or of the nation-state. There is a need for more empirical work as well as more systematic theoretical reflection on this interplay. In particular, we may want to explore the development of transnationalization as revealing complex processes of institutional construction and emergence and reflecting in turn in many different ways upon pre-existing institutional arrangements (Djelic and Sahlin-Andersson 2006; Djelic and Quack 2008). A second challenge has to do with issues of power, interests, and hegemony. We need to go beyond benign and neutral depictions of processes of deinstitutionalization and reinstitutionalization as reflecting a combination of exogenous and endogenous mechanisms. We need to inject in our readings of those processes a healthy dose of preoccupation for associated power games. We should not stop there, though. We should also explore patterns of hegemony building and hegemony contestation. Ultimately, we should probably be looking further into the complex interplay of hegemony logics and more classical and 'visible' resource-and interest-based power games. There lies, I suggest, an important dimension of contemporary institutional dynamics. A related third challenge, obviously, is our capacity to reintegrate notions of conflict and disorder into institutional perspectives. Processes of deinstitutionalization and reinstitutionalization, institutional stabilization, institutional emergence and change all imply, as argued above, individuals, engagement, interactions, interpretation, power games, and negotiation.

All those in turn are bound to generate struggle, disorder, and conflict. Struggle, disorder, and conflict are intrinsically part, I would argue here, of an institutionalist perspective of the world. One could even go one step further and argue that this is precisely what differentiates institutionalism from structural and functionalist theories, or rational action frameworks.

REFERENCES

AGLIETTA, MICHEL (1976). *Régulations et crises du capitalisme*, (Paris: Calmann-Lévy).

BECKERT, JENS (1999). 'Agency, Entrepreneurs, and Institutional Change. The Role of Strategic Choice and Institutionalized Practices in Organizations', *Organization Studies* 20(5): 777–99.

——(2002). *Beyond the Market*, (Princeton, NJ: Princeton University Press).

BOTZEM, SEBASTIAN and SIGRID QUACK (2006). 'Contested Rules and Shifting Boundaries: International Standard Setting in Accounting', in Djelic and Sahlin-Andersson (eds.), 266–86.

BURNS, TOM and HELENA FLAM (1987). *The Shaping of Social Organization*, (London: Sage).

CAMPBELL, JOHN (1997). 'Mechanisms of Evolutionary Change in Economic Governance: Interaction, Interpretation and Bricolage', in Lars Magnusson and Jan Ottosson (eds.), *Evolutionary Economics and Path Dependence*, (Cheltenham, UK: Edward Elgar), 10–32.

——(2004). *Institutional Change and Globalization*, (Princeton, NJ: Princeton University Press).

——and OVE PEDERSEN (eds.) (1996). *Legacies of Change. Transformation of Postcommunist European Economies*, (New York: Aldine de Gruyter).

CLEMENS, ELIZABETH and JAMES COOK (1999). 'Politics and Institutionalism: Explaining Durability and Change', *Annual Review of Sociology* 25: 441–66.

COMMONS, JOHN (1934). *Institutional Economics—Its Place in Political Economy*, (New York, NY: Macmillan).

CROUCH, COLIN and H. FARRELL (2004). 'Breaking the Path of Institutional Development? Alternatives to the New Determinism', *Rationality and Society* 16(1): 5–43.

DAVIS, GERALD, DOUG MCADAM, RICHARD SCOTT, and MAYER ZALD (2005). *Social Movements and Organization Theory*, (Cambridge, UK: Cambridge University Press).

DIMAGGIO, PAUL (1988). 'Interest and Agency in Institutional Theory', in L. Zucker (ed.), *Institutional Patterns and Organizations*, (Cambridge, MA: Ballinger), 3–32.

——(1998). 'The New Institutionalisms: Avenues of Collaboration', *Journal of Institutional and Theoretical Economics* 154(4): 696–705.

——and WALTER POWELL (1983). 'The Iron Cage Revisited: Institutional Isomorphism and Collective Rationality in Organizational Fields', *American Sociological Review* 48: 147–60.

————(1991). 'Introduction', in Powell and DiMaggio (eds.), 1–38.

DJELIC, MARIE-LAURE (1998). *Exporting the American Model*, (Oxford, UK: Oxford University Press).

——(2004). 'Social Networks and Country-to-Country Transfer: Dense and Weak Ties in the Diffusion of Knowledge', *Socio-Economic Review* 2(3): 341–70.

——(2006). 'Marketization: From Intellectual Agenda to Global Policy Making', in Djelic and Sahlin-Andersson (eds.), 53–73.

——and ANTTI AINAMO (2005). 'The Telecom Industry as Cultural Industry: The Transposition of Fashion Logics into the Field of Mobile Telephony', in Candace Jones and Patricia

Thornton (eds.), *Transformations in Cultural Industries*, Research in the Sociology of Organizations Series, (Burlington, MA: Elsevier), 45–82.

——and SIGRID QUACK (eds.) (2003). *Globalization and Institutions*, (Cheltenham, UK: Edward Elgar).

————(2007). 'Overcoming Path Dependency: Path Generation in Open Systems', *Theory and Society* 36: 161–186.

————(2008). 'Institutions and Transnationalization', in Greenwood et al. (eds.), 299–323.

——and KERSTIN SAHLIN-ANDERSSON (eds.) (2006). *Transnational Governance*, (Cambridge, UK: Cambridge University Press).

DOBBIN, FRANK (1994). *Forging Industrial Policy*, (Cambridge, UK: Cambridge University Press).

DOUGLAS, MARY (1986). *How Institutions Think*, (Syracuse University Press).

ENGEL, CHRISTOPH and ADRIENNE HÉRITIER (eds.) (2003). *Linking Politics and Law*, (Baden-Baden: Nomos).

EVANS, PETER, DIETRICH RUEMEYER, and THEDA SKOCPOL (eds.) (1985). *Bringing the State Back In*, (New York, NY: Cambridge University Press).

FLIGSTEIN, NEIL (1990). *The Transformation of Corporate Control*, (Cambridge, MA: Harvard University Press).

——(1997). 'Social Skill and Institutional Theory', *American Behavioral Scientist* 40: 397–405.

——and IONA MARA-DRITA (1996). 'How to Make a Market: Reflections on the Attempt to Create a Single Market in the European Union', *American Journal of Sociology* 102(1): 1–33.

FOURCADE-GOURINCHAS, MARION (2001). 'Politics, Institutional Structures and the Rise of Economics: A Comparative Study', *Theory and Society* 30(3): 397–447.

GARUD, RAGHU and P. KARNØE (eds.) (2001). *Path Dependence and Creation*, (Mahwah: Lawrence Erlbaum Associates).

——CYNTHIA HARDY, and STEVE MAGUIRE (2007). 'Institutional Entrepreneurship as Embedded Agency: An Introduction to the Special Issue', *Organization Studies* 28(7): 957–69.

——SANJAY JAIN, and ARUN KUMARASWAMY (2002). 'Institutional Entrepreneurship in the Sponsorship of Common Technological Standards: The Case of Sun Microsystems and Java', *Academy of Management Journal*, 45: 196–214.

GREENWOOD, ROYSTON and ROY SUDDABY (2006). 'Institutional Entrepreneurship in Mature Fields: The Big Five Accounting Firms', *Academy of Management Journal* 49(1): 27–48.

——CHRISTINE OLIVER, KERSTIN SAHLIN, and ROY SUDDABY (eds.) (2008). *Handbook of Organizational Institutionalism*, (London, UK: Sage).

GREIF, AVNER (2006). *Institutions and the Path to the Modern Economy*, (New York: Cambridge University Press).

GUILLÈN, MAURO (1994). *Models of Management*, (Chicago, IL.: University of Chicago Press).

HALL, PETER and ROSEMARY TAYLOR (1996), 'Political Science and the Three New Institutionalisms', *Political Studies* 44(5): 936–57.

——and DAVID SOSKICE (eds.) (2001). *Varieties of Capitalism*, (Oxford, UK: Oxford University Press).

HARDY, CYNTHIA and STEVE MAGUIRE (2008). 'Institutional Entrepreneurship', in Greenwood et al. (eds.) (2008), 198–217.

HERBST, JÜRGEN (1965). *The German Historical School in American Scholarship*, (Ithaca, NY: Cornell University Press).

HODGSON, GEOFFREY (2001), *How Economics Forgot History*, (London, UK: Routledge).

——(2004). *The Evolution of Institutional Economics*, (London, UK: Routledge).

IGGERS, GEORG (1968). *The German Conception of History*, (Middleton, CT: Wesleyan University Press).

JACOBY, WADE (2000). *Imitation and Politics*, (Ithaca, NY: Cornell University Press).

JOHNSON, J. (2001). 'Path Contingency in Postcommunist Transformations', *Comparative Politics* 33(3): 253–74.

JONES, GEOFFREY and DAN WADHWANI (2006). 'Schumpeter's Plea: Rediscovering History and Relevance in the Study of Entrepreneurship', *HBS Working Paper—06-036*, (Cambridge, MA: Harvard University).

KATO, JUNKO (1996). 'Institutions and Rationality in Politics—Three Varieties of Neo-institutionalism', *British Journal of Political Science* 26(4): 553–82.

KLEINER, THIBAUT (2003). 'Building up an Asset Management Industry: Forays of an Anglo-Saxon Logic into French Business System', in Djelic and Quack, 57–82.

KOSLOWSKI, PETER (ed.) (1997). *Methodology of the Social Sciences, Ethics and Economics in the Newer Historical School*, (Berlin: Springer).

KRASNER, STEPHEN (1983). *International Regimes*, (Ithaca, NY: Cornell University Press).

KUHN, THOMAS (1962). *The Structure of Scientific Revolutions*, (Chicago, IL.: University of Chicago Press).

LAWRENCE, THOMAS and ROY SUDDABY (2006). 'Institutions and Institutional Work', in Stewart Clegg, Cynthia Hardy, Thomas Lawrence and W. Nord (eds.), *Handbook of Organization Studies*, 2nd ed., (London, UK: Sage), 215–54.

LEVI, MARGARET (1989). *Of Rule and Revenue*, (Berkeley, CA: University of California Press).

LEVY, DAVID and MAUREEN SCULLY (2007). 'The Institutional Entrepreneur as Modern Prince: The Strategic Face of Power in Contested Fields', *Organization Studies* 28(7): 971–92.

LOUNSBURY, MICHAEL and ELLEN CRUMLEY (2007). 'New Practice Creation: An Institutional Perspective on Innovation', *Organization Studies* 28(7): 993–1012.

MAGUIRE, S., CYNTHIA HARDY, and T. B. LAWRENCE (2004). 'Institutional Entrepreneurship in Emerging Fields: HIV/AIDS Treatment Advocacy in Canada', *Academy of Management Journal* 47: 657–79.

MARCH, JAMES (1981). 'Footnotes to Organizational Change', *Administrative Science Quarterly* 26(4): 563–77.

——and JOHAN OLSEN (1984). 'The New Institutionalism: Organizational Factors in Political Life', *American Political Science Review* 78: 734–49.

MAURICE, MARC and ARNDT SORGE (eds.) (2000). *Embedding Organizations*, (Amsterdam and Philadelphia: Benjamins).

MÉNARD, CLAUDE (ed.) (2000). *Institutions, Contracts and Organizations: Perspectives from New Institutional Economics*, (Cheltenham, UK: Edward Elgar).

MEYER, JOHN (1996). 'Otherhood: The Promulgation and Transmission of Ideas in the Modern Organizational Environment', in Czarniawska and Sevón (eds.), *Translating Organizational Change*, (Berlin: de Gruyter), 241–52.

——and ROWAN, BRIAN (1977). 'Institutionalized Organizations: Formal Structure as Myth and Ceremony', *American Journal of Sociology*, 83: 340–63.

——JOHN BOLI and G. THOMAS (1994). 'Ontology and Rationalization in the Western Cultural Account', in Richard Scott, John Meyer, and associates, *Institutional Environments and Organizations*, (London: Sage).

MILGROM, PAUL, DOUGLASS NORTH, and BARRY WEINGAST (1990). 'The Role of Institutions in the Revival of Trade: The Law Merchant, Private Judges and the Champagne Fairs', *Economics and Politics* 2: 1–23.

MOMMSEN, WOLFGANG (1965). 'Max Weber's Political Sociology and his Philosophy of World History', *International Social Science Journal* 17.

MORGAN, GLENN and IZUMI KUBO (2005). 'Beyond Path Dependency? Constructing New Models for Institutional Change: The Case of Capital Markets in Japan', *Socio-Economic Review* 3: 55–82.

——R. WHITLEY, and E. MOEN (eds.) (2005). *Changing Capitalisms?*, (Oxford, UK: Oxford University Press).

——PEER HULL KRISTENSEN, and RICHARD WHITLEY (eds.) (2001). *The Multinational Firm: Organizing across National and Institutional Boundaries*, (Oxford, UK: Oxford University Press).

MUNIR, KUMAL and NELSON PHILLIPS (2005). 'The Birth of the Kodak Moment: Institutional Entrepreneurship and the Adoption of New Technologies', *Organization Studies* 26(11): 1665–87.

NORTH, DOUGLASS (1990). *Institutions, Institutional Change and Economic Performance*, (Cambridge, UK: Cambridge University Press).

——(2005). *Understanding the Process of Economic Change*, (Princeton, NJ: Princeton University Press).

——and ROBERT THOMAS (1973). *The Rise of the Western World*, (Cambridge, UK: Cambridge University Press).

OFFE, CLAUS (1995). 'Designing Institutions for East European Transition', in Jerzy Hausner, Bob Jessop, and Klaus Nielsen (eds.), *Strategic Choice and Path-dependency in Post Socialism*, (Aldershot: Edward Elgar), 47–66.

PADGETT, JOHN (2001). 'Organizational Genesis, Identity and Control: The Transformation of Banking in Renaissance Florence', in A. Cassella and J. Rauch (eds.), *Markets and Networks*, (New York: Russell Sage Foundation).

——and CHRISTOPHER ANSELL (1993). 'Robust Action and the Rise of the Medici, 1400–1434', *American Journal of Sociology* 98, 1259–319.

PARSONS, TALCOTT (1976). 'Clarence Ayres's Economics and Sociology', in William Breit and William Culbertson (eds.), *Science and Ceremony: The Institutional Economics of C.E. Ayres*, (Austin, TX: University of Texas Press).

PEMPEL, T (1998). *Regime Shift: Comparative Dynamics of the Japanese Political Economy*, (Ithaca, NY: Cornell University Press).

PERROW, CHARLES (1986). *Complex Organizations*, (New York, NY: McGraw Hill).

POLYANI, KARL (1944). *The Great Transformation*, (New York, NY: Rinehard & Company).

POWELL, WALTER and PAUL DiMAGGIO (1991). *The New Institutionalism in Organizational Analysis*, (Chicago, IL.: University of Chicago Press).

QUACK, SIGRID and GLENN MORGAN (2000). 'National Capitalisms, Global Competition and Economic Performance: An Introduction', in Sigrid Quack, Glenn Morgan, and Richard Whitley (eds.), *National Capitalisms, Global Competition and Economic Performance*, (Amsterdam and Philadelphia: Benjamins), 2–26.

SCHNEIBERG, MARC (2007). 'What's on the Path? Path Dependence, Organizational Diversity and the Problem of Institutional Change in the US Economy, 1900–50', *Socio-Economic Review* 5(1): 47–80.

——and ELIZABETH CLEMENS (2006). 'The Typical Tools for the Job: Research Strategies in Institutional Analysis', *Sociological Theory* 24(3): 195–227.

——and MICHAEL LOUNSBURY (2008). 'Social Movements and Institutional Analysis', in Greenwood et al., 650–72.

SCHNEIDER, DIETER (1995). 'Historicism and Business Ethics', in Peter Koslowski (ed.), *The Theory of Ethical Economy in the Historical School*, (Berlin: Springer), 173–202.

SCHUMPETER, JOSEPH (1947). 'The Creative Response in Economic History,' *The Journal of Economic History* 7: 149–59.

——(1949). 'Economic Theory and Entrepreneurial History.' in *Change and the Entrepreneur*, (Cambridge, MA: Harvard University Press).

SCHWEITZER, ARTHUR (1975). 'Frank Knight's Social Economics', *History of Political Economy*, 7(3): 279–92.

SCOTT, W. RICHARD (1995). *Institutions and Organizations*, (London, UK: Sage).

——(2008). *Institutions and Organizations*, 3rd ed., (London, UK: Sage).

SELZNICK, PHILIPP (1957). *Leadership in Administration*, (New York, NY: Harper & Row).

SEWELL, WILLIAM (1992). 'A Theory of Structure: Duality, Agency and Transformation', *American Journal of Sociology* 98(1): 1–29.

SHEPSLE, KENNETH (1986). 'Institutional Equilibrium and Equilibrium Institutions', in Herbert Weisberg (ed.), *The Science of Politics*, (New York, NY: Agathon Press).

SHIONOYA, YUICHI (ed.) (2001). *The German Historical School: The Historical and Ethical Approach to Economics*, (London, UK: Routledge).

SKOCPOL, THEDA (1979). *States and Social Revolutions*, (Cambridge, UK: Cambridge University Press).

SORGE, ARNDT (2005). *The Global and the Local*, (Oxford: Oxford University Press).

STARK, D. (1992). 'Path Dependence and Privatization Strategies in East Central Europe', *East European Politics and Societies* 6(1): 17–54.

STEINMO, SVEN (2001). 'The New Institutionalism', in Barry Clark and Joe Foweraker (eds.), *The Encyclopedia of Democratic Thought*, (London, UK: Routledge).

——KATHLEEN THELEN, and FRANK LONGSTRETH (eds.) (1992). *Structuring Politics*, (New York, NY: Cambridge University Press).

STREECK, WOLFGANG and KATHLEEN THELEN (eds.) (2005). *Beyond Continuity*, (Oxford, UK: Oxford University Press).

——and KOZO YAMAMURA (eds.) (2001). *The Origins of Nonliberal Capitalism: Germany and Japan in Comparison*, (Ithaca, NY: Cornell University Press).

TEMPEL, ANNE and PETER WALGENBACH (2007). 'Global Standardization of Organizational Forms and Management Practices? What New Institutionalism and the Business-Systems Approach Can Learn from Each Other', *Journal of Management Studies* 44(1): 1–24.

THELEN, KATHLEEN (1999). 'Historical Institutionalism in Comparative Perspectives', *Annual Review of Political Science* 2: 369–404.

——(2003). 'How Institutions Evolve. Insights from Comparative Historical Analysis', in James Mahoney and D. Rueschemeyer (eds.), *Comparative Historical Analysis in the Social Sciences*, (Cambridge, UK: Cambridge University Press), 208–40.

——and SVEN STEINMO (1992). 'Historical Institutionalism in Comparative Politics', in Sven Steinmo, Kathleen Thelen, and Frank Longstreth (eds.), 1–32.

VEBLEN, THORSTEIN (1901). 'Gustav Schmoller's Economics', *Quarterly Journal of Economics* 16(1): 69–93.

——(1904). *The Theory of Business Enterprise*, (New York, NY: New American Library, Mentor Books).

WEBER, MAX (1927). *General Economic History*, trans. Frank Knight from the German edition (1923), (London, UK: Allen & Unwin).

——(1949). *Max Weber on the Methodology of the Social Sciences*, trans. and ed. Edward Shils and Henri Finch, (Glencoe, IL: Free Press).

——(1978). *Economy and Society*, 2 vol., eds. Günther Roth and Claus Wittich, (Berkeley, CA: University of California Press).

WEED, FRANK (1981). 'Interpreting "Institutions" in Veblen's Evolutionary Theory', *American Journal of Economics and Sociology* 40(1): 67–78.

WESTNEY, ELEANOR (1987). *Imitation and Innovation,* (Cambridge, MA: Harvard University Press).

WHITLEY, RICHARD (1999). *Divergent Capitalisms,* (Oxford, UK: Oxford University Press).

WILLIAMSON, OLIVER (1975). *Markets and Hierarchies,* (New York: Free Press).

ZARET, DAVID (1980). 'From Weber to Parsons and Schutz: The Eclipse of History in Modern Social Theory', *American Journal of Sociology* 80(5): 1180–201.

ZEITLIN, J. and G. HERRIGEL (eds.) (2000). Americanization and its Limits, Oxford University Press.

CHAPTER 2

BEYOND COMPARATIVE STATICS: HISTORICAL INSTITUTIONAL APPROACHES TO STABILITY AND CHANGE IN THE POLITICAL ECONOMY OF LABOR

KATHLEEN THELEN

INTRODUCTION

These are turbulent times in labour markets—and in labour market research. More volatile international markets, a resurgence of neo-liberal ideology, and the secular decline of manufacturing have shaken up traditional politics in the advanced industrial countries. These developments have prompted programmatic shifts within and among the main political parties, precipitated coalitional realignments among key political-economic actors, rearranged the 'winners' and 'losers', unleashed new demands, and confronted policymakers with a host of new challenges. The same trends and dynamics have also shaken up scholarship on labour market institutions and political economy, exposing gaps and shortcomings in the frameworks on which scholars have long relied to make sense of politics and outcomes in the advanced political economies.

This chapter will consider the challenges confronting students of political economy in the contemporary period, which can be characterized as the task of moving from the analysis of comparative statics to a more genuinely dynamic model of institutional evolution and change. It considers how well two important strands of the literature on the political economy of the advanced industrial democracies deal with the theoretical and methodological challenges that recent developments pose. One highly influential stream of scholarship, the varieties of capitalism (VoC) framework, is based on national models defined by strong institutional complementarities across the various institutional arenas (industrial relations, finance, training, corporate governance) that together define distinctive models of capitalism. This theory emphasizes the constitutive power of institutions in shaping the strategies of key political-economic actors, particularly employers, and sees powerful feedback loops at work that sustain distinctive trajectories of development cross-nationally even in the face of common challenges. A second, 'pragmatic constructivist' (PC) perspective contrasts sharply with the varieties of capitalism approach on many dimensions.[1] Scholars in this school do not view political economies as coherent national models but rather as complex assemblages of often contradictory features. Against the VoC view of dynamic resiliency and strong path dependency, the PC school emphasizes agency, institutional fluidity, and historical contingency.

I use an examination of the strengths and weaknesses of these two literatures as a foundation for elaborating an alternative historical-institutional approach to stability and change in labour market and other political-economic institutions. In constructing this alternative, I underscore the problems associated with research strategies that overemphasize one component—the structural-institutional or the agentic-contingent—to the neglect of the other. The literature on VoC—while deeply attuned to the impact of institutions—is sometimes insufficiently historical in the way it conceives of these institutions and neglectful of the political (as opposed to

---

[1] The term 'pragmatic constructivism' comes from Gary Herrigel, one of its most prominent practitioners (personal communication, 2 February 2008).

efficiency-based) dynamics behind their reproduction.[2] The alternative, PC approach also falls short but for the opposite reason: while appropriately historical and more centrally concerned with issues of change, this body of work is insufficiently institutional, frequently overstating the degrees of freedom actors enjoy, and understating the extent to which existing institutions shape their strategic responses to new challenges. While the VoC perspective overemphasizes resilience and institutional robustness, the PC approach overemphasizes fluidity and contingency. When it comes to change, their strengths and weaknesses are mirror images of one another.

Moreover, as different as these two approaches are on many dimensions, scholars subscribing to each of them appear to share a common emphasis on institutions as devised and sustained by actors in order to achieve joint gains through cooperation. Conceiving institutions in this way, however, often obscures the power-political, distributional foundations of the institutions of the political economy and diverts attention from the political struggles that shape and reshape these institutions over time. In contrast to both these perspectives, I will argue that it is not the problem-solving capacities of institutions and rules but instead their power-based underpinnings and the distributional contests these inspire that hold the key to understanding both stability and change in labour market institutions. Considerations of power lie at the centre of historical-institutionalism as an approach to the study of politics, and power-distributional struggles define this approach's distinctive perspective on institutional evolution and change.

The chapter consists of four sections. I begin by sketching out the contemporary state of affairs both with respect to empirical developments in labour market institutions and especially in the theoretical apparatus on which we have traditionally relied to make sense of these. I argue that institutionalists face a new challenge to move beyond the analysis of comparative statics and into a truly dynamic institutionalism that can comprehend not just institutional effects, but institutional reproduction and change. Second, I consider the strengths and weaknesses of the VoC and PC approaches to the study of labour market institutions and political-economic change. Third, I make the case for an alternative historical-institutionalist framework for analyzing institutions and institutional change that weaves together key insights from the VoC and PC literatures, but combines these in a way that avoids both the determinism of the former and the indeterminacy of the latter. A fourth section concludes and suggests an agenda for research.

BEYOND COMPARATIVE STATICS

The past two decades have witnessed important changes in the political economies of the advanced industrial countries, particularly, but by no means exclusively, with respect to labour market institutions. Changing patterns of competition in international trade, the

---

[2] The most recent work in this vein has begun to address these weaknesses, however. See especially (Hall 2007) and (Iversen and Soskice 2009).

decline of manufacturing, demographic shifts, technological advances, and changing gender relations all contribute to defining an economic and political context that is very different from the 'Golden Age' of post-war capitalism in the 1950s and 1960s. Higher unemployment, chronic low growth, and severe budget constraints in most countries intensify the problems policymakers face and limit the room for manoeuvre they have to address these issues.

Beyond the practical and policy challenges, contemporary trends pose some formidable theoretical challenges, because these same empirical developments have been associated with some very significant changes in many of the political-economic institutions that regulate, mediate, and shape the operation of labour markets. To appreciate what this means for the study of labour markets, we must recall that, traditionally, most of the literature on the political economy of the advanced industrial countries has been organized around the analysis of comparative statics, in which institutions are invoked as a key explanatory (independent or intervening) variable shaping diverse policy and political outcomes cross-nationally. The idea, in short, has been that the institutional arrangements that characterize different models of capitalism are important for the way they mediate how countries can and will respond to various shocks.

This is a venerable tradition not just in the literature on political economy but on institutionalism more generally. The pioneering work of Peter Katzenstein, and in particular his agenda-setting *Between Power and Plenty*, was a landmark study in political economy, but also in the emergence of what became known as the new institutionalism in political science (Katzenstein 1978). The same kinds of arguments—invoking institutions to explain persistent cross-national diversity in outcomes—run though the entire literature since that time. Studies of corporatist interest intermediation in the 1970s and 1980s, for example, drew attention to the impact on macroeconomic outcomes of differences in the strength and structure of organized labour in the developed democracies (see, e.g. Cameron 1984; Schmitter 1981). Revisions to this literature by Calmfors and Driffill and, in a different way, by David Soskice, refined our understandings of these connections while also drawing attention to the role of employers and their associations in sustaining positive economic outcomes in Europe's 'organized' political economies. (Calmfors and Driffill 1988; Soskice 1990). Wolfgang Streeck's influential work on the German model as a system of 'beneficial constraints' identified at much closer range the specific mechanisms that 'forced and facilitated' employers to respond to market developments in ways that were consistent with high wages and strong unions (Streeck 1991; 1997). The common thread in all of this work was to identify the core institutional features of different models of capitalism and to show how these drove different employer strategies and policy responses which were in turn associated with distinct distributional outcomes across the advanced industrial world.

Against this backdrop, the most important aspect of the current period (both in the labour market itself but also in the scholarship designed to make sense of developments within it) is that many of the institutions that served as theoretical anchors for explanations of cross-national variation are *themselves* under increasing strain and in many cases undergoing important changes. Take for example collective bargaining institutions, a cornerstone component of virtually all accounts of cross-national diversity. Industrial relations institutions, and specifically centralized collective bargaining, have been the object of intense reform efforts, in some cases resulting in explicit formal-institutional reconfigurations (e.g. Britain and Denmark) and in other cases undergoing more subtle transformations through erosion or drift (e.g. Germany and France) (Pontusson and Swenson 1996; Wallerstein, Golden, and Lange 1997; Hassel 1999; Thelen and van Wijnbergen 2003). Likewise, vocational training institutions—so central to Streeck's original beneficial constraints arguments, as well as to the contemporary varieties of capitalism literature—are under intense strain due to technological changes and the transition from manufacturing to services (Culpepper and Thelen 2007; Thelen 2007). Welfare regimes, too, are currently undergoing significant reforms across the advanced industrial countries, as governments respond to the cumulative pressures of long-term unemployment, demographic shifts, and ongoing fiscal crisis (Hacker 2005; Palier and Martin 2007; Levy 1999; Häusermann forthcoming).

We have a situation, in other words, in which many of the institutional arrangements that scholars have traditionally invoked to explain cross-national differences in policy and political responses to common pressures are themselves in flux as a result of these same pressures. This situation poses a real intellectual challenge. Although in the meantime institutional analysis has flourished and also spawned different variants (Hall and Taylor 1996), none of these traditionally has been very adept at dealing with the question of how institutions themselves evolve and change over time.[3]

Until very recently most institutionalist scholars have fallen back on a punctuated equilibrium model that encourages us to think of change as abrupt and discontinuous, characterized by the breakdown of one equilibrium or set of institutions and practices and its replacement with another. The problem with this is that most of the changes we can observe in labour market institutions—and political-economic institutions generally—are not of a variety that can be comfortably characterized in terms of wholesale breakdown or collapse (Hacker 2005; Palier 2005; Levy 2005). Instead, they take the form of shifts that are gradual and incremental, though cumulatively transformative (Streeck and Thelen 2005b; Djelic and Quack 2003). In some cases, we observe creeping changes at the formal-institutional level, but in other cases significant shifts occur under the veneer of high levels of formal stability, as institutions are 'hollowed out' through defections, or are subtly redirected to serve purposes that are very distant from their original aims (e.g. Hassel 1999; Thelen 2004). As a result, many of these changes do not even 'register' as change in the context of many prominent theoretical frameworks (Höpner 2007; Thelen 2009).

---

[3] This is beginning to change, as a growing number of scholars confront this issue. For a more extended discussion see Mahoney and Thelen, 2010: chapter 1.

The challenge for institutionalists, in short, is to capture the processes that are subtly transforming labour market institutions in the rich democracies, and in so doing, to move institutional analysis beyond its traditional 'comfort zone' of comparative statics to generate a more genuinely dynamic account of institutional reproduction and change. The next two sections discuss two important perspectives in the literature that represent distinctive approaches to these problems, the varieties of capitalism approach and the pragmatic constructivist approach. I discuss the characteristic strengths and weaknesses of these two bodies of scholarship, before turning to my own alternative, historical-institutionalist, account.

Two Perspectives on Political Economy and Institutional Change

Varieties of capitalism

The most prominent framework in the literature has been proposed by Peter A. Hall and David Soskice in their influential book, *Varieties of Capitalism* (Hall and Soskice 2001). Hall and Soskice offer a theory built around a core distinction between 'coordinated' versus 'liberal' market economies (CMEs and LMEs, in the shorthand). The key difference between these broad families of political economy relates to differences in the capacity of employers to coordinate among themselves (and with labour) in order to achieve joint gains through cooperation. The framework is based on an equilibrium model in which CMEs and LMEs represent two distinct and robust systems with strong self-enforcing tendencies. The systemic quality of individual political economies is captured in the notion of institutional complementarities that is central to the VoC framework. Labour market institutions are embedded in, and tightly coupled with, other political-economic arrangements (including financial institutions, structures of corporate governance, and welfare institutions). Political economies thus represent coherent clusters of complementary institutions, with liberal market economies relying on markets to coordinate endeavours within these various arenas, and coordinated market economies featuring institutions that facilitate non-market coordination in these realms.[4]

The theory was conceived against the backdrop of arguments predicting that globalization and deindustrialization would undermine the more egalitarian political economies of Europe, by driving competitive deregulation in labour market and other institutions in these CMEs. In sharp contrast to these theories that foresaw convergence

---

[4] There is no claim that all countries represent 'pure types'. However, Hall and Soskice do suggest that purer types may be more efficient (Hall and Soskice 2003), and Hall and Gingerich provide some evidence that institutional coherence is associated with higher growth rates (Hall and Gingerich 2009).

on the Anglo-Saxon model, Hall and Soskice maintained that contemporary pressures would if anything enhance the difference between liberal and coordinated market economies. Where other scholars cited waning labour strength as the key variable producing convergence, VoC attributes the resiliency of distinctive models of capitalism above all to the divergent preferences of employers in LMEs and CMEs.

Because these distinctive types of political economy support different firm strategies in the market, employers and their governments will confront new challenges by seeking to strengthen the particular foundations on which their competitive national advantage is based (Hall and Soskice 2003; Hall 2007). So while firms in liberal market economies like the United States will have an interest in intensifying market pressures (deregulation), those in CMEs will seek to retain previously built coordinating capacities. Thus, for example, manufacturing employers in coordinated market economies are heavily invested in production strategies that rely on an ample supply of skilled labour. For this reason they will not abandon coordinated training and collective bargaining regimes at the first sign of labour weakness because they in fact depend on these institutions for their continued success in the market. These employers will also not necessarily seize on political opportunities to dismantle strong works councils, because such arrangements traditionally have guarded against problems of 'hold up' that can plague firms that rely on the kinds of production strategies they are pursuing. These institutions are valued because they underpin and sustain the long-term and trustful relations between workers and employers that are so important for the success of manufacturing strategies based on flexibility and high-quality production (Hall and Soskice 2001: 22–6). Although LMEs and CMEs are not immutable, they exhibit strong self-enforcing tendencies.

The varieties of capitalism perspective has considerable strengths and merits. Its influence can be measured in the outpouring of publications it has generated, as well as in the fruitful research agenda it has inspired. One of the attractions of the theory is that it provided a powerful and much needed corrective to a previous wave of theorizing that saw traditional labour institutions, especially in 'coordinated market economies', as fragile in the face of neo-liberal ideology and more volatile international markets since the 1980s. Such convergence theories have not been borne out (e.g. Kitschelt et al. 1999; Hall and Gingerich 2009). Collective bargaining institutions, for example, are important for a range of distributional outcomes including wage dispersion and income equality. Despite some important changes in CMEs, industrial relations in these countries have mostly remained quite centralized especially compared to those in LMEs (Wallerstein, Golden, and Lange 1997). In some cases where significant decentralization occurred (as in Sweden or Denmark), bargaining has re-equilibrated at a high level of coordination. Given further deregulation and ongoing declines in unionization in LMEs, VoC's predictions of a continuing gap between the two families of countries seem to be well vindicated. Welfare regimes, similarly, continue to diverge in terms of both coverage and generosity in CMEs and LMEs. Despite reforms in all countries, unemployment, disability, sick pay, and old age coverage is still much more generous in the former than in the latter (Pontusson 2005; Hall and Gingerich 2009).

Many have criticized VoC as a static model, but this charge confuses the theoretical framework with the institutional outcomes it predicts. Like other equilibrium theories, VoC provides a compelling and highly *dynamic* account of institutional reproduction. The theory draws attention to powerful feedback effects and specifically to employers' own continuing interest in the institutional arrangements around which they have organized their strategies in the market. The core claim is not that institutions survive through inertia, but rather that because comparative advantage within different countries is premissed on different production strategies relying on different institutional and policy supports, employers and policymakers will seek to retain and enhance those capacities in the face of new challenges.

Empirical research has validated many of these assertions, demonstrating that employer preferences do provide a better explanation of the sometimes surprising resilience of many of the institutions in CMEs, in the face of new competitive pressures, than rival theories that attribute these outcomes to institutional 'stickiness' or even successful union defence (e.g. Thelen 2002; Callaghan 2009). Moreover, while some have criticized VoC's over-attention to employer interests (e.g. Pontusson, Rueda, and Way 2002), it does not seem too far-fetched to think that, in capitalist economies, employers do exercise very significant powers. We can agree that employers cannot determine outcomes unilaterally, but it also seems clear that where capitalists are intent on changing institutions, even the strongest labour movements are unable to resist (as the cases of bargaining decentralization in Sweden and Denmark illustrate).

In short, the strengths of varieties of capitalism are many, particularly in explaining broad and persistent cross-national differences in institutions and policy outcomes. However, the theory has fared somewhat less well when it comes to explaining change over time within particular countries. Labour market institutions are under severe strain, and welfare policies have been considerably revamped in almost all the advanced industrial countries in the past decades. These changes are significant, even if the results do not suddenly transport countries from the CME to the LME 'column'. A part of the difficulty the VoC framework has in capturing and analysing these changes thus has to do with the rather broad and dichotomous categories on which the theory rests. Another problem, though, is rooted in the theory's equilibrium view of institutions. As Greif and Laitin have pointed out, in equilibrium models all behaviour is endogenous, which means that, short of exogenous shifts or shocks, all feedback is positive and operates to shore up existing arrangements (Greif and Laitin 2004).

Both of these features help to explain a certain tendency in the VoC literature to code many of the changes one observes in CMEs as minor adjustments undertaken to shore up an existing model rather than as a fundamental challenge to that model—a practice that sometimes imposes rather high demands on 'real' change to be recognized as such (Streeck and Thelen 2005*b*). For example, all CMEs have undertaken important reforms to their welfare and labour market institutions—introducing more stringent unemployment benefits, more vigorous activation policies, supplementary private pensions, and other measures aimed at cost containment. Clearly these welfare regimes remain distinct from LMEs, but it is also hard to write off the changes that have occurred as trivial. Based on previous research, what we know for sure is that institutional change in advanced political economies is unlikely to take the form of a direct frontal attack on traditional institutions and more likely to proceed incrementally (Palier 2005; Hacker 2005; Streeck and Thelen 2005*b*). The varieties of capitalism framework in the past seemed ill-suited to capturing and analysing the kinds of gradual and incremental, but cumulatively significant, shifts that are transforming the political economies of the advanced industrial democracies.[5]

As I have pointed out elsewhere (Thelen 2002; Thelen and Kume 2006), the core distinction around which the dichotomy between LMEs and CMEs is premissed, employer coordination, is often based on a highly composite (national-level) picture of employer interests. Thus, in this literature, employers in CMEs are seen as 'invested' in various institutions (e.g. vocational training or centralized collective bargaining) and from this it follows that they will have an interest in maintaining those institutions— among other things, as the site within which they can continue to coordinate among themselves, to the benefit of all. However contemporary market conditions do not just activate new conflicts between labour and capital (as is widely known and theorized); they also activate new tensions and strains among firms and industries that are differently situated in domestic and national markets (see, e.g. Iversen 1996, 1999; Carlin and Soskice 2009). In this context it is important to think of coordination as a political process and something that has to be constantly nurtured and patched up, and sometimes even renegotiated completely (Hall and Thelen 2009). Only by doing so can we capture the power-distributional underpinnings of coordination and the political conflicts that are crucial to understanding change in these institutions over time.

Historical accounts have amply documented that the institutional arrangements governing labour markets in the advanced industrial countries are the product of political struggles in which there are winners and losers on both sides of the class divide (Mares 2000; Swenson 2002; Thelen 2004). And as an empirical matter we know that today, as well, there are tensions at work behind many of the institutions around which the VoC framework is organized. Even setting aside conflicts between labour and capital and focusing special attention—as VoC does—on firms, it is clear that different segments of capital have different interests, and conflicts among them are likely to be constantly activated by changing international conditions. Coordination, in other words, is a deeply political outcome and the particular forms it takes reflect the exercise of political power by specific identifiable coalitions over others. This is a point that is sometimes obscured by the VoC emphasis on efficiency (but see Hall 2007; Hall and Thelen 2009; Iversen and Soskice 2009).

In sum, the varieties of capitalism literature is persuasive in laying out the institutional logic within which employers conceive of their interests and formulate their strategies. However, the approach in the past has had a tendency to overpredict stability in institutions and to neglect the political as opposed to the utilitarian or market logic on which these institutions rest. The second literature noted above provides a stark alternative.

---

[5] But see (Hall 2007) for an explication of the path dependent nature of change.

Pragmatic Constructivism

An alternative approach, which its practitioners refer to as 'pragmatic constructivism' is in some ways the mirror image of VoC. Whereas the VoC perspective emphasizes distinctive national models and broad families of capitalism defined by their institutional features, pragmatic constructivists stress institutional diversity and fluidity—within countries and over time as well as across countries. Scholars in this school insist that political economies cannot be studied as 'national models' because they embody a range of different types of arrangements that often stand in tension with one another. As Jonathan Zeitlin puts it with reference to welfare state regimes: 'Most national cases . . . do not fully correspond to a single pure type . . . but comprise instead an idiosyncratic and historically contingent mix of institutions and programs derived from different models' (Zeitlin 2003: 13). Sceptical of VoC's claims of long-standing systemic differences between CMEs and LMEs, pragmatic constructivists instead emphasize how single countries contain within them diverse forms of economic governance (Berk and Schneiberg 2005; Herrigel 2007: 482).

Following from this, pragmatic constructivists do not see a world in which the institutional arrangements governing various aspects of a country's political economy exhibit the kind of institutional complementarities or coherence that are central to the VoC framework. Instead, countries represent complex configurations featuring 'improbable combinations' of institutions and organizational forms (Herrigel 2007: 481). In this view as well, the landscapes of contemporary political economies are littered with the remnants of what Barrington Moore once called 'suppressed historical alternatives' that pragmatic constructivists see as resources that remain available to actors as they cope with new problems and challenges (Sabel and Zeitlin 1997a; Berk and Schneiberg 2005: 47). Where such internal heterogeneity might be seen by VoC scholars as a source of inefficiency (e.g., Hall and Gingerich 2009), political constructivists see this kind of diversity as a crucial 'adaptive resource', and some suggest that 'mongrel' systems may be more robust than purer models (Zeitlin 2003: 14; see also Crouch 2001).

Finally, where VoC stresses that the historically evolved institutions that characterize CMEs and LMEs (and distinguish them from one another) are resilient over time, pragmatic constructivists emphasize institutional fluidity and historical contingency. Far from being 'locked in' or subject to any particularly stabilizing feedback effects, institutions in this view are extremely fragile and constantly under reconstruction. In Herrigel's words: ' . . . complexes of rules are highly contingent constructs and are recurrently recomposed' (Herrigel 2008: 114). Pragmatic constructivists see institutional rules as temporary resting places, the products of ongoing experimentation, learning, and deliberation, devised by actors as 'corrigible' solutions to the changing problems they confront in their dealings in the market and with each other (Sabel 1994).

The strengths and weaknesses of this approach are in many ways the mirror image of those of the VoC framework. One of the strengths of the approach is that it takes account of important changes over time, and of variety within countries, that are frequently obscured in the VoC framework. In contrast to the more stylized VoC accounts that downplay sub-national or even national specifics in favour of drawing out broad patterns across the advanced industrial world as a whole, the PC literature provides richer accounts, often focusing on individual regions, sectors, companies, or specific time periods (e.g., the contributions to Sabel and Zeitlin 1997*b*; also Berk 1994; Herrigel 1996; Whitford 2005; Berk and Schneiberg 2005). PC scholars stress institutional incongruity and complexity, thus complicating the easy assignment of a country to a particular 'model' of capitalism.

Related to this, pragmatic constructivists are keenly attuned to changes, including subtle changes that do not show up on the radar screen in other approaches. Where VoC stresses historical continuity within—and durable differences between—LMEs and CMEs over time, PC scholars see institutions as more mutable, and observe as well elements of diffusion, exchange, and blending across the LME/CME divide. These studies thus uncover elements of coordination in putatatively 'liberal' market economies like the United States (Berk and Schneiberg 2005), or document intense regional differences within a single country like Germany or Italy (Herrigel 1996), or identify moments of high contingency at which either coordinated or liberal responses appeared to be equally possible (Zeitlin 1996).

Pragmatic constructivist accounts of current developments likewise downplay national homogeneity and historical continuity in favour of emphasis on 'complexity, variety, process, and recombinatory change over time within cases' (Herrigel 2007: 482). Hybridization, experimentation, deliberation, learning, and the diffusion of ideas figure prominently in these accounts as shaping policy responses and reconfiguring institutions along lines that defy easy categorization as unequivocally 'liberal' or 'coordinated' (Zeitlin 2000). Danish flexicurity is given as a contemporary example of the kind of creative combinations and institutional hybridity that PC scholarship underscores (e.g., Campbell and Pedersen 2007; also Zeitlin 2003; Crouch 2005).

Finally and again in contrast to structuralist accounts, PC assigns a prominent role to agency. Rather than responding mechanically to institutional constraints and opportunities, PC emphasizes agents who improvise, borrow freely, and learn from other actors. Indeed—and this is the constructivist part of pragmatic constructivism—these scholars suggests that agents' mutual interactions with one another can cause them to rethink not just their strategies but their own roles and identities in a more profound way. Thus, in one of the foundational texts in this genre, Sabel argues that 'discrete transactions among independent actors become continual, joint formulations of common ends in which the participants' identities are reciprocally defining... [Through deliberation and interaction] parties can reinterpret themselves and their relation to each other by elaborating a common understanding of the world' (Sabel 1994: 138). Herrigel echoes this same point in a different context: 'Actors, enacting roles that the rules are designed to govern, continually reflect upon and evaluate the adequacy of both their roles and of the governing rules as they struggle to cope with the challenges and opportunities of their situation' (Herrigel 2008: 114; see also Sabel and Zeitlin 2008 on the role of deliberation and learning; and Berk and Schneiberg 2005).

We can thus see that some of the strengths of the PC approach lie precisely in the way they illuminate issues and areas that are underdeveloped in more structuralist accounts. The weaknesses of this approach are, then, also in many ways the mirror image of those of VoC. First, in emphasizing contingency and institutional fluidity, PC scholars frequently overstate the degrees of freedom that actors typically enjoy. Pragmatic constructivists sometimes distinguish themselves from structuralists by suggesting that institutional rules are highly malleable. Actors experiment with roles and rules to reach 'provisional' solutions that they 'embrace . . . only when they help solve the problems that have been collectively identified'; in the process, roles are redefined and 'rules that prove to be inadequate or irrelevant to the emerging situation are either changed or ignored' (Herrigel 2008: 114; see also Sabel and Zeitlin 2008; Sabel 2006).

Clearly however, many of the core institutions and rules around which much of the institutionalist literature is organized, enacted politically and underwritten by sanctions, cannot be easily put aside. In the area of labour markets, the emphasis on institutional fluidity is unhelpful if it diverts attention from some of the more enduring differences, e.g. between countries with legal frameworks supporting strong unions and employer associations and those without such arrangements. We do not have to subscribe to a particularly deterministic view of institutions to appreciate how basic legal infrastructures (anchoring union rights to organize for example) shape broad distributional outcomes in rather profound ways. For example, despite inevitable deviations and informal rule-breaking, more centralized wage bargaining institutions are demonstrably associated with more egalitarian wages (Wallerstein 1999).

The work of pragmatic constructivists is valuable—and valued—as offering a more nuanced alternative to overstylized structuralist accounts. This body of work has given us fine-grained portraits of internal diversity rooted in the specificities of particular regions and sectors. Its authors usefully remind us that institutions must not be reified since institutional rules are violated at times and, as I will discuss below, often contain 'gaps' that agents can exploit creatively as they pursue their interests. These insights provide an important corrective to more deterministic structural accounts, and yet it is also hard to escape the thought that the centrality within the PC literature of notions of fluidity, complexity, and contingency itself helps explain why this body of work has not had the same impact as the VoC literature, whose broad (portable and easily testable) propositions have inspired a vast and, to my mind at least, highly productive research programme.

What is most interesting from my perspective, however, is that despite many differences, there is a somewhat surprising core similarity between the VoC and PC approaches. Both adopt a rather voluntarist and utilitarian view of institutions and rules as something that actors choose or submit to in order to solve shared problems through cooperation. The earlier scholarship in the VoC tradition was especially criticized for its functionalist overtones, i.e. for depicting various arrangements, particularly within CMEs, as solutions to collective action problems that allow firms to achieve joint gains through cooperation. For example, the kinds of corporate strategies that firms pursue in CMEs are seen in this literature as relying on coordinated industrial relations systems that discourage poaching by equalizing wages by skill levels, ensure wage restraint by linking bargaining across industries, and give workers incentives to maintain a high degree of flexibility on the shop floor. This literature has also emphasized coordination between large firms and their suppliers, for example, in training and on research and development, that redounds to the benefit of both. Trade associations, likewise, have been seen as allowing smaller firms to achieve joint gains in marketing and on other fronts.

Pragmatic constructivists characterize actors' use of institutional rules in a similar way, emphasizing collaboration to achieve mutually beneficial gains.[6] For example, in a critique of theories that attribute contemporary changes in German industrial relations to 'liberalization' and class conflict, Herrigel sees developments in very different terms, as exercises in joint problem-solving, or in his words, as 'local experiments that allow employees and managers in firms to cope with the twin pressures of innovation and cost reduction' (Herrigel 2008: 126). Not just labour and managers cooperate to solve shared problems, but supplier firms and their customers also look to one another for innovation and learning. In the process, roles and identities are worked out 'through repeated interaction and reciprocal efforts to define the possibilities and limits of a jointly defined project' (Herrigel 2008: 117; see also Berk and Schneiberg 2005). In this endeavour, actors are not bound by institutions and rules so much as they use them creatively to achieve shared objectives. The metaphor one tends to run across repeatedly in this literature is jazz improvisation, which underscores both the collaborative and the improvisational aspects of these interactions (Sabel 2006: 116; Berk and Galvan 2006: 2).

In short, there are some significant differences in the view of institutions offered by VoC and PC—above all whether they are seen as robust and resilient (VoC) or fragile and contingent (PC). But in both, the emphasis has been very much on coordination and collaboration in the interests of mutual gain. Both perspectives thus lean toward a somewhat voluntarist and utilitarian view of institutions and rules as devised or deployed by actors to achieve their shared ends.

THE HISTORICAL INSTITUTIONALIST APPROACH TO CHANGE

The alternative account of institutional change I propose shares some features with each of the two perspectives discussed above, underscoring (with VoC) the importance of structural incentives and constraints, while also (with PC) leaving room for

---

[6] Sabel explicitly suggests that the forms of experimentalist governance that he examines 'should be understood in functional rather than structural or institutional terms' (p. 7).

agency in the analysis of change. But it departs from both in its view of institutions—seeing them not simply (certainly not primarily) as coordinating mechanisms allowing actors to achieve joint gains from cooperation, but rather as deeply political and contested, as underpinned by power relations and fraught with distributional implications.

Historical institutionalists have long viewed the institutions that comprise the political economies of the advanced industrial countries as the enduring legacies of concrete political struggles (Skocpol 1985; Hall 1986; Mahoney, 2010; Thelen 1999). The emphasis on the power-political underpinnings of institutions has always distinguished this version of institutionalism from alternative accounts, both sociological perspectives on institutions as shared understandings or cognitive scripts and rationalist (one could add pragmatist) approaches to institutions as voluntary resting points held together by shared interests and mutual benefit. In the political economy literature, historical institutionalists tend to focus on arrangements that are formalized (obligatory and backed up by sanctions), emphasizing however that such arrangements are politically contested not just occasionally but on an ongoing basis (Streeck and Thelen 2005*b*). These components of the historical-institutionalist view form the basis for an alternative approach to understanding institutional change that steers a path between the VoC bias towards the seemingly inevitable reproduction in perpetuity of specific political-economic models, on the one hand, and the PC vision of a world of fluidity, contingency, and seemingly infinite possibilities for creative recombinations, on the other.

What we can take from the VoC perspective (and what indeed is suggested by any structuralist account) is the idea that formal institutions are not transient behaviours-in-equilibrium; rather, they establish a set of constraints and opportunities. For this reason they shape the strategies that actors devise to confront the challenges they face, both in the market and in politics. However, putting the distributional rather than the efficiency aspects of institutions at the core allows us to see why these institutions are not automatically self-reproducing. In CMEs, for example, employer coordination and, in some versions, 'social partnership' are held together by political settlements both among employers and between employers and labour, and thus involve the exercise of power or dominance of some groups over others. Far from being self-equilibrating, institutions sustaining such coordination must be continuously shored up against all sorts of disintegrative forces and alternative coalitions. The power-distributional aspect of institutions in fact 'builds in' pressures for change as actors seek to renegotiate the form and functions of political-economic institutions to their advantage and in response to changes in the market and political context.

What historical-institutionalist accounts share with pragmatic constructivists is the idea that institutions do not define a 'rigid matrix' to which actors mechanically respond and only ever in ways that reproduce those institutions. However, against the sometimes overly sanguine view in PC of agents 'transforming distributive bargaining into deliberative problem-solving' (Sabel and Zeitlin 2008: 280) through the creative use of institutional rules to devise novel solutions to emerging problems, historical institutionalism maintains a strong focus on the power-political biases that inhere in these institutional rules, underscoring therefore not just the opportunities but also the constraints on action that they impose within a given context. Historical institutionalism emphasizes that even in 'critical juncture' moments when it may appear that institutional outcomes are 'up for grabs' institutions and politics evolve in ways that—even if not predictable ex ante—nonetheless follow a particular logic that makes sense only against the backdrop of the structural context in which 'next steps' are inevitably negotiated.

To see clearly how the institutional context matters in terms of power-distributional outcomes one often needs to 'pan out' from the kinds of local experiments that tend to capture the attention of PC scholars, for this brings back into focus the kinds of macroinstitutional differences that structuralist theories capture. As Huber and Stephens have noted, analyses based on close examination of selected episodes in particular places or times tend systematically to privilege agency and creativity in their explanations of outcomes, because the structural constraints remain in the background, 'unchanging and therefore invisible' (Huber and Stephens 2001: 8–9). In such studies, 'researchers are likely to attribute more causal importance to the preferences and strategies of [specific] actors than warranted, or at least they lose sight of the way in which the constraints of the larger power distribution and the institutional context shape the preferences and strategies of these actors to begin with' (Huber and Stephens 2001: 30). Thus, for example, the kinds of experiments in 'collaborative cost reduction' between labour and managers that Herrigel observes in Germany are likely on average to look very different from those in, say, the United States precisely because of broad differences in the political and legal-institutional environments (above all: labour laws) in these two countries.

The challenge therefore is to inject agency into institutional accounts in a way that rises above the particular episode in question, to generate portable propositions that allow us to identify broader patterns of politics and political dynamics. One way to begin to address this problem (while also tapping the strengths of the two schools of thought discussed in this chapter) is to ask how prevailing structures influence the kinds of change-agents and change-strategies that are more likely to emerge and succeed in specific institutional contexts. In this vein, Wolfgang Streeck and I identified four commonly observed modes of change, focusing especially on forms of change that are incremental but transformative over time (Streeck and Thelen 2005a). These include displacement (the replacement of one set of rules or institutions with alternatives), layering (the addition of new potentially transformative elements on to old arrangements), conversion (the redirection of old institutions or reinterpretation of old rules to serve new ends), and drift (the purposeful neglect of old institutions in the face of changes in context).[7]

In a next step, James Mahoney and I proposed some general propositions about the conditions under which one strategy or mode of change is more likely to emerge (and succeed) than another. Our framework links particular modes of change to

---

[7] In developing this typology we drew on the work of Eric Schickler (Schickler 2001 on layering) and Jacob Hacker (Hacker 2005 on drift).

specific features of existing institutional rules and of the prevailing political context, by asking two questions that correspond, broadly, to the emphasis of the two literatures discussed in this chapter. A first question, related to the traditional structuralist concerns of VoC and other varieties of institutionalism (stressing incentives and constraints), asks: does the political context afford defenders of the status quo strong or weak veto possibilities? A second question, however, takes seriously the PC emphasis on the ambiguity of rules and the possibilities for slippage in their enactment by asking: does the targeted institution afford actors opportunities for exerting discretion in its implementation and enforcement? (Mahoney and Thelen, 2010). The answers to these questions produce the analytic space depicted in Table 2.1, which suggests several propositions about the specific strategies or modes of change that are available to actors (and/or more likely to succeed) in specific institutional contexts.

A full explication of the theory is beyond the scope of this chapter (but see Mahoney and Thelen, 2010; and for an application to political economic change in advanced industrial economies, see Thelen 2009). The general point I wish to emphasize here is that we need to move beyond the question of whether agency trumps structure or the other way around and strive instead for mid-range explanations that situate agents within a context that frames and shapes the strategies they are likely to pursue and with which they are likely to be able to effect real change.

In the historical-institutional framework sketched out above, institutions constrain action but they do not eliminate agency. Moreover, beyond the traditional (and still relevant) concern for institutions as constraints this framework incorporates an expanded conception of institutions that directs our attention to important sources of change having to do with the fact that institutions and rules, by their very

Table 2.1: Contextual and institutional sources of institutional change

		Characteristics of the targeted institution	
		Low level of discretion in interpretation/ enforcement	High level of discretion in interpretation/ enforcement
Characteristics of the political context	Stronger veto possibilities	Layering	Drift
	Weaker veto possibilities	Displacement	Conversion

Source: Mahoney and Thelen, 2010.

nature, often leave 'gaps' that actors can exploit in pursuit of their own interests and in their political struggles for advantage within existing constraints (Pierson 2004: especially chapter 4; also Thelen 2009). The sources of these gaps are several, and they include cognitive limits that prevent policymakers from fully controlling the uses to which the rules they write can be put, as well as the ambiguities to which pragmatic constructivists have drawn our attention, as changing circumstances open up possibilities for new interpretations of old rules that can transform their meaning and political functions. An analysis of political contestation within and over institutional rules that takes both these dimensions seriously can, I believe, provide a framework for the systematic study of the kind of bounded, incremental, but potentially transformative changes currently underway in the political economies of the advanced industrial countries.

Conclusion and Agenda for Research

Understanding ongoing contemporary changes in labour market institutions in the rich democracies requires subtle but important revisions to how we understand institutions—what they are, how they operate, what sustains them over time, and how they change. In particular, we have to move from an analysis of the functions of institutions to the political coalitions that support and sustain them and to political contests over the form these institutions take and the uses to which they are put. The historical-institutionalist perspective sketched out here (and elaborated in Mahoney and Thelen, 2010) places the distributional effects and the power-political underpinnings of institutions at the centre of the analysis of change. Along with PC accounts, this framework focuses on incremental and bounded changes through ongoing political manoeuvring between those who design the rules and those who are called up on to implement, interpret, enforce, and live under these rules. In so doing, it acknowledges the transformative potential of this manoeuvring, thus moving beyond rigid structuralist perspectives that cannot comprehend such change. At the same time, however, it harnesses the long-standing strengths of the VoC literature by situating the agents of change in a context in which not all moves are equally likely or even possible. In this way, it illuminates how institutional context influences the strategies these actors are apt to pursue and profoundly shapes the cooperative and conflictual interactions they have with other actors.

An historical-institutional approach thus provides a sound basis for mid-range theorizing about institutional change in labour market institutions and beyond. The empirical work is just beginning, but already a good deal of the groundwork has been laid. The framework sketched out above will not be the last word on the subject, but it might represent a first foray beyond institutionalism's traditional comfort zone of 'comparative statics' that avoids, however, what Paul Pierson has called the theoretical abyss of agency unleashed.[8]

REFERENCES

BERK, GERALD (1994). *Alternative Tracks: The Constitution of American Industrial Order*, (Baltimore: Johns Hopkins University Press).
——and DENNIS GALVAN (2006). 'Syncretism and Institutional Change Across Time, Space and Hierarchies: A Field Guide to How People Remake Institutions'. Paper read at APSA, at Philadelphia.
——and MARC SCHNEIBERG (2005). 'Varieties in Capitalism, Varieties of Association: Collaborative Learning in American Industry, 1900 to 1925', *Politics & Society* 33 (1): 46–87.
BUSEMEYER, MARIUS R. (2009). *Wandel trotz Reformstau: Die Politik der beruflichen Bildung seit 1970*, (Frankfurt: Campus).
CALLAGHAN, HELEN (2009). 'Insiders, Outsiders, and the Politics of Corporate Governance', *Comparative Political Studies* 42 (6): 733–62.
CALMFORS, LARS, and JOHN DRIFFILL (1988). 'Bargaining Structure, Corporatism, and Macroeconomic Performance', *Economic Policy* 3 (6): 13–61.
CAMERON, DAVID (1984). 'Social Democracy, Corporatism, Labour Quiescence, and the Representation of Economic Interest in Advanced Capitalist Society', in *Order and Conflict in Contemporary Capitalism*, ed. J. H. Goldthorpe, (London: Oxford University Press).
CAMPBELL, JOHN L. and OVE K. PEDERSEN (2007). 'The Varieties of Capitalism and Hybrid Success: Denmark in the Global Economy', *Comparative Political Studies* 40 (3): 307–32.
CARLIN, WENDY and DAVID SOSKICE (2009). 'German Economic Performance: Disentangling the Role of Supply-side Reforms, Macroeconomic Policy and Coordinated Economy Institutions', *Socio-economic Review* 7 (1): 67–100.
CROUCH, COLIN (2001). 'Welfare State Regimes and Industrial Relations Systems: The Questionable Role of Path Dependency Theory', in *Comparing Welfare Capitalism*, eds. B. Ebbinghaus and P. Manow, (London: Routledge).
——(2005). *Capitalist Diversity and Change*, (New York: Oxford University Press).
CULPEPPER, PEPPER D., and KATHLEEN THELEN (2007). 'Institutions and Collective Actors in the Provision of Training: Historical and Cross-National Comparisons', in *Skill Formation: Interdisciplinary and Cross-National Perspectives*, eds. K.-U. Mayer and H. Solga, (New York: Cambridge University Press).
DJELIC, MARIE-LAURE and SIGRID QUACK (2003). 'Conclusion: Globalization as a Double Process of Institutional Change and Institution Building', in *Globalization and Institutions*, eds. M.-L. Djelic and S. Quack, (Cheltenham, UK: Edward Elgar).
GREIF, AVNER and DAVID LAITIN (2004). 'A Theory of Endogenous Institutional Change', *American Political Science Review* 98 (4): 633–52.
HACKER, JACOB (2005). 'Policy Drift: The Hidden Politics of US Welfare State Retrenchment', in *Beyond Continuity: Institutional Change in Advanced Political Economies*, eds. W. Streeck and K. Thelen, (Oxford: Oxford University Press).

---

[8] Comments at a workshop on 'Explaining Change: Historical-institutionalist Perspectives,' Northwestern University, October 2007.

HALL, PETER A. (1986). *Governing the Economy: The Politics of State Intervention in Britain and France*, (New York: Oxford University Press).

——(2007). 'The Evolution of Varieties of Capitalism in Europe', in *Beyond Varieties of Capitalism*, eds. B. Hancké, M. Rhodes, and M. Thatcher, (Oxford: Oxford University Press).

——and DANIEL GINGERICH (2009). 'Varieties of Capitalism and Institutional Complementarities in the Political Economy: An Empirical Analysis', *British Journal of Political Science* 39 (3): 449–82.

——and DAVID SOSKICE (eds.) (2001). *Varieties of Capitalism: The Institutional Foundations of Comparative Advantage*, (New York: Oxford University Press).

————(2003). 'Varieties of Capitalism and Institutional Change: A Response to Three Critics', *Comparative European Politics* 2 (1): 241–50.

——and ROSEMARY C. R. TAYLOR (1996). 'Political Science and the Three Institutionalisms', *Political Studies* 44: 936–57.

——and KATHLEEN THELEN (2009). 'Institutional Change in Varieties of Capitalism', *Socio-economic Review* 7: 7–34.

HASSEL, ANKE (1999). 'The Erosion of the German System of Industrial Relations', *British Journal of Industrial Relations* 37 (3): 484–505.

HÄUSERMANN, SILJA (forthcoming). *Modernization in Hard Times: The Politics of Welfare State Reform in Continental Europe*, (New York: Cambridge University Press).

HERRIGEL, GARY (1996). *Industrial Constructions: The Sources of German Industrial Power*, (New York: Cambridge University Press).

——(2007). 'Guest Editor's Introduction: A New Wave in the History of Corporate Governance', *Enterprise and Society* 8 (30): 475–88.

——(2008). 'Roles and Rules: Ambiguities, Experimentation and New Forms of Stakeholderism in Germany', *Industrielle Beziehungen* 15 (2): 111–32.

HÖPNER, MARTIN (2007). 'Coordination and Organization: The Two Dimensions of Nonliberal Capitalism', in MPIfG Discussion Paper, (Cologne: Max Planck Institut für Gesellschaftsforschung).

HUBER, EVELYNE and JOHN D. STEPHENS (2001). *Development and Crisis of the Welfare States: Parties and Policies in Global Markets*, (Chicago: University of Chicago Press).

IVERSEN, TORBEN (1996). 'Power, Flexibility and the Breakdown of Centralized Wage Bargaining: The Cases of Denmark and Sweden in Comparative Perspective', *Comparative Politics* 28 (4): 399–436.

——(1999). *Contested Economic Institutions: The Politics of Macroeconomics and Wage Bargaining in Advanced Democracies*, (New York: Cambridge University Press).

——and DAVID SOSKICE (2009). 'Distribution and Redistribution: The Shadow from the Nineteenth Century', *World Politics* 61 (3): 438–86.

KATZENSTEIN, PETER J. (ed.) (1978). *Between Power and Plenty*, (Madison, WI: University of Wisconsin Press).

KITSCHELT, HERBERT, PETER LANGE, GARY MARKS, and JOHN D. STEPHENS (eds.) (1999). *Continuity and Change in Contemporary Capitalism*, (New York: Cambridge University Press).

LEVY, JONAH (1999). 'Vice into Virtue? Progressive Politics and Welfare Reform in Continental Europe', *Politics & Society* 27 (2): 239–73.

——(2005). 'Redeploying the State: Liberalization and Social Policy in France', in *Beyond Continuity*, eds. W. Streeck and K. Thelen, (Oxford: Oxford University Press).

MAHONEY, JAMES (2010). *Colonialism and Development: Spanish America in Comparative Perspective*, (New York: Cambridge University Press).

MAHONEY, JAMES and KATHLEEN THELEN, (2010). 'A Theory of Gradual Institutional Change', in *Explaining Institutional Change: Ambiguity, Agency, and Power*, eds. J. Mahoney and K. Thelen, (New York: Cambridge University Press).

MARES, ISABELA (2000). 'Strategic Alliances and Social Policy Reform: Unemployment Insurance in Comparative Perspective', *Politics & Society* 28 (2): 223–44.

PALIER, BRUNO (2005). 'Tracing the Political Processes of Path-Breaking Changes in French Social Policy', in *Continuity and Discontinuity in Institutional Analysis*, eds. W. Streeck and K. Thelen, (Oxford: Oxford University Press).

——and CLAUDE MARTIN (2007). 'From "a Frozen Landscape" to Structural Reforms: The Sequential Transformation of Bismarckian Welfare Systems', *Social Policy & Administration* 41 (6): 535–54.

PIERSON, PAUL (2004). *Politics in Time: History, Institutions, and Political Analysis*, (Princeton, NJ: Princeton University Press).

PONTUSSON, JONAS (2005). *Inequality and Prosperity: Social Europe vs. Liberal America*, (New York: New Century Foundation).

——DAVID RUEDA, and CHRISTOPHER WAY (2002). 'Comparative Political Economy of Wage Distribution: The Role of Partisanship and Labor Market Institutions', *British Journal of Political Science* 32 (2).

——and PETER SWENSON (1996). 'Labor Markets, Production Strategies, and Wage Bargaining Institutions: The Swedish Employer Offensive in Comparative Perspective', *Comparative Political Studies* 29 (2): 223–50.

SABEL, CHARLES F. (1994). 'Learning by Monitoring: The Institutions of Economic Development', in *The Handbook of Economic Sociology*, eds. N. J. Smelser and R. Swedberg, (Princeton, NJ: Princeton University Press).

——(2006). 'A Real Time Revolution in Routines', in *The Firm as a Collaborative Community*, eds. C. Heckscher and P. Adler, (Oxford: Oxford University Press).

——and JONATHAN ZEITLIN (1997a). 'Stories, Strategies, Structure: Rethinking Historical Alternatives to Mass Production', in *Worlds of Possibility*, eds. C. F. Sabel and J. Zeitlin, (Cambridge: Cambridge University Press).

————(eds.) (1997b). *World of Possibilities*, (Cambridge: Cambridge University Press).

————(2008). 'Learning from Difference: The New Architecture of Experimentalist Governance in the European Union', *European Law Journal* 14 (3): 271–327.

SCHICKLER, ERIC (2001). *Disjointed Pluralism: Institutional Innovation and the Development of the U.S. Congress*, (Princeton, NJ: Princeton University Press).

SCHMITTER, PHILIPPE C. (1981). 'Interest Intermediation and Regime Governability in Contemporary Western Europe and North America', in *Organizing Interests in Western Europe*, ed. S. BERGER, (Cambridge: Cambridge University Press).

SKOCPOL, THEDA (1985). 'Bringing the State Back In: Strategies of Analysis in Current Research', in *Bringing the State Back In*, eds. P. B. Evans, D. Rueschemeyer, and T. Skocpol, (New York: Cambridge University Press).

SOSKICE, DAVID (1990). 'Reinterpreting Corporatism and Explaining Unemployment: Co-ordinated and Non-co-ordinated Market Economies' in *Labour Relations and Economic Performance*, eds. R. Brunetta and C. Dell'Aringa, (New York: New York University Press).

STREECK, WOLFGANG (1991). 'On the Institutional Conditions of Diversified Quality Production', in *Beyond Keynesianism*, eds. E. Matzner and W. Streeck, (Aldershot, UK: Edward Elgar).

——(1997). 'Beneficial Constraints: On the Economic Limits of Rational Voluntarism', in *Contemporary Capitalism: The Embeddedness of Institutions*, eds. J. R. Hollingsworth and R. Boyer, (New York: Cambridge University Press).

——and KATHLEEN THELEN (eds.) (2005a). *Beyond Continuity: Institutional Change in Advanced Political Economies*, (Oxford: Oxford University Press).

————— (2005b). 'Introduction: Institutional Change in Advanced Political Economies', in *Beyond Continuity: Institutional Change in Advanced Political Economies*, eds. W. Streeck and K. Thelen, (Oxford: Oxford University Press).

SWENSON, PETER (2002). *Capitalists Against Markets*, (New York: Oxford University Press).

THELEN, KATHLEEN (1999). 'Historical Institutionalism in Comparative Politics', *The Annual Review of Political Science* 2.

——(2002). 'The Political Economy of Business and Labor in the Advanced Industrial Countries', in *Political Science: The State of the Discipline*, eds. I. Katznelson and H. Milner, (New York and Washington DC: Norton Books and the American Political Science Association).

——(2004). *How Institutions Evolve: The Political Economy of Skills in Germany, Britain, the United States and Japan*, (New York: Cambridge University Press).

——(2007). 'Contemporary Challenges to the German Vocational Training System', *Regulation and Governance* 1 (3): 247–60.

——(2009). 'Institutional Change in Advanced Political Economies', *British Journal of Industrial Relations* 47 (3): 471–98.

——and IKUO KUME (2006). 'Coordination as a Political Problem in Coordinated Market Economies', *Governance* 19 (1): 11–42.

——and CHRISTA VAN WIJNBERGEN (2003). 'The Paradox of Globalization: Labor Relations in Germany and Beyond', *Comparative Political Studies* 36 (8): 859–80.

WALLERSTEIN, MICHAEL (1999). 'Wage-setting Institutions and Pay Inequality in Advanced Industrial Societies', *American Journal of Political Science* 43: 649–80.

——MIRIAM GOLDEN, and PETER LANGE (1997). 'Unions, Employers' Associations, and Wage-setting Institutions in Northern and Central Europe, 1950–1992', *Industrial and Labor Relations Review* 50 (3): 379–402.

WHITFORD, JOSHUA (2005). *The New Old Economy: Networks, Institutions, and the Organizational Transformation of American Manufacturing*, (Oxford: Oxford University Press).

ZEITLIN, JONATHAN (1996). 'Re-forming Skills in British Metalworking, 1900–1940: A contingent failure'. Paper read at 21st meeting of the Social Science History Association, Oct 10–13 (panel on 'Skill formation in comparative-historical perspective'), at New Orleans.

——(2000). 'Americanizing British Engineering? Strategic Debates, Selective Adaptation, and Hybrid Innovation in Post-war Reconstruction, 1945–1960', in *Americanization and Its Limits*, eds. J. Zeitlin and G. Herrigel, (Oxford: Oxford University Press).

——(2003). 'Introduction: Governing Work and Welfare in a New Economy: European and American Experiments', in *Governing Work and Welfare in a New Economy: European and American Experiments*, eds. J. Zeitlin and D. Trubek, (Oxford: Oxford University Press).

CHAPTER 3

....

ACTORS AND INSTITUTIONS

....

GREGORY JACKSON

INTRODUCTION

....

A distinguishing feature of comparative institutional analysis is the emphasis on understanding actors and actor constellations. Institutional analysis is concerned with processes of isomorphism and explaining similarities among organizations within an institutional field. 'Comparative' approaches to studying institutions must, by nature, deal with the diversity of institutions across countries or over time. Comparative methodologies aim to link the similarities and differences in these institutions with a particular outcome of interest, such as economic growth, inequality, innovation patterns, and so on. But the act of comparison itself raises important questions about the nature and configurations of actors in different institutional settings, the non-identical nature of those actors, and how processes of institutionalization relate to the behaviour of those actors.

This chapter aims to give an overview of these issues from the perspective of comparative institutional analysis. The second section briefly examines the relation between actors and institutions in economics, political science, and sociology. This review does not aim to cover all schools of institutional theory (see Hall and Taylor 1996), but selectively reviews several conceptions of scholars engaged in the comparative study of institutions. This section demonstrates certain points of agreement—actors and institutions are seen as being mutually constitutive of one another. One implication is the need to adopt a more historical and process-oriented approach to studying institutions. The third section explores the non-identical nature of actors in greater detail. In particular, institutions are argued to influence processes of identity formation, the definition of interests, and the forms of organization adopted by collective actors. Two brief illustrations are provided drawing on comparative examples from two institutional domains: industrial relations and corporate governance. The fourth section raises the broader issue of how institutions influence action itself. Given the mutual interdependence of actors and institutions, institutionalization may be seen as a matter of degree. Actors respond to institutions as one element within a situation, but institutional contexts never fully determine action. The concluding section suggests a few important methodological points for the comparative study of institutions from an actor-centred perspective.

The Importance of Actors for the Comparative Study of Institutions

Institutional analysis has a rich and diverse set of traditions with different perspectives on the relationship between actors and institutions. Rational choice or game-theoretical approaches often begin the analysis with a particular constellation of actors, and see 'institutions as a strategic choice' of those actors. Institutions are seen as an outcome of a game in which multiple but known strategic equilibriums are possible. Here the constellation of actors is taken as given and institutions are described as an endogenous outcome of an economic game. Other scholars see 'institutions as the rules of the game itself'. Institutions regulate the behaviour of actors through both formal and informal rules enforced by third parties (North 1990). Here institutions have a largely constraining character, setting clear boundaries on actors' choices (Ingram and Clary 2000). Institutions are exogenous to actors, who are themselves seen as pre-existing and having stable preferences. For example, this approach has been influential in the 'law and economics' literature, which has interpreted cross-national differences in economic activity as being influenced by different legal institutions rooted in either common law or civil law traditions (La Porta et al. 1998; 1999; 2000).

The utility of seeing actors as either 'rule-makers' or 'rule-takers' often depends upon the particular research question. Yet each of these perspectives alone is incomplete in a theoretical sense. Both perspectives share assumptions of methodological individualism, which tends to conceptualize actors' identities, interests, or preferences as separate and apart from the institutions they inhabit. However, an alternative perspective has been gaining currency across the different social sciences, including economics. Namely, scholars increasingly conceptualize actors and institutions 'as being mutually constitutive of one another'. Actors may be 'rule-makers', but take existing rules as a starting point for defining their own identities and interests.

Conversely, actors may also be 'rule-takers', but nonetheless modify or even overturn those rules from time to time. Or as Karl Marx (1852) famously argued in his *The Eighteenth Brumaire of Louis Bonaparte*, 'Men make their own history but not in circumstances of their own choosing.' The main point here is that institutionalization is a dynamic process. Institutional rules must be 'enacted' by actors, but institutions themselves are produced and reproduced through these actions. Institutionally defined situations influence the interests and even identities of actors within the boundaries of institutions, and conversely institutions are rules defined in relation to stable configurations of actors with particular (institutionally defined) identities and interests. In sum, a constitutive approach conceptualizes actors and institutions as being mutually interdependent and reflexively intertwined with one another.

These arguments clearly echo developments in both 'classic' and contemporary sociological theory. For example, sociologist Georg Simmel (1955) noted the 'dual constitution' of social groups—namely, individuals are defined by social groups, but social groups are defined by the individuals who are included as members. More broadly, the social sciences have moved away from dualities such as 'structure and agency', 'micro and macro', or 'interests and ideas'. Rather than seeing one as having primacy over the other, recent sociological theory has sought to integrate these dualisms into a relational perspective where actors and social structures are mutually interdependent—for example, the theory of structuration (Giddens 1984), theories of practice (Bourdieu 1990), or theories related to social networks (White 1992).

While the constitutive view of institutions is certainly not unique to the comparative analysis of institutions, it can nonetheless be argued that the notion of actors being 'socially constructed' through their institutional settings has a very fundamental role in comparative analysis. Cross-national comparison usually involves a systematic examination of the similarities and differences in institutions either within a particular domain of the economy (e.g. corporate governance, financial systems, or labour markets), or through a 'holistic' investigation of linkages between the various domains that make up the wider political economy.[1] These sorts of comparisons face the inevitable issue that not only do the institutional rules differ across countries, but the identities, interests, and resources of the actors or players of the game differ as well. For example, the comparative institutional analysis of corporate governance might examine the legal rights and obligations of a set of actors such as shareholders. Yet the most important categories of 'shareholder' differ vastly across countries— individual shareholders or institutional investors such as pension funds are common in the United States, but in Europe or Japan shareholders also include banks, other corporations, families, the state, and so on. Likewise, a comparative analysis of

---

[1] The literature on comparative capitalism (CC) seeks to develop a holistic and synthetic comparison of national 'models' or types incorporating a number of institutional domains. This literature has made important contributions to the study of international business (Jackson and Deeg 2008), the role of state regulation and intervention (Jackson and Deeg 2008), and institutional change more generally (Deeg and Jackson 2007).

political institutions must go beyond the formal properties of electoral rules and constitutional division of powers. Different sets of actors inhabit these systems, such as political parties, interests groups and associations, social movements, the media, and so on. Moreover, different sets of rules (e.g. majoritarian vs. proportional electoral systems) may have a strong influence on the actors themselves (e.g. the dominance of two broad 'catch all' parties or a greater number of more niche issue-oriented parties). To understand an institution, one must look at both the rules and the players, seeing each as an interdependent context for the other.

Of course, comparative institutional scholars still differ in the extent they subscribe to more 'realist' and interest-driven explanations or favour emphasis on how actors develop their interests through processes of interpretation. Nonetheless, all comparative institutional analysis touches on processes of social construction in some sense. All comparative analysis involves comparing apples and oranges, since both the rules and the players of the game differ across time and space, thus requiring 'contextualized comparisons' (Locke and Thelen 1995). Indeed, Richard Hyman has argued that all comparisons involve an element of the incomparable, thus raising the issue of how far the formal logic of comparative methods (e.g. comparing most similar cases with most different outcomes) can ever be realized in practice (Jackson et al. 2008). For present purposes, however, the important implication of this apples and oranges issue is the need to see institutionalization as a dynamic and actor-centred social process, recognizing the duality of structure and agency, as well as the material and cognitive aspects of institutions. Before taking up this argument further, the remainder of this section will focus on how comparative scholars across different social science traditions have begun to address this common issue in understanding how actors and institutions are mutually 'constitutive' and interdependent.

In economics, comparative institutional analysis has undergone substantial elaboration in recent years. A pioneering example has been the work of Masahiko Aoki. His early work sought to understand the institutionalization of different forms of corporate organization in Japan and the United States (Aoki 1988). He developed a coalitional model of corporate control and internal organization of firm-internal labour markets based on the different interactions among managers, owners, and employees. This game-theoretic approach has now developed into an integrated framework for understanding how institutions constrain actors and how actors reproduce and change institutional environments (see also Greif 2005). Aoki (2001: 202) defines institutions as a 'compressed, commonly perceived representation of ways in which a game is played'. This definition incorporates elements of rational/ economic approaches and cognitive/sociological approaches such as Berger and Luckmann (1966) into a more strategic and game-theoretic perspective. Institutionalization is conceptualized as a process of feedback mechanisms represented by the Table 3.1 box and its four elements (Aoki 2001: 203–06). Subjective expectations (E) about the behaviour of other actors coordinate the strategic choices of individual agents (S). This allows individuals to economize on information, while their choices are thereby constrained. As expectations are shared and serve as stable guides for

Table 3.1: Subjective game model of institutionalization

	Exogenous	Endogenous
Micro (individual) dimension	(A) Capacities as active repertoires	(S) Strategies as best-response choice
Macro (collective) dimension	(CO) Consequences through inference rules	(E) Expectations as private beliefs
	(I) Institutions as shared beliefs	

Source: Adapted from Aoki 2001.

strategy, collective behaviour confirms and reinforces such expectations about others' strategic choices. Institutions also have consequences (CO) within a given technological and institutional environment that, in turn, constrain and shape the capacities for action accumulated by actors (A).

With regard to Simmelian 'duality' of actors and institutions, Aoki's definition has a number of notable characteristics. First, institutions are defined in terms of a dynamic process of institutionalization. Institutions are produced and reproduced by the strategic behaviour of actors, even while actors are constrained by institutions. Aoki (2007: 8) stresses this duality as follows,

An institution as a summary representation of equilibrium is produced and must be repeatedly reproduced as an endogenous outcome of the strategy interplays of all the agents in the domain . . . while it appears as if it were an external entity beyond their individual control which needs to be taken into consideration for individual choices.

Second, institutions do more than constrain actors' pursuit of material interests. Rather, institutions shape the cognitive capabilities and dispositions of actors. Aoki (2007: 8) stresses that ' . . . the rules of play can become an institution and sustained as such, only when they are deeply internalized by each individual, constituting part of his/her mind-set or belief.' Institutions are intrinsically linked to a particular constellation of actors and their capabilities, even as institutions serve to create them. A third and key consequence is the importance of history for institutional analysis. Aoki (2007: 8) argues that

Any model useful for examining the nature of an institution and conditions for its self-enforceability is likely to need to specify a player and its possible action choices beforehand . . . the existence of such a player may be rationalized as historically given. We need to acknowledge, however, then that such methodology implies that the game theoretic analysis cannot be a complete theory of institution.

While the parameters of an institution appear as exogenous and fixed to actors in the short-term, they must be considered variable in the long run. Hence, game theoretical analysis goes hand-in-hand with historical analysis (Greif 2005).

Political scientists have proposed an essentially parallel understanding of actors and institutions, even where the theoretical micro-foundations are less formalized

*historical
institutionalism*

than in economic theory. In making a case for historical institutionalism, Steinmo and Thelen (1992: 10) stress how political actors are constrained by institutions, and yet also create and change institutions. A defining aspect of this approach concerns the issue of preference formation. While rational choice approaches to institutions take preferences as given based on particular assumptions, 'historical institutionalists take the question of how individuals and groups define their self-interest as problematical' (Steinmo and Thelen 1992: 8). Institutions not only constrain the strategies of actors, but actually shape their preferences, interests, and goals in more fundamental ways. Given that preferences are not fixed, ideas play a potentially large role by influencing how groups think about their interests. Actors may be strategic, but define their goals in a historically situated fashion based on prevailing and contingent interpretation of social situations, including institutionalized values, norms, and power configurations. One important consequence is that coalitions among actors may emerge in surprising ways, not merely based on a lining up of groups based on clear pre-existing sets of interests. For example, historical perspectives to comparing institutions such as employee codetermination in Germany show how institutions may be based upon and embody political compromises, relying on symbolic agreement over ambiguous or even contradictory sets of rules (Herrigel 2008; Jackson 2005). Over time, existing institutions shape the interests and political struggles over the adaptation or further change of those institutions in the future.

Historical institutionalism thus shares a common agenda with the aforementioned economics approach in seeking to understand the dynamic process of co-constitution between actors and institutions in historical time. Rather than starting with a clean slate of pre-existing actors with assumed or fixed sets of interests, institutional analysis is informed by a fundamentally historical understanding of actors within a particular context and setting. These settings help to define actors' identities and interests, but actors also seek to transform these settings through their actions—particularly through politics and contention. Thus, historical institutionalism sees actors and institutions as mutually constitutive. One important implication is that actors and institutions also change over time in a recursive or dialectical fashion. Actors may be socialized by or consciously adapt to institutions, but actors may also deviate from or reinterpret institutions in ways that change those institutions. While different substantive research problems may lead scholars to either start with actors and move to institutions (e.g. explaining their origin) or move from institutions to actors (e.g. explaining economic outcomes), historical institutionalism stresses that these processes are ongoing and recursive social processes.

Finally, these ideas appear again or even drew inspiration from institutional analysis in sociology. In trying to understand the isomorphic character of organizations within a particular field, proponents of the 'new' institutionalism saw organizations as enacting ritualized mythologies or scripts (Meyer and Rowan 1977). By their very nature, organizations are constituted by the formal and informal rules imposed by their institutional environment. Institutions embody shared understandings, such as cognitions or interpretative frames (Scott 1995). The identity of an organization, such as a corporation or a school, is shaped by the institutional field

(Scott and Christensen 1995). Organizations thus adopt durable institutional forms that are compatible or resemble existing ones because actors interpret situations and adopt solutions from a menu of established, legitimate patterns of behaviour. Comparative scholars in this tradition have stressed how historical patterns of legitimate political authority across countries have led to different cognitive templates for corporate organizing in Europe and America (Dobbin 1994), or legitimated different logics of managerial authority across firms in East Asia (Biggart 1991). Likewise, the spread of new organizational forms such as the 'shareholder value' model of the firm in the US is linked with processes of diffusion and changing cognitive concepts of control among top managers (Fligstein 1990, 2001).

More broadly, sociologists have outlined three pillars to institutions based on a regulative or coercive dimension, a normative dimension, and a cognitive dimension (DiMaggio and Powell 1991). While these pillars are well known, recent contributions have tried to emphasize the dynamic aspects of institutions. For example, the rapid spread and institutionalization of a particular cognitive notion such as 'shareholder value' may be associated with new opportunities to mobilize actors in support of political change of existing institutions, such as through shareholder-oriented legal reforms (Davis and Thompson 1994; Gourevitch and Shinn 2005). One reason for this dynamism is that the different pillars of institutions influence one another in different ways over time—cognitive 'frames' may be used to legitimate new strategies for political reform, or coercive rules may create new interactions among professional groups in ways that reshape social norms (Campbell 2005).

A very poignant theoretical statement that encapsulates many of these ideas can also be found in the literature on actor-centred institutionalism (Mayntz and Scharpf 1995; Scharpf 1997). This literature was concerned with a comparative analysis of public policy and processes of governance across different sectors of the political economy. Reacting against some of the perceived deterministic aspects of institutional analysis, these authors see institutions as a 'context for action' within which 'constellations of actors' may interact with one another. First, institutions shape actors. This statement is particularly true in comparative analysis, which has a strong focus on collective actors, such as formal organizations. Collective actors are themselves often constituted through institutional rules, such as the legal frameworks governing the independence of central banks in different countries (Scharpf 1987), or the systems of certification that govern membership within professions such as doctors or lawyers across countries (Döhler 1993). Second, institutions define particular arenas of interaction between different collective actors. These arenas shape how actors further define their interests, and develop both normative and strategic action orientations vis-à-vis other actors. For example, electoral systems influence the strategies and coalition dynamics of political parties, or institutionalized patterns of employee participation shape the bargaining games between employers and unions.

Both of the above arguments about identities and interactions apply at multiple levels of analysis. Collective actors within a policy arena, for example, may be formal organizations such as unions or business associations. These organizations are themselves made up of other organizations or individuals, which may be important additional levels of analysis in understanding the orientation and capacity for action. Certain categories of individuals (e.g. families, ethnic groups, etc.) may also become collective actors inasmuch as they consciously aim to coordinate their actors under particular circumstances—as suggested in social movement theory (Davis et al. 2005).

One caveat regarding actor-centred institutionalism is the argument that institutions themselves never fully determine actors' identities, their perceptions, goals and orientations, or ultimately their actions. Institutions shape interaction, but actors retain scope for choice within constraints or even alter those constraints by strategic or interpretative acts. Institutional analysis is an essential but inherently incomplete explanation when applied to particular outcomes (Scharpf 1997). This stress on the role of actors and actor constellations means that institutions are considered simultaneously as both dependent and independent variables—institutions are a remote cause of an outcome, and action remains a proximate cause.

In sum, this section has aimed to show how several key strands of comparative institutional analysis have converged toward an essential theoretical point—namely, actors and institutions are co-generative. Actors' identities and interests are shaped by the broader institutional environment, and should not be considered as fixed or exogenous. Likewise, institutional analysis must take seriously the constellations of actors within a given institutional domain, and their interactions. This common principle does not deny the differences among various approaches and disciplines. Economics retains a stronger emphasis on the strategic choice aspect of institutions (e.g. actors as rule-makers), whereas sociology has tended to see organizations as enacting institutional rules (e.g. actors as rule-takers). Political science has certainly straddled both of these traditions, given its inherent focus both on the politics of how rules are made but also the enforcement of those rules. But these differences should not blind us to common themes—the importance of history, and the dynamic ways in which actors and institutions condition one another in historical time. Indeed, a broad agreement is emerging that to the extent institutional analysis neglects history, it will fall victim to functionalist fallacy (e.g. that institutions were created to serve the specific ends of the actors) or the structuralist fallacy (e.g. that institutions are immune to change even when actors face pressures to defect). The next section will develop these points further through a discussion of particular actors and actor constellations in comparative institutional analysis and then return to the relationship between actors, action, and institutions in the final section.

ACTORS AND INSTITUTIONS

In undertaking comparative institutional analysis, a key theoretical and methodological issue concerns the 'non-identical nature of actors' across different institutional contexts. This point was made perhaps most explicitly and profoundly by various authors associated with the 'societal effect' approach to studying work organization (Maurice et al. 1986; Sorge and Warner 1986). This work compared micro aspects of work organization, primarily in France, Germany, and the United Kingdom based on matched pairs of factories with the intent of isolating those shop-floor traits differing across societies attributable to societal differences and then linking these closely with an analysis of various social institutions in the respective countries. The ways in which actors were educated and socialized by firms differed systematically across countries, so that the 'qualificational space' and authority relations between shop-floor workers and middle managers were based on very different categories of qualifications in each country. Comparing organizations across societies required these authors to explore how actors construct organizations, and understand how this constructive process is influenced by the societal fabric in which the actors operate. The actors within firms, such as managers and workers, were studied in relation to their social contexts and compared in terms of several interrelated sets of institutions: organization, skill formation, industry structure, industrial relations, and innovation (Sorge 1999).

As mentioned above, the diversity of actor identity and interests is particularly important given the strong emphasis on collective actors in the study of comparative political economy. While individuals are often the focus in terms of their behaviour as consumers, employees or voters, comparative studies often examine collective actors such as business associations, unions, state agencies, and so on. Even the nature of firms as economic actors is highly variable across societies (Biggart 1991; Whitley 1999). As formal organizations, firms use authority as a means of allocating resources. But the nature and boundaries of this authority are often unclear. Firms as economic actors differ in the scale and scope of business activity and resources that they control. Firms may range from large, vertically integrated managerial hierarchies to fragmented and sometimes loosely federated business groups, such as those organized around informal kinship ties and so on. This section will now turn to several illustrations of actor configurations within comparative institutional analysis.

An illustration: comparative industrial relations

The social construction of actors is well established within the study of industrial relations, as illustrated in the discussion by Streeck (1993). He argues that the interests of employees are not objectively determined, but depend upon the individual and collective identity which those employees find to be most salient. These interests and identities form a possible basis for different forms of union organization, which reflect this diversity. Organizations themselves function in the context of institutions, which help to channel the expectations of their members and structure interactions with other parties such as employers or the state. Institutions condition politics in the sense of collective goals and the distribution of resources and life chances to the extent that those institutions constrain and enable particular decisions or strategies. These relationships are not conceived as being unidirectional whereby one is an 'independent variable', but a complex set of mutual interactions. Thus, causal sequences do not only run from identity to interest to organization, but also vice-versa so that different institutions influence the success of different forms of union organization, as well as perception of employee interests and even the socialization of employees into different identities.

Streeck illustrates these relationships with regard to three different ideal-typical institutions in the domain of industrial relations—corporatism, pluralism, and paternalism. Corporatism is grounded in a class model of union organization, where employees define their identities in terms of their position as selling labour power in the labour market (e.g. the working class). Based on these identities, employee interests are closely related to solidaristic policies that diminish differences in income and status, such as the notion 'equal pay for equal work.' Identities rooted in social class are likely to be organized in terms of encompassing industrial unions that seek to gain members and set wages for an entire industry or even nation. However, unions conversely need strong organizational incentives and sanctioning mechanisms to prevent small groups and particularistic interests of employee groups from reasserting themselves. Corporatist institutions are, in turn, important for industrial unions to establish and maintain their representational monopoly over employees and thus maintain sufficient centralization to pursue solidaristic interests.

Similar analysis could be made of other institutional configurations. *Pluralism* is, by contrast, based on an occupational model of organization. Here employee identities are linked to human capital and qualifications that comprise the individual profession or occupation. Based on their occupational identity, employees define their interests in terms of meritocratic or particularistic standards. Flowing from this, union organization is likely to take on the form of a craft union where membership is specialized and exclusive based on the status of a particular occupation. Finally, *paternalism* is based on an enterprise model of union organization. Here identity is based on the employment relation itself, typically within a large enterprise. Interests tend to be defined in terms of the stability of employment and seniority-based promotion within the internal labour market. These interests are typically organized by enterprise unions, who protect the interests of 'core' employees, and can be institutionalized by informal or formal mechanisms of participation in the decision-making of the firm.

These ideal types may be used to elucidate the more complex relation of actors and institutions when comparing particular cases. Indeed, Streeck argues that German industrial relations involves a unique configuration of class, occupational, and enterprise elements. German unions are organized as industrial unions based on broad class interests. At the same time, co-determination at the plant and in the company support enterprise-based interests. Tension exists between these dual bases for representation. On one hand, local cooperation between works councils and management at the company or workplace levels may undermine broader based class solidarity across different enterprises. On the other hand, German unions may integrate the company model by capturing seats in works councils and using them to implement, enforce, and adapt industry-wide collective bargaining agreements.

Works councils may also be strengthened by expertise and independence through 'outside' union support.

Similar arguments apply to occupational interests in the German apprenticeship-based vocational training system. Industrial unions have maintained solidarity among different occupational groups by supporting the upgrading of skills that leads to fewer and more broadly defined occupations and by encouraging further training that supports the mobility between occupations. This strategy is notably different from the politics of market closure prevalent among traditional craft unions. While this example cannot be discussed further here, it does suggest how institutions may embody divergent 'logics' or principles of rationality that reflect historical compromises between different groups of actors. Yet at the same time, institutions help stabilize and 'construct' the particular interests and identities of those actors within this context.

An illustration: comparative corporate governance

Corporate governance is often defined in terms of the relations between owners and managers, or more broadly between managers and various stakeholders. Corporate governance is traditionally studied within the framework of agency theory which views the interests of investors as being homogeneous functions of risk and returns. Comparative and historical studies have noted differences in the structure of share ownership across countries. For example, high concentration of ownership stakes influences the ability of shareholders to exert power through voting rights, while fragmentation tends to pacify shareholder voice. However, less attention has been given to the fact that various investors (e.g. banks, pension funds, individuals, insurance companies, hedge funds, private equity, etc.) possess different identities, interests, time horizons, and strategies (Aguilera and Jackson 2003). Many investors are themselves often organizations governed by institution-ally defined rules.

Investors may have different sorts of identities related to whether their relationship with companies is defined in a purely financial or more diffuse strategic fashion. For example, individual shareholders are usually motivated to invest by the prospect of financial return on investment. Individuals' relation to the firm may be more strategic in the case of an employee share ownership plans (ESOP). Still, the prevalence, form, and participation in ESOPs differ widely across countries, and are strongly influenced by related sets of institutions for employee voice within the firm (Poutsma et al. 2006). Another example concerns institutional investors, such as pension funds, whose identities are defined more directly by legal regulations regarding fiduciary duty to maximize the financial value of their shares on behalf of their beneficiaries. Again the prevalence of institutional investors and their size in terms of financial assets and shareholders differs widely across countries depending on the type of welfare state and system of pension provision (Jackson and Vitols 2001). Finally, banks and corporations typically use ownership stakes as a means to pursue the strategic interests of their organizations that go beyond purely financial relationships—such as regulating competition between firms, underwriting relational contracts, securing markets, managing technological dependence, or protecting managerial autonomy from outside shareholders. Once again, the capacities of banks to engage in long-term relationships with firms depend strongly on the regulatory traditions across countries (Roe 1994). Similarly national traditions of anti-trust regulation are one factor giving rise to wide variation in the structure, density, and shape of intercorporate shareholdings across countries (Windolf 2002).

Related to these different identities, shareholders define their interests in different ways—adopting different time horizons and seeking varying degrees of liquidity or commitment in their relationship to the firm. In more familiar terms, shareholders may differ with regard to their propensity to exercise exit or voice in the decision-making of the firm (Hirschman 1972). Traditionally, the literature on corporate governance describes individual investors as having a purely financial orientation and a high propensity to exit. The rise of institutional investors, such as pension funds, is conversely seen as leading to greater commitment and propensity to exercise voice in corporate governance (Useem 1996). These differences in interests reflect the different modes of organization of investment—whereas isolated individuals have little capacity to process information and mobilize efforts to discipline managers, the aggregation of individual investment in larger, professionally managed funds changes the capacity of shareholders to pursue such interests. However, as Hirschman pointed out, the choice between exit and voice is mediated by the degree of loyalty—and hence related to the identities of the actors.

Consequently, substantial variation may again exist across institutional contexts. In the USA, public sector pension funds are far more independent and activist than corporate pension funds, which are financed by corporate management and act less independently on corporate governance issues (Davis and Kim 2007). Meanwhile, pension funds play only a marginal or different role in corporate governance in other economies. In countries with strong and generous public pension provision, private pension funds have not yet accumulated large capital reserves or these funds remain organizationally embedded, such as the direct commitments between firms and employees in Germany or the relationship-based provision of life insurance in Japanese corporate groups (Jackson and Vitols 2001).

Complex and changing actor constellations are very important to understanding the diversity and change of corporate governance institutions, even in contexts that are often considered as similar market-based models based on the notion of 'shareholder value' such as the UK or USA. Historically, a managerialist model of the corporation emerged in both countries, where managers were strong and shareholders were weak due to the dispersed nature of ownership and consequent separation of ownership from control. The rise of new actors, such as pension funds, changed the power relations among these factors and gave rise to new corporate governance institutions. Their influence depended in turn on the emergence of other actors, such as takeover raiders engaged in leveraged buyouts. These actors sought to exploit particular weaknesses in corporate governance institutions and create new opportunities—namely, as individual investors would sell shares and follow strategies of 'exit', opportunities emerged for takeover raiders to buy corporations at a low price. This threat of hostile takeover gave institutional investors greater power and influence, as managers sought to keep investors loyal to the firm and thwart takeovers by higher share prices. Ultimately, the rise and institutionalization of corporate governance based on the logic of 'shareholder value' rests upon an uneasy or ambiguous compromise between different definitions of shareholder value and conflicting strategies for realizing value based on liquidity, commitment, and different organizational forms of shareholder activism.

Taken together, these examples illustrate the limits of using the concept of 'shareholders' or 'shareholder value' as a homogeneous category in comparative analysis. Shareholders differ not only in their capacity for control based on the dispersion or concentration of ownership stakes, but more fundamentally in terms of their overall orientation and social relationship to the firm in different national institutional contexts. The institutionalization of different models of corporate governance depends upon a particular configuration of identities, interests, and organizational forms of shareholders—but equally, shareholders as key 'actors' within the corporate governance process depend on institutionalized definitions of their interests, and institutionally enabled opportunities to pursue those interests vis-à-vis managers. Comparative and historical analysis makes obvious that this relationship between the actors and institutions is far from a static equilibrium, but a dynamic process of mutual interdependence where the emergence or decline of different types of actors is a driving factor behind institutional diversity and change.

One methodological implication of the non-identical nature of actors is that comparative studies always involves comparing apples with oranges to some degree (Locke and Thelen 1995). A common approach to comparative analysis has been to focus on a single process, such as globalization or financialization, and compare the different patterns of change across a range of countries. Similar pressures are mediated by diverse institutional contexts. Cross-national variation in outcomes is explained by the divergent features of the institutional context. As useful as this approach may be, the salience of a particular issue may, in fact, be very different across countries given the diverse nature of those actors. Actors not only have different interests, but have different identities, worldviews and cognitive maps. The point here is that institutional comparison must go beyond broad typologies of institutions, and look in a 'contextualized' way at the underlying identities and constellations of actors. A similar issue or process may result in different outcomes or struggles, and processes that may seem very different may sometimes result in similar outcomes. Consequently, comparisons that are parallel in an analytical sense may require focus on different sticking points and trigger different sorts of struggles over institutional change. In this, comparison always confronts a challenge of the incomparable and the imperfect balancing of historical uniqueness with theoretical generalization (Hyman 2001).

ACTION AND INSTITUTIONALIZATION

Institutions place constraints on economic actors through various regulative, normative, and cognitive pressures (Powell and DiMaggio 1991; Scott 1995). Regulative institutions are based on the making and enforcement of rules, such as formal laws that regulate behaviour. Normative institutions are rooted in collective moral understandings about legitimate behaviour. Cognitive institutions are those based on taken-for-granted definitions of the situation and worldviews. These categories are analytically distinct, and imply different mechanisms of institutionalization and carriers of institutional effects. Empirically, however, institutions may be underpinned by all three dimensions to various degrees.

Institutions also create opportunities for economic action in several ways. Any economic order requires a basic institutional infrastructure in order to function. International business scholars have stressed the importance of basic institutional infrastructure with regard to emerging and developing economies, particularly the importance of property rights and the rule of law (Khanna and Palepu 2006). But institutions not only give a basic framework for economic exchange, but may also solve certain collective action problems in ways that facilitate alternative modes of governance over transactions—such as markets, hierarchies, networks, associations, state regulation, and so on (Hollingsworth and Boyer 1997). Perhaps more importantly, institutions influence the collective supply of inputs (e.g. skills, capital) available to firms and other economic actors (Streeck 1992). Consequently, many scholars have argued that different countries may have comparative institutional advantages for different kinds of economic activity (Amable 2003; Hall and Soskice 2001; Whitley 1999). Institutional complementarities across functionally distinct institutional domains (e.g. finance, labour markets) may also lead to multiple, efficient combinations of institutions (Aoki 2001).

In understanding institutions as both constraining and enabling particular business strategies and models of economic growth, a large literature now exists based on various national typologies—most famously between liberal and coordinated market economies, but also using more elaborate classifications based on the Nordic, Germanic, Anglo-Saxon, Mediterranean, or Asian models. Yet a growing wave of criticism has been directed at these typologies as neglecting the dynamics of institutional emergence and institutional change (for an overview, see Deeg and Jackson 2007). In stressing the coherence and economic advantages of different institutional arrangements, comparative institutional analysis has faced growing criticism as being deterministic with regard to actors and their strategies. For example, in stressing the differences across countries, the diversity of organizational forms within national economies was seriously neglected (Lane and Wood 2009). Institutional scholars have given an 'oversocialized' account of institutions and one-sidedly stressed their isomorphic character. Consequently, scholars have recently tried to deepen comparative institutional approaches by a more systematic analysis of institutional change (Campbell 2004; Crouch 2005; Streeck and Thelen 2005), as will be discussed in the next chapter of this Handbook.

In the context of actors and institutions, it is nonetheless important to note that efforts to reclaim a less deterministic and more historically grounded understanding of institutions have led scholars to re-examine the relationship between institutions and action. If institutions are coercive, normative, or cognitively taken-for-granted rules that constrain action or enable 'efficient' strategies, why and how may actors change their relationships to those constraints in ways that transform institutions?[2] The short answer is that while institutions enable and constrain action, substantial indeterminacy and situational ambiguity remain. Yet this gap between institutional context and intentional action has not been sufficiently explored within institutional theory. Most existing theories of action rely on a teleological means–ends schema for understanding of human intentionality that leaves little scope for creativity (Joas 1992). Here action is conceived as the pursuit of pre-established ends or preferences that remain stable from context to context. The perception of the world is given, and separate from our actions. Actions are then 'chosen' by their anticipated consequences—in what might be termed 'portfolio models' of the actor (Whitford 2002). Even cognitive models of institutions stress how actors enact preconceived and taken-for-granted worldviews (DiMaggio and Powell 1991)—again bracketing how individuals might break with routine implicit understandings to change institutions.

A less deterministic theory of action[3] would see institutions as just one element of a situation—a Durkheimian 'social fact' within the situational horizon. Actors may interpret or utilize institutions in different ways, stretching their boundaries, adapting them to new contingencies, or avoiding them through deviant behaviour (Oliver 1991; Clemens and Cook 1999). No one-to-one relationship exists between an institution and its meaning in a specific situation (Friedland and Alford 1991: 255). Institutions represent situations only in a summary form as 'typifications' where under certain conditions X, a particular type of actor Y is expected to do Z (Berger and Luckmann 1966). As Mohr and White (2008) argue, 'Interpretive frames at the institutional level are not immediate and specific; they are general and abstract; and they are collective rhetorics that are known, shared, and embraced as orienting devices for the construction, consumption, and bundling of stories across different netdoms [domains of social networks].' Institutionalized values must remain general enough to be transposed across diverse situations, but specific enough for actors to mobilize control in enforcing an institution (White 1992). But this generality or gap between institutional rules and situational contingencies means that actors may

[2] Conceptualizing institutional change faces issues similar to the 'duality' of structure and agency examined by Bourdieu (1990) and Giddens (1984), who focus on how actors and social structures exist in a dialectical relation of mutual influence (Sewell Jr. 1992).

[3] A number of scholars in institutional theory and economic sociology have 'rediscovered' pragmatism and symbolic interactionism as a particularly relevant avenue for understanding *actors* and *institutions* (Beckert 1999, 2003, 2009; Sabel 1994; Sorge 1999). While a full discussion is beyond the scope of this chapter, Hans Joas (1992) suggests the concept of 'situation' as a basic category for a theory of action where actors pursue various 'ends-in-view' that emerge concretely out of situations based on judgements and assumptions about the type of situation and the possible actions that flow from it.

develop local styles or variations of an institution (White 1993) or have scope to challenge institutions through active political contestation (Zilber 2002).

A key implication here is that institutions must not be considered a fixed, objective reality outside of actors, but as a 'matter of degree' (Jepperson 1991). Particular relationships or behaviours may be more or less institutionalized. In the extreme, Erving Goffman (1961) used the metaphor of a 'total institution' where all situations are governed by an institution and action is only possible 'backstage' through deviations in the performance of fixed roles. But while some institutions may be rigidly prescriptive (actors 'must' follow a certain rule), others may establish more limited boundaries of what is not possible (actors 'must not' do something), and others may provide only loose models around which actors engage in substantial improvization (Crawford and Ostrom 1995).

If institutionalized action is understood as a matter of degree, how might this general theoretical consideration apply specifically to the comparative study of institutions? Here two points are relevant. First, in terms of institutions themselves, theoretical frameworks for comparisons should take into account not only differences in the type of institutions, but also the degree of institutionalization and corresponding level of organizational heterogeneity within the boundaries of an institution. For example, comparative analysis should move beyond national averages, and compare the scope of firm-level variation within different national systems (Jacoby 2004). Second, in terms of actors, comparisons should also take into account how institutions stem from particular historical constellations of actors who possess particular identities, interests, and capabilities. The remainder of this section develops these two points in more detail.

Institutions as ambiguous

Unlike uncertainty or vagueness, the concept of ambiguity suggests institutions can take on two or more specific meanings depending on the situational context (Jackson 2005). Such multiplicity of meanings is commonplace as institutions become part of changed situational horizons and ends-in-view. As any professional lawyer will know, everyday actors may not always know whether a strategy will be considered consistent with expected norms or values. If institutions are capable of being understood in more than one way, gaps between institutionalized expectation (e.g. rule or value) and strategic action must be filled (Clemens and Cook 1999: 448). These gaps allow scope for creative interpretation, application, and enactment through processes of iteration, projection, and evaluation (Emirbayer and Mische 1998). Actors will always face choice and be confronted by dilemmatic decisions (Sorge 2005).

One consequence is that different national, regional, or sectoral economies may be institutionalized to different degrees. No society or business system can be said empirically to consist of fully integrated and complementary elements. For example, the post-war Japanese model is often cited as one that is internally homogeneous and tightly coupled, characterized by strong institutional complementarities. However, the unwinding of cross-shareholding and weakening of main bank relationships in Japan since the mid-1990s did not lead to the rise of Anglo-Saxon-style forms of corporate governance based on 'shareholder value,' but rather a range of new hybrid forms of corporate governance that mixed and matched various elements of different models (Ahmadjian and Robinson 2001; Aoki et al. 2007). The more general point is that deinstitutionalization of older forms of organization is not always replaced by new models but may lead to more ambiguous and diverse patterns. Similarly, the adoption of shareholder-value orientated managerial practices in Germany led to a number of substantive innovations as a result of adapting these to an existing institutional context that is largely stakeholder-orientated (Buck and Shahrim 2005; Fiss and Zajac 2004; Sanders and Tuschke 2006; Vitols 2004). A more extreme case of weakly institutionalized forms of capitalism can be found in Eastern Europe or other transition economies. In studying the transition of Eastern European economies to market-oriented capitalism, Stark (2001) demonstrated how past institutions become 'ambiguous assets' that were used toward a variety of ends and different paths of future institutional development. The institutional flux of transition economies gave rise to very heterogeneous forms of organization that contrast with the more stable and institutionalized patterns in Western Europe.

Actor capabilities and institutionalized action

A flip side of ambiguity concerns the fact that actors interpret institutions not only with regard to exogenous elements of a situation, but vis-à-vis their own changing identities, interests, and capabilities for action. A very important observation is that actors often require particular social skills to act within an institutional setting (Fligstein 2001). Social skills are required for the everyday operation of an institution. Actors must be socialized into take-for-granted assumptions, and learn how prevailing norms are interpreted and applied by others. For example, the political economy literature has stressed how the different capabilities between large and small firms or across industrial sectors lead to differences in how actors are able to cope with or utilize institutions as a source of competitive advantage. In Japan, smaller firms in domestic industries are very dependent on regulatory protection, and have fewer resources to maintain other key institutions like lifetime employment in the absence of such protections. Meanwhile, larger firms with more international operations seem to have sufficient organizational buffers or strategic capability to maintain commitments to core employees even in the face of market and financial liberalization (Vogel 2006).

Likewise, the emergence of new skills and capacities may create opportunities for innovation or institutional change. An interesting example here is Silicon Valley. Whereas old economy firms in the region faced strong constraints on their behaviour, the creation of new start-up firms allowed many of these rules to be renegotiated and existing resources recombined in new ways that led to innovation in terms of property rights, inter-firm collaboration, and human resource management practices (Saxenian 1994). Ongoing processes of experimentation, learning, and emulation within and across institutional boundaries may lead to new organizational or individual capacities (Levitt and March 1988), and thereby speed deinstitutionalization or lead to the creation of alternative institutions over time. Expanding the boundaries of an institution may bring in new sorts of actors and thus introduce new capacities for action unforeseen when the institution was created (Thelen 2004). For example, a large literature exists on the role of multinational enterprises in introducing institutional innovation or having capacity to engage in institutional avoidance (Edwards and Ferner 2004). Skilled actors may borrow and blend from more than one institution to create innovative local styles.

An often forgotten point is that institutions may unravel because the necessary capabilities or skills for their operation and reproduction erode or even disappear over time. The post-war model of German capitalism, for example, is based on a particular set of value commitments often labelled in terms of the 'Social Market Economy' (Lehmbruch 2001). But such discourses may become eclipsed over time by new sets of ideologies and understandings, such as the ascendency of new models of management (Guillén 1994; Khurana 2007). These value commitments underlying institutions arise in experiences of self-formation and self-transcendence that lead to enduring modifications of the self—both through positive and negative experiences (Joas 1992). While non-economic value commitments may become important elements of economic institutions, their instrumentalization in service of utilitarian aims may erode those very values. This is precisely because the experiential basis of those value commitments fails to be reproduced, and cannot be reproduced on the basis of rational utilitarian calculation alone—as Durkheim was so insistent in pointing out (Durkheim 1984 [1893]).

By treating institutions as ambiguous and actors as skilled, comparative scholars may be reminded of the role of contestation, conflict, and coalitions in creating, reproducing, and changing institutions. Institutionalization requires efforts of control in enforcing institutional rules and understandings against deviant behaviour or political challenges. Recent work in organizational theory has attempted to draw links between organizations and social movements along these lines to better understanding of how institutionalized features of organizations result from collective action, as well as how the rise of new actors within organizations influences institutional change (Davis et al. 2005).

CONCLUSION

Institutions may be understood as a non-deterministic context for action. These contexts are inhabited by multiple actors with different skills and capacities. Actors may see and interpret the same institution in different ways. Such differences may give rise to contention or conflict over those meanings, and lead to the incremental modification of those institutions over time. This point is even more important given the fact that institutional contexts are comprised of a rich and differentiated set of institutions—notwithstanding the efforts of social scientists to understand societies as having coherent or functionally integrated sets of institutions.

One caveat is important here. If we view institutions as socially constructed by specific constellations of actors and view institutions as having an element of indeterminacy, this should not lead us to the opposite view that institutions are infinitely pliable. As Aoki (2001) suggests, institutions might be seen as a focal point for actors within an arena—while actors may define their identities or interests as being in line with or in conflict with an institution, the fact remains that actors must make these definitions 'with reference to existing institutions'. Institutions have the character of social facts, even when an institution remains one of many factors within a situational horizon.

For scholars engaged in comparative institutional analysis, the importance of actors has important conceptual and methodological implications. First, institutions need to be explored in an actor-centred fashion that allows for the non-identical nature of those actors across societies, sectors, or over time. Institutions are not the product of the same actors playing the same game with different outcomes. Equally, different actors may play different games with the same outcomes. This apples and oranges issue makes comparative analysis a perpetual challenge and one that often requires art or a 'sociological imagination' alongside the application of scientific methods. Second, actors' strategies toward institutions need to be explored empirically. Different institutions may be more or less constraining and lead to different degrees of institutionalization across societies and over time. This consideration suggests not merely comparing national averages from a static point of view, but also looking at the degree of variation around those means. Institutions should not be taken for granted by scholars of institutions, even if we discover that they are taken for granted by the actors themselves.

REFERENCES

AGUILERA, RUTH V. and GREGORY JACKSON (2003). 'The Cross-National Diversity of Corporate Governance: Dimensions and Determinants', *Academy of Management Review* 28(3): 447–65.

AHMADJIAN, CHRISTINA L. and PATRICIA ROBINSON (2001). 'Safety in Numbers: Downsizing and the Deinstitutionalization of Permanent Employment in Japan', *Administrative Science Quarterly* 46: 622–54.

AMABLE, BRUNO (2003). *The Diversity of Modern Capitalism*, (Oxford: Oxford University Press).

AOKI, MASAHIKO (1988). *Information, Incentives, and Bargaining in the Japanese Economy*, (Cambridge: Cambridge University Press).

——(2001). *Toward a Comparative Institutional Analysis*, (Cambridge, MA: MIT Press).

——(2007). 'Endogenizing Institutions and their Changes', *Journal of Institutional Economics* 3(1): 1–31.

AOKI, MASAHIKO, GREGORY JACKSON, and HIDEAKI MIYAJIMA (eds.) (2007). *Corporate Governance in Japan: Institutional Change and Organizational Diversity*, (Oxford: Oxford University Press).

BECKERT, JENS (1999). 'Agency, Entrepreneurs and Institutional Change: The Role of Strategic Choice and Institutionalized Practices in Organizations', *Organization Studies* 20: 777–99.

——(2003). 'Economic Sociology and Embeddedness. How Shall We Conceptualize Economic Action?', *Journal of Economic Issues* 37: 769–87.

——(2009). 'Pragmatismus und wirtschaftliches Handeln', MPIfG Working Paper 09/04.

BERGER, PETER L. and THOMAS LUCKMANN (1966). *The Social Construction of Reality: A Treatise in the Sociology of Knowledge*, (Garden City, NY: Doubleday).

BIGGART, NICOLE WOOLSEY (1991). 'Explaining Asian Economic Organization. Toward a Weberian Institutional Perspective', *Theory and Society* 20: 199–232.

BOURDIEU, PIERRE (1990). *The Logic of Practice*, (Stanford: Stanford University Press).

BUCK, TREVOR W. and A. SHAHRIM (2005). 'The Translation of Corporate Governance Changes Across National Cultures: The Case of Germany', *Journal of International Business Studies* 36: 42–61.

CAMPBELL, JOHN L. (2004). *Institutional Change and Globalization*, (Princeton, NJ: Princeton University Press).

——(2005). 'Where do we Stand? Common Mechanisms in Organizations and Social Movements Research', in *Social Movements and Organization Theory*, eds. Gerald F. Davis, Doug McAdam, W. Richard Scott, and Mayer N. Zald, (Cambridge: Cambridge University Press), pp. 41–68.

CLEMENS, ELISABETH S. and JAMES M. COOK (1999). 'Politics and Institutionalism: Explaining Durability and Change', *Annual Review of Sociology* 25: 441–66.

CRAWFORD, SUE and ELINOR OSTROM (1995). 'Grammar of Insitutions', *American Political Science Review* 89(3): 582–99.

CROUCH, COLIN (2005). *Capitalist Diversity and Change. Recombinant Governance and Institutional Entrepreneurs*, (Oxford: Oxford University Press).

DAVIS, GERALD F. and E. HAN KIM (2007). 'Business Ties and Proxy Voting by Mutual Funds', *Journal of Financial Economics* 85: 552–70.

——DOUG McADAM, W. RICHARD SCOTT, and MAYER N. ZALD (eds.) (2005). *Social Movements and Organization Theory*, (Cambridge: Cambridge University Press).

——and TRACY A. THOMPSON (1994). 'A Social Movement Perspective on Corporate Control', *Administrative Science Quarterly* 39: 141–73.

DEEG, RICHARD and GREGORY JACKSON (2007). 'Towards a More Dynamic Theory of Capitalist Variety', *Socio-Economic Review* 5(1): 149–80.

DIMAGGIO, PAUL J. and WALTER W. POWELL (1991). 'The Iron Cage Revisited: Institutional Isomorphism and Collective Rationality in Organization Fields', in *The New Institutionalism in Organizational Analysis*, eds. Walter W. Powell and Paul J. DiMaggio, (Chicago, IL: University of Chicago Press), pp. 63–82.

DOBBIN, FRANK (1994). *Forging Industrial Policy. The United States, Britain, and France in the Railway Age*, (Cambridge, UK: Cambridge University Press).

DÖHLER, MARIAN (1993). 'Comparing National Patterns of Medical Specialization: A Contribution to the Theory of Professions', *Social Science Information* 32(4): 185–223.

DURKHEIM, EMILE (1984 [1893]). *The Division of Labor in Society*, (New York: The Free Press).

EDWARDS, TONY and ANTHONY FERNER (2004). 'Multinationals, Reverse Diffusion and National Business Systems', *Management International Review* 24(1): 51–81.

EMIRBAYER, MUSTAFA and ANN MISCHE (1998). 'What is Agency?' *American Journal of Sociology* Vol.103, No.4, pp. 962–1023.

Fiss, Peer C. and Edward Zajac (2004). 'The Diffusion of Ideas over Contested Terrain: The (Non)adoption of a Shareholder Value Orientation among German Firms', *Administrative Science Quarterly* December(49): 501–34.

Fligstein, Neil (1990). *The Transformation of Corporate Control*, (Cambridge, MA: Harvard University Press).

——(2001). *The Architecture of Markets: An Economic Sociology of Capitalist Societies*, (Princeton NJ: Princeton University Press).

——(2001). 'Social Skill and the Theory of Fields', *Sociological Theory* 19(2): 105–25.

Friedland, Roger and Robert R. Alford (1991). 'Bringing Society Back In: Symbols, Practices, and Institutional Contradictions', in *The New Institutionalism in Organizational Analysis*, eds. Walter W. Powell and Paul J. DiMaggio (Chicago, IL: University of Chicago Press), pp. 232–66.

Giddens, Anthony (1984). *The Constitution of Society*, (Berkeley: University of California Press).

Goffman, Erving (1961). *Asylums: Essays on the Social Situation of Mental Patients and Other Inmates*, (Garden City, NY: Doubleday Anchor).

Gourevitch, Peter A. and James Shinn (2005). *Political Power and Corporate Control: The New Global Politics of Corporate Governance*, (Princeton, NJ: Princeton University Press).

Greif, Avner (2005). *Institutions: Theory and History*, (Cambridge, UK: Cambridge University Press).

Guillén, Mauro F. (1994). *Models of Management: Work, Authority and Organization in Comparative Perspective*, (Chicago, IL: University of Chicago Press).

Hall, Peter A. and David Soskice (eds.) (2001). *Varieties of Capitalism: The Institutional Foundations of Comparative Advantage*, (Oxford: Oxford University Press).

——and Rosemary C. R. Taylor (1996). 'Political Science and the Three New Institutionalisms', *Max-Planck-Institut für Gesellschaftsforschung*, Discussion Paper(6).

Herrigel, Gary (2008). 'Roles and Rules: Ambiguity, Experimentation and New Forms of Stakeholderism in Germany', *Industrielle Beziehungen* 15(2): 111–32.

Hirschman, Albert O. (1972). *Exit, Voice, and Loyalty: Responses to Decline in Firms, Organizations, and States*, (Cambridge, MA: Harvard University Press).

Hollingsworth, J. Rogers and Robert Boyer (1997). *Contemporary Capitalism: The Embeddedness of Institutions*, (Cambridge, UK; New York: Cambridge University Press).

Hyman, Richard (2001). 'Trade Union Research and Cross-National Comparison', *European Journal of Industrial Relations* 7(2): 203–32.

Ingram, Paul and Karen Clary (2000). 'The Choice-Within-Constraints: New Institutionalism and Implications for Sociology', *Annual Review of Sociology* 26: 525–46.

Jackson, Gregory (2005). 'Contested Boundaries: Ambiguity and Creativity in the Evolution of German Codetermination', in *Beyond Continuity: Institutional Change in Advanced Political Economies*, eds. Wolfgang Streeck and Kathleen Thelen, (Oxford: Oxford University Press), pp. 229–54.

——(2008). 'From Comparing Capitalisms to the Politics of Institutional Change', *Review of International Political Economy* 15(4): 680–709.

——and Sigurt Vitols (2001). 'Between Financial Commitment, Market Liquidity and Corporate Governance: Occupational Pensions in Britain, Germany, Japan and the USA', in *Comparing Welfare Capitalism. Social Policy and Political Economy in Europe, Japan and the USA*, eds. Bernhard Ebbinghaus and Philip Manow, (London: Routledge), pp. 171–89.

——and Richard Deeg (2008). 'Comparing Capitalisms: Understanding Institutional Diversity and Its Implications for International Business', *Journal of International Business Studies* 39(4): 540–61.

——MARI SAKO, CHRISTEL LANE, and RICHARD HYMAN (2008). 'Dialogue on Comparative Institutional Analysis and International Business', in *Corporate Governance and International Business: Strategy, Performance and Institutional Change*, eds. Roger Strange and Gregory Jackson, (London: Palgrave), pp. 151–67.

JACOBY, SANFORD M. (2004). *The Embedded Corporation: Corporate Governance and Employment Relations in Japan and the United States*, (Princeton, NJ: Princeton University Press).

JEPPERSON, RONALD L. (1991). 'Institutions, Institutional Effects, and Institutionalism', in *The New Institutionalism in Organizational Analysis*, eds. Walter W. Powell and Paul J. DiMaggio, (Chicago, IL: University of Chicago Press), pp. 143–63.

JOAS, HANS (1992). *Die Kreativität des Handelns*, (Frankfurt am Main: Suhrkamp).

KHANNA, TARUN and KRISHNA PALEPU (2006). 'Stategies that Fit Emerging Markets', *Harvard Business Review* 84(June): 60–9.

KHURANA, RAKESH (2007). *From Higher Aims to Hired Hands: The Social Transformation of American Business Schools and the Unfulfilled Promise of Management as a Profession*, (Cambridge, MA: Harvard Business School Press).

LA PORTA, RAFAEL, FLORENCIO LOPEZ-DE-SILANES, and ANDREI SHLEIFER (1999). 'Corporate Ownership Around the World', *Journal of Finance* 54(2): 471–517.

——————and ROBERT W. VISHNEY (1998). 'Law and Finance', *Journal of Political Economy* 106(6): 1113–55.

————————(2000). 'Investor Protection and Corporate Governance', *Journal of Financial Economics* 58: 3–27.

LANE, CHRISTEL and GEOFFREY WOOD (2009). 'Introducing Capitalist Diversity and Diversity in Capitalism', *Economy and Society* 39(4):530–50.

LEHMBRUCH, GERHARD (2001). 'The Institutional Embedding of Market Economics: The German "Model" and its Impact on Japan', in *The Origins of Nonliberal Capitalism: Germany and Japan in Comparison*, eds. Wolfgang Streeck and Kozo Yamamura, (Ithaca, NY: Cornell University Press), pp. 39–93.

LEVITT, B. and JAMES G. MARCH (1988). 'Organizational Learning', *Annual Review of Sociology* 14: 319–40.

LOCKE, RICHARD M. and KATHLEEN THELEN (1995). 'Apples and Oranges Revisited: Contextualized Comparisons and the Study of Comparative Labor Politics', *Politics and Society* 23(3): 337–67.

MAURICE, MARC, FRANCOIS SELLIER, and JEAN-JACQUES SILVESTRE, (1986). *The Social Foundations of Industrial Power: A Comparison of France and Germany*, (Cambridge, MA.: MIT Press).

MAYNTZ, RENATE and FRITZ W. SCHARPF, (1995). 'Der Ansatz des akteurzentrierten Institutionalismus', in *Gesellschaftliche Selbstregelung und politische Steuerung*, eds. Renate Mayntz and Fritz W. Scharpf, (Frankfurt am Main: Campus), pp. 39–72.

MEYER, JOHN M. and B. ROWAN (1977). 'Institutionalized Organizations: Formal Structure as Myth and Ceremony', *American Journal of Sociology* 83: 340–63.

MOHR, JOHN W. and HARRISON C. WHITE (2008). 'How to Model an Institution', *Theory and Society* 37(5): 485–512.

NORTH, DOUGLASS C. (1990). *Institutions, Institutional Change and Economic Performance*, (Cambridge: Cambrige University Press).

OLIVER, CHRISTINE (1991). 'Strategic Responses to Institutional Processes', *Academy of Management Review* 16: 145–79.

POUTSMA, ERIK, PANU KALMI, and ANDREW PENDLETON (2006). 'The Relationship between Financial Participation and Other Forms of Employee Participation: New Survey Evidence from Europe', *Economic and Industrial Democracy* 27(4): 637–67.

POWELL, WALTER W. and PAUL J. DiMAGGIO (eds.) (1991). *The New Institutionalism in Organizational Analysis*, (Chicago, IL: University of Chicago Press).

ROE, MARK J. (1994). *Strong Managers, Weak Owners: The Political Roots of American Corporate Finance*, (Princeton, NJ: Princeton University Press).

SABEL, CHARLES F. (1994). 'Learning By Monitoring: The Institutions of Economic Development', in *The Handbook of Economic Sociology*, eds. Neil J. Smelser and Richard Sweberg, (Princeton, NJ: Princeton University Press).

SANDERS, W. M. GERARD and ANJA CHRISTINE TUSCHKE (2006). 'The Adoption of Institutionally Contested Organizational Practices: The Emergence of Stock Option Pay in Germany', *Academy of Management Journal* 50(1): 33–56.

SAXENIAN, ANNALEE (1994). *Regional Advantage: Culture and Competition in Silicon Valley and Route 128* (Cambridge, MA.: Harvard University Press).

SCHARPF, FRITZ (1987). *Crisis and Choice in European Social Democracy*, (Ithaca, NY: Cornell University Press).

——(1997). *Games Real Actors Play: Actor-Centered Institutionalism in Policy Research*, (Boulder, CO: Westview Press).

SCOTT, W. RICHARD (1995). *Institutions and Organizations*, (London: Sage Publications).

——and SOREN CHRISTENSEN (eds.) (1995). *The Institutional Construction of Organizations: International and Longitudinal Studies*, (Thousand Oaks, CA: Sage).

SEWELL Jr., WILLIAM H. (1992). 'A Theory of Structure: Duality, Agency, and Transformation', *American Journal of Sociology* 98(1): 1–29.

SIMMEL, GEORG (1955). *Conflict and the Web of Group Affiliations*, (New York: Free Press).

SORGE, ARNDT (1999). 'Organizing Societal Space within Globalization: Bringing Society Back In', MPIfG Working Paper, 99/10.

——(2005). *The Global and the Local: Understanding the Dialectics of Business Systems*, (Oxford: Oxford University Press).

——and MALCOM WARNER (1986). *Comparative Factory Organization: An Anglo-German Comparison of Manufacturing, Management and Manpower*, (Aldershot: Gower).

STARK, DAVID (2001). 'Ambiguous Assets for Uncertain Environments: Heterarchy in Postsocialist Firms', in *The Twenty-First-Century Firm. Changing Economic Organization in International Perspective*, ed. Paul DiMaggio, (Princeton, NJ: Princeton University Press), pp. 69–104.

STEINMO, SVEN and KATHLEEN ANN THELEN (1992). 'Historical Institutionalism in Comparative Politics', in *Structuring Politics: Historical Institutionalism in Comparative Analysis*, eds. Sven Steinmo, Kathleen Ann Thelen, and Frank Longstreth, (Cambridge, UK: Cambridge University Press), pp. 1–32.

STREECK, WOLFGANG (1992). *Social Institutions and Economic Performance: Studies of Industrial Relations in Advanced Capitalist Economies*, (London; Newbury Park, CA: Sage).

——(1993). 'Klass, Beruf, Unternehmen, Distrikt: Organisationsgrundlagen industrieller Beziehung im Europäischen Binnenmarkt', in *Innovation und Beharrung in der Arbeitspolitik*, eds. Burkhard Strümpel and Meinold Dierkes, (Stuttgart: Schäffer-Poeschel Verlag), pp. 39–68.

——and KATHLEEN THELEN (eds.) (2005). *Beyond Continuity: Institutional Change in Advanced Political Economies*, (Oxford: Oxford University Press).

THELEN, KATHLEEN, (2004). *How Institutions Evolve: The Political Economy of Skills in Germany, Britain, the United States and Japan*, (Cambridge, UK: Cambridge University Press).

USEEM, MICHAEL (1996). *Investor Capitalism: How Money Managers are Changing the Face of Corporate America*, (New York: Basic Books).

VITOLS, SIGURT (2004). 'Negotiated Shareholder Value: The German Version of an Anglo-American Practice', *Competition and Change* 8(4): 1–18.

VOGEL, STEVEN K. (2006). *Japan Remodeled: How Government and Industry are Reforming Japanese Capitalism*, (Ithaca, NY: Cornell University Press).

WHITE, HARRISON C. (1992). *Identity and Control: A Structural Theory of Social Action*, (Princeton, NJ: Princeton University Press).

——(1993). *Careers and Creativity. Social Forces in the Arts*, (Boulder, CO: Westview Press).

WHITFORD, JOSH (2002). 'Pragmatism and the Untenable Dualism of Means and Ends: Why Rational Choice Theory Does Not Deserve Paradigmatic Privilege', *Theory and Society* 31(3): 325–63.

WHITLEY, RICHARD (1999). *Divergent Capitalisms: The Social Structuring and Change of Business Systems*, (Oxford: Oxford University Press).

WINDOLF, PAUL (2002). *Corporate Networks in the United States and Europe*, (Oxford: Oxford University Press).

ZILBER, TAMMAR B. (2002). 'Institutionalization as an Interplay Between Actions, Meanings, and Actors: The Case of a Rape Crisis Center in Israel', *Academy of Management Journal* 45(1): 234–54.

CHAPTER 4

INSTITUTIONAL REPRODUCTION AND CHANGE

JOHN L. CAMPBELL[1]

INTRODUCTION

How and why do political-economic institutions change or remain the same? This chapter explores a variety of theories and empirical studies that seek to answer this question. It concentrates primarily on political-economic institutions in advanced capitalist democracies. And it focuses on literatures in comparative political economy and organizational analysis rather than, for instance, social movements theory, which is also interested in institutional stability and change but not necessarily with respect to the sorts of political-economic institutions that are of primary concern in this volume.[2]

The scholarship in question here is largely a product of the last thirty years or so. Interest in institutional change began to grow significantly in the 1970s. Stagflation emerged as a worldwide problem and both governments and firms began to alter their institutional arrangements in order to cope with it. Moreover, transnational investment, trade, and other forms of economic activity (i.e. globalization) began to develop around the same time and accelerated after the mid-1980s. National forms of

---

[1] Glenn Morgan and Ove Pedersen provided helpful comments on an earlier draft.

[2] That said, there are important parallels between the social movements literature and the literature on institutional analysis and change such that a dialogue between them may be fruitful for better understanding the processes of institutional stability and change (e.g. Campbell 2005).

capitalism began to change in response. As scholars saw what was happening around them they became interested in researching and theorizing the conditions under which institutions changed or not.

To put things into perspective however, first, I begin by reviewing some historical antecedents of this scholarship. Second, I examine theories of institutional reproduction and stability, which focus predominantly on the concept of path dependence. Third, I discuss theories of institutional change and do so at greater length because this is where comparative institutional analysis has had the most to offer. There are several of these theories and I present them more or less in chronological order so that readers can appreciate the debates that have evolved within this literature. Fourth, I address briefly the ontology of institutional change, that is, what we mean by institutions and how we know if they have changed or not. Finally, I conclude with a few remarks about where the study of institutional reproduction and change seems to be headed. Among other things, we are now beginning to realize that the processes of institutional reproduction and change are mutually constitutive in the sense that many of the forces that change institutions also stabilize them. This is why I address both theories of institutional reproduction and change in this chapter.

It is worth highlighting in advance some of the more important points made here. First, the processes of institutional reproduction and change are contested. They involve considerable struggle, conflict, and negotiation. Power is central to all of this. Second, scholars have gradually come to recognize that theories of institutional reproduction and change must pay close attention to the mechanisms by which institutions are stabilized or transformed. Unless they do this, theories risk lapsing into functionalist tautology. Third, there is a growing tendency for researchers and theorists to think about institutional change in terms of the changing functions that institutions may come to perform. While it is important to understand what institutions do, to equate institutional change with a change in the functions they perform is a dangerous analytic precedent that is fraught with difficulties.

HISTORICAL ANTECEDENTS

For a long time comparative institutional analysis was not concerned with either institutional change or reproduction per se. Instead most scholarship focused on how fixed institutions varied across countries, and how cross-national variation in these institutions affected a variety of national-level outcomes, such as economic policy, unemployment, inflation, and growth (e.g. Katzenstein 1978; Gourevitch 1986). Some recognized that there was considerable institutional variation across sectors within national political economies and that these variations also had important effects on sector-level policies and performance (Hollingsworth et al. 1994). For the most part, this was all in the spirit of a comparative statics approach to institutional analysis. That is, cross-national institutional variations were viewed as the critical independent variables used to explain political-economic outcomes (Thelen and Steinmo 1992). Little attention was paid to how or why the institutions themselves changed or remained the same.

This is not to say that nobody was concerned with institutional reproduction and change. During the 1950s and 1960s modernization theorists wrote about how democratic and capitalist institutions would spread around the world thanks to the wonders of technological change and industrialization, and how these modern societies would be preferable to and eventually replace the alternatives like socialism (e.g. Rostow 1960). Conversely, during the 1960s and 1970s, neo-Marxists developed theories about how capitalist institutions were reproduced in the short run, but would eventually be transformed into socialism in the long run thanks to the forces of class struggle and the structural contradictions that permeated capitalist democracies (e.g. O'Connor 1973; Poulantzas 1974). By the 1980s, both of these perspectives were largely discredited by world events, but also by the realization that there were significant institutional differences among advanced capitalist societies and that these differences mattered for their performance—an insight closely associated with a Weberian renaissance among political scientists and sociologists (e.g. Evans et al. 1985). Finally, and foreshadowing this renaissance, some scholars offered conjunctural theories about the political and ideological conditions under which capitalist institutions were likely to develop (Gershenkron 1962). But this perspective was more concerned with the development of capitalism per se than with institutional variation and transformation within capitalism.

As noted above, beginning in the 1980s all of this began to change. Scholars began to call for an analysis of the conditions under which institutional variations within capitalism emerged and changed historically (Campbell et al. 1991; Thelen and Steinmo 1992). To a degree, this was sparked in comparative political economy by the notion that the so-called Fordist model, based on mass production and mass consumption institutions like the multidivisional firm and Keynesian welfare state, had started to give way to a post-Fordist model, based on much different institutions, such as less hierarchical and more flexibly organized firms, smaller welfare states, and less economic regulation (Lash and Urry 1987). It was also driven by recognition that some of these institutions had come under considerable pressure to change in response to the problems of stagflation, globalization, and the rise of neo-liberalism (Campbell and Pedersen 2001).

One branch of institutional analysis—that associated with sociology and organization studies—became interested in institutional change at about the same time, but for reasons largely unrelated to the late twentieth-century political-economic climate. These researchers were interested more in the long historical view and why, in their view, a worldwide political culture was emerging in which nation-states began to adopt a common set of institutional practices, such as similar educational systems, democratic institutions, and rational scientific modes of thought (Thomas et al. 1987). Based on this work, scholars began to theorize about how national institutions adapted to this emergent world culture.

The point is that by the late 1980s social scientists became increasingly interested in institutional stability and change. Much of this work has adopted a cross-national focus.

INSTITUTIONAL REPRODUCTION

As researchers began to turn their attention to the analysis of change, they recognized that institutions typically do not change rapidly—they are sticky, resistant to change, and generally only change in 'path dependent' ways. The concept of path dependence refers to a process where contingent events or decisions result in institutions being established that tend to persist over long periods of time and constrain the range of options available to actors in the future, including those that may be more efficient or effective in the long run. In other words, latter events are largely, but not entirely, dependent on those that preceded them (e.g. Nelson 1994: 132; North 1990: 93–5; Pierson 2000b; Roe 1996). Scholars who argue that institutional and policy 'legacies' constrain change make very similar arguments (e.g. Berman 1998; Dobbin 1994; Guillén 2001; Steinmo et al. 1992).

The path dependence concept is now commonplace and has been discussed extensively elsewhere (e.g. Ebbinghaus 2005; Djelic and Quack 2007; Mahoney 2000). It has been used, for example, to characterize the development of economic institutions in China (Guthrie 1999) and post-communist Europe (Stark and Bruszt 1998) as well as in the advanced capitalist countries (North 1990). It has also been used to describe a variety of welfare and other public policy developments (Korpi 2001; Pierson 2000b; Prasad 2006).

Scholars have complained that the path dependence concept is used without a clear specification of the causal mechanisms involved (Knight 1998: 97; North 1998: 21–2; Thelen 1999). But when they are specified, a variety of mechanisms can come into play (Deeg 2005: 22–5). For instance, political scientists often argue that path dependence occurs in politics as a result of feedback mechanisms through which actors gain increasing returns for behaving in ways that are consistent with how they have acted in the past. As a result, institutions and the behaviour associated with them become locked into a particular path of historical development (Pierson 2000a, 2000b). Why? First, political institutions have large start-up costs so that once they are established actors are not likely to seek to change them, especially if they perceive that the chances of other actors joining them to innovate are increasingly slim given the costs involved. Second, sometimes politicians deliberately build institutions in ways that make them difficult to change. They may, for instance, impose procedural obstacles, such as super majority voting rules, to prevent others from later changing the institutions that they create. Third, once a particular policy style or decision-making approach has been institutionalized, actors accumulate knowledge about how it works. The more familiar and comfortable they become with it, the more hesitant they are to deviate from it. Fourth, beneficiaries of legislative or institutional largesse reinforce institutional behaviour that will continue to provide them with benefits. Senior citizens, for example, will support politicians who promise to protect the social security systems upon which seniors depend. Arguments about lock in, feedback, and the like are typically derived from the work of economic historians, who have maintained that these sorts of mechanisms restrict actors to a particular path of economic or technological development (e.g. Arthur 1994; David 1985).

Another version of the path dependence argument comes from sociologists who argue that principles and practices become institutionalized to the extent that they are taken for granted by the actors involved in them (Jepperson 1991). Notably, Dobbin (1994) argued that the development of railroad systems in Britain, France, and the United States resulted in very different organizational forms, but that they were entirely consistent with the organizational forms of earlier turnpike and canal systems within each country. This was due to the fact that decision-makers in each country had certain taken-for-granted assumptions about the appropriate way to build a transportation system. The French, for example, assumed that it should be done in a very centralized fashion with strong direction from the national government. The Americans assumed that it should be done in a more decentralized fashion with much control being delegated to the private sector. The point is that within each country transportation systems developed in path dependent ways as a result of the normative and cognitive mindset of the actors involved. These are rather different mechanisms from those involving sunk costs, strategic obstacles, vested knowledge, or institutional constituents, although none of these are necessarily mutually exclusive in practice.

Finally, comparative political economists have written much lately about institutional complementarities and how they lead to institutional reproduction. The idea here is that any political economy consists of several institutions, such as those governing finance, labour-management relations, corporate governance, labour markets, and more. Over time, these institutions develop in ways that functionally complement one another and that tend towards institutional stability. The classic formulation is by Hall and Soskice (2001), who distinguish between two varieties of capitalism: liberal and coordinated market economies. This approach is referred to as the 'varieties of capitalism' approach. They argue that institutions complement each other to the extent that the functioning of one enhances the functioning of another. For instance, the returns from stock market trading may be enhanced more by rules requiring fuller exchange of information about corporate activity than by rules requiring less transparency. The implication is that the interconnectedness of institutions, and the complementarities or synergies that result, make it very difficult to change one institution because changing one implies changing others as well since they are tightly coupled. And changing one could undermine the benefits resulting from institutional complementarity. Hence, the institutional configuration of different types of national political economies tend to be rather stable even in the presence of considerable pressures for change (Aoki 2001; Crouch 2005: 30–1).

All of these literatures are well suited to explaining institutional reproduction and persistence. However, many scholars have used the concept of path dependence to explain why institutional change tends to be slow and incremental. Things change slowly, they say, precisely because these sorts of path dependent processes are operating. Hence, change typically occurs only at the margins, which in turn means that institutions tend to change only in incremental or evolutionary ways (e.g. North 1990; Pierson 2000a; Roe 1996).[3] But here we run into a problem. How can we explain change by relying on an analysis of mechanisms that block change? This is a logical trap into which many path dependent explanations of institutional change fall (Campbell 2004, chap. 3; Thelen 1999, 2000a, 2000b). In this sense, path dependence arguments are often very deterministic (Ebbinghaus 2005; Haydu 1998).

Some researchers have tried to theorize change mechanisms in arguments about path dependence by introducing the concept of critical junctures—that is, major exogenous shocks and crises that disrupt the status quo and trigger fundamental institutional changes (Haydu 1998; Thelen 1999). Things like wars and energy crises are good examples of critical junctures in so far as the transformation of political institutions is concerned. Such arguments often invoke the notion of punctuated equilibrium where institutions are stable until disrupted suddenly by a shock, which triggers a major institutional adjustment and eventually a new equilibrium (Krasner 1984). But there are at least three problems with this approach. First, shocks and crises of the sort that constitute critical junctures explain why major, revolutionary changes occur, but not why more incremental or evolutionary (i.e. path dependent) change happens (Thelen 2000a, 2000b). Second, the critical junctures approach assumes that the impetus for institutional change comes in the form of an exogenous shock. There is little recognition that the internal inconsistencies and contradictions of an institutional arrangement may also spawn crises that result in its transformation (Haydu 1998; Schneiberg 1999). Third, the critical junctures approach tends to focus our attention on the key events that create pressures for change, but not on the complex search process that follows whereby actors actually determine what institutional changes to make, if any (e.g. Campbell and Lindberg 1991). It would appear, then, that we need a more nuanced approach to explain institutional change than those found typically in arguments about path dependence.

INSTITUTIONAL CHANGE

Several schools of thought can be identified that seek to explain how institutions change cross-nationally. These include arguments that emphasize functionalism and technical efficiency, diffusion, conflict and power, bricolage and translation, gaps

---

[3] There are strong and weak versions of the path dependence argument with the weaker ones being more open to the possibilities of incremental change along relatively fixed paths. For further discussion of the difference between strong and weak versions, see Djelic and Quack (2007) and Ebbinghaus (2005).

between intentions and outcomes, and institutional complexity. It is important to note that while these approaches differ in many respects, most of them avoid the punctuated equilibrium view of change.

Functionalism and technical efficiency

Early work in comparative political economy on institutional change stemmed from a critique of efficiency-based or functionalist theories. In particular, scholars criticized two streams of work. One was Alfred Chandler's (1977) research on the rise of the modern corporation in the United States. Chandler argued that in the United States managers shifted from a uni-divisional to a multidivisional firm structure in response to improvements in communication and transportation technologies, which led to the development of national and international markets for mass produced goods. Multidivisional firms were better equipped organizationally to manage the vast inputs and outputs required in order to achieve economies of scale. Hence, they were more efficient and, thus, more likely to survive in this new environment. Scholars have extended Chandler's logic by arguing that new innovations in communication and transportation technologies, such as the Internet and overnight delivery service, create larger and more volatile markets, which have elicited a functional response in the form of new, decentralized, and networked inter-firm arrangements (Powell 1987, 1990).

The other stream of scholarship receiving criticism was that of Oliver Williamson (1985), who argued that when specialized assets were required for manufacturing or marketing, and when inputs or outputs tended to be procured repeatedly from the same firm, the most efficient way to organize production and distribution was through hierarchically organized firms, such as those that Chandler studied, rather than through market contracting. This was because under these conditions hierarchies reduced transaction costs relative to what they would be in the market. Thus Chandler, Williamson, and their followers believed that institutional change was a functional response to changes in the technical environments within which firms operated, and that the most functionally efficient institutions tended to prevail over time.

Much of this work was based on analyses of the United States. However, subsequent criticisms were often based on cross-national research, which raised serious questions about the adequacy of these theories and suggested that had Chandler and Williamson been more sensitive to cases from other countries, they might have been more circumspect in their arguments. For instance, it is apparent that the organization of industries with similar technical requirements and markets can vary considerably across countries. One reason for this may have to do with cultural differences. British and American managers may be much less inclined to trust managers in other firms with whom they have to deal than is the case with Japanese managers, because Japanese culture places a greater premium on honourable behaviour than does Anglo-Saxon culture. Hence, the incentives to move contracting out of the market and into large vertically integrated, multidivisional firms in order to mitigate opportunistic behaviour and reduce transaction costs may be greater in Britain and the United States than in Japan. And this may be why the auto industry, for example, has traditionally been more vertically integrated in Britain and the United States whereas it has involved much more long-term sub-contracting and outsourcing in Japan (Dore 1983). This may also be one reason why, despite the rise of economic globalization and increased international competition, national political economies have not demonstrated much convergence towards common modes of corporate governance, human resource management, or other institutionalized business practices as globalization has advanced (Dore 2000; Jacoby 2005). In other words, cultural and social relations may mediate the degree to which changes in the technical environment necessarily precipitate institutional transformations (see also Granovetter 1985).

Researchers have also criticized the functionalist view for neglecting the role of the state and politics in explaining institutional change (Campbell and Lindberg 1990; Fligstein 1990; Guillén 1994; Perrow 2002). Much research shows that the state influences how the economy is organized. One example is Dobbin's work on railroads. But other studies show that for political as well as cultural reasons political leaders can inhibit the development of certain types of economic arrangements and facilitate others. This is one reason why, for instance, Taiwan developed a form of capitalism based on networks of family-owned firms; South Korea developed the chaebol form of capitalism; and Japan developed business groups consisting of many firms, connected through complex cross-shareholding arrangements (Hamilton and Biggart 1988). It is also why Italy has become famous for its industrial districts, which are an artefact of the post-war Christian Democratic Party's efforts to encourage the development of small and medium-sized firms (Weiss 1988). Especially important in all of this are national legal systems, which can affect the institutional arrangement of firms in the economy as well as their relationships with investors and other stakeholders (Roe 1994, 2003).

Despite the important insights of these criticisms of functionalist and efficiency-based arguments, few of them spend much time addressing the issue of change. Rather they engage in the sort of comparative statics approach discussed earlier where cross-national institutional variations, this time in either culture or political systems, account for the degree to which economies tend to follow the developmental trajectories specified by efficiency theorists.

Theories that emphasize functional or efficient outcomes are frequently rooted in rational choice theory. Williamson's theory of institutional change is a good example. However, some rational choice theorists have offered theories of institutional change that are neither functionalist nor assume that institutions tend necessarily toward efficiency. Notably, Douglass North (1990) argued that actors sometimes seek to renegotiate institutional arrangements as their preferences change. New institutions may or may not emerge and, if they do, they may or may not be more efficient. It depends, according to North, on the relative bargaining strength of the actors involved, their perceptions and interpretations of the situation and possibilities for change, and the prevailing institutional arrangements, which may be resistant to change as a result of various mechanisms that tend to lock them into place in path dependent ways.[4] This sort of argument has also been used recently to explain the dramatic deterioration of institutions in ways that severely compromise efficient economic growth. In particular, Robert Bates (2008) showed how many African states turned toward corrupt and predatory policies when, in the face of declining state revenues, their leaders moved to line their own pockets and reinforce their political power in ways that ruined the national economy.

Sceptics would argue that theories such as these ignore how things like values, ideologies, and other types of ideas may also affect institutional change (e.g. Blyth 2002; McNamara 1998). In his more recent work, North (2005) deliberately tackles these issues. He explains that one cannot understand institutional change without theorizing how the culturally and ideologically filtered perceptions of individuals set normative and cognitive constraints on their ability to change institutions in ways that yield more efficient outcomes. And he argues that explaining these constraints is essential because actors typically face situations marked by considerable uncertainty and incomplete information, which means that their ability to calculate rationally is limited. Hence, they must resort to a variety of cognitive schema in order to make sense of their situations and figure out what institutional changes to make. The fact that North points towards the importance of ideas, cognition and perception, offers a bridge to another and very different view of institutional change.

Diffusion

In contrast to rational choice arguments, John Meyer and several of his colleagues at Stanford University and elsewhere developed the idea that institutions and institutional change are not the result of either efficiency considerations or functionalist imperatives. Rather they are the result of organizations seeking legitimacy from their peers within a field of related organizations (Thomas et al. 1987). In other words, organizations operate according to a logic of appropriateness rather than a logic of instrumentality (March and Olsen 1989). They showed through a series of empirical studies that western institutional practices diffuse among nation-states such that over time countries tend to converge on common institutional norms that is, a set of principles and practices that are deemed appropriate and legitimate by their peers within the field. Hence, a decentralized world culture emerged gradually during the twentieth century. For instance, nation-states have adopted common educational, environmental, human rights, scientific, and other practices that have been codified through international codes of conduct, treaties, and transnational organizations, such as the United Nations (e.g. Meyer et al. 1997a, 1997b).

---

[4] Within rational choice theory, bargaining strength, power relations, and negotiation have become increasingly important for theories of institutional change (e.g. Knight 1992, 2001; Ostrom 1990; Scharpf 1997).

Debate revolves around the mechanisms by which this sort of diffusion occurs, particularly in so far as it leads to the spread of institutions modelled after the advanced capitalist nations. The Stanford School typically argues that convergent or isomorphic outcomes stem from either a normative process, whereby organizations learn what the normatively appropriate practices are and then move to adopt them, or a mimetic process, whereby organizations observe the surrounding organizations, evaluate which ones are performing best, and then copy what they do in the hope that so doing will enhance their own performance (DiMaggio and Powell 1983). Research on developing countries, however, points to the fact that western practices are often coercively imposed on countries by international organizations, such as the International Monetary Fund or World Bank, in exchange for loans and other valuable resources (Haggard and Kaufman 1995; Stallings 1992).

The diffusion perspective has been criticized on several grounds. First, despite claims that the mimetic and normative processes of isomorphic change are the most common, much of the research does not convincingly make the case due to methodological flaws. In particular, these mechanisms are imputed rather than demonstrated empirically because researchers have been more concerned with investigating how much isomorphism occurs, rather than testing competing theories of how it occurs (Mizruchi and Fein 1999). This situation has started to improve lately as researchers have begun, for example, to study how particular actors, such as international non-governmental organizations, influence the policies and practices of nation-states through combinations of normative and coercive pressures (Boli and Thomas 1999; Keck and Sikkink 1998). Recent studies of globalization have also begun to test the mechanisms by which political and economic institutions have diffused internationally. They have found that all three mechanisms noted above (coercive, normative, and mimetic) have been operating, but that a fourth mechanism—competition—has also been evident where countries change because they believe that if they do not match the institutions of competitor states, then they will lose out (Dobbin et al. 2007; Simmons et al. 2008).[5] In this work it is clear that the mechanisms postulated by diffusion theorists are not mutually exclusive explanations because combinations of these mechanisms may operate in particular cases (e.g. Babb 2001; Campbell 2001; Halliday and Carruthers 2007).

Second, critics have charged that diffusion models are too simple; they fail to take seriously the notion that diffusing institutional practices are modified and transformed when adopted by receiving countries (Djelic 1998; Duina 2006; Soysal 1994; Westney 1987). This is so even when a group of countries agrees to adopt a common practice, such as directives from the European Union, which are often modified by member states during their initial translation into national law, and again during implementation, in order to fit their unique institutional traditions (Duina 1999).

---

[5] The identification of competition as a fourth diffusion mechanism is not a new discovery, although it is one that is often neglected by diffusion theorists. Indeed, the classic article by DiMaggio and Powell (1983) that is generally credited with bringing coercive, normative, and mimetic diffusion mechanisms to the attention of scholars also recognized the importance of competition.

Thus, what may appear initially to be a case of isomorphic diffusion often involves considerable cross-national variation.

Finally, and following the last point, the diffusion perspective often dwells on cross-national similarities rather than differences. In other words, it turns a blind eye towards the important institutional differences that may exist across countries, the origins of these differences, the mechanisms that reproduce them, and therefore the significant effects that they may have for political-economic performance. This is in sharp contrast to theories of institutional change that focus on how conflict and power shape the institutional profiles of different countries in different ways.

Conflict and power struggles

Taking exception with the idea that institutional change is driven by a logic of appropriateness, a third perspective argues that institutional change is determined largely by conflicts and struggles to control valued resources, dominate markets, and otherwise obtain power (Amable 2003; Campbell 2004, ch. 6). Those who are most powerful get the institutions they want and are best able to change them to fit their purposes. For instance, Mark Roe (1994, 2003) showed that cross-national differences in corporate governance institutions resulted from political struggles among contending interest groups. In the United States, large insurance companies, investment banks, pension funds, and mutual funds have long been prevented by law from owning large blocks of stock in a firm. This is because politicians, banks, and other interested actors at the state and local levels feared the emergence of monopolistic financial intermediaries and passed legislation limiting stock ownership by these organizations. Hence, stock has long been held by a plethora of small, fragmented shareholders—a situation that affords corporate managers tremendous autonomy from shareholders and, thus, control over the firm. In other countries, such as Japan and Germany, the constellation of interests and political power was very different so legal obstacles to concentrated ownership were largely absent and shareholders gained more control vis-a-vis managers over firms.

Much of the literature on institutional change within this perspective pays close attention to the relationship between the state and economy, often arguing that economic institutions are embedded in and thus largely determined by the political context within which they operate (Campbell and Lindberg 1990). So, for instance, researchers have shown that political fights led to changes in property rights and anti-trust law and, therefore, changes in institutionalized corporate practices (Fligstein 1990; Guillén 1994), inter-firm relations (Campbell and Lindberg 1990), industrial arrangements (Best 1990; Perrow 2002), and the trajectory of capitalism per se (North 1981). Conversely, scholars have argued that the resilience of shareholder and stakeholder forms of corporate governance in the face of stiff global pressures to change stems from the efforts of powerful vested interests to maintain the institutional status quo—an argument that resonates with some of the path dependence literature discussed previously (Dore 2000; Jacoby 2005).

Some rational choice theorists have argued that power struggles over the distribution of resources are the driving force behind institutional change (Knight 1992, 2001; Scharpf 1997).[6] However, researchers closely associated with the Stanford school have also started to see the relevance of this point of view. In particular, organizational sociologists are beginning to argue that institutional change resembles social movements in so far as it involves the strategic framing of issues and interests, mobilization of resources, and coalition building (Davis et al. 2005). In their view, this is a promising way to tease out the mechanisms underlying the coercive, normative, and perhaps even mimetic processes that they have often imputed to account for institutional change.

One of the most important insights recently about power and institutional change concerns competing models. Several scholars have shown that even though a particular set of institutions, such as a set of property rights or a particular form of corporate governance, may come to dominate the landscape, its proponents often had to defeat those advocating other models. For instance, small-firm industrial districts were commonplace during the early to mid-1800s in the textile and armaments industries in the United States, but eventually gave way to large vertically integrated firms (Best 1990; Perrow 2002). State owned utility and transportation systems often suffered the same fate (Roy 1997; Schneiberg 2007). These transformations often involved much political deal making, power brokering, and corruption. Competition among different institutional models has marked other countries as well (e.g. Djelic 1998; Weiss 1988). The point is that as a result of power struggles it is by no means guaranteed that the most efficient institutional models will win out in the end, or that institutions will change at all, even when they are found to be deficient in important ways (Perrow 2002; Schneiberg 2007). Proof of this is that multiple models may exist simultaneously for extended periods within a particular national political economy or industry (Campbell and Lindberg 1990; Deeg and Jackson 2007). This also suggests that the processes of institutional reproduction and change are mutually constitutive. That is, many of the forces that change institutions—that is, conflict and struggle—also stabilize them.

Bricolage and translation

The possibility that multiple models may exist side by side suggests that national political economies may be less homogeneous institutionally than is generally recognized by those who specify different ideal types of capitalism, such as liberal and coordinated market economies as posited by the varieties of capitalism approach (Campbell et al. 1991; Crouch 2005; Zeitlin 2003). As Campbell (2004, ch. 3) explains, this suggests that the process by which institutions change may often involve the rearrangement or recombination of institutional principles and practices in new and creative ways, or, similarly, the blending of new elements into already existing

---

[6] As noted earlier, this is a departure from other rational choice theorists who suggest that institutional change is a more or less inevitable response to shifting environmental conditions by actors who are interested in achieving an efficient institutional equilibrium (e.g. Calvert 1998; Shepsle 1986).

institutional arrangements. The former is known as bricolage; the latter is known as translation because new elements must often be modified to properly blend with the old institutions (see also Crouch 2005, ch. 3). This should not be surprising because even within well-established institutional orders there is much institutional flotsam and jetsam—bits and pieces of previously attempted models and parallel paths—that actors can use to fashion new institutional arrangements (Hancké and Goyer 2005; Schneiberg 2007).

There is considerable cross-national work using this perspective to explain, for instance, the evolution of national vocational training (Thelen 2004), post-communist inter-firm relations (Stark 1996), the emergence of Germany's coordinated market economy (Sorge 2005), translation of the American model into post-war Europe (Djelic 1998), translation of EU directives into national practice (Duina 1999), and the adoption of post-national citizenship in Europe (Soysal 1994). There are also excellent case studies of this process in single countries, such as the revival of the mid-western American metal working industry (Whitford 2005).

This approach has several advantages over the others reviewed here. First, it is not functionalist and does not assume that efficiency considerations drive institutional change. This is because power is important. Second, this approach is not excessively deterministic as, for instance, efficiency theories and some diffusion theories are. Actors exercise a degree of autonomy to pick and choose from their repertoires as they see fit. Third, this view sees institutions as dynamic. It does not view them only as constraints on action. It also views them as resources that actors can use to facilitate and enable action. Fourth, this is an approach that can account for change that is path dependent. Through bricolage and translation actors create new institutional combinations, but combinations that still resemble their predecessors to a significant degree in so far as they are made up of institutional principles and practices that entrepreneurs have inherited from the past (Campbell 2004, 2006).

That said, there is room for improvement in this approach. In particular, more work is required to understand where institutional entrepreneurs get their repertoires from and, thus, why they create one bricolage rather than another. At the micro level, one would want to understand the interpersonal networks within which entrepreneurs are embedded in order to know what sorts of ideas they are exposed to and likely to incorporate into their repertoires. Arguably, the most creative ideas come from people in networks spanning different institutional locations where they are exposed to multiple models thus providing relatively more possibilities for experimenting and creating hybrid institutional forms (Campbell 2004, ch. 3; Schneiberg and Clemens 2006: 218–19). One reason, for instance, that Italy did not embrace the American model of corporate organization and governance as much as Germany or France, after the Second World War, was because Italy had weaker ties to the United States through which the diffusion of ideas could flow. Thus, Italian political leaders were less supportive and accommodating of the American model than leaders in other European countries (Djelic 1998). Similarly, early twentieth-century institutional reform in the United States in agriculture, welfare, and urban planning stemmed from the interpersonal ties among politicians, social activists, and intellectuals on both sides of the Atlantic by which European models were found by American policymakers who often translated them into the American context (Rodgers 1998).

At the macro level, to explain bricolage one would want to know the range of alternative institutional models that had been tried or advocated previously in a certain location in order to understand the range of historically given alternatives that entrepreneurs might consider in the future. This is important, for example, in understanding why a cooperative model of production, which is quite different from the traditional American model, spread during the early twentieth century across infrastructure industries like electricity generation, insurance, and banking in the mid-western United States (Schneiberg 2007). It is also important for understanding how the Dutch pension system shifted from public towards private provisions, drawing upon dormant or suppressed historical alternatives that had been experimented with briefly immediately after the Second World War (Ebbinghaus 2005). And it helps explain how French firms in the 1980s reduced their dependence on the state and capital markets and decentralized labour relations and economic planning to increase productivity. The inspiration for these institutional innovations came from a largely unsuccessful earlier effort by the state to deregulate, decentralize, and privatize financial and other markets (Hancké and Goyer 2005).

Gaps between intentions and outcomes

Recall that the varieties of capitalism literature argues that national political economies consist of rather stable sets of complementary institutions falling into two basic types, liberal and coordinated market economies. In this view, stability stems from the presence of institutional complementarities, by which interconnected institutions reinforce each other, thereby deterring actors from changing any one of them for fear of triggering change in the rest. But the evidence is clear that national political-economic institutions are changing, if often in only incremental ways (Morgan et al. 2005). As a result, some scholars have tried to push this perspective in a more dynamic direction that is better equipped to explain institutional change (e.g. Crouch 2005; Deeg and Jackson 2007; Ebbinghaus 2005). In some cases, this has led to a cataloging of different patterns and mechanisms of institutional change in advanced capitalist economies during the late twentieth century.

Streeck and Thelen (2005) offer a typology of change that is perhaps the most well-known example of this approach. They identify five patterns and mechanisms of change. To begin with, institutions change when new institutional layers are grafted on to existing institutions, or when new institutional models appear and replace old ones. They refer to these processes as layering and displacement, respectively. To a degree, they resemble bricolage and translation. Under layering, actors perceive that their interests would be better served by adding new institutional principles, or practices, to old ones in the hope that the new ones will grow and eventually reduce the salience of the old ones. So, for instance, private pension schemes were added on to public social security systems in the hope that the former would grow in popularity to such an extent that public pensions would no longer be needed by most citizens. Under displacement, actors operate from a similar calculus but simply abolish old institutions and add new ones. In both cases, actors deliberately reform institutions.

Streeck and Thelen also argue that institutions change when the functions they serve change (see also Deeg and Jackson 2007; Ebbinghaus 2005: 23). They identify three possibilities. First is drift, a situation where the environment surrounding an institution changes in ways that alter the scope, meaning, and function of the institution. Sometimes this happens by accident, but sometimes it happens because actors deliberately neglect to keep an institution current vis-à-vis its environment. This might happen, for instance, when the national birth rate rises but policymakers do not increase funding for family allowances and daycare. Second is conversion, a situation where formal institutions per se do not change, but are redirected toward new goals, functions, or purposes. German vocational training was initially intended to undermine the social democratic labour movement, but eventually became a source of strength to that movement vis-à-vis employers. Third is exhaustion, a situation where an institution gradually withers away because it no longer functions as intended. That is, it no longer produces enough significant returns or benefits relative to costs. Germany's early retirement system, for instance, was established to deal with the unemployment associated with a few declining industries. But over time it was used to cope with rising unemployment more generally, especially during reunification. As a result, the demands on the programme outpaced the growth of its budget thereby threatening its very existence.

Identifying drift, conversion, and exhaustion as three types of institutional change is Streeck and Thelen's most innovative contribution. In particular, it focuses on the idea that institutional change is associated with the gap that may emerge between the intentions and actual outcomes of institution building. A substantial literature on policy implementation exists that takes off from the recognition that such a gap exists (e.g. Pressman and Wildavsky 1984). But few have incorporated this insight into an analysis of institutional change. We will return to this point later.

Creating typologies like this one is admirable in so far as it alerts us to the possibility that there may be a variety of mechanisms and processes involved in institutional change, not just one. However, this approach suffers in an important respect. The argument is framed as a sympathetic corrective to the varieties of capitalism literature (Streeck and Thelen 2005: 5–6). But while the notion of institutional complementarities is the core principle upon which the varieties of capitalism approach rests—and the source of institutional stability—Streeck and Thelen's approach to change actually says very little about how institutional complementarities or the interconnections among institutions more generally may provide important dynamics for institutional change. Their five types of change focus either on a single institution in isolation from others (drift, conversion, exhaustion), or on multiple institutions but with little regard for the complementarities that may or may not be involved (displacement, layering). Thus, their approach provides important insights about institutional change over all, but not about how institutional change is derived from or based on institutional complementarities and interconnectedness.

Recently, and in response to their critics, proponents of the varieties of capitalism approach have taken it upon themselves to develop an analysis of institutional change that is compatible with the notion of institutional complementarity (e.g. Hancké et al. 2007*a*; Thelen this volume). In brief, they argue that exogenous shocks, such as increased international trade, capital flows, and competition, create pressure for national economies to adjust their institutions in order to compete effectively—pressure that mounts as gaps between intentions and outcomes materialize, such as when firms or industries lose their competitive edge. However, these adjustments occur within constraints presented by cross-class coalitions, intra-firm relations, informal networks among business and policymakers, and state institutions—all of which played key roles in the development of national institutions and institutional complementarities in the first place. As a result, adjustments normally follow an incremental path-dependent process, not deviating radically from past practices. Why? Actors may seek institutional and functional equivalents to pre-existing forms of coordination. For instance, German centralized wage bargaining persists but has adopted a cost-competition wage model. Or significant institutional changes may occur in one sector of the economy without spilling over into others, thus preserving many of a country's institutional legacies and complementarities. However, if cross-class coalitions or networks have changed dramatically since they created current institutions, then more radical institutional change can occur as pressure mounts. And it may spread from one sector to another if they are tightly linked. While all of this is said to hold for all types of capitalism, there is a certain asymmetrical quality to the argument. Several scholars argue that change is more arduous in national political economies that have high levels of institutional coordination, such as Germany or Switzerland, because change there requires negotiation, compromise, and arm twisting among social partners, related businesses, and policymakers. Where such coordination is lacking, as in Britain or the United States, institutional change can take place faster and easier (Hall 2007; Hancké et al. 2007*b*).

Institutional complexity

Many critics of the varieties of capitalism approach have argued that it oversimplifies institutional reality. Real-world national political economies are in varying degrees complex institutional hybrids. They consist of a variety of interrelated institutions, some typical of liberal market economies and some typical of coordinated market economies (Amable 2003; Campbell et al. 1991; Crouch 2005; Zeitlin 2003). Moreover, institutions (i.e. rules) are rarely specified or understood absolutely clearly. As a result, they are ambiguous and open to interpretation by actors (Halliday and Carruthers 2007: 1149; Streeck and Thelen 2005: 14). All of this opens up the possibility that institutions are not as stable or locked in as the concept of institutional complementarity suggests (Deeg and Jackson 2007; Ebbinghaus 2005; Streeck and Thelen 2005; Djelic and Quack 2007). These insights have led to several new theoretical moves to explain institutional change.

The first move involves insights about the institutional variety and hybrid nature of political economies. As already discussed, real-world political economies are institutionally complex. There are a variety of institutional principles and practices available for actors to use when they want to change institutions. Bricolage, layering, translation, and displacement are the processes that are enabled by such institutional variety and hybridization (Campbell 2004; Crouch 2005). In this sense, institutions should be viewed as resources that actors can use in the pursuit of their interests (Hall and Thelen 2009; Streeck and Thelen 2005). Some have gone so far as to argue that the more institutional heterogeneity there is in a situation, the more likely it is that actors will engage in truly innovative institutional changes. Hence, contrary to the varieties of capitalism view (e.g. Hall and Gingerich 2004), heterogeneity and hybridization in national political economies may be beneficial because it yields institutional flexibility and innovation—that is, institutional change—that can improve socio-economic performance (Crouch 2005: 71).

The second theoretical move involves institutional interconnectedness. This is the premiss underlying the varieties of capitalism argument that strong complementarities prevent widespread change because actors are hesitant to change one institution for fear of starting ripple effects in others (Deeg and Jackson 2007: 167; Hall and Thelen 2009). The critical insight is that understanding institutional change requires a relational approach. That is, one cannot understand change simply by focusing on a single institution; it can only be understood by focusing on the relationships among institutions. This is not because a change in institution A necessarily triggers a functional response in institution B. Rather this is because actors in institution B have learned to live with institution A in ways that yield certain benefits, such as those derived from institutional complementarity. So when institution A changes, actors in institution B may suddenly have incentives to make changes in B in order to preserve these benefits or develop new ones.

For instance, changes in property rights institutions often precipitate changes in other institutions (Campbell and Lindberg 1990). Fligstein (1990) showed that in the United States every time policymakers made major changes to anti-trust law, the institutions of corporate organization and management changed as well, first from horizontally integrated firms, then to vertically integrated firms, and finally to conglomerates. This was because corporate managers wanted to avoid the penalties associated with violating new anti-trust laws and so changed their own institutions. As one institution changed it created new incentives for actors in another institution to change as well. Managers avoided the costs that would have been incurred by leaving a mismatch between the new law and the old corporate practices, which would have now been illegal. In fact, this was a reciprocal or co-evolutionary relationship because corporate practices initially precipitated changes in anti-trust law, which then precipitated further changes in corporate practices, and so on (see also Djelic and Quack 2007; Halliday and Carruthers 2007).

It follows that the more tightly coupled institutions are, the more likely it will be that a change in one will precipitate a change in another. For example, during the 1980s international financial organizations embraced and institutionalized a new set of normative principles—neo-liberalism. When the communist regimes in Eastern Europe collapsed, those countries that were more indebted to these orga- nizations (e.g. IMF, private banks, national governments) were more likely to institutionalize neo-liberal practices themselves than countries that were less in- debted (Campbell 2001). In other words, post-communist countries that were more tightly coupled to western financial organizations were more susceptible to the institutional changes favoured by those organizations. Of course, proponents of the varieties of capitalism view and others have made the opposite argument, suggest- ing that tight coupling (i.e. strong complementarities) tends to prevent widespread change (Djelic and Quack 2005: 159, 2007). We need better specifications of exactly what constitutes loose and tight coupling and then empirical research to settle the issue (Deeg 2005).

These last examples also illustrate a third theoretical move regarding institutional complexity and change—a move that emphasizes the connections among different institutional levels. The varieties of capitalism literature, among others, focuses on how the interconnectedness of institutions at the national level may affect change. Put differently, they stress the horizontal connections among institutions within a particular level of analysis. But others have shown that the vertical connections among institutions across local, regional, national, and international levels are also important. For instance, Halliday and Carruthers (2009) examined how after the 1997 Asian financial crisis various international professional and non-governmental organizations promulgated general guidelines for bankruptcy legislation in the hope that national governments would adopt them, standardize the law across countries, and thus enhance international commerce. However, the degree to which countries like China, Indonesia, and South Korea did so depended in large measure on how much leverage international organizations, multinational corporations and other states had over them and how legitimate these governments perceived the guidelines to be. In other words, institutional change at the national level was very much conditioned by forces related to institutional change at the transnational level. The importance of international guidelines, standards, and other forms of 'soft law' has gained increasing attention among scholars interested in how transnational institu- tions cause change at the level of nation-states (e.g. Djelic and Sahlin-Andersson 2006). But causality can work in both directions. Transnational institutions are often shaped according to various national institutional precedents. Nation-states helped create Halliday and Carruthers's transnational bankruptcy guidelines. And transna- tional markets including the European Single Market, Mercosur in South America, and the North American Free Trade Agreement, were all shaped according to the legal precedents of their member states (Duina 2006). Furthermore, changes in national institutions may be very much influenced by institutional changes at the sub-national level as occurred when the US government modelled its welfare institutions on those developed earlier by state governments (e.g. Skocpol 1992). That is to say, things both trickle down and trickle up.

The fourth theoretical move stems from the notion of institutional ambiguity, which implies that the meaning of an institution is always open to interpretation. The exact meaning of an institution is never completely clear because social norms and rules are never unequivocal or capable of speaking for themselves. And inter-pretations of what an institution is are contested and may change over time. Indeed, what an institution makes possible, or not, is continuously redefined by what might be called interpretive entrepreneurs (Streeck and Yamamura 2003: 44). The possibility for such interpretive flux is exacerbated by the fact that actors are situated simultaneously in multiple and complex institutional locations, which makes it difficult for them to define their interests and strategies for action (Weir 2006).

It follows that the nature of institutional complementarity is also open to interpretation.[7] That is, actors may perceive for various reasons that a certain institutional configuration no longer yields benefits associated with institutional complementarity and, therefore, move to change it. Such an interpretation would be based on the belief of some actors that the institutions in question were not serving their interests in a satisfactory manner any longer, or that they were otherwise inappropriate (Hall and Thelen 2009). That said, institutions may generate different levels of complementarity for different groups of actors (Deeg and Jackson 2007: 168). Assuming that institutions are settlements born from struggle and bargaining (Campbell 2004: 1), then those in power are most likely to hold sway over the situation and, thus, it is their interpretations that may matter the most in the end. But this will involve considerable struggle, bargaining, and negotiation over these interpretations.

Comparative political economy has taken up issues of interpretation by analysing how ideas and discourse affect institutional change. Blyth (2002), for example, showed how different interpretations of the 1970s stagflation problem led to changes in taxation and welfare institutions in Sweden and the United States. And Schmidt (2001, 2002) showed how policymakers use different discursive strategies in different countries to facilitate change depending on the institutional configuration of their political economies. As noted above, even rational choice theorists, who have not typically paid much attention to the issue of interpretation, have started to recognize how important this is for explaining institutional change (e.g. Knight and North 1997; North 2005).[8] Central to much of this work is the notion that ideas and

---

[7] Indeed, even among researchers, there is disagreement on just what institutional complement-arity means and how it should be measured (e.g. Crouch 2005; Hall and Gingerich 2004; Kenworthy 2006).

[8] Perhaps the most extreme turn in this direction from within rational choice theory comes from North (2005), who advocated recently the cognitive approach to understanding institutional change noted earlier.

discourse can be used strategically by actors as tools in struggles to change institutions, but that they also exert effects structurally by constraining how actors perceive their interests and options in the first place (Campbell 1998).

Some of the most innovative work in this area stems from the recognition that perceptions and interpretations themselves can change according to changes in patterns of interactions among policymakers and others. For instance, one reason that the institutions governing German business are changing is that young corporate managers in Germany, who were formally trained in the United States, have started to develop different world views regarding how business systems ought to be organized that are more in line with their Anglo-American counterparts than with traditions in their own country (Lane 2005: 93). In addition to formal training, managers may have different perceptions of their firm's interests depending on how much interaction they have with other firms in their industry through business and employer associations (Martin 2005, 2006). Similarly, researchers have found that when groups with apparently diametrically opposed interests are granted authority to cooperatively make regulatory policy themselves, rather than lobby the state for it, long-term dialogue ensues, which leads actors to reinterpret their interests. In the end, previously adversarial, zero-sum conflicts become consensual, positive-sum negotiations that lead to cooperative trial-and-error experimentation, and incremental institutional change (Dorf and Sabel 1998; Karkkainen et al. 2000). Much the same occurred in Germany as firms learned that benefits could be gained through codetermination legislation, which forced them to cooperate with labour (Streeck 1997). The point is that the nature of the interactions that occur among actors from different institutional spheres may affect their interpretations of problems and interests and, in turn, institutional change itself (Fligstein 2001).

Finally, a fifth theoretical move involves the origins of change. Some scholars assume that institutional change is triggered initially by exogenous shocks of various sorts. This is common, for example, among scholars who argue for path dependent accounts of change of the punctuated equilibrium form, and among researchers who view institutional change as a functional response to technological innovations. But recognizing that there is much institutional variety in the world raises the possibility that the incentives or logics of action associated with different institutions may create tensions or otherwise contradict one another (Friedland and Alford 1991; Orren and Skowronek 1994). People may be motivated to ease these tensions or resolve these contradictions by changing institutions. Similarly, the ambiguities associated with interpreting institutional rules create opportunities for reinterpretation, which can then lead to institutional change. Hence, change is not necessarily precipitated by exogenous shocks but can also be triggered by endogenous processes. Theorists and researchers have started to incorporate this realization into their theories of institutional change (e.g. Campbell 2004, ch 6; Sorge 2005).

THE ONTOLOGICAL NATURE OF
INSTITUTIONAL CHANGE

Despite the amount of attention paid to explaining institutional change, surprisingly little effort has been devoted to defining exactly what we mean by institutional change in the first place. What exactly constitutes evolutionary or revolutionary change, incremental or rapid change, and so forth? And how do we know it empirically when we see it?

Some researchers have argued that institutions are multidimensional sets of rules so it is important to track all the important dimensions over an appropriate period of time in order to determine how much and what kind of change has occurred in specific cases. In comparative political economy this has led recently to the use of quantitative techniques, such as cluster analysis, in order to identify different institutional types of capitalism (e.g. Amable 2003; Boyer 2004). Combining cluster analysis with longitudinal techniques like event history analysis or interrupted time-series analysis is a way to more precisely identify the degree to which different dimensions of an institution change over time. The logic of tracking institutional dimensions can be used in qualitative as well as quantitative analysis (Campbell 2004, ch. 2).

Another recent approach is to focus on institutional functions. Here institutions are considered to have changed if the functions they are said to perform shift or are otherwise transformed. Streeck and Thelen (2005) illustrate the approach especially in so far as they see institutional change where unintentional drift, conversion, or exhaustion occurs, meaning that an institution's function has changed but its formal rules have not.[9] But taking a functionalist approach to measuring institutional change is fraught with difficulties. First, determining precisely what functions an institution performs can be a devilishly tricky business, especially if we take seriously the notion that some functions may be less obvious than others (e.g. Merton 1967). Second, picking important functions is not always straightforward. Even proponents of the institutional complementarities perspective seem to disagree about which functional indicators are most important to track (e.g. Hall and Gingerich 2004; Kenworthy 2006), if for no other reason than that selecting the 'most important' functions is partly a normative matter. Third, it is easier to determine the degree to which institutional rules have changed than it is to determine the degree to which these changes have affected functional performance. This is because it is often hard to determine precisely how much institutions, rather than other factors, affect national political-economic performance (Schwartz 2001). Fourth, if institutions actually

---

[9] There is a tension within their argument regarding how they define institutions. They write that institutions are 'formalized rules that may be enforced by calling upon a third party' (p. 10), a definition that is consistent with that used by many people, including most comparative political economists. But they also write that 'the practical enactment of an institution is as much part of its reality as its formal structure' (p. 18), which points to the importance of institutional functions.

consist of both rules and functional outcomes, then the question becomes how much change has occurred if the rules but not the function change, or if the function but not the rules change? Are these two possibilities equivalent or somehow significantly different? This is a tough question left unanswered.

All of this has implications for contemporary debates about the degree to which capitalist institutions are changing as a result of rising transnational economic activity. Some suggest that national institutions are beginning to converge on a common set of principles and practices while others say they are not. Part of this debate revolves around exactly which institutions are being examined. But part of it revolves around whether institutions are defined in terms of their rule structures or functions. A review of this literature is well beyond the scope of this chapter, but my guess is that those who dwell on institutional functions may find more change than those who dwell on rules per se (e.g. Campbell 2004; Streeck and Thelen 2005).

In sum, definitions matter. The definition of an institution has major implications for how researchers can study institutional change and how much institutional change they find. Most researchers would accept that changes in rules qualify as institutional change. I suspect that many would be less inclined to accept that changes in function also qualify.

CONCLUSION

Several things have become clear as the literature on institutional reproduction and change has evolved. First, where early theories emphasized functional or technical imperatives as the driving force behind institutional change, more recent theories have paid more attention to how actors are involved in the process—as institutional entrepreneurs, bricoleurs, and so on. As such, theorists and researchers have incorporated the notion of struggle, conflict, and negotiation over institutions into their understandings of institutional change. This is especially important because it reveals how institutional reproduction and change are flip sides of the same coin. That is, institutions are contested. So, depending on the balance of power among those contesting them, they may change or not. In this sense the processes of institutional reproduction and change are mutually constitutive—many of the forces that change institutions also stabilize them.

Second, with an increased emphasis on actors, there is also increased attention being paid to how actors perceive and interpret their situations vis-à-vis institutions. Similarly, institutions are seen not only as constraints that limit the range of choices available to actors, but also as malleable resources that actors can use to achieve their objectives. The notions of bricolage and translation are especially important in this respect. And the malleability of institutions is enhanced to the extent that they are ambiguous and open to interpretation by actors in the first place.

Third, the notion of path dependence is becoming understood in a more dynamic way. On the one hand, we now understand how institutions provide resources and opportunities that creative and innovative actors can use to alter institutional arrangements, albeit in incremental and evolutionary ways. In this regard, the punctuated equilibrium view of change has been supplanted by more nuanced views. On the other hand, we also understand how institutions constrain—but do not completely determine—the choices available to actors. So the concept of path dependence is more useful for explaining the process of change—better still, constrained change—than has previously been the case.

Finally, we now recognize that institutions are multidimensional phenomena and that in political-economic settings a variety of institutions are in place. This has led to a greater appreciation for the interconnectedness and complexity of institutional settings. In turn, this has led researchers to inquire about how interconnectedness, institutional complementarities, and tight and loose coupling affect institutional change. It has also led scholars to recognize that institutions at the national level are connected to institutions at the transnational and sub-national levels in ways that affect change. Better understanding of these relationships is probably the area we know least about and that requires the most attention in the future.

REFERENCES

AMABLE, BRUNO (2003). *The Diversity of Modern Capitalism*, (New York: Oxford University Press).

AOKI, MASAHIKO (2001). *Toward a Comparative Institutional Analysis*, (Cambridge, MA: MIT Press).

ARTHUR, W. BRIAN (1994). *Increasing Returns and Path Dependence in the Economy*, (Ann Arbor: University of Michigan Press).

BABB, SARAH (2001). *Managing Mexico*, (Princeton, NJ: Princeton University Press).

BATES, ROBERT (2008). *When Things Fell Apart: State Failure in Late-Century Africa*, (New York: Cambridge University Press).

BERMAN, SHERI (1998). *The Social Democratic Movement: Ideas and Politics in the Making of Interwar Europe*, (Cambridge, MA: Harvard University Press).

BEST, MICHAEL (1990). *The New Competition: Institutions of Industrial Restructuring*, (Cambridge, MA: Harvard University Press).

BLYTH, MARK (2002). *Great Transformations*, (New York: Cambridge University Press).

BOLI, JOHN and GEORGE M. THOMAS (eds.) (1999). *Constructing World Culture: International Nongovernmental Organizations Since 1875*, (Stanford: Stanford University Press).

BOYER, ROBERT (2004). 'New Growth Regimes, but Still Institutional Diversity', *Socio-Economic Review* 2: 1–32.

CALVERT, RANDALL L. (1998). 'Rational Actors, Equilibrium, and Social Institutions', in *Explaining Social Institutions*, eds. Jack Knight and Itai Sened, (Ann Arbor: University of Michigan Press), pp. 57–94.

CAMPBELL, JOHN L. (2006). 'What's New? General Patterns of Macro-Institutional Change', in *Innovation, Science, and Institutional Change*, eds. Jerald Hage and Marius Meeus, (New York: Oxford University Press), pp. 505–24.

——(2005). 'Where Do We Stand? Common Mechanisms in Organizations and Social Movements Research', in *Social Movements and Organization Theory*, eds. Gerald F. Davis, Doug McAdam, W. Richard Scott, and Mayer N. Zald, (New York: Cambridge University Press), pp. 41–68.

——(2004). *Institutional Change and Globalization*, (Princeton, NJ: Princeton University Press).

——(2001). 'Convergence or Divergence? Globalization, Neoliberalism and Fiscal Policy in Postcommunist Europe', in *Globalization and the European Political Economy*, ed. Steven Weber, (New York: Columbia University Press), pp. 107–139.

——(1998). 'Institutional Analysis and the Role of Ideas in Political Economy', *Theory and Society* 27: 377–409.

——and LEON N. LINDBERG (1991). 'The Evolution of Governance Regimes', in *Governance of the American Economy*, eds. John L. Campbell, J. Rogers Hollingsworth, and Leon N. Lindberg, (New York: Cambridge University Press), pp. 319–55.

————(1990). 'Property Rights and the Organization of Economic Activity by the State', *American Sociological Review* 55: 634–47.

——and OVE K. PEDERSEN (eds.) (2001). *The Rise of Neoliberalism and Institutional Analysis*, (Princeton, NJ: Princeton University Press).

——J. ROGERS HOLLINGSWORTH, and LEON N. LINDBERG (eds.) (1991). *Governance of the American Economy*, (New York: Cambridge University Press).

CHANDLER, Jr. ALFRED D. (1977). *The Visible Hand: The Managerial Revolution in American Business*, (Cambridge, MA: Harvard University Press).

CROUCH, COLIN (2005). *Capitalist Diversity and Change*, (New York: Oxford University Press).

DAVID, PAUL A. (1985). 'Clio and the Economics of QWERTY', *American Economic Review* 75(2): 332–7.

DAVIS, GERALD F., DOUG MCADAM, W. RICHARD SCOTT, and MEYER N. ZALD (eds.) (2005). *Social Movements and Organization Theory*, (New York: Cambridge University Press).

DEEG, RICHARD (2005). 'Path Dependency, Institutional Complementarity, and Change in National Business Systems', in *Changing Capitalisms?*, eds. Glenn Morgan, Richard Whitley, and Eli Moen, (New York: Oxford University Press), pp. 21–52.

——and GREGORY JACKSON (2007). 'Towards a More Dynamic Theory of Capitalist Variety', *Socio-Economic Review* 5(1): 149–79.

DIMAGGIO, PAUL J. and WALTER W. POWELL (1983). 'The Iron Cage Revisited: Institutional Isomorphism and Collective Rationality in Organizational Fields', *American Sociological Review* 48: 147–60.

DJELIC, MARIE-LAURE (1998). *Exporting the American Model: The Postwar Transformation of European Business*, (New York: Oxford University Press).

—— and KERSTIN SAHLIN-ANDERSSON (eds.) (2006). *Transnational Governance: Institutional Dynamics of Regulation*, (New York: Cambridge University Press).

——(2005). 'Rethinking Path Dependency: The Crooked Path of Institutional Change in Post-War Germany', in *Changing Capitalisms?*, eds. Glenn Morgan, Richard Whitley, and Eli Moen, (New York: Oxford University Press), pp. 135–66.

——and SIGRID QUACK (2007). 'Overcoming Path Dependency: Path Generation in Open Systems', *Theory and Society* 36: 161–86.

DOBBIN, FRANK, BETH SIMMONS, and GEOFFREY GARRETT (2007). 'The Global Diffusion of Public Policies: Social Construction, Coercion, Competition, or Learning?', *Annual Review of Sociology* 33: 449–72.

——(1994). *Forging Industrial Policy*, (New York: Cambridge University Press).

DORE, RONALD (2000). *Stock Market Capitalism, Welfare Capitalism: Japan and Germany versus the Anglo-Saxons*, (New York: Oxford University Press).

——(1983). 'Goodwill and the Spirit of Market Capitalism', *British Journal of Sociology* 34: 459–82.

DORF, MICHAEL C. and CHARLES F. SABEL (1998). 'A Constitution of Democratic Experimentalism', *Columbia Law Review* 98: 267–473.

DUINA, FRANCESCO (1999). *Harmonizing Europe: Nation States within the Common Market*, (Albany: State University of New York Press).

—— (2006). *The Social Construction of Free Trade*, (Princeton, NJ: Princeton University Press).

EBBINGHAUS, BERNHARD (2005). 'Can Path Dependence Explain Institutional Change? Two Approaches Applied to Welfare State Reform'. Discussion paper 05/2. Cologne, Germany: Max Planck Institute for the Study of Societies. Available on-line at www.wpifg.de.

EVANS, PETER, DIETRICH RUESCHEMEYER, and THEDA SKOCPOL (eds.) (1985). *Bringing the State Back In*, (New York: Cambridge University Press).

FLIGSTEIN, NEIL (1990). *The Transformation of Corporate Control*, (Cambridge, MA: Harvard University Press).

——(2001). 'Social Skills and the Theory of Fields', *Sociological Theory* 19: 105–25.

FRIEDLAND, ROGER and ROBERT A. ALFORD (1991). 'Bringing Society Back In: Symbols, Practices and Institutional Contradictions', in *The New Institutionalism in Organizational Analysis*, eds. Walter Powell and Paul DiMaggio, (Chicago: University of Chicago Press), pp. 232–64.

GERSCHENKRON, ALEXANDER (1962). *Economic Backwardness in Historical Perspective*, (Cambridge, MA: Harvard University Press).

GOUREVITCH, PETER (1986). *Politics in Hard Times: Comparative Responses to International Economic Crises*, (Ithaca, NY: Cornell University Press).

GRANOVETTER, MARK (1985). 'Economic Action and Social Structure: The Problem of Embeddedness', *American Journal of Sociology* 91: 485–510.

GUILLÉN, MAURO (1994). *Models of Management*, (Chicago: University of Chicago Press).

——(2001). *The Limits of Convergence: Globalization and Organizational Change in Argentina, South Korea, and Spain*, (Princeton, NJ: Princeton University Press).

GUTHRIE, DOUG (1999). *Dragon in a Three-Piece Suit: The Emergence of Capitalism in China*, (Princeton, NJ: Princeton University Press).

HAGGARD, STEPHAN and ROBERT R. KAUFMAN (1995). *The Political Economy of Democratic Transitions*, (Princeton, NJ: Princeton University Press).

——(1992). 'Institutions and Economic Adjustment', in *The Politics of Economic Adjustment*, eds. Stephan Haggard and Robert R. Kaufman, (Princeton, NJ: Princeton University Press), pp. 3–37.

HALL, PETER A. (2007). 'The Evolution of the Varieties of Capitalism in Europe', in *Beyond Varieties of Capitalism*, eds. Bob Hancké, Martin Rhodes, and Mark Thatcher, (New York: Oxford University Press), pp. 39–88.

——and DANIEL GINGERICH (2004). 'Varieties of Capitalism and Institutional Complementarities in the Macroeconomy: An Empirical Analysis'. Discussion paper 04/5, Cologne, Germany: Max Planck Institute for the Study of Societies. Available on-line at www.wpifg.de.

HALL, PETER A. and DAVID SOSKICE (2001). 'An Introduction to Varieties of Capitalism', in *Varieties of Capitalism: The Institutional Foundations of Comparative Advantage*, eds. Peter A. Hall and David Soskice, (New York: Oxford University Press), pp. 1–70.

——and KATHLEEN THELEN (2009). 'Institutional Change in Varieties of Capitalism', *Socio-Economic Review* 7(1).

HALLIDAY, TERENCE and BRUCE CARRUTHERS (2007). 'The Recursivity of Law: Global Norm Making and National Lawmaking in the Globalization of Corporate Insolvency Regimes', *American Journal of Sociology* 112: 1135–1202.

——(2009). *Bankrupt: Global Lawmaking and Systemic Financial Crisis*, (Stanford: Stanford University Press).

HAMILTON, GARY and NICOLE BIGGART (1988). 'Market, Culture, and Authority: A Comparative Analysis of Management and Organization in the Far East', *American Journal of Sociology* 94: S52–S94.

HANCKÉ, BOB and MICHEL GOYER (2005). 'Degrees of Freedom: Rethinking the Institutional Analysis of Economic Change', in *Changing Capitalisms?*, eds. Glenn Morgan, Richard Whitley, and Eli Moen, (New York: Oxford University Press), pp. 53–77.

——MARTIN RHODES, and MARK THATCHER (eds.) (2007a). *Beyond Varieties of Capitalism*, (New York: Oxford University Press).

——————(2007b). 'Introduction: Beyond Varieties of Capitalism', in *Beyond Varieties of Capitalism*, eds. Bob Hancké, Martin Rhodes, and Mark Thatcher, (New York: Oxford University Press), pp. 3–38.

HAYDU, JEFFREY (1998). 'Making Use of the Past: Time Periods as Cases to Compare and as Sequences of Problem Solving', *American Journal of Sociology* 104: 339–71.

HOLLINGSWORTH, J. ROGERS, PHILIPPE C. SCHMITTER, and WOLFGANG STREECK (eds.) (1994). *Governing Capitalist Economies: Performance and Control of Economic Sectors*, (New York: Oxford University Press).

JACOBY, SANFORD (2005). *The Embedded Corporation: Corporate Governance and Employment Relations in Japan and the United States*, (Princeton, NJ: Princeton University Press).

JEPPERSON, RONALD L. (1991). 'Institutions, Institutional Effects, and Institutionalism', in *The New Institutionalism in Organizational Analysis*, eds. Walter W. Powell and Paul J. DiMaggio, (Chicago: University of Chicago Press), pp. 143–63.

KARKKAINEN, BRADLEY, ARCHON FUNG, and CHARLES SABEL (2000). 'After Backyard Environmentalism: Toward a Performance-Based Regime of Environmental Regulation', *American Behavioral Scientist* 44(4): 690–709.

KATZENSTEIN, PETER J. (ed.) (1978). *Between Power and Plenty: Foreign Economic Policies of Advanced Industrial States*, (Madison: University of Wisconsin Press).

KECK, MARGARET and KATHRYN SIKKINK (1998). *Activists Beyond Borders: Advocacy Networks in International Politics*, (Ithaca, NY: Cornell University Press).

KENWORTHY, LANE (2006). 'Institutional Coherence and Macroeconomic Performance', *Socio-Economic Review* 4: 69–91.

KNIGHT, JACK (1992). *Institutions and Social Conflict*, (New York: Cambridge University Press).

——(2001). 'Explaining the Rise of Neoliberalism: The Mechanisms of Institutional Change', in *The Rise of Neoliberalism and Institutional Analysis*, eds. John L. Campbell and Ove K. Pedersen, (Princeton, NJ: Princeton University Press), pp. 27–50.

——(1998). 'Models, Interpretations, and Theories: Constructing Explanations of Institutional Emergence and Change', in *Explaining Social Institutions*, eds. Jack Knight and Itai Sened, (Ann Arbor: University of Michigan Press), pp. 95–120.

KNIGHT, JACK and DOUGLASS NORTH (1997). 'Explaining Economic Change: The Interplay Between Cognition and Institutions', *Legal Theory* 3: 211–226.

KORPI, WALTER (2001). 'Contentious Institutions: An Augmented Rational-Action Analysis of the Origins and Path Dependency of Welfare State Institutions in Western Countries', *Rationality and Society* 13(2): 235–83.

KRASNER, STEPHEN D. (1984). 'Approaches to the State: Alternative Conceptions and Historical Dynamics', *Comparative Politics* 16(2): 223–46.

LANE, CHRISTEL (2005). 'Institutional Transformation and System Change: Changes in the Corporate Governance of German Corporations', in *Changing Capitalisms?*, eds. Glenn Morgan, Richard Whitley, and Eli Moen, (New York: Oxford University Press), pp. 78–109.

LASH, SCOTT and JOHN URRY (1987). *The End of Organized Capitalism*, (Madison: University of Wisconsin Press).

MCNAMARA, KATHLEEN R. (1998). *The Currency of Ideas: Monetary Politics in the European Union*, (Ithaca: Cornell University Press).

MAHONEY, JAMES (2000). 'Path Dependence in Historical Sociology', *Theory and Society* 29: 507–48.

MARCH, JAMES G. and JOHAN P. OLSEN (1989). *Rediscovering Institutions: The Organizational Basis of Politics*, (New York: Free Press).

MARTIN, CATHIE J. (2005). 'Corporatism from the Firm Perspective', *British Journal of Political Science* 35(1): 127–48.

——(2006). 'Corporatism in the Post-Industrial Age: Employers and Social Policy in the Little Land of Denmark', in *National Identity and the Varieties of Capitalism: The Danish Experience*, eds. John L. Campbell, John A. Hall, and Ove K. Pedersen, (Montreal: McGill-Queen's University Press), pp. 271–94.

MERTON, ROBERT (1967). 'Manifest and Latent Functions', in *On Theoretical Sociology*, (New York: Free Press), pp. 73–138.

MEYER, JOHN W., JOHN BOLI, GEORGE M. THOMAS, and FRANCISCO O. RAMIREZ (1997*a*). 'World Society and the Nation State', *American Journal of Sociology* 103(1): 144–81.

——DAVID FRANK, ANN HIRONAKA, EVAN SCHOFER, and NANCY B. TUMA (1997*b*). 'The Structuring of a World Environmental Regime, 1870–1990', *International Organization* 51: 623–51.

MIZRUCHI, MARK S. and LISA C. FEIN (1999). 'The Social Construction of Organizational Knowledge: A Study of the Uses of Coercive, Mimetic, and Normative Isomorphism', *Administrative Science Quarterly* 44: 653–83.

NELSON, RICHARD R. (1994). 'Evolutionary Theorizing about Economic Change', in *The Handbook of Economic Sociology*, eds. Neil J. Smelser and Richard Swedberg, (Princeton, NJ: Princeton University Press), pp. 108–36.

NORTH, DOUGLASS (1981). *Structure and Change in Economic History*, (New York: Norton).

——(1990). *Institutions, Institutional Change and Economic Performance*, (New York: Cambridge University Press).

—— (2005). *Understanding The Process of Economic Change*, (Princeton, NJ: Princeton University Press).

——(1998). 'Five Propositions about Institutional Change', in *Explaining Social Institutions*, eds. Jack Knight and Itai Sened, (Ann Arbor: University of Michigan Press), pp. 15–26.

O'CONNOR, JAMES (1973). *The Fiscal Crisis of the State*, (New York: St. Martin's Press).

ORREN, KAREN and STEPHEN SKOWRONEK (1994). 'Beyond the Iconography of Order: Notes for a "New Institutionalism"', in *The Dynamics of American Politics*, eds. Lawrence D. Dodd and Calvin Jillson, (Boulder: Westview Press), pp. 311–30.

OSTROM, ELINORE (1990). *Governing the Commons: The Evolution of Institutions for Collective Action*, (New York: Cambridge University Press).

PERROW, CHARLES (2002). *Organizing America: Wealth, Power, and the Origins of Corporate Capitalism*, (Princeton, NJ: Princeton University Press).

PIERSON, PAUL (2000a). 'Not Just What, but When: Timing and Sequence in Political Processes', *Studies in American Political Development* 14 (Spring) 72–92.

——(2000b). 'Increasing Returns, Path Dependence, and the Study of Politics', *American Political Science Review* 94(2): 251–67.

POULANTZAS, NICOS (1974). *Political Power and Social Class*, (London: New Left Books).

POWELL, WALTER (1987). 'Hybrid Organizational Arrangements', *California Management Review* 30(1): 67–87.

——(1990). 'Neither Market Nor Hierarchy: Network Forms of Organization', *Research in Organizational Behavior* 12: 295–336.

PRASAD, MONICA (2006). *The Politics of Free Markets: The Rise of Neoliberal Economic Policies in Britain, France, Germany and the United States*, (Chicago: University of Chicago Press).

PRESSMAN, JEFFREY and AARON WILDAVSKY (1984). *Implementation*, (Berkeley: University of California Press).

RODGERS, DANIEL (1998). *Atlantic Crossings*, (Cambridge, MA: Belknap Press).

ROE, MARK J. (1994). *Strong Managers, Weak Owners*, (Princeton, NJ: Princeton University Press).

——(1996). 'Chaos and Evolution in Law and Economics', *Harvard Law Review* 109(3): 641–668.

——(2003). *Political Determinants of Corporate Governance*, (New York: Oxford University Press).

ROSTOW, W. W. (1960). *The Stages of Economic Growth: A Non-Communist Manifesto*, (New York: Cambridge University Press).

ROY, WILLIAM G. (1997). *Socializing Capital: The Rise of the Large Industrial Corporation in America*, (Princeton, NJ: Princeton University Press).

SCHARPF, FRITZ W. (1997). *Games Real Actors Play: Actor-Centered Institutionalism in Policy Research*, (Boulder: Westview Press).

SCHMIDT, VIVIEN A. (2002). *The Futures of European Capitalism*, (New York: Oxford University Press).

——(2001). 'Discourse and the Legitimation of Economic and Social Policy Change in Europe', in *Globalization and the European Political Economy*, eds. Steven Weber, (New York: Columbia University Press), pp. 229–72.

SCHNEIBERG, MARC (1999). 'Political and Institutional Conditions for Governance by Association: Private Order and Price Controls in American Fire Insurance', *Politics and Society* 27(1): 67–103.

——2007. 'What's on the Path? Path Dependence, Organizational Diversity and the Problem of Institutional Change in the U.S. Economy, 1900–1950', *Socio-Economic Review* 5(1): 47–80.

——and ELISABETH CLEMENS (2006). 'The Typical Tools for the Job: Research Strategies for Institutional Analysis', *Sociological Theory* 24(3): 195–227.

SCHWARTZ, HERMAN (2001). 'The Danish "Miracle"? Luck, Pluck, or Stuck?' *Comparative Political Studies* 3(2): 131–55.

SHEPSLE, KENNETH A. (1986). 'Institutional Equilibrium and Equilibrium Institutions' in *Political Science: The Science of Politics*, ed. Herbert Weisberg, (New York: Agathon), pp. 51–81.

SIMMONS, BETH, FRANK DOBBIN, and GEOFFREY GARRETT (eds.) (2008). *The Global Diffusion of Markets and Democracy*, (New York: Cambridge University Press).

SKOCPOL, THEDA (1992). *Protecting Soldiers and Mothers: The Political Origins of Social Policy in the United States*, (Cambridge, MA: Belknap/Harvard University Press).

SORGE, ARNDT (2005). *The Global and the Local: Understanding the Dialectics of Business Systems*, (New York: Oxford University Press).

SOYSAL, YASEMIN (1994). *Limits of Citizenship*, (Chicago: University of Chicago Press).

STALLINGS, BARBARA (1992). 'International Influence on Economic Policy: Debt, Stabilization and Structural Reform', in *The Politics of Economic Adjustment*, eds. Stephan Haggard and Robert Kaufman, (Princeton, NJ: Princeton University Press), pp. 41–88.

STARK, DAVID (1996). 'Recombinant Property in East European Capitalism', *American Journal of Sociology* 101: 993–1027.

——and LASZLO BRUSZT (1998). *Postsocialist Pathways: Transforming Politics and Property in East Central Europe*, (New York: Cambridge University Press).

STEINMO, SVEN, KATHLEEN THELEN, and FRANK LONGSTRETH (eds.) (1992). *Structuring Politics: Historical Institutionalism in Comparative Perspective*, (New York: Cambridge University Press).

STREECK, WOLFGANG (1997). 'Beneficial Constraints: On the Economic Limits of Rational Voluntarism', in *Contemporary Capitalism: The Embeddedness of Institutions*, eds. J. Rogers Hollingsworth and Robert Boyer, (New York: Cambridge University Press), pp. 197–219.

——and KATHLEEN THELEN (2005). 'Introduction: Institutional Change in Advanced Political Economies', in *Beyond Continuity: Institutional Change in Advanced Political Economies*, eds. Wolfgang Streeck and Kathleen Thelen, (New York: Oxford University Press), pp. 1–39.

——and KOZO YAMAMURA (2003). 'Introduction: Convergence of Diversity? Stability and Change in German and Japanese Capitalism', in *The End of Diversity? Prospects for German and Japanese Capitalism*, (Ithaca, NY: Cornell University Press), pp. 1–50.

THELEN, KATHLEEN (2000a). 'Timing and Temporality in the Analysis of Institutional Evolution and Change', *Studies in American Political Development* 14 (Spring), 101–08.

——(2000b). 'How Institutions Evolve: Insights from Comparative-Historical Analysis', unpublished manuscript. Department of Political Science, Northwestern University.

——(1999). 'Historical Institutionalism in Comparative Politics', *Annual Review of Political Science* 2: 369–404.

——(2004). *How Institutions Evolve*. New York: Cambridge University Press.

——and SVEN STEINMO, (1992). 'Historical Institutionalism in Comparative Politics', in *Structuring Politics: Historical Institutionalism in Comparative Analysis*, (New York: Cambridge University Press), pp. 1–32.

THOMAS, GEORGE M., JOHN W. MEYER, FRANCISCO O. RAMIREZ, and JOHN BOLI (eds.) (1987). *Institutional Structure: Constituting State, Society, and the Individual*, (Newbury Park: Sage).

WEIR, MARGARET (2006). 'When Does Politics Create Policy? The Organizational Politics of Change', in *Rethinking Political Institutions*, eds. Ian Shapiro, Stephen Skowronek, and Daniel Galvin, (New York: New York University Press), pp. 171–86.

WEISS, LINDA (1988). *Creating Capitalism: The State and Small Business Since 1945*, (New York: Basil Blackwell).

WESTNEY, ELEANOR D. (1987). *Imitation and Innovation: The Transfer of Western Organization Patterns to Meiji Japan*, (Cambridge: Harvard University Press).

WHITFORD, JOSH (2005). *The New Old Economy*, (New York: Oxford University Press).

WILLIAMSON, OLIVER E. (1985). *The Economic Institutions of Capitalism*, (New York: Free Press).

ZALD, MAYER N. and PATRICIA DENTON (1963). 'From Evangelism to General Service: The Transformation of the YMCA', *Administrative Science Quarterly* 8(2): 214–34.

ZEITLIN, JONATHAN (2003). 'Introduction', in *Governing Work and Welfare in a New Economy: European and American Experiments*, eds. Jonathan Zeitlin and David Trubek, (New York: Oxford University Press).

CHAPTER 5

....

COMPLEMENTARITY

....

COLIN CROUCH[1]

INTRODUCTION

....

The idea of complementarity is of considerable use in studies of institutions, because if it can be correctly applied it enables analysts to consider when and how certain institutions 'belong' together to form a *Gestalt* or overall shape,[2] or in contrast to indicate when two or more institutions might be incompatible with each other. If it is possible to reach conclusions of this kind, not only is institutional analysis placed on a scientific basis, but it can also acquire relevance to policymakers and other institution builders. For example, assume that policymakers in country A notice, say, a form of industrial relations working very effectively in country B. They will be tempted to imitate that institution in their own country. If institutional experts could pronounce on whether such an imitation is likely to be complementary to the surrounding institutions, they would be able to advise on whether such an imitation would be likely to succeed. Unfortunately there are considerable limitations to the applicability of the idea of complementarity in this way, or at least limitations in our knowledge of how it might operate. Because of both the attractiveness of the concept and its risks, it is essential that any study of comparative institutions should have a clear idea of this term, its potentiality, and its weaknesses.

[1] I am grateful to John L. Campbell and to Glenn Morgan for comments on earlier drafts of this chapter.
    [2] It was German scholars, working principally in psychology, who first considered in depth the way that disparate elements tend to come together in a limited number of overall figures or shapes. The German word, *Gestalt*, therefore carries this meaning in a way that is not fully captured in the English 'figure' or 'shape'.

The following discussion will distinguish between three different usages of the concept to be found in the literature, and will analyse that literature as it falls within these different usages.[3] Some problems and weaknesses will then be identified. The overall tendency of the argument will be to advise caution in the use of complementarity in institutional research, though the concept is not rejected, as a distinct role will be found for it.

COMPLEMENTARITY AS COMPONENTS
COMPENSATING FOR EACH OTHER'S DEFICIENCIES

This is the strictest but also the most everyday sense of the idea of complementarity. It defines two or more phenomena (in our case institutions) as complementary when each can be defined in terms of what is lacked by the other(s) in order to produce a defined whole.[4] A perfect example is found in the nursery rhyme:

> Jack Sprat could eat no fat.
> His wife could eat no lean.
> So, between the two of them,
> They licked the platter clean.

Jack Sprat and his wife complemented each other in the achievement of a clean platter.

Setting aside the world of nursery rhymes, complementarity is most often encountered where mathematics can be used, as this can give a formal meaning to the idea of complementarity; Höpner (2005) cites the instance of the computer scientist's concept of complementary binary numerical series. Two hemispheres that together form a sphere constitute a further example. Another is Nils Bohr's discovery that the transmission of light requires both point-like and linear characteristics—features that earlier scientists had considered to be mutually incompatible. For Bohr it was precisely the contrast afforded by such incompatible principles that made the phenomenon possible.[5]

We can find examples of discoveries of such complementarity in the social sciences. Legal theory often speaks of the complementarity of two different jurisdictions (say, the European Court and national legal systems), in the sense that they deal with different kinds of problem, rather than either clashing or overlapping (Cherednychenko 2007; Kleffner 2003). Democracy and liberty have been seen to

---

[3] An earlier, shorter, version of this discussion will be found in Crouch (2005: 50–60).

[4] For the sake of simplicity, in this discussion we shall normally talk in terms of two institutions being complementary to each other, but in reality there is no limit to the number of components that might be considered to constitute complementary parts of a whole.

[5] I am indebted to Rogers Hollingsworth for drawing my attention to Bohr's work on this.

be complementary, in the sense that the former deals with the rights of the many and the latter with those of the individual (Vanberg 2008). Campbell and Pedersen (2001c: 257) have identified contrary elements in some institutions to 'compensate' for the establishment of neo-liberalism in others: '... the development of neo-liberal institutions in one area was compensated for by institutions based on different principles in other areas...; the adoption of neo-liberalism was heavily mediated by other institutional principles.'

In Sweden, statutory and voluntary social services have been found by research to be complementary, in that they each seem to address needs that the other misses (Dahlberg 2005). In the same vein, Elke Viebrock (2004), in a study of different forms of unemployment benefit systems, has shown how Sweden—usually the absolute paradigm case of the social democratic welfare state—has for reasons of political history retained a role for voluntary associations alongside the state in the organization of its unemployment insurance system. Kristensen (1997), comparing the development of management systems in England, Germany, and Denmark, finds the last to be dominated by a 'personal reputational' system, which does not feature in any of the usual stereotypes of Scandinavian countries, and which might play a role in compensating for those features.

Another example would be the study by Streeck et al. (1987) of the highly portable skill qualifications of the German vocational training system, which offset the tendency towards low labour mobility of many other German labour market institutions. The opposite role might be played by non-transferable company pension schemes in US corporations, which offset the tendency towards the high labour mobility of many other US labour market institutions. A further example would be the role of big institutional investors in the US economy, whose individual impact on a firm or whole sector can be so large that they cannot behave as in a pure market, but need to act strategically, often engaging in dialogue with firms' managements. They thereby offset the bias towards spot markets of some other US financial institutions, and make possible a supply of patient capital.

In a lengthy study of the changes that took place in the political economy of the UK during the 1980s, Gamble (1994) examined the relationship between the 'free economy' and the 'strong state'. The idea seems contradictory, as a 'free' economy is one in which governments do not intervene in markets, while a strong state would seem to be one that intervenes strongly in society. However, a strong state is not required to act everywhere; it can demonstrate its strength by choosing where to intervene and where not to do so. Gamble showed how a 'free' economy could be constructed in late twentieth-century Britain only through considerable exercise of state power to resist pressures from groups in society whose interests would be harmed by stronger use of free markets. The relationship between the free economy and the strong state was a paradox, not a contradiction, the two operating in a complementary manner.

A similar puzzle was considered by Lütz (2003), who studied the reform of financial regulation in the UK and Germany in the 1980s and 1990s. These reforms were, like the general change processes that took place in Britain, part of a move to free markets. Part of the process took the form of establishing a strong level of legal regulation, replacing a more informal system in both countries. This might appear to contradict the idea of freeing markets, but free markets require a high level of transparency, clear rules, and easy entry by new players. International firms from outside the countries concerned could not understand the informal financial systems of Germany and the UK, but they could understand a clear set of formal legal rules established by the respective governments according to some internationally recognized principles. Statutory regulation and market liberation were complementary.

Similar again, in showing the complementarity of strong legal rules and free markets, is the study by Carruthers, Babb, and Halliday (2001), showing how, across the world, central bank rules have become stricter while bankruptcy laws have become softer. The authors conclude:

> ... [bankruptcy law] is the institution that constitutes the legal preconditions for market pressure! Indeed, bankruptcy laws are being altered so as to ameliorate the market pressures that distressed corporations face. This does not invalidate the idea of institutional efficiency, but it casts doubt on the idea that market pressures drive institutions in the direction of ever-greater efficiency.   (ibid. 119–120)

Similarly, a family pattern complementary to a free-market economy might be one that provides resources of emotional support and maintenance of the worker to offset the rigours and insecurities of the labour market (Parsons and Bales 1955). Whitley (2005) talks of how in the Netherlands the links between the corporate governance system, state policies, and the organization of business groups are so strong as to outweigh the relatively arm's-length bank–firm relationships. He also points out (ibid.) how there are likely to be contradictions between dominant institutional arrangements with respect to firm governance, strategies, authority sharing, and employer–employee commitments, these contradictions giving managers the chance to develop idiosyncratic strategies and capabilities.

To turn to an institution of a very different kind, Renate Mayntz (2004) has drawn attention to the combination of hierarchy and network as modes of governance within terrorist organizations. These were not 'designed' as complements to each other, but coexist as coincidental diversity. In a hostile environment the capacity to switch from one to the other becomes a complementarity. This is typical of the unpredictable and non-designed character of complementarity in institutions. A difference becomes a complementarity when it 'works'. But this requires specification of a goal; for terrorist organizations trying to survive under pressure, goals are clear. But one of the ways in which normal life differs from terrorist organizations is that it has multiple, contested and uncertain goals.

These, and many other examples, all take the basic form: $X = y + z$, where $X =$ the whole and y, z the component parts. In terms of institutional design, if we know what X is, and already have y, then we would seek to complete our institution by finding a component that had the characteristics of $X–y$. So, in the Jack Sprat example, if our objective is a clean platter, we know that the food on it constitutes lean meat and fat, and we already have an eater of lean meat, then we know that the complement we seek must be an eater of fat.

In complex institutional analysis, however, it is often very difficult to specify what would constitute a whole, and therefore not easy to specify what would be complementary components of it. As in all sciences that have (complementary!) empirical and theoretical components, there is a constant interaction between theoretical ideas and empirical observation. The former cannot develop purely deductively, as they might in mathematics, but repeatedly feed on knowledge of facts. In the various examples cited above, the case of liberalism and democracy comes closest to being purely deductive, as one does not need much empirical evidence in order to discern a distinction, and possible conflict, between group and individual interests. However, to turn to another of the examples, it is not possible to work out in theory the sum total of needs to which social services might respond, in order to establish which of the specified totality are served by statutory and which by voluntary services. One starts with the observation that these services tend to serve different needs, and then develops a theory that the two are therefore complementary. The other studies cited come part way between the two: the authors have some ideas of how the coexistence of two apparently contradictory institutions can be explained, but they depend on their research to show exactly how the complementarity seems to work. Having done so, they can refine the theory.

In the cases cited here, the authors do not go beyond presentation of the relationship they have discovered, and some do not actually use the concept of complementarity. But for many scholars identification of these relationships has raised the possibility of specifying systematic links, to the extent that we might develop a body of knowledge of which combinations of institutions are likely to be successful, and to seek 'necessary' complementarities among social structures. This raises a number of methodological and theoretical problems. These will be addressed below, but we must first consider the other uses of the term, as similar objections apply to them.

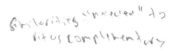

COMPLEMENTARITY AS SIMILARITY

Although the everyday meaning of complementarity implies contrasts and differences in the constitution of elements deemed to be involved, these differences are clearly nested in certain kinds of similarity, or they would not 'fit'. To revert to one of the mathematical examples, the two hemispheres that together form a sphere contrast, in that, in order to make the sphere, they have to face different directions. But they are both hemispheres; it would not work if one were a cube.[6] Some studies of

---

[6] It would not 'work' on the assumption that the expected whole is a sphere. It is however possible to imagine some applications (say, in engineering) where a desired shape was a combination of a hemisphere and a cube. This draws our attention to the fact that complementarity analysis assumes that

complementarity stress the idea of similarity embedded in the idea, and either explicitly or implicitly reject the idea of contradiction and difference.

For example, Amable used the concept to support the assumption that national systems must possess an overall internal congruence, or else different components will give contradictory signals to agents (Amable 2000: 6, 57). The same applies to Whitley (2005), when he defines complementarity as the degree to which social institutions encourage similar kinds of economic actors to behave in similar ways and reinforce each other's effects. This refers to situations where the existence of one institution provokes that of another, which in turn strengthens the first, and so on. The idea of difference and contrast has disappeared here. Later, Amable (2005: 372) was to consider that complementarity should not be reduced to similarity (or what he calls 'isomorphism'). By adopting the economist's approach to complementarity (*vide infra*) he was able to use the concept in a way that can include both similarities and differences.

The logic of similarity has been strongly asserted by Goodin et al. (1999: 6) in a study of different kinds of welfare regime:

These clusters [of different forms of welfare capitalism] . . . represent intellectually and prag-matically unified packages of programmes and policies, values and institutions. It is between these whole packages—these welfare regimes as a whole—the social engineers are obliged to choose. It is the performance of these welfare regimes, taken as a whole, that we ought to try to compare.

For Hall (1999), similarity emerges from the way in which a given set of national, regional, or sectoral institutions tends to create equilibrium forms of firm behaviour, combined with a broader set of factors that include the presence of specific public policies, social coalitions, and socio-economic conditions. Hall and Gingerich (2004) take this further to argue that systems mixing institutions of different fundamental types will under-perform pure types. In other words, pedigree dogs will out-perform mongrels. Their theoretical argument is supported by impressive quantitative evidence on national economic performances. It belongs in the class of 'U-curve' theories which, disconcertingly for most policymakers, predict that extreme cases will out-perform compromises and hybrids. As Hay (2002) has pointed out, having derived theoretical reasons for producing a set of types, authors tend to regard as somehow 'incoherent' those cases whose histories have happened not to place them in the theorist's boxes. He cites the instance of Garrett (2000), who, having set up Scandinavia and the so-called Anglo-Saxon model as his theoretically 'pure' cases of different forms of welfare state and political economy has to insist that Germany and the Netherlands are 'incoherent'.

The idea of *Wahlverwandschaft* (elective affinity),[7] is often used to describe this process whereby institutions across many different parts of a society find some kind

we know the identity of the whole to which the parts contribute. This might be obvious from the context, but it might also raise problems of functionalism, which will be discussed later in this chapter.

[7] Max Weber was the first to use this concept in social science. It originated from eighteenth-century German chemistry, where it was used to describe the process by which certain elements seemed to be

of intellectual fit together, mainly through cognitive processes and social learning (Powell and DiMaggio 1991: 63–82). Both formal and informal sources, regulation and cultural cognitive processes might induce this isomorphism. Kitschelt et al. (1999*b*: 3), for example, see *Wahlverwandschaft* linking types of production regime, patterns of socio-economic inequality and protection through welfare states, and the constitution of corporate political actors in parties and interest groups. Whitley (1997) does not use the term elective affinity, but describes the same phenomenon, when he argues that patterns link the training system and the role of employers and workers' organizations in running it, the academic stratification of the labour market, the strengths and policies of the state concerning the integration of the pre-industrial training system, the extent to which owners are locked into the fate of the firms into which they invest, their trust in the formal institutions governing property rights and other economic issues, and systemic trust in general, which is in turn linked to types of financial markets, and the nature and form of legitimation of authority relations.

For Hall and Soskice (2001*b*), the political system in a liberal market economy, being located in a system where markets are strong, should also function like a market, with a large number of actors pursuing their goals in a system which achieves balance through the sheer number of transactions, and the incapacity of any one group to dominate. This is pure isomorphism with no subtle balances of contrast. As Hall and Soskice (ibid: 17–21) put it, particular institutions develop similar capacities in neighbouring spheres, such as corporate governance, vocational training, and collective bargaining. Such assumptions have, for example, enabled proponents of neo-liberal labour market reform in Europe to argue that intensified product-market competition will be a spur to such reform because, if firms are competing intensively in product markets, they will find it difficult to cooperate in labour markets (Blanchard 2004). But often authors achieve their generalizations about such links by looking at a few components of an institution and falsely assuming that all others are isomorphic with it. For example, in examining types of welfare state, Goodin et al. (1999), in the study quoted above, consider only their tax transfer aspects. As a result they are not required to confront such apparent anomalies as the major role of public investment and public institutions in the US education system, or the universalist national health service that still endures in the UK.

If we set the findings of these studies alongside those cited earlier, which showed the role of the first, opposed, meaning of complementarity, we are presented with a problem: theory-builders, rather than recognize the coexistence of the two opposed processes, will move between opposite logics—similarity and complementarity—as makes theory seem more convincing; presenting an overall account which looks plausible but which is not vulnerable to counter-factual test.

attracted to each other. It was then used by Goethe to describe certain forms of romantic attachments—though here there is a subtle mix between elements of similarity and contrast that tends to elude scientific inquiry. See Crouch (2005: 48–50.)

There is an approach to complementarity that is able to incorporate elements of both similarity and difference without recourse to such ruses, and that is to apply the term analogously to its use in economic theory.

[handwritten margin note: Complementarity use part of production function]

COMPLEMENTARITY IN THE ECONOMIST'S SENSE

Economists see complementarity as part of the production function, defining it clearly in terms of two goods, a fall in the price of one of which will lead to a rise in the demand for the other. Elsewhere (Crouch 2005: 52–3), I have used the example of how a rise in demand for the flour used in making pizza might lead to a rise in the price of tomatoes. Bacon and eggs are also often cited as instances of products related in this way.

Aoki (1994, 2000, 2001), an institutional economist, was probably the first systematically to extend this concept to institutions, defining institutions as complementary when the enhancement of one would assist provision of the other. To grasp this concept, one has to imagine a kind of market for institutions, such that if one of them grows, there will be an increased demand for those that help to sustain it. Aoki's initial point of reference was the various institutions that seem to go together to constitute the ensemble of the Japanese economy. He was thinking in particular of the way in which contingent company monitoring by main banks of large firms was complementary to the team-oriented lifetime employment system of those firms. Team-oriented production is difficult to monitor, as individuals' performance is not assessed. However, the lifetime employment system that used to be dominant in Japan meant that it was very difficult for employees to find a job in a new firm; as a result employees feared the liquidation of their firm and had a strong incentive themselves to ensure that no one's performance was putting its viability at risk. The risk of liquidation would appear if the firm's main bank started to enquire in detail into its performance; but it would carry out such enquiries only if the firm were performing poorly. Provided employees and managers collaborated on ensuring good overall performance, they need not fear that this would happen. A cluster of features of the institutions surrounding the Japanese firm therefore reinforced a particular pattern of behaviour. If something were to change—say a shift to a short-term shareholder system of ownership, which to a limited extent did start to occur during the 1990s (Dore 2000; Jackson 2001)—the whole network of incentives would change, and different institutions would be needed to ensure economic success.

[handwritten margin note: Japanese firms in 1990s an example]

One has here all the elements of a complementarity approach. Different institutions are brought together, not because they remedy deficiencies in each other (as in the Jack Sprat form), nor because they embody some kind of similarity or affinity, but because when they occur together they produce a stable model that is mutually reinforcing.

Amable, Ernst, and Palombarini (2005) have formalized the theory behind this approach, taking the example of Aoki's hypothesized relationship between different types of corporate finance and systems of industrial relations, but not limiting its application to Japan. Drawing on the firm-centred approach of Hall and Soskice (2001*a*), their analysis of long-term and short-term oriented financial systems, and Crouch's (1993) analysis of western European industrial relations systems, they use game theory to show that in systems of long-term, 'patient' capital, managers and unions alike will prefer strong, coordinated systems of industrial relations, as they can take the long-term viability of the firm for granted. Where capital has short-term horizons, the identity of a firm is vulnerable to rapid change; neither managers nor unions will adopt a long-term approach to the firm, and the former has an incentive to ensure that unions are weak.[8]

This approach is pregnant with possibilities for comparative institutionalists, as it holds out the same promise as embodied in the first, everyday meaning of complementarity, but without the requirement of finding a way in which the components somehow remedy deficiencies in each other. There might be complementarity in this sense, but there might also be elements of similarity, isomorphism, or the subtle mix of true elective affinity. One requires a theoretical expectation that two institutions are likely to be found together, supported by empirical evidence of an association. It then becomes in principle possible to build up a strong edifice of knowledge about systematic associations between different types of institution, ultimately enabling us to identify a limited number of types of society, as the shapes or *Gestalten* formed by these associations that come together in a limited number of typical ensembles. It then becomes possible to predict the overall pattern of institutions likely to be found in a society on the basis of knowledge of just one or two. Even more ambitiously, it may be possible to predict which ensembles will be associated with superior economic performance. This latter has long been an aspiration of institutional analysts, enabling them to rival the economic forecasting claims of economists. Unfortunately social scientific knowledge is rarely sufficiently advanced for us to make the *ex ante* predictions on this base that should in principle be possible; we usually have to make do with *ex post* reasoning about some empirical observations.

Amable (2003) used it to derive a typology of forms of capitalism, based on a wide range of quantitative data and a large number of cases. Deeg (2005) used the concept of 'coherence' rather than complementarity in his study of the components of national business systems, but his intentions are similar (if more cautious). As will be discussed in more detail below, various authors of the *régulationiste* school have used it, together with the almost conflicting idea of institutional hierarchy, to develop typologies of different types of capitalism over time and space.

If the idea of complementary associations among institutions that make for economic success can be established, it should also be possible to identify 'bad' matches, of where one institution exists but not the partner institutions that are known to be complementary to it. The most systematic and explicit study of this

---

[8] Amable et al. could also have made use of the fact that in coordinated industrial relations systems, the firm is not the basic unit, but the industry or sector. Unions at least are required to believe only in the long-term viability of the industry, not so much an individual firm.

kind to date has been Hall and Gingerich's (2004) account of the association among various components of corporate governance and industrial relations. This showed a negative association between economic success and countries with mixed institutional patterns. However, Kenworthy (2006) used the same data to explore a more inclusive set of variables, reaching very different conclusions. Campbell and Pedersen (2007) took his arguments further to explore the case of Denmark, demonstrating superior performance possibilities in certain forms of institutional 'hybrid'.

To date, research of this kind has focused on a relatively narrow range of institutions and national cases, considerably narrower than those where complementarity in the first sense has been used or implied. There has been a particular concentration on the relationship between financial systems and corporate governance on the one hand and industrial relations and other labour issues on the other (Aoki's starting point), and on comparisons between Germany and the USA/UK in particular. Other, more isolated, topics have however concerned the relationship between scientific and economic organisation (Whitley 2006), social capital, and economic performance in central and eastern Europe (Haerpfer, Wallace, and Raiser 2005).

PROBLEMS WITH COMPLEMENTARITY STUDIES

There are a number of difficulties with using the idea of complementarity in research on institutions. Some apply to all three of the approaches discussed here, others to only one or two of them. These now need to be addressed.

Defining survival and success

Complementarity research tends to make much use of the idea of the 'success' of institutions. This is not simple. Societies and economies do not have aims or goals; an external observer can impose such on them, and evaluate the relative success of their different institutions at achieving economic growth, or quality of life, or social equality, or anything else in which the observers are interested and for which they can construct more or less plausible indicators. But these are external impositions of the observer, and we have no idea how these might relate to some idea of evolutionary success.[9]

Amable, Ernst, and Palombarini (2005: 313) suggest that success may have two meanings in complementarity research. It is often associated with the idea of economic success (Amable 2003; Hall and Soskice 2001a), but, as in evolutionary theory, success for a pattern of institutions might mean mere survival and resistance

---

[9] See Quack and Morgan (2000) for a good discussion of the endogenous definition of 'performance'.

to change. Indeed, Amable (2005: 372) suggests as a means of operationalizing the idea of success in this sense 'that two institutions are compatible if their coexistence does not set in motion a process of change'. But the most successful institutions are those that embody within their structure a capacity to change, though we have not yet advanced far in our study of how these processes relate to complementarity (Deeg 2007). This then raises the question that, if conditions change, successful complementarity in this sense might mean inability to adapt to change. In evolutionary theory, this is similar to the difference between species that successfully adapt to a particular environment, and those that develop a capacity to change environments.

There is then the problem that biological evolution takes place with very large numbers of cases over very long periods of time. Studying a few countries over three or four decades does not provide this. Here institutional analysts seem to be able to take advantage of a functional equivalent for a large number of iterations: the role of social actors in being able to perceive successful associations and to work at them, short-cutting as it were the market or evolutionary process. The market and evolution are blind processes, operating without purposeful intervention, which is why they require such large numbers of cases to sort out relative efficiency. However, while this solves one problem, where the economic analogy of complementarity is concerned it opens the door to that already discussed of the conscious creation of some human institutions.

These problems do not mean that it is inappropriate or wrong to use the idea of complementarity, but that institutional analysts should be careful to specify clearly what they are claiming and its limitations, and to be aware, when they use the analogy of the economics version of the concept, of when the conditions of that analogy do not apply to their case.

Problems of the economics analogy

Next, and with particular reference to extensions of the economist's use of the term, we must note certain changes in the claims made for it as it moves from the original to the extended application. To return to the pizza ingredients illustration, economists do not claim, on the basis of their empirical observations, that the combination of flour and tomatoes will be more 'successful' than other uses of tomatoes, or that if eggs are eaten with something other than bacon the diner will have an unpleasant experience. All they would want to claim is that there is something successful in these associations, otherwise they would not persist. The economic theory of complementarity has nothing to say about the quality of the associations it finds. In some cases, as with pizza or eggs and bacon, they are purely the results of human tastes, and dependent on the continuity of those tastes for survival. (A rise in tomato allergies would lead to a rise in demand for *pizza bianca*, a pizza made without tomatoes, breaking the complementarity.) Other complementarities observed by economists are more functional, such as the demand for nuts and bolts; though technical change producing the boltless nut would change that association too. Complementarities are highly contingent on a variety of different causes of the association.

Institutional theorists need to be similarly cautious in their claims, but they tend not to be. They frequently wish to draw conclusions about which combinations of institutions are more or less 'successful', and often want to account for different levels of national economic success in terms of whether or not a country's combination of economic institutions is acting complementarily or not. This may be stretching the knowledge conveyed by the observation that two institutions are complementary in a number of cases further than it can go. Also, as Höpner (2005: 340) points out: 'identification of complementarity cannot tell us anything about directions of causality'. For example, to take the most cited case: do certain patterns of corporate governance 'cause' (in the sense of make possible) certain kinds of industrial relations? Is it vice versa? Or are both produced by something else—like the interests of an elite? Without some knowledge of this, it would be difficult to give policy advice about institutional change.

Second, institutionalists must also remember that if they are using economics analogies, they are using the concept of a market. Associations between the demand for one product and another emerge out of very large numbers of transactions, repeated over time: it needs rather more than thirty people eating bacon and eggs to make these into complementary goods. The market for institutions does not have this character of a mass of transactions. Research on the advanced economies of the world is unlikely to have more than thirty-two cases (the number of current member states of the Organisation for Economic Cooperation and Development), and in practice often features considerably fewer. This is not enough to make confident claims about the strength of associations. What we observe may be little more than coincidence, combined with some direct imitation. Also, unlike an economic market, transactions in the market for institutions are not repeated many times; once institutions have been set on a path, they are likely to remain on it for a long time.

This also applies to the related idea of an association between institutions being the result of an evolutionary process. Evolution and the market share the characteristic of having very large numbers of iterations, all slightly different, some of which turn out to have survival value, others of which do not.[10] Complementary institutions are often depicted as those that have survived, while many others will have failed, indicating that the complementary ones are successful. However, as Knight has argued (2001: 37):

for economic institutions competitive selection can often be invoked as the primary causal mechanism, because markets with vast numbers of transactions are assumed; but for institutions the numbers of cases and actors are too small to be considered to constitute a market, the

[10] There are however important limits to the association between the market and evolution, particularly in relation to the nature of 'survival' in the two processes. People often talk of market competition as a 'Darwinian' struggle for survival, but Darwin's model of evolutionary survival does not necessarily imply a head-to-head conflict between different species or species forms.

fundamental market condition of anonymity is not respected, and the intentions of actors can [at least to a certain extent] therefore serve as the basis for explanations of change.[11]

We therefore need to watch closely if political institutional theories make use of arguments concerning evolution through competition that they cannot sustain.

Closely related to this is the point that has been very well demonstrated by Höpner (2005): direct human agency may select two institutions, not through a mass of choices in a market, but through a small number of strategic decisions by powerful elites. He argues that this does not constitute complementarity in the economists' market-based meaning of the term. This is so for two reasons. First, the elites might make mistakes when they establish a certain pattern of institutions. Given the difficulty of making changes in institutions once they have been established, they may persist despite not being particularly successful. Other actors may over time take a number of measures that will ensure that the connection does work, without changing the observable institutional form. They do this either because it is too difficult to make major institutional change, or because the elite will not let them try. To an outside observer the two institutions are succeeding well alongside each other, but in practice it is a series of informal practices that makes the ensemble succeed. This is a finding very familiar to the sociology of organizations, where, for example, what at first sight appears to be a well-functioning bureaucracy in reality works well only because employees subvert rigid formal structures with their own informal work practices. Such things can be discovered only in intensive case studies, which unfortunately rank low in the hierarchy of social science research methods in comparison with large quantitative studies that make use of straightforward indicators, which are usually based on formal attributes of institutions alone. Important theoretical issues concerning how institutions actually function are concealed by this problem of a distorted choice of methodology.

Further, the elites may not be wholly innocent in their institution construction, but may seek to extract certain gains for themselves in the way that things are organized. Again, people trying to make the institutions work will have to leave the structure in place, because powerful elites draw their rents from it, but may find invisible, informal ways round it. Complementarity theorists have a tendency to ignore issues of the pursuit of interests and conflicts between interests in their study of institutions.

The problem of functionalism

Höpner's second argument takes in a problem with all uses of complementarity in institutional analysis: its tendency towards functionalism, explaining the existence of institutions in terms of their outcomes rather than their initial causes. Separate from, though often appearing alongside, such a tendency is adoption of the 'innocent' view that institution-creators seek generally desirable outcomes rather than special

---

[11] Knight has political institutions particularly in mind, but the point is capable of extension to national economies as institutional forms, the principal institutions involved in complementarity studies.

privileges for themselves. The two become related in that accounts which explain institutions in terms of their contribution to solving various problems—the outcome of which is a functionalist account—tend also to describe the roles of leading actors as motivated solely by attempts to solve the problems concerned.

Complementarity theory is vulnerable to taking these paths because of the need to specify a whole and to account for components in terms of their contribution to its maintenance. However, the problem can be avoided, and some complementarity theorists have been aware of it and have built the possibility of conflict, contradiction, and various possibilities of upheaval and inefficiency into their models. To do this one needs to speak from a more general theory of institutions and how they work, going beyond the complementarity theme; otherwise the concept is likely to collapse into so many exceptions that it has no meaning.

Indeed, how do we know whether two institutions are 'complementary' or 'contradictory'? We might say that they are the former when the consequences of the combination are benign, and the latter when they are malign. Sometimes that will be clear enough, but the relationship will change over time, and evaluation of it may vary with different social interests. For example, for several years increasing mortgage and credit card debt and the development of derivatives markets in the British and US economies were highly complementary. The debts enabled consumers on moderate incomes to buy many goods and services that they would otherwise have not been able to afford, while the derivatives markets traded the debt. Eventually however the relationship became over-strained, leading almost to a collapse of the financial system (see Engelen and Konings, this volume, for a detailed discussion). What had at one time seemed a benign relationship now appeared as a toxic mix. However, from the point of view of many people working in the financial sector, the arrangements had been extremely profitable. From what perspective can we gain a view of a 'whole', the impact on which various institutional combinations can be seen as positive or negative? Similarly, many authors have argued that emerging contradictions between institutions can serve as catalysts for change, the grit in the oyster that makes the pearl. But how are we to know whether such change should be evaluated positively or negatively without a concept of what constitutes the 'good of the whole', especially when the change might also alter what we regard as the whole. For example, globalization is a process of change that makes it increasingly difficult to view the nation-state as an individual whole.

It is therefore not surprising that the authors who have made perhaps the most convincing use of this kind of approach have been the French *régulationiste* school (e.g. Boyer 2000, Boyer and Saillard 1995), as they start from a strong general theoretical position. Starting originally from Marxist theory, with a rather rigid approach to how different systems of production succeeded each other historically, they have recently produced nuanced studies in which complementarity vies with hierarchy (seen as the imposition of institutional forms by higher levels on to lower ones, not necessarily producing the most functionally efficient outcomes). This also enables them to see institutions co-evolving through trial and error, with mutual adjustment until they are 'made' compatible with each other—not necessarily by top-down elite action, but by institutional entrepreneurs at various levels.

This remains vulnerable to Höpner's objections (discussed above) to mixing accounts based on strategic action with those using the idea of a market, but it helpfully widens the range of potential combinations that retrospectively seem to constitute complementarities. For example, Streeck (2005: 364) has pointed out that certain combinations of financial regime and forms of industrial relations that writers have deemed to be impossible because not complementary on the basis of German experience have actually been developed by deliberate strategy of a wide range of actors in recent years in Denmark, where they seem to have operated with considerable effectiveness. In a different argument, but pointing to the same ends, Streeck also points out (ibid: 364) that claims to identify complementarity must allow for the fact that different elites and interests might dominate different institutional spheres, not necessarily permitting matching institutions, and that this will be particularly the case as internationalization affects many institutions.

Streeck and Yamamura (2001; Yamamura and Streeck 2003) find another means of avoiding functionalism, while rescuing the complementarity idea. Elites might establish institutions for a number of motives. However, once the institutions are in existence, they might be used for a variety of purposes, and might indeed become part of complementarities as other actors in the society (institutional entrepreneurs, *vide infra*) start to use them. These examples might fit the economists' concept: through a kind of market, actors at various levels of a system look, in a non-strategic and certainly not all-knowing way, for institutions that might fit together to solve some problems. Gradually, repeated success at making certain links leads to a strong association between the institutions concerned. Streeck and Yamamura use this kind of discussion to account for various distinctive features of historical German and Japanese capitalisms as they emerged from the late nineteenth century onwards.

Writing more generally along similar lines, Streeck (2005: 363) has pointed out that, a high level of slack exists in most economic institutions, and institution building is a very slow process; this reduces the likelihood that we shall find many really tightly structured complementarities. In the language of the present discussion, institution-building is not really a market process and is carried out in a context of considerable lack of knowledge. This is an approach that fits very well into the gradualist forms of institutional theory developed by Campbell (2004) and Crouch (2005) in their adaptation and extension of Levi-Strauss's concept of *bricolage*, where institutions are seen as being constructed and reconstructed as different actors search around among the bits of institutions that surround them and try to fashion them into somewhat new shapes. Similar points emerge from studies by Streeck and Thelen (2005), Thelen (2002) and Ebbinghaus and Manow (2001) of the ways in which major institutional changes might emerge through 'layering' and branching, with major changes emerging slowly out of successions of minor adjustments.

This again introduces into the argument the problematic role of human agency in complementarity, in the form of institutional entrepreneurs. Entrepreneurs are people (or groups) who innovate by making new combinations of things to make a new product. Institutional entrepreneurs put together different institutional components in order to produce new ones. (It must also be kept in mind that they will be seeking their own ends by so doing.) They can only do this if there are institutions 'lying around' within their society that do not fit into an existing scheme, but which they can use to construct a new one—as envisaged in the idea of institutional *bricolage.*

This is important for the study of institutional change. Consistently with their tendency to functionalism, some complementarity analyses present societies as so hard-wired that it seems impossible that any change could take place in such precisely integrated structures. Indeed, as already noted, one of Amable's (2005) definitions of successful complementarity almost seemed to require lack of change. This is probably a source of variation among societies (or parts of societies). Some may be relatively hard-wired, such that large numbers of institutions are closely linked together, and change becomes very difficult: the countries of the former Soviet bloc probably took this form, which is why change in them was so slow. But others will be more loosely wired, with not all institutions neatly integrated at any one time. However, these would emerge from some versions of complementarity theory as 'unsuccessful' cases at any one point in time, because their institutions do not 'fit together'.

Höpner provides an example of this in his account of how (contrary to the expectations of more rigid theorists) the German co-determination system is finding surprising new complementarities with a more Anglo-American style of corporate governance (2005: 348; see also Jackson, Höpner, and Kurdelbusch 2005). Höpner concludes with an observation that is useful and instructive for all attempts to use the idea of complementarity in institutional research (ibid: 350):

> ... [I]f, in the end a complementary relationship of shareholder orientation and co-determi-
> nation seems at least conceivable, must the theoretical consequence be that complementarity
> may be possible in any given institutional configuration? This would be misleading as not
> every conceivable institutional configuration is functionally promising... Elective affinities
> between institutions actually exist. But the interplay of shareholder orientation and co-
> determination in Germany shows that the range of possible complementarities may be larger
> than the number of already existing configurations.

CONCLUSIONS

In the face of these difficulties for strong complementarity theory, it is not surprising that some authors have produced a far weaker model of complementarity as merely 'mutual effects'. Pierson (2000: 78) refers to configurations of complementary in-stitutions as being those 'in which the performance of each is affected by the existence of others'. This is weak in its implications, but many authors use complementarity in this sense. We can go further, provided we remain aware of the various traps discussed above.

Identification of complementarity in the first, 'Jack Sprat' sense used here of institutional components that seem to coexist because they compensate for each other's deficiencies or overemphases will always be valuable, partly because this usage of the word corresponds to its everyday meaning, and partly because such paradoxical demonstrations are fascinating in themselves. The use of complementarity as similarity is more difficult, and methodologically dubious if combined in apparently ad hoc ways with the opposing principle, but can be made to work if combined with a further underlying theory. This could be the economics meaning of complementarity, provided there are grounds for identifying a market for institutions in the context concerned. The alternative, hinted at a number of times in the above account, is to relate institutional formations to the interests of human agents—whether strategic decision-makers, or institutional entrepreneurs practising institutional *bricolage*, or compromises between groups of powerful actors.

For example, the *régulationiste* literature was able to propose a homogenization of coherent Fordist principles across a wide range of institutions, because it was fundamentally related to Marxist theory, which in turn sustains a thesis that all the institutions of a social formation will reflect the interests of a dominant class. (There is of course considerable diversity and ambiguity in Marxist theory whether an actor-centred or a functionalist account should be given of how this domination comes to be expressed.) Esping-Andersen's (1990) model of welfare-state formation is an example of a logic of stylized compromises between opposed social and political forces, as the designation of the types in terms of political models implies. (See also Korpi 1983 for a general formulation of this power-relations approach to social analysis; for an application aimed specifically at the study of capitalist diversity while also bringing power into a game-theoretic approach, see Amable 2003: 9–10, 46, 66–73.) It is also possible to depict the establishment of particular kinds of governance as an outcome of socio-political struggle.

Similar again is North's (1990) account of the emergence of the Anglophone model of capitalism: a liberal but non-democratic political settlement that favoured the interests of bourgeois property owners over both aristocratic elites and the property-less masses. Steinmo, Thelen, and Longstreth (1992); Thelen (1999); Kristensen (1997); and Streeck and Yamamura (2001) and other 'historical institutionalists' (Campbell and Pedersen 2001*b*) have similarly looked at the role of conflict and contention in the establishment of particular national sets of institutions. Teubner (2001) has drawn attention to the way in which incompatibilities between different legal principles in a complex system provide useful 'irritants' from which innovation can result. From a different theoretical perspective, Pierre Bourdieu also considered 'fields' of action as *both* arenas of purpose and of conflict (Bourdieu, Chamboredon, and Passeron 1973). Therefore the organizational field becomes an important source of constraints and patterns, denying simple rational choice models (Scott 2001: 140).

If we do not adopt a functionalist approach we shall want to postpone the search for such links to the empirical application of a theory rather than its initial formulation (Streeck 2001). For example, it is possible to show how South African and Northern Irish capitalism took advantage respectively of racial and religious segregation to segment and maintain dominance over the labour force, even though such segregation in itself contradicts market principles—cases of complementarity rather than *Wahlverwandschaft*. It would however be an error to move from that observation to the thesis that segregation was functionally necessary to capitalism—though South African and Irish Marxists used to make such an analysis. Capitalists were certainly able to *make use* of racial and religious discrimination and to bind it into their economic system, but this was the result of skilful action, not system requirements. And eventually they were able to shed their dependence on these forms of labour control when their negative features outweighed their (for them) positive ones.

The study of complementarity is primarily a study of institutional stability, especially when use is made of functionalist assumptions. However, at various points in the discussion we have encountered processes of change. Some of these have been built into the concept of complementarity itself as institutions encounter changing environments: the 'grit in the oyster' as complementarities become contradictions, possibly favouring endogenous change; evolution as minor *bricolage* changes beget further minor changes that eventually become major ones through layering and branching; trial and error experimentation; strategic design by dominant elites and institutional entrepreneurs. Others are exogenous, such as the selection of 'superior' institutional forms through market competition. The study of social stability set apart from change is often necessary for heuristic purposes of analysis, but it is important to remember that it is an illusion, as Deeg (2007) and Deeg and Jackson (2007) have demonstrated in comparative studies of economic institutions, distinguishing among processes at macro, meso, and micro levels. Institutions are constantly adapting and adjusting, with some minor processes having major consequences. The stability of institutions and their complementarities is the stability of the person riding a bicycle, not that of the person standing still. This chapter therefore has to be read in conjunction with the section of this book that deals with theories of institutional change.

REFERENCES

AMABLE, B. (2000). 'Institutional Complementarity and Diversity of Social Systems of Innovation and Production', *Review of International Political Economy*, 7/4: 645–87.
——(2003). *The Diversity of Modern Capitalism*, (Oxford: Oxford University Press).
——(2005). 'Complementarity, Hierarchy, Compatibility, Coherence', *Socio-Economic Review* 3, 2: 371–3.
——E. ERNST and S. PALOMBARINI (2005). 'How do Financial Markets Affect Industrial Relations: An Institutional Complementarity Approach', *Socio-Economic Review* 3, 2: 311–30.
AOKI, M. (1994). 'The Contingent Governance of Teams: Analysis of Institutional Complementarity', *International Economic Review* 35/3: 657–76.

——(2000). *Information, Corporate Governance, and Institutional Diversity*, (Oxford: Oxford University Press).

——(2001). *Towards a Comparative Institutional Analysis*, (Cambridge, MA: MIT Press).

BLANCHARD, O. J. (2004). 'The Economic Future of Europe'. MIT Economics Working Paper No. 04–04, (Cambridge, MA: MIT Press).

BOURDIEU, P., J.-C. CHAMBOREDON, and J.-C. PASSERON (1973). *Le métier de sociologue: préalables épistémologiques*, (Paris: Mouton).

BOYER, R. (2000). 'Is a Finance Led Growth Regime a Viable Alternative to Fordism? A Preliminary Analysis', *Economy and Society* 29: 111–45.

——and Y. SAILLARD, (1995). *Théorie de la régulation. L'état des savoirs*, (Paris : La Découverte).

CAMPBELL, J. L. (2004). *Institutional Change and Globalization*, (Princeton, NJ: Princeton University Press).

——and O. K. PEDERSEN (eds.) (2001*a*). *The Rise of Neoliberalism and Institutional Analysis*, (Princeton, NJ: Princeton University Press).

————(2001*b*). 'The Rise of Neoliberalism and Institutional Analysis', in J. L. Campbell and O. K. Pedersen (eds.) (2001*a*), q.v., 1–23.

————(2001*c*). 'The Second Movement in Institutional Analysis', in J. L. Campbell and O. K. Pedersen (eds.) (2001*a*), q.v., 249–82.

————(2007). 'The Variety of Capitalism and Hybrid Success: Denmark in the Global Economy', *Comparative Political Studies* 40, 3: 307–32.

CARRUTHERS, B. G., S. L., BABB, and T. C. HALLIDAY (2001). 'Institutionalizing Markets, or the Market for Institutions? Central Banks, Bankruptcy Law, and the Globalization of Financial Markets', in J. C. Campbell and O. K. Pedersen (eds.) (2001*a*), q.v., 94–126.

CHEREDNYCHENKO, O. O. (2007), 'Fundamental Rights and Private Law. A Relationship of Subordination or Complementarity?', Utrecht Law Review, 3, 2: 1–25.

CROUCH, C. (1993). *Industrial Relations and European State Tradition*, (Oxford: Oxford University Press).

——(2005). *Capitalist Diversity and Change: Recombinant Governance and Institutional Entrepreneurs*, (Oxford: Oxford University Press).

DAHLBERG, L. (2005). 'Interaction between Voluntary and Statutory Social Service Provision in Sweden: A Matter of Welfare Pluralism, Substitution, or Complementarity?', *Social Policy and Administration* 39, 7: 740–63.

DEEG, R. (2005). 'Path Dependency, Institutional Complementarity, and Change in National Business Systems', in G. Morgan, R. Whitley, and E. Moen (eds.) (2005), q.v., 21–52.

——(2007). 'Complementarity and Institutional Change in Capitalist Systems', *Journal of European Public Policy* 14, 4: 611–30.

——and G. JACKSON (2007). 'Towards a More Dynamic Theory of Capitalist Variety', *Socio-Economic Review*, 5: 149–79.

DORE, R. (2000). *Stock Market Capitalism: Welfare Capitalism*, (Oxford: Oxford University Press).

EBBINGHAUS, B. and P. MANOW (2001). 'Introduction: Studying Varieties of Welfare Capitalism', in B. Ebbinghaus and P. Manow (eds.) (2001), *Comparing Welfare Capitalism: Social Policy and Political Economy in Europe, Japan and the USA*, (London: Routledge).

ESPING-ANDERSEN, G. (1990). *The Three Worlds of Welfare Capitalism*, (Cambridge: Polity Press).

GAMBLE, A. (1994). *The Free Economy and the Strong State: The Politics of Thatcherism*. 2nd edn., (Basingstoke: Macmillan).

GARRETT, G. (2000). *Shrinking States? Partisan Politics in the Global Economy*, (Cambridge: Cambridge University Press).

GOODIN, R., B. HEADEY, R. MUFFELS, and H.-J. DIRVEN (1999). *The Real Worlds of Welfare Capitalism*, (Cambridge: Cambridge University Press).

HAERPFER, C. W., C. WALLACE, and M. RAISER, (2005), 'Social Capital and Economic Performance in Post-Communist Societies', in Koniordos, S. M. (ed.) Networks, Trust and Social Capital, 243–78.

HALL, P. A. (1999). 'The Political Economy of Europe in an Era of Interdependence', in H. Kitschelt, P. Lange, G. Marks, and J. Stephens (eds.) (1999a), q.v.

——and D. W. GINGERICH (2004). 'Varieties of Capitalism and Institutional Complementarities in the Political Economy: An Empirical Analysis'. MPIfG Discussion Paper 04/5 (Cologne: Max-Planck-Institut für Gesellschaftsforschung).

——and D. SOSKICE (eds.) (2001a). *Varieties of Capitalism: The Institutional Foundations of Comparative Advantage*, (Oxford: Oxford University Press).

————(2001b). 'Introduction', in P. A. Hall, and D. Soskice (eds.) (2001a), q.v., 1–68.

HAY, C. (2002). 'Common Trajectories, Variable Paces, Divergent Outcomes? Models of European Capitalism under Conditions of Complex Economic Interdependence'. Conference of Europeanists, (Chicago, Mar. 2002).

HÖPNER, M. (2005). 'What Connects Industrial Relations and Corporate Governance? Explaining Institutional Complementarity', *Socio-Economic Review* 3, 2: 331–59.

JACKSON, G. (2001). 'The Origins of Nonliberal Corporate Governance in Germany and Japan', in W. Streeck and K. Yamamura (eds.) (2001a), q.v.

——M. Höpner, and A. KURDELBUSCH (2005). 'Corporate Governance and Employees in Germany: Changing Linkages, Complementarities and Tensions', in H. Gospel and A. Pendleton (eds.), *Corporate Governance and Labour Management in Comparison*, (Oxford: Oxford University Press), 84–121.

KENWORTHY, L. (2006). 'Institutional Coherence and Macroeconomic Performance', *Socio-Economic Review* 4: 69–91.

KITSCHELT, H., P. LANGE, G. MARKS, and J. STEPHENS (eds.) (1999a). *Continuity and Change in Contemporary Capitalism*, (Cambridge: Cambridge University Press).

—————————(1999b). 'Convergence and Divergence in Advanced Capitalist Democracies', in H. Kitschelt, P. Lange, G. Marks, and J. Stephens, (eds.) (1999a), q.v.

KLEFFNER, J. K. (2003). 'The Impact of Complementarity on National Implementation of Substantive International Criminal Law', *Journal of International Criminal Law*, 1, 1: 86–113.

KNIGHT, J. (2001). 'Explaining the Rise of Neoliberalism: The Mechanisms of Institutional Change', in J. L. Campbell and O. K. Pedersen (eds.) (2001a), q.v., 27–50.

KORPI, W. (1983). *The Democratic Class Struggle*, (London: Routledge Kegan Paul).

KRISTENSEN, P. H. (1997). 'National Systems of Governance and Managerial Prerogatives in the Evolution of Work Systems: England, Germany, and Denmark Compared', in Whitley and Kristensen (eds.) (1997), q.v.

LÜTZ, S. (2003). 'Convergence within National Diversity: A Comparative Perspective on the Regulatory State in Finance'. MPIfG Discussion Paper 03/7 (Cologne: Max-Planck-Institut für Gesellschaftsforschung).

MAYNTZ, R. (2004). 'Organizational Forms of Terrorism: Hierarchy, Network, or a Type sui generis?'. MPIfG Discussion Paper 04/4 (Cologne: Max-Planck-Institut für Gesellschaftsforschung).

MORGAN, G., R. WHITLEY, and E. MOEN (eds.) (2005). *Changing Capitalisms? Complementarities, Contradictions and Capability Development in an International Context*, (Oxford: Oxford University Press).

NORTH, D. C. (1990). *Institutions, Institutional Change, and Economic Performance*, (Cambridge: Cambridge University Press).

PARSONS, T. and R. F. BALES (1955). *Family, Socialization and Interaction Process*, (New York: Free Press).

PIERSON, P. (2001). 'The Limits of Design: Explaining Institutional Origins and Change', *Governance* 13, 4: 475–99.

POWELL, W. and P. DIMAGGIO (1991). *The New Institutionalism in Organizational Analysis*, (Chicago: Chicago University Press).

QUACK, S. and G. MORGAN (2000). 'National Capitalisms, Global Competition and Economic Performance: An Introduction', in S. Quack, G. Morgan, and R. Whitley (eds.) (2000), *National Capitalisms, Global Competition and Economic Performance*, (Amsterdam: Benjamins), 2–26.

SCOTT, W. R. (2001). *Institutions and Organizations*, 2nd edn., (Thousand Oaks, CA: Sage).

STEINMO, S., K. THELEN, and F. LONGSTRETH (1992). *Structuring Politics: Historical Institutionalism in Comparative Analysis*, (Cambridge: Cambridge University Press).

STREECK, W. (2001), 'Introduction: Explorations into the Origins of Neoliberal Capitalism in Germany and Japan', in W. Streeck and K. Yamamura (eds.) (2001), q.v.

——(2005). 'Requirements for a Useful Concept of Complementarity', *Socio-Economic Review* 3, 2: 363–6.

——and K. THELEN (eds.) (2005). *Beyond Continuity: Institutional Change in Advanced Political Economies*, (Oxford: Oxford University Press).

——and K. YAMAMURA (eds.) (2001). *The Origins of Nonliberal Capitalism: Germany and Japan in Comparison*, (Ithaca, NY: Cornell University Press).

——J. HILBERT, K. H. VAN KEVELAER, F. MAIER, and H. WEBER (1987). *The Role of the Social Partners in Vocational Training and Further Training in the Federal Republic of Germany*, (Berlin: CEDEFOP).

TEUBNER, G. (2001). 'Legal Irritants: How Unifying Law Ends up in New Divergences', in P. Hall and D. Soskice (eds.) (2001a), q.v., 417–41.

THELEN, K. (1999). 'Historical Institutionalism in Comparative Politics', *Annual Review of Political Science* 2: 369–404.

——(2002). 'How Institutions Evolve: Insights from Comparative-Historical Analysis', in J. Mahoney and D. Ruschmeyer (eds.) (2002), *Comparative Historical Analysis in the Social Sciences*, (New York: Cambridge University Press).

VANBERG, V. J. (2008). 'On the Complementarity of Liberalism and Democracy: A Reading of F. A. Hayek and J. M. Buchanan', *Journal of Institutional Economics* 4: 139–61.

VIEBROCK, E. (2004). 'The Role of Trade Unions in Intermediary Institutions in Unemployment Insurance: A European Comparison'. PhD thesis (Florence: European University Institute).

WHITLEY, R. (1997). 'The Social Regulation of Work Systems: Institutions, Interest Groups, and Varieties of Work Organization in Capitalist Societies', in R. Whitley and P. H. Kristensen (eds.) (1997), q.v.

——(2005). 'How National Are National Business Systems? The Role of States and Complementary Institutions in Standardising Systems of Economic Coordination and Control at the National Level', in G. Morgan, R. Whitley, and Moen, E. (eds.) (2005), q.v.

——(2006). 'Understanding Differences: Searching for the Social Processes that Construct and Reproduce Variety in Scientific and Economic Organization', *Organization Studies* 27, 8: 1153–79.

——and P. H. KRISTENSEN (eds.) (1997). *Governance at Work. The Social Regulation of Economic Relations*, (Oxford: Oxford University Press).

YAMAMURA, K. and W. STREECK (eds.) (2003). *The End of Diversity? Prospects for German and Japanese Capitalism*, (Ithaca, NY: Cornell University Press).

QUALITATIVE COMPARATIVE ANALYSIS OF SOCIAL SCIENCE DATA

BRUCE KOGUT[1]

INTRODUCTION

This chapter explores two topics: comparative methods and methodological responses to contingent 'truth' claims of social science. Social science methodology is an iteration between a researcher and physical and social facts, to which we attach a domain of plausible logical relations. The objective of comparative research is, by this approach, to investigate truth claims across a subset of all possible worlds. For many researchers in the field of comparative social science, these worlds are inhabited by nation-states, but they could be, of course, any type of organization or collective.

The kind of truth claims that interest researchers of the study of comparative institutions is the identification of those institutions whose efficacy is universalistic or specific to a country. For example, the question does the institution of democracy

[1] I would like to thank Glenn Morgan and Charles Ragin for their comments on an earlier draft.

lead to growth poses an inquiry into whether the condition, democracy, is sufficient to cause growth: this is the truth claim to be investigated. These causal claims are essentially qualitative insofar that the results pertain to a discrete quality, namely an institution. The methodology may be based on intensive field research or case research conducted in a library, generating rich analyses of one or a small number of cases. Often, this research falls under the rubric of 'Small-N research' (small number of cases). The object of this research is frequently less concerned with the finding that 10 per cent more of democracy creates .5 per cent more growth. Instead, the object is to understand if countries belonging to the category of democratic countries experience higher growth.

The word qualitative has often been reserved for case studies, but clearly an argument can be made, as King, Keohane, and Verba (1994) do, that statistical approaches are appropriate methodologies for qualitative research. There are thus two different but not exclusive ways to understand the term qualitative: a research method focused on contextual understanding of a case and a method that is concerned with differences between different 'kinds' of things. For purposes of clarity, we will adopt the terminology of Ragin (1987) to refer to analyses done in the spirit of small-N research as qualititative comparative analysis (QCA) and larger-N research as statistical—even though the number of countries can be deceptively similar for reasons discussed below.

The objective of comparative research to investigate the domain and validity of a truth claim faces at least four challenges. The first is that the relationship among causal factors is likely to be 'complex' and thus comparisons can often not fully identify the validity of a truth claim. By complex, we mean that explanatory factors interact theoretically and empirically. In the language of experimental design, main effects will not be sufficient to determine causality.

Consider an argument that claims a linear causal relationship. In the important law and finance literature on corporate governance, a claim made in the 1990s was that Anglo law leads to more developed capital markets than French law or that of any other legal system (La Porta et al. 1997). This argument states that no matter the country, the legal system will linearly influence capital market development. An argument that states the directional effect of a legal system will depend on other elements in a country is contingent and expresses a non-linear prediction. It suggests that the legal system 'interacts' with other institutional features in a country, such as ownership patterns. In other words, institutions are often complements of each other and their efficacy depend upon their joint presence.[2] As a result, the comparative analysis must consider countries as 'configurations' of interacting institutions. This perspective has

---

[2] We alert the reader that complements have two meanings relevant to our discussion. One is the set theoretic definition of the complement of set X is not X (or 1-X). The other is derived from the formal literature on production functions in the context of complementary elements in a production system such that doing *more* of one thing *increases* the returns to doing *more* of another. See Milgrom and Roberts, 1991.

been popularized in recent years under the research umbrella of the 'varieties of capitalism' to which we return below.

The second challenge is the 'limited diversity' of cases given all possible permutations (Ragin 2000). Limited diversity is related to complexity, since the demands on data increase with complexity. To account for all possible interactions, the rule for the number of cases is 2^n, where n is the number of explanatory factors. Because it is time consuming to iterate between case and concept or because data are not easily available, it is very common in comparative research that the number of dimensions leads to a demand for cases greater than the number of observed 'independent' cases. Thus, causal inference cannot be made in the context of a 'fully saturated design', by which all possible combinations of conditions are observed.

The third challenge is that cases are in fact often not independent—a problem more troubling to qualitative designs such as QCA than to statistical approaches. The term 'Galton's Problem' stems from the observation of the nineteenth-century statistician Francis Galton (1889) who observed that societies are often contaminated by diffusion and hence not independent. We cannot thus treat them as independent and fully controlled experiments. Whereas a statistical solution to this challenge is to control for this contamination, it too suffers from unobserved sources of correlation. The suspicion is frequently that the unobserved heterogeneity (i.e. the factors not explicitly treated) may be conceptually important. Not surprisingly then, efforts to treat explicitly these unobservables can lead to 'complex' arguments. The recent research on law and economics described above has blossomed into proposals for common language, religion, and even genetic similarities as causal factors in economic differences among countries, often without explicit rationales. But perhaps these traits are not independent, but rather the willingness of countries to adopt new institutions indicates a degree of indigenous innovation that itself is the source of economic difference. Berkowitz, Pistor, and Richard (2002), for example, argue that legal systems are frequently adopted from other countries but their efficacy depends on their proximity to national traditions. Thus, a similar legal system in two countries may have common origins but result in different financial market outcomes due to unobserved 'interactions' with other national features.

This last issue points to a common architecture in institutional analysis, namely its multilevel design. It is common to try to explain important social outcomes, such as the welfare state, by macro-institutions, e.g. unions or political parties. However, clearly social outcomes are also influenced by the behaviour of individuals who desire and support welfare transfers and services. These individuals may act differently depending upon whether they are in a country which has organized labour or not, a strong church or not, whether they live in a conservative or liberal village. There is thus an institutional level and an individual behavioural level. Related to multilevel settings is a specific scourge to analysis, the so-called 'ecological fallacy'. This fallacy is expressed by the departure of results conducted at the level of aggregates (e.g. the country, region, nation-state) and those conducted at the level of individuals making up the aggregates. This problem, deeply explored by Przeworski and Teune (1970), has developed into a substantial literature on tests of ecological validity; see, for example, King (1997). This problem is common to statistical and to qualitative comparative research, though QCA type approaches have not currently addressed this fallacy.

Each of these challenges to comparative research deserves attention. There are many more challenges of course, one of the most important being the distinction between 'etic' and 'emic' knowledge, that is knowledge known by outsiders and that known to insiders to a culture. This distinction has significant implications for the design and implementation of research strategies, e.g. the use of double translated questionnaires or reliance on bilingual experts. Oddly, since these controls are 'dyadic', it cannot be assumed that transitivity holds, namely that we can 'order' these dyadic relations to extend to triplets or higher number of societies. This violation of transitivity means that a Swahili concept translated into French and then into English will not be equivalent to the translation of Swahili to English.

For reasons of comparing QCA and statistical approaches, we focus on the four challenges and leave aside the important issue of ascertaining meaning. We concentrate on the small-N approach of Charles Ragin to causal inference in such settings. We briefly address the statistical approaches in order to highlight differences and relative points of strength and weakness. Finally, we will briefly discuss the use of simulation in future research.

Classical Model of the Nineteenth Century

Comparative analysis would be greatly facilitated if the classical experimental research design could be applied. In the teaching of research methods, we are increasingly expanding the arsenal of statistical tools. It is good to remember, though, that this arsenal is needed in many cases because experimental conditions are not met. What then are these conditions?

Claude Bernard (1865) in France and John Stuart Mill (1843) in the nineteenth century set out early statements on the experimental method which could isolate cause and effect. The simplest case is a two by two factorial design. This design asks given a disease, does a treatment X generate an outcome Y. The variable X takes on two states: the treatment is given or not given; variable Y takes also two states: the outcome is positive (the disease is eradicated) or negative. Obviously, in order to evoke causality, we have to obey Hume's strictures on causality—treatment precedes temporally the outcome and the treatment is in spatial proximity to the outcome. In order to make an inference, we must observe cases in which the treatment is given and not given and in which the disease has variance in response. By populating all cells in the two by two table formed by evoking all possible combinations of X and Y, we generate a fully saturated design.

The advances in statistics in the late 1800s and the first half of the 1900s provided statistical methods by which to decide if X caused Y. It will prove instructive, though, to abide by the more deterministic spirit of the nineteenth century to ask if we can logically infer causality. By Mill's method of agreement and difference, we can state clearly the conditions for logical inference, specifically in reference to necessary and sufficient conditions. Consider the question: do I observe X when I see outcome Y? This question asks whether the requirements to establish necessity are met. Or we can ask, when we see the outcome X, do we observe also Y? Here we are asking if X is sufficient for Y.

The logic of necessary and sufficiency conditions is a statement about the set-theoretic relationships between cause (X) and effect (Y). A necessary condition always subsumes the set of outcomes. There are cases in which a necessary cause is present but there is no effect, but there is never a case in which the effect is present but the necessary cause is not. In other words, there is no case in which Y but not X. Sufficiency implies that the outcome also includes the set of sufficient causes. There may be cases where an outcome exists but a sufficient cause is missing, but a sufficient cause cannot be present without the presence of the outcome. In other words, there is no case in which X but not Y.

Thus a cause (X) that is sufficient or necessary for a given effect (Y) implies the following relationships:

$$X \text{ is a necessary condition} : Y \subseteq X \text{ if } Y \Rightarrow X$$
$$X \text{ is a sufficient condition} : Y \supseteq X \text{ if } Y \Leftarrow X$$

In the case that Y and X are subsets of each other, then we can infer that X is a necessary and sufficient cause of Y.

Mill considered the ideal comparison to be between cases that differed on one cause but shared otherwise identical traits. In current parlance, this design is called a comparison among the 'most similar' cases; the opposing design is the 'greatest difference' in which the choice of cases is motivated by seeking variance. A good example of Mill's method is Weber's use of ideal types—which can also be called a configuration. Weber famously argued that capitalism arose in the West due to the diffusion of a Protestant Ethic that supported savings and investment in economic activities. Consider four causes {A,B,C,D} and an outcome X. Let us use capital letters to indicate 'presence' and lower case to indicate 'absence'. Cause D is the presence of a Protestant Ethic; outcome X is capitalism. If we observe capitalism (X) is present whenever we see ABCD but do not see capitalism when we see ABCd, then Mill concluded D is causal. Formally, we can describe this argument as 'if ABC, then $D \rightarrow X$'.[3]

Indeed D is causal. However, we don't know if it is necessary or sufficient. If we think through this problem of causal reduction, we have $3^4 - 1$ possibilities, since each cause can cause capitalism by being present (e.g. D) or by being absent (d), or it can be irrelevant (it does not matter if it is present or not). (See Ragin, 2000: 137, for an explanation.) The number one is subtracted since the case of four irrelevant causes

---

[3] Of course, there may be other combinations that produce capitalism (e.g. aBCd), a point to which we return below.

is not of interest. In effect, we would have to test each possibility. In the case of an argument testing four causes, we would need to test 80 distinct cases—this would in essence be the power set of the four factors that can take one of three values. Weber only looked at a handful of countries or regions: the West, China, India, and Judaism (the latter unfinished). The paucity of cases given the multiplicity of causes is a common feature of comparative research.

Using implicitly Mill's method, Weber avoided this problem by creating an ideal type in which causes A, B, and C were present in all cases, such that only variations in D (ethic) could matter. This approach is then very much in the spirit of a 'controlled experiment' in which the controls are held fixed. Weber's method is then a very sparse form of the experimental method factorial design. Given the controlled sample, the truth table consists of one treatment, religious values, and thus there are 2 combinatorial possibilities (2^1); of course, there is always also the null case that it simply doesn't matter to the outcome. There is a difference between 'not Protestant' as a cause for capitalism compared to 'it doesn't matter if Protestant or not'.

Let's say we loosen up the controls and add one of them, say agricultural surplus or A, to the causal factors. We now have a 2^2 combinatorial set: {AD}, {Ad}, {aD} and {ad}. For each combination, we determine the outcome of savings and investments being present or absent. By logical inference, or statistical analysis, we can make an assessment of the causal claims. Of course, this procedure becomes more complicated when the number of factors increased. Accordingly, Weber's use of ideal types was to choose one combination and then vary one factor to see if it held. Thus, the Chinese had agricultural surplus but they did not have values to promote savings (rather they tended towards acquisitions of landed estates to mimic the amateur functionary).

For Weber, this strategy worked well, but in fact it left open the question could capitalism be created if there was no Protestant Ethic and no agricultural surplus. From an empirical perspective, the data given to us for social science research rarely are sufficient to establish this justification of just one factor varying—which might explain why Weber's magnificent study falls in and out of favour. We obviously can do better, and here, with the assistance of another nineteenth-century philosopher, George Boole, Charles Ragin introduced a powerful set of tools by which to explore multiple causation.

CHARLES RAGIN AND MULTIPLE CONJUNCTURAL ANALYSIS: CONFIGURATIONS

We have seen so far that when the number of causal candidates (factors) become large and the ideal type is not defensible to fix all their values save one, Weber's method fails. In many ways, the reasoning of the nineteenth century was to find, deterministically, the necessary cause for an event. The twentieth century grew, however, increasingly at home with inherent uncertainty and multiple causes. Thus, the paramount nineteenth-century social science, economics, began to deviate from unique equilibrium to considerations of multiple equilibria; all social sciences began to consider 'non-ergodic' processes characterized by path dependence.

Whereas sometimes the weak of heart fell back upon old ways—such as the law and economics tradition in corporate governance discussed earlier, powerful concepts, such as complementarities, became more formal and the basis for multiple causal configurations. Another way to understand complementarities is to recall Robert Merton's (1957) concept of 'functional equivalence' whereby an outcome can be achieved by different factors, sometimes in conjunction with other causal combinations. In the famous example of the anthropological study of Malinowski, the father did not play the Freudian authority figure in the primitive society under study; rather the uncle did. The relevance of this observation to complementarities is that it is possible that two distinct combinations of factors can nevertheless produce similar outcomes.

In a landmark book (1987), Charles Ragin proposed a research methodology called qualitative comparative analysis (QCA) that provided a clear and simple foundation to these ideas of complementarities and multiple causation arising in subsequent work. Elaborated in subsequent books, his methodology consisted of a few steps:

1. The researcher should have deep knowledge of the case material and be willing to engage in a dialogue between this knowledge and the logical inferences.
2. Theory should dictate the choice of cases and variables, and substantive knowledge should guide their binary (0,1) coding or what we early signified through the use of capital and lower case letters. (Later, values lying on the open line between 0 and 1 would be considered using a fuzzy set method.)
3. Truth tables should be built that provide a census of all possible cases and the cells of this table should be populated by what the researcher has been able to observe. Often, the table will not be fully populated, indicating a less than fully saturated experimental design—a condition Ragin called 'limited diversity'.
4. Logical contradictions indicate the presence of 'unobserved' variables and theorizing should be expanded to identify and to include these variables.
5. The truth tables should be tested by the application of Boolean operators for necessary and sufficient conjunctural causality given the available data, resulting in a set of possible causal combinations.
6. The 'limited diversity' of cases relative to the set of all possible causes may lead to undesirable complexity in the analysis and thus the set of inferred causes should be further reduced by the use of parsimonious 'simplifying assumptions'.
7. The results can be compared to the initial hypotheses to determine if they are logically equivalent.
8. The robustness of the results can be checked against counterfactuals.
9. The results can be used to inform the initial substantive reasoning and may lead to new understanding of the primary case material. Thus there is a dialogue between etic and emic interpretations.

Table 6.1: Truth table: Ragin and Sonnett data on the welfare state

Strong Unions (U)	Strong Left Parties (L)	Generous Welfare State (G)	N of Cases
Yes	Yes	Yes	6
Yes	No	No	8
No	No	No	5
No	Yes	?	0

Consider a theory that says strong unions and left-wing parties cause generous welfare states. There are $2^2 = 4$ possibilities; we observe only 3.

Let's consider the data analysed by Ragin and John Sonnett, reported in Table 6.1. These data follow from a theory that a generous welfare state is caused by the conjunction of two causes, strong unions and strong left parties. Since the table already shows a selection of variables, the data have already passed step 1. Step 2 is the hypothesis, or truth claim, to be investigated. Using our earlier script, we hypothesize that UP =>W. We would like to test this proposition against the data we have. Since we have 2^2 combinations, the truth table lists four combinatorial possibilities, with one combination unobserved. To say that the combination of strong unions and strong left parties causes generous welfare states is logically equivalent to stating that their intersection is causally associated with a particular truth condition. By intersection, we mean that strong unions 'AND' strong left parties must be jointly present to cause the generous welfare state. This causal conjunction is an example of a 'configuration' and we can say that this configuration is sufficient to cause the outcome. There may be another causal configuration and thus causality may be multiple. If it were the case that strong unions 'OR' strong left parties cause separately generous welfare states, we would denote this by U + P => W.

This stylization may seem counterintuitive but it is consistent with Boolean algebra. Under Boolean algebra, we would write UP = W as $1 * 1 = 1$ and U + P = W as $1 + 1 = 1$. This algebra becomes very useful in sorting out causality through a process of minimizing the causal possibilities to the fewest possible.

Boolean minimization relies upon two principal operations:

Absorption: U + UP = U
Reduction: UP + Up = U(P+p) = U(1) = U

The second operation is derived directly from the distributive and complement laws of Boolean algebra.[1] The first operation derives from the laws of subset. If UP is the intersection of the sets U and P, then this intersection must be equal to, or be a subset of, U.

We should choose cases then that fully 'saturate' the four logical possibilities. The cases chosen should conform to type of random draw to assure independence. If they share a feature (perhaps due to a Galton-like previous diffusion of a common institution), then a variable should be added that controls for this effect. An easy way to violate this rule is to choose one country for two cases, thinking that Russia of 1905 is different than Russia of 1917 (see the discussion in Ragin 1987: 38, of this point). A recent study in globalization chose Argentina at two different points of time as comparison. In this case, independence is most assuredly violated and given the multiplicity of contamination (after all, Argentina in 2000 is conditional on Argentina 1990), the comparison is bound to be troubled. An exception may be if the theory concerns social development or economic growth; below, we give an example how to treat this problem.

By step 3, we are now ready to organize our cases into a truth table (as in Table 6.1). There are missing observations on one causal combination and thus there is limited diversity; the choice of cases has not saturated all possibilities. The good news is, under step 4, that there are no logical contradictions: for all cases assigned to a logical possibility, their causal configurations always predict the same outcome. Thus we do not need to consider, on this basis, other factors to resolve the contradiction.

Step 5 is the application of these two rules to the truth table we assemble. In the case of Figure 6.1, it is easy to see that minimization results in the conjunction of UP as the sufficient and unique configuration that causes the welfare state.

Whereas this reduction appears as pretty obvious in this simple case, the utility of these operators (which are really algorithms) can be surely appreciated if the number of factors are many; 5 factors has $2^5 = 32$ possibilities in the truth table and $3^5 - 1 = 242$ possible causal solutions.

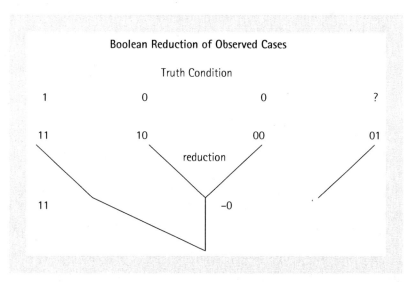

Figure 6.1: Causal tree: illustrating the effect of limited diversity on causal inference

Solutions: 11 = U * L = Generous welfare state
−0 = 1= not-generous state
*Means interaction or complements; + means separate configurations
Lower case means = 0 or absence of the factor (e.g. not left-wing party)

In this case, the result is so simple, we don't need to worry about step 6 and simplifying assumptions. This step is very close to the counterfactual discussed later in any event. It is easy to see that the logical inference supports exactly the hypothesis, so that by step 7, we can claim perfect consistency between the data and the hypothesis. This is jolly good and we could end right here and claim victory. We have achieved an important result. The results indicate that strong unions and strong left parties are *complementary*, i.e. both must be jointly present to cause a generous welfare state. When one is present and the other is not, we do not observe the welfare state; when both are missing, we do not observe the outcome. Thus there is no single cause; causality is conjunctural. The unique configuration is then UP, conforming to the theory.

COUNTERFACTUALS

Step 8 is the investigation of counterfactuals, which is one of the most interesting subjects to 're-emerge' in recent years. The great David Hume erred in stating first his famous definition of causation and then overlooking the distinction posed by a counterfactual when he wrote: 'We may define a cause to be "an object followed by another, and where all the objects, similar to the first, are followed by objects similar to the second". Or, in other words, "where, if the first object had not been, the second never had existed".' (1748, section VII; cited in Menzies 2008.). One can understand why it took more than two centuries before logicians and social science turned again seriously to counterfactuals, for if empirical observation no longer serves, by definition, to limit the set of possible counterfactual antecedents, then how could the problem then be bounded? Then anything might serve as a counterfactual.

Here, the philosopher David Lewis provides a helpful analysis that lies at the heart of current counterfactual methodologies. He starts off his book on *Counterfactuals* by this example: ' "If kangaroos had no tails, they would topple over" seems to me to mean something like this: in any possible state of affairs in which kangaroos have no tails, and which resembles our actual state of affairs as much as kangaroos have no tails permits it to, the kangaroos topple over' (Lewis 1973: 1). A counterfactual then is a case, or possible world, similar to actuality but differing in important details. This condition is surprisingly close to Mill's method of choosing the 'most similar' cases discussed earlier. A possible world is defined by its 'comparative similarity' to the actual world. A possible world is said to be 'closer to actuality' than another if the first better matches the actual world (Menzies 2008).

Thus, Weber's method is a kind of counterfactual reasoning, though grounded on observable worlds. If the ideal type exists in many countries except for variance in one feature (Protestant Ethic), a counterfactual test is to ask, does capitalism prevail when all relevant causal conditions are present save the presence of a Protestant

Ethic. Weber did not satisfy himself by the evidence that the West conforms to his theory; he showed counterfactually that the prediction fails to be obtained when the Protestant Ethic is not present. In this sense, a counterfactual is a type of 'robustness' test. The theoretical claim is confirmed when counterfactuals do not produce the relevant result.

A more radical use of the concept of counterfactual is to make use indeed of possible worlds that are not observable. The concept of a counterfactual has an interesting role to play in relation to the problem of limited diversity that Ragin (2000) emphasizes. Limited diversity is the incompleteness of our observations on all possible combinations, due either to incomplete data collection or to the absence of such experiments in the world. We have seen already that Figure 6.1 presents an incomplete truth table showing limited diversity and yet we were able to make a causal inference.

We might wonder if the result is really robust and thus we might be troubled by that missing observation on causal combination 4. If we believed that history optimizes, we might treat this combination as inefficient. If the outcome variable were economic growth, this belief might then justify that we assign causal outcome a value of 0—for such inefficient outcomes might be eliminated by learning or selection. This type of 'survivor bias' reasoning is quite frequently made, and only sometimes with justification. It surely does not seem appropriate to the study of the determinants of the welfare state.

One way to visualize the implication of limited diversity on causal inference is to convert the truth table in Table 6.1 into a causal tree given in Figure 6.1. The top row states the truth condition, using Boolean binary digits to indicate that whether the welfare state obtains (W=1) or does not (w=0). The second row from the top presents each possible combination as a final node. Here 11 indicates UP, 10 indicates Up, etc. We want to walk down (i.e. make a logical inference) to know if we might reduce these combinations by Boolean minimization to a reduced causal statement. Figure 6.1 indicates that we are clearly handicapped by the missing case.

Ragin and Sonnett (2004) posed the following counterfactual: what would happen if the unobserved combination existed and if the outcome variable was positive, that is if up =>1? Using our causal tree technique, Figure 6.2 illustrates the implications of the counterfactual for causal inference.

Now all the logical possibilities are considered and the truth table is saturated. Our logical inference is now changed, since the left side of the tree reduces to one condition: only strong left-wing parties matter. Thus, the counterfactual has shown our inference to be poorly robust and we have been able to simplify our causal findings to a single condition. Parenthetically, we can see also how counterfactuals can (in the presence of limited diversity) be an example of a 'simplifying assumption' (step 6), since the assumption that Up =>1 simplified the causal conclusion.

The right side of the causal tree considers the cases where the result of a generous welfare state does not obtain. We made no use of these results in our analysis. How can we be sure that an analysis of the 'no generous welfare state' will produce results consistent with the left-side of the graph? Let's remember De Morgan's Law in which UP=>1 is

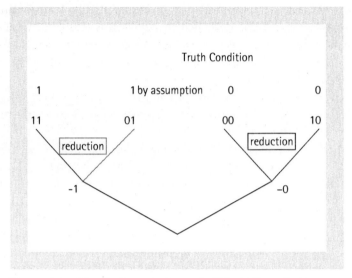

Figure 6.2: Simple Counterfactual: What if a missing case would have caused a welfare state

Solutions: -1 = L = Generous welfare state
-0 = 1 = Not-generous welfare state

equivalent to $(u + p) => o$. In our very simple example, $-o$ (or $-p$) $=> o$ becomes equivalent to -1 (or $-P$) $=> 1$, consistent with the left-side.

In Figure 6.3, we provide the causal tree for the counterfactual where we assign a causal implication of o to the missing configuration.

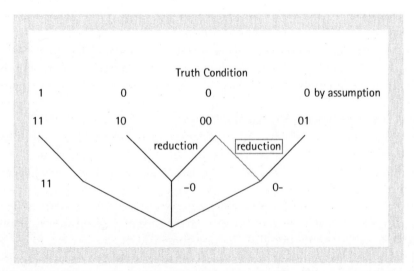

Figure 6.3: Simple Counterfactual: What if a missing case would not cause a welfare state

Solutions: 11 = U*L = Generous welfare state
0- or -0 = u or l = Not-generous state

We can then proceed to analyse this possibility as well, following the same procedure. The more interesting counterfactual, however, is given in Figure 6.2, for it leads most dramatically to a refinement of the original analysis constrained by limited diversity.

COUNTERFACTUALS, PAUL TETLOCK, AND LARS-ERIK CEDERMAN

Ragin and Sonnett's counterfactual approach expresses a methodology that is approachable and relies upon a 'most similar' design by which only non-observed cases that are similar are chosen. This type of reasoning often is called a *ceteris paribus* assumption: everything else stays the same. We have seen that the admission of new cases and a presumption of their truth value results in a causal cascade that can reduce the solution to simpler causal claims. However, we may also wonder if proximity to observed worlds is the only criteria.

Paul Tetlock and Aaron Belkin (1996) offer an appealing guideline consisting of six criteria by which to evaluate counterfactual arguments. Three of these criteria are consistent with historical facts, theoretical arguments, and statistical consistency. By the latter, they mean the argument should be consistent with statistical findings of other studies. The other three are particularly interesting: clarity, cotenability, and projectability. A strength of the Boolean approach is clarity. The variables that guide the analysis are transparent and 'flipping' the value on a variable leads easily to identifying the causal implications along the causal tree.

Cotenability requires that counterfactual experiment be logically consistent. For example, running the thought experiment of the consequences for Napoleonic France to have acquired nuclear weapons is not cotenable with the sort of background knowledge presumed in any non-experimental setting. Clearly, knowledge of nuclear technology in the late eighteenth century necessitates many other changed relationships. In this sense, the counterfactual is not cotenable with the type of a *ceteris paribus* design. Again, the Boolean approach is unlikely to run afoul of this argument, since the counterfactual is not assuming a new causal factor but only admitting an unobserved case.

The last factor of projectability means that a causal factor should be indeed causal and not simply a state description. Though Tetlock and Belkin do not make this observation, it is best to consider projectability as allied to the problem of spurious causation. It might be true that Napoleon wore black the day the French assaulted Moscow; however, the causal connection might be simply that Napoleon was present that day on the battlefield, regardless of the colour of his clothes. Again, the Boolean approach should rule out this spurious causality (with sufficient variety), since an outcome would be produced when the cause was not present and the 'true' cause was present. Of course, if the spurious factor is a proxy for an unobserved cause (that is, it is correlated with a true cause), then assigning it causality is an improper inference.

The counterfactual framework presented by a causal tree analysis is, in some ways, a microcosm of the computational solutions offered by simulations. Lars-Erik Cederman (1996) illustrates the potential offered by complex adaptive systems (CAS) to generate a causal mapping from a set of factors to outcomes.[4] Using his work on whether multipolarity in international relations leads to conflict or not, Cederman argues that his computational approach agrees closely with the criteria of clarity, cotenability, and projectability. This claim seems at first less obvious for cotenability and projectability, since CAS permits a search over many possible worlds, some of which may seem highly unlikely and unreasonable. However, since CAS, like Ragin's method, relies on causal rules between factors and mechanisms (rules), cotenability is preserved. Projectability is also preserved, since spurious effects will wash away through the pooling of many runs and across many iterations.

The challenge of such simulations is agreement with statistical facts. One solution is to compare the predicted patterns to observed macro patterns (if there is enough data). Cederman (2003), for example, starts off his analysis of the frequency of wars by showing a power law distribution of conflict over time, and then shows that the simulation generates the outcome. Another, far less used approach, is to bootstrap the simulation from actual data. This approach appears to fall between two chairs of pure thought experiments and statistical analysis, but it is otherwise an attractive combination of methods consistent with the idea of using 'comparative similarity' discussed above; that is, to initialize the simulation on an observed world, and then explore the causal implications by imposing new rules or new parameter values. The spirit of this approach is similar to counterfactual statistical approaches, to which we now turn.

COUNTERFACTUALS AND GARY KING

Counterfactuals are frequently used in statistical research. The estimation of a regression equation produces coefficient values which stipulate the relationship between the explanatory and dependent variables. The estimates are dependent upon the observed but counterfactuals are still possible. To run a counterfactual, one can ask what would happen if the observed variable took on a different value. The estimated model produces a prediction, which may be then

---

[4] See also Cusack and Stoll (1990).

contrasted against the observed model. When is this use of a counterfactual reasonable?

Lewis's comparative similarity is useful in judging its reasonableness in two ways. Gary King and Langche Zeng (2007) have proposed the following diagnostic, which is in fact an interesting application of Lewis's comparative similarity and possible worlds. The first part of the proposal is to vary only one value at a time (similar to Mill's method) and the second is to ask if the value of the variable lies within the minimum and maximum values of the observed data. Consider a traditional case of interpolation and extrapolation in which the variable, a strong left party, has an observed range of, say, 2 to 6; the value 5 is not observed. By setting the value of the variable to 5, the counterfactual is based on 'interpolation'; if the value of the variable is set at 0, then this choice lies outside the range of the observed values and the counterfactual is an extrapolation. The greater the extrapolation, the more likely the counterfactual suffers model specification error. They develop a number of diagnostics to isolate the bias of such errors.

Ragin and Sonnett's approach permits a finer grain analysis of the causal implications of a counterfactual. As illustrated by the causal trees, changing the value of an independent variable or imposing a value on an unobserved value in a configuration results in a causal waterfall. Ultimately, the reasonableness of the intervention depends upon the theoretical prior of the research (and researchers) as well as the gain in causal reduction.

The concept of 'net effects' summarizes the philosophical difference between Ragin and statistical approaches. King and Zeng propose a measure of causal contribution to be the difference of the predicted value under observed data and the prediction under the counterfactual; the counterfactual is calculated as changing the value of one factor—again in accordance with the Mill and Weber reasoning we discussed above. This difference is a net effect and is measurable.

Ragin's approach would ask how would a change in a variable influence the multiple conjunctural analysis—that is the solution space. The absence of an observed configuration in a truth table invites a counterfactual intervention, namely, the researcher may impose a value on the unobserved. This intervention results in a cascade along the causal chain, which may modify dramatically the configurational solutions. Whereas this intervention is extrapolation and thereby model dependent under King and Zeng's analysis, the set-theoretic approach of Ragin views this intervention as testing more thoroughly the solution space under different hypotheticals on unobserved worlds. This difference in counterfactual reasoning illustrates nicely the philosophical difference between a statistical approach concerned about model specification and data fitting and a set-theoretic approach concerned about improving the inferential basis of theory development by a more rigorous treatment of unobserved counterfactuals than found in more casual theorizing.

COMPARISON TO STATISTICAL APPROACHES: EXAMPLE OF VARIETIES OF CAPITALISM[5]

A comparison of an approach to common data and theory permits a contrast between statistical and configurational approaches. In the following, we consider a statistical treatment of panel data and reanalyse the data using QCA. This contrast indicates how QCA handles over-time data and the gain to using both qualitative approaches.

In recent years, there has been considerable attention paid to institutional complementarities in economics, sociology, and political science. QCA is one of many approaches to the comparative study of institutions. It is a useful methodology for two important reasons. The first is that the concept of configuration is the methodological equivalent to the economic concept of complementarity developed by Milgrom and Roberts (1990). It is not far-fetched to see QCA is to economic complementarities what structural models are to formal models in industrial organization.

A contribution of QCA methodology is its ability to make causal inference from small-N data sets where the researcher brings a lot of contextual knowledge to the analysis. Very often, the audience for the research also cares about the countries and is less interested in the estimated quantitative relation between democracy and growth than how democracy in Greece caused growth. QCA appears to reconcile somewhat better this trade-off between the universal and the specific than most methodologies by permitting different logics of causation to be suited to countries depending upon their assignment to a configuration.

Comparative institutional analysis has been a major growth industry in recent years due to the transfer of analytical focus on the competition between capitalism and welfare states (or communism) towards a wider interest in the ways by which institutions vary and influence important social and economic outcomes. The 'Varieties of Capitalism' approach proposed by Hall and Soskice is a prominent example of this interest. Their approach is primarily a theory of distributive bargaining, with equal primacy given to non-statal actors, such as labour unions and business associations. While this reweighting of the importance of actors is an important shift in political economy, it converges with the broader treatment of institutional configurations found in other disciplines. A number of studies have proposed institutional complements as a way to understand national configurations. Boyer (1996), in particular, classifies countries into several types, representing various complementarities among macroeconomic systems (e.g. Keynsian macroinstitutions) and work practices (e.g. mass production). Amable (1999) also proposes that labour markets and macroeconomic policies reveal complementarity. Boyer and Amable are agnostic as to how many possible distinctive configurations there may be.

---

[5] This section draws from Kogut and Ragin (2006).

The broader and more ambitious claim is that these bargaining institutions guide the formation of country capabilities that define a country's comparative advantage. Berger and Dore (1996) aptly name this a theory of 'institutional advantage'. These claims are broadly held across many literatures. The claim that is not broadly held is the following: these complementarities consist of two defined sets, one called 'coordinated market economies', the other 'liberal market economies' (Hall and Soskice 2001). This claim, associated with the label 'Varieties of Capitalism', has a distinctive methodological implication: because common institutions produce common outcomes, the nation is no longer the qualitative unit of analysis, but the quantitative degree to which nations have achieved the set of institutional complements associated with the two modal cases.

The perspective of institutional complementarities has an attractive trait. It looks at the compatibility of institutions and markets, and hence opens the policy question of whether 'cookbook' recommendations are independent of national conditions. In the great rush to advise the transition economies, papers proposed the idea of 'policy complementarities' and indeed the IMF has a menu of 'best practices for corporate governance' that must be enacted in toto. But the issue of policy complementarities not only is an ancient echo, it reveals a stunning blindness: countries already have existing institutions. It is not enough that policies be complements with each other; they also have to be complements with existing institutions.

Configurational analysis provides the important caveat that imported pieces confront an indigenous system of institutions. But then have we not fallen into the trap that there are as many theoretical configurations as countries if indigenous conditions matter? The claim of Hall and Soskice is that countries fall along a continuum between two polar types, where 'coordinated market economies' anchor one and 'not-coordinated market economies' (to use Boolean logic) anchor the other. Indigenous conditions may matter, but if a country cannot conform to one of the two prototypes (i.e. coordinated or market), then it will suffer in economic performance. This is a theoretical claim that deserves empirical testing.

Hall and Gingerich (2001) provide this service by looking at the institutional complementarities and their relationship to growth for twenty rich OECD countries in the period 1971 to 1997. Using factor analysis, they construct two types of complementarities: labour and corporatist. Since capitalisms can be many, but only a few institutional configurations (or complements) result in high economic performance, they want to show that conformity to their two theorized ideal types leads to more growth. Countries that are jointly high on both scales of labour and corporatist coordination are 'coordinated market economies'; those jointly low are 'liberal market economies'. Mixtures of the two scales (i.e. labour and corporatist indices) should result in poor performance, once controlling for other economic variables. These variables are changes in the terms of trade, the rate of inflation, international growth conditions (weighted according to trade openness), dependency ratio (a measure of demographic structure), and the log of a country's per capita income in 1971. Using a sophisticated panel analysis, they find that countries located in the middle of these two institutional configurations do less well than those that adhere to them.[6] Thus, they find evidence that deviations from these two theoretical proto-types decay performance.

The advantage of a panel analysis is that the number of observations is NxT, such that a dataset of twenty countries over twenty-seven years becomes quite large for statistical testing of a few parameter values. The danger is not simply the problem of outliers (for which there are reasonable tests), but the obscure status of the nation as the unit of analysis. The data consist of economic observations that vary by year, plus country fixed effects captured by time-invariant measures of the degree to which a country is a coordinated market economy or a liberal market economy. Because other country effects would be captured by these time-invariant measures, they apply statistical refinements to correct for the problem.

To translate Hall and Gingerich's interval-scale variables to crisp sets, we first converted their pooled time-series data set to a cross-sectional set by averaging the values for each case over the entire time period.[7] For example, instead of receiving a score on economic growth rate for each year, each country received a single score—its average rate of growth over the entire period. To create conventional binary sets from these variables, we dichotomized them at or near their median values. The resulting binary scores for growth and the six measures of corporate gover-nance (shareholder power, dispersion of control, size of stock market, level of wage coordination, labour turnover, and degree of wage coordination) are reported in Table 6.2.

Before proceeding to the analysis of these scores, it is important to point out that our analysis is very different in character from Hall and Gingerich's, not only because of the difference in technique, but also because of the difference in structure—pooled cross-sectional time series analysis versus cross-sectional analysis. For example, the correlation between the log of initial GDP per capita (which is constant across time in their analysis) and average growth rates is very strong, $r = -.816$. The scatterplot of these two variables reveals a near-perfect inverse relationship. It is clear, therefore, that explaining average growth rates over the entire period is not the same as addressing year-to-year fluctuations in growth rates. In fact, the relationship between average rate of growth and log of initial GDP per capita demonstrates that most economic growth over this period involved a convergence among the rich countries. The less rich of the rich countries grew faster than the richer rich countries, indicat-ing a trend toward the equalization of levels of wealth among the richest countries of the world.[8]

---

[6] This relationship is detected by building the construct called 'coordinated market economy' and then taking its square. The quadratic estimation shows negative and positive signs on the two respective constructs, suggesting a U-shaped relationship between conformity to ideal types and growth.

[7] Fuzzy set analysis would avoid the messiness of dichotomizing the variables, and also preserve the relation of identity and membership grade. However, for purposes of illustrating QCA, we restrict our analysis to crisp sets.

[8] Initial conditions may proxy for other factors, such as the stock of physical and human capital. It is an implicit claim of the varieties of capitalism approach that capital investments are endogenous; institutions determine the attractiveness of investment in equipment and in education.

Table 6.2: Mapping limited diversity and assessing simplifying assumptions*

		Configurations of Labour Institutions							
		dlt	dlT	dLt	Dlt	dLT	DlT	DLt	DLT
Configurations of	psc	5	0	0	0	0	0	0	1
Corporate	psC	0	0	0	0	0	0	0	0
Institutions	pSc	1	0	0	0	0	0	0	0
	Psc	0	0	0	0	0	0	0	1
	pSC	1	0	0	0	0	0	0	1
	PsC	0	0	0	0	2	0	0	0
	PSc	0	0	0	0	0	0	1	0
	PSC	0	0	0	0	3	1	1	2

Corporate Institutions (upper case denotes corporatist elements):
P = low shareholder power; p = high shareholder power
S = small stock market; s = large stock market
C = low dispersion of control; c = high dispersion of control
Labour Institutions (upper case denotes corporatist elements):
D = high degree of wage coordination; d = low degree of wage coordination
L = high level of wage coordination; l = low level of wage coordination
T = low level of labour turnover; t = high level of labour turnover
*Shaded portion of the table shows cells covered by the equation for high growth.

QCA takes advantage of the time invariance of the six coordination variables by analysing the cross-section of average growth rates, dichotomized into faster growing versus slower growing. There is no point in looking at the impact of initial GNP per capita, because of its near-perfect negative relationship with average growth rates. In effect, the analysis of average growth rates (faster versus slower growth) is also an analysis of initial levels of wealth, in reverse (lower versus higher initial wealth). Similar to the dichotimization of the dependent variable, the six coordination variables are also all dichotomized. Hall and Gingerich's four control variables (international demand conditions, change in the terms of trade, the rate of inflation, and change in the dependency ratio) are excluded, since they make sense only in the context of an analysis that has an explicit longitudinal component, focusing on variation in growth rates over time.

We begin by noting that with six causal conditions—the six coordination variables—a saturated experimental design would require the examination of sixty-four unique combinations. Obviously, with an N of twenty it is impossible to cover all sixty-four combinations. However, it is worth noting that twelve different combinations are evident among the twenty cases in Table 6.3, indicating considerable diversity among the cases with respect to institutional configurations.

The only uniform clustering is the five liberal countries with market coordination: Australia, Canada, New Zealand, United Kingdom, and the United States. While only two countries, Germany and Austria, have the full complement of corporatist institutions, an additional six countries have five of the six features.

Table 6.3: Hall and Gingerich's data converted to Boolean values

Country	Growth	Degree of wage coordination	Level of wage coordination	Labour turnover	Shareholder power	Stock market size	Dispersion of control
Austria	1	1	1	1	1	1	1
Germany	1	1	1	1	1	1	1
Italy	1	1	0	1	1	1	1
Belgium	1	0	1	1	1	1	1
Norway	1	1	1	0	0	1	1
Finland	1	1	1	0	1	1	1
Portugal	1	0	1	1	1	1	1
Sweden	0	0	1	1	1	0	1
France	0	0	1	1	1	1	1
Denmark	1	1	1	0	1	1	0
Japan	1	1	1	1	1	0	0
Netherlands	0	0	1	1	0	0	1
Switzerland	0	1	1	1	1	0	0
Spain	1	0	0	0	0	1	1
Ireland	1	0	0	0	0	1	0
Australia	0	0	0	0	0	0	0
New Zealand	0	0	0	0	0	0	0
Canada	0	0	0	0	0	0	0
United Kingdom	0	0	0	0	0	0	0
United States	0	0	0	0	0	0	0

The coordination dichotomies are all coded in the same direction, with a score of 1 signalling conformity with 'coordinated' market economies and a score of 0 signalling conformity with 'liberal' market economies.

Viewed configuration by configuration, only one of the twelve existing combinations of the six coordination dichotomies is causally 'contradictory'—linked empirically to both slower and faster growth rates. The combination in question involves all but one of the six elements of corporatist coordination—the three cases with this combination have a low degree of wage coordination, despite having all the other corporatist elements. Two cases with this combination, Belgium and Portugal, had higher growth rates, while France had a lower growth rate. In the analysis that follows, France is treated as an unexplained outlier, in line with the thrust of Hall and Gingerich's theory.

The next step in the analysis is to make logical inference, first by avoiding simplifying assumptions altogether, second by allowing the use of simplifying assumptions. Consider first the maximum use of the evidence. For every logically possible combination (sixty-four), there is an associated truth value. With Hall and Gingerich's data, the truth value is 1 if linked to faster growth (nine combinations, embracing eleven cases) and 0 if linked to slower growth (three combinations, embracing eight cases).[9] The remaining fifty-two combinations (those lacking empirical cases) are coded as 'either 1 or 0,' and the minimization algorithm is free to use them to simplify the results (see Ragin 1987). The resulting equation is not 'obligated' to cover all the configurations lacking cases; it covers only those that help produce more parsimonious results.

For example, assume that configurations ABC and aBc both lead to high growth. (As before, upper-case letters indicate the presence of a causal condition; lower-case letters indicate its absence; multiplication indicates combined conditions; and addition indicates alternative causal combinations). These two cannot be reduced because neither of the two minimization rules, absorption and reduction, can be applied. Assume configurations ABc and aBC lack cases and the analysis permits simplifying assumptions. These two configurations could be used as assumptions to simplify 'ABC + aBc' to 'B', as follows:

$$Y = ABC + aBc + ABc + aBC$$
$$= (ABC + aBC) + (aBc + ABc)$$
$$= (BC) + (Bc)$$
$$= B$$

When the number of existing configurations is small relative to the number of logically possible configurations, the impact of simplifying assumptions is substantial. Generally, researchers should check the plausibility of each simplifying assumption that is made. However, the analysis of plausibility of the simplifying assumptions made in the subsequent reanalysis of Hall and Gingerich's data is far beyond the scope of this brief discussion of method. However, we do sketch the nature of this analysis. Table 6.3 shows our coding of each country's configuration of institutional structures.

---

[9] Recall that we are treating France as an outlier, so the total number of cases is nineteen.

Table 6.4: Configurational analysis of causal determinants of growth for Hall and Gingerich data

a) Solution for High Growth/Low Initial GDP per capita, *without* simplifying assumptions:

Degreewc levelwc turnover sharehld STOCKMKT +
DEGREEWC LEVELWC turnover SHAREHLD STOCKMKT +
DEGREEWC LEVELWC TURNOVER STOCKMKT DISPERSN +
DEGREEWC TURNOVER SHAREHLD STOCKMKT DISPERSN +
LEVELWC TURNOVER SHAREHLD STOCKMKT DISPERSN +
DEGREEWC LEVELWC TURNOVER sharehld stockmkt dispersn

b) Solution for High Growth/Low Initial GDP per capita, *with* simplifying assumptions:

STOCKMKT +
One of the following:
DEGREEWCH sharehld + LEVELWC sharehld + TURNOVER sharehld

c) Solution for Low Growth/High Initial GDP per capita, *without* simplifying assumptions:

degreewc levelwc turnover sharehld stockmkt dispersn +
DEGREEWC LEVELWC TURNOVER SHAREHLD stockmkt dispersn +
Degreewc LEVEL WC TURNOVER SHAREHLD stockmkt DISPERSN

d) Solution for Low Growth/High Initial GDP per capita, *with* simplifying assumptions:

degreewc stockmkt +
SHAREHLD stockmkt +

Key for Table 6.4a to 6.4d:

DEGREEWC = degree of wage coordination (upper case indicates a high degree)
LEVELWC = level of wage coordination (upper case indicates a high level)
TURNOVER = labour turnover (upper case indicates a low level)
SHAREHLD = shareholder power (upper case indicates a low level)
STOCKMKT = share markets size (upper case indicates a smaller stock market)
DISPERSN = dispersion of control (upper case indicates a low level)

Variable names in upper case indicate conformity to corporatist coordination; lower-case indicates conformity to liberal coordination.

The results of our analysis of these data are presented in Table 6.4.

Panel a) shows the solution for high growth, without simplifying assumptions. There is one mixed liberal configuration, the first, with four liberal elements and one corporatist. This mixed combination is specific to Ireland and Spain. The next one is also mixed, with four corporatist elements and one liberal. It is specific to Denmark and Finland. The next three configurations, all uniformly involving five of the six corporatist elements and no liberal elements, embrace Austria, Germany, Italy, Belgium, Norway, Finland, and Portugal. These three configurations provide the strongest support for Hall and Gingerich with respect to the importance of corporatist coordination for economic growth. The final configuration is specific to Japan and is completely inconsistent from Hall and Gingerich's perspective. It combines all the corporatist labour relations elements and all the liberal corporate governance elements. According to Hall and Gingerich's theory, Japan should have suffered very poor economic performance over this period.

Panel b) of Table 6.4 shows the results of this same analysis, permitting simplifying assumptions. Because there are so many combinations of conditions lacking cases, the reduction from panel a) to panel b) is substantial. In essence, this analysis constitutes an attempt to pinpoint the decisive differences between the high-growth and the low-growth countries, based upon information about their economic institutions. The first term is simply smaller stock market size, a characteristic shared by all the high-growth countries except Japan. (As noted in the table, upper case indicates values consistent with corporatist coordination.) For the second term, there is a choice among three configurations, each with two conditions. Essentially, these are three different ways to capture Japan's distinctiveness from the low-growth countries, given that it has a larger stock market (a feature not shared by the other high-growth countries). Japan can be seen as different from the low-growth countries in its combination of lower shareholder power with any of the three elements of corporatist labour institutions.

Overall, the results in panel b) indicate that the most decisive single difference between low-growth and high-growth countries is stock market size, with smaller stock markets linked to superior economic performance. One possible interpretation of this finding is that smaller stock market size is a defining feature of economies with corporatist institutions, which in turn are strongly linked to superior economic performance, at least over the period studied by Hall and Gingerich.

Panel c) of Table 6.4 shows the results of the analysis of the low-growth countries. There are three configurations linked to slower relative growth. The first is perfectly consistent with liberal labour relations and liberal corporate governance, an institutional configuration that should be *high*-growth according to Hall and Gingerich. This configuration embraces Australia, New Zealand, Canada, the United Kingdom, and the United States. The second, which covers only Switzerland, combines elements of corporatist labour relations with two out of the three elements of liberal corporate governance. It thus resembles Japan in five of six aspects. However, this case, unlike Japan, experienced low growth over this period. The third low-growth configuration, which embraces Sweden and the Netherlands, is also mixed with four corporatist elements and two liberal elements. While the low-growth experience of these three countries with mixed configurations supports Hall and Gingerich's theory, the most striking finding from the analysis of the low-growth countries is the cluster of five countries with uniformly liberal characteristics. This pattern directly contradicts their theory.

Finally, panel d) of Table 6.4 shows the results of this same analysis using simplifying assumptions. Once again, the results are parsimonious because of the very large number of simplifying assumptions that have been made, which again reflects the fact that only twelve of the sixty-four logically possible combinations are found among these twenty countries. There are two configurations linked to slower relative growth: lower degree of wage coordination combined with larger stock market, and less shareholder power combined with larger stock market. The first configuration embraces the five liberal countries; the second embraces three countries: Sweden, the Netherlands, and Switzerland.

It is important to point out that the results reported in panel d) are a perfect negation of one version of the results of panel b). Specifically, it is possible to completely reverse (negate) the results in panel d) by applying De Morgan's Law to this equation, as follows. First, state the equation for low growth:

$$low\_growth = degreewc*stockmkt + SHAREHLD*stockmkt$$

Next, apply De Morgan's Law by reversing the outcome, changing all upper-case to lower-case, and vice versa, and then also changing intersection to union, and vice versa:

$$high\_growth = (DEGREEWC + STOCKMKT)*(sharehld + STOCKMKT)$$

Finally, simplify the terms using Boolean algebra:

$$high\_growth = STOCKMKT + DEGREEWC*sharehld$$

This application of De Morgan's Law indicates that the most logically consistent result in panel b) given the findings of panel d) is the first of the three alternatives listed. This choice makes the results for high growth the perfect inverse of the results for low growth, when simplifying assumptions are used. Of course, if all sixty-four possible configurations were present and there were no contradictions, then the logical inferences derivable from the high-growth configurations would be the same as those derivable from the low-growth configurations. However, given limited diversity, this is unlikely to be the case. Hence, the finding of a perfect inverse provides indirect evidence in support of the simplifying assumptions that have been made in panels b) and d).

As noted previously, it is important to assess simplifying assumptions, that is, to not make them mechanistically. Table 6.2 offers a guide to this assessment. It cross-tabulates the eight logically possible combinations of labour institutions against the eight logically possible combinations of corporate institutions. The cells of this table report the number of empirical instances of each of the sixty-four logically possible combinations. Of course, most cells are empty. The only cell with a substantial number of cases is the combination of consistently liberal labour institutions with consistently liberal corporate institutions (which we have shown to be a 'low'-growth configuration).

The shaded portion of Table 6.2 shows the cells that are consistent with our equation for high growth:

$$high\_growth = STOCKMKT + DEGREEWC*sharehld$$

(i.e. small stock market size or the combination of a high degree of wage coordination and greater shareholder power). It is clear that most of the shaded cells, those embraced by the equation for high growth, lack cases. Thus this table makes transparent the dependence of parsimonious statements on simplifying assumptions in situations of limited diversity. To assess the impact of limited diversity, it would be necessary to evaluate the plausibility of the inference that cases in these shaded cells, if they in fact existed, would experience high growth. Generally, it is best to make these assessments cell by cell. Note that all the unshaded cells are covered by the equation for low growth reported in panel d) of Table 6.4. To assess the plausibility of the simplifying assumptions for low growth, it would be necessary to follow the same procedure—examine the unshaded empty cells one at a time and evaluate the empirical plausibility of the assumption that cases in these cells would be low growth—if they existed.

While it might be tempting to divine a linear causality from the results in panels b) and d) in Table 6.4 (focusing on stock market size, shareholder power, and degree of wage control), it would be a mistake to do so. The goal of the analyses presented in panels b) and d) is to provide maximum logical parsimony, based on key differences between positive and negative cases. However, the larger goal of this reanalysis of Hall and Gingerich's data is to focus on configurations of institutions and to make configurational comparisons of empirical patterns. For these interpretive purposes, the results in panels a) and b) are clearly more useful.

Overall, the findings support only part of Hall and Gingerich's argument. High growth is linked to consistently corporatist configurations, but it is linked to several mixed configurations as well, including one that is completely discordant (Japan, with corporatist labour relations and liberal corporate governance). In contrast to their reasoning, low growth is clearly linked to consistently liberal configurations. Even the reduced equations reported in panels b) and d) reveal that mixed (inconsistent) configurations are linked to both high growth and low growth.

CRITICISM OF QCA

The above analysis by QCA of the treatment of institutions in terms of configurations casts considerable doubt on the idea that having either coordinated *or* liberal institutional complements is the key to economic growth among rich countries. Whether other configurations that are theoretically grounded can be identified is open to investigation, but the configurational inferences from the analyses presented in Table 6.4 suggest principally one: Anglo-Saxon (i.e. liberal) stock markets are bad for growth.

However, surely, QCA has itself important limitations.[10] First, by dichotomizing variables, it pushes all measurements to polar ends. The central claim of Hall and Gingerich is that countries in the middle will do worse, but there is no middle on any one variable. In Table 6.2, wage coordination in Sweden and the Netherlands is coded

---

[10] I would like to thank Peter Hall for help in thinking through the drawbacks to QCA.

at 0, the same level as the US, which is surely a bad description of the status quo, as might well be the 0 given Belgium here.

There is of course a middle configurational position, and it is this claim that the in-between configuration will do worse that the QCA analysis rejected. Even here though, the Hall and Gingerich approach was more subtle in suggesting that particular types of coordination will do better than just simply all types of coordination. QCA quickly becomes limited when the number of variables exceeds the data.

It might also be claimed that QCA did not make good use of the over-time variation, whereas the panel design could estimate the contribution of varying state variables and invariant institutions. However, this criticism seems a bit to be the sword of Damocles. For the panel analysis gains significance through treating the twenty countries by twenty-seven years as five hundred and forty records. Still at the end of the day, there are twenty countries, the institutions—if they are to qualify as institutions—are time invariant, and thus the variation is not remarkably strong, even though it permits estimation. The QCA design remained faithful to the primacy of the country and the constancy of its institutions as stable units of analysis.

FUZZY SET LOGIC[11]

It is an obvious objection that the world rarely conforms to a binary, or crisp, characterization. Fuzzy set methodology relies on an inference engine that permits graded membership in a set. An element may have a membership in a set between 0 and 1; Boolean logic requires crisp membership in which an orange is either a fruit or not a fruit. Charles Ragin (2000) proposed a robust application of fuzzy logic to the analysis of social science data, which relies upon a combination of the satisfaction of a few logical conditions and probabilistic assessment.

Fuzzy logic is of interest because it also captures important theoretical concepts in social science concerning identities and categories. Kogut and Ragin (2006) and Kogut (2008) have pointed out that people have multiple identities, to which they belong with varying degrees of fuzzy membership. These identities are defined, analytically, by categories in relation to various social affinities, such as religion. For example, sexual membership as male or female is, biologically, relatively crisp, i.e. binary, in some respects, but less so in others. It is clearly not crisp if the question is sexual preference or sexual identification.

It is common in social science research to rely on categories to offer discrete approximations of a continuum. For example, rich countries have per capita income in excess of $15000, middle income is less than $15,000 but more than $5,000, and the income of poor countries is less than $5000. Possible labels for these categories

---

[11] The empirical material in this section draws upon Kogut, MacDuffie, and Ragin (2004).

are developed, emerging, and poor countries. It is possible to code each of these discrete categories as three binary variables. Under a QCA crisp Boolean approach, three additional variables adds explosively to the analytic task of inferring causality, since the space of possible configurations increases by 2^n.

Ragin (2000) proposed a fuzzy set methodology that has three merits. The first two are methodological: fuzzy sets permits variables to take on values between 1 and 0 and it also avoids the proliferation of binary variables to code for essentially discrete intervals along a common continuum, such as suggested above by the example of per capita income. The third merit is that fuzzy sets introduces a careful examination of the theoretical meaning of variables and their measures, thus opening up a powerful way to let the fuzzy measurement of a category parallel the fuzzy membership in multiple identities.

The interesting insight of fuzzy set logic is that semantics matter. For example, the category of rich and not rich is not simply the inverse of not-poor and poor. Thus the researcher is forced carefully to think about the theoretical meaning of the semantic labels that are often too easily assumed in social science research. The way people categorize and label become essential to the theoretical task of understanding identities and memberships.

Since people can have multiple identities which may be correlated, it is reasonable to think then of a synthetic identity, defined by fuzzy membership in several different social engagements. The proposal of creating synthetic identities leads quickly to the concept of treating configurations as types of prototypes, along the lines proposed by Eleanor Rosch (1975). Prototypes are the best examples of members belonging to the same category. For example, Kogut, MacDuffie, and Ragin (2004) analysed the concept of the 'Toyota Production System' as a prototype to which manufacturing plants belonged more or less. We will use their analysis as an illustration of the use of fuzzy set inference.

The usage of prototypes implies that the degree of membership is a gradient, with more distant members holding lower degrees of membership.[12] Using this concept, we define membership in a fuzzy set of a given member x in the fuzzy set of A as

$$m_A(x) = Degree(x \in A)$$

Degree of membership can be geometrically portrayed by a hypercube in which a set is no longer constrained to be located at one of the 'crisp' vertices. The simple case is a straight line:

0_____.5_____1

The two end points are the crisp values of 1 or 0, in or out of the set. Values in between identify fuzzy membership, e.g. fairly rich countries or not very rich countries (Klir and Yuan 1995). The mid-point, .5, is of interest, for it defines

---

[12] We flag that there is a debate regarding prototype theory and fuzzy logic. For example, Lakoff (1973) sees fuzzy logic as insufficient for fully accounting for observed categorization heuristics.

maximal fuzziness (or what Kosko (1993) refers to as maximal entropy) and it represents a natural cognitive anchor.

A prevailing practice in statistical work is to combine like-items into a scale by imposing a functional transformation. For example, the data can be factor analysed, or transformed into z-scores while testing for their inter-item discrimination. Membership values in a fuzzy set can also be subjected to scaling. The caveat to scaling is that since the causal analysis (as described below) relies upon greater than, or less than, relations (rather than correlations), the results are very sensitive to the data values.

Partially as a consequence of this sensitivity, the assignment of membership can be strongly influenced by linguistic hedges (Klir and Yuan 1995: 230–1). Zadeh (1972) proposed that such a hedge as 'very' signifies that membership values should be squared (what he called concentration). The hedge 'fairly' is naturally captured by taking the square root of membership (or what he referred to as 'dilation'). These transformations have a common sense property. Clearly, an apple that has a membership value of .5 in the set of red apples should have a lower membership value in the set of very red apples.

The above example relies intuitively upon a notion of subsets. An important property that we rely heavily upon in the analysis below is that membership of x in a subset of A is less than or equal to membership in the set of A:

$$m_{B \leq A}(x) \leq m_A(x)$$

Figure 6.4 provides a graphic illustration that membership of X in the subset of A, defined by a two-dimensional space, lies in the domain of the set of A.

Fuzzy set logic

The categorization of entities by their degree of membership means that categories are not exclusive. This property has the attractive feature of conforming to common-sense notions of categories: people can be somewhat religious or somewhat moral. Manufacturing plants similarly have high membership in new work practices, but low membership in team organization. This property of membership, however, poses the question of how should we define the intersection and union of fuzzy sets. What is the membership value of a plant in the intersection of new work practices and work organization? This logical problem is the analogue of trying to find the factor score of a plant, except the operators are derived from a first-order logic.

Because membership values are binary, logical operations on fuzzy sets are more complicated than crisp operations, though fairly simple. The key difference is that membership values in a fuzzy set lies in the interval of [0,1]. As a result, the operations of negation, union, and intersection must heed the membership values.

Negation: In crisp logic, the set of A has the complement of the set of not-A. (See Klir and Yuan 1995: 50). This operation applies also to fuzzy sets. Consider the set A whose element X has a fuzzy membership denoted by a point along the unit interval. Then, negation is simply

$$m_{\bar{A}}(x) = 1 - m_A(x)$$

This definition is technically intuitive, and yet deserves a note of caution. For while the complement of rich is not rich, we would not want to say that the complement of rich is poor. We may view Portugal as holding a membership value of .4 in the set of rich countries, and hence the value of .6 in the set of not rich countries. Yet, we may assess its membership in the set of poor countries as considerably less than .6. Language clearly matters in understanding fuzzy sets, and the use of a predicate logic does not eradicate the ambiguity in linguistic terms and quantifiers.

Union: The union of two sets is logically denoted as an 'or' operation. The union of A and B implies that x belongs to A or B. However, this denotation is complicated in the context of fuzzy logic, because the membership of x in A or B can take on any value between, and including, 0 and 1. Fuzzy logic applies the union operator by taking the maximum of the membership value of X in each of the two sets:

$$m_{A \cap B}(x) = \max\ (m_A(x), m_B(x))$$

If X is short and smart with membership values of .5 and .8 respectively, in these two sets, X has then a membership value of .8 in the set of people who are short or smart. This definition corresponds intuitively with the implication of an 'or' operation. That is, x is a member of set A or set B with degree of membership equal to its maximum membership in each set.

Intersection: Fuzzy logic defines the intersection operator as the minimum of the membership degree of X in each of the two sets:

$$m_{A \cap B}(x) = \min\ (m_A(x), m_B(x))$$

The intersection of two sets is logically denoted as an 'and' operation. To belong to two sets means that X is member of both set A and set B. If X is not jointly a member, then it does not belong to the intersection. Again, we see a complication that X is likely to have different membership degrees in the two sets. It is unappealing that X's membership in the intersection should be greater than its membership in either of the individual sets.

The application of the minimum operator makes intuitive sense and is consistent with a prototype theory of membership. Consider the adjectives of big and furry to describe dogs. A given dog can be furry and very small, and it has membership values of .9 and .10 in the respective sets of furry and big. To average these membership values would give the misleading impression that furry can linearly compensate for being small. It might be surprising, having purchased a dog by the internet without a photo and who bore only the characterization as 'a more or less' member in the set of big and furry dogs, to open a big box containing a Pekinese. To most, a Pekinese has a low degree membership in the club of dogs who are both furry and big.[13] The

---

[13] Hampton (1997) summarizes some of the objections from cognitive psychology to fuzzy set definitions of prototypes. Part of these objections consist of problems of taking intersections among nested sets, a classic paradox in set theory. We empirically avoid these operations below.

minimum operator also makes formal sense. Recall the earlier definition of complementarities as supermodular. Since the value of doing two things together is higher than when they are apart, it makes sense to guarantee that the arguments to the function are all increasing. Taking the maximum would neglect the inferior argument. The minimum clearly indexes increases in the joint presence of two variables by the least value. This permits a direct test of whether the minimum of doing two (or three or more) is associated with increases in performance.

Fuzzy causal inference

Assigning membership values to all possible combinations constitutes the first step in the analysis. The second step is to derive those combinations, or complements, that explain the causality of observed outcomes. Causality in fuzzy logic shares some of the intuitive properties commonly confronted in statistical work. In linear specifications, we ask how does y vary with more of x. Fuzzy causal inference relies upon the set-theoretic definitions of necessity and sufficiency to identify factors that satisfy the subset axioms (Ragin 2000). For necessity, the outcome is a subset of the causal factor. Necessity implies, then, that the membership degree of a case in a causal factor should be associated with a 'smaller' membership value in an outcome. For sufficiency, the causal factor is a subset of the outcome. Sufficiency implies, then, that the membership degree of a case in the causal factor should be associated with a 'larger' membership value in an outcome.

A graphic illustration of determining necessary and sufficient conditions can be given by graphing the degree of membership in a hypercube in which a set is no longer constrained to be located at one of the 'crisp' vertices. Figure 6.5 shows a hypothetical relationship between lean buffers and the causal outcome of high performance.

Lean buffers satisfies the axiomatic definition of a necessary condition, because all cases have larger membership degrees in it than in the causal outcome.

Figure 6.6 portrays the analysis of sufficiency. Since the membership value in work teams uniformly is less than the membership degree in the causal outcome for all cases, we conclude that lean buffers is sufficient. The same analysis can be used for a configuration of two factors (lean buffers and work teams). Since we are looking at their joint effect (or intersection), we take the minimum of each case's membership value in these two factors. The minimum effectively must move the distribution of dots to the left in Figure 6.5, except for the unlikely case that the membership values in the two causal factors are the same.

It is obvious that a given factor cannot be both sufficient and necessary, except for the cases when the causal factor and causal outcome share the same membership values. Empirically, we expect that a causal factor or configuration will not be found only above or below the diagonal. The statistical formula to calculate the z-score (developed in Ragin 2000) permits an assessment of the statistical significance of

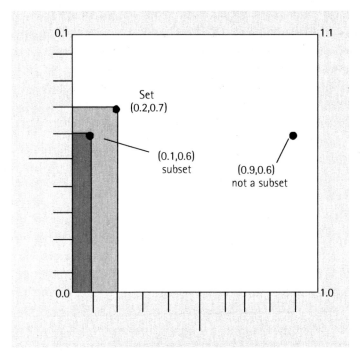

Figure 6.4: Fuzzy logic and subsets

necessity and sufficiency.[14] Moreover, since, for fuzzy set logic, every case has a membership value in a configuration, the problems of small sample size are much less severe than for crisp logic.

The calculation of the z-score requires the researcher to state a benchmark. Here the linguistic hedge suggests the choice of the benchmark proportionality. To ask, for example, if the observed proportion is significantly greater than 'usually necessary' indicates a benchmark of .65. A benchmark of 'very necessary' implies a value slightly greater than .7 benchmark. (The linguistic hedge of 'very' is mathematically equivalent to squaring the membership value, as discussed earlier; the square of .71 is approximately .5, the cognitive anchor where a member is maximally more or less a member of the set of 'very necessary' causes. We use the value of .65 in the following analysis.) Whereas these benchmarks may seem arbitrary (but no more arbitrary than the conventions governing questionnaire scaling such as a Cronbach alpha or significance tests), sensitivity analysis around the benchmark easily provides a way to assess robustness. In addition, sensitivity of measurement error can be examined by

---

[14] Ragin (2008) revised his method, replacing a statistical approach with a refined measure of consistency. Similarly, consistency replaces the diagonal classifier proposed in the 2000 book.

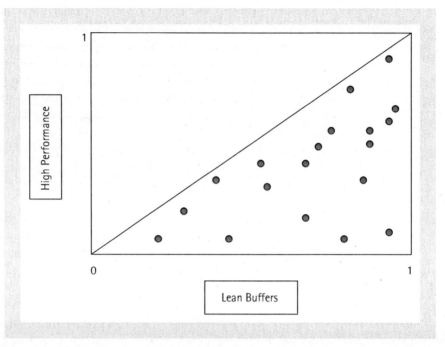

Figure 6.5: Plot of fuzzy relationship of necessary condition and causal effect

adjusting the diagonal to accept errors that differ by a stated percentage off the diagonal.

The determination of fuzzy sets proceeds, then, by statistically identifying necessary causes. Cases that reveal zero membership in the necessary causes are eliminated (by definition, they cannot satisfy the logical condition of necessity). Sufficient causes are then found by identifying causal configurations that statistically satisfy the requirement that their membership values are less than the causal outcome.[15] This analysis generates then a listing, or union, of sufficient configurations, conditioned on the initial identification of necessary causes. To achieve a global assessment of the statistical strength of the analysis, a membership score in the sufficient configurations for each case can be calculated. The comparison of this membership degree against the observed membership in the causal outcome serves to generate a test statistic to determine the significance of the classification success of the method.

Any cause that is individually sufficient is also sufficient jointly.[16] Necessity of one cause does not mean, however, that two necessary causes are jointly necessary.

---

[15] Theoretically, if enough cases lie exactly on the diagonal, a cause can be found to be both sufficient and necessary.

[16] For a proof, see Kogut, 2008: 262–3. In Ragin (2008), this approach is now subsumed in his treatment of 'coverage'.

However, any jointly necessary conditions are also individually necessary. It is thus justified to apply rules of Boolean absorption to fuzzy sets. Since the configuration Ab is a subset of the configuration of A (i.e. Ab is an intersection and hence a subset of A), the union of two configurations Ab and A logically implies that x will have a membership value equal to its membership value in A. Thus, Ab + A logically reduces to A. In fuzzy sets, absorption can produce awkward results (see footnote 13). Ragin (2008) chose to replace absorption by treating each test of fuzzy subset-hood as a statement and then constructing the truth table of this collection, which is then reduced by crisp set logic. For example, the statement that tall men must shave can be absorbed into the statement men must shave. To a great extent, this rule captures the meaning of a radial category. Peripheral members are absorbed into more basic representations of the category.

However, the rule of Boolean reduction does not apply. Since (B + b) equals max (B,b) and not 1—as in crisp logic, the crisp law of complements does not hold and Ab + AB does not reduce further. Fuzzy set analysis consequently loses some of the logical sharpness of the crisp method, since configurations do not easily reduce to more general and simpler causal factors.

This loss of sharpness is compensated for partly by the statistical analysis that tests each configuration for significance. Since all cases (e.g. car plants) are members 'to some degree' in each configuration, each configuration has a sample size equal to the number of all plants in the sample.[17] This property greatly facilitates the application of statistical methods, as described above. The configurations that pass significance can then be minimized by the absorption rule that applies to both crisp and fuzzy sets.

The final step of the analysis then assigns cases to configurations by choosing the maximum membership value of that case in the minimized configurations. For example, an analysis of car plant productivity might find that technology and human resource management constitute one configuration and technology and high scale form another. A given plant has a membership score of .4 in the first and .7 in the second (each score is derived by taking the intersection, or minimum, of the two practices constituting that configuration). The assignment rule would then assign this plant to the second configuration.

This reduction can obviously assign plants that are bad examples of a particular configuration. It makes little sense, for example, to claim that a given plant is characterized by high performance work practices when it belongs weakly to every attribute set that defines this configuration. This possibility conforms with a proto-type theory of classifications whereby an ostrich is a bad example of a bird. It also reflects a methodological weakness in fuzzy sets insofar that operations of intersec-tions can assign members to classes that are not commonsensical. Lazarfeld (1937) offers, as noted before, a proposed solution to this type of problem by ruling out implausible combinations. (This intervention is broadly standard in statistical

---

[17] For the analysis of necessity, we lose cases whose outcome values are 0; the Ragin (2008) approach no longer confronts this issue.

methodologies, such as in confirmatory factor analysis or model specification.) In a similar fashion, Ragin proposes to allow for the use of commonsense and theoretical intervention in two forms. First, in the interpretation of the configurations, we look at the 'better' examples, that is, those cases that score .5 or more in a configuration; these are what Kogut, MacDuffie, and Ragin (2004) would call prototypical examples.

Secondly, to reduce the overall solution space, the analysis identifies 'simplifying assumptions' that eliminate configurations that grossly violate theoretical and commonsensical relationships. As in the case of Boolean comparative analysis, the fuzzy set methodology faces the problem of limited diversity. Consider Figure 6.4 again that provides a two dimensional representation of operations on fuzzy sets.

Imagine that the graph is divided into four quadrants from each of the midpoints at .5. The corners represent the crisp sets, and in this way, each quadrant is associated with a given crisp configuration. Limited diversity arises when there is no case in a quadrant. For Boolean analysis, limited diversity is obvious, as no case will show the configuration.

For fuzzy sets, since all cases have membership in all configurations, it is necessary to be especially careful to check that a causal configuration is not derived from an assumption that is not strongly justified by the empirical data. This verification is conducted by assessing the degree of membership of each case in every combination of causal conditions and identifying those that have no cases with membership values greater than .5. This list can be used to isolate the combinations of factors for which

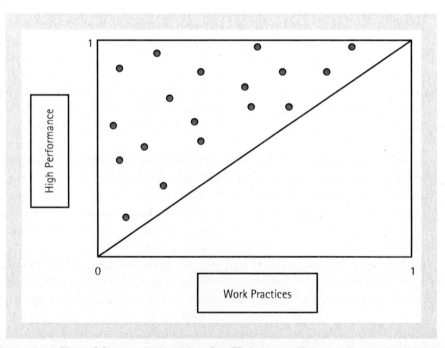

Figure 6.6: Plot of fuzzy relationship of sufficient condition and causal outcome

there is little empirical evidence. This then poses the question whether these combinations, that Ragin (2000) labels simplifying assumptions, are justified to play a role in deriving the minimized configurations. To check robustness, the researcher can check if these assumptions have been incorporated into the results of the sufficiency analysis. If this is the case, the researcher can either eliminate the simplifying assumption, which may change the results, or decide for theoretical reasons that the assumption should be retained. Both of these strategies have analogues in other methods. Econometrics often infers from the absence of a condition that decision makers did not choose a configuration because it was not profit maximizing. This provides information and can be used in the estimations (see Athey and Stern 1996, for an example). The second strategy is more common and arises in multiple variable regressions when one factor is not significant, but contributes to the overall estimation. An advantage with the Boolean and fuzzy set methodologies is that the researcher can explicitly identify the simplifying assumptions used in the minimization and decide, based on theory or field knowledge, if they should be eliminated or retained.

Multi-level Analysis

In recent years, there has been considerable attention paid to institutional complementarities in economics, sociology, and political science. Very frequently, the analysis considers only macro-institutions (e.g. political parties, unions, central bank) and the impact on, say, economic growth. Such analysis, often justified, does present problems. After all, what do such aggregates mean? Do they mean that unions are actors, but this is not precisely true—people act and thus union leaders act or people belonging to a union act? It is easier if we are thinking of a central bank headed by 'a' Central Banker. But this is often not the case.

In his famous last book before his death, the renowned sociologist James Coleman (1990) argued that at the art of good sociological analysis is a resolution of the micro–macro problem. Using the celebrated argument by Weber regarding capitalism, Coleman said a good analysis considers how the macro-institution of Protestantism influences the beliefs held by micro-actors (e.g. individuals) who then act (e.g. they save and invest) which feeds back positively on Protestantism and its ethic. There is thus a causal chain, which has positive feedback.

This framework of micro–macro analysis seeks to establish greater clarity in the causal argument but at the cost of shifting the causal attention to a lower level (individuals) who act in reference to institutions. The data requirements thus change as well. For example, in the case argued by Ragin and Sonnett, we would no longer be satisfied with comparing parties and unions and their outcomes across countries. Instead, we would have to ask how do individuals in countries where strong left parties and strong unions behave versus in countries where parties are weak, etc.

Let's take a case of the impact of the diffusion of new ways to produce cars, called the Toyota System; this case has been examined in MacDuffie (1994) and by QCA (or more precisely, qualitative fuzzy set analysis) by Kogut, MacDuffie, and Ragin (2005). The unit of analysis is the car plant (micro-level) whose efficiency depends upon its method of manufacturing (Toyota System or not) and the macro-institutions of a country where the plant is located. Since we are not looking at over-time data, we do not consider any feedback loops.

To make our example simple, we would like to know if a plant that uses the Toyota System or not (coded T or t) and is located in a country with strong unions or not (U or u) results in high performance or not (P or p). One research strategy is to look at all plants in a weak union country and strong union countries and ask: did the Toyota System diffuse to particular countries and how do we explain this? Or could we ask did TS plants perform better than other plants? Most likely the two questions are related and we might assume that countries that did not adopt it did not do so because the plants were not efficient. There are though other explanations, such that TS relies on teams that threaten the power of unions in the shop floor and thus unions object to the adoption of TS, regardless of the efficiency properties.

The only way to resolve this conflict in interpretation is to consider both the macro-institutional and micro-level performance. An easy way out is to code a variable for each country and add these binary variables (which append a string of 'o's with one '1' to the micro-level description of each plant). This approach clearly adds exponential burden to the required number of cases to saturate the truth table. More importantly, it does not add a lot of theoretical insight. This is similar to adding country dummies to a regression and then to change the intercept for each plant located in different countries.

The more theoretically satisfactory approach is to decide, as Weber did, what are the control and theoretical variables of interest. It would be great if we could fix the control values at the same values for all countries (as Weber tried to do) but most likely they will vary. Thus, there must be great parsimony in the choice of these controls. The good news of this approach is that since there are many more car plants than there are countries that have car plants, the sample size is larger and it is possible to more fully populate the truth table.

Summing up, an approach to designing the research strategy that we described is to identify the key institutional variables (such as unions), the control variables (e.g. economic development), micro-level causal factors (T), and then the performance outcome. QCA can then be applied as before. The analytical result will be to indicate if TS alone is sufficient for causing high performance ($T \Rightarrow P$), or whether it is contingent on the institution ($UT \Rightarrow P$ or U or T do not cause U).

The above is fairly simple and we can do somewhat better. It is likely that the above approach will produce logical contradictions, cases in which UT produce both high and low performance. Earlier, we said that such contradictions lead to a rethinking of the theory and indicate usually the need to add additional variables. In the context of this study, an approach is simply to decompose the Toyota System into discrete practices, such as quality control (Q) and efficient inventory buffers (B).

In this case, we might find that institutions interact differently with the practices and it is possible to have multiple configurations. For example, it is logically possible that both UB and uQB will produce high performance, thus there are two configurations whose complementarities produce equivalent results. Not surprisingly, the QCA analysis of the car plant data shows such variations, indicating that plants in different countries make the choice of which practice to adopt with an (implicit or explicit) understanding that the causal outcome is contingent on the local institutions.

The above observation has a very powerful lesson for comparative research on the diffusion of new methods and ideas. Some methods and ideas diffuse rapidly because they are 'institutionally neutral' in relation to many countries (Kogut 2002). Thus, unions may not object to efficient inventory but they do care about who runs the quality circles in the plants. Thus, B is institutionally neutral (showing up in both configurations) but Q is not (absent where unions are strong and the outcome is high performance). The subtle implication is that the Toyota System might be adopted *adaptively*, if first efficient buffers are adopted, and then overtime quality circles are adopted. There is a catch to this example. If UB is not efficient, then efficient buffers will not be adopted or maintained either, and the Toyota System cannot adaptively (or incrementally) diffuse over time in a country.

An interesting analysis would be to complete the Coleman cycle, and then ask if the feedback is positive or negative. If quality circles do erode union power, we could expect negative feedback, weakening unions and thus easing the institutional constraint preventing the diffusion of quality circles. The Boolean algebra of QCA has, therefore, a nice property of clarifying the arguments, requiring arguments to state clearly their static causality and dynamic adaptive causality assertions. This property of the comparative method is useful, no matter if the causal analysis subsequently relies upon logical inference or statistical methods.

STATISTICAL APPROACHES: MULTI-LEVEL ANALYSIS AND THE ECOLOGICAL FALLACY

This macro–micro reasoning suggests a hierarchical or multi-level analysis. Such an analysis is principally approached statistically if the goal is to account for the sources of variability in the dependent variable of interest. This type of analysis faces a trade-off between pooling data across different units (e.g. counties or countries) or relying on aggregate averages. Multi-level analysis seeks to find a weighting between these extremes such that variations at the upper level are combined with variations at the lower level in order to avoid spurious estimations and to assign proper causality (see for example the discussion in Gelman and Hill 2007). Causal inference across multi-levels poses complex statistical problems due to endogeneity. For example, unioni-zation can appear as an institutional factor, but in fact, it can be also be the outcome of preferences of individuals who share common traits and who populate differen-tially geographic units, such as countries.

Multi-level analysis also confronts the problem of the ecological fallacy, or the error of assigning causal relations at the upper hierarchical level to the subjects of the lower level. This fallacy is sometimes called the 'Robinson effect' after the study by Robinson. Robinson studied the relation of race and illiteracy in nine geogra-phies in 1930. The ecological correlation between the nine geographies was .95 but only .2 at the individual level. Clearly, the sampling was not randomized and there is a selection bias due to common unobserved traits 'within' the group.

This kind of problem has recently received renewed interest (King 1997). The traditional approach has been a bounds solution. The unknowns are the proportions of the type of individual on interest (e.g. gender, socio-economic class, etc.). A bounds approach recognizes that the probability of an individual belonging to a type must lie on the [0,1] interval, thereby permitting lower and upper bounds to be established for the proportion. King has proposed to do better by random effects model, treating the proportions as drawn from a specific probability distribution. Neither approach has been shown to be consistently reliable (Cho 1998).

Looking Forward: Mechanisms and Simulation

QCA is not suited to redressing this type of problem. However, by and large, as long as the conclusions at one level are not ascribed as motives to another, QCA avoids committing the fallacy. The fallacy occurs primarily when statements about what Jan Elster (1979) calls 'mechanisms' at the lower level are inferred via patterns at the aggregate level. The avoidance of this fallacy also means that QCA is limited in its ability to assign accountability. As we saw in the illustrative application of QCA to the Toyota Production System, the configurational focus of QCA means that it has greater flexibility in matching individual and institutional factors but at the cost of complexity.

Another way to sort out the complexity due to endogeneity and causal inference in absence of complete data is to rely on simulations to investigate more thoroughly the solution space. The analysis of counterfactuals relies upon simulations, however restricted, to test the robustness in deviations in the values or causal roles assigned to key variables. A broader use of simulations would specify more clearly the behavioural mechanisms at the individual level to see if the macro-institutional relations may be 'grown' and dynamically feed back into the behaviours of individuals. (See for example Hedström 2005, and Epstein 2006.) This approach allows for a more complete treatment of Coleman's micro–macro relationship, for it investigates more fully the feedback of beliefs and behaviours on structures.

The traditional statistical and comparative qualitative methods can never fully resolve the problem of inference in face of limited diversity. However, limited diversity is not an error, such as an omitted variable bias, but philosophically is fundamental to comparative analysis in two ways. The first is that static comparisons will not adequately determine the causes of social dynamics. For this, the concept of mechanisms is far less restrictive and insightful. The second is that an empirical isolation of all possible combinations of factors is never feasible. For every theory that succeeds in the mapping of factors to the power set of all causal factors, there remains all the theories, known and to be discovered, that identify additional factors. In this state, it is best to think of comparative analysis as the exploration of possible worlds and statements of causality restricted to those that we know and those that we can simulate counterfactually. This agenda is far less ambitious than the classic seeking of 'truth'—as in a truth table—but represents a new opening in social science towards explorations of worlds that 'could be' and perhaps even 'should be'.

REFERENCES

ATHEY, SUSAN and SCOTT STERN (1996). 'An Empirical Framework for Testing Theories About Complementarity in Organizational Design,' Cambridge, MA: NBER Working Paper 6600.

AMABLE, BRUNO (1999). 'Institutional Complementarity and Diversity of Social Systems of Innovation and Production', Review of International Political Economy 7(4): 645–87.

BERGER, SUZANNE and RONALD DORE (eds.) (1996). National Diversity and Global Capitalism, (Ithaca, NY: Cornell University Press).

BERNARD, CLAUDE (1865). Principes de médecine expérimentale, éditions ebooks France, http://www.laphilosophie.fr/ebook/Bernard,%20Claude%20-%20Principes%20de%20m%E9decine%20experimentale.pdf.

BERKOWITZ, DANIEL, KATHARINA PISTOR, and JEAN-FRANCOIS RICHARD (2002). 'Economic Development, Legality, and the Transplant Effect,' European Economic Review 47: 165–95.

BOYER, ROBERT (1996). 'The Convergence Hypothesis Revisited: Globalization but still the Century of Nations?', in Suzanne Berger and Ronald Dore (eds.), National Diversity and Global Capitalism, (Ithaca, NY: Cornell University Press).

CEDERMAN, LARS-ERIK (1996). 'Rerunning History: Counterfactual Reasoning in World Politics,' in Paul Tetlock and Aaron Belkin (eds.), Counterfactual Thought Experiments in World Politics: Logical, Methodological, and Psychological Perspectives, (Princeton, NJ: Princeton University Press).

——(2003). 'Modeling the Size of Wars: From Billiard Balls to Sandpiles', American Political Science Review 97: 135–50.

CHO, WENDY K. TAM (1998). 'Iff the Assumption Fits . . . : A Comment on the King Ecological Inference Solution,' Political Analysis, 7: 143–63.

Cusack, Tom and Richard Stoll (1990). *Exploring International Relations Theory with Computer Simulation,* (Boulder: Lynne Rienner Publications).

Epstein, Joshua (2006). *Generative Social Science: Studies in Agent-based Computational Modeling,* Princeton studies in complexity, (Princeton, NJ: Princeton University Press), pp. xx, 356.

Galton, Francis (1889). 'Comment on Edward B. Tylor's "On a Method of Investigating the Development of Institutions: Applied to Laws of Marriage and Descent"', *Journal of the Royal Anthropological Institute* 18: 245–69.

Gelman, Andrew and Jennifer Hill (2007). *Data Analysis Using Regression and Multilevel/ Hierarchical Models,* (Cambridge: Cambridge University Press).

Hall, Peter A. and Daniel Gingerich (2001). 'Varieties of Capitalism and Institutional Complementarities in the Macroeconomy: An Empirical Analysis.' Unpublished. Department of Government, Harvard University.

——and David Soskice (2001). 'Varieties of Capitalism: The Institutional Foundations of Comparative Advantage', (Oxford: Oxford University Press).

Hampton, James (1997). 'Conceptual Combination', in Koen Lamberts and David Shanks (eds.), *Knowledge, Concepts, and Categories,* (Cambridge: MIT Press), pp. 133–60.

Hedström, Peter (2005). *Dissecting the Social: On the Principles of Analytical Sociology,* (Cambridge; New York: Cambridge University Press), pp. x, 177.

King, Gary (1997). *A Solution to the Ecological Inference Problem,* (Princeton, NJ: Princeton University Press).

——and Langche Zeng (2007). 'When Can History Be Our Guide? The Pitfalls of Counter-factual Inference,' *International Studies Quarterly* 51: 183–210

——Robert O. Keohane, and Sidney Verba (1994). *Designing Social Inquiry: Scientific Inference in Qualitative Research,* (Princeton, NJ: Princeton University Press).

Kling, Jeffrey (1995). 'High Performance Work Systems and Firm Performance,' *Monthly Labor Review, Washington,* 118: 29–36.

Klir, George J. and Bo Yuan (1995). *Fuzzy Sets and Fuzzy Logic: Theory and Applications,* (Upper Saddle River, NJ: Prentice Hall PTR).

Kogut, Bruce (2002). 'The Transatlantic Exchange of Ideas and Practices: National Institutions and Diffusion,' Les Notes de l'IFRI No. 26, Institut français des relations internationales, Paris.

——(2008). *Knowledge, Options, and Institutions,* (Oxford: Oxford University Press).

——and Charles Ragin (2006). 'Exploring Complexity when Diversity is Limited: Institutional Complementarity in Theories of Rule of Law and National Systems Revisited', *European Management Review* 3: 44–59.

——John Paul MacDuffie, and Charles Ragin (2004). 'Prototypes and Strategy: Assigning Causal Credit Using Fuzzy Sets' *European Management Review* 1: 132–44.

Kosko, Bart (1993). *Fuzzy Thinking: The New Science of Fuzzy Logic,* (New York: Hyperion).

Lakoff, George (1973). 'Hedges: A Study in Meaning Criteria and the Logic of Fuzzy Concepts', *Journal of Philosophical Logic* 2: 458–508.

——(1987). *Women, Fire, and Dangerous Things. What Categories Reveal about the Mind,* (Chicago: University of Chicago Press).

La Porta, Rafael, Florencio Lopez-de-Silanes, Andrei Shleifer, and Robert W. Vishny (1997). 'Legal Determinants of External Finance', *Journal of Finance* LII (3): 1131–50.

Lazarsfeld, Paul (1937). 'Some Remarks on Typological Procedures in Social Research', *Zeitschrift fuer Sozialforschung* 6: 119–39.

Lewis, David (1973). *Counterfactuals,* (London: Blackwell).

MENZIES, PETER (2008). 'Counterfactual Theories of Causation', *The Stanford Encyclopedia of Philosophy (Winter en.)*, Edward N. Zalta (ed.), URL = <http://plato.stanford.edu/archives/win2008/entries/causation-counterfactual/>.

MERTON, ROBER (1957). *Social Theory and Social Structure*, revised and enlarged (London: The Free Press of Glencoe).

MILGROM, PAUL and JOHN ROBERTS (1990). 'The Economics of Modern Manufacturing: Technology, Strategy and Organization', *American Economic Review* 80: 511–28.

MILL, JOHN STUART (2002). *A System of Logic*, Honolulu: University Press of the Pacific.

PRZEWORSKI, ADAM and HENRY TEUNE (1970). *The Logic of Social Inquiry*, (New York: John Wiley).

RAGIN, CHARLES (1987). *The Comparative Method: Moving Beyond Qualitative and Quantitative Strategies*, (Berkeley: University of California Press).

——(2000). *Fuzzy-Set Social Science*, (Chicago: University of Chicago Press).

——(2008). *Redesigning Social Inquiry*, (Chicago: Chicago University Press).

——and JOHN SONNETT (2004). 'Between Complexity and Parsimony: Limited Diversity, Counterfactual Cases, and Comparative Analysis', in Sabine Kropp and Michael Minkenberg (eds.), *Vergleichen in der Politikwissenschaft*, (Wiesbaden: VS Verlag fuer Sozialwissenschaften).

ROBINSON WILLIAM (1950). 'Ecological correlations and the behavior of individuals', *American Sociological Review* 15: 351–57.

ROSCH, ELEANOR (1978). 'Principles of Categorization,' in Eleanor Rosch and BB Lloyd (eds.), *Cognition and Categorization*, (Hillsdale, NJ: Lawrence Erlbaum Associates).

TETLOCK, PAUL and AARON BELKIN (1996). 'Counterfactual Thought Experiments in World Politics: Logical, Methodological, and Psychological Perspectives', in Paul Tetlock and Aaron Belkin (eds.), *Counterfactual Thought Experiments in World Politics: Logical, Methodological, and Psychological Perspectives*, (Princeton, NJ: Princeton University Press).

ZADEH, LOFTI (1972). 'A Fuzzy Set Interpretation of Linguistics Hedges', *Journal of Cybernetics* 2: 4–34.

PART II

INSTITUTIONS, STATES, AND MARKETS

CHAPTER 7

THE STATE IN THE ECONOMY: NEOLIBERAL OR NEOACTIVIST?

LINDA WEISS

INTRODUCTION

This chapter discusses key approaches to the state's role in the contemporary economy in the light of several different bodies of research drawn from the literature on comparative capitalism and international political economy.

The state's influence in the economy has been a major topic of theoretical debate and empirical enquiry since the rise of capitalism and a market society. Where the state's nurturing of infant industries was seen by some as essential to climbing the ladder of development at home (List 1841), its encouragement of international commerce or 'free trade' was hailed by others as the key to prosperity and peace among nations (cf. Hirschman 1997). Though widely cited today as the poster children for unfettered ('free') markets, Adam Smith and his contemporaries, the Scottish moralists, considered the idea of a market society divorced from social norms and legal and political rules as outlandish, if not utopian. As Hungarian political economist Karl Polanyi (1944) would later famously put it, the modern market economy works because of its institutional 'embeddedness'.

The pre-eminent or macro-institution in this regard is that political complex we call 'the state', whose allocative and regulatory powers set it apart from the micro-institutions of the economy. The state's capacity to define, allocate, and enforce property rights, for example, gives it a distinctive source of market-shaping power, enabling state actors to alter the organization of the economy (Campbell and Lindberg 1990). This is not to deny the importance of other economy-shaping structures—including systems of corporate governance, labour market regulation, education and training—but these are effectively second-order institutions in so far as they depend on specific regulatory regimes (and infrastructural resources) that are the preserve of the nation-state (Hall and Soskice 2001: 4).

In this respect, the two-hundred year history of market society is at once a story of the state's generally increasing role in economic affairs—helping to establish markets and enabling them to work—*and* a history of each state's specific institutional evolution. Thus, states have not only grown more links with their economies over this period, they have also grown such links in distinctive ways that give rise to diverse traditions of economic governance. As various scholars have observed, there is no such thing as a generic state. Rather, nation-states 'vary dramatically in their internal structure and relations to society. Different kinds of state structures create different capacities for action' (Evans 1995: 127).

Scholars working in the field of comparative capitalism have identified three such state traditions associated with modern market economies—liberalism, corporatism, and statism (Schmidt 2002). While these labels are intended as ideal types rather than perfect representations of reality, nonetheless, in each case, the orientation of state actors, their organizational structure, and the mode of interaction with economic actors are held to differ systematically, creating different patterns of economic governance, each distinguished by the extent to which development (*aka* structural change, technological upgrading, or innovation) is market-led, government-sponsored, or coordinated by organized economic actors themselves. In this context, liberalism and statism occupy the two ends of the spectrum, the first typified in the literature by the United States and Britain (Hall and Soskice 2001; Lutz and Eberle 2004), the latter more commonly associated with the political economies of Japan, Korea, Taiwan, and Singapore in Asia (Woo-Cumings 1999), and France in Europe (Schmidt 2003; Loriaux 2003). In the Anglo-Saxon liberal market economies (LMEs) the state is held to play a basic regulatory or 'market facilitating' role, underwriting market relationships, maintaining the competitive rules of the game, and intervening only to correct market failure. In so-called statist or, what we might term, 'governed market economies' (GMEs), state actors use the powers of the state to achieve the developmental goals of structural transformation and technology catch-up (Johnson 1982; Amsden 1989; Wade 1990). In between these two types are the coordinated market economies (CMEs) in which states pursue more extensive social policies, creating a framework for organized actors (employers and employees) to coordinate their own economic endeavours and enable cooperative responses to pressures for change (Katzenstein 1984; Hall and Soskice 2001; Pontusson 2005).

The rationale for much of this literature emerges from a dual set of concerns that are seen to be broadly connected, one focused on the rise of neoliberalism as an ideology and policy regime, the other on the impact of economic globalization on the role of the state and the viability of non-LME systems. What role if any can/should states play in the market economy and in particular, how can they promote development? To what extent if at all are state traditions of economic governance being homogenized? Does the global economy valorize one state type over others and are state types necessarily 'pure'? If such questions are insistent it is because of a modern belief that the world has fundamentally altered, that states face unprecedented challenges, which shrink policy space and curtail their role in the economy. Among the more pertinent challenges, compliance with the multilateral rules of the global trade regime, responsiveness to capital mobility, and conformity with the dominant economic ideology of market fundamentalism are often singled out for their restrictive impacts on state activity in the domestic economy.

Our interest here lies in the main perspectives on the role of the state as researchers seek to deal with these issues. Not surprisingly, that role is contested. What is perhaps more surprising (we shall see), is the gap between the strength of the (neoliberal) perspective that has come to dominate debate and the strength of the evidence to support it. As Theda Skocpol (1985) famously argued more than two decades ago, the state's autonomy and capacity, including its catalytic role in economic change, has long been downplayed in the social sciences in favour of a society-centred paradigm. The roots of that paradigm have been traced to Cold War politics (Ciepley 2000). While all sorts of theories have been invented to suggest that states and markets inhabit conflicting realms and to justify why the state cannot, does not, or should not be involved in the economy, it appears that the 'state versus market' dichotomy emerged not out of theorizing, but from geopolitical imperatives.[1] Contemporary debates have been framed and informed by that paradigm.

This chapter discusses three perspectives on the state–economy relationship. These range from a priori claims that view states as impediments to markets, to hypotheses that posit a world of neoliberal states restricted to creating the best environment for transnational capital, to arguments that seek to conceptualize actually existing states as solutions to the problem of development. First, the discussion begins with a brief sketch of the state's role in neoliberal theory. Next it examines how the theory is believed to play out in practice as a result of globalization and the rise of neoliberalism. Third, it considers the debate on the rise of governed market economies, and their challenge to the free-market paradigm. Finally, we revisit the proposition that the global economy valorizes a minimalist (neoliberal) state. This time, however, we focus on the recent experience of one so-called LME, asking how far the US state–economy relationship itself conforms to the one depicted by the standard label. Here we approach the limits of our comparative capitalism typologies as they apply to state practice.

---

[1] Ciepley (2000) argues that due to its unsavoury associations with militarism, communism, and nazism, the idea of state autonomy that was prominent in the social sciences prior to 1945 took on a more sinister meaning after the war, not only in Europe, but also, especially, in the United States.

The state was quickly dropped from social science treatments as US–Soviet relations soured in 1947 and a new conceptual dichotomy of 'capitalism–weak state' and 'communism–strong state' took hold in academic and political discourse; this construction served the important political purpose of allowing maximum differentiation between the Western 'free-market' and the Soviet 'totalitarian' systems.

THE STATE AS PROBLEM: THE NEOLIBERAL ARGUMENT

The state as an economic actor has long occupied an ambiguous role in the social science literature, viewed by some as readily serving the public good by intervening to correct market failure, and by others as fundamentally self-serving, venal, or inefficient unless heavily restrained. In much of the economics (and some of the political-economy) literature, it is the latter view—referred to here as the 'neoliberal' argument—that has come to dominate academic and political debate.

The neoliberal argument concerning the role of the state—often associated with the work of Milton Friedman and the Chicago School economists—gained a robust political following in the late 1970s and early 1980s in conjunction with the so-called Thatcher revolution in Britain and its US variant led by the Reagan administration (Gamble 1988). As an economic theory emphasizing deregulation and the reduction of the state, its attack on 'big government' had particular resonance in the context of an expanding welfare state, budget deficits, and slow growth. The neoliberal argument that emerges in this 'pre-globalized environment' centres on what the state 'should or should not' do in the domestic market economy. One may note that in later years, as the world economy becomes much more integrated ('globalized'), the neoliberal emphasis shifts to what the state 'can or cannot' do (discussed in the subsequent section).

The basic claim—that the state should minimize its role in the economy—is premised on different assumptions about the respective attributes of markets and states. The neoliberal view of the market shares some ideas with economic liberalism classically associated with the work of Adam Smith, namely that only markets produce an efficient allocation of resources and that market competition will best serve the public interest, in so far as it allows individuals to express their choices freely and prices to be determined by supply and demand. But it adopts a more extreme approach to the market than classical liberalism, advocating maximum expansion of transactions so that as many areas of social life as possible are organized through markets, unfettered by state intervention.[2]

The state, by contrast, is believed to have little capacity or motivation to benefit society. In the tradition of neoclassical economic theory, the state is seen as normally incompetent or corrupt. State actors are held to be chiefly motivated by self-serving behaviour. Bueaucrats are perceived either as a collection of self-serving revenue-maximizers or, alternatively, they are susceptible to the political machinations of vote-maximizing politicians whose interventions generate rents that private agents seek to capture. Even when not directly self-serving, government interventions are almost always inefficient since they distort the market and inhibit entrepreneurship,

---

[2] The key policy prescriptions, defined originally in 1989 by John Williamson as the 'Washington consensus' came to be applied much more broadly (see Williamson 1993 for an account).

ultimately producing outcomes far worse than the ones they were designed to correct (*aka* 'government failure'). As a result of this a priori reasoning, the neoliberal argument concludes that states should refrain or withdraw from all forms of intervention that would interfere with the free operation of the market, whether through public ownership, environmental and labour regulation, government spending, tariffs and so on.[3] In theory, the state is only necessary for the prevention of behaviour that interferes with the free market (such as monopolies), or for the enforcement of reforms that ensure the market's expansion.

As one study of the theory and practice of neoliberalism observes,

> Neoliberals are particularly assiduous in seeking the privatisation of assets. . . . Sectors former-ly run or regulated by the state must be turned over to the private sphere and be deregulated (freed from any state interference). . . . The free mobility of capital between sectors, regions, and countries is regarded as crucial. All barriers to that free movement (such as tariffs, punitive taxation arrangements, planning and environmental controls, or other locational impediments) have to be removed, except in those areas crucial to 'the national interest', however that is defined.   (Harvey 2005: 65–6)

Translated into government practice and promoted through global governance institutions, including the WTO, the World Bank and the IMF, the package of reforms that ranged from deregulation of labour and capital markets to privatization of public services and assets, was intended to withdraw the state from all but a minimal role in the economy (Biersteker 1990). US President Reagan's refrain: 'Government is not a solution to our problem; government is the problem', has been the political leitmotif for neoliberal theory.

In neoliberal theory, then, the best government is the least government. In practice, the neoliberal state must therefore set about freeing enterprise from regulations, reducing taxes, balancing budgets—in short, providing the best macro-economic environment for encouraging investment. This particular theme takes on especial importance in the context of globalization, examined next.

GLOBALIZATION AND THE TRANSFORMED STATE: NEOLIBERALISM IN PRACTICE

For the past three decades or so, the global economy has grown in tandem with a major policy drive in many countries throughout the world—a pattern comprising liberalization, deregulation, and privatization—known as the neoliberal paradigm. In the context of globalization, neoliberalism is often described as a 'political project'

---

[3] For an overview of the arguments about government failure, see Weiss (1998: 17–20).

concerned with sweeping institutional changes. Campbell and Pedersen (2001: 1), for example, argue that neoliberalism has sought 'to transform some of the most basic political and economic [postwar] settlements... including labor market accords, industrial relations systems, redistributive tax structures, and social welfare programs'.

In tandem with these policy and institutional shifts, researchers have observed the emergence of new structures of governance that appear to elevate the importance of other power actors—especially private economic networks—in the legislative and policy determinations once considered the preserve of elected governments. As Harvey (2005: 76) writes, 'Neoliberalization has entailed... increasing reliance on public-private partnerships' in which business collaborates with state actors in formulating and implementing policies, in setting the regulatory frameworks and sometimes in writing the legislation. Similar observations on public-private policy networks have been reported in the context of international trade and multilateral rule-setting (Shaffer 2003).

For many observers, this global diffusion and uptake of neoliberal reforms has called into question the very idea of the state as an economic and political actor, giving rise to a vigorous debate that—until the 2008 global financial meltdown—had shown few signs of abating: what were its drivers, how extensive was its reach, and how uniform has been its impact (see e.g. Lutz and Eberle 2004; Soederberg et al. 2005; Simmons et al. 2008)? In tackling these and similar questions, both enthusiasts and critics of economic integration were inclined to posit a fundamental conflict between globalization and the state. More often than not they concluded that the marriage of neoliberalism and the expansion of global markets had dramatically narrowed the state's policy space. As national economies grew more interconnected, they argued, the state's role in economic governance necessarily becomes more severely restricted to 'tinkering around the edges'. After all, they reasonably concluded, if capital is mobile and nation-states are not, what is left for the state to do in the economic arena—other than to facilitate competition and provide the most attractive investment environment for transnational capital via low taxes, easy labour laws, and a generally permissive regulatory system (Cerny 1995; Hirst and Thompson 1996; Held et al. 1999).

The core of the so-called 'transformationalist' (*aka* 'constrained state') argument is the idea that openness to the global economy produces a 'constraining effect' on macroeconomic policies around the world by inducing increased budgetary pressure. The reasoning behind the constraints hypothesis runs as follows. Trade and financial liberalization exert downward pressure on government's taxing and spending activity by increasing the mobility of finance capital and production factors, which creates direct arbitrage effects. By allowing firms to seek out the most cost-friendly environments in which to conduct their activities, globalization thereby generates increased tax competition among nation-states (in its most extreme form, a global tax 'race to the bottom') in order to retain and attract investment. Thus, if policymakers in one or more jurisdictions introduce tax reforms to encourage growth-inducing investment, policymakers in other countries will be pressured to follow suit. In addition to the direct competitive logic, in a different version of the argument, there is also a *structural* logic that impacts on macroeconomic policy: if governments assume that international capital flows are important for national economic growth and believe that investors respond negatively to poor fiscal and monetary policies, they will be induced to shape their macroeconomic policies accordingly, avoiding inflation and deficit spending. On this point, economists as diverse as Stanley Fischer (1998) and Joseph Stiglitz (2000) appear to agree. Either way, as a result of the constraints effect, it is anticipated that global interdependence gradually erodes the income and capital tax bases of the more developed (higher taxing, higher spending) countries, resulting in the state's diminishing ability to finance public spending programmes, especially the welfare state. As a consequence, predicts the constraints hypothesis, governments claw back not only protective labour regulations but also social spending, which results in welfare retrenchment.

The 'constrained state' argument is reminiscent of the Friedmanesque idea of the 'golden straitjacket' according to which national governments who seek to grow their economies must generally abide by the neoliberal rule book to create the most favourable environment for transnational capital (Friedman 2000). Beyond these path-clearing measures, state efforts to govern the economy are either bound to fail, to warn off investors, or to incur trade sanctions.

Taken to its logical conclusion, the globalization of neoliberalism would therefore create a more *homogeneous* world in which diverse state traditions and political economy approaches would start to look the same. Thus in a related argument, many of the same analysts posited the erosion of varieties of capitalism and the concomitant diffusion of the so-called American or LME model (based, theoretically, on a minimal state, deregulated markets, and business-driven innovation). Homogenization arguments have been applied to all states outside the American neoliberal model—as much to the European welfare state model as to the East Asian developmental version. In such arguments the LME model is often posited, by globalization enthusiasts and critics alike, as the most viable one for a global economy (cf. Kay 2004: 310–11).

A virtual academic industry thus took shape debating the various ways in which the state's economic role was being restricted or reconstituted by market forces at home and abroad and, in the process, giving rise to a 'transformed' institution to which the label 'neoliberal' was widely applied. While there has been much debate over the nature and extent of the changes, many agree that the state has undergone some fundamental 'transformation' and that neoliberal globalization lies behind it (Crouch and Streeck 1997; Held et al. 1999; Cerny 1997).

With the neoliberal label comes a useful, sometimes important—though essentially partial—perspective on the nature of state–economy relations in an international environment. The problem arises when what is true for a part of the policy apparatus is effectively generalized to the whole; and when the existence of a 'tendency' is conflated with wholesale transformation. Critically, what this means is that the idea of the state as a 'polymorphous' beast (Mann 1986) appears to be all but forgotten. Put differently, as a complex of political institutions whose parts have *changes in different stages.*

evolved at different stages in response to different issues and constituencies, the state may well be neoliberal in one sphere (like trade unions), yet developmental in another (e.g. technology), a promoter of free trade in some sectors (financial services), yet mercantilist in others (agriculture or textiles).

As scholars begin more carefully to test the claims of homogenization and state transformation (e.g. Bell 2005), some important reminders of that complexity have begun to emerge from cross-national analysis of institutional and policy change: '...states are much less incapacitated by the rise of neoliberalism than is often appreciated', observe one group of writers. 'Instead, states can block, adapt to, mediate, and in some cases even reverse neoliberal tendencies' (Campbell & Pedersen 2001:1). Below we discuss four main ways in which the hypothesis of 'neoliberal state transformation' has been challenged.

Taxing and spending: the 'disciplined' state?

Not surprisingly, there is a substantial empirical literature devoted to testing the constrained state hypothesis. Important contributions examining the tax competition and welfare effect of trade and financial liberalization include Garrett (1998); Garrett and Mitchell (2001); Quinn (1997); Swank (1998, 2003, 2006), Kaiser and Laing (2001); Hobson (2003); and Dreher et al. (2008). However, after more than a decade of research, the results of both quantitative and econometric studies are inconclusive: some studies report a constraints effect, while several others find no significant effect from exposure to economic openness. Schulze and Ursprung's (1999: 345–47) survey of the literature on the relationship between international market exposure, the tax structure and government spending (which included several of the studies cited here), concluded that: 'The general picture...does not lend any support to an alarmist view.' At least at an aggregate level 'many of these studies find no negative relationship between globalization and the nation states' ability to conduct independent fiscal policies'. Almost ten years later, a more disaggregated econometric study of the impact on diverse social spending categories in the OECD over a thirty-year period similarly concluded that 'globalization has not affected the composition of government expenditures' (Dreher et al. 2008: 265). On the state's fiscal activity over the forty-year period 1965–2006, for example, social expenditure in the OECD countries as a percentage of GDP increased from 16 per cent to 20.6 per cent (OECD 2007); while state spending overall in the OECD remained relatively robust, averaging 40 per cent of GDP (World Bank *Development Report* 2004). Looking beyond the rhetoric of 'retrenchment' and 'rolling back of government', what has changed, some writers suggest is that 'the "growth" of the size of the state has been halted' (Prasad 2006: 6)—at least for the moment.

In short, although the constrained state hypothesis is often presented as a fact of life, the relationship between international market exposure, macroeconomic policy, and the tax and spending structure is not established. IMF economists Tytell and Wei (2004: 35) note that 'there are in fact surprisingly few tests of the constraints or "discipline effect", none of which match theoretical plausibility with robust causal evidence'. Reporting on their own results, they conclude cautiously that 'there is some *modest* evidence that financial globalization "may" have induced countries to pursue "low-inflation" monetary policies. However, there is "no evidence" that it has encouraged *low budget deficits*' (emphasis added). Indeed, interviews with financial investors suggest an overall neutrality towards government spending on welfare unless it involves massive budget deficits that have to be funded by inflationary borrowing (Mosley 2000). Harvard economist Dani Rodrik dismisses the constraints effect more emphatically. The idea that 'governments might be less inclined to squander their societies' resources if such actions were to spook foreign lenders' is disingenuous, he argues. 'In practice ...the discipline argument falls apart. Behavior in international capital markets is dominated by mood swings unrelated to fundamentals' (Rodrik 2001).

It should also be noted that from a theoretical perspective, the effects of global integration are ambiguous. This is because, as others have argued, the constraints hypothesis ignores the politically 'enabling' dynamic of globalization, which may neutralize the effects of an external discipline. The enabling effect is made manifest at the level of domestic politics via resistance to welfare retrenchment or demands for compensatory expenditure. The so-called enabling effect thus appears to create new political incentives and economic opportunities for state involvement in the economy (Quinn 1997; Swank 2003; Weiss 2003). According to the 'enabling' hypothesis, the costs and benefits of neoliberal responses are conditioned by domestic institutional structures through which social preferences are framed, organized and expressed: the expected expenditure shift under globalization might thus be neutralized, minimized or reversed by political action (Swank 2003; 2006). Studies in this vein have pointed out that for all the talk of lean governments donning the 'golden straitjacket', the practical outcome of the global neoliberal agenda over the past three decades or so has not been, in most cases, to diminish either the state's infrastructural power or its revenue base (e.g. Hobson 2003). If anything, they argue, globalization has impacted diversely in different institutional settings, helping either to restructure, reinforce, or expand state spending on social protection and to strengthen the power of many nation states to intervene in economic affairs. As one of the more recent studies concludes, 'the effects of globalization might [thus] be exaggerated in the popular discussion and might simply not exist' (Drehrer et al. 2008).

New governance structures: the regulatory state

A similar question has been raised regarding the idea of the state's dramatic withdrawal from the market economy. Here the literature, using two eyes rather than one, shows that while the withdrawal of the state as 'direct' producer of goods and services (*aka* 'privatization') has been an important general trend, so too has been the 'growth' of the apparatus of 'regulation' in those same sectors. Christopher Pierson (2004: 105) notes: 'One of the most keenly felt ironies of the "withdrawal" of the state from its role as a direct producer of goods and services has been the mushrooming of the apparatus of "regulation" through which it seeks to exercise a continuing control over its divested functions.' In short, deregulation has been accompanied by a process of reregulation, or in the words of Steven Vogel (1996): 'freer markets' mean 'more rules'.

A number of authors have thus emphasized the paradox of the deregulation trend: namely, an unexpectedly larger role for the state and a new arena for state activism (Levy-Faur and Jordana 2003; Cioffi 2005). Far from removing the state from the market, the neoliberal drive has required national authorities to set new rules of the economic game—whether devising competition policy for telecoms and other recently privatized utilities, or setting prudential norms for deregulated financial institutions (and sometimes failing to set these at all!). In turn, this has meant the creation of new governance structures to set and apply the rules (sometimes referred to as new forms of governance). In this context, a number of studies draw attention to the plethora of decentralized regulatory agencies and hybrid public–private structures which, being effectively removed from democratic oversight, in principle give the state more rather than less scope for action (Levy-Faur and Jordana 2003; Harvey 2005).[4]

However, while the growth of regulatory bodies has been a broadly observed pattern, the outcomes do not appear to support a convergence or homogenization trend. Vogel's study of the Japanese experience (2006) encapsulates some of the key findings in the comparative literature with the notion of 'patterned innovation' to indicate that the process and outcomes of reregulation remain heavily informed by specific state traditions. In one of the most comprehensive comparative studies to date, Vogel (1996) found that in spite of implementing pro-competitive regulatory reforms similar to those adopted in Britain and the United States, in practice, Japan's policymakers sought to preserve their authority in order to manage the terms of competition after reform—a conclusion reaffirmed in his follow-up study ten years later. Even financial liberalization, it appears, was not a jacket cut everywhere from the same cloth. In pace as well as approaches, states often differed, setting the rules of market opening to align with national development orientations and legitimacy needs (Thurbon 2003). Similar findings have been reported for trade and investment strategies (Thurbon and Weiss 2006), as well as for market opening in the telecommunications sector (Jho 2007; Yoo 2004).

While regulatory activism is perhaps one of the most widely discussed countertrends to the neoliberal (*qua* minimal) state, it is by no means the only one. Several new state missions have been identified in the affluent democracies, ranging from 'making systems of social protection and labour markets more employment friendly' to 'repairing the main varieties of capitalism' (Levi 2006). In Levi's terms, this is 'market-supporting'—as distinct from 'market-steering'—intervention. According to this argument, 'market-steering intervention' best describes what states did before globalization took hold. Such distinctions are most useful when applied to specific

---

[4] Sometimes referred to as new forms of governance.

activities in specific sectors, but as a general descriptor of what states do now, compared with what they did in the recent past, the 'steering versus supporting' language is perhaps too blunt as an analytical instrument. Even when utilities were under state ownership, for example, there was very little actual state 'steering' of these entities. By the same token, however, when national authorities select a technology or sector for special sponsorship and resource allocation, as they do presently—e.g. in biotechnology, nanotechnology, new energy (see below)—the dividing line between 'steering' and 'supporting' breaks down. States have always done both and the mix in any context is a matter of empirical enquiry.

The activist technology state

Another important test of the neoliberal state argument relates to the state's industrial activities. According to an influential view, states no longer do industrial policy (e.g. select or 'target' particular sectors for promotion and thus resource allocation) because this would involve interventions in the market that are no longer acceptable under the WTO. In this connection, the creation of the multilateral trade regime under the WTO, which has overseen extensive trade liberalization, is viewed as a key pillar of the neoliberal order. Where developing countries are concerned, for example, it has been powerfully argued that the WTO has been 'kicking away the ladder' by prohibiting the very policy tools—tariffs, subsidies, and capital controls, and the imposition of local content requirements on foreign companies—that industrialized countries once used in order to to grow their own economies (Chang 2002; Reinert 2007).

The ladder kicking metaphor is useful, however, only up to a point. While making it more difficult for those lower down the ladder, the rich states have been busy adding new rungs to aid their own (continuous) high-technology climb—promoting what they see as the foundation of the new knowledge economy. Under the rubric of S & T (Science and Technology) policy, the developed democracies have carved out ample room in which to grow their own industries within the multilateral framework—chiefly by setting subsidy rules that mesh with their own technology profile, which is knowledge-intensive. In such sectors, the new infant industries include biotechnology, microelectronics, and information technology, new materials, and nanotechnology. For example, the EU has doubled financial support for innovation in biotech under programmes which will run from 2007 to 2013. In most cases, the key directions are being forged and the programmes run in various forms of partnership with private-sector participants, including cofinanced VC funds, R & D consortia, and biomanufacturing facilities to assist fledgling biotechs through clinical trials. Even in 'free-market' Britain, the government has taken 'proactive steps' to greatly increase support to its biotech sector, in response to the industry's own strategic assessment, expanding R & D subsidies, developing world-class manufacturing facilities, and forging public–private collaboration between the NHS and bioscience sector.

This is, in short, infant industry promotion, high-tech style, with a renewed role for state activism (i.e. not just passively setting tariffs as in the pre-WTO period). The multilateral regime may require states to abandon certain protectionist instruments, but right across the OECD, national authorities are actively seeking ways to foster their infant industries in the leading knowledge-intensive sectors, sponsoring initiatives in biotechnology, ICT, and the fledgling nanotechnology and new energy sectors in the belief that these are fundamental to future prosperity. The rules certainly seek to discipline states to lay off specified protectionist instruments; but this does not mean that states are taking a back seat. Rather, they have shifted gear to accommodate new needs: old-style import controls and subsidized production may be largely off the agenda, but the industrialized nations (who conveniently wrote the WTO rules in the first place) now have less need of these policy tools as they embark on a technology race. For their purposes, the more appropriate forms of techno-industry promotion include R & D subsidies and cost-shared partnerships, intellectual property licensing and protection, technology procurement, standard setting, and sponsorship of venture capital funds (Weiss 2005).

The careful WTO relabelling of this activity as S & T policy is important—because language matters. But it does not hide the fact that it is effectively open economy industry policy. Otherwise put, S & T policy is a means of developing the knowledge-intensive infant industries central to the advanced industrial nations; it uses measures that are essentially *functional equivalents* of the *old infant industry* policies—once widely utilized to establish industries (in the traditional labour- and capital-intensive sectors)—but which are now largely prohibited. Thus although the WTO would appear to restrict policy space for those lower down the development ladder, the rules provide ample policy scope for those still at the top.

Varieties of capitalism: the institution-sustaining state

A fourth rejoinder to the idea of the neoliberalizing state derives from the varieties of capitalism perspective associated with the work of Peter Hall and David Soskice (2001). It offers an important theoretical challenge to the homogenization thesis (the idea that states and varieties of capitalism (VoC) are converging on the neoliberal model). VoC scholars develop a firm-centred institutional approach in order to show why global competition is not a zero-sum game in which one kind of capitalism is selected as the winner. Their perspective allows them to pinpoint different institutional strengths in each system that underpin their respective innovation capacities; moreover, these writers argue, because the national innovation system is based on institutional complementarities, a change in one arrangement that might be desirable (e.g. the welfare state) would necessitate changes in other areas (e.g. labour relations), which might be economically undesirable or politically impracticable. The general argument is that there is no one best system of political economy for generating growth in a global economy. In this framework, CMEs offer an efficient and stable alternative to LMEs (*qua* neoliberal capitalism), and firms with their distinctive national innovation capacities, which in turn rely on distinctive institutional complexes, are the central actors generating persistent differences across countries. Thus some nations maintain strong labour regulations and high welfare spending because firms find this arrangement to be most efficient for their technology profile. Firms specializing in highly engineered high-cost products, as in Germany, for example, require highly skilled labour; this implies lengthy training, long-term commitment and stable employment relations. Employers in such countries can therefore be expected to support the institutions that complement their production profile (Hall and Soskice 2001).

Although the VoC thesis offers a rigorous theoretical rebuttal of the neoliberal homogenization thesis, it has certain shortcomings of its own. Some critics charge that it overstates the systemic coherence and 'locked in' nature of national institutions and thus presumes a degree of stability that ignores the transformative role of agency (see e.g. Crouch 2005). Another limitation of the VoC perspective is a tendency to portray the role of the state in largely passive, functional terms. Its proponents see the world as a two-forms-of-capitalism game in which the state remains in the background, supporting the status quo in conformity with firms' requirements (Schmidt 2002). Governed market economies in which economic and political actors together coordinate change are not part of its framework. Even for CMEs, this neglect has led analysts to overlook the important ways in which these political economies adjust to economic and social challenges. It has been argued, for example, that the Dutch and German states played a critical role in supporting their innovation systems by reforming social policy, labour-market policy, and wage policies in the context of slow growth and fiscal austerity, sometimes working within existing corporatist frameworks, at other times, suspending or dismantling them in order to secure urgently needed reforms (Hemerijck and Vail 2006). Such criticisms regarding the overstatement of systemic coherence and the neglect of the state's more active role can also be applied more broadly to the way in which LMEs are constructed in the comparative capitalism literature, a theme to which we return in the final section.

THE STATE AS SOLUTION: THE RISE (AND DEMISE?) OF GOVERNED MARKET ECONOMIES

A third perspective on the state in the economy sees state power not as a problem, nor as tightly constrained by economic integration, but as a potential source of solutions to the problem of national economic development. In the post-war period a number of countries in East Asia—beginning with Japan in the 1970s, followed soon after by its former colonies Korea and Taiwan, then further south, by Singapore—achieved the highest sustained growth rates ever recorded as they speedily transformed their industrial structures. How had they risen so far and so fast, out of poverty into the rich-country OECD club virtually within a generation, building successful industries from scratch and rapidly closing the technology gap? In the normal scheme of things, climbing the ladder of industrial development meant steadily acquiring prowess in traditional labour-intensive sectors like food, textiles, steel, and the like; but East Asian firms went further and faster—eventually creating a swathe of high-technology industries, which included super-computers, robotics, semiconductors, and flat panel displays. By any stretch, this was an exceptional achievement in the history of industrialization.

It is no exaggeration to say that the rise of East Asia posed a serious challenge for economic theory with its market-led view of economic development.[5] For exceptional results quite plausibly raise the possibility that something 'out of the ordinary' has produced them. Development scholars and area specialists proposed that the non-ordinary factor consisted in the role of the state. State actors in each setting, they argued, took a prominent and proactive role in coordinating structural change and the upgrading of technology (Johnson 1982, 1987; Amsden 1989; Wade 1990; Evans 1995; Chang 2002). From these analyses, the East Asian four emerged as different instances of a distinctive type of political economy, to which the terms 'developmental state' and 'governed market' system were applied. Using different methods, national authorities in each setting pursued an industrial strategy (i.e. selective or sectoral industrial policies) that combined import substitution with export orientation, while focusing on raising the investible surplus and shifting the technology profile upstream.

However, given the prevailing theoretical assumptions about government failure (and indeed the fact that industrial policies in various parts of the world were often associated with failure or lacklustre results), much subsequent debate centred on why, in these settings, such policies seemed to succeed more often than fail. Some studies drew attention to the importance of an incentive structure in which state support was conditioned by performance requirements:

rather than simply offered as handouts, subsidies were made conditional on exports and protection was time-limited (Johnson 1982; Amsden 1989). Conditionality thus had the positive feature of ensuring that the incentives were captured by firms that were able to compete in international markets, rather than going scatter-gun fashion to the strugglers. Others drew attention to much 'below the radar' ('administrative guidance') activity in which engineering-trained bureaucrats worked with domestic producers to identify new export opportunities and to remove obstacles, often 'nudging' international companies to work with potential local suppliers rather than source abroad.   (Wade 1990)

But in spite of their different emphases, these studies also enjoined us to look behind the policies to the state's institutional structure and normative political environment. Key to understanding why East Asian policies were largely effective, they argued, was the role of a competent economic bureaucracy, imbued with a catch-up mission and sufficiently insulated from the push and pull of special interests. Thus, keeping

---

[5] For accounts that try to squeeze East Asia into free-market theory, and their counter-critique, see Wade (1992). The Japanese-funded World Bank (1993) reassessment of the whole East Asian development experience is widely viewed as a striking example of the attempt at paradigm maintenance and efforts to square the circle. For a balanced critique, see Lall (1994) and Cassen and Lall (1996).

definitions to a minimum, a developmental state could be defined partly by what it looks like—reliance on a pilot agency or network of agencies with Weberian characteristics of bureaucracy (competent, cohesive, mission-oriented, relative political autonomy or independence from special-interest pressures); and partly by what it does—technology catch-up and strategic (sectoral) industry policy. In its original formulation, the developmentalism of the developmental state was thus linked to its centralized bureaucratic control. But this understanding of the dynamics of the developmental state's effectiveness changes as industrial development proceeds, as the research discussed next makes clear.

In further refinements of the idea of state effectiveness, the developmental state—while relatively autonomous from political pressures—is at the same time highly embedded in the surrounding economy, and connected to the private sector via trade associations. Its 'embedded autonomy' (Evans 1995) is what keeps it from capture on the one hand and predation on the other. In other words, if it is to be at all effective, the developmental state needs not just an independent sense of purpose; it also needs access to and information from the economic actors it seeks to influence. Although often using different language, a good deal of comparative research has offered support for this idea, highlighting the regularized forms of interaction and constant tailoring of policies to meet the changing needs of firms not only as economies opened up to international markets, but also as the tasks of technological innovation have become more complex (e.g. Anchordoguy 1988: 513; Weiss 1998; Amsden and Chu 2003; Wade 2003; Weiss and Thurbon 2004; Jho 2007).

The results of this body of research suggest that in moving up the technology ladder, the developmental state's ability to 'impose' its decisions is of diminishing relevance to its transformative capacity. Of greater importance is a governance structure through which the state is able to institute a continuing conversation with economic actors about the opportunities for innovation and the obstacles to be overcome, and not least, the capacity to pursue such opportunities with a performance-based incentives structure that disciplines its beneficiaries. 'Governed interdependence' (Weiss 1998) is one way of conceptualizing the dynamics of this goal-directed governance structure, prevalent in the industrial bureaucracies of East Asia, but not necessarily confined to that region. In the case of the East Asian four, theorists of the developmental state argue that because of their normative and institutional equipment, these states had the capacity to produce effective outcomes with more consistency than most other developing countries. Thus, when looking to the much more 'mixed' development records of, say, Brazil and India or the countries of Southeast Asia and Latin America more generally, the difference they argue lies not in the presence or absence of industry policies per se, but in the character and purposiveness of their bureaucracies, in the extent of their political cohesion, and in the manner of their public–private linkages (e.g. Kohli 2004; Evans 1995).[6]

---

[6] Both Kohli and Evans analyse comparative economic outcomes in several developing countries, offering different versions of state efficacy.

Accordingly, the idea of the developmental state does not entail either state dominance *over* business or timeless institutions for governing the economy (Johnson 1999). More generally, the relations between government and business in the neodevelopmental state differ from the more top-down model of the 1960s and 1970s. In the updated ('open economy industrial policy') version, the state actively engages a wide range of public and private actors in technology-focused networks, both domestic and international, which are tasked with the formulation and implementation of policies (Jho 2007; Pereira 2008; Weiss and Thurbon 2004; Ritchie 2002: 19–20). In Korea, for example, techno-nationalist ambitions continue to flourish in agencies most closely connected to the nation's industrial strength in ICT, in particular, the Ministry of Information and Communications (MIC). No longer commanding economic outcomes from the heights, state agencies like MIC now coordinate a network of policymakers, local and international firms. In such cases, the state's effectiveness in coordinating more complex industrial upgrading in the context of increasing openness has come to rely more heavily on a governance structure involving intense policy dialogue and partnering with the private sector and on the coordination of inter-firm networks for product development. Thus, while some have posited a neoliberal restructuring of the developmental state (Moon and Rhyu 1999; Pirie 2005), the contrasting hypothesis of 'liberalization as a development strategy' (Jho 2007) seems closer to the mark. Moving outside the Asian setting, a parallel argument has been applied to the state's high-technology role in Ireland. Indeed some see Ireland as a new ('networked') type of DS (e.g. O'Riain 2004). Whether such new labels are warranted, they should not be allowed to blind us to important parallels with the neodevelopmental states of East Asia.

More generally, there is one common ingredient of developmental states that lies beyond the grasp of all such new labels, namely, the political 'will' to pursue transformative projects. Although it is fashionable to emphasize state capacity constraints in a globally interconnected environment, the prior importance of political will is much more easily overlooked or taken for granted.[7] Yet political will (*qua* commitment to industrial transformation) is the fundamental ingredient of state developmentalism. In its absence, the capacity to meet new demands under changing conditions (e.g. via new governance structures) will come to naught. As the most comprehensive study of Japan's remodelled capitalism observes, for all the liberalizing reforms, what remains in place, is: 'a [bureaucratic] commitment to promoting Japanese industry, a tradition of working closely with the private sector, and a fierce determination to preserve its own authority' (Vogel 2006: 218). In this light, the argument that 'governments are most constrained when they believe themselves to be powerless, and least constrained when they do not' (Vogel 1996), deserves to be taken seriously.

Debate over the developmental state argument has been both broad and deep, covering issues ranging from the sources of state developmentalism to its

---

[7] The self-conscious articulation of this principle by the industry policy arm of the Taiwanese state is discussed in Weiss and Thurbon (2004).

consequences and, most recently, to its institutional viability in a global economic environment.[8] Although for many the developmental state 'has been one of the most compelling explanations' for Asian economic development, the question of how far this depended on a particular kind of governmental bureaucracy is difficult to determine because of the coexistence of several other factors, including favourable international political and economic conditions (Pempel 1999: 136). More contentious however is the extent to which developmental strategies have paid off. Indeed, the debate over the effectiveness of industrial policy is inconclusive because of a deficient methodology, as a result of which econometric models fail to capture the policy effects (Rodrik 2008).[9] Criticisms of the developmental state interpretation of East Asia's rise have thus ranged from sweeping claims that intervention made no difference to East Asian growth, to the opposite assertion that these economies would have grown even faster without government guidance.[10] While it is reasonable to approach with caution claims about the effectiveness of the developmental state's industrial policies, this is a far remove from the neoclassical assertion that the East Asian four industrialized by following free-market prescriptions. At the very least, the fact that industrial policies were used abundantly throughout the 'miracle' economies of East Asia in their fast-growth phase belies the 'failure' assumptions of the neoliberal interpretation (Chang 2007).

In the most recent version of the neoclassical/neoliberal[11] critique, commentators have suggested that the Asian financial crisis of the late 1990s demonstrates the ultimate failure of the GME or developmental state model of development and that Taiwan, South Korea, and Japan have been discarding their governed market system, reforming themselves along the lines of the American market-led model. Thus, this reasoning continues, whatever validity that governed markets, sectoral-industrial policy, and the developmental state may have possessed in earlier times, their time is past.[12] Two points are in order here. First, regarding the demise of East Asia's erstwhile governed market economies, suffice it to note that the more sustained empirical research in the region—much of which has been discussed earlier—suggests that developmental states have been reinvented rather than retired (e.g. Woo-Cumings 1999; Amsden and Chu 2003; Vogel 2006: 219). Many of the

---

[8] For an overview of the main issues, see the important collection edited by Woo-Cumings (1999).

[9] For example, as indicated earlier, the East Asian approach typically involved two important features, neither of which are captured by existing econometric models. The first was the existence of engineer-type bureaucrats who, in a sustained dialogue with industry actors, regularly analysed the import profile in order to identify the higher-value added items that could, with sufficient public encouragement (e.g. 'nudging') and support, be made locally for export (Wade 1990). The second feature was the attachment of incentives to measurable performance conditions. The point is that these policy measures are hard to capture in econometric models, which are more at home dealing with such items as tariffs and official subsidies (see e.g. Noland and Pack 2003).

[10] See n. 5.

[11] The terms are sometimes used interchangeably to indicate the association of neoclassical economic theory with neoliberal policies.

[12] Wade summarizes this critique in the Introduction to his 2003 edition of *Governing the Market*. For an assessment of the book's arguments and their applicability to the East Asian region post-Asian financial crisis, see the 2004 edition of @@@*Issues & Studies* 40(1), ed. Andrew Marble.

same analysts have also observed that—from China to India and South Africa—their developmental strategies continue to offer a point of reference and model for emulation. Second, a very large dose of caution is warranted when issuing comparative judgements that elevate the virtues of one model over others. This point is vividly underlined by the sudden swing by many of its former admirers against the American system. Laid low by the 2007–8 financial collapse and by its spectacular failure to curb widespread abuses and corruption (Altman 2009), the free-market model is increasingly the object of scorn rather than admiration or emulation.

This leads to our final question as to how well the United States fits its own label. An emerging literature on this topic throws into doubt the idea of a coherent neoliberal model to which other states are allegedly conforming.

Theory versus Practice: In Search of the Neoliberal State

....

Analysts often hesitate when classifying countries as this or that type of capitalism led by this or that type of state. Yet they have hesitated less when applying the neoliberal label, regularly treating the United States (along with Britain) as a clear instance of a liberal political economy in which the state remains mostly aloof from the market. In practice, of course, the American neoliberal model of free-market-minimal state is not a plausible description of how any market economy 'works'. Indeed, it more aptly describes countries where markets are dysfunctional or weak, such as Nigeria or Haiti. Ironically, however, it 'is' a plausible description of how the US financial sector worked—where since 1999, three critical prudential regulations have been stripped away or rejected[13]—at least until its spectacular collapse and bailout in 2008. Beyond the (albeit major) exception of the state's regulatory approach to the financial sector, the reality of the United States and the market systems of Western Europe is not the

---

[13] Among the most important regulatory acts of omission and commission were: (a) the 1999 repeal of the Glass Steagall Act which separated commercial banks and investment banks, thus enabling the growth of a vast unregulated shadow banking industry; (b) the 2002 Congressional exemption from regulation of numerous derivatives (including credit default swaps), enabling massive expansion of unregulated financial products; and (c) the 2004 decision of the Securities and Exchange Commission to remove an old regulation limiting the amount of debt that the big Wall Street investment banks could take on, thus unshackling billions held in reserve to cushion against losses. The *New York Times* Editorial 'Don't Blame the New Deal', 28 September 2008, gives an instructive account of regulatory failure; some excellent pieces of *NYT* investigative journalism are reported in the months of September and October, including Stephen Labaton's 'Agency's '04 Rule Let Banks Pile Up New Debt', October 2. For a broader discussion of the repercussions and responses to the US financial breakdown see Simon Johnson (2009).

minimal state but 'the embedded market', for these economies have 'the largest, most powerful and most influential governments the world has ever seen' (Kay 2004: 311). Beyond the general truism that all modern markets are politically embedded, however, there is more to the American model than meets the neoliberal eye. This 'something more' has often been noted with regard to aspects of its labour market (Blyth 2003), its social spending (Galbraith 2007) and its home-ownership model (Seabrooke 2006; Schwartz 2008), where state intervention has been significant in shaping the ways that these markets work.

Perhaps even more at odds with the neoliberal tag is the US innovation model and the public–private networks that sustain it. In this context, what deserves emphasis is not the state's liberalism, but its *developmentalism*, which in some major respects pushes it towards the governed market end of the spectrum (Block 2008; Weiss 2008). Although virtually invisible in the story that is normally told of post-war US development, the federal state has been deeply involved in governing the market, financing techno-industry development, licensing, protecting, and procuring its firms' innovations, as well as helping to create and expand their markets at home and abroad. A substantial research output on US innovation shows that most of the high-technology sectors in which the US economy now leads—from computers and software technologies to semiconductors and aeronautics—owe their start to the funding, infrastructure, and purchasing programmes of the state (Mowery and Nelson 1999). Even the development of a commercial biotechnology industry is a state-led story whose strategic origins have only recently come to light through archival analysis of declassified material (Hurt 2008). In particular, it is difficult to overstate the developmental importance of federal 'technology procurement' as an engine of US innovation. In other words, to the question: 'where do US innovations come from?' a very large part of the answer would include: 'government contracting to buy things from the private sector that do not yet exist or which need to be adapted for public use' (Weiss 2008). That, in essence, is the meaning of technology procurement. Its role in promoting the IT sector and the emergence of Silicon Valley has been well documented, notwithstanding the myth of pure market development (Kenney 2000). If the early stages of Silicon Valley had no need of private venture capital or stock markets, it was because it could rely on 'the biggest angel of them all' (Leslie 2000)—namely, the US government—which provided both the capital and the demand pull of a huge federal market. Today, armed with an annual procurement budget of $450 billion—more than $1 trillion if the states are included—the state plays a very large role in the economy, not least through proactive, innovation-led procurement.

Lacking the broad political legitimacy and hence 'normalization' of the East Asian version, US developmentalism has nonetheless remained relatively 'hidden' (Block 2008). Indeed, one may observe that in the very period when neoliberal theory became globalized in political discourse, US policy began to diverge more markedly in practice: in the course of the 1980s when the United States, challenged by Japan, began to lose its lead in one advanced technology after another, the federal agencies began imparting directional thrust to the economy, fostering a series of public–private R & D partnerships, fielding a host of manufacturing extension services, and establishing a federally-funded innovation programme that now disperses more than US$2 billion annually as the world's largest venture capital fund (Weiss 2008).

The problem with labels

Does this mean that the United States is no longer an LME? Or does it mean that such comparative capitalism typologies have more limited value? Analysts whose work was discussed earlier have developed the notion of institutional complementarity to justify their systemic labels and to explain why national systems are unlikely to converge. As well as drawing attention to the benefits of retaining existing institutional arrangements, the idea of complementarity draws attention to the attendant costs and difficulties of making changes to the rules of the game in one area without affecting all the other interconnected elements (Hall and Soskice 2001; cf. Amable 2000). However, as we saw, critics charge that this approach overstates systemic coherence, thereby ignoring or dismissing the significance of institutional anomalies or hybrid forms (Campbell 2004; Crouch 2005). Much of this discussion about institutional complementarity, however, relates to the micro-institutions of the economy, not to the state.

The state is a different story. For one thing, it is internally a quintessentially, non-unitary configuration whose various components have crystallized at different points in time, experienced often separate histories, and become linked to different constituencies. Complementarity among the various parts (agencies) is therefore likely to be rare rather than typical. Thus even in the same issue area (the economic–industrial bureaucracy for example), actors in one part of the institution may be, or become, state-power averse and laissez-faire in their approach to economic advancement (notably, for example, in the US financial administration and its regulatory bodies); in another agency, however, state actors may be quite differently oriented, basing their approach on the understanding that national (*qua* economic) security and government involvement are tightly coupled (e.g. the network of US agencies involved in technology procurement, for example, the Department of Defense, the CIA, NASA, the Department of Energy, the National Institutes of Health, the Department of Agriculture).

The problems raised by tying polymorphous institutions like states to particular labels are thus especially apparent in the US context where one finds both liberal and networked statist (governed market) components in those parts of the state that interface with the private sector. In the US setting, this internal disjuncture between liberalism and statism—between opposition to and support for the use of state power for economic development—is reflected in a normative environment that regularly demonizes industry policy for strictly commercial results, unless framed in the language of national security and linked to its pursuit. The result is often a hybridization of the state whereby national security agencies take on private-sector characteristics (e.g. the CIA becomes an angel investor taking equity in private companies in order to fund the commercialization of security-relevant projects).[14] Alternatively, a quasi-hybridization takes place via the reconstruction of national-security agency missions to encompass commercial goals (see e.g. Fong 2000).

In considering the implications for identifying the neoliberal state or even its developmental counterpart, Colin Crouch's comments seem appropriate: it is not that we can or should abandon labelling as such, since it is useful, even necessary, but labels should come with a cautionary note attached so that instead of asking 'to what type does this case correspond?' one would ask 'examples of what type do I find in this case and in what proportions?' (2008: 533, 535). Whether there are now so many elements of the governed market type that the US state can no longer be considered an example of the neoliberal type that it was once thought to be remains a question for systematic empirical research. But the point remains that even considering the United States as the most widely recognized exemplar of an LME, there is more scope for variety 'within' a state type than existing comparative capitalism categories allow. As global integration proceeds and as economies approach the technological frontier, so the role of state agencies appears to take on renewed importance. Some governance structures and practices of the governed market economies as they evolved in East Asia are now diffusing to the major economies, perhaps more markedly in the United States than in other Anglophone economies, some of whose institutional innovations now depart substantially from the standard LME model.

CONCLUSION

The theory of neoliberal state transformation that has dominated the social science literature in recent decades is in part prescriptive (states 'should' act in certain ways and not others), and in part deductive (given certain conditions, states 'must' act in given ways). Empirically, however, the idea of a neoliberal or laissez-faire state, a developmentally inert state—encaged by global markets and confined to the role of market facilitator-cum-competition regulator—is not established.

There is no question that liberalizing reforms—from privatization via the sale of state-owned companies to trade, investment and financial liberalization via the negotiation of bilateral and multilateral treaties—have been widely diffused throughout the globe. Significant policy liberalization, however, has not retired the state from transformative economic tasks. Even so-called liberal states at the technological frontier are deeply if not widely engaged in governing the market for high technology, targeting knowledge-intensive sectors for special promotion as the global technology race intensifies. Climbing the ladder of technology development is a continuous enterprise and where the stakes are high, states rarely leave things to

---

[14] The CIA's hybridized model of technology procurement is discussed in Weiss (2008).

the market. More significant than the pressures of the international environment are those emanating from the normative environment that informs and sustains state purpose. Despite some cracks in the latter, there remains a greater degree of legitimacy for economic activism than for neoliberalism.

Arguably, the neoliberal state is a fiction because it treats the state as unitary and thereby misidentifies the part for the whole. (The United States—neoliberal in finance, but interventionist in national innovation—is the exemplary case.) Yet the fiction has been *influential.* One reason why it has been so influential is that the challenges of globalization that allegedly *constrain* state activism are very well publicized (though not necessarily well established—as we saw in the case of the relationship between capital mobility and macroeconomic policy); whereas the challenges of globalization that *valorize* state activism are much less widely discussed, let alone well understood. One reason for this lopsidedness, I have suggested in the introduction to this chapter, bears on the sociology of knowledge, namely, the intellectual legacy of cold-war politics.

We can expect some of this analytical lopsidedness to be rectified as the worst financial crisis in history begins to demand rather more, not less, capacity from state authorities over the coming years. Such new circumstances should prompt a research agenda that delivers a more nuanced understanding of the ways in which the maintenance and growth of the global economy—far from precluding an active role for the state—tends increasingly to demand it.

REFERENCES

ALIC, J., DAVID C. MOWERY, and EDWARD S. RUBIN (2003). 'U.S. Technology and Innovation Policies: Lessons for Climate Change', Pew Center on Global Climate Change, Nov. 2003.

ALTMAN, ROGER C. (2009). 'The Great Crash, 2008', *Foreign Affairs* 88 (Jan/Feb).

AMABLE, BRUNO (2000). 'Institutional Complementarity and Diversity of Social Systems of Innovation and Production', *Review of International Political Economy* 2/4: 645–87.

AMMAN, EDMUND and JOAO CARLOS FERRAZ (2004). 'Ownership Structure in the Post-privatized Brazilian Steel Industry: Complexity, Instability and the Lingering Role of the State', Centre on Regulation and Competition, *Working Paper Series, No. 75*, University of Manchester.

AMSDEN, ALICE (1989). *Asia's Next Giant: South Korea and Late Industrialisation,* (New York: Oxford University Press).

——and WAN-WEN CHU (2003). *Beyond Late Development: Taiwan's Upgrading Policies,* (Cambridge, MA: MIT Press).

ANCHORDOGUY, MARIE (1988). 'Mastering the Market: Japanese Government Targeting of the Computer Industry', *Industrial Organization* 42(3): 509–43.

BELL, STEPHEN (2005). 'How Tight are the Policy Constraints? The Policy Convergence Thesis, Institutionally Situated Actors and Expansionary Monetary Policy in Australia', *New Political Economy* 10(1): 67–92.

BIERSTEKER, THOMAS J. (1990). 'Reducing the Role of the State in the Economy: A Conceptual Exploration of IMF and World Bank Prescriptions', *International Studies Quarterly* 34(4): 477–92.

BLOCK, FRED (2008). 'Swimming Against the Current: The Rise of a Hidden Developmental State in the United States', *Politics & Society* 36: 169–206.

BLYTH, MARK (2003). 'Same as it Never was? Typology and Temporality in the Varieties of Capitalism', *Comparative European Politics* 1(2): 215–25.

CAMPBELL, JOHN L. (2004). *Institutional Change and Globalization*, (Princeton, NJ: Princeton University Press).

——and LEON N. LINDBERG (1990). 'Property Rights and the Organization of Economic Activity by the State', *American Sociological Review* 55(5): 634–47.

——and OVE K. PEDERSEN (2001). 'Chapter 1: The Rise of Neoliberalism and Institutional Analysis', in Campbell and Pedersen (eds.), *The Rise of Neoliberalism and Institutional Analysis*, (Princeton, NJ: Princeton University Press).

CASSEN, ROBERT and SANJAYA LALL (1996). 'Lessons of East Asian Development', *Journal of the Japanese and International Economies* 10(3): 326–34.

CERNY, PHILIP (1995). 'Globalization and the Changing Logic of Collective Action', *International Organization* 49(4): S39–S64.

——(1997). 'International Finance and the Erosion of State Policy Capacity', in Colin Crouch and Wolfgang Streeck (1997).

CHANG, HA-JOON (2002). *Kicking Away the Ladder. Development Strategy in Historical Perspective*, (London: Anthem Press).

——(2007). *The East Asian Development Experience: The Miracle, the Crisis, and the Future*, (London: Palgrave Macmillan).

CIEPLEY DAVID (2000). 'Why the state was dropped in the first place: A prequel to Skocpol's "bringing the state back in"'. *Critical Review*, 14 (2&3): 157–213.

CIOFFI, JOHN W. (2005). 'Corporate Governance Reform, Regulatory Politics, and the Foundations of Finance Capitalism in the United States and Germany', *CLP Research Paper No. 6*, Working Paper Series.

COLEMAN, WILLIAM D. and C. CHIASSON (2002). 'State Power, Transformative Capacity and Adapting to Globalization: An Analysis of French Agricultural Policy, 1960–2000', *Journal of European Public Policy* 9(2): 168–85.

CROUCH, COLIN (2005). *Capitalist Diversity and Change: Recombinant Governance and Institutional Entrepreneurs*, (Oxford: Oxford University Press).

——and W. STREECK (1997). *Political Economy of Modern Capitalism: Mapping Convergence and Diversity*, (London: Sage).

DREHER, AXEL, JAN-EGBERT STURM, and HEINRICH W. URSPRUNG (2002). 'The Impact of Globalization on the Composition of Government Expenditures: Evidence from Panel Data', *Public Choice* 134: 263–29.

——J-E STURM, and H. W. URSPRUNG (2008). 'The impact of globalization on the composition of government expenditures: Evidence from panel data', *Public Choice*, 134 (3–4): 263–292.

EVANS, PETER (1995). *Embedded Autonomy: States and Industrial Transformation*, (Princeton, NJ: Princeton University Press).

FISCHER, STANLEY (1998). 'Capital Account Liberalization and the Role of the IMF': http://www.imf.org/external/np/speeches/1997/091997.htm.

FONG, GLENN (2000). 'Breaking New Ground or Breaking the Rules: Strategic Reorientation in U.S. Industrial Policy', *International Security* 25(2): 152–86.

FRIEDMAN, THOMAS (2000). *The Lexus and the Olive Tree*, (New York: Basic Books).

GALBRAITH, JAMES K. (2007). 'What is the American Model Really About? Soft Budgets and the Keynesian Devolution', *Industrial and Corporate Change* 16(1): 1–18.

GAMBLE, ANDREW (1988). *The Free Economy and the Strong State: The Politics of Thatcherism*. London: Macmillan.

GARRETT, GEOFFREY (1998). 'Global Markets and National Politics: Collision Course or Virtuous Circle?', *International Organization* 52(4): 787–824.

——and DEBORAH MITCHELL (2001). 'Globalization, Government Spending, and Taxation in the OECD', *European Journal of Political Research* 39:145–77.

HAGGARD, STEPHAN (2004). 'On Governing the Market', *Issues and Studies* 40(1): 14–45.

HALL, PETER A. and D. SOSKICE (2001). 'An Introduction to Varieties of Capitalism', in P. A. Hall and D. Soskice (eds.), *Varieties of Capitalism: The Institutional Foundations of Comparative Advantage*, (New York, NY: Oxford University Press), pp. 1–70.

HARVEY, DAVID (2005). *A Brief History of Neoliberalism*, (New York: Oxford University Press).

HELD, DAVID, ANTHONY McGREW, DAVID GOLDBLATT, and JONATHAN PERRATON (1999). *Global Transformations*, (Cambridge: Polity Press).

HEMERIJCK, ANSTON and MARK VAIL (2006). 'The Forgotten Center: State Activism and Corporatist Adjustment in Holland and Germany', in Jonah Levy (ed.), *The State After Statism*, (Cambridge, MA: Harvard University Press).

HIRSCHMAN, ALBERT (1997). *The Passions and the Interests: Political Arguments for Capitalism before its Triumph*, (Princeton, NJ: Princeton University Press).

HIRST, PAUL and G. THOMPSON (1996). *Globalization in Question*, (Cambridge: Polity Press).

HOBSON, JOHN M. (2003). 'Disappearing Taxes of the "Race to the Middle"? Fiscal Policy in the OECD', in L. Weiss (ed.), *States in the Global Economy*, (Cambridge: Cambridge University Press).

HURT, SHELLEY (2008). 'The Military's Hidden Hand: Examining the Dual-Use Origins of Agricultural Biotechnology in the American Context, 1969–1976'. Paper presented at the Berkeley Workshop on 'The US as a Hidden Developmental State', UC Berkeley, June.

JAYASURIYA, KANISHKA (2005). 'Beyond Institutional Fetishism: From the Developmental to the Regulatory State', *New Political Economy* 10(3): 381–97.

JHO, WHASUN (2007). 'Liberalisation as a Development Strategy: Network Governance in the Korean Mobile Telecom Market', *Governance* 20(4): 633–54.

JOHNSON, CHALMERS (1982). *MITI and the Japanese Miracle: The Growth of Industrial Policy, 1925–1975*. Stanford, CA: Stanford University Press.

——(1987). 'Political Institutions and Economic Performance: The Government–Business Relationship in Japan, South Korea, and Taiwan', in Frederic Deyo (ed.), *The Political Economy of the New Asian Industrialism*, (Ithaca, NY: Cornell University Press).

——(1999). 'The Developmental State: Odyssey of a Concept', in Woo-Cumings (1999).

JOHNSON, SIMON (2009). 'The Quiet Coup', *The Atlantic Online*, May.

KAISER, EDGAR and AARON MATTHEW LAING (2001). 'Have We Overestimated the Effects of Neoliberalism and Globalization? Some Speculations on the Anomalous Stability of Taxes on Business', in Campbell and Pedersen (eds).

KATZENSTEIN, PETER (1984). *Corporatism and Change*, (Ithaca, NY: Cornell University Press).

KAY, JOHN (2004). *The Truth About Markets: Their Genius, Their Limits, Their Follies*, (London: Penguin).

KENNEY, MARTIN (ed.) (2000). *Understanding Silicon Valley: The Anatomy of an Entrepreneurial Region*. Stanford, CA: Stanford University Press.

KOHLI, ATUL (2004). *State-directed Development: Political Power and Industrialization in the Global Periphery*, (New York: Cambridge University Press).

LALL, SANJAYA (1994). 'The East Asian Miracle: Does the Bell Toll for Industrial Strategy?', *World Development* 22(4): 645–54.

LESLIE, STUART W. (2000). 'The Biggest "Angel" of Them All: The Military and the Making of Silicon Valley', in Kenney (2000).

LEVY-FAUR, DAVID and JACINT JORDANA (eds.) (2003). *The Politics of Regulation*, (London: Edward Elgar).

LIST, FRIEDRICH (1841). *The National System of Political Economy*, trans. Sampson S. Lloyd, 1885.

LORIAUX, MICHAEL (2003). 'France: A New "Capitalism of Voice"?', in L. Weiss (ed.), *States in the Global Economy*, (Cambridge: Cambridge University Press).

LÜTZ, SUSANNE and DAGMAR EBERLE (2004). 'From National Diversity Towards Transnational Homogenization? Corporate Governance Regulation Between Market and Multi-Level Governance'. Paper prepared for the ARCCGOR Inaugural Workshop, Amsterdam, 17–18 Dec.

MANN, MICHAEL (1986). *The Sources of Social Power: A History of Power from the Beginning to A.D. 1760*, vol. I. (Cambridge: Cambridge University Press).

MOON, CHUNG-IN and SANG-YOUNG RHYU (1999). 'The State, Structural Rigidity, and the End of Asian Capitalism', in R. Robison, M. Beeson, K. Jayasuriya, and H-Rae Kim (eds.), *Politics and Markets in the Wake of the Asian Crisis*, (London: Routledge), 77–98.

MOSLEY, LAYNA (2000). 'Room to Move: International Financial Markets and National Welfare States', *International Organization* 54: 737–73.

MOWERY, DAVID C. and RICHARD R. NELSON (1999). 'Explaining Industrial Leadership', in D. C. Mowery and R. Nelson (eds.), *Sources of Industrial Leadership*, (New York: Cambridge University Press).

NOLAND, M. and H. PACK (2003). *Industrial Policy in an Era of Globalization: Lessons from Asia*, (Washington DC: Institute for International Economics).

O'RIAIN, SEAN (2004). *The Politics of High-Tech Growth: Developmental Network States in the Global Economy*, (Cambridge: Cambridge University Press).

PEMPEL, T. J. (1999). 'The Developmental Regime in a Changing World Economy'. In M. Woo-Cumings (ed), *The Developmental State*. Ithaca, NY: Cornell University Press.

PEREIRA, ALEXIUS (2008). 'Whither the Developmental State? Explaining Singapore's Continued Developmentalism'. *Third World Quarterly*, 29(6): 1189–203.

PIERSON, CHRISTOPHER (2004). *The Modern State*, 2nd edn. (London: Routledge).

PIRIE, IAIN (2005). 'The New Korean State', *New Political Economy* 10(1): 25–42.

POLANYI, KARL (1944 [2001]). *The Great Transformation: The Political and Economic Origins of our Times*, (New York: Rinehart & Co) (version in print: Beacon Press, 2001).

PONTUSSON, JONAS (2005). *Inequality and Prosperity: Social Europe Vs. Liberal America*, (Ithaca, NY: Cornell University Press).

PRASAD, MONICA (2006). *The Politics of Free Markets: The Rise of Neoliberal Economic Policies in Britain, France, Germany, and the United States*, (Chicago: University of Chicago Press).

QUINN, DENNIS (1997). 'The Correlates of Change in International Financial Regulation', *American Political Science Review* 91: 531–49.

REINERT, ERIK S. (2007). *How Rich Countries Got Rich and Why Poor Countries Stay Poor*, (London: Constable and Robinson).

RITCHIE, BRYAN K. (2002). 'Foreign Direct Investment and Intellectual Capital Formation in Southeast Asia', OECD Development Centre Working Paper No. 194. Paris.

RODRIK, DANI (2007). *One Economics, Many Recipes: Globalization, Institutions, and Economic Growth*, (Princeton, NJ: Princeton University Press).

——(2008). 'Normalizing Industrial Policy', Commission on Growth and Development Working Paper No. 3, Washington DC.

RUTTAN, VERNON W. (2004). 'Military Procurement and Technology Development'. Febr. 2004 Draft, Department of Applied Economics, Hubert H. Humphrey Institute of Public Affairs, University of Minnesota.

Schmidt, Vivienne (2002). *The Futures of European Capitalism*, (Oxford/New York: Oxford University Press).

Seabrooke, L. (2006). *The Social Sources of Financial Power: Domestic Legitimacy and International Financial Orders*, (Ithaca, NY: Cornell University Press).

Schwartz, Herman (2008). 'Housing, Global Finance, and U.S. Hegemony: Building Conservative Politics One Brick at a Time'. *Comparative European Politics*, 6: 262–84.

Shaffer, Greg (2003). *Defending Interests: Public–Private Partnerships in W.T.O. Litigation.* (Washington, DC: Brookings Institution Press).

Simmons, Beth A., F. Dobbin, and G. Garrett (2006). 'Introduction: The International Diffusion of Liberalism', *International Organization* 60 (Fall): 781–810.

——Frank Dobbin, and G. Garrett (eds.) (2008). *The Global Diffusion of Markets and Democracy*, (Cambridge: Cambridge University Press).

Skocpol, Theda (1985). *Bringing the State Back In*, (Cambridge: Cambridge University Press).

Smith, Adam (1776). *An Inquiry into the Causes of the Wealth of Nations*, ed. Edward Cannan 1904. 5th edn. (London, Methuen & Co).

Soederberg, Susanne, Georg Menz, and Philip G. Cerny (eds.) (2005). *Internalizing Globalization: The Rise of Neoliberalism and the Erosion of National Varieties of Capitalism*, (London: Palgrave Macmillan).

Stiglitz, Joseph (2000). 'Capital Account Liberalization, Economic Growth, and Instability', *World Development*, 6(28): 1075–86.

Swank, Duane (1998). 'Funding the Welfare State: Globalization and the Taxation of Business in Advanced Market Economies'. *Political Studies* 46: 671–92.

——(2003). 'Withering Welfare? Globalization, Political Economic Institutions, and Contemporary Welfare States', in Linda Weiss (ed.), *States in the Global Economy: Bringing Domestic Institutions Back In*, (Cambridge: Cambridge University Press).

——(2006). *Global Capital, Political Institutions and Policy Change in Developed Welfare States*, (Cambridge: Cambridge University Press).

Thurbon, Elizabeth (2003). 'Ideational Inconsistency and Institutional Incapacity: Why Financial Liberalization in Korea went Horribly Wrong', *New Political Economy* 8(3): 341–62.

——(2007). 'The Developmental Logic of Financial Liberalization in Taiwan', in W. R. Garside (ed.), *Institutions and Market Economies: The Political Economy of Growth and Development*, (London: Palgrave).

——and Linda Weiss (2006). 'Investing in Openness: The Evolution of FDI Strategy in South Korea and Taiwan', *New Political Economy* 11(1): 1–22.

Tytell, Irina and Shang-Jin Wei (2004). *Does Financial Globalization Induce Better Macro-economic Policies?* IMF Working Paper No. WP/04/84.

Vogel, Steven (1996). *Freer Markets, More Rules: Regulatory Reform In Advanced Industrial Countries*, (Ithaca, NY: Cornell University Press).

——(2006). *Japan Remodeled. How Government and Industry are Reforming Japanese Capitalism*, (Ithaca, NY: Cornell University Press).

Wade, Robert (1990). *Governing the Market: Economic Theory and the Role of Government in East Asian Industrialisation*, (Princeton, NJ: Princeton University Press).

——(1992). 'East Asia's Economic Success: Conflicting Perspectives, Partial Insights, Shaky Evidence', *World Politics* 44(2): 270–320.

——(2003): 'Introduction to the 2003 Edition', *Governing the Market* [1990]. (Princeton, NJ: Princeton University Press).

Weiss, Linda (1998). *The Myth of the Powerless State*, (Ithaca, NY: Cornell University Press).

——(2003). 'Introduction: Bringing Domestic Institutions Back In', in Linda Weiss (ed.), *States in the Global Economy*, (Cambridge: Cambridge University Press).

——(2005). 'Global Governance, National Strategies: How Industrialized States Make Room to Move under the WTO', *Review of International Political Economy* 12(5): 723–49.

——(2008). 'Crossing the Divide: From the Military-Industrial Complex to the Development-Procurement Complex'. Paper presented at the Berkeley Workshop on 'The U.S. as a Hidden Developmental State', UC Berkeley, 19–21 June. Reprinted as Working Paper 1. Institute of Governmental Affairs, UC-Davis, Dec. 2008.

——and ELIZABETH THURBON (2004). 'Where there's a "Will", there's a Way: Governing the Market in Times of Uncertainty', Roundtable on Robert Wade's 2003 edition of *Governing the Market: Issues and Studies*, 40(1): 61–72.

WILLIAMSON, JOHN, (1993). 'Democracy and the "Washington Consensus"', *World Development* 21: 1329–36.

WOO-CUMINGS, MEREDITH (ed.) (1999). *The Developmental State*, (Ithaca, NY: Cornell University Press).

WORLD BANK (1993). *The East Asian Miracle: Economic Growth and Public Policy*, (Oxford: Oxford University Press).

YOO, CHRISTOPHER S. (2004). 'The Unfulfilled Promise of Korean Telecommunications Reform', in T. Ginsburg (ed.), *Legal Reform in Korea*, (London: Routledge).

CHAPTER 8

MONEY AND MARKETS

GLENN MORGAN[1]

INTRODUCTION

In his early study of the economics of capitalism, Oliver Williamson wrote that 'in the beginning there were markets' (Williamson 1975: 20). By contrast, institutionalist analysis begins from the assumption that in the beginning there were social relations out of which emerged, in specific contexts and forms, market processes (see for example, Durkheim's classic account of the social origins of contract in contrast to Spencer's individualism, Durkheim 1997). Comparative institutionalist analysis aims to investigate different patterns of markets, how they emerged, are reproduced, managed and changed. Markets do not exist in a state of nature. There have to be social and institutional rules which underpin contracts and market exchanges. Five particular sets of rules can be distinguished that can be used to interrogate and investigate any market situation;

- *Who* sets the rules in markets?
- *What* are the rules in particular markets?
- *How* are the rules implemented, sanctioned, and enforced?
- *When* are market exchanges allowed to take place?
- *Where* are markets situated?

These are the themes around which this chapter develops.

[1] I would like to thank John L. Campbell and Colin Crouch for their insightful and invaluable comments on earlier versions of this chapter.

This chapter begins by providing an initial framework for identifying market processes. It then describes the conditions of existence of such processes and the embeddedness of such processes in social relations and social institutions. This requires a historical perspective in order to distinguish the emergence of local market relations within non-market societies from the development of market societies per se. Market societies imply the existence of relatively stable institutional orders that facilitate the formation and operation of markets in a wide range of domains. The legitimacy of this mode of organizing economic activity and arguments about its scope are considered as part of a general question about the morality of market societies. In keeping with the comparative perspective of this book, an important aspect is that different forms of market society emerge and these reflect the politics and institutional formation of particular societies at key historical moments of development. However, this focus on specific territorially bounded and state organized market systems is not in itself sufficient. Adapting John Donne's words, 'no market society is "an island entire of itself"; every market is "a piece of the Continent, a part of the main. . . . And therefore never send to know for whom the bell tolls; It tolls for thee."' Different markets and market societies are tied together, no matter how differently their institutions may be organized; disjunctures in one market ripple through and impact on others, a point also recognized in the work of the nineteenth-century economist, Walras, in terms of developing a 'general equilibrium' model of markets. In this sense there is one single global market differentiated and demarcated in many complex ways but nevertheless tied together and interdependent (Arrighi 1994, 2007; Wallerstein 2004).[2] A comparative institutionalist analysis of markets therefore has to be about, firstly, particular markets and how they are socially embedded, secondly how particular market societies (the national level) influence and shape this embeddedness process and thirdly how markets spread across national boundaries and develop forms of embedding that are global or international in scope. This is very clearly the case in the current period because of the influential role of the diffusion of a particular model of market society, that associated with neo-liberalism, and its role in pressurizing societies to change their social institutions in order to allow markets to operate more on the free market liberal model. The chapter therefore considers the debate on the diffusion of the neo-liberal market model and examines the ways in which particular models of markets are becoming embedded in international and global processes. In this respect, the question arises as to whether there is a market for markets, how such a market might be said to operate and in particular how political factors structure that market by making certain forms of market structure more legitimate than others.

[2] Although there are arguments to this effect particularly in Marxist scholars like Wallerstein and Arrighi, it was Colin Crouch in particular who helped me to understand the significance of this for my own analysis in this chapter. I return to this issue in the final section of the chapter.

WHAT ARE MARKETS?

For most economists, the concept of 'the market' is an analytical category separate from any temporal or spatial embodiment. By contrast, historians and sociologists take a different starting point beginning with the idea that markets are embedded in societies. Braudel, for example, expresses some of the key themes in this transition:

> Without [the market] there would be no economy... only a form of life 'embedded' in self-sufficiency or the non-economy. The market spells liberation, openness, access to another world.... Men's activities, the surpluses they exchange, gradually pass through this narrow channel to the other world with as much difficulty at first as the camel of the scriptures passing through the eye of the needle. Then the breaches grow wider and more frequent, as society finally becomes a 'generalized market society'. 'Finally': that is to say with the passage of time, and never at the same date or in the same way in different regions. So there is no simple linear history of the development of markets.   (Braudel 1985: 26)

Braudel emphasizes the need for the historical analysis of how markets emerge in specific institutional contexts and it is this interplay between institutions, historical path dependencies, and market processes that is the main object of this chapter. However, Braudel also emphasizes another aspect of the commonality of markets, the sense of something singular yet diverse underneath particular manifestations of markets. This is the specifically moral and political embeddedness of the emergence of markets. Hirschman, for example, argued that the initial proponents of markets perceived themselves as having a 'civilizing' mission (Hirschman 1977, 1982). Markets were a way of taming the 'passions' in societies built around warfare and military activity by engaging instead the 'interests' of various key social actors. Whereas 'passions' know no bounds beyond the achievement of their goals, 'interests' are calculable, capable of compromise and negotiation. Hirschman is interested in how societies make this shift from passion and warfare to interests and trade. In this model, trade and markets grew in ways which tie people together across boundaries and make their interests interdependent. For many theorists of market liberalism, this interdependence of interests is central to undermining the potential for armed conflict. Helleiner states that the early market liberals such as John Stuart Mill and Cobden 'viewed this cosmopolitan case for free trade as ultimately much more important than Ricardo's economic case. As Mill put it, "the economical benefits of commerce are surpassed in importance by those of its effect which are intellectual and moral". Free trade was, in his words, "the principal guarantee of the peace of the world" which would contribute to "uninterrupted progress of the ideas, the institutions and the character of the human race"' (Helleiner 2002: 313).

What is termed the *doux commerce* thesis associated with Adam Smith and the early economic liberals argues that 'markets nurture a long list of bourgeois virtues including integrity, honesty, trustworthiness, enterprise, respect, modesty and responsibility' (Fourcade and Healy 2007: 4) through freeing the individual from the constraints of feudalism and encouraging creativity and innovation.

Furthermore, these virtues are not externally imposed but arise from the pursuit of self-interest.

Undoubtedly, the *doux commerce* thesis has gone through multiple mutations and as broader social conditions changed it became asserted in a new language that challenged growing state intervention, most notably in Hayek's 'The Road to Serfdom' first published in 1944 but increasingly influential in the broader rise of neo-liberalism in economics and politics during the 1970s and 1980s (Hayek 1944). Nevertheless, this aspect of the market still remains significant. For example, in their recent effort to identify the 'new spirit of capitalism', Boltanski and Chiapello argue that 'to be capable of mobilizing people, the spirit of capitalism must incorporate a moral dimension' (Boltanski and Chiapello 2005: 486). They identify this as emerging from various forms of critique where the market becomes the object of analysis. On the one hand the market is a site of inequality and exploitation but it is also a site of liberation, excitement, and freedom. The tension between these two forces is expressed in the elaboration of various historically specific forms of critique that drive capitalism into new forms of organization. The liberatory elements of the market were also shown in the way in which neo-liberalism in the 1980s constituted the appeal of markets and democracy against the faltering Soviet system. The collapse of the Soviet alternative left the neo-liberal cause as dominant on a global scale, leading Fukayama to pronounce 'the end of history'(Fukuyama 1992). If markets were triumphant, however, their legitimation was not utilitarian or even efficiency based but inherently moral as it had been when Adam Smith sought to articulate a vision of market society. As Fourcade and Healy state 'the discourse of the market is increasingly articulated in moral and civilizational terms, rather than simply in the traditional terms of self-interest and efficiency' (Fourcade and Healy 2007: 27). In this sense, specific market forms partake of, respond and reshape this morality, with the consequence that the making and managing of markets is an arena of multiple dimensions of conflict and debate. In this respect, the specific combination under the Bush presidency of neo-liberal economics and the use of military as well as economic and political power to spread approved forms of democracy and markets indicates another twist in the relationship between markets and morality. Institutionalist analysis of markets, therefore, needs to grasp this dynamism at the same time as it searches for the sources of stability in markets.

In terms of approaching such a complex and diverse topic, a useful place to begin is with Weber who with his usual perspicacity offers a definition of the 'market situation for any object of exchange' that sets a framework for further analysis. He states that by the term 'market situation' is meant all the opportunities of exchanging it (the object of exchange) for money which are known to the participants in exchange relationships and aid their orientation in the competitive price struggle' (Weber 1978: 227). The following section considers each of these in turn as features of markets before moving on to consider the social institutions that underpin these processes.

Markets as distinctive sites of exchange

Historical research emphasizes that in pre-modern societies markets generally had a specifically confined spatial and temporal existence. In Europe and elsewhere, kings and princes gave permission for markets to take place in particular places and at particular times of the year (Braudel 1985). Markets were carefully bounded off in time and space from the rest of social life. Whilst the conditions under which such boundaries are made and monitored has considerably changed, it is nevertheless the case that markets still tend to be confined spatially and temporally in various ways. Consider, for example, financial markets. The major stock exchanges of the world still have their trading hours. Whilst the traders themselves can in theory trade 24 hours a day now that their screens keep them in touch with exchanges throughout the world, the exchanges themselves have limited opening hours (Knorr Cetina and Preda 2005). Up until around the 1980s, these markets were still associated with a fixity of place; if a person wanted to trade shares in a company quoted on the London Stock Exchange, they had to come to the floor of the exchange and do so (or more likely instruct their broker to do so). Trading pits where the market is made still exist in some financial markets even if most trading can now be done through the virtual space of computerized networks (MacKenzie 2006; Zaloom 2006). The spatial and temporal fixing of market transactions has the advantage that it makes visible to all participants what is going on—what objects are being traded, the supply and demand for the objects, and the impact on prices. Once market relations move away from this model (which they have done across a range of transactions in modern societies) and visibility and transparency is reduced, new risks and uncertainties arise. This is even more the case when buyers and sellers are not buying and selling in order to use what is being exchanged but in order to trade it on to others.[3] We can therefore expect to see multiple conflicts and negotiations between buyers, sellers, and intermediaries around the conditions under which markets are spatially and temporally confined and how this relates to conditions of transparency and competition.

Market objects

What can be exchanged on markets? Markets require that there be objects of exchange that are alienable, i.e. they can be transferred from the buyer to the seller. A key issue here is that a set of property rights in the object have to be established. Somebody has to own something before they can legitimately sell it on the market. Commodities need to have the characteristic that they can be passed cleanly from one actor to the other in a market transaction without trailing behind a web of other

[handwritten margin note: Alienable objects required for markets.]

---

[3] The complexity of these secondary markets, particularly as they have developed in sophisticated financial markets for options and derivatives, needs special attention, since in Marxist terminology, the use value of the object of exchange may be simply as an item of exchange and its connection with any material object capable of being consumed is entirely fictional.

diffuse obligations. For markets to exist, there have to be property rights in objects and commodities, which enabled the seller to sell on the marketplace and the buyer to buy. The commodity has to be constituted so that there can be property rights in it. This requires that the commodity can be treated as though it had a separate, finite existence reflected in alienable ownership. As Callon says: 'one is not born a commodity, one becomes it' (Callon 1998: 19). Nothing is automatically a commodi-ty, i.e. a package of clearly related qualities that are standardized (and therefore available for comparison and pricing), measurable, and ownable. In Callon's terms, the commodity 'must be decontextualized, disassociated and detached'. For Callon, the commodity has to be given a set of qualities that attach it in a material way to markets. Callon et al. state that: 'The characteristics of a good are not properties which already exist and on which information simply has to be produced so that everyone is aware of them. Their definition, or in other words, their objectification, implies specific metrological work and heavy investment in measuring equipment' (Callon, Meadel, and Rabeharisoa 2002: 198–9).

Callon emphasizes what he terms systems of calculation and the technostructures that enable commodities to take shape in markets. Other sociological accounts of the emergence of products tend to focus more on issues of culture and morality as determining what can and cannot be put up for sale. Shifting morality has shaped and changed markets for a large number of other commodities ranging from tobacco, alcohol and drugs through to markets for blood, sex, body parts, and children (Healy 2006). Zelizer, for example, examined how the establishment of a market for life insurance in the US required that potential consumers saw this as a matter of prudent risk management rather than a gamble on somebody's life (Zelizer 1983). In later work, she has continued to explore the inter-relationship between money, markets and intimate aspects of social life, revealing the conditions under which personal acts such as sex, having children, bringing children up, looking after the ill and the elderly become subject to market relations, where prices are given and exchanges can be made (Zelizer 1985, 1994, 2005).[4] MacKenzie and Millo (2003) show also how the early derivatives markets were affected by similar debates; so long as these products were seen as essentially a gamble on the forward movement of prices, they were considered as not appropriate for financial markets. It was only after it became possible to argue that there was a rational scientific basis to their pricing (provided by the Black-Scholes formula) that they rid themselves of this stigma and were really able to expand. This sort of intertwining of science, politics, and morality is characteristic of the formation of new markets in the contemporary period (Strathern 2002).

---

[4] It is worth noting in passing that there is more complexity here that could be addressed. For example, things can be sold on legal markets but in illegal ways (through misrepresentation, fraud etc.). Other things may be sold in the informal economy where issues of legality are less significant than questions of reputation, reciprocity, and possibly coercion. Finally there are many things which are sold on illegal markets such as prohibited drugs. This chapter concentrates on legal markets.

The idea that there are things which cannot be sold on the market, that there is a sphere of social and economic relations outside the market is important both historically and in relation to more contemporary processes. It is important to know what is outside market relations in order to understand what is inside and more importantly how and why the boundaries shift. In historical terms, exchange per se has played a limited role in human subsistence and where it has emerged it has taken many different forms. Anthropological studies of systems of reciprocity and barter have revealed that these can contain highly complex mechanisms of exchange in which calculations about honour, status, and prestige can carry obligations over time and place through various symbolic and oral means. Mostly, however, as Braudel states: 'the world of the peasants was of course *par excellence* the zone excluded (or at least half-excluded) from the market; this was the world of self-sufficiency, autarky, a self-contained life. Peasants had to be content their lives long with what they produced with their own hands, or what their neighbours could give them in exchange for a few goods or services'. (Braudel 1985: 55).

If the position of market exchange in historical terms is limited, it is also important to recognize that the advent of modern capitalism constitutes a new form of non-market transactions—those associated with the redistributive function of the state. States in modern societies are legitimized through their claim to represent the will of the people as expressed through the institutions of democracy and equality before the law and characterized by citizenship claims. These set up a fundamental tension in capitalism between forms of equality under systems of liberalism and democracy and forms of inequality emergent under market conditions (see also the chapters by Streeck and Weiss in this volume). T. H. Marshall identified this as the source of debates about how far citizenship rights could be expanded into spheres of social and economic life (Marshall 1950), through state provision of rights to health, education, and welfare as ways of overcoming the inequality of outcomes generated by market relations. This distinction between market and non-market forms of distribution and how the boundaries between the two are organized, negotiated, and reconstructed is central to the debate on comparative capitalisms as societies manage these tensions in different ways depending on their history, the challenges which they face at particular times, and the characteristic pattern of social relations and power.

The medium of exchange in markets: money

Market exchange is based on money (for the best comprehensive discussion of money from a sociological point of view, see Ingham 2004). Standard economic accounts define money as 'a means of exchange, a store of value and a unit of account'. As a unit of account, money becomes the medium through which all goods and services become commensurable and comparable. Generalized systems of exchange require money as a unit of account in order to come into being. In this context, money is a unit of measurement. Money as a means of exchange expresses a different dimension; it implies a materialized existence in some form—traditionally metal and paper—that is accepted in a particular context as a relatively stable store of value. In principle, money can be held without losing value; it can be spent anywhere within a particular currency area or it can be saved and used at a later date. Carruthers states that 'as a unit of account', 'money permits comparisons and evaluations; it measures the relative worth of commodities and services. Money commensurates alternatives and promotes rational decision-making' (Carruthers 2005: 356). Weber similarly places central weight on the way in which money works stating that 'from a purely technical point of view, money is the most 'perfect' means of economic calculation' (Weber 1978: 86). Money enables the competitive price struggle to emerge as buyers and sellers compare prices and adjust according to supply and demand.

Because money is 'abstract' and 'fictitious', it can only work effectively if people trust that its ability to act in the expected way is somehow secure. For centuries, this security was based on combining two characteristics. Firstly, coins were struck in precious metals; they could therefore be melted down into the precious metal and sold on if necessary. For this reason 'debasement of the coinage' by adding non-precious metals or 'clipping coins' was a serious crime in pre-capitalist England carrying a maximum penalty of death. Ironically, at this time, governments were most guilty of debasement and clipping as ways to create more money for themselves. This reflects the fact that the security of the currency relied also upon the nature of the issuer. Coins were pressed with a symbol of the ruling power on one of the sides. The ruler was in effect guaranteeing that the coin was the proper weight for the value shown on it. It also designated the territory of the ruler within which the coin was currency. In pre-modern Europe and the post-Columbus Americas, it was common for coins of relatively high worth to circulate across state or imperial boundaries because their precious metal component gave them a common value.

Ferguson, for example, notes that there were seven different forms of coinage in circulation in the medieval trading centre of Pisa (Ferguson 2008). This, however, reveals the second element of money which is that historically it has rarely been confined into a specific material form. In order for a system to work which had multiple currencies, there had to be intermediaries willing to trade back and forth across different currencies. This was done by developing bills of exchange, in effect promises to pay in the future, which allowed the holder to convert the paper into a currency at a discounted rate. Thus what might be described as paper money existed alongside previous metal coins, expressing a situation of credit and debt between two parties. The issuance of paper money by states developed this process further, particularly when paper money was no longer backed by a promise to pay the bearer in a precious metal.

Money is not therefore a simple intermediary in markets, solely a neutral arbiter for a way of measuring value and a unit of exchange. It constitutes its own specific set of social forces that shape markets. Of particular importance is the way in which money both stabilizes and destabilizes broader social relations. Money is the primary way in which markets are released from the bounds of face-to-face bargaining and instead become disaggregated across time and space. The expansion of money more widely meant that social actors did not have to literally meet in a market and exchange money for goods. As the forms of money became more diverse and methods of storing and transferring money more complex and virtual, so market relations moved away from being fixed in particular spaces and times. However, this leads to the problem of realizing values in markets when time and space separate buyers and sellers, which in turn is managed through the provision of money and credit and the development of various sorts of intermediaries and agents. Market situations are complex bindings of different time horizons and different geographical spaces that are mediated through the mechanisms of money and credit. Money is the way in which market exchange breaks through temporal and spatial boundaries to interconnect societies and economies. However localized markets may appear, through the mechanism of money and credit, they are integrated into wider networks that span spatial and temporal boundaries and gradually connect all the parts together. It is impossible to examine any form of market without examining how money and credit is implicated into the exchange relationship. As Swedberg has recently stated 'money and markets ... belong together' (Swedberg 2005: 250).

Money is essential to setting prices in markets. However as Swedberg notes 'few sociological studies of how prices are set exist' (Swedberg 2005: 249). Recent work in the social studies of finance has emphasized the material aspect of money and the technology required to bring a 'price' into being. Beunza et al. state that 'a price is a thing. . . . The forms of embodiment of prices are various . . . but are always material. If a price is to be communicated from one human being to another, it must take a physical form' (Beunza, Hardie, and MacKenzie 2006: 729; see also Beunza and Stark 2004). The 'embodiment of prices' identified by Beunza et al. requires a technostructure of different sorts of agents, both human and non-human. Preda describes the key linkages in the following way;

money essential for setting prices.

This perspective requires abandoning the notion of price as something abstract in favour of price data, produced in specific settings under specific conditions. Concomitantly it opens up a programme of research about (a) the assumptions of veridicality, robustness and reliability implied in the production of price data; (b) the cognitive activities—such as observation, classification, memorization—without which data production cannot take place; (c) the technologies that endow data with specific properties. In short, price data are treated as a practical problem for market actors and not as the given or natural basis of financial transactions.   (Preda 2007: 519)

Markets and the competitive price struggle

The outcome of the creation of markets as defined spaces with commodities available for exchange and mechanisms for the revelation of prices is the creation of competition. How do competitive markets reveal themselves? Economists have generally identified a single model of a competitive market in which there is perfect transparency enabling prices to reflect supply and demand conditions at particular times; those firms succeed which are able to match their supply to demand most efficiently. From this perspective, there are a variety of ways in which free and efficient markets can be distorted, e.g. through state activity, information asymmetries, asset specificities, natural monopolies etc.

Campbell et al. developed a typology of mechanisms through which markets were organized (Campbell, Hollingsworth, and Lindberg 1991). They distinguished between two dimensions—the degree of formal integration in the market and the range of interaction between actors in the market context. From this they provide what may be considered as Weberian ideal types for how competition and prices are managed in specific markets. Firstly, they identify the ideal type of the free market which is low on formal integration and primarily bilateral in nature. In these markets, prices emerge from the interaction of actors in the market. They are likely to move rapidly depending on supply and demand within the market. The opposite end to this consists of the Williamsonian organization in which transactions are administered and there is no competition. However, as Williamson argues (Williamson 1975), this contrast can be overdrawn. Many organizations set up shadow markets or internal markets both as a pressure towards pricing transactions according to exemplars in outside markets, but also in order to enable transactions to be outsourced on to the market in circumstances where it appears that the market can provide the required product cheaper. Between these two extremes, however, are a variety of forms of managing the market, reducing uncertainties and risk through different forms of collective action. Campbell et al.'s framework identifies four such intermediary market forms:

[handwritten margin note: Intermediary market forms]

1. Monitoring contexts: these contexts are characterized by extensive corporate interlocks for information sharing, market-sharing agreements, and dominant-firm pricing. They may be described in terms of levels of cartelization. Firms within the cartel are price-makers rather than price-takers.
2. Obligational bilateral networks: these networks are characterized by long-term relationships between actors at connecting points in the value chain. In these contexts, prices and the setting of prices are embedded in broader obligational relationships which may involve joint design and collaborative innovation. Prices are negotiable, not transparent to the outside world as they are specific to the relationship. They are likely to change by negotiation and slowly, rather than quickly.
3. Promotional multilateral networks; Campbell et al. argue that 'Promotional networks typically bring together diverse actors from different parts of the production or service delivery chain for the common promotion of a product' (Campbell et al. 1991). Such networks consist of firms from different parts of the value chain trying to stabilize the market for the final product on which they are all dependent. They may cooperate on a range of activities up to and including price collusion.
4. Associations: trade associations and other forms of formalized cooperation between multiple actors describe contexts in which prices are agreed and set by members of the association. This form of price setting, which characterized medieval and early modern guilds before it was made illegal in most societies, remained in existence in a number of important areas of the economy through to

the late twentieth century, e.g. in the fixed commission systems on stock broking which characterized the New York and London stock exchanges until deregulation in 1975 and 1986 respectively.

What are the forces determining which sorts of competitive struggles emerge in different contexts? The following section considers this question.

Shaping Market Situations: Influences and Institutions

There are certain key influences in the shaping of markets which can be identified. These can be identified broadly as firstly the state, secondly firms and their networks, thirdly social movements, and fourthly models of markets and their socio-technical capacities. Each of these is examined in turn.

States and markets

The centrality of states to providing the conditions for the expansion of the market is a constant theme of institutionalist approaches, particularly through drawing on and developing the ideas of Polanyi (2001). Block, for example, has used the phrase 'the always embedded market economy' to emphasize the impossibility of conceiving of markets without social institutions. He also makes the further move to emphasize that the key actor in this 'always embedded' context is the state in particular. He argues that:

The always embedded concept makes it very hard to gloss over or hide the state's fundamental role in shaping actually existing economies. Because the state establishes the noncontractual bases of contract and is centrally involved in constructing the markets for the fictitious commodities of land, labor and money, it becomes impossible to imagine how the economy would run if only the state would cease its unnecessary meddling.   (Block 2003: 301)

Krippner and Alvarez (2007) have also emphasized the importance of the link between embeddedness of the market and the state: 'Although the Polanyian litera-ture is quote diverse, what nearly all writers in this tradition share is an emphasis on the mutual constitution of state and economy. . . . For Polanyians, the notion that markets could exist outside of state action is simply inconceivable' (Krippner and Alvarez 2007: 233).

This tradition of research flows into a concern with how particular states and markets are constituted in specific historical contexts. Elsewhere, Block re-empha-sizes the point when he states: 'Markets are always politically embedded. They require a set of legal rules, a set of institutions and so on. Such political embeddedness exists at both the national and the global levels; there are at particular times these global regimes that are politically structured' (Block in Krippner et al. 2004: 118).

Finally, Krippner summarizes this argument clearly, emphasizing the processual and conflictual elements:

Every transaction, no matter how instantaneous, is *social* in the broader sense of the term: congealed into every market exchange is a history of struggle and contestation that has produced actors with certain understandings of themselves and the world which predispose them to exchange under a certain set of social rules and not another. In this sense, the state, culture and politics are 'contained' in every market act; they do not invariably exert their influence on some kinds of markets more than others.   (Krippner et al. 2004: 112)

States have a central influence over all the aspects of the market situation previously described.

States and market sites

In pre-modern societies, the political authorities determined how and when markets could be established. This can be seen clearly in Braudel's analysis of what he terms 'elementary markets'. Such markets existed in urban areas and were characterized by clear and fixed rules about who was allowed to trade, spaces where they could trade from, which hours and which days they could trade. Medieval fairs were similar in form though larger in scale and less frequent, attracting participants from in some cases hundreds of miles away because of their reputations. Urban authorities supervised and taxed markets and fairs. On the one hand, they competed to attract merchants to them but on the other hand, they faced problems of public order arising from these events. Urban areas could overflow with unruly and disruptive outsiders during these events and they could become the site for social unrest and even rebellion. Markets and fairs were face-to-face events where merchants and consumers met and prices were negotiated. Some of these merchants had networks which as Braudel and Greif both reveal, were managed through the use of bills of exchange and merchants' leagues (such as the Hanseatic League) drawing traders and producers into webs of interconnectedness across the European landmass and into Asia, as well as across the sea routes around Europe and Africa and into Asia and the Americas (Braudel 1985; Greif 2006). Such systems were dependent on 'friendly' rulers willing to accept and protect merchants, in return for taxation and other economic benefits. Contemporary societies still set rules for certain sorts of markets concerning where and when they may trade, though frequently these are negotiated with the state by social actors rather than imposed by the state, e.g. in relation to financial markets.

States and the objects of exchange

States set limits on what can be exchanged on markets. Human beings can no longer be sold as slaves on markets. Most states do not allow the sale of babies to potentially adopting parents. In the current period of development around biotechnology and medical innovation, states engage in complex ethical and moral debates about the degree to which organs, genes, stem-cells, eggs, and sperm can be bought and sold on the market. A key issue here is that of property rights. Polanyi's use of the idea of fictitious commodities in relation to labour reveals part of the problem here. Developing the Marxist analysis of labour power, Polanyi argues that the idea that labour is a commodity is a fiction for two reasons. Firstly, labour power cannot be separated from the labourer and yet, except under slavery (which is primarily a coercive relationship and not an exchange one even though characteristically slaves are bought and sold), it is not the labourer who is being bought but the potential to labour. Secondly because it is this potential to labour that is being bought, the buyer of labour power has to put the labourer to work and the outcome of this, the 'effort bargain', is uncertain. Labour is a fictitious commodity in the sense that it is ultimately not alienable; it cannot be separated from a host of other considerations, which in turn are not calculable in advance. The emergence of capitalism requires wresting peasants out of subsistence agriculture and turning them into landless labourers willing and able to sell their labour power on markets. Historical sociology is full of classic studies of how this process has been achieved in different countries, the role of the state and the effect that this had on the subsequent formation of particular political economies (Marx 1990; Moore 1973; Polanyi 2001). Furthermore what Polanyi described as the great transformation continues to reshape peasant subsistence across the globe, most notably in the current period in China and India (Arrighi 2007; Glyn 2007). Capitalism requires subsistence forms of agriculture to decline and markets to emerge as the arena in which money and goods are exchanged, not just for subsistence but in their own right.

One of Polanyi's other 'fictitious' commodities is land. Land clearly exists prior to its articulation with the commodity form. In fact, all societies have established complex systems of rights over land which reflects its different uses. In current UK law, the rights to all gold and silver belong to the sovereign, not what might be termed the 'landowner'. During the industrial revolution, it was common for landowners to sell off the land but retain the mineral rights beneath the soil. It was also possible to lease the land over very long terms but to retain ownership of the freehold. Land could be entailed, i.e. it could not be sold or mortgaged but had to be kept in the possession of the family for which it had been entailed. Landowners may find their rights to land compromised by other types of rights, such as common rights, footpath and bridle rights, etc. The right to private property in land emerged only gradually in societies that were defined by the warlike traditions of feudalism. Property was held by grace of the liege lord, who could withdraw that right and confiscate land and other goods subject to force of arms. Macfarlane argues that a specifically English model of individualism developed very early from the struggles to establish private property and that this influenced the speed with which England was able to develop capitalism (Macfarlane 1978, 1987).

North and Weingast focus on the later period of the Restoration in order to present their analysis of when rights to private property are most firmly established in the new United Kingdom in terms of establishing credible commitments on the part of the sovereign and the Parliament to respect each other's rights (North 1990;

North and Weingast 1989). The history of the establishment of individual property rights and their security from the depredations of the more powerful or from the state has varied depending on traditions of land-holding and labour in agricultural societies and how these were transformed in the shift to an industrial market economy (see, for example Beckert's discussion of inheritance law and how the individual's right to pass on property was constituted: Beckert 2008). Societies that became communist in this process either through civil war or through conquest placed another layer of collective ownership rights over and across existing mixtures of individual and traditional collective rights. The shift of these societies out of the socialist system into a system of private ownership has involved further permutations in and conflicts over property rights, whilst in developing countries the effort to formalize property rights in informal housing settlements has been a significant debate (Soto 2000).

For markets to exist, therefore, there had to be property rights in objects and commodities that enabled the seller to sell on the marketplace and the buyer to buy. These rights had to be established by the state. Thus something like stocks or shares in a company are not natural phenomena; the joint stock company, which was owned by its shareholders, had to be legally created and socially accepted. Early attempts to achieve this in the UK were through chartered companies such as the Hudson Bay Company and the East India Company. Only gradually did the idea of limited liability emerge so that ownership could be spread more widely. The rate at which this emerged varied as did the limiting conditions of the nature of property in corporations, with the Anglo-American version being more shareholder driven than that of most other countries where rights of certain sorts were given to other stakeholders.

States and money

States are central actors in the provision of money. Money is key to the power of the state; states that lose control of money tend to be inevitably weakened and their sovereignty compromised. States require money to fund their activities. In the early modern age, this related particularly to the need to fund military activity through borrowing and it was this nexus that gave rise to the formation of national paper currencies, central banking institutions, and the development of stock and bond markets (Ferguson 2001, 2008). The ability to raise revenue in a consistent manner, to the level required to sustain a military force and to do it in a relatively consensual way that avoided generating rebellion, was crucial to the formation of the modern state (Mann 1986; Tilly 1990). In this period, various bodies (not just states and monarchs but also private actors such as banks and merchants) began to issue 'paper' money, which could be turned into gold on presentation at the appropriate location. Paper money required trust that it could reliably act as a store of value and means of exchange since it could in theory be made valueless by the collapse in the legitimacy of the originating issuer (whether that be a bank or a state). Paper money also meant that the holders of notes had a clearer limit than previously to the generalizability of their currency. Whereas coins based on precious metals could in theory be valid in any context, since they could be melted down and turned into any currency, paper money could only ever be valid within the geographical confines where it was issued and accepted. The crucial exception to this was that market intermediaries could act to convert money from one currency to another. The rate at which this conversion took place was fundamental as it affected the abilities of nations, firms and individuals to engage in trade across borders. Paper money, therefore, created a new hierarchy separating those who controlled the 'real' store of value, (i.e. the gold and other metals that had a more universal trading value) from those who had such access only at second hand. This impacted in two ways. States could tighten conditions for creditors or for debtors. 'Loose' money reduced the cost of borrowing and therefore potentially benefited debtors; it would likely weaken the currency thus increasing inflation and make it more difficult for the state and others to borrow internationally. 'Tight' money on the other hand would benefit the 'money interest' and those concerned with stability of the currency. These differences influenced cleavages in societies between creditors and debtors creating what can be considered as a specific form of monetary politics that in turn impacted on the operation and functioning of markets.

This politics of money has been frequently hidden under efforts to imply natural solutions to money supply questions derived from the technical analyses of economists. During the early part of the twentieth century, this was linked into the analysis of the gold standard. 'Paper' money issued by the state, was, under the gold standard and its predecessors, until the collapse of the international currency system between the two world wars, based on a promise to pay the bearer in gold. It was in effect a form of credit that the holder of the paper provided to the issuer of the paper. The problem with this 'credit' was that its value was not stable for the reasons already outlined. The issuer could in theory issue as much or as little paper money as it wanted, the result of which would be either inflation and the effective devaluation of the paper money people actually held or deflation and the rise of endebtedness and unemployment. In the nineteenth century, as nation-states strengthened in Western Europe, control of the issuance of paper money was centralized into the national bank and the national mint. Only in nineteenth-century USA with its combination of the ready availability of precious metals (following gold and silver discoveries in the west) and a populist anti-bank politics did this process lead in a serious way to a challenge to the gradual centralization and concentration of control over money and the money supply (Goodwin 2004). In theory, inflationary temptations were controlled by states adhering to the gold standard, which meant that there were sufficient gold reserves held in the national bank to pay out to any individual who wanted to exchange paper currency for gold. Gold reserves were, however, also meant to be the means for paying for foreign imports that were not balanced by exports. Where, as a result, gold flowed out of a country, deflationary pressures emerged, reducing prices and pushing down consumption whilst countries with high gold surpluses were likely to suffer from price rises and higher demand. The result would be a reversal of the previous situation. Thus the gold standard contributed to the creation of a moving equilibrium to maintain international trade (Eichengreen 2008).

In the First World War, countries went off the gold standard and the previous system effectively broke down creating the potential for periods of raging inflation and subsequent deflations. Following the Second World War, the Bretton Woods system aimed to create an alternative adjustment mechanism to gold that depended increasingly on the US dollar as the base in which the value of other currencies could be calculated. When this system proved incapable of containing inflationary pressures, control of money was shifted to a combination of central banks and financial markets in which adjustments between currencies and within national economies were facilitated by monetary supply and interest rates, though the dollar continued to play a central role. Central to the development of paper money has been control of the money supply and the impact of this on inflation and deflation. Expectations about inflation and deflation, particularly in social contexts characterized by intensive monitoring and measuring of these phenomena and high reflexivity about their impact and consequences, enter into markets continuously.

Money is not therefore a simple intermediary in markets, a way of measuring value and a unit of exchange. It constitutes its own specific set of social forces that shape markets (Simmel 2004). The ability of states to control money is limited by endogenous and exogenous factors. Endogenous factors relate to the ability of social actors to create credit. Credit is a surrogate form of money. Credit is a means of creating money; it therefore impacts on processes of inflation. It impacts not just directly on markets, by making them more flexible, but indirectly, by making them more subject to instabilities arising from inflation.

In the modern era, the difference between money and credit has become more complex. Carruthers seeks to distinguish between the two by describing money as 'generalized, immediate and transferable legitimate claims on value' in contrast to credit which he defines as 'non-generalized, deferred and variably transferable legitimate claims on specific value' but as he recognizes 'intermediate forms exist. As credit becomes more general, uniform, and transferable, it approximates money. No hard-and-fast distinction separates the two kinds of claims' (Carruthers 2005: 356). The development of 'securitization' technologies in the financial markets, whereby providers of credit parcel up individual loans on mortgages etc. and sell them as a package to another financial institution further elided this distinction. Credit providers turned the loans, which they had made, back from non-generalized claims into money with its 'generalized' claims, allowing them to lend again and expand further the credit available. States therefore lose control of the money supply and with that access to key levers of control.

This is exacerbated by exogenous factors. Money and the national currency provide the link between one society and another. When exchange rates float, as they do currently, differences in economic performance are reflected in exchange rate movements, causing changes in pricing. Whilst governments are theoretically able to control their own currency and can print as much money as they want, the consequence is to devalue the currency in relation to others, creating price inflations and a resultant scarcity of commodities. In these circumstances, citizens may look for other forms of hard currency that retain their value better, generating parallel markets, a process that can be encouraged by governments desperate for such hard currency, as was the case in state socialist regimes in the 1980s. States may even accept the loss of their currency sovereignty entirely and simply allow the use of a more stable currency for many transactions, as happens with the use of the US dollar in many Latin American and African societies. These processes reflect the way in which politics and economics become entwined with monetary politics (Cohen 1998, 2006; Ingham 2004). This interaction is present in the development of non-national currencies such as most notably the Euro which stands in a complex relationship to the member states and the European institutions themselves (Dyson 2002; Fligstein 2008; Jabko 2006). A recognition of this also underlies Hayek's radical proposal for competitive currencies in which the state's monopoly of currency issuance and legal tender was to be swept away to allow individuals to choose between different currencies, an argument which he evolved later to incorporate the idea of allowing private actors to issue their own money (Hayek 1990). In effect, whilst states need money, money per se does not need the state; it can (and does) exist in a variety of forms that are only partially kept in check by states.

States and the rules of competition

States are also powerful actors in shaping the rules of competition in markets.[5] Three particular aspects can be considered. Firstly, states constitute the boundaries of market activity in the sense that they exist as non-market entities. Their legitimacy derives from political processes. In the current period, there have been strong arguments put forward as to why state activities should be marketized so that citizens become consumers who choose and pay for their health, education, etc. in the same way as they purchase food or clothes. However, historical path dependencies as well as more recent political developments make the scale of state activities per se and the role of markets in the provision of state services highly variable across societies. Secondly and related to this is the way in which, and the purposes for which, different societies regulate markets. The way in which financial services, for example, has been regulated and deregulated varies across economies even in the recent period of neo-liberal dominance (Jordana and Levi-Faur 2004; Knights and Morgan 1997; Laurence 2001; Morgan and Engwall 1999). Finally, and associated with these issues, is the way in which states seek to regulate competition and the positions taken towards issues like monopoly and cartelization.

Fligstein's initial work on the multi-divisional form and how it was influenced by the US anti-trust movement demonstrated the extent to which competition law could impact on market structure in the US (Fligstein 1990). In later work (Fligstein 2001), he points to formal legal arrangements and informal cooperative endeavours. Formal legal arrangements relate to the ways in which competition and anti-trust law shape the conditions under which firms can engage in markets. The increased centrality of forms of competition law and the effect of this on firms and markets

---

[5] This is not to discount the influence of other factors on the rules of competition—cartels, monopolies, oligopolies, monpsonies, private interests such as business associations, etc.

has become a central interest particularly in the context of the relationship between national and international forms of regulation and competition (Djelic 1998, 2002).

Fligstein argues that 'conceptions of control reflect market-specific agreements between actors in firms on principles of internal organization (i.e. forms of hierarchy), tactics for competition or cooperation (i.e. strategies) and the hierarchy or status ordering of firms in a given market.'

It is worth at this stage adding a note of caution in that the recent decades have seen the development of other forms of political authority beyond the state level that are impacting on the organization of markets. Two particular features can be identified that will be discussed further later in the chapter. The first is the construction of cross-national political entities that have developed rules concerning markets. Duina, for example, compares NAFTA, Mercosur and the EU in terms of how they create free markets within their geographical space (Duina 2006). He demonstrates that the nature and extent of the rules and regulations that they develop vary immensely, even whilst they all have some sort of impact on market organization processes (on the EU see in particular Fligstein 2008; Jabko 2006; Stone Sweet, Sandholtz, and Fligstein 2001). The second is the construction of international organizations, which have an impact on how markets are organized through their role in monitoring trade and sanctioning countries that engage in unfair practices. By far the most important organization in this is the World Trade Organization (WTO), which has engaged in strenuous efforts to get states to agree on the appropriate set of rules for trade in goods and services. Although the extension of WTO principles to areas such as agriculture and intellectual property has been fraught with conflict and difficulty, nevertheless it has exercised an influence in shaping expectations of free markets. Both regional entities and global entities such as the WTO emerge out of negotiations between states but they evolve to varying degrees their own power and influence, their own procedures and processes and in this way impact not just on relations between states but also on the construction of markets.

Firms and networks

Although firms and networks of firms have influence over the sites of market activity and the objects of market exchange, they are most important in relation to shaping the competitive structure of the market. This section will therefore concentrate on this point.

The idea that competition and price setting is mediated through network relationships has become an increasingly fertile field of research (for overviews see Smith-Doerr and Powell 2005; Thompson 2003). Much of this begins from Harrison White's work, which has focused on production markets characterized by relationships between firms as both buyers and sellers (White 1992, 2002). White argues that in producer markets where there are relatively small numbers and firms tend to act as both buyers and sellers, there is a large amount of signalling which going on. Firms watch each other's behaviour and in particular respond in order to maintain their own distinctive position within the market. Thus the market is not an anonymous site but it possesses a structure that emerges out of these inter-firm networks. Leifer and White state that:

the shape and location of the structural context of market activity are dependent on specific sets of producers and cannot be defined apart from them. The structural context of a schedule of niches sums up market possibilities and thereby provides a guide for producer behavior. In a viable market, producer behavior is guided in such a way that it functions to reproduce the structural context from which it derives. . . . In our model, markets are real structures with definite boundaries. Producers are position holders whose behavior reaffirms their position in the market, marked by a distinct reputation in the 'culture' associated with a market.   (Leifer and White 2004: 319, 321–2)

This idea that networks of relationships provide markets with distinctive structures that impact on prices and competitive behaviour has also been developed by Granovetter in his analysis of embeddedness (Granovetter 1985, 2005). He summarizes his argument as follows:

Social structure, especially in the forms of social networks affects economic outcomes for three main reasons. First social networks affect the flow and quality of information. Much information is subtle, nuanced and difficult to verify so actors do not believe impersonal sources and instead rely on people they know. Second, networks are an important source of reward and punishment since these are often magnified in their impact when coming from others personally known. Third trust, by which I mean the confidence that others will do the 'right' thing despite a clear balance of incentives to the contrary emerges, if it does in the context of a social network.   (Granovetter 2005: 33)

Granovetter's insights have led to the analysis of a variety of empirical contexts, market structures and the influence of networks.

One sort of market structure that has been identified is that discussed by Podolny in terms of the distinction between high status and low status providers (Podolny 2005). His observation, drawn from the analysis of investment banks, is that high status providers have advantages. They are able to spend less than other banks on persuading clients and others to do business with them. Their status and reputation attracts others to them and because they are trusted, other transaction costs in terms of contracts, etc. are likely to be less. Secondly, because of their reputation they are able to charge higher fees without necessarily losing business. Clients believe that they are paying for skills, networks, experience, and higher levels of certainty. He describes this as the 'Matthew Effect' after the biblical phrase 'to him that hath shall be given'. Again this suggests that markets do not work simply on the basis of price competition but have an underlying network structure, in this case based on perceptions of reputation and trust. One of the central dynamics in this context concerns how the borders between high and low status providers shift and how individual producers may strategize to move higher in the status rankings or alternatively may fall because of mistakes or crises. Maintaining a desired position in a market structure requires careful management and adaptation to changing circumstances and Podolny seeks to identify the features that enable or constrain these processes. He suggests that this sort of structure may characterize other markets where there are sharp differences between high value products and more commoditized and lower value goods and services, (also on status groups in financial markets see Preda 2005; on the art market see Velthius 2005). Burt identifies similar processes in his analysis of networks and 'structural holes' (Burt 1992). In networks of firms, there is a possibility that value can be captured by mediating between two members of the network who are currently unconnected. Bridging such a structural hole generates new possibilities for all the actors in the network, e.g. bringing together two firms that have complementary technologies that can be used to build something new or bringing a venture capitalist together with a firm that needs more capital.

In a variation on this argument, Uzzi has shown how personal relationships impact on prices. In his study of the relationship between banks and corporate borrowers (Uzzi 1997, 1999), he found that where actors know and trust each other, they are willing to moderate their expectations on market prices because they offset this against reliability. Participants in markets therefore tend to have two sorts of ties, one set of diffuse and longer terms ties with those they know and trust and another set of ties with those with whom they transact on a one-off basis. In their study of price formation in the corporate law market, Uzzi and Lancaster found that:

embeddedness affects prices by adding unique value to exchanges. This value can include lower transaction costs, more efficient production, better product differentiation or conspicuous consumption. Embeddedness promotes these values by facilitating private information exchange and the creation of informal governance arrangements that are unavailable through market processes.   (Uzzi and Lancaster 2004: 340)

These studies emphasize that markets are not arenas of anonymous transactions in which prices emerge through the spontaneous interaction of buyers and sellers (for similar points see Abolafia 1996, 1998). On the contrary, social actors position themselves in markets through the medium of their social ties and the nature and diversity of these ties leads them into a variety of forms of action. Prices which emerge in these contexts and forms of competition are shaped by the strength and weakness of these social ties. The nature of these social ties is influenced by the sorts of products and services that are being exchanged, the sort of strategies pursued by firms, but more importantly the way in which social relationships have emerged and been sustained over time within particular contexts. These are likely to include personal ties formed through kinship, friendship, and other forms of social solidarity (e.g. ethnic and neighbourhood groupings), as well as those formed by long-term business relationships and the reputations, status and rankings emerging out of these processes.

Social movements and markets

Social movements particularly impact on markets with respect to constructing the objects of exchange in markets and shaping the rules of competition that occur.

In relation to the objects of exchange, two examples are particularly important. The first which has already been mentioned is in terms of the category of labour and the nature of labour markets. Labour is a commodity that has to be brought in to being through the interaction of actual existing labourers and managerial processes. This struggle over the effort bargain or the contested terrain as described by Edwards (1979) takes place in particular social and industrial contexts and has generated path-dependent industrial relations structures that shape the nature of the labour market in particular contexts (Crouch 1993). The power of different sorts of trade union structures and movements, the way in which they are involved in the development of states and politics and their relevance inside firms shapes the qualities of labour as a commodity in different contexts. This can also be related to the gendered nature of labour as a commodity. The nature of the labour which is brought to the labour market is affected by the division of labour within the family and the way in which feminist social movements in different periods and contexts have shaped expectations about work and labour.[6]

The second more general point about social movements is how they act to shape cultural expectations around the sorts of things that can be sold on the market (Davis 2005; Schneiberg and Lounsbury 2008). This has already been discussed as a feature of debates about the object of exchange but it is clear that social movements play a central part here. For example, the nature of markets in energy is being reshaped by social movements concerned with the ecological and global warming impact of fossil fuels. Pressures towards finding new forms of energy are creating new market opportunities (Garud and Karnøe 2001; Rao 2009) and new market forms, e.g. the carbon trading system in the EU (Engels 2006). Zelizer in her recent work shows how market relations evolve and penetrate into personal lives as expectations and technologies change (Zelizer 2005). As Boltanski and Chiapello suggest, capitalism is often driven forward by criticism and critique; new markets emerge in response to demands for freedom, autonomy, ethical sourcing, corporate social responsibility, etc. (Boltanski and Chiapello 2005).

Models of markets: expertise, technostructures and performativity

The final major influence on market situations derives from the interaction between explicit models of how markets work, their implementation in particular contexts, and the technostructures that make them possible. It is clear that markets do not and have not needed models of how they work in order to establish themselves. However, there is an increasing body of work, which illustrates that such models are increasingly used even in relatively simple settings. A well-known example of how even simple markets can be seen as performing economic models appears in the article where Garcia-Parpet examines the

---

[6] It is also relevant to note that 'capital' can be represented in social movements, for example, the development of shareholder activism during the 1980s onwards can be seen as a form of social movement, see e.g. Useem 1993, 1996; also Gourevitch and Shinn 2007.

creation of a strawberry auction at Fontaines-en-Sologne in France (Garcia-Parpet 2007). She shows how this auction had to be created by standardizing the products (i.e. the strawberries), persuading buyers and sellers to be present in the auction room, creating a technostructure for the auction (that included digital displays of prices for the Dutch auction format, which was used, as well as rooms provided for the various parties to the auction and equipped with the technical means to enable them to participate), and gaining support for the auction from local cooperatives of strawberry growers and from local government in the region. She states that 'the practices which constitute the market are not market practices' (p. 37) and further that 'the trading practices that characterize this market were not given in advance. Rather they were the product of work, of investment in two senses of the term. First, there was financial investment in a site, a building and personnel. . . . Second, there was a further form of psychological investment: the work that went into creating an association and a collective identity for its members' (p. 44). Garcia-Parpet emphasizes that a central element in the construction of this market was a theory of markets. The way in which the physical structure of the market was created, the emphasis given to transparency of prices and homogeneity and standardization of products were all designed to create a 'perfect market'. A key agent in this process was an economic adviser who, in the words of the author, 'allowed the enterprise to benefit from his legal and social capital which derived from a training in biology, law and neo-classical economics'. Garcia-Parpet states that 'the market is better conceived as a field of struggle than as the product of mechanical and necessary laws inscribed in the nature of social reality' (p. 46). The market was 'performed' according to the theory rather than the theory reflecting the realities of the market.

The recent work of MacKenzie on the relationship between finance theory and the development of financial markets has been particularly influential in revealing this interaction. He contrasts the view that finance theory is simply a reflection and representation of what goes on in the markets with his own view that 'those markets simply could not function on anything like the scale that they currently do without a technical and communicative infrastructure incorporating models that can be traced back to option theory' (MacKenzie 2006: 253). From this perspective, financial markets are made over time to work in accordance with the model because the participants in the markets and the calculative mechanisms, which have become part of their actor network, are built to conform to the model developed by finance theory. The market is in effect performed by the theory rather than the theory being defined by the market. Referring to the key innovation which provided a mechanism for pricing options, the Black-Scholes model, MacKenzie states that 'the model's relation to the market was not always passive, but sometimes active; . . . its role was not always descriptive but sometimes performative. . . . An engine, not a camera' (MacKenzie 2006: 259; see also MacKenzie 2009).

This inter-relationship has also been studied in terms of auctions, particularly with reference to the field of telecommunications (Guala 2006; Nik-Khah 2006; Mirowski and Nik-Khah 2007). In these auctions, two groups of economists took on important roles. Firstly, game theorists were important in arguing that creating a specific sort of auction process would generate high returns. The Federal Communications

Comisssion (FCC) explicitly involved academic game theorists in advising it on how to conduct the auction and this was rapidly followed by game theorists being employed by the main participants in the auction process, in order to help them lobby for a format to the auction that would most suit their interests. Eventually the FCC agreed to a suggestion from some of the game theorists to what was termed as a 'simultaneous-multiple round-independent auction (SMRI)'. However, it remained unclear exactly how this would work and therefore a second group of economists, the experimental economists, were brought in. This group had expertise derived from laboratory settings and concentrated on resolving inconsistencies and ambiguities of the SMRI auction.

Muniesa and Callon (2007) focus more generally on how these performativity effects emerge through a complex process of experimentation in different sorts of contexts ranging from economic laboratories through to platform configurations (which are essentially models of how complex markets work that are then used to reconfigure existing practices through to what they describe as 'in vivo experiments' (Guala 2007; Muniesa and Callon 2007). In Callon's terms, economics is performative but the way this works depends on the level of experimentation involved. Each of these levels constitutes its own reality, its own world. In order to be moved from one world to another, for example from the laboratory setting to the design of a platform, he states that 'the sociotechnical *agencement* that "goes with it" has to be transported as well' (Callon 2007: 331). In this sense

the performativity approach makes it possible to exhibit the struggle between worlds that are trying to prevail; it makes the struggle for life between statements visible. Each statement, each model, struggles to exist. . . . In reality this struggle between statements is a struggle between sociotechnical *agencements*. It is not the environment that decides and selects the statements that will survive; it is the statements that determine the environment required for their survival.   (Callon 2007: 332)

It can be argued that this approach comes to 'increasingly resemble neoclassical economics, if not serve as its cheerleader' (Nik-Khah 2006: 19), that it assumes that markets along the lines of the neo-classical model do come into existence, and that in the process social influences on how markets operate disappear (Miller 2002; Mirowski and Nik-Khah 2007). Mirowski and Nik-Khah suggest that this approach by 'isolating the economists as the key protagonists . . . tends to distract attention from those who may be major players involved in the construction and shoring up of the economy. . . . It might even end up as prettified neoliberalism decked out in new rags' (2007: 217). On the other hand, the value of this work is to open up the study of the concrete interactions between models of the market as developed by economists, the technostructures of particular markets, and the dynamics of activity and process in such markets. In this way, this approach has made a major contribution to the study of markets by drawing attention to the inter-relationship between economics and markets. As Callon says:

To make a formula or auction system work, one has to have tools, equipment, metrological systems, procedures and so on. To establish relations that 'exist' between monetary masses and price levels, to act on the one in order to control the others, there have to be institutions, systems of observation, codification and data collection, tools for analyzing large numbers and so on. A host of professions, competencies and nonhumans are necessary for academic economics to be successful. Each of these parties 'makes' economics. They are engaged in the construction of a world described and performed by statements and models that we readily agree belong to the world of economics, in the strict sense of the word. The world conveyed by the statement is realized only after a long collective effort, which one could call economic research, involving 90 percent engineering and 10 percent theory.   (Callon 2007: 333)

This argument becomes more complex and central when it is used to consider the development of neo-liberal markets in the period since the 1970s. While there are many political and economic conditions that underpin this process, it is also possible to see how central particular models of the economy were to this process. In her analysis of the growth of the economics profession world-wide, Fourcade, for example, argues that 'the state itself has been redefined as a key professional terrain for economists . . . it has been reconstructed and governmentalized so as to legitimate the claims of economists', which she describes as 'the economicization of the tech-nocracy' and the 'institutionalization of economic knowledge within the state' (Fourcade 2006: 167). Economics in this context refers to a specific form of abstract reasoning in which 'economic problems are detached from their local (historical and geographical) context and are generally understood to be instances of some universal phenomena' (ibid: 160). Economics is established as a universal form of reasoning partly based on a rhetoric of quantification that gives it scientific status in a world of competing forms of expertise and legitimate authority. This universalism enables the creation of clear hierarchies of academic expertise, which facilitate the diffusion of the key ideas and practices as well as the creation of strong networks and reputational communities based around particular universities, departments and individuals. Economists have played a central role in reconstituting competition law and competition agencies as they have imported their specific forms of knowledge into these contexts. Ways of understanding anti-competitive behaviour have become more technical as have efforts to evolve new market structures for introducing competition into utilities and the privatization of public services.

In so doing, economists have also changed the rules of inter-professional competition, particularly in relation to lawyers. Dezalay and Garth (2002a: 5; see also Dezalay and Garth 2002b), for example, examine how neo-liberalism was transferred in the 1980s and 1990s and note that 'economics has been relatively more successful than law' in terms of framing new institutions and practices. Traditional forms of law in relation to competition and the formation of markets have been transformed in the USA and this is reflected in the development of a law-and-economics framework that generates professionals with expertise in both areas around the common discourse of neo-liberal economics. It has been argued that this has led to two other movements in the construction of markets—the process of judicialization and the expansion of adversarial legalism. Stone Sweet defines judicialization as follows:

Judicialization of dispute resolution is the process through which a TDR [Third Party Dispute Resolution] mechanism appears, stabilizes and develops authority over the normative structure governing exchange in a given community. . . . Once individuals have moved to the triadic level, the internal dynamics of TDR will drive processes of judicialization. The dispute resolver will seek to balance the competing claims of disputants but will also generate precedent to legitimize decisions. Triadic rule-making will gradually reconfigure normative structure and, in so doing, reconstruct social relation.   (Stone Sweet in Shapiro and Stone Sweet 2002: 72)

The judicialization of the market opens the door for what has been described as legal adversarialism. This term was developed by Kagan to describe what he refers to as the American Way of Law (Kagan, 2001). He defines the term in relation to 'formal legal contestation' and 'litigant activism'. Formal legal contestation refers to the way in which participants in a dispute are likely to assert their legal rights and engage in action in the courts for remedy (as opposed to other forms of negotiating over conflicts informally or outside the court system). Litigant activism emphasizes that it is the parties to the dispute and not the court itself who pursue the action, seeking out supporting evidence and argument. Adversarial legalism has two main effects. Firstly it is potentially very costly; secondly, it creates high levels of legal uncertainty as the way in which precedents, argument, and evidence can be marshalled and developed can be highly varied and will frequently be innovative and dependent on what can be termed legal entrepreneurialism. Keleman and Sibbitt argue that legal adversarialism 'manifests itself in detailed prescriptive rules, substantial transparency and disclosure requirements, formal and adversarial procedures for resolving disputes, costly legal contestation involving many lawyers and frequent judicial intervention in administrative affairs' (Keleman and Sibbitt 2004: 103). This new judicialization of market regulation has impacted most directly on competition law, placing decisions about concentration and centralization of markets away from the hands of politicians into those of economists, lawyers, and courts.

Thus, whilst in some ways economists are more influential than lawyers in shaping markets, the influence of lawyers returns as judicialization increases. Further, judicialization is not neutral in its effects; it gives rise to forms of legal adversarialism as market actors challenge interpretations and seek to change decisions. Legal adversarialism is highly expensive and therefore access is predominantly available for those individuals and corporations that are wealthy enough to afford the costs, though this can be ameliorated by certain forms of lawyering such as class actions and payment by results. Under judicialization, challenges to regulatory agencies have to be legitimated through appeals to the law and not to politics; they have to be argued using transparent information, which is broadly available to the public. Whilst the agencies are subject to political oversight, they are also increasingly subjected to judicial review. Markets then are performed in particular ways by these professional groups who are significant actors in shaping both the rules of markets and the processes through which the rules are interpreted.

UNDERSTANDING MARKETS
IN COMPARATIVE TERMS

What may be termed the 'neo-Polanyian' perspective emphasizes that there is no separation of the market from social institutions. Markets are never disembedded; they are, rather, embedded in different ways and this process of embedding revolves centrally around the relationship between the state and the market. This is a central topic in the comparative study of institutions. Many of the chapters in this book deal with specific aspects of this relationship and how they vary across different forms of capitalism, e.g. labour (Rubery), the law (Morgan and Quack), financial systems and corporate governance (Deeg, Goyer, Engelen and Konings) and the state more generally (Weiss). Rather than repeat these discussions, the following section is concerned with the idea that the recent period has seen the growing dominance of a particular model of the market known as the liberal market model and that this has caused a significant reshaping of market processes in the major economies, undermining differences and creating convergence.

Markets and deregulation in neo-liberal economies

*realised
deregulation*

The rise of neo-liberal economics has been couched in the language of deregulation. As neo-liberalism emerged, it aimed its critique at state control and state regulation of the market which, it was argued, created perverse incentives for actors to look to the state for ways to extract rent from their positions rather than engage in competitive behaviour in markets that would generate profit and efficiency. Only if the state was taken out of markets and actors were provided with incentives to compete directly with each other rather than look for state support would economies become more efficient. The areas of economic activity that had fallen under state influence ranged from labour markets through to capital and money markets, product markets (retail, wholesale, and commodities markets), markets for corporate control as well as in areas of production and consumption (such as utilities, health, education, social services, etc.). In most developed countries in the post-war period, a range of activities had either been removed from market competition or had been allowed to grow massively within the non-market environment of state provision, e.g. education, health, social services. These were deemed to create spheres of inefficiency and wage inflation and cause higher state spending and increased taxation. The actions of the state were also seen as inimical to market development because they allowed political considerations to enter into what should be 'market decisions'. Thus politicians facing elections were considered likely to use economic policy tools to boost the economy irrespective of the longer term consequences. Therefore, efforts needed to be made to keep politicians out of key areas of decision-making that affected markets. One of the most important such areas was in relation to interest rates where it was argued that independent central banks were better able to provide monetary stability and avoid inflation than were politicians. Underlying these arguments was the belief that markets were the best means to aggregate the preferences of individuals and therefore the role of government should be minimal.

Neo-liberal economists and their political supporters, therefore, pressed the case for deregulating markets. Given the way in which many societies had resolved their social and economic problems following 1945, this gave the neo-liberals a large target at which to aim. Forms of coordinated capitalism, state directed capitalism, corporatism existed across the developed economies of Europe and Asia in the 1970s and 1980s, and even to a degree were present in part of the US. Most developing economies also heavily relied on the state to direct and guide economic activity and the creation of markets. The rise of politicians such as Reagan and Thatcher who espoused these arguments and gradually began to put them into practice in a range of areas of economic activity served to sharpen up the tools and policies available in all contexts where neo-liberal voices were heard. Once the Berlin Wall fell and the Soviet system collapsed, the matter of building forms of capitalism in this image became pressing, a process furthered by the increasingly rapid rise of forms of market capitalism in China and later India.

What became clear in the process, however, was that whilst removing the state from these processes might be the key objective, in order to achieve it the state had to be brought back in. New rules had to be put into place in order to stop politicians and others slipping back into old habits and to encourage everyone instead to concentrate on making markets work (Majone 1990). In effect, deregulation swapped one form of regulation (with one set of purposes and associated social relations) with another (this time one made from the neo-liberal vision of how markets should work). The central elements of this new form of regulation concerned making, monitoring, and adjusting the market so that competitive behaviour was incentivized and other forms of behaviour associated with rent seeking were outlawed. This required the establishment of new sets of rules, new actors, new institutions and new forms of monitoring, enforcement, and sanctioning. As Vogel notes, 'we have wound up with freer markets and *more* rules. In fact, there is often a logical link: liberalization requires reregulation' (Vogel 1996: 3; Vogel 2007). Levy discusses this in terms of a shift from the state taking a role in market direction to engaging in market support. He identifies what he calls two constructive state missions that have emerged in the era of deregulation. These are 'recasting regulatory frameworks to permit countries to cross major economic and technological divides and expanding market competition in industry and services at home and abroad' (Levy 2006: 3). He argues that:

framing the issue in terms of whether the state is growing or shrinking misses what is perhaps a more important set of changes—a shift in the purposes and modalities of contemporary state intervention . . . state activism is an essential component of the move to the market. Instead of an eclipse of the state, economic liberalization is perhaps best conceived of as a redeployment of state energies on behalf of new missions. It is an agenda for state activism, not withdrawal.   (Ibid. 2006: 11, 28)

What are the new ways in which the neo-liberal state intervenes and shapes markets? One important feature is the centrality of specialist regulatory agencies placed at arm's length to the state. This is associated with a number of processes. Firstly it reflects the neo-liberal agenda to take politics out of regulation, at least to the extent that the impact of electoral cycles and the temptation for politicians to shape policies in terms of short-term electoral interests is reduced. Secondly, the agencies are supposed to be a reservoir of technocratic expertise which is used to reach decisions. Thirdly, the development of this technocratic expertise combines a certain delegation of authority to the agencies, within a broad model of public accountability and transparency and executive responsibility. Fourthly, the range of instruments that can be used by the regulators have expanded from coercion and formal law through to forms of soft law. Knill and Lenschow, for example argue that 'instead of hierarchy, these regulations emphasize participation, self-initiative, and voluntarism' (Knill and Lenschow 2004: 221). Fifthly, market participants are drawn into the ambit of the regulatory agencies through consultation, joint working parties, and the sharing of resources and personnel.

Central to the neo-liberal agenda is that such agencies are concerned with what Jordana and Levi-Faur (2004) describe as regulation-*for*-competition and regulation-*of*-competition. They note that regulation-*of*-competition tends to be the task of national regulatory authorities, while regulation-*for*-competition is usually the re-sponsibility of sector specific agencies. The former are mainly concerned with acting to avoid anti-competitive practices from emerging due to levels of concentration in the economy. The latter are more concerned with making sure that in areas that have in the past, for public interest reasons, had a single monopoly provider or a limited number of providers, the conditions are created that open up market participation to a wider group of actors, e.g. in the public utilities.

The argument for a new form of state regulation depends on a contrast with other forms. The neo-liberal model was developed primarily in the US in terms of both its theory and its practice, though it is important to recognize that the US model also includes massive corporate lobbying, a weakening of anti-trust to permit the growth of monopolies, and a lot of political trade protectionism—especially at state level. As described in the chapters in this book, most other societies have evolved historically different forms of relationships between states and the regulation of markets and therefore the shift towards this new model requires a substantial change of institu-tions. One example is that described by Moran in his discussion of the British system of regulation. He uses the term 'club regulation' to describe the way in which market regulation mostly took place in the UK prior to the last two decades. He describes the characteristics of this system as follows:

First, its operations were oligarchic, informal and secretive. Secondly it was highly pervasive.... It . . . shaped government in the over-lapping spheres of self-regulation and the vast, labyrinthine world of quasi-government. Third, it was anachronistic and deliberately so . . . it protected elites from more modern forces: from the threats posed by the new world of formal democracy and from an empowered and often frightening working class.   (Moran 2003: 4)

Central to the 'club' was a form of self-regulation in which insiders decided on how the market was to be managed with very little outside scrutiny. Professional groups like lawyers were able to set fixed prices for their services as were brokers and jobbers on the London Stock market. Fixing prices guaranteed a living for the market participants and limited competitive pressures. The state delegated responsibility and took little interest in the efficiency consequences of these decisions. Competition legislation was weak; many areas were excluded from its terms of reference; the capacity to undertake investigations and enforce changes was limited. Confusingly all of this took place in a context where 'the market' remained a dominant discourse of legitimation going back to nineteenth-century liberalism and before that to Adam Smith. However, the key contrast in this discourse was with state ownership per se, as practised in the UK nationalized industries or in continental Europe and the Soviet bloc. 'The market' as a technical construct, measured by distinctive competitive processes and monitored by economists and others, barely came into this discussion. 'Markets' were ideological constructs in the battle between left and right that characterized the initial post-war period in the UK. In this respect, Moran identifies the sources of 'club' regulation in the social basis of British society whereby the traditional elite had to come to terms with the advent of democracy by sustaining key sources of power away from the direct scrutiny of the public and politicians. As well as fighting as much as it could in public arenas to sustain its power and influence, and drawing on new forms of legitimacy such as education to reinforce this, the elite defended itself by trying as far as possible to retain control over areas of activity that could be legitimated as semi-private and dependent on the goodwill of practitioners. Only with the advent of Thatcherism and the range of changes associated with the rise of neo-liberal economics and the new regulatory state was this model seriously challenged, having survived, in Moran's view, since the Victorian age.

Clearly other countries had different historical traditions. In most European countries, the market had never been given the ideological prominence that it received in the UK. Recent discussions of 'economic nationalism' (Helleiner 2003; Helleiner and Pickel 2005) suggest that 'national identities and nationalism shape economic policies and processes' (p. 221) and that this is reflected in different ways depending on the timing involved and the countries concerned. These arguments are supported by the vast array of studies referred to in the chapters in this book which reveal the depth of divergence between national contexts due to institutional legacies and path-dependencies. Thus in relation to Germany, the regulation of the market reflects a conflict between the legacy of List's ideas and the commitment to competitive processes embedded in the German tradition of 'ordo-liberalism'. Under the Listian perspective, cartels, which agreed prices and market shares amongst member firms, were an acceptable way of building the economic strength of the country even though they required protectionist customs barriers and had the consequence of high prices for consumers. However, proponents of free trade and markets rejected this and in the post-war period, there was increased debate about introducing competition to markets, not least from the pressure of the US to ensure that Germany adopted an open market model. Djelic and Quack (Djelic and Quack 2005; Quack and Djelic 2005; see also Sorge 2005) argue that the impact of these debates was complex. Cartel processes in production markets were gradually overcome but the result was the creation of oligopolies rather than open competitive markets. In other areas such as banking, the effort to create free markets failed almost entirely. Also important to these discussions of the post-war German social market was a perceived need to ensure a market in which small and medium-sized firms could thrive, not just for economic reasons but also to sustain a strong middle class (believed to be a bulwark against communism and fascism). In Germany, therefore, the two approaches to competition coexisted and the impact of the neo-liberal model was different from the UK and the US.

These examples could be increased by looking at other countries. In each country, the way in which markets are constituted, managed, and regulated is a path-dependent process, reflecting political, economic, and social struggles over long periods of time. As institutionalists emphasize, this creates an inertia effect, a resistance to change. What does this mean for the argument that the neo-liberal model of markets and how to regulate them has been diffused more generally across contexts?

Fourcade-Gourinchas and Babb (2002) argue that what they term the 'rebirth of the liberal creed' varied across national contexts due not just to national institutions and path-dependencies but also due to internal social change and external economic change (for a similar discussion focusing on Sweden, the US and the UK see Blyth 2002; also Prasad 2006). In particular, they examine how the old ways of managing markets were challenged by developments in the world economy, leading to specific types of economic crisis, which reflected the way in which particular societies were inserted into that economy. Internally, what appeared to be important in the four cases that they examined was the degree to which the elite in charge of the old system had managed to adapt itself to new circumstances (in particular by becoming more technocratic and expert, particularly in the field of economics) or was challenged from the outside by the emergence of such a group. Fourcade-Gourinchas and Babb argue that 'market policies were constructed as providing a ready-made 'solution' for combining the constraints imposed by the global economic and financial order with a "workable" national strategy' (p. 569).

Simmons et al. (2008) emphasize the external context of these shifts, arguing that the liberal market model was diffused as a result of four processes—coercion, competition, learning, and emulation. Coercion essentially refers to the ability of the USA and the international financial institutions to enforce on countries the liberal market model and its distinctive mode of regulation. However the ability to coerce along these lines is always likely to be constrained by the sorts of internal path-dependencies described earlier. Thus Djelic shows how even when the US had coercive power through being the victor of the Second World War it still could not entirely reshape the institutions of the defeated powers; the result was hybridization and adaption rather than adoption per se (Djelic 1998, 2002). Similarly the use of conditionality clauses by the international financial institutions may have a major impact but it does so in a pre-existing context and the result is not likely to be the installation of the market model without modification. Competition is described in Simmons et al. in terms of how the incentives to liberalize increase after key competitors open their markets. Failure to follow this may lead to a country slipping behind in economic terms as investors, in particular, switch their funds to competitor countries. The range of market issues that can affect this process is wide, e.g. tax systems, regulatory requirements, opening up capital markets, installing systems of transparency, managing inflation through creating an independent central bank, etc. Learning refers to the idea that economies which have been successfully opened up and liberalized enable other economies to learn important lessons about the relative merits of free markets as well as the techniques, practices, and knowledge that facilitates making them work successfully. Simmons et al. are sceptical about the role of learning because the relationship between institutional change and economic outcomes is extremely complex when it comes to the detail. More important in their view is what they term 'emulation', which refers to the generalized belief that a particular way of acting is appropriate even where the evidence-base for such an assertion is relatively weak and where the specific relevance of the example to a particular context is not clear. Emulation is particularly associated with the development of cross-national epistemic communities of experts where a shared cognitive and normative framework emerges and is the basis for exporting particular models of markets and regulation. Drori et al. for example, argue that there is a consolidation of world culture where:

we now have the global conception of a more abstract and universal rationality. There are generally right ways to do things, carried, among others, by social science professionals whose instructions have widespread and rapidly increasing authority . . . these principles and models are universal—not seen as linked to racial, historical, religious or accidental virtues of particular peoples.   (Drori, Meyer, and Hwang 2006: 37)

Among these correct ways of doing things, they identify economic development and the role of modern economic theory. Djelic (2006) develops this argument in terms of what she describes as the 'global diffusion of marketization' though she also notes that there are limits to this process arising from overt resistance and covert forms of local translation, editing, and hybridization (see, for example, the collections of papers in Djelic and Quack 2003; Djelic and Sahlin-Andersson 2006).

These approaches emphasize the role of private actors in establishing the rules of the global and international markets. However, it is clear that these private actors also interact and cooperate with different types of public actors, some of which are nationally based but others of which are international in various ways. Thus institutionalizing the rules of neo-liberal markets in the international context is a multi-actored and multi-levelled process. The collection edited by Djelic and Sahlin-Andersson (2006) provides a number of examples where private rule-setting has been important. Botzem and Quack, for example, have examined how international standard setting in accounting developed from the moves of various private professional associations to overcome problems in the standardizing of auditing procedures (Botzem and Quack 2006). Gradually these initiatives have been incorporated into the deliberations of public actors and have led, following conflict between EU-level rules and those of the US, to the establishment of global International Accounting Standards. The development of competition law also reflects these interactions, particularly in terms of potential conflicts between the EU and the US and the potential role of the WTO in mediating disagreements. Morgan, for example, shows how US law firms and the US government sought to influence EU decisions on competition law to shape a convergence of approach (Morgan 2006; see also Morgan 2008 on the interaction of public and private actors in international financial markets). Failure to achieve this led to more emphasis being placed on creating a transnational community of experts where common cognitive and normative frameworks could become established (Djelic and Kleiner 2006). Quack examines the way in which lawyers become involved in this process by virtue of the way in which their contractual innovations across borders on behalf of international clients lead to the creation of new forms of private rules that gradually become institutionalized, a process she describes as one of 'distributed agency' (Quack 2007).

In these contexts, the rules of the market are emergent from the interaction of national and international actors and private and public actors. These processes tend to be driven by neo-liberal views of how markets work and the sort of institutions in which the markets are embedded tend to be concerned with ensuring the stability of the market itself. Nevertheless, it is important to note that this is an arena of struggle in which different types of actor can have an impact (see, for example, Kahler and Lake 2003). National governments can delay the opening up of markets. Multinational companies can use their power to negotiate favourable deals. Transnational organizations can develop strong support from civil society movements to establish new sorts of rules, e.g. in relation to various forms of sustainability and corporate responsibility debates. International governmental organizations can become sites of conflict between different national interests. Transnational communities of expert groups can establish new frameworks for understanding global problems in markets. Market uncertainty and risk can turn upside down expectations about ordering processes as has occurred in the financial crisis of 2007–8. Nevertheless in all these cases, what is of interest is how central rules and institutions are to understanding markets and their functioning even in arenas where economists might argue that markets are self-regulating and self-contained.

CONCLUSIONS

This chapter has sought to provide an overview of how markets can be analysed using an institutional and comparative lens. It began by showing how market situations are embedded in social relations. They cannot exist without social rules and the role of research is to understand how these rules are created and sustained and with what effect. Drawing on Weber's definition of a market situation, the first part of the chapter examined how market processes could be understood in terms of their social underpinning. All markets are dependent on these processes but the way in which they work will differ according to different market contexts.

The second part of the chapter looked at the forces influencing the development of specific market forms, focusing particularly on the roles of the state, firms, social movements, and expert groups. Finally the chapter considered how the development of the neo-liberal market model diffused across different national and sectoral settings and impacted on different groups of firms and social actors. Institutional influences and path-dependencies introduce resistances and lead to processes of adaptation and hybridization. Rather than simplifying market processes and purging them of state influence and social concerns, the neo-liberal model of the market has created more diverse arenas for debate and conflict over how markets should be structured.

The chapter revealed certain common features in all markets and these common-alities suggest an agenda for further research on markets.

Firstly, markets depend on agreements about rules but these agreements are embedded in different social relationships. Some are embedded in legal frameworks and the role of the state in sustaining such agreements is clearly central. When it comes to a phenomenon such as money, the state has a central role in guaranteeing confidence in money as a unit of account and a store of value. Other markets are embedded in informal and private agreements that emerge among market partici-pants; some markets are local, others are localized but internationally and globally linked; still others are mainly national in scope. Historical path-dependencies mean that these rules often reflect specific developmental trajectories of particular societies. Increasingly under processes of globalization, these rules are subject to broader scrutiny both from a disciplinary point of view (e.g. do they create unfair rules of competition prohibiting the entry of foreign companies?) and from a policy point of view (are they the most appropriate rules to have in a context of open markets?), Explaining how rules emerge and change in these different arenas remains a central task for comparative institutional research.

Secondly, markets have specific structures that shape their dynamics. These struc-tures reflect how specific actors take positions in markets, respond to each other, and seek to control how the dynamics of the market emerge. In these processes, actors bring differential power resources and market rules reflect the ability of actors to make their own interests count in relation to others. Clearly the structures that are created are temporary. They are subject to change as power relations change and through competitive processes but what is also clear is that they can be relatively robust and long-lasting. What are the factors that enable these structures to emerge and reproduce and what disrupts them?

Thirdly, markets are material things. They require various forms of materialization in order to exist. Money is a form of materializing a market that relates also to the materialization of price, a system of calculation, exchange, and settlement. This materialization is not simply an intermediary between the buyer and the seller; rather it is a specific route through which exchange must pass and is therefore to be studied in its own right. Traditionally, markets were materialized in face-to-face interactions between buyer and seller. Some markets retained these features even as their role grew, e.g. financial markets were mainly open outcry markets until the 1970s and 1980s. Increasingly, however, markets are instantiated in the materiality of computer systems and software, in a technostructure where humans and machines form an actor network that has the capacity for complex calculations, exchanges, and settlements. How do particular materializations affect this passage between buyer and seller?

Fourthly, it is increasingly difficult to study markets without simultaneously studying economists and the models of markets which economists construct. In a context where markets are seen as the most efficient and effective form of resource allocation available to a society and where scientific, credentialized knowledge of a process has high status and influence, it should be unsurprising that economics as a profession and a discipline has come to play a central role in the making of markets. Economists are not passive observers of a phenomenon external to themselves; increasingly they are involved in constructing those markets through their role in competition law, in designing auctions to sell off government assets at the highest possible figure, in designing new financial markets, in advising governments on how to implement a neo-liberal market model. The argument that economics is performative requires to be taken seriously in any market context.

Understanding specific market processes requires a combination of all these different levels of analysis. However, even having taken such a broad overview of the field, it is clear that there are some areas that will require more sustained attention in the future. Two interconnected issues can be mentioned in this respect.

The first is the issue of market outcomes. Underpinning the whole discourse of markets remains the original insight of Adam Smith that through the pursuit of self-interest, the most efficient distribution of resources can be achieved. Clearly the development of political economy as a field of study was shaped by the Marxist response to this argument in which the outcomes of markets was seen in terms of intensified and growing inequality between capital and labour. Polanyi's idea of the double movement of market society described a context in which those suffering from the inequality of the market sought to develop different resources, i.e. those of the language of democracy in order to build a protection from the market. Studies of different forms of capitalism are generally concerned with how these outcomes vary across particular contexts where different political and social histories have led to distinctive state policies (see the chapter by Kenworthy). More recently the debate on financialization has sought to show how the establishment of new financial markets has contributed to increasing forms of inequality (see the chapter by Engelen and Konings). Studies of the emergence of international markets have frequently noted that the general public is excluded from processes that are based on expert networks and that the interests represented in these discussions are narrowly defined, although in certain cases, global civil society movements may break through these restrictions. However, few studies of markets take the issue of outcomes on board explicitly. Few of them 'follow the money' to see who benefits, why and how. In the light of the collapse of confidence in the idea of a universal benefit accruing to all from the adoption of the neo-liberal model of market, it may be an important time to place the issue of outcomes more firmly at the centre of studies of markets.

Related to this is the problem of how markets interact and are interdependent. This is particularly clear in relation to the interaction within financial markets and between financial markets and other markets. Financial institutions that trade in a number of distinct markets, e.g. the wholesale and the retail money markets, may find that failures in one soon start to impact on the other. Because of the high levels of leverage possible in financial markets, losses by just one trader in one market can destroy an entire bank, wiping out its reserve capital in a single stroke, as was the case with Barings and the 'rogue trader', Nick Leeson. In the more recent financial crisis, the logics of action inscribed into the growth of the derivatives markets created interdependencies on a scale not seen before and when the key elements sustaining this market disappeared, the contagion like a virus[7] spread rapidly through the financial system destroying some actors and weakening others. The failure of one bank affects all the other banks with which it does business and for this reason, systemic risk of contagion is a key concern for central banks and regulators. Failures or rumours of failures in the wholesale market can be compounded by retail depositors withdrawing their money in fear that a bankruptcy will lead to the loss of their deposits. In the US as part of the New Deal, there was an effort to keep commercial and wholesale banking apart to avoid such contagion but by the 1990s this separation had practically disappeared. In the UK, it was Northern Rock's dependence on the wholesale markets and concern that it could not secure refinancing that led to depositors seeking to withdraw their funds and the subsequent run on the bank leading eventually to nationalization in 2008. In general, central banks and financial regulators are expected to avoid systemic failure, to insulate other financial institutions from the failure of one and to protect the broader economic system from the consequences of such a breakdown. The crash of Autumn 2008 reveals how much governments are willing to do in order to avoid systemic failure. Ideological positions had been turned on their head in a matter of days, vast sums of public money had been promised to reintroduce stability into the financial system and the whole neo-liberal model has suffered a huge blow to its prestige from which it may not recover for some time.

Crashes in financial markets have varying impacts on what is termed 'the real economy'. The inter-war depression spread rapidly from Wall Street as the loss of

---

[7] The metaphor of virus as a way of understanding the financial crisis has been taken up in official circles, see e.g. the speech on 'Rethinking the Financial Network' by Andrew Haldane, Executive Director of the Bank of England (Haldane 2009).

funds there led to reduced consumption and consequent reduced internal demand for goods and services. In the more highly financialized economy of the contemporary period, there are likely to be similar impacts, even if governments and economic policymakers are better able to respond to events. The way in which the contagion spreads around an economy through different market sectors is not yet clear. Contagion effects can derive from different sources. Price rises in a significant market such as energy can have an impact on many other markets. Similarly significant price falls such as those that have occurred in computer technology can create whole new possible markets. Contagion effects also raise issues of time and space. In spatial terms, how and why does a market fall in one country impact on other countries? In terms of time, how quickly do contagion effects occur? In financial markets, as the crash of Autumn 2008 has shown, media attention focuses minute by minute on the rise and fall of the FTSE, the Dow Jones, the DAX, etc. Response times of market participants have to be measured in seconds if they are to make money in contexts where prices are gyrating wildly.

Interdependencies of markets across sectors, geographies, and time periods appears to be growing. Part of this relates to the creation of new machines of calculation, exchange, and settlement, but it is also implicit in the drive coming from the various sources described in this chapter to operationalize a particular view of the neo-liberal markets. Debates and conflicts in one market flow through into others. The vision of a free market economy provides a court of appeal for all those who believe they are facing unfair competition whatever the market sector, and suggests pressure for markets to converge in their operation creating a form of cognitive and normative interdependence that may be shaken by particular resistances or crises.

In conclusion, the comparative institutional perspective on markets has delivered a range of new perspectives on how markets work. This research constitutes a strong challenge to those determined to sustain a model of markets as self-regulating. The discussion in this chapter has shown that this is not the case. Markets are institutionally embedded. This is what gives them their diversity as well as their interest. Now that the neo-liberal model of the market is beginning to lose its aura of invincibility, the opportunity arises to develop further the comparative institutionalist agenda as developed in this chapter and this book.

REFERENCES

ABOLAFIA, M. (1996). *Making Markets: Opportunism and Restraint on Wall Street*, (Cambridge, MA: London: Harvard University Press).

——(1998). 'Markets as Cultures: An Ethnographic Approach', in M. Callon (ed.), *The Laws of the Markets*, (Oxford: Blackwell Publishers) 69–85.

ARRIGHI, G. (1994). *The Long Twentieth Century: Money, Power, and the Origins Of our Times*, (London: Verso).

——(2007). *Adam Smith in Beijing: Lineages of the Twenty-first Century*, (London; New York: Verso).

BECKERT, J. (2008). *Inherited Wealth*, (Princeton, NJ: Princeton University Press).

BEUNZA, D. and D. STARK (2004). 'Tools of the Trade: The Socio-Technology of Arbitrage in a Wall Street Trading Room', *Industrial and Corporate Change* 13(2): 369–400.

——I. HARDIE, and D. MACKENZIE (2006). 'A Price is a Social Thing: Towards a Material Sociology of Arbitrage', *Organization Studies* 27(5): 721–45.

BLOCK, F. (2003). 'Karl Polanyi and the Writing of The Great Transformation', *Theory and Society*, 32(3): 275–306.

BLYTH, M. (2002). *Great Transformations: Economic Ideas and Institutional Change in the Twentieth Century*, (Cambridge: Cambridge University Press).

BOLTANSKI, L. and E. CHIAPELLO (2005). *The New Spirit of Capitalism*, (London; New York, NY: Verso).

BOTZEM, S. and S. QUACK (2006). 'Contested Rules and Shifting Boundaries: International Standard-setting in Accounting', in M.-L. Djelic and K. Sahlin-Andersson (eds.), *Transnational Governance: Institutional Dynamics of Regulation*, (Cambridge: Cambridge University Press) 266–86.

BRAUDEL, F. (1985). *The Wheels of Commerce*, (London: Fontana Press).

BURT, R. S. (1992). *Structural Holes: The Social Structure of Competition*, (Cambridge, MA; London: Harvard University Press).

CALLON, M. (1998). 'Introduction: The Embeddedness of Economic Markets in Economics', in M. Callon (ed.), *The Laws of the Markets*, (Oxford: Blackwell Publishers), 1–57.

——(2007). 'What does it Mean to Say that Economics is Performative?', in D. MacKenzie, F. Muniesa, and L. Siu (eds.), *Do Economists Make Markets? On the Performativity of Economics*, (Princeton, NJ: Princeton University Press), 311–57.

——C. MEADEL, and V. RABEHARISOA (2002). 'The Economy of Qualities', *Economy and Society*, 31(2): 194–217.

CAMPBELL, J. L., J. ROGERS HOLLINGSWORTH, and L. N. LINDBERG (eds.) (1991). *Governance of the American Economy*, (Cambridge: Cambridge University Press).

CARRUTHERS, B. G. (2005). 'The Sociology of Money and Credit', in N. Smelser, and R. Swedberg (eds.), *The Handbook of Economic Sociology*, 2nd edn. (Princeton, NJ: Princeton University Press; Russell Sage Foundation), 355–78.

COHEN, B. J. (1998). *The Geography of Money*, (Ithaca, NY; London: Cornell University Press).

——(2006). *The Future of Money*, (Princeton, NJ; Oxford: Princeton University Press).

CROUCH, C. (1993). *Industrial Relations and European State Traditions*, (Oxford: Clarendon Press).

DAVIS, G. F. (2005). *Social Movements and Organization Theory*, (Cambridge: Cambridge University Press).

DEZALAY, Y. and B. G. GARTH (2002a). *Global Prescriptions: The Production, Exportation, and Importation of a New Legal Orthodoxy*, (Ann Arbor: University of Michigan Press).

————(2002b). *The Internationalization of Palace Wars: Lawyers, Economists, and the Contest to Transform Latin American States*, (Chicago: University of Chicago Press).

DJELIC, M.-L. (1998). *Exporting the American Model: The Post-war Transformation of European Business*, (Oxford: Oxford University Press).

——(2002). 'Does Europe mean Americanization? The Case of Competition', *Competition and Change* 6(3): 233–50.

——(2006). 'Marketization: From Intellectual Agenda to Global Policy-making', in M.-L. Djelic and K. Sahlin-Andersson (eds.), *Transnational Governance: Institutional Dynamics of Regulation*, (Cambridge: Cambridge University Press), 53–73.

Djelic, M.-L. and T. Kleiner (2006). 'The International Competition Network: Moving towards Transnational Governance', in M.-L. Djelic and K. Sahlin-Andersson (eds.), *Transnational Governance: Institutional Dynamics of Regulation*, (Cambridge: Cambridge University Press), 287–307.

——and S. Quack (2003). *Globalization and Institutions: Redefining the Rules of the Economic Game*, (Cheltenham: Edward Elgar).

————(2005). 'Rethinking Path Dependency: The Crooked Path of Institutional Change in Post-War Germany', in G. Morgan, R. Whitley, and E. Moen (eds.), *Changing Capitalisms: Internationalization, Institutional Change and Systems of Economic Organization*, (Oxford: Oxford University Press), 190–231.

——and K. Sahlin-Andersson (2006). *Transnational Governance: Institutional Dynamics of Regulation*, (Cambridge: Cambridge University Press).

Drori, G. S., J. W. Meyer, and H. Hwang (2006). *Globalization and Organization: World Society and Organisational Change*, (Oxford: Oxford University Press).

Duina, F. G. (2006). *The Social Construction of Free Trade: The European Union, NAFTA, and MERCOSUR*, (Princeton, NJ: Princeton University Press).

Durkheim, E. (1997). *The Division of Labor in Society*, (New York, NY: Free Press).

Dyson, K. H. F. (2002). *European States and the Euro: Europeanization, Variation, and Convergence*, (Oxford: Oxford University Press).

Edwards, R. (1979). *Contested Terrain: The Transformation of the Workplace in the Twentieth Century*, (New York: Basic Books).

Eichengreen, B. J. (2008). *Globalizing Capital: A History of the International Monetary System*, 2nd edn., (Princeton, NJ: Princeton University Press).

Engels, A. (2006). 'Market Creation and Transnational Rule-making: The Case of CO_2 Emissions Trading', in M.-L. Djelic and K. Sahlin-Andersson (eds.), *Transnational Governance: Institutional Dynamics of Regulation*, (Cambridge: Cambridge University Press), 329–348.

Ferguson, N. (2001). *The Cash Nexus: Money and Power in the Modern World, 1700–2000.* (London: Allen Lane).

——(2008). *The Ascent of Money*, (London: Allen Lane).

Fligstein, N. (1990). *The Transformation of Corporate Control*, (Cambridge, MA; London: Harvard University Press).

——(2001). *The Architecture of Markets: An Economic Sociology of Twenty-First-Century Capitalist Societies*, (Princeton, NJ: Princeton University Press).

——(2008). *Euroclash: the EU, European Identity, and the Future of Europe*, (Oxford: Oxford University Press).

Fourcade, M. (2006). 'The Construction of a Global Profession: The Transnationalization of Economics', *American Journal of Sociology* 112(July): 145–94.

——and K. Healy (2007). 'Moral Views of Market Society', *Annual Review of Sociology*, 33.

Fourcade-Gourinchas, M. and S. L. Babb (2002). 'The Rebirth of the Liberal Creed: Paths to Neoliberalism in Four Countries', *American Journal of Sociology* 108(3): 533–79.

Fukuyama, F. (1992). *The End of History and the Last Man*, (London: Hamish Hamilton).

Garcia-Parpet, M.-F. (2007). 'The Social Construction of a Perfect Market: The Strawberry Auction at Fontaines-en-Sologne', in D. MacKenzie, F. Muniesa, and L. Siu (eds.), *Do Economists make Markets? On the Performativity of Economics*, (Princeton, NJ: Princeton University Press), 20–53.

Garud, R. and P. Karnøe (2001). *Path Dependence and Creation*, (Mahwah, NJ; London: Lawrence Erlbaum Associates).

GLYN, A. (2007). *Capitalism Unleashed: Finance, Globalization, and Welfare*, (Oxford: Oxford University Press).

GOODWIN, J. (2004). *Greenback: The Almighty Dollar and the Invention of America*, (London: Penguin Books).

GOUREVITCH, P. and P. SHINN (2007). *Political Power and Corporate Control: The New Global-Politics of Corporate Governance*, (Princeton, NJ: Princeton University Press).

GRANOVETTER, M. (1985). 'Economic Action and Social Structure: The Problem of Embeddedness', *American Journal of Sociology* 91: 481–510.

——(2005). 'The Impact of Social Structure on Economic Outcomes', *Journal of Economic Perspectives* 19(1): 33–50.

GREIF, A. (2006). *Institutions and The Path to the Modern Economy: Lessons from Medieval Trade*, (Cambridge; New York: Cambridge University Press).

GUALA, F. (2006). 'Getting the FCC Auctions Straight: A Reply to Nik-Khah', *Economic Sociology_The European Electronic Newsletter* 7(3): 23–8.

——(2007). 'How to do Things with Experimental Economics', in D. MacKenzie, F. Muniesa, and L. Siu (eds.), *Do Economists make Markets? On the Performativity of Economics*, (Princeton NJ: Princeton University Press), 128–63.

HALDANE, A. G. (2009). 'Rethinking the Financial Network'. Downloadable from http://www.bankofengland.co.uk/publications/speeches/2009/speech386.pdf.

HAYEK, F. A., VON (1944). *The Road to Serfdom*, (London: Routledge).

——(1990). *Denationalisation of Money: The Argument Refined: An Analysis of the Theory and Practice of Concurrent Currencies*, 3rd edn. (London: Institute of Economic Affairs).

HEALY, K. (2006). *Last Best Gifts: Altruism and the Market for Human Blood and Organs*, (Chicago: University of Chicago Press).

HELLEINER, E. (2002). 'Economic Nationalism as a Challenge to Economic Liberalism? Lessons from the 19th Century', *International Studies Quarterly* 46: 307–29.

HIRSCHMAN, A. O. (1977). *The Passion and the Interests*, (Princeton NJ: Princeton University Press).

——(1982). 'Rival Interpretations of the Market: Civilizing, Destructive or Feeble?', *Journal of Economic Literature* 20: 1463–84.

INGHAM, G. (2004). *The Nature of Money*, (Cambridge: Polity Press).

JABKO, N. (2006). *Playing the Market: A Political Strategy for Uniting Europe, 1985–2005*, (Ithaca, NY: Cornell University Press).

JORDANA, J. and D. LEVI-FAUR (eds.) (2004). *The Politics of Regulation: Institutions and Regulatory Reforms for the Age of Governance*, (Cheltenham, UK: Edward Elgar Publishing).

KAGAN, R. A. (2001). *Adversarial Legalism: The American Way of Law*, (Cambridge, MA; London: Harvard University Press).

KAHLER, M. and D. A. LAKE (eds.) (2003). *Governance in a Global Economy: Political Authority in Transition*, (Princeton, NJ: Princeton University Press).

KELEMAN, R. D. and E. C. SIBBITT (2004). 'The Globalization of American Law', *International Organization* 58(winter): 103–36.

KNIGHTS, D. and G. MORGAN (1997). *Regulation and Deregulation in European Financial Services*, (Basingstoke: Macmillan Business).

KNILL, C. and A. LENSCHOW (2004). 'Modes of Regulation in the Governance of the European Union: Towards a Comprehensive Evaluation', in J. Jordana, and D. Levi-Faur (eds.), *The Politics of Regulation*, (Cheltenham, UK: Edward Elgar Publishing), 218–44.

KNORR CETINA, K. and A. PREDA (eds.) (2005). *The Sociology of Financial Markets*, (Oxford: Oxford University Press).

KRIPPNER, G. and A. S. ALVAREZ (2007). 'Embeddedness and the Intellectual Projects of Economic Sociology', *Annual Review of Sociology* 33: 219–40.

——M. GRANOVETTER, F. BLOCK, N. BIGGART, T. BEAMISH, Y. HSING G. HART, G. ARRIGHI, M. MENDELL, J. HALL, M. BURAWOY, S. VOGEL, and S. O'RIAIN (2004). 'Polanyi Symposium: A Conversation on Embeddedness', *Socio-Economic Review* 2: 109–35.

LAURENCE, H. (2001). *Money Rules: The New Politics of Finance in Britain and Japan,* (Ithaca, NY: Cornell University Press).

LEIFER, E. M. and H. C. WHITE (2004). 'A Structural Approach to Markets', in F. Dobbin (ed.), *The New Economic Sociology,* (Princeton, NJ: Princeton University Press), 302–24.

LEVY, J. D. (ed.), (2006). *The State after Statism: New State Activities in the Age of Liberalization,* (Cambridge, MA: Harvard University Press).

MACFARLANE, A. (1978). *The Origins of English Individualism: The Family, Property and Social Transition,* (Oxford: Blackwell).

——(1987). *The Culture of Capitalism,* (Oxford: Blackwell).

MACKENZIE, D. (2006). *An Engine, not a Camera: How Financial Models Shape Markets,* (Cambridge, MA; London: MIT Press).

——(2009). *Material Markets: How Economic Agents are Constructed,* (Oxford: Oxford University Press).

——and Y. MILLO (2003). 'Constructing a Market, Performing Theory: The Historical Sociology of a Financial Derivatives Exchange', *American Journal of Sociology* 109: 107–45.

MAJONE, G. (ed) (1990). *Deregulation or Re-regulation: Regulatory Reform in Europe and the United States,* (London: Pinter).

MANN, M. (1986). *The Sources of Social Power* Vol. 1: *A History of Power from the Beginning to A.D. 1760,* (Cambridge: Cambridge University Press).

——(1993). *The Sources of Social Power* Vol. 2: *The Rise of Classes and Nation-states,* (Cambridge: Cambridge University Press).

MARSHALL, T. H. (1950). *Citizenship and Social Class: And other Essays,* (Cambridge: University Press).

MARX, K. (1990). *Capital: A Critique of Political Economy.* vol. 1. (Harmondsworth: Penguin in association with New Left Review).

MILLER, D. (2002). 'Turning Callon the Right Way Up', *Economy and Society* 31(2): 218–33.

MIROWSKI, P. and E. NIK-KHAH (2007). 'Markets Made Flesh: Performativity and a Problem in Science Studies, Augmented with Consideration of the FCC Auctions', in D. MacKenzie, F. Muniesa, and L. Siu (eds.), *Do Economists make Markets? On the Performativity of Economics,* (Princeton, NJ: Princeton University Press), 190–224.

MOORE, B. (1973). *Social Origins of Dictatorship and Democracy: Lord and Peasant in the Making of the Modern World,* (Harmondsworth: Penguin).

MORAN, M. (2003). *The British Regulatory State: High Modernism and Hyper-Innovation,* (Oxford: Oxford University Press), 250.

MORGAN, G. (2006). 'Transnational Actors, Transnational Institutions, Transnational Spaces: The Role of Law Firms in the Internationalization of Competition Regulation', in M.-L. Djelic and K. Sahlin-Andersson (eds.), *Transnational Governance: Institutional Dynamics of Regulation,* (Cambridge: Cambridge University Press), 139–60.

——(2008). 'Market Formation and Governance in International Financial Markets: The Case of OTC Derivatives' *Human Relations* 61(5): 637–60.

——and L. ENGWALL (1999). *Regulation and Organizations: International Perspectives,* (London: Routledge).

MUNIESA, F. and M. CALLON (2007). 'Economic Experiments and the Construction of Markets', in D. MacKenzie, F. Muniesa, and L. Siu (eds.), *Do Economists make Markets? On the Performativity of Economics,* (Princeton, NJ: Princeton University Press), 163–89.

NIK-KHAH, E. (2006). 'What the FCC Auctions can Tell us about the Performativity Thesis'. *Economic Sociology_The European Electronic Newsletter* 7(2): 15–21.

NORTH, D. C. (1990). *Institutions, Institutional Change and Economic Performance*, (Cambridge: Cambridge University Press).

——and B. C. WEINGAST (1989). 'The Evolution of Institutions Governing Public Choice in 17th-century England', *Journal of Economic History* 49: 803–32.

PODOLNY, J. M. (2005). *Status Signals: A Sociological Study of Market Competition*, (Princeton, NJ: Princeton University Press).

POLANYI, K. (2001). *The Great Transformation: The Political and Economic Origins of Our Time*, (2nd Beacon pbk. edn.). (Boston, MA: Beacon Press).

PRASAD, M. (2006). *The Politics of Free Markets: The Rise of Neoliberal Economic Policies in Britain, France, Germany and the United States*, (Chicago: University of Chicago Press).

PREDA, A. (2005). 'Legitimacy and Status Groups in Financial Markets', *British Journal of Sociology* 56(3): 451–71.

——(2007). 'The Sociological Approach to Financial Markets', *Journal of Economic Surveys* 21(3): 506–33.

QUACK, S. (2007). 'Legal Professionals and Transnational Law-Making', *Organization* 14(5): 643–66.

——and M.-L. DJELIC (2005). 'Adaptation, Recombination and Reinforcement: The Story of Antitrust and Competition Law in Germany and Europe', in W. Streeck and K. Thelen (eds.), *Beyond Continuity: Institutional Change in Advanced Political Economies*, (Oxford: Oxford University Press), 255–81.

RAO, H. (2009). *Market Rebels: How Activists Make or Break Radical Innovations*, (Princeton, NJ: Princeton University Press).

SCHNEIBERG, M. and M. LOUNSBURY (2008). 'Social Movements and Institutional Analysis', in R. Greenwood, C. Oliver, K. Sahlin, and R. Suddaby (eds.), *The SAGE Handbook of Organizational Institutionalism*, (London: Sage), 650–72.

SHAPIRO, M. and A. STONE SWEET (2002). *On Law, Politics, and Judicialization*, (Oxford; New York: Oxford University Press).

SIMMEL, G. (2004). *The Philosophy of Money*, (London: Routledge).

SIMMONS, B. A., F. DOBBIN, and G. GARRETT (eds.) (2008). *The Global Diffusion of Markets and Democracy*, (Cambridge: Cambridge University Press).

SMITH-DOERR, J. and W. W. POWELL (2005). 'Networks and Economic Life', in N. J. Smelser and R. Swedberg (eds.), *The Handbook of Economic Sociology*, 2nd edn. (Princeton, NJ: Princeton University Press), 379–402.

SORGE, A. (2005). *The Global and the Local: Understanding the Dialectics of Business Systems*, (Oxford: Oxford University Press).

SOTO, H. DE (2000). *The Mystery of Capital: Why Capitalism Triumphs in the West and Fails Everywhere Else*, (London; New York: Bantam Press).

STONE SWEET, A., W. SANDHOLTZ, and N. FLIGSTEIN (2001). *The institutionalization of Europe*, (Oxford: Oxford University Press).

STRATHERN, M. (2002). 'Externalities in Comparative Guise', *Economy and Society* 31(2): 250–67.

SWEDBERG, R. (2005). 'Markets in Society'. in N. Smelser and R. Swedberg (eds.), *The Handbook of Economic Sociology*, 2nd edn. (Princeton, NJ: Princeton University Press; Russell Sage Foundation), 233–54.

THOMPSON, G. F. (2003). *Between Hierarchies and Markets: The Logic and Limits of Network Forms of Organization*, (Oxford: Oxford University Press).

TILLY, C. (1990). *Coercion, Capital, and European States, A.D. 990–1990*, (Oxford: Blackwell).

USEEM, M. (1993). *Executive Defense: Shareholder Power and Corporate Reorganization*, (Harvard, MA: Harvard University Press).

——(1996). *Investor Capitalism: How Money Managers Are Changing the Face of Corporate America*, (New York: HarperCollins).

UZZI, B. (1997). 'Social Structure and Competition in Interfirm Networks: The Paradox of Embeddedness', *Administrative Science Quarterly* 42: 35–67.

——(1999). 'Social Embeddedness in the Creation of Financial Capital', *American Sociological Review* 64: 481–505.

——and LANCASTER R. (2004). 'Embeddedness and Price Formation in the Corporate Law Market', *American Sociological Review*, 69(June): 319–44.

VELTHIUS, O. (2005). *Talking Prices: Symbolic Meanings of Prices on the Market for Contemporary Art*, (Princeton, NJ: Princeton University Press).

VOGEL, S. K. (1996). *Freer Markets, More Rules: Regulatory Reform in Advanced Industrial Countries*, (Ithaca, NY; London: Cornell University Press).

——(2007). 'Why Freer Markets Need More Rules', in N. H. Barma and S. K. Vogel (eds.), *The Political Economy Reader*, (London: Routledge), 341–54.

WALLERSTEIN, I. M. (2004). *World-systems Analysis: An Introduction*, (Durham: Duke University Press).

WEBER, M. (1978). *Economy and Society: An Outline of Interpretive Sociology*, (Berkeley; London: University of California Press).

WHITE, H. C. (1992). *Identity and Control: A Structural Theory of Social Action*, (Princeton, NJ: Princeton University Press).

——(2002). *Markets from Networks: Socioeconomic Models of Production*, (Princeton, NJ: Princeton University Press).

WILLIAMSON, O. E. (1975). *Markets and Hierarchies: Analysis and Antitrust Implications: A Study in the Economics of Internal Organization*, (New York: Free Press Collier Macmillan).

ZALOOM, C. (2006). *Out of the Pits: Traders and Technology from Chicago to London*, (Chicago: University of Chicago Press).

ZELIZER, V. A. R. (1983). *Morals and Markets: The Development of Life Insurance in the United States*, (New Brunswick: Transaction Books).

——(1985). *Pricing the Priceless Child: The Changing Social Value of Children*, (New York: Basic Books).

——(1994). *The Social Meaning of Money*, (New York: Basic Books).

——(2005). *The Purchase of Intimacy*, (Princeton, NJ: Princeton University Press).

CHAPTER 9

TRANSNATIONAL INSTITUTIONS AND INTERNATIONAL REGIMES

LEONARD SEABROOKE[1]

INTRODUCTION

This chapter provides a review of the debates about how transnational institutions and international regimes have influence in the international political economy. How transnational institutions and international regimes are formed, through which actors and networks they operate, and how they emerge are all questions for comparative institutional analysis. In the international relations (IR)/international political economy (IPE) literature, which is the basis for this chapter, answers to these questions reflect different traditions and approaches to the study of states and non-state actors as well as to the methodological and conceptual tools of analysis. Similarly these traditions vary in the degree to which they focus concern on specific formal organizations (such as the IMF and the World Bank, the WTO, the EU) or they take a

[1] I thank Ole Jacob Sending, Kate Weaver, André Broome, Swati Chaudhary, and Antje Vetterlein for discussions concerning this chapter's content.

more sociological view of institutions in terms of routines and practices that have become the basis for action in specific fields. Many of these differences have become embedded in the strong theoretical divides have that defined IR/IPE along the lines of realism, liberalism, Marxism, 'neo'-versions of all these, and more recently the rise of rational choice and constructivist approaches to the discipline (see Hobson 2000 for an overview). This chapter does not attempt to review all these different positions. Instead it focuses on what are identified as the 'rationalist' and 'constructivist' approaches and how they address the question of transnational institutions. Rationalist approaches prefer parsimonious deductive methods that focus on explaining the behaviour of a limited range of actors in terms of their preferences, their options, and how to create efficient mechanisms to achieve goals; in so doing they draw on various forms of rational choice and game theory, building bridges into economics and quantitative style research. These approaches are mostly state-centric and focus on explaining the conditions by which states accept an international regime's conditions or proposed policies. Constructivists choose to stress an inductive approach that seeks to understand a diverse range of actors in overlapping networks; they tend to emphasize the power of normative sanctioning from international organizations and transnational institutions. Constructivists draw from neo-institutionalist analyses of how transnational institutions emerge. They are more open to a diverse range of actors being involved in this process and consider not just formal organizations but wider networks of shared practices. Rationalist approaches look for explanations of transnational institutions and international regimes in terms of market failures, requiring the building of new institutions, with the emphasis on states as actors negotiating to produce such an outcome. Constructivists focus more on the open-ended nature of institution-building at the international level, the diversity of actors involved in the process, and the intricate inter-relationships between these processes and national contexts. From the point of view of comparative institutional analysis, the interest in these theoretical positions lies in how they help in understanding wider processes of institutional change at the national and international levels, partly through their focus on the mechanisms of particular international organizations, e.g. the World Bank, the IMF etc., and partly through their understanding of the mechanisms, which determine transnational institution-building in informal and private arenas away from the direct shaping force of the state.

With this context in mind, this chapter is organized as follows: 1. I outline the origins of these debates and early efforts at 'bridge-building' between the different positions; 2. definitions are then provided for international regimes and transnational institutions, and I reflect upon how their meaning in the literature has changed over the years; 3. I provide a review of the current state of play in rationalist literature, highlighting the emphasis on policy diffusion; 4. the same treatment is provided with reference to the turn to organizational sociology and the emphasis on norms in constructivist literature; 5. I examine some recent literature on understanding international regimes and transnational institutions that draws upon sociology, social theory, and anthropology; and, finally, 6. I reflect on how the study of international regimes and transnational institutions has developed since different calls for bridge-building.

ORIGINS OF DEBATES AND EARLY EFFORTS
AT BRIDGE-BUILDING

....

Traditionally the focus within IR/IPE has been shaped by an emphasis on states, in a field that is tied primarily to political science and its long-held view of the state as holding ontological primacy. Since the 1970s, however, there have been efforts to build bridges between political and economic analyses of world politics that previously sat in mutual neglect, as Susan Strange famously commented (1970: 315). Scholars such as Katzenstein also sought to mix political and economic analysis and processes of socialization through a stress on 'ideology' that gradually shifted into understanding 'norms' within domestic and international contexts (Katzenstein 1976, 1978, 1985, 1996). Bridge-building activity to understand how state and non-state actors were changing world politics and the global economy was an enterprising activity in the 1970s and opened up new intellectual trends. The study of international regimes and transnational institutions emerged from a desire to understand the role of non-state actors (Keohane and Nye 1971), and the impact of international economic change on world order (Strange 1970) in the face of a field overly concerned with geopolitics and 'high politics'. Two legacies for understanding international regimes and transnation- al institutions must be highlighted since the issues and themes they touch upon have been reproduced in different forms from a variety of scholars.

The first is work by Keohane and Nye (1971, 1974) on transnational politics and, especially, 'complex interdependence' (Keohane and Nye 1977) that provided a powerful way to understand greater complexity in world politics by highlighting the extent of networking and the role of non-state actors. Keohane and Nye high- lighted how the world was not particularly characterized by the role of military force, that there was often an absence of a clear hierarchy of issues in world politics, and that multiple channels of communication were present for non-state actors to exploit. Keohane and Nye provided an ideal type model of change—posed against the dominance of realism in studying world politics (cf. Gilpin 1976)—that sought to highlight the role of new transnational actors, the extent to which intergovernment- alism had emerged, and to which the state had to compete for influence.

The second legacy is that of Susan Strange and the body of work she developed over decades on international monetary, finance and trade systems, as well as her original call for bringing together a study of international politics and international economics (Strange 1970). Strange's key concept was that of 'structural power' (Strange 1988), which she considered to be the power to 'decide how things shall be done, the power to shape frameworks within which states relate to each other, relate to people, or relate to corporate enterprises' (Strange 1988: 24–5). Structural power operates across a range of fields, including knowledge, production, security, and finance. In this concept, and especially through the development of case studies in her later work on firms' behaviour (e.g. Strange 1996), Strange highlighted the importance of more informal transnational institutions that influenced change in international political economy. Strange (1987) was extremely critical of the narrowing of the study of international regimes into the form proposed by Keohane, Krasner, and others, arguing that the concept was 'woolly' while the theoretical apparatus for understanding world politics was becoming far too narrow. She later complained that IPE was increasingly favouring more formal modelling and missing out on counter-intuitive insights from a more eclectic analytic tool kit, 'better catholic complexity than protestant parsimony!' (1994: 218). The concept of structural power was intended as a counterpoint to what Strange viewed as an excessive concern with paradigm maintenance in guarding Realism, Liberalism, and Marxism as the three approaches to the study of world politics (her 1988 *States and Markets* was a challenge to Gilpin's 1987 popular text *The Political Economy of International Relations*).

The original 1970s spirit of bridge-building found itself in a more hostile environment in the 1980s as intellectual positions became more entrenched. In the US, in particular, 1980s debates concerning international regimes were distinct in developing parsimonious 'neo' versions of realism and liberalism head-to-head, with scholars such as Joseph M. Greico (1990) and Robert Keohane (1984, 1991) occupying lead positions, while dissent was raised by scholars like Strange (1982, 1987) against the field 'aping' microeconomics (Strange 1995: 164). In the UK, Strange's lead was followed more closely in that the role of firms in relation to states and processes of globalization became of central concern and the integrated study of the political and the economic at the international level flourished (see e.g. Hirst and Thompson 1996, which remains highly influential and was published in a revised new edition in 2009). Interest in hegemony within the international system also led to an interest in the UK and Canada in Gramscian analysis and even to some degree, Foucauldian approaches (Gill 1995). Influential analyses of private actors using their structural power at the international level through the development of formal and informal transnational institutions emerged (e.g. Cutler et al. 1999).

During the 1990s dissatisfaction with the continued state-centrism of the international-regimes literature, therefore, led to new work on 'private authority' and transnational institutions (Hall and Bierstecker 1999; Cutler, Haufler and Porter 1999). As researchers identified how transnational institutions were constructed, they began to emphasize more the diffusion and spread of norms (e.g. around ideas such as 'human rights' or more pertinently for this volume, 'free markets') and how this in turn trickled down to influence and reshape national institutions (Katzenstein 1996; Checkel 1998), an approach that became gradually identified as constructivism. In response to this challenge, the decade-long debate about the relative merits of neo-realism or neo-liberalism was more or less dropped and an approach developed that is now commonly identified as a rationalist perspective (Koremenos et al. 2001, Simmons et al. 2008; Hawkins et al. 2006). As suggested above, rationalist scholars stress the importance of specifying the likely conditions under which international regimes will foster cooperation, which states are likely to cheat or defect, and how institutions will generate path dependencies for a regime's success. While the 1980s and much of the 1990s featured debates between 'neos' of various forms (neo-liberalism, neo-realism, neo-Gramscianism, neo-Marxists, neo-Weberians, etc), these more recent developments have led many scholars into two broad categories of rationalism and constructivism, with the former dominating the field (Katzenstein, Keohane, and Krasner 1998).

In an effort to take the middle ground in this field, a number of scholars, most prominently Checkel (1997), have stressed what they explicitly refer to as a 'bridge-building' movement, connecting the rationalist and the constructivists in some way. While Strange's 1970 call for bridge-builders was between political and economic analyses of world politics, this modern bridge-building movement is between rationalist and constructivist mechanisms of change. If transnational institutions are seen as developing new forms of discourse and practice, then the key questions concern how the actors involved within these institution-building processes select and internalize norms (Checkel 2005; Zürn and Checkel 2005). Neo-institutionalists and constructivists emphasize that it is a logic of appropriateness that informs actors' selection or internalization of norms (Checkel 2001; March and Olsen 1998; Sending 2002; Müller, 2004) and that we therefore need to understand the social context, how norms develop, how they get diffused and with what effects. March and Olsen state:

The logic of appropriateness is a perspective that sees human action as driven by rules of appropriate or exemplary behavior, organized into institutions. Rules are followed because they are seen as natural, rightful, expected, and legitimate. Actors seek to fulfill the obligations encapsulated in a role, an identity, a membership in a political community or group, and the ethos, practices and expectations of its institutions. Embedded in a social collectivity, they do what they see as appropriate for themselves in a specific type of situation.   (March and Olsen 2004: 1)

This approach also fits with those authors examining how intersubjective dynamics such as arguing (Risse 2000), persuasion (Payne 2001), and rhetorical entrapment (Schimmelfennig 2001) differ across different types of institutions and regimes.

By contrast, more rational choice-driven approaches emphasize a logic of consequences, i.e. that actors identify alternatives, preferences etc. and then choose the most cost efficient approach to achieving those preferences. This approach, in turn, fits in with the typical Principal–Agent model of rational choice in which rational design of incentives is capable of producing an institutional system that meets actors' preferences. Thus the principal designs a system of incentives, which is structured in such a way as to ensure that the agent carries out actions in a way commensurate with the interests of the principal. The focus is on preferences, options, rational design, and cost efficiency. Thus transnational institutions are solutions to problems of market failure that are resolved by rational design.

How do these different approaches help in understanding the development of international regimes and transnational institutions?

DEFINING INTERNATIONAL REGIMES AND
TRANSNATIONAL INSTITUTIONS

Krasner defines an international regime as 'principles, norms, rules, and decision-making procedures around which actors' expectations converge in a given area'. His extended definition provides greater clarity:

Regimes can be defined as sets of implicit or explicit principles, norms, rules, and decision-making procedures around which actors' expectations converge in a given area of international relations. Principles are beliefs of fact, causation, and rectitude. Rules are specific prescriptions or proscriptions for action. Decision-making procedures are prevailing practices for making and implementing collective choice.   (Krasner 1982b: 186)

What is striking about Krasner's definition of international regimes, more than 25 years since its conception, is its breadth. During the 1980s, other prominent scholars argued that international regimes occupied 'an ontological space somewhere between the level of formal institutions on one hand and systemic factors on the other' (Kratochwil and Ruggie 1986: 760). The potential for transnational social movements, or similar groups, to be understood through this frame was therefore difficult. In any case, the breadth of this earlier understanding of international regimes was narrowed to studying international cooperation problems among public authorities, and then to understanding how domestic political decision-making affected the design and transformation of extant regimes. This was some distance from the original 'complex interdependence' conception by Keohane and Nye.

For transnational institutions, the concept itself begs of us to include a great deal of analytic flexibility. Morgan (2006: 142–3) argues that transnational institutions are 'distinctive emergent properties from the actions of public and private actors across diverse national contexts and across diverse spatial levels'. While the international regimes literature was analytically closed in how it viewed the power of non-state actors, scholars who have stressed the importance of transnational institutions have demonstrated how non-states actors can create new fields of governance that generate influence in more diffuse and subtle ways (Djelic and Quack, 2003; Djelic and Sahlin-Andersson 2006). Transnational institutions reach beyond the nation-state in being comprised of actors who form links and networks to provide regulation and reduce uncertainty. They may take the form of non-governmental organizations (NGOs) or transnational advocacy networks (TANs) (Keck and Sikkink 1998; Meyer and Jepperson 2000), business associations (Braithwaite and Drahos 2000), and groups that are able to move between public and private spheres to create transnational governance (Tsingou 2007). Transnational institutions may reflect the interests of one dominant national group, but may also emerge from more multiple sources, in which case negotiations, deliberation, and reasoning are more important (Morgan 2006: 143).

Both the literature on international regimes and transnational institutions are concerned with understanding how the two exert influence. For earlier rationalist scholars the motivation was reasonably straightforward: states participate in regimes from which they derive benefit (Keohane 1991). Long-term engagement with regimes leads to sunk costs, which explains why international regimes rarely 'die'; they just fall into disuse instead. Rationalist scholars have also examined how international regimes reflect the rational design of states to the extent that socialization does not divorce self-interest from decision-making (Koremenos et al. 2001).

Constructivist scholars have tended to understand international regimes and transnational institutions through the concept of 'norms'. Norms have been understood in a variety of ways; as a function of identity construction, the regulation of behaviour, and as inter-subjective recognition of 'social facts' (Jepperson et al. 1996; Guzzini 2000). Most of the constructivist literature related to IPE and IR has concentrated on how norms do 'good' things. In the typical relationship, an external actor (entrepreneur) working through an international regime or transnational institution introduces an 'international norm' such as 'anti-apartheid' (Klotz 1995), 'anti-nuclear weapons' (Tannenwald 1999), or 'pro-human rights' (Risse, Ropp, and Sikkink 1999) to a domestic audience. This norm is then adopted and internalized by those within the domestic setting or within the relevant policy community, creating a logic of appropriateness on how to behave. Within the sphere of economic sociology, however, much more attention has been paid to the construction of norms around 'free markets' under conditions of neo-liberalism and how these have been spread and diffused (see e.g. Blyth 2002; Djelic 2006; Fourcade 2009; also Morgan this volume).

Finnemore (1996) argues that relevant policy communities within states will often adopt international norms through their engagement with international regimes and transnational institutions in order to be viewed as civilized. Since this earlier work, other constructivists have outlined the importance of understanding deliberation and argumentation for the formation of norms (Risse 2000; cf. Kratochwil 1989). One strand of research has focused on 'ideational entrepreneurs' who use ideas as weapons during moments of radical uncertainty (Blyth 2002; Parsons 2002; for a review see Seabrooke 2006: ch. 2) to steer institutional change and realign it with a new normative agenda. Checkel, has also sought to identify when actors shift from a logic of consequences to a logic of appropriateness, differentiating types of 'internalization' to map which factors become active and when (Checkel 2005; Zürn and Checkel 2005). This view, however, has also been criticized. For example, Sending's work (2002) argues that understanding norms within a 'logic of appropriateness' removes a great deal of agency from actors, since once norms have been 'internalized' following appropriate standards becomes automatic. Seabrooke (2007a) has also challenged the stress on the use of ideas and norms during periods of uncertainty, as well as their external introduction, seeking to highlight how norms may change within a society during a period of 'normality' in ways that provide impulses to political coalitions and ideational entrepreneurs for change in the direction of policy.

RATIONALIST APPROACHES TO THE ORIGINS
OF INTERNATIONAL REGIMES

The key shift in the literature that established the rationalist perspective can be found in Keohane's development of a deductive framework for understanding international regime based on theories of market failure borrowed from economics. Keohane (1982) explained that the demand for international regimes from states comes from the need to regulate the international political economy, to reduce 'negative externalities', increase information exchange, lower transaction costs, and produce order. Keohane's (1984) classic *After Hegemony* developed this further, especially given the prominence of Hegemonic Stability Theory (HST) in IPE and IR due to concerns that the US was in decline and that Japan was starting to dominate (see, especially, Giplin 1987). In contrast to the broad definition of regimes presented above by Krasner, Keohane interpreted regimes as formed by governments. He argued:

Two features of the international context are particularly important: world politics lacks authoritative governmental institutions, and is characterised by pervasive uncertainty. Within this setting, a major function of international regimes is to facilitate the making of mutually beneficial agreements among governments, so that the structural condition of anarchy does not lead to a complete war of all against all.   (Keohane 1991: 106)

The contemporary literature on international regimes, and indeed the development of this stream of scholarship since the mid-1980s, has more or less followed this understanding of international regimes as formed by states to reduce uncertainty in world politics and in the international economy. Here the influence of economic theorizing has been important, and the role of new institutional economics especially important (Cohen 2007: 107). From this perspective, states' participation in international regimes could be understood in terms of the potential gains from the institution, and states' lack of defection from international regimes could be understood by sunk costs and path-dependence (Keohane 1991). States therefore choose to engage in international regimes according to self-interested preferences. International regimes then constrain states—this is the basic relationship (Martin and Simmons 1999). Koremenos et al.'s (2001) work on the 'rational design' of international institutions provides the most developed framework based on rationalist premisses. They discuss how the design of an international institution for decentralized cooperation problems will differ due to the incentives states have to engage with the institution in the first place. The institution, or regime, will then be 'locked-in', depending on its design, to follow mandates that will make it a viable regime or a 'dead letter' regime. Koremenos et al. identify membership rules, the scope of issues, the centralization of duties, mechanisms of deliberation, and the flexibility of institutional reform as important. They also consider what forms of uncertainty are pervasive within the institution, such as uncertainty about the world, about other states' intentions, etc.

Why states choose to enter an international regime is explained by similar means with a range of US-based scholars working on the 'international-domestic research frontier', in which the domestic foreign policy of states is explained by interests that fight through domestic political institutions, further substantiated by a study of strategic interaction between states (Cohen 2008: 126, 148). Drezner's (2007) 'revisionist' model of world politics provides a clear statement that international regimes and transnational institutions are at the mercy of the great powers, and that states will 'forum shop' for the institution or organization that will best reflect their interests—despite broader normative concerns. For example, Drezner points to the marginalization of the IMF in the process of setting international financial standards following the Asian financial crisis and the empowerment of a select club of major states through the central role played by the Financial Stability Forum of central bankers as an example of great power politics.

The importance of domestic politics has also informed recent trends in the study of international regimes concerned with legalization (Abbott et al. 2000) and policy diffusion (Simmons and Elkins 2004; Simmons, Dobbins, and Garrett 2008; Weyland 2007). Within these studies, the stress is on understanding the conditions under which policy diffusion or legalization occurs. For legal regimes, states' participation requires an alignment of self-interests. For studies of policy diffusion, domestic politics is also important in understanding which states are able to receive policies from international regimes, such as capital account liberalization, tax reform, public utilities privatization, social reforms, trade liberalization, and others. The scholars working on policy diffusion seek to understand how coercion and competition operate between states and international regimes, following the power politics and interest-driven dynamics discussed above.

However, these authors move more towards constructivist approaches in that they emphasize the role of emulation and learning, in which states seek to be seen as legitimate by others through the adoption of a standard (cf. Finnemore 1996; Bowden and Seabrooke 2006), and by which states seek to improve their information about uncertainties, but are required to rethink their standard operating procedures to do so (Simmons, Dobbins, and Garrett 2008; cf. Culpepper 2008). It is therefore noteworthy that much recent literature is 'bridge-building' in some way in that social learning can bring in new normative orders and change conceptions of self-interest—notions that are more commonly discussed in constructivist literature (Blyth 2002). The rationalist work on international regimes may be coming around from new institutional economics and moving increasingly towards tools more associated with constructivist efforts to understand knowledge production and the causal effect of norms on institutional change. In many ways this harks back to Ruggie's ambitions for the study of international regimes. In the mid-1980s he wrote with Friedrich Kratochwil that:

In the international arena, neither the process whereby knowledge becomes more extensive nor the means whereby reflection on knowledge deepens are passive or automatic. They are intensely political. And for better or worse, international organizations have maneuvered themselves into the position of being the vehicle through which both the types of knowledge enter onto the international agenda.   (Kratochwil and Ruggie 1986: 773)

The Social Construction Of International Regimes And Transnational Institutions

Particularly important for the development of the earlier constructivist literature was inspiration from sociologists such as John Meyer and the 'world culture' or 'world polity' perspective, which demonstrated how states and communities would recognize and internalize norms from the world system in order to gain recognition from their peers within the international community (Meyer et al. 1997). Meyer's approach to institutions is to focus on broad patterns of culture and the governance and organization of the state and the economy. Particular formal organizations are of less interest than the inter-relationship between the world culture defined particularly in terms of individualism, accountability, responsibility, statehood, governance, scientific expertise and the isomorphic pressures, which this creates on particular organizations (Drori et al. 2006). Formal and informal transnational institutions are mechanisms for the transmission and diffusion of these norms.

The key constructivist scholar to push this perspective has been Martha Finnemore (1996), who stressed the importance of norms from policy communities within international regimes and transnational institutions that are then adopted by states, which seek to be seen by the international community as having attained a 'standard of civilization' (see also the studies in Djelic and Quack 2003 and Djelic and Sahlin-Andersson 2006). The stress here from constructivist scholars is that the decision to engage in a transnational institution or international regime is not just made on a cost-benefit calculus, but is also deeply symbolic and reflective of intersubjective understandings within a peer community (Sharman 2008: 646–7) where networks of experts engage in problem solving at the transnational level, building up protocols, procedures, and soft laws to act together with, or supplementary to, formal transnational organizations such as the IMF etc.

A particularly important development in the understanding of norms was provided by Finnemore and Sikkink (1998) with their delineation of a norm 'life cycle' based around the properties of norm emergence, norm cascades, and norm internalization. The typical relationship here was that a norm entrepreneur (or 'ideational entrepreneur') would engage in 'strategic social construction' to introduce a norm to a community, seeking to embed the norm (Finnemore and Sikkink 1998: 888). Once the norm was taken up, it then proceeded through a 'cascade' and was internalized. Once internalized, the norm is assumed to form a logic of appropriateness that guides actors' behaviour. Work by Keck and Sikkink (1998) provided a wealth of empirical material on how transnational advocacy networks (TANs) seek to introduce norms to various communities, stressing how they can effectively challenge both international regimes and states in altering the normative order.

Criticisms of the norm life cycle model have also been put forward. For example, Campbell (2009) has argued that the mechanisms by which norms are introduced need to be more effectively tested against rationalist arguments concerning competition and coercion (he recommends Bartley 2007 as an example of such a study). Park and Vetterlein (2010) argue that the norm life cycle provides too linear a view of normative change, seeing normative change as a progressive march when, in fact, norms may be more circular, relying on social feedback. Furthermore, as noted above, Sending (2002) has provided an important critique that the view of norms as internalized and setting a 'logic of appropriateness' effectively robs actors of their agency. The point here is to assess which norms are selected and why, who carries norms into new arenas (and why), how actors in these new arenas respond, resist or adapt, how norms are implemented and internalized, and with what consequences.

There is now an increased emphasis on the role of norms, with a range of works emerging that are explicitly constructivist (Blyth 2002; Parsons 2002), or 'economic constructivist' (Seabrooke 2006) or 'critical constructivist' (Best 2005). To date, the stress within this literature has been on norm entrepreneurs and ideational entrepreneurs who carry forward ideas during a period of uncertainty. The emphasis is also on domestic actors and how they interact with international regimes and transnational institutions. Parsons (2002), for example, examines how ideas can be understood as having an independent causal effect when there is a period of uncertainty, which creates external pressures that cuts across all political and economic coalitions and permits ideas to generate a new 'mainframe' that can introduce ideational path dependence. Blyth's (2002) work specifies how ideas can be used as weapons by entrepreneurs during periods of radical uncertainty, so that elite actors such as economists and politicians can realign conceptions of not only their own self-interest, but the interests of society, which then leads to a change in the broader intersubjective understanding (Blyth 2007). Blyth relates the use of ideas and the resetting of self-interest within domestic normative orders to broader changes in the international political economy, such as the rise and fall of Keynesianism, as well as the rise of neo-liberalism. More recently, researchers have sought to outline mechanisms of persuasion not only between elite actors, but also the role of mass discourses, seeking to highlight how everyday politics matters for norm change (Widmaier, Blyth, and Seabrooke 2007; Widmaier 2010 forthcoming; Bukovansky 2002; Seabrooke 2006).

There has also been work on the rise of private authority and transnational institutions that has developed along constructivist lines. Work by Rodney Bruce Hall has been particularly prominent here, including his work on how transnational networks and international regimes were mobilized in order to discursively demolish the Asian development model (Hall 2003), as well as studies on how private transnational institutions can generate authority (Hall and Bierstecker 1999; cf Abdelal 2007), and on the importance of shared ideas and norms for monetary authorities (Hall 2008).

A key contribution to the constructivist analysis of formal transnational organizations has been made by Barnett and Finnemore (1999, 2004) in detailing bureaucratic 'pathologies' within international organizations. They provide a comparative frame for examining how staff within international organizations can distort policy outcomes and set in practices that become part of the organizational culture. Barnett and Finnemore (1999) specify five mechanisms for how bureaucracies generate pathologies. They include: 'irrationality of rationalization' (where the rules become the ends in themselves), 'bureaucratic universalism' (one-size-fits-all policies), 'normalization of deviance' (where exceptions become the rule in practice), 'organizational insulation' (where staff are protected from negative feedback, be it from professionalism or from their organizational environment), and 'cultural contestation' (where parts of the organization compete over its aims and norms). Barnett and Finnemore discuss an array of international organizations in order to illustrate their argument. The International Monetary Fund (IMF) is identified as a case of bureaucratic universalism in how it handled the Asian financial crisis of 1997–8 through the application of models designed for countries with current rather than capital account troubles. The World Bank is considered as a case of insulation as the staff has a particular way of 'seeing' different states that created distortions when customizing policy advice (cf. Broome and Seabrooke 2007).

However, a criticism that has been raised here is the extent to which staff within international organizations can be seen as operating as a conventional public bureaucracy—when in fact many staff may belong to looser transnational institutions and networks that float between the public and private sphere, importing and exporting practices from both. In such a case of 'revolving doors' the pathologies may not emerge from within the organizational environment but from those operating within 'linked ecologies' for the transnational public and private spheres (Abbott 2005; Tsingou and Seabrooke 2008).

Another important constructivist contribution has been made by Best (2005) in her work on the role of ambiguity in international finance, highlighting the importance of how elite actors provide normative benchmarks (such as Keynes) and especially how different actors interpret agreements between states (see also Abdelal 2007). Best's key contribution is the argument that if international organizations, such as the IMF, seek to impose transparency then they are doomed to failure, since politics operates best in situations where there is ambiguity. In short, ambiguity permits political manoeuvring and an insistence on standards that denies these options will lead states to defect, cheat, or to provide merely 'lip service' (as often happens with the IMF, see Seabrooke 2007b). As Best states, ambiguity can foster communication between actors and is particularly useful in 'encouraging greater institutional flexibility, political negotiability, and discursive self-reflexivity' (2005: 8). For example, Best highlights how the IMF's Articles of Agreement lacked a precise definition of 'fundamental disequilibrium' that permitted political actors flexibility in how they then translated their participation with the international regime back to their domestic audiences, as well as providing them with greater autonomy (Best 2005: 56, 84). Best's work is important in highlighting the perils of standard-setting and benchmarking within transnational institutions that has been discussed with increased fervour.

Fourcade's work on professionalization among economists also shows how ideas, norms, and their institutional manifestations (in professional education, in associations, in distinctive bodies of knowledge and methods, in career structures, and standardized methods of assessment) emerge in national contexts and are then reshaped as more intensive international connections are developed (Fourcade 2006; 2009; see also Morgan 2002 on business communities). The point of departure here from earlier work by Meyer and others is an emphasis on practical mechanisms that assist the 'creative destruction' of transnational institutions and how they relate to broader economic and social transformations (Fourcade 2006: 152). In doing so, Fourcade and others are pointing to the fragility of norms and to stronger conceptions of interests than are found in the earlier literature.

New alternatives

In recent years, a number of scholars have sought to develop new analytic tools and drawn upon a diverse range of concepts from sociology, social theory, anthropology, and even linguistics to understand the transformation of international regimes and transnational institutions. The key departure here is that norms are increasingly treated as contingent and contested rather than internalized or institutionalized. As such, this new scholarship provides both a challenge to existing scholarship on international regimes and transnational institutions, as well as potential means to extend some bridges.

First of all, it is noteworthy that there is something of an anthropological or ethnographic turn in how IPE and IR scholars are studying international regimes and transnational institutions. For example, Chwieroth's (2007a, 2007b) work provides a detailed mapping of how ideas are carried from educational institutions to international organizations and then into national governments. In particular, Chwieroth has shown how neo-liberal ideas in Latin American countries can be traced back to international regimes and transnational networks of scholars, including revealing how, for example, a Latin American scholar is trained at Chicago as an economist, spends his or her early career at the IMF, and then at home as a neo-liberal economist who has power within the Treasury or can lend support as a 'technopol' (who have 'hybrid status as technocrats and politicians', Chwieroth 2008: 449). Chwieroth's methods are qualitative and quantitative, with a stress on the latter. In a more qualitative vein, Pouliot's work (2007, 2008) seeks to understand the 'logic of practicality' behind security communities such as NATO. Pouliot borrows a framework from Bourdieu to understand how actors involved in international regimes and transnational institutions generate a 'habitus' in how they operate that later informs decision-making (see also Vetterlein 2006 on 'organizational personality' in the IMF and the World Bank).

A good example of the power of ethnographic research is provided by Weaver (2008) in her work on the World Bank and 'hypocrisy traps' (see also Park 2005). Weaver's work seeks to understand how ideas and practices are institutionalized through observation, including non-participant observation of meeting, 'brown-bag' discussions, and the learning of what she refers to as the local language, 'Bankese' (Weaver 2008: 14). The result is a finely detailed analysis of how hypocrisy creates distortions but also keeps the organization running. Such research augments the themes highlighted by Barnett and Finnemore discussed above. To take an example, the benefits of ethnographic research can be found in statements such as the following:

The internal governance advocates I interviewed between 2000 and 2005 argue that the strategic framing of governance in terms amenable to the Bank's resistant economists worked insofar as governance ideas made significant inroads into the Bank's discourse. The choice of linguistic, theoretical, and methodological ways for talking about governance and corruption seem to matter. And once 'on the table,' staff members argue, ideas can be debated and definitions can be broadened. Yet, even three years after the PREM was created as the main home for governance work, staff continued to complain that the Bank's *official* view of the state noticeably lacked a theory of politics and had no forthright examination of power. This has affected the way in which governance concepts have been articulated and diffused inside the Bank. Much of its research and operations continue to focus on technocratic ingredients of state capacity, while ignoring overtly cultural or political factors.   (Weaver 2008: 112–13)

Weaver is thereby able to elaborate on tensions between staff, and discuss transformation within the international regime alongside elements such as the staff's need for external prestige and recognition from academic research communities (as is also the case with the IMF, see Momani 2007). Weaver's stress on language also reflects a more prominent theme in new literature.

For example, Sharman's (2006, 2008) work on tax havens and anti-money laundering campaigns concentrates on the role of reputation, rhetoric, and shaming in international regimes and transnational institutions (see also Broome 2009). Sharman borrows from J. L. Austin and John Searle to emphasize the concept of a 'speech act', that words have the capacity to shape behaviour, to see 'words as deeds' (Sharman 2006: 13, 115). In his work on tax havens, Sharman discusses how the Organisation for Economic Co-Operation and Development's (OECD) attempt to 'blacklist' non-member tax havens for 'harmful tax competition' was turned back on itself through 'rhetorical jujitsu' by small state tax havens, who argued that the OECD was surely pro-competition. Through the use of speech acts, the small state tax havens were able to avoid complete isolation and most were able to cooperate with the OECD in a new international regime. Within Sharman's understanding norms are highly contested and rather than being internalized provide ammunition for rhetorical battles.

In recent years the influence of postmodernism has been more apparent. Originally the conventional literature was not adverse to such perspectives (see Keeley 1990), but during the past fifteen years many constructivists' drive to establish themselves among orthodox political science by 'showing ideas as causes' led them to dismiss postmodernists as not attempting to 'assess how ideas relate to objective pressures' (Parsons 2002: 49). Of course postmodernists would suggest that the establishment of an objective position or the independent causal effect of ideas grossly misinterprets notions such as *dispositifs*, where discourses establish conduct in practice that is reinforcing and not objectively critiqued by those affected. Among the new range of perspectives informed by postmodernism, the work on governmentality is becoming perhaps most prominent. For example, Sending and

Neumann's (2006) work on governmentality argues that their Foucauldian-inspired analyses tell us more about how international regimes and transnational institutions work in practice than work concerned with 'global governance'. In particular, they argue that global governance work tends to oppose state and non-state actors, providing a conception of power as a zero-sum game. By contrast, they argue that a governmentality perspective does not automatically see how groups such as TANs provide more power to civil society and take it from the state but, instead, focuses on how TANs seek to make society governable. Rather than replicating an opposition between the state and non-state actors, Sending and Neumann argue that it is more useful to discuss *governmental rationalities* that transform over time. They provide case studies on population policy and landmines that demonstrate that effective governance strategies occur when the population is actively engaged as subjects rather than treated as passive objects. This work also ties into more recent work on 'everyday life' (Langley 2008) and 'everyday politics' (Hobson and Seabrooke 2007) in the international political economy that, respectively, seeks to highlight potential and actual forms of agency for how non-elites can transform their economic and social environments. In this sense norms are treated not as value goals or logics of appropriateness, but more as 'practices' (Pouliot 2008) or 'doing things' (Seabrooke and Sending 2009).

A Bridge Too Far?

This chapter has reviewed the origins and key developments on international regimes and transnational institutions, particularly as represented in IR/IPE literature. The original work on international regimes and transnational institutions sought to build bridges by understanding international political and economic processes together, as well as by seeking to understand the role of non-state actors and informal transnational institutions. The modern invocation of 'bridge-building' that is represented by Checkel (2005) in IPE and IR and others seeks to fuse together rationalist and constructivist insights to understand when actors will enter into an international regime or transnational institution, whether that entry accords to a logic of consequences or a logic of appropriateness and whether, over time, the balance between these two forces changes and leads to a restructuring of the actors and the institution. This literature is making great strides in getting constructivists and rationalists to talk to each other rather than criticizing each other for overplaying either material self-interest or norms. However, there is a warning to be made here as well.

As suggested at the beginning of the chapter, many of the themes and issues discussed by the 'complex interdependence' framework of Keohane and Nye are back. The same is true for Strange's concern with structural power and how it can assist us in understanding how international regimes and transnational institutions can have influence 'behind the scenes' rather than in direct power relationships. As reviewed, the complex interdependence literature transformed into regime theory in the 1980s in a manner that removed much of the 'noise' from the sample, but which increased the number of assumptions about what actors matter in world politics— namely, the state. The literature that emerged on private authority, on TANs, on governmentality etc., tells us that there is more going on with international regimes and transnational institutions than state–non-state or public–private dichotomies of old would suggest. 1990s work on bureaucratic pathologies is increasingly becoming refined by scholars who are drawing upon on a diverse range of interdisciplinary analytical tools. Much of the recent bridge-building scholarship may benefit from analytical pragmatism rather than rehearsing known theories on known topics (see Katzenstein and Sil 2008). Comparative institutional analysis of international regimes and transnational institutions requires this mix to increase its capacity for original and counterintuitive insights. While bridge-building is a progressive movement, it will only remain so while those involved in its engineering operate with an open mind.

REFERENCES

ABBOTT, ANDREW (2005). 'Linked Ecologies: States and Universities as Environments for Professionals', *Sociological Theory* 23(3): 245–74.

ABBOTT, KENNETH, ROBERT O. KEOHANE, ANDREW MORAVCSIK, ANNE-MARIE SLAUGHTER, and DUNCAN SNIDAL (2000). 'The Concept of Legalization', *International Organization* 54 (3): 401–19.

ABDELAL, RAWI (2007). *Capital Rules: The Construction of Global Finance*, (Cambridge, MA: Harvard University Press).

BAKER, ANDREW (2006). *The Group of Seven: Finance Ministries, Central Banks and Global Financial Governance*, (London: Routledge/Warwick Studies in Globalization).

BARNETT, MICHAEL and MARTHA FINNEMORE (1999). 'The Politics, Power, and Pathologies of International Organizations', *International Organization* 53(4): 699–732.

——(2004). *Rules for the World: International Organizations in Global Politics*, (Ithaca, NY: Cornell University Press).

BARTLEY, TIM (2007). 'Institutional Emergence in an Era of Globalization: The Rise of Transnational Private Regulation of Labor and Environmental Conditions', *American Journal of Sociology* 113(2): 297–351.

BEST, JACQUELINE (2005). *The Limits of Transparency: Ambiguity and the History of International Finance*, (Ithaca, NY: Cornell University Press).

BLYTH, M. (2002). *Great Transformations: Economic Ideas and Institutional Change in the Twentieth Century*, (Cambridge: Cambridge University Press).

——(2007). 'Powering, Puzzling, or Persuading? The Mechanisms of Building Institutional Orders', *International Studies Quarterly* 51(4): 761–77.

BOWDEN, BRETT and LEONARD SEABROOKE (2006). *Global Standards of Market Civilization*, (London: Routledge/RIPE Studies in Global Political Economy).

BRAITHWAITE, JOHN and PETER DRAHOS (2000). *Global Business Regulation*, (Cambridge: Cambridge University Press).

BROOME, ANDRÉ (2008). 'The Importance of Being Earnest: The IMF as a Reputational Intermediary', *New Political Economy* 13(2): 125–51.

——and LEONARD SEABROOKE (2007). 'Seeing Like the IMF: Institutional Change in Small Open Economies', *Review of International Political Economy* 14(4): 576–601.

BUKOVANSKY, MLADA (2002). *Legitimacy and Power Politics: The American and French Revolutions in International Political Culture*, (Princeton, NJ: Princeton University Press).

CAMPBELL, JOHN L. (2009). 'What Do Sociologists Bring to International Political Economy', in Mark Blyth (ed.), *Routledge Handbook of International Political Economy*, (London: Routledge). forthcoming.

CHECKEL, JEFFREY T. (1997). 'International Norms and Domestic Politics: Bridging the Rationalist-Constructivist Divide', *European Journal of International Relations* 3(4): 473–95.

——(1998). 'The Constructivist Turn in International Relations Theory', *World Politics* 50(2): 324–48.

——(2001). 'Why Comply? Social Learning and European Identity Change', *International Organization* 55(3): 553–88.

——(2005). 'International Institutions and Socialization in Europe: Introduction and Framework', *International Organization* 59(4): 801–26.

CHWIEROTH, JEFFREY (2008). 'Normative change from within: the International Monetary Fund's approach to Capital Account Liberalization', *International studies quarterly*, 5(1): 129–158.

——(2007*a*). 'Testing and Measuring the Role of Ideas: The Case of Neoliberalism in the International Monetary Fund', *International Studies Quarterly* 51(1): 5–30.

——(2007*b*). 'Neoliberal Economists and Capital Account Liberalization in Emerging Markets', *International Organization* 61: 443–63.

COHEN, BENJAMIN J. (2008). *International Political Economy: An Intellectual History*, (Princeton, NJ: Princeton University Press).

COOPER, RICHARD N. (1968). *The Economics of Interdependence*, (New York: McGraw-Hill).

CULPPER, PEPPER D. (2008). 'The Politics of Common Knowledge: Ideas and Institutional Change in Wage Bargaining', *International Organization* 62(1): 1–33.

CUTLER, A. CLAIRE, VIRGINIA HAUFLER, and TONY PORTER (eds.) (1999). *Private Authority and International Affairs*, (Albany: State University of New York Press).

DIMAGGIO, PAUL and WALTER POWELL (1983). 'The Iron Cage Revisited: Institutional Isomorphism and Collective Rationality in Organizational Fields', *American Sociological Review* 48(1): 147–160.

DJELIC, MARIE-LAURE (2006). 'Marketisation: From Intellectual Agenda to Global Policymaking', in Djelic and Sahlin-Andersson (2006) pp. 53–73.

——and SIGRID QUACK (eds.) (2003). *Globalization and Institutions: Redefining the Rules of the Economic Game*, (Cheltenham: Edward Elgar Publishing).

——and KERSTIN SAHLIN-ANDERSSON (eds.) (2006). *Transnational Governance: Institutional Dynamics of Regulation*, (Cambridge: Cambridge University Press).

DREZNER, DANIEL W. (2007). *All Politics Is Global*, (Princeton, NJ: Princeton University Press).

DRORI, GILI, JOHN W. MEYER, and HOKYU HWANG (2006). *Globalization and Organization: World Society and Organizational Change*, (Oxford: Oxford University Press).

FINNEMORE, MARTHA (1996). *National Interests in International Society*, (Ithaca, NY: Cornell University Press).

——and KATHRYN SIKKINK (1998). 'International Norm Dynamics and Political Change', *International Organization* 52(4): 887–917.

FOURCADE, MARION (2006). 'The Construction of a Global Profession: The Transnationalization of Economics', *American Journal of Sociology* 112(1): 145–94.

——(2009). *Economists and Societies: Discipline and Profession in the United States, Britain and France, 1890s to 1990s,* (Princeton, NJ: Princeton University Press).

GILL, STEPHEN (1995). 'Globalisation, Market Civilisation and Disciplinary Neoliberalism', *Millennium* 24(3): 399–423.

GILPIN, ROBERT (1976). *U.S. Power and the Multinational Corporation: The Political Economy of Foreign Direct Investment,* (London: Macmillan).

——(1987). *The Political Economy of International Relations,* (Princeton, NJ: Princeton University Press).

GRIECO, JOSEPH M. (1990). *Cooperation among Nations,* (Ithaca, NY: Cornell University Press).

GUZZINI, STEFANO (2000). 'A Reconstruction of Constructivism in International Relations', *European Journal of International Relations* 6(2): 147–82.

HAAS, ERNST B. (1983). 'Words can Hurt you; Or, Who Said What to Whom about Regimes', in Stephen Krasner (ed.), *International Regimes,* (Ithaca, NY: Cornell University Press), 23–60.

HALL, RODNEY BRUCE (2003). 'The Discursive Demolition of the Asian Development Model', *International Studies Quarterly* 47(1): 71–99.

——(2008). *Central Banking as Global Governance,* (Cambridge: Cambridge University Press).

——and THOMAS J. BIERSTEKER (eds.) (1999). *The Emergence of Private Authority in Global Governance,* (Cambridge: Cambridge University Press).

HAWKINS, DARREN G., DAVID A. LAKE, DANIEL L. NIELSON, and MICHAEL J. TIERNEY (eds.) (2006). *Delegation and Agency in International Organizations,* (Cambridge: Cambridge University Press).

HIRST, PAUL and GRAEME THOMPSON (1996). *Globalization in Question,* (London: Polity Press).

HOBSON, J. M. (2000). *The State and International Relations,* (Cambridge: Cambridge University Press).

——and L. SEABROOKE (eds.) (2007). *Everyday Politics of the World Economy,* (Cambridge: Cambridge University Press).

JEPPERSON, RONALD L., ALEXANDER WENDT, and PETER J. KATZENSTEIN (1996). 'Norms, Identity and Culture in National Security', in Peter J. Katzenstein (ed.), *The Culture of National Security,* (New York: Columbia University Press), 33–75.

KATZENSTEIN, PETER J. (1976). 'International Relations and Domestic Structures: Foreign Economic Policies of Advanced Industrial States', *International Organization* 30(1): 1–45.

——(ed.) (1978). *Between Power and Plenty,* (Madison: University of Wisconsin Press).

——(1985). *Small States in World Markets,* (Ithaca, NY: Cornell University Press).

——(1996). *Cultural Norms and National Security,* (Ithaca, NY: Cornell University Press).

——(2005). *A World of Regions: Asia and Europe in the American Imperium,* (Ithaca, NY: Cornell University Press).

——and RUDRA SIL (2008). 'The Contributions of Eclectic Theorizing to the Study and Practice of International Relations,' in Chris Reus-Smit and Duncan Snidal (eds.), *Oxford Handbook of International Relations,* (Oxford: Oxford University Press).

——ROBERT O. KEOHANE, and STEPHEN D. KRASNER (1998). 'International Organization and the Study of World Politics', *International Organization* 52(4): 645–85.

KECK, MARGARET E. and KATHRYN SIKKINK (1998). *Activists Beyond Borders,* (Ithaca, NY: Cornell University Press).

KEELEY, JAMES F. (1990). 'Towards a Foucauldian Analysis of International Regimes', *International Organization* 44(1): 83–105.

KEOHANE, ROBERT O. (1982). 'The Demand for International Regimes', *International Organization* 36(2): 325–55.

——(1984). *After Hegemony: Cooperation and Discord in the World Political Economy*, (Princeton, NJ: Princeton University Press).

——(1991). *International Institutions and State Power: Essays in International Relations Theory*, (Boulder: Westview Press).

——(2009). 'The Old IPE and the New', *Review of International Political Economy*, 16(1): forthcoming.

——and JOSEPH S. NYE (1971). 'Transnational Relations and World Politics: An Introduction', *International Organization* 25(3): 329–49.

————(1974). 'Transgovernmental Relations and International Organizations', *World Politics* 27(1): 39–62.

————(1977). *Power and Interdependence*, (Boston: Little Brown).

KLOTZ, AUDIE (1995). *Norms in International Relations: The Struggle Against Apartheid*, (Ithaca, NY: Cornell University Press).

KOREMENOS, B., C. LIPSON, and D. SNIDAL (2001). 'The Rational Design of International Institutions', *International Organization* 55(4): 761–99.

KRASNER, STEPHEN D. (1976). 'State Power and the Structure of International Trade', *World Politics* 28(3): 317–47.

——(1982a). 'Regimes and the Limits of Realism: Regimes as Autonomous Variables', *International Organization* 36(2): 497–510.

——(1982b). 'Structural Causes and Regime Consequences: Regimes As Intervening Variables', *International Organization* 36(2): 185–205.

KRATOCHWIL, FRIEDRICH (1989). *Rules, Norms and Decisions*, (Cambridge: Cambridge University Press).

——and JOHN G. RUGGIE (1986). 'International Organization: A State of the Art on the Art of the State', *International Organization* 40(4): 753–75.

LAKE, DAVID A. (2009). 'TRIPs across the Atlantic: Theory and Epistemology in IPE', *Review of International Political Economy* 16(1): 47–57.

LANGLEY, PAUL (2008). *The Everyday Life of Global Finance*, (Oxford: Oxford University Press).

LEAVER, RICHARD (1994). 'International Political Economy and the Changing World Order: Evolution or Involution', in Richard Stubbs and Geoffrey R. D. Underhill (eds.), *Political Economy and the Changing Global Order*, (London: Macmillan), 130–41.

MCNAMARA, KATHLEEN R. (2009). 'Of Intellectual Monocultures and the Study of IPE', *Review of International Political Economy*, 16(1): 72–84.

MARCH, JAMES G. and JOHAN P. OLSEN (1984). 'The New Institutionalism: Organizational Factors in Political Life', *American Political Science Review* 78(3): 734–49.

——(1998). 'The Institutional Dynamics of International Political Orders', *International Organization* 52(4): 943–69.

————(2004). 'The Logic of Appropriateness', ARENA Working paper no. 04/09.

MARTIN, LISA L. and BETH A. SIMMONS (1999). 'Theories and Empirical Studies of International Institutions', in Peter J. Katzenstein, Robert O. Keohane, and Stephen D. Krasner (eds.) *Exploration and Contestation in the Study of World Politics*, (Cambridge, MA: MIT Press), 89–117.

MEYER, JOHN W. and BRIAN ROWAN (1977). 'Institutionalized Organization: Formal Structure as Myth and Ceremony', *American Journal of Sociology* 83(2): 340–63.

——and RONALD L. JEPPERSON (2000). 'The "Actors" of Modern Society: The Cultural Construction of Social Agency', *Sociological Theory* 18(1): 100–20.

——John Boli, George M. Thomas, and Francisco O. Ramirez (1997). 'World-Society and the Nation-State', *American Journal of Sociology* 103(1): 144–66.

Momani, Bessma (2007). 'IMF Staff: Missing Link in Fund Reform Proposals', *Review of International Organizations* 2(1): 39–57.

Morgan, Glenn (2002). 'Transnational communities and business systems', *Global Networks* 1(2): 113–30.

——(2006). 'Transnational Actors, Transnational Institutions, Transnational Spaces: The Role of Law Firms in the Internationalization of Competition Regulation', in Marie-Laure Djelic and Kerstin Sahlin-Andersson (eds.) (2006), *Transnational Governance: Institutional Dynamics of Regulation*, (Cambridge: Cambridge University Press), pp. 139–60.

Müller, Harald (2004). 'Arguing, Bargaining and all that: Communicative Action, Rationalist Theory and the Logic of Appropriateness in International Relations', *European Journal of International Relations* 10(3): 395–435.

Nielson, Daniel L. and Michael J. Tierney (2003). 'Delegation to International Organizations: Agency Theory and World Bank Environmental Reform', *International Organization* 57(2): 241–76.

Park, Susan (2005). 'Norm Diffusion within International Organizations: A Case Study of the World Bank', *Journal of International Relations and Development* 8(1): 111–41.

——and Antje Vetterlein (2010) (eds.) forthcoming. *Owning Development*, (Cambridge: Cambridge University Press).

Parsons, Craig (2002). 'Showing Ideas as Causes: The Origins of the European Union', *International Organization* 56(1): 47–84.

Payne, Rodger A. (2001). 'Persuasion, Frames and Norm Construction', *European Journal of International Relations*, 7(1): 37–61.

Pouliot, Vincent (2007). ' "Sobjectivism": Toward a Constructivist Methodology', *International Studies Quarterly* 51(2): 359–84.

——(2008). 'The Logic of Practicality: A Theory of Practice of Security Communities', *International Organization* 62(2): 257–88.

Reus-Smit, Christian (1999). *The Moral Purpose of the State: Culture, Social Identity, and Institutional Rationality in International Relations*, (Princeton, NJ: Princeton University Press).

Risse, Thomas (2000). ' "Let's Argue!"—Communicative Action in World Politics', *International Organization* 51(1): 1–41.

——Stephen C. Ropp, and Kathryn Sikkink (eds.) (1999). *The Power of Human Rights: International Norms and Domestic Change*, (Cambridge: Cambridge University Press).

Ruggie, John Gerard (1975). 'International Responses to Technology: Concepts and Trends', *International Organization* 29(3): 557–83.

——(1982). 'International Regimes, Transactions, and Change: Embedded Liberalism in the Postwar Economic Order', *International Organization* 36(2): 379–415.

——(1998). 'What Makes the World Hang Together? Neo-utilitarianism and the Social Constructivist Challenge', *International Organization* 52(4): 855–85.

Schimmelfennig, Frank (2001). 'The Community Trap: Liberal Norms, Rhetorical Action, and the Eastern Enlargement of the European Union', *International Organization* 55(1): 47–80.

Seabrooke, L. (2006). *The Social Sources of Financial Power: Domestic Legitimacy and International Financial Orders*, (Ithaca, NY: Cornell University Press).

——(2007a). 'The Everyday Social Sources of Economic Crises: From "Great Frustrations" to "Great Revelations" in Interwar Britain', *International Studies Quarterly* 51(4): 795–810.

——(2007*b*). 'Legitimacy Gaps in the World Economy: Explaining the Sources of the IMF's Legitimacy Crisis', *International Politics* 44(2/3): 250–68.

——and OLE JACOB SENDING (2009). 'Norms as Doing Things vs. Norms as Things to Do: Reason and Interest in World Politics', unpublished paper, Norwegian Institute for International Affairs, (March).

SENDING, OLE JACOB (2002). 'Constitution, Choice and Change: Problems with the "Logic of Appropriateness" and its Use in Constructivist Theory', *European Journal of International Relations* 8(4): 443–70.

——and IVER B. NEUMANN (2006). 'Governance to Governmentality: Analyzing NGOs, States, and Power', *International Studies Quarterly* 50(3): 651–72.

SHARMAN, J. C. (2006). *Havens in a Storm: The Struggle for Global Tax Regulation*, (Ithaca, NY: Cornell University Press).

——(2008). 'Power and Discourse in Policy Diffusion: Anti-Money Laundering in Developing States', *International Studies Quarterly* 52(3): 635–56.

SIMMONS, BETH A. and ZACHARY ELKINS (2004). 'The Globalization of Liberalization: Policy Diffusion in the International Political Economy', *American Political Science Review* 98(1): 171–189.

——FRANK DOBBINS, and GEOFFREY GARRETT (eds.) (2008). *The Global Diffusion of Markets and Democracy*, (Cambridge, MA: Cambridge University Press).

SINCLAIR, T. J. (2005). *The New Masters of Capital: American Bond Rating Agencies and the Politics of Creditworthiness*, (Ithaca, NY: Cornell University Press).

STRANGE, SUSAN (1970). 'International Economics and International Relations: A Case of Mutual Neglect', *International Affairs* 46(2): 304–15.

——(1982). '*Cave! hic dragones*: a critique of regime analysis', *International Organization* 36(2): 479–496.

——(1987). 'The persistent myth of lost hegemony', *International Organization* 41(4): 551–74.

——(1988). *States and Markets*, (London: Pinter Publishers).

——(1994). 'Wake up, Krasner! The world *has* changed', *Review of International Political Economy* 1(2): 209–19.

——(1995). 'Political Economy and International Relations' in Steve Smith (ed.), *International Relations Theory Today*, (Cambridge: Polity Press), 154–74.

——(1996). *The Retreat of the State: The Diffusion of Power in the World Economy*, (Cambridge: Cambridge University Press).

——(1998). 'Why Do International Organizations Never Die?' in Bob Reinalda and Bertjan Verbeek (eds.), *Autonomous Policy Making by International Organizations*, (London: Routledge), 213–20.

TANNENWALD, NINA (1999). 'The Nuclear Taboo: The United States and the Normative Basis of Nuclear Non-Use', *International Organization* 53(3): 433–68.

TSINGOU, ELENI (2007). 'Transnational Private Governance and The Basel Process: Banking Regulation and Supervision, Private Interests and Basel II', in Jean-Christophe Graz and Andreas Nölke (eds.), *Transnational Private Governance and its Limits*, (London: Routledge), 58–68.

——and LEONARD SEABROOKE (2008). 'Revolving Doors and Linked Ecologies in the International Political Economy: Private Authority and the Public Roles Behind International Financial Reform', paper presented to the British International Studies Association, University of Exeter, (Dec.).

VETTERLEIN, ANTJE (2006). 'Change in International Organizations: Innovation or Adaptation? A Comparison of the World Bank and the International Monetary Fund', in Diane

Stone and Christopher Wright (eds.), *The World Bank and Governance: A Decade of Reform and Reaction*, (London: Routledge), 125–44.

WEAVER, CATHERINE (2008). *Hypocrisy Trap: The World Bank and the Poverty of Reform*, (Princeton, NJ: Princeton University Press).

WEYLAND, KURT (2007). *Bounded Rationality and Policy Diffusion: Social Sector Reform in Latin America*, (Princeton, NJ: Princeton University Press).

WIDMAIER, WESLEY W. (2010). *Anxiety in Everyday Economies*, forthcoming.

——MARK BLYTH, and LEONARD SEABROOKE (2007). 'Exogenous Shocks or Endogenous Constructions? The Meanings of Wars and Crises', *International Studies Quarterly* 51(4): 747–59.

ZÜRN, MICHAEL and JEFFREY T. CHECKEL (2005). 'Getting Socialized to Build Bridges: Constructivism and Rationalism, Europe and the Nation-State', *International Organization* 59(4): 1045–79.

CHAPTER 10

LAW AS A GOVERNING INSTITUTION[1]

GLENN MORGAN

SIGRID QUACK

INTRODUCTION

Law, that is the formal codification and application of norms and values of society as crafted by politicians and judges, is a central institution in modern economies. Law constitutes economic organization, framing the nature of categories such as firms, property, contract, labour, and capital. It defines and facilitates the powers that can be claimed by different actors in the economy—the rights of firms, shareholders, managers, employees, etc. It regulates the ways in which these collective agents can act and provides a means for remedying disputes (Edelman and Suchman 1997: 101). It leads to processes through which instabilities, conflicts, and uncertainties can be dealt with. It does this by reference to precedents, procedures, and theories of justice that constrain what is possible to actors as they enter the juridical field. As Bourdieu says 'entry into the juridical field implies the tacit acceptance of the field's fundamental law . . . that. . . . conflict can only be resolved juridically—that is, according to the rules and conventions of the field itself' (Bourdieu 1987: 831). Thus, even though

[1] We thank John L. Campbell, Grahame Thompson, Richard Whitley, and Jonathan Zeitlin for helpful comments on an earlier version of this chapter.

the law is integrally related in the modern period to the state and relies to a crucial extent on the state's monopoly of the legitimate use of force as its ultimate form of sanction, it cannot simply be reduced to being an 'arm' of the state. The law is politically and professionally mediated. It therefore has its own specific conditions of existence that relate to the form of law (manifested in statute, case law, and systems of regulation), the arenas of law and their rules of action and procedure (public courts as well as private settings), the agents of law, their social position and their licensing system (lawyers, law firms, and judges; professional associations), the technology and artefacts of law (documentation, standards, cases, statutes), and the body of knowledge that underpins the law (the role of jurisprudence and academic legal theorizing that crosses the boundaries between universities, courts, and politics). These conditions of existence constitute obligatory passage points through which other actors such as the state, organizations, and individuals have to pass in order to engage with the law and under certain circumstances change and reform law and the legal system. Law is defined by this dynamic between its internal structuring and conditions of existence and its external impact. The fact that the internal and the external conditions of existence change means that the legal field is not fixed or defined but ever-shifting and moving, extending, and contracting. This dynamic has important consequences which Bourdieu describes as follows:

As is true of any 'field', the constitution of the juridical field is a principle of the constitution of reality itself. To join the game, to agree to play the game, to accept the law for the resolution of the conflict, is tacitly to adopt a mode of expression and discussion implying the renunciation of physical violence and of elementary forms of symbolic violence. . . . It is above all to recognize the specific requirements of the juridical construction of the issue . . . a complete retranslation of all of the aspects of the controversy is necessary.   (Bourdieu 1987: 831–2)

The logic of judicial fields derives from complex historical path dependencies. We can expect therefore that because law as a social institution has occupied a distinctive place within different trajectories of social and economic development, we will find judicial fields constituted differently across various contexts and that this will be consequential for economic organization. In simple terms, this is why comparative institutional analysis has to take account of law. However, this leads to three possible dangers that we seek to avoid in this chapter. The first danger is to fall into a linear evolutionary perspective based on functionalist principles. For example, there is a long tradition of arguing that in order for a capitalist economy to exist, there must be an appropriate set of legal institutions, e.g. in terms of property rights, contract law, etc. (see for example North and Thomas 1973; North 1990 and in the more policy-oriented debates on the promotion of the rule of law in developing and transition economies, Dam 2006; for a critical assessment in the case of China see Peerenboom 2002; for Eastern Europe see Murell 2001). The problem with such accounts is that they tend to assume a certain outcome and ignore the variety of different historical developments and the continued diversity between countries in terms of legal systems.

Emphasizing differences between legal systems, however, leads to the second set of dangers because the arena of law has never been a purely nationally defined arena.

For example, all western legal systems (including those established elsewhere through colonialism and imperialism) can be traced back to Roman Law and the debates across Christian Europe in the medieval period concerning *ius commune*, natural law, and the nature of canon law. These debates reflected upon efforts to create a single underlying set of principles of law to underpin (and, to a degree, shape, constrain, and civilize) the more variable systems of customary and local law imposed in particular jurisdictions on the back of the coercive power and, frequently, personal preferences of the local ruler. Even as nation-states became more powerful and societies more secularized, this ambition for a universal basis for law did not disappear, reaching its Enlightenment apogee in Kant's essay on Perpetual Peace in the effort to ground the principles of law in the operation of Reason. Such efforts to create a public international law became significant in the post-1945 environment following the foundation of the United Nations and its various principles, charters, and associated bodies. Later processes of economic globalization gave this thrust towards international law a more pragmatic, technical, and functionalist impetus, undermining the Kantian moral imperatives (see Koskenniemi 2007 for an exposition of these tensions). Thus national law is embedded within networks of international law and the exchange, imitation and diffusion of laws, legal principles, and practice and jurisprudence.

The third danger is that law is treated as an independent variable, which determines economic and social organization. Whilst on the one hand, law is constitutive and shaping of economic and social relations, it is not independent of those relations. Most obviously economic actors seek to change the law to accommodate it more to their interests. Legal actors themselves have positions within wider social and economic structures that affect how they are organized, how law is implemented, and for whose benefit. Actors within the legal field mediate and articulate these tensions between law as a field in itself and the broader context. Edelman and colleagues (Edelman 2004, 2007; Edelman and Stryker 2005; Edelman and Suchman 1997; Suchman and Edelman 2007) have been particularly insistent on the importance of seeing law as endogenous to the social order, not standing outside it but continuously interacting. The law moves on and changes because of the way in which those inside the legal field influence and are influenced by those outside it, such as clients, the state, social movements, and economic, social and technological innovations.

In order to avoid these dangers, this chapter is structured around these themes to suggest how they may be combined to give a more complete view of law as a governing institution. The first section of the chapter, therefore, examines classical institutionalist accounts of the role of law. This reveals the tension between evolutionary, functionalist driven notions of law and more historical and contingent accounts of the emergence of particular legal systems, practices, and forms. The second section builds on this by examining how forms of economic organization and economic outcomes are determined by law and in particular by national legal systems. The third section problematizes this argument by showing how law in the contemporary period that impacts on economic organization is moving and dynamic, national and international, public and private, soft and hard. This requires a focus on three phenomena; firstly, the internal structure of legal systems and the sorts of powers and capacities that particular actors accrue in those contexts and how they use this power to shape and innovate in law; secondly, the development of law as a business and what this means for the dynamism of law from different national contexts; thirdly, how this dynamism has led to new forms of innovation and internationalization in law that challenge any deterministic ideas of the relationship between law and economic organization.

Law, Economy and Society in Classical Institutional Theory

Classical institutionalist accounts of law tended to be constructed from an evolutionary point of view. What were the forms of law present in the emergent capitalist societies of the nineteenth and early twentieth centuries and how and why did these differ from those characterizing pre-capitalist society? In *Ancient Law*, Maine (1861) argued that law and society had developed from status to contract. Whilst in ancient times, the main function of contract was to tightly bind persons to traditional status groups, the invention of private contract in modern times enabled economic exchange and association between individuals, which were viewed as autonomous and free in their choice of contract partner and not constrained by their membership of a particular status group. Durkheim ([1893] 1997), also emphasized the importance of contract as part of the expansion of what he called restitutive law, i.e. law that provides general rules of conduct towards which individuals re-orient their behaviour. In contrast to his arch-enemy, the English utilitarian Herbert Spencer, however, these rules were—as Durkheim showed in his famous analysis of the non-contractual elements of contracts—embedded in a wider societal context, where social actors sustained reciprocal moral expectations that contracts should be fulfilled. Thus law evolves towards a more individualistic and contractual form as societies become more capitalist but it remains underpinned by social norms, not simply utilitarian compliance.

Marx and Engels also took an evolutionary view of law as adapting and changing in response to broader environmental processes even if they emphasized the class interests which drove these changes more than most other authors. In *The German Ideology*, for example, they saw the rise of capitalism as inseparably intertwined with legal guarantees of private ownership of the means of production and the employment relationship: 'Whenever, through the development of industry and commerce, new forms of intercourse have been evolved (e.g., insurance companies, etc.) the law has always been compelled to admit them among the modes of acquiring property' (Marx and Engels 1976: 92, cited in Stone 1985: 52).

The American institutional economist and labour historian John Commons in the *Legal Foundations of Capitalism* ([1924] 1995), developed similar arguments examining the process by which English courts from the sixteenth to the eighteenth century validated business practices, and thereby converted ideas relating to property.

These evolutionary accounts tended to see law as a dependent variable in the broad historical transition to capitalism; the law was subject to irresistible pressure to change in a way which made it more functional for the emerging new order. Once in place, however, the law as an institution becomes itself determining; it reinforces the particular pattern of economic organization by putting in place rules and sanctions that are functional for and fit the structure of the economy.

By contrast, another strand of analysis focused more specifically on the nature of the law as an institution and the place of this institution in the broader social context. The dominant influence here is Weber. In particular, Weber was well aware of the indeterminacy in the relationship between legal and economic phenomena. In his view, law reflected not only economic but also ethical, religious, social, and political influences. Therefore, economic phenomena could have at best a partial impact on legal phenomena. It could not determine the law and the law should not be seen as evolving from one state to another because of purely economic factors. For Weber, the relationship between the economy and law was strongly mediated by the legal system, legal thought and the dominant types of 'legal honoratiores' in different countries, or in his own words: 'Economic factors can therefore be said to have had an indirect influence only . . . we shall frequently see that those aspects of law which are conditioned by political factors and by the internal structure of legal thought have exercised a strong influence on economic organizations' (Weber [1921] 1978: 655).

The law as a specific set of social relations with its own conditions of existence emerges strongly in Weber's analysis. Legal norms and rules, according to Weber, differ from other social norms and rules because they are made, imposed, and sanctioned by a staff of people especially holding themselves ready for this purpose (*Rechtsstab*). Rational legal authority, as compared to other forms of authority, is based on an abstract legal order that grants formal treatment to all subjects and violations of which are sanctioned by the *Rechtsstab*. But it also depends on the legitimacy beliefs of those subjected to authority in the legality of the order. Apart from legislation 'from above', Weber's analysis, therefore, highlights the role of 'legal honoratiores' and judicial procedures in charge of making and enforcing the law (Weber [1921] 1978: 784ff). In his comparison of common and civil law systems, Weber pointed to the influence of the social composition and training of lawyers, judges, and other law specialists in different societies on the development of legal thought and its affinities with the substance and form of law as well as the operation of the legal system. His arguments therefore reject the notion of the law as determined and evolving in order to meet the 'needs' of the economy[2] and instead focus

---

[2] This is not to neglect the unresolved ambiguities inherent in Weber's work between his assessment of civil law as formally more rational than common law and his analysis of the complexity of the

on the necessity for a detailed analysis of the legal system in its own right in order to disentangle the subtleties inherent in the relationship between law and economy (Rheinstein 1954).

Weber's rejection of simple evolutionary accounts of law is reflected also in the work of Eugen Ehrlich, a law professor born in Bukowina in 1862 and living in Czernowitz until his death in 1922, both cities located in a part of the former Austrian-Hungarian Empire that fell under several, changing legal jurisdictions over the course of his lifetime. Ehrlich started from the observation that the rules, which guide the behaviour of actors in economy and society, often diverge significantly from the rules that are laid down in statutory law and court rulings. Therefore, his writing was dedicated to the analysis of 'a practical concept of law' (Ehrlich [1913] 2002: 3ff) which would help to fill the 'blind spot' of jurisprudence (Ziegert [1913] 2002: xxvii) and to replace the assumptions of evolutionary and functionalist accounts of the law with an alternative empirical sociology of the law. Ehrlich's *Fundamental principles of the sociology of law* ([1913] 2002) was, like Weber's *Economy and Society* ([1921] 1978), constitutive for the formation of the sociology of law and socio-legal studies.[3] The fragility of the legal authorities under which Ehrlich lived led him to particularly appreciate that in transnational contexts, there are often various overlapping and competing private and state actors claiming legitimacy for law-making and law enforcement (Quack 2007). For Ehrlich ([1913] 2002), legal rules are only followed by people because they are supported by pre-existing social orders of living. It is only within the context of social norms, which tie members of a society together through a web of mutual expectations and potential social sanctions, that we can understand why legal rules are followed or not, hence, the author's critique of the positivist position that ascribed legal propositions an effect in their own right. Ehrlich's plea for a study of the 'living law' (Ehrlich [1913] 2002: 81), instead, drew attention to the methodological need for an empirical study of the interactions between legal and social rules in practical life. It also pointed to routines and practices of social life as a source for legal decision-making rules and state law. In Ehrlich's view, legal rules are distinct from social rules in so far as they emerge from a specialized social structure aimed at developing a system of legal decision-making and/or the state as legislator. While the legal decision-making system includes lawyers and judges as those who apply and further develop the law in individual case decisions, state law encompasses all the rules, which are devised by state functionaries and politicians, passed through the parliament or decreed by a ruler. In sum, the work of Ehrlich like that of Weber highlights the importance of studying the legal system itself in order to understand better the effects of legal rules on

intermediating role of the legal system (for a long-standing debate see for example Trubek 1972, Hunt 1978, and Ewing 1987). Our view, however, is that the 'English problem' can be also seen as a case of equifinality in which the English and continental legal systems represent 'two kinds of administration of justice' (Weber [1921] 1978: 892).

[3] Interestingly, Ehrlich was translated into English (in 1936) much earlier than Weber's and Durkheim's writings on law and was very influential for socio-legal research in the US under the promotion of Roscoe Pound at the Harvard Law School (Ziegert [1913] 2002: pp. xxvi).

economic coordination. Ehrlich, more than Weber, prepared the ground for a profound understanding of the reflexivity of legal in response to social norms (and vice versa) highlighted in modern socio-legal theories, such as Nonet and Selznick (1978), Luhmann (1985) and Teubner (1983).

Law Shaping National Differences in Economic Organization

The previous section has shown that institutionalist analysis has an ambivalent legacy in respect of law as a governing institution. Contemporary discussions on law in institutional analysis do reflect some of these ambiguities. While both the analysis of business systems (Whitley 1999) and the varieties of capitalism approach (Hall and Soskice 2001) highlight distinctive legal systems as an important institutional dimension shaping economic organization in different societies (and thereby question the notion of universally valid development trajectories), they remain largely silent on how the law itself evolves and how it specifically affects economic organization as compared to other institutions. As Stryker (2003) critically remarks, institutional and socio-economic studies are often very unspecific about the nature of institutions and do not separate out the effects of law from other institutions' effects (see Swedberg 2003 for economic sociology). Whitley (1999) refers to law under the broad category of state regulation and introduces it predominantly as an institutional factor shaping forms of economic organization. Similarly, Hall and Soskice (2001a) in the presentation of their analytical framework refer to contract law as an institutional element, which is complementary to specific types of inter-company relations that are regarded as typical of liberal and coordinated market economies (LME and CME). Contributions to their volume illustrate the complementary effects of legal regulations with specific forms of corporate governance, inter-company relations, and innovation in LMEs and CMEs (Vitols 2001; Casper 2001). In both approaches, law is treated as an exogenous factor with determining effects on economic organization, reinforcing a particular institutional framework. Little consideration is given to the actual interpretation and adaptation of legal rules by the actors in question, the interaction of legal and non-legal institutions, and the recursivity of law.[4] This sort of comparative institutionalist analysis focuses on how different legal systems have constituted firms as legal entities, and have shaped the rights of collective

[4] The chapter by Teubner (2001) represents an exception since it deals with the question of how legal irritants affect cross-border transfers of legal concepts from a perspective that acknowledges the recursivity of law.

actors in relation to firms and rules on how collective actors may behave in market contexts.

There is no doubt that this approach has yielded a range of important insights into the relationship between law and different forms of capitalism and the impact of law on economic performance outcomes. The relevance of law for the constitution of corporate and collective actors has been highlighted by institutional and legal scholars with regard to national differences in the incorporation of the large modern enterprise (Hopt 2007), small- and medium-sized enterprises (Bagnasco and Sabel 1995; Lane 1995), including those prevalent in banking and finance (Deeg 1999; Vitols 2005; Lütz 2002), formal association and the interest organization of capital (Schmitter and Streeck 1985) and labour (Ferner and Hyman 1998), the prevalence of intermediary organizations (Morgan and Quack 2005), and the capacity of local public administration and government in relation to the central political authorities of a country (Putnam 1994; Zeitlin 1995). Less often treated in the varieties of capitalism and business system approach—though arguably of similar importance for the comparative institutional analysis of economic systems—are the professions (Abbott 1998; Lane et al. 2002), 'third sector' organizations (Anheiner and Seibel 1990; Evers and Laville 2004) and civil society organizations (Della Porta 2007). Another factor, which is highly relevant for shaping the constitution of economic actors and their resources, is inheritance law (Beckert 2008) which also has broader consequences for the distribution of wealth within societies.

In the field of financial economics, the relationship between law and corporate governance has become of major interest. La Porta and colleagues have argued that the degree of legal protection accorded to outside shareholders is crucial to understanding the growth of financial markets and through this financial development more generally (for an extensive overview of the debate, see La Porta et al. 2008; also Goyer in this volume). They argue that where this protection is high, outsiders are encouraged to invest in financial markets, thus making these markets broader and deeper and overall more efficient in terms of their allocation process. By contrast, where these protections are weak, insiders dominate companies and seek the private benefits of control. The result is less efficient allocation of capital. La Porta et al. ascribe these different forms of protection to differences between common law systems (where protection is high) and civil law systems (where protection is low). On the basis of quantitative analysis based on cross-country comparisons, they argue that there is clear evidence that better shareholder protection is associated with higher income per capita. The arguments of La Porta et al. are based on a strong view of the determining effect of law and in particular on the nature of law at a high level of abstraction, i.e. in terms of the comparison between civil and common law.

Taking this issue more broadly, however, the constitutive function of law for the formation of identities, preferences, and strategies of economic actors may be illustrated with a focus on the role of capital and labour in the corporate governance of large public companies in Japan, Germany, and the United States (see Morck 2000, 2005 and O'Sullivan 2003 for a comparison of a broader range of countries). Historically, the emergence of the large modern corporation in the nineteenth century (that is a company with legal personality, limited liability, and transferable shares) soon led to a series of crisis and scandals, which quickly drew public attention to the need for regulation of the corporation. The company law codifications of the second half of the nineteenth century in the Western industrialized countries and subsequent reforms over the last 100 years were attempts to find a balance between protection of owners, as individuals and as a class, and the public interest. With increasing separation of ownership and control (Berle and Means 1932, Roe 1994), finding a balance between delegation of decision-making to directors and management and ensuring control over them by legal rules and liability became another focus of attempts to regulate the public corporation in company law, bankruptcy law, and other fields of law. While entailing a fair amount of cross-border borrowing and learning (Hopt 2007), legal specifications of the rights and duties of different groups of stakeholders in public companies still show significant variations between countries.

Aguilera and Jackson (2003: 453) highlight how the property rights arising from these historical developments in the contemporary period 'shape capital specifically by establishing rights that favour different types of shareholders'. According to these authors, Japanese law entails a 'shareholder sovereignty model', where voting rights follow a majority principle and shareholders' meetings retain broad powers. German law, too, privileges majority voting, but its 'constitutional model' differs from Japanese law in so far as it legally mandates two-tier board structures with substantial supervisory functions being delegated from general shareholder meetings to a supervisory board, since the latter tends to give disproportionate power to owners of large blocs of shares and thereby favours their strategic interests. Legislation in the United States, in contrast, is characterized by a 'liberal market approach', which provides minority shareholders with strong protection by means of high disclosure requirements and norms of one-share-one-vote.[5] However, the federal structure in the US and the competition between states means that the actual operation of these processes is more complex. The state of Delaware has become the favoured place of incorporation for US companies because Delaware law has been relatively open to executives creating protective mechanisms against hostile takeover, such as 'poison pill' defences. Income from incorporation is essential to the Delaware state budget and this requires the approval of senior managers in firms; elements of the legal system that favour incumbent management versus shareholders constitute an informal quid pro quo. In sum, by granting differential rights, legal stipulations in the three countries favour different interest groups in their influence on corporate governance (see also Goyer in this volume; Coffee 2006; Gourevitch and Shinn 2005; Morgan 2007; Roe 2003).

On the labour side, too, corporate governance in public companies shows considerable variation in the types of collective actors involved and the degree to which they are entitled to representation in company decision-making (Gospel and Pendleton

[5] But note that shareholders in the US historically have little direct influence over company management, such as nomination for corporate boards of directors or control over their pay.

2005; Pistor 2001; Streeck 2009). These reflect historical struggles of labour to organize at the firm-level and other channels of influence on corporate management, which in some countries resulted in representation being guaranteed by statutory law (like co-determination in Germany), while in other countries being written into collective bargaining agreements (like joint consultation practices in France) which are derived from statutory collective bargaining rights, and again in other countries being very weak (as in the USA) (Aguilera and Jackson 2003). The degree and the form of representation rights (co-determination, information, or consultation) give employees and unions distinctive channels to influence companies' decisions, which in turn shape the collective identity of representation bodies and unions in the different countries. One area in which the impact of different forms of employee representation becomes visible is in the restructuring of large companies where the legal rights of employees to representation and consultation slows down the sort of quick takeover process which is characteristic of the US and the UK (Ahlering and Deakin 2007; Deakin 2009; Deakin et al. 2006).

In addition to providing a legal identity, law also shapes larger patterns of economic organization by defining the rules which should govern the relationships between corporate and collective actors within the economy. In this way legislation and court decisions shape broader 'patterns of competitive and/or cooperative relations between economic actors' with significant implications for industry structures, models of production, and innovation, and for what Fligstein (2002) called the 'control conception' of an industry or economy. Property relations are also significant in this respect since they define social spaces in which companies determine their business models, develop patterns of inter-firm cooperation, and strategize for market control (see Campbell and Lindberg 1990 for different American industries; Carruthers and Ariovich 2004).

Anti-trust and competition legislation has historically played an important role in institutionalizing such control conceptions. In many countries, it reflects social struggles that took place during formative historical periods that became enshrined into law and subsequently influenced the economy in substantial ways. In the USA, the discussions and conflicts preceding the passing of the Sherman Antitrust Act in 1890 and following during the years up to the Clayton Act in 1914 represents such a formative period (Berk 1994). In the struggle between big corporations and small producers, cartels and loose agreements became denounced as unreasonable restraints of trade and were therefore outlawed in principle while mergers between firms, as long as they increased efficiency, remained a legitimate form of economic behaviour (Djelic 1998). Alternative patterns of control, such as associational systems, (see Berk 1994 for the railroad industry; Schneiberg 2007 for infrastructure industries) became undermined by government anti-trust cases against such small-firm trade associations in the 1920s.

US anti-trust policy made, as emphasized by Chandler (1977, 1990), a major contribution to the growth of mergers and concentrations in US industry. Jurisdictional actions played an equally important role in the struggle about the legitimacy of different production models (Berk 1994). While overall, the American economy was fostering mergers leading to large concentrations, oligopolistic market control, and mass production, there always remained loopholes and exceptions, and legislation also had sometimes unintended effects. Zeitlin (2007: 229) highlights how localized speciality producers were able to informally organize the provision of collective services and information exchange, enabling collective learning at the industry level (Scranton 1997; see also Whitford 2006). Drawing on Berk (2009) he also points to exceptional court decisions, which allowed associations in the printing industry information sharing as long as they refrained from coordinated pricing policies. Finally, anti-trust decrees obliging large firms to licence technology to competitors became the basis for the development of new industrial clusters in the Silicon Valley (Borrus and Zysman 1997, cited in Zeitlin 2007: 229). In sum, however, US anti-trust legislation can be said to have fostered for a long time large corporations and mass production at the expense of such alternative forms of production.

The development of competition law in Europe, and particularly in Germany, provides an interesting comparison to the US case. Historically, cartels have been regarded much more favourably by German policy-makers, industry, and the larger public well into the period after the Second World War than they have in the US (Herrigel 1996). Attempted transfers of US competition law to Europe (Djelic 1998) in the early post war period were partially successful. However, as the reform of the German competition law in 1957 shows, social struggles over what would represent acceptable forms of cooperative behaviour and what should be outlawed as inappropriate restraints on competition took their own dynamics within a distinctive historical, social, and institutional context (Quack and Djelic 2005). While outlawing cartels, the Law against Restraints on Competition (*Gesetz gegen Wettbewerbsbeschränkungen*), passed in 1957, excluded certain types of company agreements from the general ban. In particular, term-fixing, rebate, and specialization agreements remained legal and provided small- and medium-sized firms with the possibility of information sharing and collective learning at the industry level (Herrigel 1996: 170–4). Furthermore, industries in which full competition was not regarded as possible were excluded from the application of the law. This applied not only to the public and infrastructure sector but also to banking and insurance (Djelic and Quack 2005, 2007). In sum, a break with cartels was combined with legal stipulations, which subsequently allowed German industry to reinvent previously existing forms of social coordination in a modern associational form. While certainly not the only factor, the development of German competition law after the Second World War can be nevertheless plausibly considered as a constitutive influence on the persistence of a decentralized industrial order (Herrigel 1996) and the success of diversified quality production in the 1970s and 1980s (Streeck 1991). The importance of competition law in fostering or hindering the provision of common or public goods at the disposal of all or a group of companies has been more generally highlighted in research on the success of Italian, German, and Danish industrial districts in comparison to their decline in Britain and the US (Zeitlin 1995, 2007).[6]

---

[6] France would be another negative case though not caused by competition law.

LAW IN THE CONTEMPORARY PERIOD:
COMBINING THE WEBERIAN PERSPECTIVE
AND COMPARATIVE ANALYSIS

The previous section examined the ways in which law could be seen to determine and shape economic organization. In that perspective, law is given a classic 'black box' status where its inner workings are bracketed off in order to concentrate on its effects on other institutions. However, as we illustrated at the start, there is an alternative approach to law as an institution that derives from the historical and sociological accounts of law initiated by Weber and Ehrlich. From this perspective, we need to get inside the 'black box' and understand how it is constituted and reconstituted under specific historical conditions in order to appreciate the co-evolution and interaction of law, and economic organization. This requires three steps: firstly an historical understanding of how the legal field became constituted in different social contexts and the impact of this on relations between law, lawyers, and economic organization; secondly, an analysis of how and where the law evolved from being structured by political and social relations into becoming a business in its own right and the consequences of this for economic organization; thirdly, how, as law became a particular form of business, it changed the conditions under which international economic activity takes place, becoming highly innovative in shaping and reshaping legal rules and constraints at different levels of action (national, regional, global) and through distinct modalities of law (soft law, hard law, private law, lex mercatoria, etc.). In this way, the interactive nature of the relationship between law, political authority, and economic organization can be identified, leading away from deterministic and evolutionary models towards a social and political concept of law as an institution.

The social constitution of legal fields

In this section, we examine how the actors in the legal field became constituted and the implications of this for economic organization. The focus is particularly on the relationship between lawyers on the one hand and on the other hand, firstly the state and secondly, the private actors in society (particularly those with economic power). The basic issue that we explore is the degree to which lawyers identified with the state as a political entity, with the private actors as clients, or with law as a set of principles and processes above and beyond the state and private interests. It is this identification and its embeddedness in practices of law and the social relations of law that shapes how law as an institution interacts with economic organization.

If we take the example of England, what became identified as the common law tradition emerged from the combination of a tamed monarchy, an independent legislature controlled by the rich and powerful, and a legal profession with its own structure (Osiel 1990). This arose from the long and tortured process of political and social change from the late medieval period into the early modern age. As early as the signing of the Magna Carta in 1215, the rights of nobles against the monarchy were enshrined and kingship became the centre of long running battles between different noble families. The efforts of the Tudors were to create a system of national administration freed from the influence of Rome where monarchical power could be asserted in any part of the kingdom. This reduced the powers of feudal lords but faced other challenges such as those arising from religious and commercial change, both of which could find outlets in disputation in the parliamentary and legal systems (Braddick 2000). The Civil War of the mid-seventeenth century and the Glorious Revolution of 1688 created a new balance between monarchy and parliament, which worked against the imposition of a system of law controlled from above and led to a relatively flexible approach in which case law, disciplined by systems of appeal and legislative oversight, adapted to changing circumstances.

Under these conditions, lawyers claimed to be guardians of liberty by using the common law and the system of precedents to legitimize rights (particularly of property) and to guard against state despotism (on lawyers and liberalism in general see Halliday and Karpik 1997; Halliday, Karpik, and Feeley 2007). On the other hand, the liberty which was being protected was the liberty of the individual property owner. Thus the English lawyer was always firmly tied to the client (invariably drawn from the rich and powerful classes) against threats to the property of the client, either from the monarch or later from the propertyless masses either through theft, revolution, or the actions of a redistributive state.

Lawyers were not part of the emerging state apparatus; in theory they were an 'independent' profession with the power to control their own systems of recruitment, qualification, remuneration, and ethical values. Even though judges were appointed by the monarch and later the government, they had to be chosen from the profession where they had spent many years practising as independents in return for fees from clients. In so far as they were dependent, they were dependent on their clients rather than the state. This contributed to a particular vision of the law and the role of lawyers. They sought to serve their clients' interests by interpreting the law creatively. Such creativity could be tempered by the judiciary or the legislature but the overall consequence was that the common law evolved gradually but continuously as circumstances changed, as clients faced new problems and lawyers developed new solutions. Common law was a pliable instrument for the wealthy and for their legal advisers.

Most European societies evolved a different dynamic primarily because monarchical power lasted longer and therefore legal systems were imposed much more powerfully from the top with very little restraint from either a legislature or an independent judiciary. This was formalized in the Codes of law imposed by Napoleon across much of Europe in the early nineteenth century and although the defeat of Napoleon led to their repeal, many European nations eventually produced their own codes. Although nineteenth-century Codes achieved political legitimacy through the adapted forms of political authority, which European states were establishing in this period, the principle of the Code remained unchanged—to place in an orderly manner in statute the law which governed all particular actions. In civil code law systems, judicial decision-making focused on the statute and commentaries on the statute rather than cases. The law could only respond to changing circumstances by statutes themselves being changed. Associated with this, legal advice was cautious and constraining. If statute and the scholarly exegeses associated with statute did not explicitly give permission for a particular course of action, then it would be considered illegal and not to be undertaken.

Code law systems had two effects. On the one hand, lawyers in these systems became guardians of those rights, which had been established against monarchical control or were established in the Code itself, and the principles underlying the Code. On the other hand, lawyers faced the problem of being embedded within the state, being effectively servants of the state. Therefore where the state was illiberal, they were unable to practise the doctrines of liberalism (Halliday and Karpik 1997) and became potentially complicit in the coercive nature of the state (as happened with German lawyers in the Nazi period). Either way, the legal profession in these systems was at arms' length from private clients. In a number of contexts, judges were appointed by the state without any period as independent practitioners. The independent fee-earning lawyer was of relatively low status compared to the lawyer as a civil servant or even, later, as an employed adviser inside firms.

The development of the legal profession in Germany illustrates the impact of this. During the nineteenth century, German states spearheaded by Prussia and Bavaria sought successfully to bring lawyers under state control (Siegrist 1996). The Prussian model of a closed and state-regulated legal bar in which lawyers as well as judges had the status of civil servants became crucial for the further development of the legal profession in the unified Germany. Even after the establishment of an independent and self-governing German bar association in 1878, the professional prototype of the lawyer continued to be modelled on the civil servant. This was intensified by the development of civil law regulations concerning trade and economy, such as the German Civil Code of 1896 that provided comprehensive legal codification. The German Empire built on the Prussian authoritarian state tradition regarded law as an unquestioned order to which citizens had to comply (Rueschemeyer 1990, 1997). The professional and legal system in the German Empire, thus, offered fewer opportunities for lawyers to develop entrepreneurial qualities than in the British context. There was also less demand for market-based legal advice, as large German corporations and banks established in-house legal departments that internalized a considerable part of legal work.

The majority of the German legal profession maintained a strong social and cultural distance from the needs and interests of industry and commerce (Siegrist 1996) that was reflected in the status-group orientated approach, a critical attitude towards the expansion of law firms in scale and scope, and an emphasis on professional standards that focused on the single practitioner (Blankenburg and Schultz 1989; McClelland 1991). Legal education reflected this with a predominant emphasis on constitutional and administrative law and little on areas like contract drafting or tax law. Osiel summarizes that the dominant view of law in the German case saw it as a:

purely analytical, intellectual construct, a sealed system of logically interconnected propositions impermeable to the economic pressures of the business world. . . . Whatever new opportunities for work and wealth the evolving social needs of the time presented to lawyers
were thereby lost.   (Osiel 1990: 2052–3)

An important element in this discussion is what Bourdieu refers to as 'the general
position of the juridical field within the broader field of power' (Bourdieu 1987: 823).
In common law systems, lawyers established themselves as independent practitioners
serving the interests of their clients. From early on, this brought them into close
alliance with the rich and powerful. In the USA, Perrow in his analysis of the
development of the American economy in the nineteenth century labelled lawyers
as the 'shock-troops of capitalism' (Perrow 2002) for the ways in which they served
the robber barons of the gilded age. In the UK, these linkages were more subtle. A key
group of law firms (later forming the nucleus of the Magic Circle firms) worked in
the City of London, facilitating the development of the stock market and associated
activities as well as working with the Bank of England and the UK Treasury. Members
of these firms were part of a social and political elite of British society (Morgan and
Quack 2005).

   Although there were business law firms in Germany, they were outnumbered by
lawyers working inside the state or inside companies and banks. Rueschemeyer
describes the Prussian bar in the mid-nineteenth century as 'as close to being
Prussian civil servants as an attorney can be. And legally they were considered to
be members of the royal Civil Service, with all the obligations this entailed for their
professional and personal conduct, including restrictions on political activity'
(Rueschemeyer 1997: 210). They did not exercise the influence of US and UK lawyers.
They were a part of the German corporate system, not independent of it nor
particularly influential within it.

   In France, also, the state played a central role in shaping the position of lawyers in
the broader social structure. What differentiated this civil law system from Germany, however, was that French lawyers had played a role in the downfall of the
Ancien Regime and became associated with the new state. Karpik identifies French
lawyers as central actors in the building of a 'liberal political society' (Karpik 1997,
1999). Lawyers identified the rule of law with the principles of a liberal state and the
rights of the individual as expressed in the Declaration of the Rights of Man passed
by the French National Assembly convened after the fall of the Bastille in 1789. For
Karpik,

The relationship with the political sphere had become the dominant organizing principle of
the profession. . . . It is the priority given to political action together with the distance the
collectivity maintained with respect to capitalist accumulation of wealth . . . which enables us
to understand the presence of a profession . . . characterized by self-government, a rigorous
code of ethics, a moderate economics, primacy of the courts and of the pleadings, a preponderance of individual clients.   (Karpik 1997: 122)

In these different societies, therefore, the position of being a lawyer was constructed
in distinctive national ways. In England, lawyers were closely allied to dominant

economic interests, using their knowledge to advise firms and wealthy individuals on how they could act. This advice was entrepreneurial, business oriented, case law based. In Germany on the other hand, lawyers were mostly employed by the state and only a small number were engaged in advising clients on an independent fee basis. Further the law was treated as something embedded in statute not something that could be adapted and remade by lawyers in response to changing economic circumstances. In France, lawyers were strongly embedded in the development of political liberalism, standing aloof in most cases from economic activity.

Law as a business: the rise of the mega-law firm[7]

These developments had implications for the way in which lawyers organized their activities through to the mid-twentieth century. In France, for example, lawyers tended to work as sole practitioners or in small partnerships. Their individual clients rarely required more resources. Even where lawyers took on corporate work, this was of a limited scale. Only gradually, in the period after 1945, did a small number of firms become more specialized in corporate work but even then their size remained limited.

Germany was also characterized by relatively small firms of lawyers. Lawyers were only admitted to practice in their local court and therefore law firms were highly localized. The growing complexity of legal issues and growing demand for private legal advice raised repeatedly controversial debates within the German Chamber of Attorneys, particularly in the 1920/30s and in the 1960/70s, about the degree to which lawyers should become engaged in commercial activities and whether the operation of large law firms was consistent with the ethics of a liberal profession (Siegrist 1996). The existing rules of self-regulation were criticized by business law firms in various local Chambers of Attorneys as limiting innovation and being dominated by the interests of sole practitioners (Rogowski 1994, 1995) but there was no majority to achieve a fundamental change. The practice of lawyers remained restricted to the locality in which they were registered at a court. Though cooperation between lawyers (and lawyers and accountants) was possible and took place in the legal form of civil law association (*Gesellschaft bürgerlichen Rechts, GbR*), the size of these firms remained limited by the 'location principle'. Few German law firms had more than ten partners in the early 1980s, long after restrictions on partnership size had been removed in England. It was not until the late 1980s that this situation changed. Following a decision of the Federal Court of Justice in 1987 that declared the

---

[7] While in the following section we focus on law firms as important actors in the legal field, other authors have highlighted the influence of legal scholars and judges in generating ideas and legal constructs. In a very interesting comparison of the historical evolution of American and German corporate law, Klages (2009) demonstrates how legal actors in each country produced law doctrines, which oscillated between institutionalism and individualism and thereby established an elective affinity of law and economic interests. Rehder (forthcoming) provides an in-depth analysis of an epistemic community of labour judges, which reshaped legal doctrines in German labour law.

existing code of professional rules for lawyers as invalid, a number of reforms have taken place that liberalized the practice of law firms significantly. The admission of supra-local law firms led to the establishment of national law firms through mergers between law firms from different regions. Whereas none of the largest corporate law firms had employed more than fifty lawyers (including partners and associates) in 1989, many of them doubled in size during the following three years, the largest one reaching the number of one hundred and twelve lawyers in 1992 (Rogowski 1995: 125).

It is interesting to compare these developments to those in the US. The nature of US economic and political development from early on placed its legal profession on a distinctive trajectory. Abel and Lewis (1988) argue that nineteenth-century Americans were already more likely to use law and litigation to maintain a sense of moral order than their counterparts in England and Western Europe. This was related to the more pluralistic and transient nature of the American society, considerable mistrust of citizens in any concentration of government power and their strong rights-orientation. In the context of an eventually evolving weak and fragmented American state, lawyers and judges represented—to use Alexis de Tocqueville's expression—the 'aristocracy' of pre-revolutionary America. Tocqueville also provided one of the earliest descriptions of what much later would be labelled the judicialization of politics (Shapiro and Stone Sweet 2002b) when he wrote that 'scarcely any political question arises in the United States that is not resolved, sooner or later, into a judicial question' (1945: 290).

Within this context, the economic development of the United States, at the beginning of the twentieth century, laid the ground for the triumphal procession of private practitioners and their influential role in the development of the American legal profession. The transformation of American capitalism from a small producer society into a world of large industrial corporations and big business was largely facilitated by lawyers. American business lawyers developed an unparalleled scope of professional activity, both inside and outside the court room. The anti-trust legislation that attempted to combat the misuse of economic power, for example, gave responsibility for judgements to the courts and thereby opened the floor for spectacular 'legal wars' between industrial giants each represented in the courts by an army of lawyers (Roy 1997). At the same time, lawyers expanded their activities from legal advice into adjacent fields, such as the intermediation of financial and corporate deals. Overall, their focus shifted from representation at the courts to negotiations in the board room and to contract work in their offices. According to Galanter and Palay (1991: 1), American lawyers started to 'do more things for more clients and in more settings (not only the courts) than do their counterparts elsewhere'. The growth of big business in the 'gilded age' of American capitalism thus stimulated and was stimulated by the emergence of the big law firm.

The crucial thing about the growing size of law firms was that it enabled specialization. It was Paul Cravath who in the first decade of the twentieth century established the new organization of the law firm by employing highly qualified associates from law schools on an understanding that they might progress to partnership after having worked as associates for an extended period. Under the up or out system, only a small number each year would succeed yet all the associates would work long hours in an effort to win the tournament. This employment system quickly spread across American law firms and allowed them to achieve growth in size and specialization. The number of law firms with more than four lawyers increased significantly in the first two decades of the twenieth century. In the early 1940s, it was not unusual for the largest American law firms to employ forty or fifty lawyers—though most of them were still operating only in one city or region. According to Galanter and Palay (1991: 14) 'the large law firm—and with it the organization of law practice around the "promotion to partnership" pattern—became the industry standard'.

From the 1970s onwards, the large American law firm underwent a further change as it adapted to the increasing internationalization of US business and the expansion of capital markets. Galanter described this as the rise of mega-lawyering (Galanter and Dingwall 1983), a term that has since been taken up to describe changes in other countries such as the UK (Flood 1989, 1996). The size and geographical scope of law firms increased from the 1980s onwards, partly through inter-state mergers and the establishment of offices outside the US, to an extent that formalized management methods were introduced to govern their activities. American mega-law firms, in short, became increasingly driven by commercial considerations of how to increase turnover and profitability through high partner-to-associate (leverage) ratios, maximizing the rain-making capacities of their partners and having the legal work done by numerous associates and employees.

The emergence of the mega-law firm resulted from a 'conjunction between the growth imperative inherent in the big firm's organizational form and a set of changes in the business and legal environment' (Galanter and Palay 1991: 76). Among the latter, the merger and acquisition waves of the 1980s and the increasing financialization of corporate governance in the US deserve mentioning. Another important factor was the growth in litigation, with a significant number of cases involving increasingly complex issues and higher stakes than in earlier periods. Robert Kagan coined the term 'adversarial legalism' to describe the dramatic increase in judicialization and litigation that the US has experienced since the 1970s (Kagan 2001). Adversarial legalism is characterized by two key features: formal legal contestation, e.g. competing interests and disputants readily invoking legal rights, duties, and procedural requirements, and litigant activism, e.g. a style of legal contestation dominated by disputing parties or interests, acting primarily through lawyers (Kagan 2001: 9). Kagan argues that the emergence of adversarial legalism relates to the inability of powerful actors—most obviously the state but also social groups such as the civil rights movement, trade unions, and employers' associations—to impose their goals on others, in other words where 'authority is fragmented and in which hierarchical control is relatively weak' (ibid). The US federal system with multiple jurisdictional levels coupled with a market system that sustains diversity of forms of economic organization is crucial to this adversarial legalism. Within this environment of adversarial legalism, mega-law firms with their abilities to search systematically for precedents, to gather evidence on a large scale, and to develop aggressive arguments, prospered and grew to a previously unforeseeable extent while also expanding their reach to foreign markets (Dezalay 1990, 1995; Dezalay and Garth 1996, 2002a, b).

The process of mega-lawyering proceeded more slowly in the UK. After the Second World War, a small number of law firms based in the City of London became integrally involved in facilitating the construction of financial products and aiding in their legal constitution. Although this led to some jurisdictional disputes, particularly with merchant banks (less so with accountants who were generally low status in this particular corner of the English class system), in the main, the symbiotic relationship between the City and these firms worked highly effectively in providing a legal environment in which financial institutions could experiment and develop new products. However the relatively small scale of the City compared to the environment of Wall Street and the US where large corporations were becoming predominant in the economy meant that there was limited pressure for growth and the Cravath system was not really used. Until 1967, the UK maintained a ceiling of twenty on the number of partners that could join together in one law firm so even the richest and most profitable law firms stayed relatively small. Once the ceiling was removed, firms could grow in size and the possibility of national and international expansion became a reality. It was not until the mid-1980s when a series of political and institutional changes occurred in the UK that there opened up huge new areas of business for corporate lawyers (Flood 1989, 1996). These included the Big Bang deregulation of the Stock Exchange, the Financial Services Act, the privatization of state enterprises, the transformation of building societies' assets from mutual to private ownership, and a pension reform giving rise to increased private investment. These changes were followed up with the opening of Eastern and Central Europe to business and financial markets and later by the rise of China and India. For the US and UK mega-law firms' internationalization was the obvious way forward. From the 1980s, US and UK law firms' set up offices in new locations and engaged in mergers with other lawyers in the main centres of financial, political, and economic power (Spar 1997; Warf 2001). German firms were particularly favoured targets for mergers as they offered access both to the German market itself and to much of Central and Eastern Europe (Morgan and Quack 2005; Quack 2008).

The rise of the mega-law firm is a crucial point in the development of law as a governing institution for two reasons. Firstly, the capacity of law firms to shape the law on behalf of their clients increases exponentially because of the resources being deployed. The important point here as will be described in the following section is that the mega-law firm can effectively 'attack' the law, finding ways round it and through it for clients, finding ways to influence legislation, finding new ways of avoiding state law and replacing it with forms of private, soft law. It can engage legal procedures at new levels—international, regional, global, as well as national. The mega-law firm has the capacity for this in a way that previous types of law firms have not. Further they have access to multinational clients for whom this sort of activity is deemed valuable and economically rewarding. Thus the mega-law firm reconstitutes the relevant economic law in its own image as multilevelled, multifaceted and multi-jurisdictional.

Secondly, the mega-law firm is a US invention; it is a product of adversarial legalism and in important ways a carrier of adversarial legalism. It requires vast numbers of cases, conflicts, litigations, and above all fees to be economically viable. However in its power it threatens other models of law firms by winning their clients, accessing their markets, and shaping a new international arena of law. Thus the model of the small independent lawyer is undermined as national, regional, and international mergers and acquisitions creates new global law firms.

Internationalization and innovation

The growth of mega-lawyering brings into sharp relief the development of the entrepreneurial side of legal activities. It reveals law in the making, shifting and developing at multiple levels and in multiple arenas as mega-law firms and their clients develop a more activist and interventionist position on law, defining it as much as a facilitator as a constraint. From this perspective, the law as stable, predictable, and determining of economic action breaks down. Instead the law itself has to be seen as endogenously positioned with economic and social fields evolving and changing in response to actors and circumstances within those fields. Similarly the fields cannot be conceptualized using a national lens; they are frequently international in scope, with overlapping forms of jurisdiction, disputation, and adjudication that the mega-law firms coordinate and manage. Large law firms with intense forms of specialization, high numbers of lawyers, developed systems of support, dense networks of offices across jurisdictions cooperating together are active on behalf of their corporate clients in solving problems and developing solutions for problems clients did not even realize they had. Powell argues that:

the role of lawyers in shaping cases and manipulating the law to fit their clients' interests becomes central.... Lawyers not only interpret and transform the law in their daily practice but also create new devices... lawyers use novel legal arguments and courtroom advocacy to change the common law or case law that governs relations among private interests... lawyers contribute to lawmaking by the development of new legal practices and devices such as novel tax shelters, new arrangements for the ownership and leasing of property, new types of securities and bonds and even new forms of corporate organization.   (Powell 1993: 426–8)

The entrepreneurialism and innovation of law firms increases not just because of the capabilities arising from scale but also because of the new opportunities, which emerge from internationalization. McBarnett identifies what she describes as the problems posed for global business in terms of:

- clashes between jurisdictions in terms of basic legal concepts as well as their interpretation and application,
- multiple requirements being imposed... [e.g.] different accounting rules,
- gaps, where there are emergent markets, for example, but no legal infrastructure within them appropriate to market dealing (McBarnett 2002: 100).

In terms of law firms and their multinational clients, the goal is to recognize variations across jurisdictions, levels, and arenas and to use these effectively for the economic benefit of both the clients and the law firms. This is partly about arbitrage, where difference is taken for granted and used to maximize advantages. It is also partly about the opposite, i.e. creating standard rules which apply across jurisdictions. These two practices go together, in creating value for clients and profits for the law firms, at the same time as generating a vortex of activity, innovation, and uncertainty that sucks more and more actors in.

In relation to arbitrage, the global law firm is able to advise clients about how to utilize the diversity of national legal systems in order to both manage their affairs and maximize their advantage. In the field of merger and acquisitions, for example, global deals require that relatively large numbers of national competition authorities agree to the terms. This is a complex process of coordination, which can break down particularly if key competition authorities such as those in the US or Europe decide that a deal is inappropriate (Morgan 2006). Global law firms aim to overcome client problems and develop solutions. This has the potential to create a new product/solution that can then be sold to other clients. McBarnett states that:

Law is not just an obstacle to business but a material which can be worked on to its advantage. If creative means can be found to overcome legal obstructions to global deals, then those obstructions—still in existence, at least for a time, for others—become not an obstruction but an opportunity, and a route to competitive advantage. There is therefore a constant drive for new legal constructs to solve the global problem not just at the collective level but at the level of the individual business.   (McBarnett 2002: 101)

At the global level then, law firms have multiple opportunities to develop new ways into the problems and gaps that exist in dealing across jurisdictions. Flood, for example, provides a range of illustrations of how law firms develop new products for banks, investors, and multinationals in order to provide a legal framing for new problems (Flood 2002, 2007, 2008; Flood and Skordaki 2008; Flood and Sosa 2008).

This places global law firms in a complex relationship to movements to harmonize and standardize laws across national boundaries. It might, for example, be argued that it is in the interests of global business to establish stability and predictability through creating forms of 'global law'. Indeed, there is plenty of evidence that at least in the form of privately agreed international rules and regulations (soft law) this is occurring in many arenas (Djelic and Sahlin-Andersson 2006). For example, Morgan describes how the private association, the International Securities and Derivatives Association (ISDA), made up of the largest participants in the over-the-counter derivatives markets, created a model contract that became the common template for all such transactions. Two major law firms from the UK and the US played a significant role in drawing up the contract and identifying potential areas of problems where national jurisdictions might contradict the rules which ISDA sought to provide. Local legal opinions were therefore sought and efforts made to lobby for change in national systems in order to bring them in line with the international model contract (Morgan 2008). This works against arbitrage techniques, but by reducing costs and uncertainty brings another set of gains for clients.

This interplay between national and international, hard and soft law has become a central arena for global law firms and for firms and regulators in many different sectors (Applebaum, Felstiner, and Gessner 2001; Djelic and Quack 2003; Djelic and Sahlin-Andersson 2006; Gessner 2009; Graz and Nölke 2008; Likosky 2002; Quack and Djelic 2005). At one level, these studies reflect the emergence of what Hedley Bull described as 'the new medievalism' (Bull 2002). Bull identified the decline of the sovereignty of the nation-state as a return to a sort of medieval order in which there existed multiple forms of authority and legitimation with overlapping spheres of jurisdiction. Although Bull's metaphor overplays the decline of the nation-state and neglects the long-term existence of Kantian forms of theorizing about international law and their embeddedness in certain international institutions such as the UN with the idea of a constitutionalized international legal system (Koskenniemi 2007), it nevertheless captures some of the new environment, which is being created by the interactions between law and global law firms with multinational clients and new forms of transnational solidarity.

In her analysis of this form of legal pluralism, Riles emphasizes what she describes as 'stepping outside Weber's shadow' (Riles 2006), i.e. the absolute association of law with the state and instead recognizing that the nation-state's ability to define the nature of the law that is relevant for its subjects has never been absolute. It has always been mitigated by transnational and global arenas of law as well as national and local (see also Halliday 2004). It is about other actors besides the state and other arenas besides those defined by the nation-state. The confluence of international mega-law firms, multinational clients, global economic processes, and new forms of international law-making in the public and the private domain and at various levels of collectivity (the EU, the WTO on the public side and the plethora of private standard setting bodies on the other) has created a new environment. As Watt states: 'Such changes suggest multiple polyvalent perspectives from which law can be perceived: beyond the perspective of the national court, law is evolving under the impetus of private arbitrators, mobile capital seeking to invest, transnational communities of interests, international courts or non-governmental organizations' (Watt 2006: 585; see also Applebaum et al. 2001; Gessner 2009).

For example, there is no doubt that the legislative institutions of the European Union have generated a dense net of European regulations and directives which have direct and indirect effects on national law in the member states. As a result, comparing the law of different nation states as independent and separate entities within the EU is increasingly misleading. Instead, the development of the law in the member states needs to be considered as interconnected and co-evolving in various ways (Alter 2001; Craig and De Búrka 2007). This opens space and opportunities for economic actors to strategize on multiple levels of the policy and law-making process. Furthermore, networked governance within the EU generates various types of voluntary rules and standards as potential sources of formalized law

(Tömmel and Verdun 2009). In addition, European law has become interconnected through various treaties with international law (Oberthür and Gehring 2006).

Beyond an analysis of the multilayered nature of the legislative process in the EU, it is important to consider a number of related elements of the transnationalization of law. The first element concerns the shift of decision-making into legal arenas and out of the political context. The second concerns the nature of the process of decision-making in this arena and the sort of knowledge that is effective in this arena. The third element concerns the construction of a global elite to manage these processes.

With regard to the shift of decision-making into legal arenas, this has been articulated as a process of judicialization (Shapiro and Stone Sweet 2002a). At one level, this enables actors to take out of the political arena controversial issues that seem incapable of solution and instead place them in a context where they can be resolved according to specific rules and procedures. This creates a different logic, one that is driven by technical expertise and the ability to marshal legal resources rather than being driven by debates on broader values and norms. In an era where these values and norms are subject to contestation and there are a plurality of interests articulated in the political realm, there are significant institutional blockages to resolving many issues through the political process. Increasingly, therefore, this gap has been filled by the development of formal and informal legal rules and practices. Dezalay and Garth, for example, have shown how the International Court of Arbitration in Paris became an increasingly important site for the resolution of disagreements between companies and countries (Dezalay and Garth 1996) and has filled this gap. The Court was drawn from notable lawyers from the US and Europe who developed their own rules of procedure. The Court was convened on the instruction of the parties to the disagreement and proceeded on the basis of minimal publicity in order not to create wider conflict between two commercial actors who would in the future want to work together again. Dezalay and Garth show how gradually US global law firms, primarily because of their mega-law capabilities and their common law competences became dominant actors in this process representing multinational clients and sovereign states and providing increasing numbers of arbitrators.

Similar developments have occurred in the arena of trade law where the formation of the WTO led to a judicialization of disputes between countries via the creation of the Appellate Court of the WTO, where aggrieved nations could seek remedy on the grounds that their ability to conduct free trade according to WTO rules was being obstructed by the actions of a government (Garth 2008). In the EU, the European Court of Justice has become increasingly involved in interpreting the relationship between European law and national law. Contrary to initial expectations, the ECJ has evolved a significant constitutional role and in so doing has taken some issues away from the politics of the Council of Ministers and moved them into a judicial form (Alter 2001, 2008; Cohen and Vauchez 2007). In these arenas, the model of process and litigation developed in the US, which requires legions of lawyers working in a highly concentrated way on particular cases and bringing these cases to court and representing them, has become dominant—leading some authors to identify a global transfer of Kagan's adversarial legalism (Keleman 2006; Keleman and Sibbitt 2004).

The second issue concerns the nature of the legal knowledge, which counts in these transnational arenas. Here, there is a strong argument that the dominant form of knowledge is one based on US law and in particular on the development of a particular conjuncture of economic knowledge and law that has characterized the US over the last few decades. The Law and Economics movement pioneered in the US, and in Chicago in particular, involved a drawing together of free market economics with a focus on law as both a contributor to the free market and as also subject to the efficiency requirements of the free market. These arguments linked together common law, free market economics, and issues of economic development into the neo-liberal discourse that became a dominant feature of international economic policy from the 1980s to the impact of the credit crisis of 2008. Faust, for example, quotes Posner, one of the founders of the economic analysis of law, stating that 'the common law is best (not perfectly) explained as a system for maximizing the wealth of society' (Faust 2006: 839). Dezalay and Garth explored how this combination of legal and economic analysis became spread throughout the world (Dezalay and Garth 2002a, b). Key features of this concerned the investment that the US made in providing education and training in law for the elites of other countries (Silver 2000, 2002, 2007), often by providing scholarships to the best and the brightest students from foreign systems into the US legal education world. European legal elites had been badly tainted by their involvement and sometime collusion with the Nazis. By contrast, the US in the era post-1945 was seen as the bringer of the rule of law in a benign liberal environment. Elites seeking to study law therefore turned to the US in a way which they had not previously. In the US, these elites learnt the nature of the law and economics perspective, many of them in the most high status and well connected of the law schools. Some of them took this knowledge back to their home countries where over time they became increasingly influential conduits for the flow of these ideas and practices into their home systems. Others stayed in the US and acted from there to spread such ideas by using their networks in their original locations, while at the same time increasing the diversity inside the US firms sufficient to allow them to deal more effectively with different legal systems.

This spread had impacts on many areas of law. In competition law, for example, the US model with its emphasis on the technical analysis of economic impacts and its rejection of simple concentration models and definitions of anti-competitiveness has been of major significance. It has led a shift in competition policy away from the politics of producers and small firms and into the judicial arena where economic analysis has become the key deciding factor (Djelic 1998, 2002; Djelic and Kleiner 2006; Gerber 2006; Morgan 2006; Quack and Djelic 2005). In financial markets law, the combination of US (New York) law and UK law has been the dominant force (Morgan 2008).

These arguments about the Americanization of the transnational arena may ultimately over-estimate the process. The creation of transnational rule systems remains relatively decentralized with a wide range of participants. Halliday and Carruthers, for example, have looked at the development of bankruptcy law in different national contexts and whilst they identify certain common actors, they also emphasize that there is an element of uncertainty in the process of transplanting rules across contexts. Actors in national contexts react back and create loops of recursivity in which changes and adaptations are made to systems (Carruthers and Halliday 2006; Halliday and Carruthers 2007, 2009; Halliday and Osinsky 2006). Similarly, law firms may take different forms in the global arena and do not necessarily follow the US model of mega-law and adversarial legalism (Morgan and Quack 2005; Quack 2008). Duina (2007) shows how different national legal traditions had a significant influence on how different transnational market systems (the European Single Market, NAFTA, and Mercosur) were built. His analysis demonstrates that the law influenced how transnational markets are organized and that law at one level (national) affected economic activity at another level (transnational). In a multipolar world characterized by diverse legal actors, traditions, and arenas, there remains a high level of complexity and indeterminacy even within a context where US law has many sources of dominating power (Quack 2007).

CONCLUSION

In this chapter, we have examined law as a governing institution. Contrary to some institutionalist accounts in which law is taken as a given, an exogenous factor determining economic organization, we have emphasized the dynamic, endogenous nature of law. As we have shown, there are many useful insights about institutional reproduction and change that can be developed through treating the law as stable and then comparing the impact of distinctive national systems of law on aspects of economic organization. There is now, for example, a flourishing field in relation to issues of corporate governance where analyses of shareholder protections and the claims of various legally constituted actors to particular assets or to particular rights are clearly affected by the law. Similarly, laws relating to markets and competition impact strongly on how firms evolve and develop in relation to merger and takeover activity, price fixing and profit-taking in markets and incentives for innovation associated with the protection of intellectual property rights and the vesting of claims to IPR in various entities. There is no doubt that continued research along these lines can yield dividends in terms of understanding differences across nations and firms and the impact of these processes on the growth of firms and national economies.

However, throughout this chapter, we have emphasized that this approach needs to be balanced by a view which recognizes that law is always something in the making. It has its own trajectory of development, which is historically embedded. This embeddedness is reflected in the nature of law itself, in the organization of the legal profession, and in the position of law and lawyers in the broad political and social structure of the society. These actors in the juridical field or on its margins engage in shaping and reshaping the law as part of their regular activity and business. It is therefore essential to understand the internal dynamics of the business of law and how it is evolving and with what purpose.

In this respect, we have emphasized three features. Firstly, we have shown how the growth of mega-law firms speeds up the dynamics of legal innovation and internationalization since these firms have the capability to explore multiple legal environments and engage in arbitrage as well as standardization in order to serve their multinational corporate clients. Secondly, we have demonstrated that this reflects the emergence of a multilayered world of law where there are overlapping jurisdictions and judicial and quasi-judicial bodies ranging from the national through the regional (especially the EU) to the global (most prominently in the WTO). Thirdly, we have highlighted the growth in this multilayered system of soft law and private agreements between actors as ways of resolving potential legal problems (e.g. in the establishment of the International Commercial Court of Arbitration or in the work of the International Swaps and Derivatives Association). An understanding of how law is evolving is therefore crucial to our analysis of institutional change and stability. It is necessary to 'open the black box' of law in the way in which other such issues have been opened for analysis. Once this is done, what appeared to be stable and objective is revealed to be subject to contestation and change.

References

Abbott, A. (1998). *The System of Professions: An Essay on the Division of Expert Labor*, (Chicago: University of Chicago Press).

Abel, R. L. and P. Lewis (1988). *Lawyers in Society*, (Berkeley: University of California Press).

Aguilera, R. and G. Jackson (2003). 'The Cross-national Diversity of Corporate Governance: Dimensions and Determinants', *Academy of Management Review* 28 (3): 447–65.

Ahlering, B. and S. Deakin (2007). 'Labor Regulation, Corporate Governance and Legal Origin: A Case of Institutional Complementarity?', *Law and Society Review* 41: 865–908.

Anheiner, H. K. and W. Seibel (1990). *The Third Sector: Comparative Studies of Nonprofit Organizations*, (Berlin: De Gruyter).

Alter, K. J. (2001). *Establishing the Supremacy of European Law: The Making of an International Rule of Law in Europe*, (Oxford: Oxford University Press).

——(2008). 'The European Court and Legal Integration: An Exceptional Story or Harbinger of the Future?', in K. E. Whittington, R. D. Keleman, and G. A. Caldeira (eds.), *The Oxford Handbook of Law and Politics*, (Oxford: Oxford University Press) 209–28.

APPLEBAUM, R. P., W. FELSTINER, and V. GESSNER (eds.) (2001). *Rules and Networks: The Legal Culture of Global Business Transactions*, (Oxford: Hart Publishing).

ARMOUR, J., S. DEAKIN, and S. KONZELMANN (2003). 'Shareholder Primacy and the Trajectory of UK Corporate Governance', *British Journal of Industrial Relations* 41: 531–55.

BAGNASCO, A. and C. F. SABEL (eds.) (1995). *Small and Medium-Size Enterprises*, (London: Pinter).

BECKERT, J. (2008). *Inherited Wealth*, (Princeton, NJ: Princeton University Press).

BERK, G. (1994). *Alternative Tracks. The Constitution of American Industrial Order 1865–1917*, (Baltimore and London: Johns Hopkins University Press).

——(2009). *Louis D. Brandeis and the Making of Regulated Competition, 1900–1932*, (Cambridge: Cambridge University Press).

BERLE, A. and G. MEANS ([1932] 1991). *The Modern Corporation and Private Property*, (New York: Transaction Publishers).

BLANKENBURG, E. and U. SCHULTZ (1989). 'German Advocates: A Highly Regulated Profession', in R. L. Abel and P. S. Lewis (eds.), *Lawyers in Society*, vol. II *The Civil Law World*, (Berkeley: University of California Press) 124–159.

BORRUS, M. and J. ZYSMAN (1997). 'Globalization with Borders,' *Industry & Innovation* 4 (2): 141–66.

BOURDIEU, P. (1987). 'The Force of Law: Toward a Sociology of the Juridical Field', *Hastings Law Journal* 38: 805–53.

BRADDICK, MICHAEL J. (2000). *State Formation in Early Modern England c. 1550–1700*, (Cambridge: Cambridge University Press).

BROUWER, M. (2006). 'Reorganization in US and European Bankruptcy Law', *European Journal of Law and Economics* 22: 5–20.

BULL, H. (2002). *The Anarchical Society: A Study of Order in World Politics*, 3rd edn. (New York: Columbia University Press).

CAMPBELL, J. L. and L. N. LINDBERG (1990). 'Property Rights and the Organization of Economic Activity by the State', *American Sociological Review* 55: 634–47.

CARRUTHERS, B. G. and L. ARIOVICH (2004). 'The Sociology of Property Rights', *Annual Review of Sociology* 30: 23–46.

——and T. HALLIDAY (1998). *Rescuing Business. The Making of Corporate Bankruptcy Law in England and the United States*, (Oxford: Clarendon Press).

————(2006). 'Negotiating Globalization: Global Scripts and Intermediation in the Construction of Asian Insolvency Regimes', *Law & Social Inquiry* 31(3): 521–84.

CASPER, S. (2001). 'The Legal Framework for Corporate Governance: The Influence of Contract Law on Company Strategies in Germany and the United States', in P. Hall and D. Soskice (eds.), *Varieties of Capitalism: The Institutional Foundations of Comparative Advantage*, (Oxford: Oxford University Press), 387–416.

CHANDLER, Jr., A. D. (1977). *The Visible Hand: the Managerial Revolution in American Business*. (Cambridge, MA: Harvard University Press).

——(1990). *Scale and Scope: The Dynamics of Industrial Capitalism*, (Cambridge, MA: Harvard University Press).

COFFEE, J. (2006). *Gatekeepers: The Professions and Corporate Governance*, (Oxford: Oxford University Press).

COHEN, A. and A. VAUCHEZ (2007). 'Introduction: Law, Lawyers and Transnational Politics in the Production of Europe', *Law & Social Inquiry* 32(1): 75–82.

COMMONS, J. R. ([1924] 1995). *Legal Foundations of Capitalism*, (Edison, NJ: Transaction Publishers).

COMMONS, J. R. ([1950] 1970). *The Economics of Collective Action*, (Madison, WI: University of Wisconsin Press).

CRAIG, P. P. and D. DE BÚRCA (2007). *EU law: text, cases, and materials*, (Oxford: Oxford University Press).

DAM, K. W. (2006). *The Law-Growth Nexus: The Rule of Law and Economic Development*, (Washington, DC: Brookings Institution Press).

DEAKIN, S. (2009). 'Legal Origin, Juridical Form and Industrialisation in Historical Perspective: The Case of the Employment Relationship and the Joint Stock Company', *Socio-Economic Review* 7: 35–65.

——R. HOBBS, S. KONZELMANN, and F. WILKINSON (2006). 'Anglo-American Corporate Governance and the Employment Relationship: A Case to Answer?', *Socio-Economic Review* 4(1): 155–174.

DEEG, R. (1999). *Finance Capitalism Unveiled. Banks and the German Political Economy*, (Michigan: University of Michigan Press).

DELLA PORTA, D. (ed.) (2007). *The Global Justice Movement*, (Boulder; London: Paradigm Publishers).

DEZALAY, Y. (1990). 'The Big Bank and the Law: The Internationalization and Restructuration of the Legal Field', in M. Featherstone (ed.), *Global Culture*, (London: Sage), 278–93.

——(1995). '"Turf Battles" or "Class Struggles"; The Internationalization of the Market for Expertise in the "Professional Society"', *Accounting, Organizations and Society* 20(5): 331–44.

——and B. G. GARTH (1996). *Dealing in Virtue: International Commercial Arbitration and the Construction of a Transnational Legal Order*, (Chicago: University of Chicago Press).

————(2002a). *Global Prescriptions: The Production, Exportation, and Importation of a New Legal Orthodoxy*, (Ann Arbor: University of Michigan Press).

————(2002b). *The Internationalization of Palace Wars: Lawyers, Economists, and the Contest to Transform Latin American States*, (Chicago: University of Chicago Press).

DJELIC, M.-L. (1998). *Exporting the American Model: The Post-War Transformation of European business*, (Oxford: Oxford University Press).

——(2002). 'Does Europe Mean Americanization? The Case of Competition', *Competition and Change* 6(3): 233–50.

——and T. KLEINER (2006). 'The International Competition Network: Moving Towards Transnational Governance', in M.-L. Djelic and K. Sahlin-Andersson (eds.), *Transnational Governance: Institutional Dynamics of Regulation*, (Cambridge: Cambridge University Press), 287–307.

——and S. QUACK (eds.) (2003). *Globalization and Institutions*, (Cheltenham: Edward Elgar).

————(2005). 'Rethinking Path Dependency: The Crooked Path of Institutional Change in Post-war Germany', in G. Morgan, E. Moen, and R. Whitley (eds.), *Changing Capitalisms?*, (Oxford: Oxford University Press), 137–66.

————(2007). 'Overcoming Path Dependency: Path Generation in Open Systems', *Theory and Society* 36: 161–86.

——and K. SAHLIN-ANDERSSON (2006). *Transnational Governance: Institutional Dynamics of Regulation*, (Cambridge: Cambridge University Press).

DONAHUE, C. (2008). 'Comparative Law before the Code Napoleon', in M. Reimann and R. Zimmermann (eds.), *The Oxford Handbook of Comparative Law*, (Oxford: Oxford University Press), 3–32.

DUINA, F. (2007). *The Social Construction of Free Trade: The European Union, NAFTA, and Mercosur*, (Princeton, NJ: Princeton University Press).

DURKHEIM, E. ([1893] 1997). *The Division of Labor in Society*, (New York: Free Press).

EDELMAN, L. B. (2004). 'Rivers of Law and Contested Terrain: A Law and Society Approach to Economic Rationality', *Law & Society Review* 38(2): 181–97.

——(2007). 'Overlapping Fields and Constructed Legalities: The Endogeneity of Law', *ESRC/ GOVNET Workshop The Dynamics of Capital Market Governance*. Australian National University, Canberra.

——and R. STRYKER (2005). 'A Sociological Approach to Law and the Economy', in N. J. Smelser and R. Swedberg (eds.), *The Handbook of Economic Sociology*, (Princeton NJ: Princeton University Press), 527–51.

——and M. SUCHMAN (1997). 'The Legal Environments of Organizations', *Annual Review of Sociology* 23: 479–515.

EHRLICH, E. ([1913] 2002). *Fundamental Principles of the Sociology of Law*, (Edison, NJ: Transaction Publishers).

EVERS, A. and J.-L. LAVILLE (eds.) (2004). *The Third Sector in Europe*, (Cheltenham: Edward Elgar).

EWING, S. (1987). 'Formal Justice and the Spirit of Capitalism: Max Weber's Sociology of Law', *Law & Society Review* 21(3): 487–512.

FAUST, F. (2006). 'Comparative Law and the Economic Analysis of Law', in M. Reimann and R. Zimmermann (eds.), *The Oxford Handbook of Comparative Law*, (Oxford: Oxford University Press), 837–65.

FERNER, A. and R. HYMAN (eds.) (1998). *Changing Industrial Relations in Europe*, (New York: Wiley-Blackwell).

FLIGSTEIN, N. (2002). *The Architecture of Markets: An Economic Sociology of Twenty-First-Century Capitalist Societies*, (Princeton, NJ: Princeton University Press).

FLOOD, J. (1989). 'Megalaw in the UK: Professionalism or Corporatism? A Preliminary Report', *Indiana Law Journal* 64: 569–92.

——(1996). 'Megalawyering in the Global Order: The Cultural, Social and Economic Transformation of Global Legal Practice', *The International Journal of the Legal Profession* 3(2): 169–213.

——(2002). 'Capital Markets, Globalisation and Global Elites', in M. Likosky (ed.), *Transnational Legal Processes: Globalisation and Power Disparities*, (London: Butterworth), 114–34.

——(2007). 'Lawyers as Sanctifiers: The Role of Elite Law Firms in International Business Transactions', *Indiana Journal of Global Legal Studies* 10.

——(2008). 'Ambiguous Allegiances in the Lawyer–Client Relationship: The Case of Bankers and Lawyers', School of Law, University of Westminster.

——and SKORDAKI E. (1997). 'Normative Bricolage: Informal Rule-making by Accountants and Lawyers in Mega-insolvencies'. in G. Teubner (ed.) *Global Law Without a State*, (Aldershot: Dartmouth), 109–31.

————(2008). 'Structuring Transactions: The Case of Real Estate Finance', in V. Gessner (ed.), *Contractual Certainty in International Trade: Empirical Studies and Theoretical Debates on Institutional Support for Global Economic Exchanges*, (London: Hart Publishing), 157–72.

——and F. P. SOSA (2008). 'Lawyers, Law Firms and the Stabilization of Transnational Business', *Northwestern Journal of International Law and Business*, 28: 489–525.

GALANTER, M. and R. DINGWALL (1983). *Mega-Law and Mega-Lawyering in the Contemporary United States*, (London: Macmillan).

——and T. M. PALAY (1991). *Tournament of Lawyers: The Transformation of the Big Law Firm*, (Chicago ; London: University of Chicago Press).

GARTH, B. (2008). 'The Globalization of the Law', in K. E. Whittington, R. D. Keleman and G. A. Caldeira (eds.), *The Oxford Handbook of Law and Politics*, (Oxford: Oxford University Press), 245–64.

GERBER, D. J. (2006). 'Comparative Antitrust Law', in M. Reimann and R. Zimmermann (eds.), *The Oxford Handbook of Comparative Law*, (Oxford: Oxford University Press), 1194–1224.

GESSNER, V. (ed.) (2009). *Contractual Certainty in International Trade: Empirical Studies and Theoretical Debates on Institutional Support for Global Economic Exchanges*, (Oxford: Hart Publishing).

GLENN, H. P. (2006). 'Comparative Legal Families and Comparative Legal Traditions', in M. Reimann and R. Zimmermann (eds.), *The Oxford Handbook of Comparative Law*, (Oxford: Oxford University Press), 421–40.

GOSPEL, H. F. and A. PENDLETON (eds.) (2006). *Corporate Governance and Labour Management: An International Comparison*, (Oxford: Oxford University Press).

GOUREVITCH, P. and J. SHINN (2005). *Political Power and Corporate Control: The New Global Politics of Corporate Governance*, (Princeton, NJ: Princeton University Press).

GRAZ, J.-C. and A. NÖLKE (eds.) (2008). *Transnational Private Governance and Its Limits*, (London; New York: Routledge).

GRAZIADEI, M. (2006). 'Comparative Law as the Study of Transplants and Receptions', in M. Reimann and R. Zimmermann (eds.), *The Oxford Handbook of Comparative Law*, (Oxford: Oxford University Press), 441–75.

HALL, P. and D. SOSKICE (2001a). 'An Introduction to the Varieties of Capitalism Approach', in P. Hall and D. Soskice (eds.), *Varieties of Capitalism: The Institutional Foundations of Comparative Advantage*, (Oxford: Oxford University Press), 1–70.

——(eds.) (2001b). *Varieties of Capitalism: The Institutional Foundations Of Comparative Advantage*, (Oxford: Oxford University Press).

HALLIDAY, T. (2004). 'Crossing Oceans, Spanning Continents: Exporting Edelman to Global Lawmaking and Market-Building', *Law & Society Review* 38(2): 213–20.

——and B. CARRUTHERS (2007). 'The Recursivity of Law: Global Norm Making and National Lawmaking in the Globalization of Corporate Insolvency Regimes', *American Journal of Sociology* 112(4): 1135–1202.

——(2009). *Bankrupt: Global Lawmaking and Systemic Financial Crisis*, (Stanford: Stanford University Press).

——and L. KARPIK (1997). *Lawyers and the Rise of Western Political Liberalism*, (Oxford: Clarendon Press).

——and M. FEELEY (2007). *Fighting for Political Freedom*, (Oxford: Hart Publishing).

——and P. OSINSKY (2006). 'Globalization of Law', *Annual Review of Sociology*, 32: 447–70.

HERRIGEL, G. (1996). *Industrial Constructions: The Sources of German Industrial Power*, (Cambridge: Cambridge University Press).

HOBSON, J. M. (2000). *The State and International Relations*, (Cambridge: Cambridge University Press).

HOPT, K. J. (2007). 'Comparative Company Law', in M. Reimann and R. Zimmermann (eds.), *The Oxford Handbook of Comparative Law*, (Oxford: Oxford University Press), 1161–92.

HOVENKAMP, H. (1990). 'The First Great Law & Economics Movement', *Stanford Law Review* 42(4): 993–1058.

HUNT, A. (1978). *The Sociological Movement in Law*, (New York: Macmillan).

KAGAN, R. A. (1995). 'What Socio-Legal Scholars should do when there is too much Law to Study', *Journal of Law and Society* 22(1): 140–8.

——(2001). *Adversarial Legalism: The American Way of Law*, (Cambridge, MA: Harvard University Press).

KARPIK, L. (1997). 'French Lawyers and Politics', in T. Halliday and L. Karpik (eds.), *Lawyers and the Rise of Western Political Liberalism*, (Oxford: Clarendon Press), 101–23.

——(1999). *French Lawyers: A Study in Collective Action 1274 to 1994*, (Oxford: Clarendon Press).

KELEMAN, R. D. (2006). 'Suing for Europe: Adversarial Legalism and European Governance', *Comparative Political Studies* 39(1): 1–27.

——and E. C. SIBBITT (2004). 'The Globalization of American Law', *International Organization* 58(winter): 103–36.

KLAGES, P. (2009). 'Juristische Akteure zwischen Ökonomie und Recht. Eine Untersuchung zur rechtlichen Institutionalisierung ökonomischen Wandels am Beispiel der Aktienrechtsentwicklung in Deutschland und den USA'. PhD Dissertation, (Cologne: Max Planck Institute for the Study of Societies).

KOSKENNIEMI, M. (2007). 'The Fate of Public International Law: Between Technique and Politics', *Modern Law Review* 70(1): 1–30.

LANE, C. (1995). *Industry and Society in Europe: Stability and Change in Britain, Germany, and France*, (Cheltenham: Edward Elgar).

——W. LITTEK, and M. POTTON (2002). 'The Professions between State and Market', *European Societies* 4(2): 235–60.

LA PORTA, R., F. (LOPEZ-DE-SILANES), and A. SHLEIFER (2008). 'The Economic Consequences of Legal Origins', *Journal of Economic Literature* 46(2): 285–332.

LIKOSKY, M. (ed.) (2002). *Transnational Legal Processes: Globalisation and Power Disparities*, (London: Butterworths).

LÜTZ, S. (2002). *Der Staat und die Globalisierung von Finanzmarkten: regulative Politik in Deutschland, Großbritannien und den USA*, (Frankfurt/Main: Campus).

LUHMANN, N. (1985). 'A Sociological Theory of Law', (London: Taylor and Francis).

McBARNETT, D. (2002). 'Transnational Transactions, Legal Work, Cross-border Commerce and Global Regulation', in M. Likosky (ed.), *Transnational Legal Processes: Globalisation and Power Disparities*, (London: Butterworth), 98–113.

McCLELLAND, C. (1991). *The German Experience of Professionalism*, (Cambridge: Cambridge University Press).

MAINE, H. S. (1861). *Ancient Law: Its Connection with the Early History of Society, and Its Relation to Modern Ideas*, (London: John Murray).

MATTEI, U. and PES L. G. (2008). 'Civil Law and Common Law: Toward Convergence?', in K. E. Whittington, R. D. Keleman, and G. A. Caldeira (eds.), *The Oxford Handbook of Law and Politics*, (Oxford: Oxford University Press), 267–80.

MARX, K. and F. ENGELS (1976). 'The German Ideology', in K. Marx and F. Engels, *Collected Works*, vol. 5, (New York: International Publishers).

MICHAELS, R. (2006). 'The Functional Method of Comparative Law', in M. Reimann and R. Zimmermann (eds.), *The Oxford Handbook of Comparative Law*, (Oxford: Oxford University Press) 339–82.

MITCHELL, W. C. (1924). 'Commons on the Legal Foundations of Capitalism', *American Economic Review* 14(2): 240–53.

MORCK, R. K. (ed.) (2000). *Concentrated Corporate Ownership*, (Chicago: University of Chicago Press).

——(ed.) (2005). *A History of Corporate Governance Around the World*, (Chicago: University of Chicago Press).

MORGAN, G. (2006). 'Transnational Actors, Transnational Institutions, Transnational Spaces: The Role of Law Firms in the Internationalization of Competition Regulation', in M.-L. Djelic and K. Sahlin-Andersson (eds.), *Transnational Governance: Institutional Dynamics of Regulation*, (Cambridge: Cambridge University Press) 139–60.

MORGAN, G. (2007). 'M & A as Power', in D. Angwin (ed.), *Mergers and Acquisitions*, (Oxford: Blackwell Publishing) 116–52.

——(2008). 'Market Formation and Governance in International Financial Markets: The Case of OTC Derivatives', *Human Relations* 61(5): 637–60.

——and S. QUACK (2005). 'Institutional Legacies and Firm Dynamics: The Growth and Internationalization of UK and German Law Firms', *Organization Studies* 26(12): 1765–86.

MURRELL, P. (2001). *Assessing the Value of Law in Transition Economies*, (Michigan: Michigan University Press).

NONET, P. and P. SELZNICK ([1978] 2001). *Law & Society in Transition*, (Edison, NJ: Transaction Publishers).

NORTH, D. C. (1990). *Institutions, Institutional Change and Economic Performance*, (Cambridge: Cambridge University Press).

——and R. P. THOMAS (1973). *The Rise of the Western World. A New Economic History*, (Cambridge: Cambridge University Press).

OBERTHÜR, S. and T. GEHRING (2006). *Institutional Interaction in Global Environmental Governance: Synergy and Conflict Among International and EU Policies*, (Cambridge, MA: MIT Press).

OSIEL, M. J. (1990). 'Lawyers as Monopolists, Aristocrats and Entrepreneurs', *Harvard Law Review* 103: 2009–66.

O'SULLIVAN, M. (2003). 'The Political Economy of Comparative Corporate Governance', *Review of International Political Economy* 10 (1): 23–72.

PARSONS, K. H. (1942). 'John R. Commons' Point of View', *Journal of Land & Public Utility Economics* 18(3): 245–66.

PEERENBOOM, R. (2002). *China's Long March toward Rule of Law*, (Cambridge: Cambridge University Press).

PERROW, C. (2002). *Organizing America: Wealth, Power, and the Origins of Corporate Capitalism*, (Princeton, NJ; Oxford: Princeton University Press).

PISTOR, K. (2001). 'Law as a Determinant for Equity Market Development: The Experience of Transition Economies', in P. Murrell (ed.), *Assessing the Value of Law in Transition Economies*, (Michigan: Michigan University Press), 249–84.

POWELL, M. J. (1993). 'Professional Innovation: Corporate Lawyers and Private Lawmaking', *Law & Social Inquiry* 18(3): 423–52.

PUTNAM ROBERT D., ROBERT LEONARDI, RAFFAELLA Y. NANETTI (1994). *Making Democracy Work: Civic Traditions in Modern Italy* (Princeton NJ; Princeton University Press).

QUACK, S. (2007). 'Legal Professionals and Transnational Law-Making', *Organization* 14(5): 643–66.

——(2008). 'Combining National Variety: Internationalisation Strategies of European Law Firms', Mimeo, Cologne: Max Planck Institute for the Study of Societies.

——and DJELIC M.-L. (2005). 'Adaptation, Recombination and Reinforcement: The Story of Antitrust and Competition Law in Germany and Europe', in W. Streeck and K. Thelen (eds.), *Beyond Continuity: Institutional Change in Advanced Political Economies*, (Oxford: Oxford University Press) 255–81.

REUS-SMIT, C. (2004). *The Politics of International Law*, (Cambridge: Cambridge University Press).

REHDER, B. forthcoming. 'Die Politik der Rechtsprechung. Der Beitrag des Bundesarbeitsgerichts zum Werden und Wandel des deutschen Kapitalismus', Mimeo, Cologne: Max Planck Institute for the Study of Societies.

RHEINSTEIN, M. (1954). 'Introduction' in Max Weber, *On Law in Economy and Society*, (Cambridge, MA: Harvard University Press), pp. xxv–xxvii.

RILES, A. (2006). 'Comparative Law and Socio-Legal Studies', in M. Reimann and R. Zimmermann (eds.), *The Oxford Handbook of Comparative Law* (Oxford: Oxford University Press) 775–813.

ROE, M. (1994). *Strong Managers, Weak Owners: The Political Roots of American Corporate Finance*, (Princeton, NJ: Princeton University Press).

——(2003). *The Political Determinants of Corporate Governance*, (Oxford: Oxford University Press).

ROGOWSKI, R. (1994). 'Auditors and Lawyers in Germany: Co-evolution, not Competition', *The International Journal of the Legal Profession* 1(1): 13–29.

——(1995). 'German Corporate Lawyers: Social Closure in Autopoietic Perspective', in Y. Dezalay, D. Sugarman, and P. Bourdieu (eds.), *Professional Competition and Professional Power*, (London: Routledge) 114–35.

ROY, W. G. (1997). *Socializing Capital : The Rise of the Large Industrial Corporation in America*, (Princeton, NJ: Princeton University Press).

RUESCHEMEYER, D. (1990). 'Comparing Legal Professions: A State-Centred Approach', in R. Torstendahl and M. Burrage (eds.), *The Formation of Professions: Knowledge, State and Strategy*, (London: Sage), 289–321.

——(1997). 'State, Capitalism and the Organization of Legal Counsel: Examining an Extreme Case—the Prussian Bar 1700–1914', in T. Halliday and L. Karpik (eds.), *Lawyers and the Rise of Western Political Liberalism*, (Oxford: Clarendon Press), 207–27.

SCHMITTER, P. and W. STREECK, (1985). 'Community, Market, State—and Associations? The Prospective Contribution of Interest Governance to Social order', *European Sociological Review* 1(2): 119–38.

SCHNEIBERG, M. (2007). 'What's on the Path? Path Dependence, Organizational Diversity and the Problem of Institutional Change in the US Economy, 1900–1950', *Socio-Economic Review*, 5: 47–80.

SCRANTON, P. (1997). *Endless Novelty: Specialty Production in American Industrialization, 1865–1925*, (Princeton, NJ: Princeton University Press).

SHAPIRO, M. and A. STONE SWEET, (2002a). *On Law, Politics, and Judicialization*, (Oxford; New York: Oxford University Press).

————(2002b). *On Law, Politics, and Judicialization*, (Oxford: Oxford University Press).

SIEGRIST, H. (1996). *Advokat, Bürger und Staat*, (Frankfurt am Main: Vittorio Klostermann).

SILVER, C. (2000). 'Globalization and the US Market in Legal Services—Shifting Identities', *Law and Policy in International Business* 31(4): 1093–150.

——(2002). 'The Case of the Foreign Lawyer: Internationalizing the US Legal Profession', *Fordham International Law Journal*, 25: 1039–83.

——(2007). 'Local Matters: Internationalizing Strategies for US Law Firms', *Indiana Journal of Global Legal Studies* 14(1): 6793.

SPAR, D. L. (1997). 'Lawyers Abroad: The Internationalization of Legal Practice', *California Management Review* 39(3): 8–28.

STONE, A. (1985). 'The Place of Law in the Marxian Structure-Superstructure Archetype', *Law & Society Review* 19(1): 39–68.

STREECK, W. (1991). 'On the Institutional Conditions of Diversified Quality Production', in E. Matzner and W. Streeck (eds.), *Beyond Keynesianism: The Socio-Economics of Production and Full Employment*, (Cheltenham: Edward Elgar), 21–61.

——(2009). *Re-Forming Capitalism. Institutional Change in the German Political Economy*, (Oxford: Oxford University Press).

STRYKER, R. (2003). 'Mind the Gap: Law, Institutional Analysis and Socioeconomics', *Socio-Economic Review* 1: 335–67.

SUCHMAN, M. C. and EDELMAN L. B. (2007). 'The Interplay of Law and Organizations', in L. B. Edelman and M. C. Suchman (eds.), *The Legal Lives of Private Organizations*, (Aldershot: Ashgate).

SWEDBERG, R. (2003). 'The Case for an Economic Sociology of Law', *Theory and Society*, 2: 1–37.

TEUBNER, G. (1983). 'Substantive and Reflexive Elements in Modern Law', *Law & Society Review* 17(2): 239–85.

——(2001). 'Legal Irritants: How Unifying Law Ends up in New Divergences'. in P. Hall and D. Soskice (eds.), *Varieties of Capitalism: The Institutional Foundations of Comparative Advantage*, (Oxford: Oxford University Press), 417–41.

TOCQUEVILLE, A. de ([1835] 1945). *Democracy in America*, (New York: Vintage Books).

TÖMMEL, I. and A. VERDUN (eds.) (2009). *Innovative Governance in the European Union: The Politics of Multilevel Policymaking*, (Boulder, CO: Lynne Rienner Publishers).

TRUBEK, D. M. (1972). 'Max Weber on Law and the Rise of Capitalism', *Wisconsin Law Review* 3: 720–53.

——(1986). 'Max Weber's Tragic Modernism and the Study of Law in Society', *Law & Society Review* 20(4): 573–98.

VAN DE VEN, A. H. (1993). 'The Institutional Theory of John R. Commons: A Review and Commentary', *Academy of Management Review* 18(1): 139–52.

VITOLS, S. (1995). 'Changes in Germany's Bank-Based Financial System: Implications for Corporate Governance', *Corporate Governance* 13(3): 386–96.

——(2001). 'Varieties of Corporate Governance: Comparing Germany and the UK', in P. Hall and D. Soskice (eds.), *Varieties of Capitalism: The Institutional Foundations of Comparative Advantage*, (Oxford: Oxford University Press) 337–60.

——(2005). (German corporate governance in transition: Implications of bank exit from monitoring and control) *International Journal of Disclosure and Governance*, Volume 2, Number 4, 1 December 2005, pp. 357–367(11).

WARF, B. (2001). 'Global Dimensions of US Legal Services', *The Professional Geographer* 53(3): 398–406.

WATT, H. M. (2006). 'Globalization and Comparative Law', in M. Reimann and R. Zimmermann (eds.), *The Oxford Handbook of Comparative Law*, (Oxford: Oxford University Press), 579–607.

WEBER, M. ([1921] 1978). *Economy and Society*, (Berkeley: University of California Press).

WHITFORD, J. (2006). *The New Old Economy: Networks, Institutions, and the Organizational Transformation of American Manufacturing*, (Oxford: Oxford University Press).

WHITLEY, R. (1999). *Divergent Capitalisms*, (Oxford: Oxford University Press).

ZEITLIN, J. (1995). 'Why are there no Industrial Districts in the United Kingdom', in A. Bagnasco and C. F. Sabel (eds.), *Small and Medium-Size Enterprises*, (London: Pinter), 98–171.

——(2007). 'The Historical Alternatives Approach', in G. Jones and J. Zeitlin (eds.), *The Oxford Handbook of Business History*, (Oxford: Oxford University Press) 120–40.

ZIEGERT, K. A. ([1913] 2002). 'Introduction to the Transaction Edition', in E. Ehrlich (ed.), *Fundamental Principles of the Sociology of Law*, (Edison, NJ: Transaction Publisher).

C H A P T E R 11

INSTITUTIONAL CHANGE IN FINANCIAL SYSTEMS

RICHARD DEEG

INTRODUCTION

For many comparative institutional scholars the financial system stands at the heart of each nation's system of capitalism. How and to whom capital is distributed by the financial system is taken as constitutive of the economy more generally and plays a major role in deciding which firms are successful, as well as the distribution of resources to groups in society and the overall pattern of economic growth. While change in financial systems has been widely documented, the interpretation of change—what does it mean?—and the explanation of change—why and how did this happen?—remain open to debate. We will argue that a meaningful answer to these questions begins with a typology of financial systems. Each system will be characterized by certain structural features, patterns of behaviour, and an overall system 'logic'. Once this is established, we can begin to characterize the significance of observed changes.

This chapter will concentrate on the advanced capitalist economies since the early 1980s. It does not focus directly on the development of international financial markets per se, though developments in this area are intricately linked with institutional change in domestic financial systems. The chapter has four sections. The first reviews alternative approaches to comparing financial systems and conceptualizing their broader political-economic functions. The second section provides a brief empirical summary of key changes in financial systems. The third addresses debates on how to explain change in financial systems. The final section revisits the issue of financial system typologies, looks more closely at the changing function of financial systems vis-à-vis the real economy and the financial crisis of the late 2000s, and concludes with an agenda for future research in the field. The chapter suggests that simple typologies of national financial systems are increasingly difficult to sustain in light of common trends toward increased financialization and internationalization of finance, even as remaining differences in national financial systems are quite evident in the differential impact of the global financial crisis.

DEFINING AND COMPARING NATIONAL FINANCIAL SYSTEMS

Following Schmidt et al. (2002), we conceive the financial system as constituted by three dimensions. First is the 'structure of financial markets and their regulation'. This includes the nature of financial firms and distribution of activity among them, as well as the diverse market segments in which financial products are sold, consumed, or traded. Second, financial systems are also distinguished by 'financing patterns', that is, the type and extent of credit extended from the financial sector to firms, households, and governments. Finally, the financial system is understood to include the 'corporate governance' system, since firm financing patterns and the structure of financial markets are affected by (or affect) corporate governance. Corporate governance refers to the rules (formal and informal) that determine 'how authority is distributed among [firm] owners, the board of directors, senior managers, and employees' (Bebchuk and Roe 1999; see also Goyer in this volume). What defines and unifies all three dimensions into the financial system is the existence of institutional complementarity (here in the sense of functional interdependence) among them. It is also important to note that the constitution and evolution of a financial system is driven both by choices on the demand side—market choices made by consumers of financial products—and the supply side—innovators of new products and markets. All of these actors also shape the rules and regulations (institutions) that govern financial markets through political processes.

While some analysts may not use the word 'revolution' to describe changes in financial systems, all would agree that there have been dramatic changes since the late 1970s in all advanced capitalist economies. Between the 1930s and early 1970s national financial systems were in a period of relatively autonomous development due to the near collapse of international capital markets in the Depression and their slow revival in the post-war period (Helleiner 1994). The global economy was characterized by 'embedded liberalism' in which global trade was promoted while global finance was restricted through capital controls. The latter was a requisite of the fixed exchange rate regime under Bretton Woods (Ruggie 1982). During this period, the distinctive paths of national financial systems intensified in many respects, as they were more deeply embedded in the post-war national economic models that emerged. In some cases, such as France and Italy, the state used both bank ownership and credit regulation to channel capital according to state-defined goals. In other cases, such as Germany, banks remained relatively independent of state control but were embedded deeply in corporate governance through extensive corporate lending, equity ownership, and active monitoring of firms in corporate boards. In cases such as the UK and US, where securities markets were comparatively more important and banks had more arms-length relations to firms, market competition in finance was nonetheless muted through extensive regulation designed to limit systemic risk (Zysman 1983). Limitations on international finance and the strengthening of institutional complementarities between financial systems and the broader national economies held these systems relatively stable through the 1970s.

The present era of financial internationalization is generally dated to the rise of the Eurodollar market in the 1960s, the collapse of the Bretton Woods system at the beginning of the 1970s, and the subsequent removal of capital controls in the 1970s and 1980s. Change in domestic financial systems was slow at first, but accelerated over time. By the turn of this century, the changes have been sufficiently far-reaching that the distinctive characteristics of national financial systems are less readily apparent, and we begin to ask whether the typologies of financial systems developed in the post-war era to characterize them are still useful. If not, what typologies are now meaningful? Or, do we need to see financial systems as converging to a more or less homogenous model?

Probably the most common typology of financial systems divides them into two ideal types—bank-based and market-based (Allen and Gale 2000). In bank-based systems banks dominate all aspects of financial markets, including corporate finance, retail banking, and underwriting and trading in securities markets. Financial intermediation ratios are high, as household savings are channelled largely through the banking system. In such systems banks also typically engage in 'relational banking' with corporate clients, meaning a long-term relationship based on reciprocity (Aoki 2001). The use of equity for firm finance is typically circumscribed and reliance on bank loans relatively high.[1] In many cases banks play a prominent role in corporate governance, exercising influence over firms via large equity stakes and seats on company boards. Bank-based systems have been characterized as systems of 'patient capital' with a comparative advantage in financing long-term investment in relatively stable technologies and industries (Rajan and Zingales 2003; Allen and Gale 2000).

---

[1] Though a number of studies suggest the differences between the two systems have generally been exaggerated (Corbett and Jenkinson 1994).

In market-based financial systems, on the other hand, borrowers rely much more on markets for equities, bonds, or other instruments to secure their external finance (as opposed to bank loans). In market-based systems ownership of firms tends to be more widely dispersed. Diffuse ownership, in turn, makes management more vulnerable to market sanctions in the form of declining share price (which they usually feel compelled to correct) or external takeover of the firm by another group of owners. The greater use of markets also means that deal-based, rather than relationship-based, banking is predominant. Market-based finance is typically ascribed with a comparative advantage in financing risky investments in new technologies and growth sectors.

Until the late 1990s an important variant of this typology was commonly used. This typology added a 'state-dominated' financial system to the categories of bank- and market-based (Zysman 1983). This third ideal-type category captured financial systems in which the state played a central strategic role in allocating capital to specific firms or categories of investment. In some cases this was achieved through state ownership of important banks; in other cases it was achieved through indirect methods in which bureaucracies used monetary regulation, 'guidance', subsidies, etc. to direct capital towards targeted firms, sectors, or technologies. The value in this third category of financial systems is that it not only captured important aspects and dynamics of several European countries (France, Spain, Italy) but also of many East Asian economies (notably Japan, South Korea, and China in the current era).

A final important typology focuses on the corporate governance and firm owner-ship dimension to distinguish among financial systems. This typology also divides systems into two basic types, alternately labelled insider versus outsider systems, concentrated versus dispersed ownership systems, or stakeholder versus shareholder systems (Franks and Mayer 1990; see also Goyer in this volume).[2] An insider or stakeholder system is characterized by many features. First, all major stakeholders— owners, managers, employees, and perhaps even supplier firms—are viewed as having a 'stake' in the firm and thus a legitimate right to participate (not necessarily equally) in the key decisions affecting the firm's strategy and the distribution of firm income. Second, since employees are stakeholders, firms have a strong commitment to employment security. Stakeholder corporate governance systems are typically strong when equity markets are weak, since the latter tend to encourage a focus on shorter-term profitability, which often can only be achieved through the ready dismissal of labour.[3] The commitment to long-term employment and focus on long-term investment is further facilitated by the concentration of ownership. Major block-holders constitute a core of stable, long-term investors that work with management towards long-term success (usually defined more in terms of revenue growth and market share than profitability). In such systems there has traditionally

---

[2] These different labels reflect the fact that different scholars focus on different aspects of systems, but generally speaking, insider systems are those with concentrated ownerships and stakeholders; outsider systems have dispersed ownership and shareholder orientation.

[3] In stakeholder systems, employees may have a formal, statutory role in firm management, as in Germany through the institutions of co-determination and works councils.

been a bias against small, minority shareholders (Roe 2003; Gourevitch and Shinn 2005). Stakeholder systems are often characterized by equity links (and interlocking directorates) among groups of firms, with the Japanese _keiretsu_ perhaps being the most famous example. Banks are often part of these equity and personal networks, which facilitates relational banking (and patient capital).

In outsider or shareholder-oriented corporate governance systems ownership tends to be more widely dispersed. Corporate governance rules do not typically accord stakeholders such as labour a voice in firm management. In principle, firms are managed in the interest of owners alone. In reality, though, when ownership is widely dispersed firm managers frequently have a high degree of autonomy in managing the firms. To make the interests of owners and managers coincide, starting in the 1980s it became common to pay managers to a significant degree with performance-related forms of compensation such as stock options. Outsider systems are characterized by rules that protect minority shareholders, e.g. by curtailing or eliminating shares with unequal voting rights. To encourage investment and create liquid markets for shares, these systems traditionally also have more stringent accounting rules that increased the transparency of corporate finances. Because of the prominence of equity finance, management is more oriented towards maintaining a higher share price and maximizing the return on owner equity (that is, maximizing 'shareholder value'). This management focus is further strengthened by a 'market for corporate control,' especially in the form of hostile takeovers.

Stakeholder corporate governance typically coincides with a bank-based financial system (and outsider with market-based) because of institutional complementarities. However, in the last decade there is evidence that these two dimensions of financial systems are changing in different directions,[4] or at least at different speeds, with important consequences for how we characterize and understand differences among financial systems. Finally, it is worth stressing that even during the era of relatively stable evolution in the mid-twentieth century, these typologies elided substantial differences among financial systems even within the same type. The importance of these differences becomes apparent as we analyse systemic change in recent decades.

Financial systems, models of capitalism, and firm behaviour

In much of the comparative political economy literature institutional complementarities between the financial systems and other key institutions are seen as central to constituting the overall character of the political economy (for a review, see Jackson and Deeg 2008). There is, however, no simple correspondence between typologies of financial systems and typologies of capitalism. Comparative institutional theories of

---

[4] For example, in several European countries (France is a notable example) there is a clear decline in large firm dependence on bank-intermediated finance, but concentrated ownership or insider control persists in many cases.

capitalism postulate anywhere from two to six types of capitalism, whereas institutional theories of finance typically postulate two or three types (a notable exception is Whitley 2008). Thus for the purpose of simplifying discussion, we use the parsimonious Varieties of Capitalism (VoC) typology (Hall and Soskice 2001) to illustrate some of the key linkages between the financial system and firm behaviour (financing patterns and market strategies) that are posited in the literature.

The VoC approach divides national political economies into two ideal types—liberal market economies (LME) and coordinated market economies (CME). Both types rest on a distinct set of complementarities among the institutions governing finance, firms, and labour markets that, in turn, lead to diverse firm and national competitive advantages. In LMEs, firms generally coordinate with internal and external actors—workers, suppliers, owners, and financiers—through competitive market arrangements or hierarchical control. Firms in LMEs have a comparative advantage in 'radical innovation', that is, innovations that entail major changes in the production process or the development of entirely new products (and firm start-ups). Firms pursue production strategies based on general assets and thus the ability to quickly switch assets to new purposes. This strategy and the radical innovation that follows profits from flexible labour markets—hence the advantage of low or minimal employment protection laws, as found in the US—and market-based finance, which provides a higher level of risk-oriented capital and the ability to quickly reallocate capital to new purposes and technologies. The high level of risk-oriented venture capital funding the US and UK, for instance, is complemented by NASDAQ-type stock exchanges which enable venture capitalists to sell their company stakes to new investors who, in turn, infuse innovative firms with new capital. The diffusion of ownership, deep and liquid equity markets, and active market for corporate control—as found most prominently in the UK and US—also facilitate innovation through the acquisition or recomposition of corporate assets. Thus in LMEs it is more common to find firms such as the American firm DuPont, which remade itself in the late 1990s through divisional sales, spin-offs, and acquisitions from a chemicals manufacturer into a life sciences firm.

In coordinated market economies (CME) firms rely more on non-market governance mechanisms, such as less formal 'relational' or 'incomplete contracting' to solve their coordination problems. A prominent example would be joint R & D arrangements between German car manufacturers and key supplier firms such as Bosch. Firm networks and associations, such as the German industry associations, also play a prominent role as coordination mechanisms. Firms pursue production strategies that rely more on specific assets (whether capital or labour) which take advantage of these cooperative institutions. Thus, CME firms exhibit a comparative advantage in 'incremental innovation', understood as continuous but smaller changes in products and production processes. CMEs are thus associated with bank-based financial systems, which are superior in providing 'patient capital'. Long-term finance enables firms to make long-term employment commitments and investments with delayed returns or those based heavily on the utilization of specific assets. Because these are also stakeholder systems, labour has an institutionalized role within firms, commonly via works councils or in some cases, as most prominently in Germany, board-level co-determination, and relatively high levels of job security. This is said to facilitate higher levels of investment in human capital formation and labour–management cooperation. Markets for corporate control (especially hostile takeovers) and shareholder value are anathema to CMEs because they raise incentives for management to maximize shorter-term profits over longer-term investments.

In sum, understanding the role of the financial system for the broader economy can be usefully done by understanding how systemic characteristics of finance complement the organizational and market strategies of non-financial firms. That said, the extensive and rapid change in financial systems over the last two decades raises questions about the extent to which such characterizations are still accurate and whether changes in finance are leading to notable changes in the strategies of non-financial firms. Moreover, as a business sector, finance has grown much more rapidly than the general economy and increasingly followed a developmental logic independent of the needs of the real economy (see Engelen and Konings in this volume).

Change in Financial Systems

All financial systems in advanced capitalist economies have changed substantially over the last two decades, though bank-based systems are typically viewed as having undergone more radical change, and many see them as converging on a market-based system (Rajan and Zingales 2003). While they have all changed in different ways and to varying degrees, common trends can be identified across all of the advanced economies and we briefly summarize them here before turning to alternative explanations of change.

Bank disintermediation

While the share of financial claims held by all financial intermediaries has remained steady or increased in most cases (Schmidt et al. 2002), for banks there has been a clear decline since the early 1990s in asset intermediation ratios, that is, investors are increasingly bypassing banks and holding assets in bonds, equities, and other investments (Byrne and Davis 2002). In many countries firms are also borrowing less from banks (Byrne and Davis 2002). To be clear, though, relative to GDP, conventional banking business has also grown in the last twenty-five years (see Table 11.1) but not as rapidly as securities markets.

Table 11.1: Comparative data on financial systems for selected countries (percentage of GDP)

Country	Private Credit by Deposit Money Banks		Total Market Capitalization		Stock Market Capitalization		Bond Market Capitalization	
	1979	2004	1975*	2004	1975*	2004	1975*	2004
France	67	88	27	181	11	81	16	100
Germany	83	113	43	122	13	42	30	80
Italy	57	85	72	176	7	42	65	134
Netherlands	58	160	44	208	24	97	20	111
Sweden	40	103	74	183	15	97	59	86
UK	25	148	84	217	41	173	43	44
USA	32	44	102	289	45	132	57	157
Japan	82	99	70	255	29	73	41	182

Table from Deeg and O'Sullivan (2006).
Original sources: Data on private credit by deposit money banks from International Financial Statistics, line 22d; 1975 data for stock and bond market capitalization from Vittas, 1978, p. 30; 2004 data for stock and bond market capitalization from Standard & Poor's Emerging Market Database, compiled in Beck and Hussainy, 2006, Financial Structure Database.

Growth of securities markets

Bank disintermediation is caused by the expansion of securities markets and a shift in financial activity to non-bank financial institutions. The relative growth of such markets is nearly universal among advanced capitalist economies and has been promoted from the demand side through changes in regulation, tax laws, pension systems, etc. that encourage households to shift their assets from bank deposits to securities, whether held directly or indirectly.[5] Increasingly this capital is collected and invested by institutional investors—banks, insurance firms, pension, and investment or mutual funds. The introduction and promotion of private pension savings in many nations has been a major boost to the demand side for securities. The growth of markets is also promoted on the supply side through the deregulation of markets and the proliferation of new financial products that are traded on markets, such as stock options, futures, and other derivatives. Table 11.1 reveals an overall rapid expansion of financial markets vis-à-vis the real economy, a process that falls under the broader concept of financialization (see Nölke and Perry 2007; and Engelen and Konings in this volume). In many countries the financial industry

[5] For supporting data see Byrne and Davis (2002) and http://stats.oecd.org/WBOS/index.aspx.

was—at least until 2008—an increasingly important source of employment and contributor to GDP.[6]

Securitization

This refers to the process of transforming liabilities into tradable securities, thus supplying securities markets with more products (commonly known as 'asset-backed securities') to be purchased and traded among investors. Much of these originate from banks securitizing their loans, including corporate loans and mortgages. For banks this is attractive because it removes these loans as liabilities from their balance sheets, thus freeing up capital to be used for other new business (see Schmidt et al. 2002). In principle, borrowers benefit from this process because it leads to increased funds available for loans and—through better risk management—better priced loans. In Europe, for example, the value of securitized assets rose from €47 billion in 1997 to €320 billion in 2005 (European Securitization Forum 2006 www.euro-peansecuritisation.com). The growth of securities markets also substantially shifted the function of rating and monitoring debt from banks to the three dominant credit ratings agencies, which in effect represents a substantial global centralization of the debt rating process (Sinclair 2005).

Financial centre deregulation and stock exchange consolidation

The increased mobility of capital not only enhanced direct competition among financial institutions but also among national financial centres, such as New York, London, Tokyo, Frankfurt, and Paris. A globally competitive financial centre is widely seen by domestic economic and political actors as increasing the efficiency of investment flows, lowering the cost of capital, and ensuring adequate supply of capital for domestic demands. To compete, governments sought to enhance the attractiveness of their financial centres by making them more profitable for investors, especially institutional investors. In practice this means deregulation of financial products and reduction of the costs associated with securities issuing and trading (among other things). Virtually all securities exchanges have been transformed into joint-stock corporations in order to enhance their innovative capacity, but also to open the door to cross-border cooperation and/or mergers among exchanges, such as that between NYSE and Euronext.

---

[6] In the UK, for example, finance's contribution rose from 5.5% of GDP in 2001 to 10.1% in 2007 with more than one million employed in financial services (IFSL 2008).

Changing content and process of financial regulation

Another common change across advanced economies is a shift from a high degree of self-regulation by financial sectors to a more mixed system in which self-regulation is increasingly overseen and codified in state supervision (Moran 1991; Lütz 2004). Domestic regulation of financial markets has also become increasingly shaped and constrained by international regulatory processes. Perhaps most prominent are the Basel capital regulations issued by the Bank for International Settlements. International or transnational regulation occurs to a substantial degree via governance networks involving both public and private actors (Djelic and Sahlin-Andersson 2006). On the whole, however, international financial regulation was relatively limited and based more on voluntary compliance, though the global crisis of 2008 suggests this will change.

Weakening of relational banking

In bank-based financial systems there has also been a notable weakening of relational banking, especially in Germany but also in Japan (Beyer and Höpner 2003; Aoki, Jackson, and Miyajima 2007). This occurred as banks increasingly shifted their market activities from traditional commercial banking to more profitable investment banking. Relational banking also weakened in part because many banks responded to growing competitive pressures by selling long-term equity stakes they held in corporate clients—which served as an important basis for their relationship—in order to free up capital to invest in more profitable ventures. Finally, relationship banking is weakened by declining bank borrowing by big firms and their increased use of securities for external finance.

Structural change in the finance industry

The financial industry itself has also undergone considerable change as an industry. Privatization of financial institutions has been widespread, thus state-dominated financial systems have become uncommon among the advanced capitalist economies (though are still common among emerging markets such as China). As a result of competition, deregulation, and privatization, there has also been a general trend toward consolidation among banks and concentration in the distribution of financial assets. In most countries there has also been a desegmentation of financial markets, i.e. restrictions limiting financial institutions to a limited set of financial activities have been loosened or eliminated. Thus universal banking has become more widespread. Finally, non-bank financial institutions, such as hedge, equity, and venture capital funds, and most importantly institutional investors, have become increasingly important actors in financial markets and also in corporate finance and equity markets.

Financial internationalization

It goes without saying that the most obvious change in financial markets is the growth of cross-border financial networks and flows of capital. Though internationalization is widely dated in its origins to the emergence of the Eurodollar market in the 1960s (Helleiner 1994), financial internationalization really only grew in relative terms after 1994: from 1980 to 1994 total global cross-border capital flows remained roughly steady at 4–5 per cent of global GDP; after 1994 this grew rapidly to 17.2 per cent (equal to $8.2 trillion) in 2006 (Farrell et al. 2008: 14). Internationalization also takes the form of financial firms from one country taking up activities in others, either through cross-border mergers and acquisitions or the establishment of new offices.

The risk revolution

Perhaps the most profound set of changes in financial markets might be summed up as a revolution in the management of financial risk. Before the 1980s, most forms of credit risk were carried on the balance sheets of the original issuer of the financial instrument (typically equities, bonds, loans, and mortgages). Over the last twenty or so years, financial risks have been increasingly divided and shared, sold and resold, through an ever-growing number of financial instruments, broadly known as derivatives. Derivatives are commonly defined as instruments whose value is derived from the value of an underlying asset, such as equities, bonds, or currencies. In essence, derivatives are financial contracts between two parties in which one pays the other to assume a specific risk. The most common derivatives include futures, options, foreign exchange contracts, interest rate contracts, collateralized debt obligations, and credit default swaps.

Financial markets have become increasingly constituted and shaped by the exponential growth of derivatives products: The notional value of derivatives (futures and options) traded on organized exchanges rose from $730 billion in 1987 to $7.8 trillion in 1993, and to $87 trillion as of early 2007; derivatives traded in the much larger (and less regulated) over-the-counter (OTC) market grew even greater, rising from $80.3 trillion in 1998 to $415 trillion (notional value) in 2006.[7] Derivatives are attributed with improving financial markets by helping investors hedge their risks, improving market liquidity, and also with creating a new class of investment instruments. Derivatives have also become important risk management tools for non-financial firms. Exporters, for example, benefit from the use of foreign currency options. Given these benefits and light regulation, there was rapid innovation of new kinds of derivatives in recent years. In an environment of low inflation and high global liquidity, financial speculation in exotic new derivatives grew tremendously, helping to produce housing bubbles in the United

---

[7] Data from Bank for International Settlement (BIS) (tables 19 and 23) and author's own calculations. Notional value is the total value of the underlying assets: 'gross market value'—the cost of replacing all derivatives contracts—is much smaller at around $10 trillion in 2006. Adjusting this number further to reflect netting agreements means that the net credit exposure or truly at risk assets amounts to about 1% of global GDP (Farrell et al. 2008: 20).

States and the UK. However, the financial crisis of the late 2000s revealed that derivatives markets had grown so large and complex that risks were in fact much greater than most investors believed. It also revealed the tremendous depth of global financial market interdependence and systemic risks created through the explosion of derivatives and securitized assets, as the default risk from sub-prime debt originated in the US housing market spread through the global financial system.

The expansion of derivatives markets was driven largely by investment banks, and to a lesser extent, commercial banks trading on their own accounts. This reflects in part their effort to replace dwindling traditional sources of interest income and boost profit ratios. The growth of derivatives has also been driven by the emergence and growth of hedge funds (many of which are run by investment banks). Hedge funds collect money from wealthy investors, banks, and institutional investors and, among many other investments, use much of these funds to invest in derivatives. Like many other aspects of financial markets, growth in hedge funds has been explosive; from well under 1,000 funds managing less than $150 billion in assets in 1996, the industry grew to more than 9,000 funds managing $1.75 trillion at the end of 2006 (IFSL 2008). Hedge funds, and especially private equity funds, have also become important actors in corporate restructuring in North America and Europe via equity stakes or purchases of firms. More generally, private equity funds have become significant alternative channels for large investors to achieve higher rates of return on their investments in equities. Like hedge funds and investment banks, their tremendous expansion in the 2000s was built substantially on using ample cheap money to conduct leveraged buyouts.[8]

The financial crisis and ensuing regulation intend to rein in a good deal of the most egregious practices that emerged during the preceding years. Derivatives, hedge funds, and credit rating agencies are all subject to greater regulation. This raises the question of whether financialization, especially securitization and the proliferation of derivatives, will reverse course and decline in relevance. During and immediately after the crisis this is obviously the case. However, over the longer term many of the market and political forces that drove these processes are likely to reassert themselves.

EXPLAINING CHANGE IN FINANCIAL SYSTEMS

The obvious question at this point is what explains this dramatic transformation in financial systems? It used to be possible to draw a rather sharp line between explanations of financial system change based on level of analysis. On one hand,

---

[8] Private equity investment follows a highly cyclical pattern, though from the mid-1990s to 2007 there was clearly a substantial upward trend. After rising to a peak of about $200 billion invested in 2000, private equity dropped into the $100 billion per annum range until booming again in 2006 when total investments reached $365 billion globally (IFSL 2008).

we find those that see change in domestic financial systems largely as a response to pressures arising from the changing terms of international economic competition and power relations among states (see Cohen 1996; Djelic and Quack 2003; Andrews 1994; Strange 1996; Simmons et al. 2008). On the other hand, we find explanations emphasizing domestic markets and politics independent of international pressures as primary causes of change, thus implying that the global financial system is essentially the summation of domestic financial systems (Sobel 1994; Perez 1998; McNamara 1998; Kapstein 1994). Although there is still significant utility in parsing out international from domestic sources of change, there has been a blurring of the distinction between these two types of explanations as scholars have—rightly—focused increasingly on the 'interaction' between international and domestic factors in their analyses of financial system change (for example, Jabko 2006; Posner 2005, 2009). Lines of debate now run significantly along ontological differences, and we therefore organize the literature along structural, institutional, and ideational (or constructivist) lines rather than level of analysis. It is important to note that these categories are not necessarily mutually exclusive and that within them we still find many scholars who emphasize either the domestic or international level.

Structural explanations

Structural or systemic explanations attribute change and stability in finance to inevitable and irreversible market forces or the structure of the international state system. The first common structural explanation can be labelled the 'capital mobility thesis' which, in essence, argues that increasingly mobile capital shifts the balance of power from states to market actors, and from holders of relatively fixed assets, especially labour, to holders of mobile assets, such as financial capital (Frieden 1991). As the structural economic power of mobile capital rises, global investors demand reforms in capital markets that deepen and open securities markets, thus providing expanded investment opportunities and even greater capital mobility. Change in financial markets is therefore driven by a self-reinforcing structural market process. The ensuing competition for capital forces states to adapt their market regulations in line with the leading states (Cerny 1993; Andrews 1994; Strange 1996; Simmons et al. 2008). While rising capital mobility is a fact, the extent to which it serves as a causal explanation for financial system change is disputed. For some, it is disputed on the grounds that rising capital mobility does not coincide chronologically with important financial market reform measures (Oatley 1997). For others it is disputed on the grounds that capital market pressures can be—and have been—met through a variety of responses, not all of which push financial systems toward greater marketization (Jabko 2006).

A second structural argument emphasizes the distribution of state power in the international political system. Powerful states coerce other states into capital market deregulation. Much of this literature emphasizes the preferences of the United States because it is best positioned to organize international cooperation via such organizations as the IMF, OECD, or IOSCO that promote capital openness and market integration (Pauly 1997; Simmons 2001). And when cooperation in multilateral settings fails, or does not lead to the outcome preferred by the US, it has frequently used bilateral arrangements to impose its preferences (Lütz 2004; Posner 2006). Alongside the direct application of power, coercion can also occur when a dominant state achieves 'first mover' advantages, forcing others to follow suit, or when powerful states act as focal points that solve coordination problems when multiple equilibriums exist (Simmons et al. 2008). The decision by the EU to model its monetary union and central bank along the lines of the German Bundesbank and German monetary policy preferences is a prime example of the latter.

A third structural explanation emphasizes technological change, especially in communications and information technology, as the driving force of financial system change (e.g. Herring and Litan 1995; O'Brien 1992). Technological changes facilitate financial product innovation (such as collateralized debt obligations) which tends to undermine existing market structures and regulatory restrictions (including those on cross-border capital flows). In time, regulators are forced to reform regulation in recognition of the market realities. One variant of the technology argument, which received surprisingly scant attention until the financial crisis of 2007–9 (an early exception to this is Whitley 1986), analyses the impact of formal knowledge for pricing market risk, and thus facilitating financial product innovation (e.g. index funds). MacKenzie's (2006) study of the Black–Scholes–Merton option pricing model suggests that the application of this model in practice made the actual market processes more like their theoretical depiction (for a while, at least). This, in turn, gave market actors more confidence in their ability to accurately price new forms of risk, thus boosting the expansion of such markets to previously improbable levels. More generally, as financial market activity increasingly comprises swaps, securitized assets, and derivatives of all stripes, the pricing of risk has become highly complex and mathematical, making such technologies indispensable to these markets. One thing, however, that distinguishes formal knowledge as a technology is that it works well (if at all) only if market actors *believe* they are correct models of reality. Thus confidence in such technologies was an important contributing factor to the expansion of collateralized debt obligations resting on mortgages in the US. In hindsight, it becomes clear—and painfully so—that when confidence in their accuracy collapsed, so did asset prices.

A final structural argument is strongly functional in character, resting on the belief that capitalist systems evolve through stages of development. Prominent early work in this vein was done by Gerschenkron (1962), who explained differences in national financial systems in the late nineteenth century on the basis of the timing of industrialization relative to other nations. A more recent example is that of Eichengreen (2006), who argues that financial system change in Europe stems from a structural shift from extensive to intensive growth patterns. In the latter, generating innovation is paramount but technology also becomes more uncertain, and success is greater when 'bets' on technologies are undertaken by financial markets rather than banks. Thus Europe moved toward market-based and globalized finance out of a functional need to maintain competitiveness. Rajan and Zingales (2003) see this transformation in Europe as a natural process of 'financial development', while arguing that structural factors are necessary but insufficient to explain systemic transformation. They note that most actors (including central banks) will prefer the insider rents of bank-based systems rather than the more competitive environment of markets. Thus some kind of agency by political actors or an exogenous shock must play a catalyzing role.

Institutionalist explanations

What defines institutional explanations is their emphasis on the interaction between actors' pursuit of self-interest (and shifts in those interests) and pre-existing institutions in shaping both domestic and international financial market structures and regulation. Several scholars of international political economy have suggested that international institutions, such as the IMF, can be important for diffusing particular norms (e.g. capital market openness) and policy approaches across national settings (Simmons et al. 2008: 30–1; Abdelal 2007). Such institutions can also be important in fostering cooperation among states around financial policy. Scholars whose analyses focus on international factors have tended to see domestic institutions as filters that shape national responses to common exogenous pressures. Thus during the 1990s many believed that increased capital mobility would—in spite of these institutional filters—lead to convergence across national economies in financial market structure and regulation (e.g. O'Brien 1992). However, such approaches are offset by a substantial body of scholarship, which emphasizes the preferences of domestic actors and their success in forming political coalitions for, or against, financial market reform. Thus it is competition among organized interests within national economies that drives (or hinders) financial globalization and financial system change (Sobel 1994; Moran 1991). Since institutional context shapes actor preferences, and which political coalitions are likely to prevail, equivalent actors in different countries may have different preferences regarding financial market change. What we also commonly find in this type of explanation is that patterns of change and stability reflect path dependent processes. Over the last two decades there has been considerable work within this category, ranging from the early work of Moran (1991) and Sobel (1994) to more recent work by Lütz (2004) and others. In explaining institutional change in financial systems (including corporate governance), three distinct approaches have been much discussed in recent years: the legal origins cum quality of corporate law approach, the varieties of capitalism approach, and a coalitional approach.

In the legal approach, the expansion of securities markets and dispersion of ownership are contingent upon the quality of the legal context and regulation. In other words, securities markets are underdeveloped where the legal framework and the courts' capacity to support private contract enforcement between (dispersed) owners and managers (e.g. laws regarding disclosure, liability standards, and private enforcement incentives) are weak. Thus the risks for small investors are high and the incentive is to hold large blocks of shares in order to have direct influence over management. Further, it is argued that common law countries are better than civil law countries in contract enforcement and therefore have much stronger equity markets (La Porta et al. 2000). Thus if countries get the laws 'right,' securities markets expand (see also Goyer in this volume). The problem with this approach is that there are countries with 'good' laws but still concentrated ownership and weak securities markets, and 'good' laws do not in themselves eliminate other incentives for concentrated ownership (Roe 2003: 160). Moreover, securities markets have expanded dramatically in 'both' common and civil law countries since the early 1990s, though historical differences in relative market size remain.

A 'varieties of capitalism' approach suggests that the structure and change of the financial and corporate governance system is connected to the broader model of production employed in the economy (Hall and Soskice 2001). Due to high levels of institutional complementarity, institutional change will either ripple throughout the system, or will be rather marginal because the competitive advantages rooted in the existing system lead actors to resist more radical change. The reliance of firms in CMEs on specific assets for competitive advantage works better when capital mobility, in the broadest sense, is restrained through non-market coordination (Gourevitch and Shinn 2005). Hence, under these conditions domestic actors—owners, managers, and workers—prefer block-holding ownership, limited securities markets, and the retention of a bank-based financial system. This framework may help explain the more limited transformation of financial systems in certain countries such as Germany and Italy (Vitols 2004). However, even in many CMEs there has been considerable change in the direction of a market-based financial system, and this has generally been attributed to the shifting preference of large financial institutions and multinational enterprises (Culpepper 2005; Aoki, Jackson, and Miyajima 2007).

A third institutional approach focuses on the endurance or breakdown of socio-political coalitions (Amable 2003). Mark Roe (2003), for example, argues that countries with a politically dominant 'social democratic' coalition will have insider corporate governance systems with weak securities markets. The reason is that when labour is protected—through institutions like co-determination and employment protection laws—owners want to hold large blocks of shares in order to counter the pressure from workers on management to stabilize employment, focus on growth rather than profitability, and avoid high risk investments. This approach suggests that changing formal laws and regulations to promote securities markets, shareholder value, etc. will have limited impact so long as the social democratic coalition dominates. Real change is more likely to arise from an increase in market competition for firms that force managers to focus on profitability in order to ensure firm survival. Hence firms in sectors more exposed to international competition will press for (or in the case of workers, tolerate) changes in the financial system that enhance firm profits and thus their viability.

Over the last decade or so another literature has emerged that analyses the emergence of transnational governance regimes arising from the dynamic interaction between actors engaged in market reform across multiple levels of governance. In these regimes, myriad state and private actors together make rules—formal and informal (norms, standards, voluntary codes)—that regulate financial activity. Scholars who study these regimes emphasize that compliance mechanisms are based not just on state authority but also on socialization with incentives for voluntary compliance coming from access to membership, resources, or certification (Djelic and Quack 2003; Djelic and Sahlin-Andersson 2006). Put another way, a complex web of transnational institutions shape global financial markets in ways not captured by conventional international relations approaches. Much of this literature is inspired by financial market integration in Europe. A prime example is provided by Jabko (2006), who acknowledges that rising global capital mobility and external pressures for reform were important causes of the liberalization of European financial markets. However, the specific European response to these pressures was not foreordained and, moreover, financial market reform in Europe went further than many European governments initially preferred. Thus countries like Italy were induced to reform their financial markets beyond what would probably have otherwise occurred. Jabko explains this outcome in terms of the European Commission's successful propagation of the idea that the market was a 'constraint' that was best met by a united European effort to take a proactive response to market developments. Posner (2005: 7) finds a similar process behind the emergence of new, NASDAQ-style stock exchanges in Europe during the 1990s in which 'civil servants in Brussels—by forging new interests, embedding themselves in supportive coalitions, liberally interpreting Europe-wide laws, and framing political discourse to make their behavior seem legitimate and useful to others—create autonomy for themselves from other key actors and craft the political landscape in which they operate.' In both accounts the Commission successfully exploited the European decision-making process to build cross-national coalitions among governments and market actors in favour of its reform agenda.

Ideational explanations

Ideational or constructivist explanations have become increasingly influential in recent years. These explanations analyse a variety of cognitive influences, from the role of ideological and belief systems to norms, identities and aspirations, to information and ideas as catalysts for, or obstacles to, change in financial systems. Within this category we find two common types of arguments; first, those that emphasize the constitutive dynamic, i.e. 'focuses on processes through which the preferences and subsequent strategies of actors (such as corporations and states) are socially constructed, varying over time and space, and defining the identity or nature of the actors in relation to others' (Sinclair 2005: 11). One widespread thesis roots the now dominant financial orthodoxy around the efficacy and desirability of open, competitive financial markets with minimal state interference in the broad ideological shift in many advanced industrial countries from the interventionist and Keynesian approaches dominant after to the war to the rise of monetarism and neoliberal ideology (Cerny 1993; McNamara 1998).

Even many structuralist and institutionalist accounts of financial system change acknowledge the importance of shifting beliefs about not only what is desirable, but what is possible (Helleiner 1994; Andrews 1994). Within financial markets, for example, much has been written about the diffusion of 'shareholder value' as the new global norm for the rules governing financial and especially securities markets (Fiss and Zajac 2004). What has sometimes been lacking in such accounts are specifics about the causal mechanisms and pathways through which such ideas diffuse. That said, there is notable recent work that focuses on identifying the mechanism for the construction and spread of new norms about financial system governance (e.g. Simmons et al. 2008: 31–40). Work on the accounting industry, for example, has traced the rise of international financial reporting and accounting standards and the spread of fair value accounting as the preferred approach (Botzem and Quack 2006; Nölke and Perry 2007).

The other type of constructivist arguments are captured well by Jabko's (2006) label of 'strategic constructivism' in that they attempt to combine rationalist and constructivist accounts. In such accounts, the preferences of some actors appear as exogenously determined, but uncertainty among actors about cause and effect means that ideas and discursive processes matter in determining the outcomes (which cannot be reduced to an initial set of actor preferences). Thus Jabko, in his explanation of the European Commission's role in fostering financial markets and monetary integration in Europe, argues that the Commission used the idea of the 'market' in alternative ways to build winning political coalitions behind market reforms. Using a similar approach, Abdelal (2007) seeks to explain the process through which international bureaucracies (EU, IMF, OECD) generated and spread liberal rules for global finance. While material incentives for compliance were significant, 'The process of social construction through which international organizations produced new scripts and joining countries drew lessons—an essentially sociological process— was critical' (38–9). An important twist in Abdelal's work is his argument that countries did not adopt capital market openness as a result of the spread of neo-liberal ideas, as is commonly argued, but rather as the result of key European actors adopting new ideas about how to achieve their preferred social and political objectives within a changed global context.

There are useful lessons to draw from this recent constructivist literature. One is that an understanding of the causes of financial system change benefits from consideration of both the social construction of preferences as well as the strategic use of ideas. But the way in which (and when) ideas matter should perhaps be determined inductively, through careful process trace methodologies, rather than deductively. A second lesson is that demonstrating the relevance of ideas and discursive processes is likely to be most successful in studies focused on specific causal pathways, such as in accounting harmonization or in ratings.

In conclusion, it is not clear that the literature is further along in resolving the question about the causes of financial system change and globalization than Cohen (1996) noted more than a decade ago (also Deeg and O'Sullivan 2009). Nonetheless, there has been considerable progress in mid-range theorizing and research.

Noteworthy in this respect are the literatures on corporate governance, trans-national regulation, and on financial market integration and transformation in the EU. These literatures tell us much about the causal (intermediate, if not original) forces behind, and the mechanisms shaping, the evolution of the financial systems in the modern era.

DISCUSSION

Given all the changes in financial systems discussed in this chapter, we might ask whether the distinction between bank and market-based 'national' financial systems is still useful, or whether we need new typologies. If anything, the literature is moving away from the use of any typology. This is most obviously the case for those who see convergence in financial systems. Yet even for those who believe convergence is overstated, the characterization of any given national financial system appears less and less accurate if one applies a single label to it, even when one acknowledges that ideal types always elide differences in their instantiation in any one specific country. Specifically, as financial systems have grown, become more complex and interdependent, it becomes more fruitful to break the analysis and characterization of national financial systems into major dimensions; this preserves some of the utility of conventional typologies.

If we examine and compare 'patterns of firm finance' cross-nationally, the bank versus market distinction becomes difficult to sustain without further differentiation. At the aggregate level, there has been a long-term trend toward increasing self-finance and market finance by European firms (Byrne and Davis 2002; Murinde, Agung, and Mullineux 2004). However, in most countries this trend is much more pronounced for larger firms. When looking at SME finance the old distinction has more merit, that is, in traditionally bank-based systems SMEs continue to rely heavily on bank finance (Deeg 2009). The picture varies, though, from country to country. In Germany, for instance, firm financing for SMEs still fits the bank-based description well, while for large firms it does not (Rivaud-Danset, Dubocage, and Salais, 1998; Schmidt et al. 2002; Hackethal, Schmidt, and Tyrell 2005: 9). In France, on the other hand, both large and small firm finance has moved dramatically in the direction of market-based financing (O'Sullivan 2007; Schmidt et al. 2002; Culpepper 2005). But perhaps the most striking change in France is the overall rise in self-financing by firms, which has brought the French pattern of firm financing (bank borrowing, self-finance, and shareholder equity) much closer to that of the UK (Byrne and Davis 2002).

In contrast, if we examine 'patterns of household savings and investment', the bank versus market distinction holds up better. There is a common long-term trend in Europe away from holding assets in bank deposits and, with the exception of Germany, system distinctions no longer appear meaningful for this category (Byrne and Davis 2002).

However, in other major asset categories considerable national differences remain. Household investment in bonds (government and corporate) is notably greater in Germany and Italy than in the UK and France, for instance. Conversely, equity investment (including unquoted shares) is much higher in the UK and France than in Germany and Italy. Thus, in terms of household investment patterns, Germany and Italy retain a strong bank orientation, while France has moved quite substantially toward the UK market-based pattern. Though in France two-thirds of household equity investment is in unquoted shares—most likely in family firms (Byrne and Davis 2002: 88, 93; also, Vitols 2004; Gourevitch and Shinn 2005).

We might ask how it is that national firm financing patterns might deviate from household investment patterns. One likely reason is that firms' access to capital is no longer limited to domestic sources; thus how they finance themselves can diverge from household asset patterns (e.g. domestic investors may not buy much corporate equity, but foreigners might). This also points to different national patterns of corporate ownership and thus corporate governance. More market-oriented finance for large firms is, in many cases, now 'married' with still relatively concentrated ownership patterns, such as in Germany and Italy (Mengoli, Pazzaglia, and Sapienza 2007; Vitols 2004). This too highlights the disutility of trying to apply a single descriptor—bank or market-based—to the entire national financial system.

The widespread phenomenon of financialization also raises questions about the utility of national distinctions in financial systems (see Engelen and Konings, this volume).This concept captures the rising impact of financial markets and financial actors on non-financial firms and the real economy. Nölke and Perry (2007) usefully divide the process of financialization into two components. The first is *profit* financialization, which consists of two sub-types: the first is the relative growth in profitability of the financial sector, and the second is the growing proportion of profits that non-financial firms (in aggregate) are making from financial transactions and investments rather than the sale of goods or services. Taking the US as an example, the financial sector's share of all profits rose from 10 per cent in the early 1980s to 40 per cent in 2007 (*Economist* 22 March, 2008: 79; also Krippner, 2005). Other studies suggest similar trends across OECD countries (Epstein and Jayadev, 2006; Duménil and Lévy 2004). Similarly, studies suggest that as much as 40 per cent of non-financial corporate sector profits in the mid-2000s were derived from financial activity—an increase from roughly 10 per cent during the 1950s and 60s (Krippner, 2005; Duménil and Lévy 2004; Crotty 2006). The second component of financialization is 'control' financialization. It refers to 'the process by which the maximization of shareholder value (SV) has become the primary objective of firms' managers' (Nölke and Perry, 2007: 8). The increased orientation to SV is itself driven by pressures from financial investors. With greater financialization both shareholders and managers begin to view the firm as a collection of assets, with the primary criterion for managing each of those assets being maximum profit extraction (Froud et al. 2006; also Fligstein 1990).

While financialization is a widespread phenomenon, even at its peak the degree of financialization varied considerably across national economies thus leaving important national distinctions. The importance of such distinctions was manifest during the late 2000s crisis. The US and UK financial systems were by far the two systems exhibiting the highest degree of financialization and securitization before the crisis and suffered most during it. Meanwhile, continental countries such as France and Italy remained relatively unaffected because of the comparatively domestic and conventional orientation of their financial systems. German banks absorbed very heavy losses from sub-prime assets and several failed, but the financial system as a whole was not threatened due in large measure to the large market share of public savings banks and cooperative banks. In Spain there was a housing boom like in the US and UK, which ended in a bust yet the financial system remained relatively strong, due to pro-cyclical capital adequacy regulations.

Financial system changes and financialization also have implications for the broader patterns of economic coordination in national economies. For many scholars financialization is associated with asymmetric pressures on bank-based systems and their associated coordinated systems of capitalism (for example, Beyer and Höpner 2003). The general argument is that the 'patient capital', which under-girded coordinated approaches to production and innovation, is diminishing due to the transformation of financial markets. Germany is the pivotal case for this debate.

Germany has long been regarded as a prime example of bank-based finance and insider-dominated corporate governance. Since the early 1990s, banks have become less central in the financial system based on intermediation ratios. Household savings flow increasingly into securities and the stock market grew substantially in size relative to GDP, but in comparative perspective these are still modest. Moreover, bank lending to firms in aggregate has remained fairly constant over the past two decades. Thus on several key measures Germany remains a relatively bank-oriented financial system. Simultaneously, there have been many changes in the relationship between firms and their shareholders. Most important in the German case are an increased orientation to shareholder value (though not for all large firms), increased transparency, and investor protection and some decline of block-holding and inter-firm equity links (Fiss and Zajac 2004; Culpepper 2005; Deeg 2009). While overall measures of ownership concentration remain comparatively high in Germany, the number and size of block-holdings in several of the largest German firms have declined substantially. The large German banks in particular have been selling off or drastically reducing their large block-holdings and dramatically reducing their role in corporate governance. Despite considerable research, there is still no consensus in the literature on whether Germany's bank-based system and coordinated economy have undergone evolutionary or revolutionary change.

In the case of France, there is both more radical change in most dimensions of the financial system and also greater consensus that these changes amount to a systemic transformation. In France, change began with the decline during the 1980s in the role of the state and state-controlled banks in enterprise finance and ownership. From the late 1980s to the mid-1990s, France approximated a German system of corporate ownership with large domestic block-holders retaining important stakes in most large French firms. However, this system unwound in the late 1990s and ownership in

French firms became more widespread and held to a considerable extent by foreign investors.[9] Commensurate with this was a significant shift from bank to securities financing by firms (Schmidt et al. 2002, O'Sullivan 2007, Culpepper 2005). Household investing behaviour also shifted dramatically from bank to securities. Consequently, the French stock market exhibited a dramatic expansion since the early 1980s, and especially over the last ten years (Table 11.1). In terms of corporate governance, like Germany, there is some controversy over how to interpret recent changes. Some see a shift to an outsider system (Goyer 2003), while to others it appears to sit somewhere between an insider and outsider system (O'Sullivan 2007). With fewer block-holders and little role for labour in corporate governance, there is good reason to argue against a strong insider system (or at least a stakeholder system). Yet control over management through market mechanisms also does not appear strong in the French case (O'Sullivan 2007). And foreign institutional investors, even those with substantial blocks in French firms, appear to be relatively passive vis-à-vis management. Nor have French firms adopted the same level of transparency and disclosure as in many other continental systems, such as Germany or even Italy. At the moment it appears the French financial and corporate governance system has evolved into one with a higher degree of market finance but a hybrid corporate governance system.[10]

The global financial crisis of the late 2000s represented an important break in many of the trends we have discussed and raised many questions about future patterns of financial system change and financialization. On one hand, long-term studies on financialization suggest it has been a steady trend for several decades, coinciding with the rise of financial globalization (Krippner 2005). This suggests it is a sustainable process so long as there is not a widespread return to protectionism. On the other hand, in the mid-2000s profit financialization was driven to new highs in large part by lax monetary policy and excessive leveraging, securitization, and trading (especially of derivatives) to boost income (Nölke and Perry 2007). The global crisis obviously reversed these trends and it is unclear what the new long-term patterns will be.

In sum, while many of the consequences of financial system change are still much debated, there is little doubt that financial markets have undergone tremendous change since the 1980s and financial markets and actors have expanded their broader impact on the global and national economies. The financial and economic crisis of recent years notwithstanding, the importance of understanding financial system changes for the changing context of firm activity and political-economic organization of national capitalisms continues to rise.

---

[9] For the 38 largest companies in France, the average percentage of shares held by the top two shareholders declined from 50.4% in 1993 to 32% in 2000 (Culpepper 2005). Foreign ownership of French shares rose from 10% in 1985 to 42% by 2002 (O'Sullivan 2007: 14).

[10] A similar argument about rising managerial autonomy has also been made about German corporate governance (Hackethal et al. 2005).

REFERENCES

ABDELAL, R. (2007). *Capital Rules: The Construction of Global Finance*, (Cambridge, MA: Harvard University Press).

ALLEN, F. and GALE, D. (2000). *Comparing Financial Systems*, (Cambridge, MA: MIT Press).

AMABLE, B. (2003). *The Diversity of Modern Capitalism*, (Oxford: Oxford University Press).

ANDREWS, D. M. (1994). 'Capital Mobility and State Autonomy: Toward a Structural Theory of International Monetary Relations', *International Studies Quarterly* 38/2: 193–218.

AOKI, M. (2001). *Toward a Comparative Institutional Analysis*, (Cambridge, MA: MIT Press).

——G. JACKSON, and H. MIYAJIMA (2007). *Corporate Governance in Japan: Institutional Change and Organization Diversity*, (Oxford: Oxford University Press).

BECK, T., and E. AL-HUSSAINY (2006). 'Financial Structure Database'. Washington, DC: The World Bank. Downloaded from: http://go.worldbank.org/X23UD9QUX0

BEBCHUK, L. A. and M. J. ROE (1999). 'A Theory of Path Dependence in Corporate Governance and Ownership', Columbia Law School: Center for Law and Economic Studies. Working Papers No. 131.

BEYER, J. and M. HÖPNER (2003). 'The Disintegration of Organized Capitalism: German Corporate Governance in the 1990s', *West European Politics* 26: 179–98.

BOTZEM, S. and S. QUACK (2006). 'Contested Rules and Shifting Boundaries: International Standard-Setting in Accounting', in M. Djelic and K. Sahlin-Andersson (eds.), *Transnational Governance: Institutional Dynamics of Regulation*, (Cambridge, MA: Cambridge University Press).

BYRNE, J. P. and P. E. DAVIS (2002). 'A Comparison of Balance Sheet Structures in Major EU Countries', *National Institute Economic Review* 180.

CERNY, P. G. (ed.) (1993). *Finance and World Politics: Markets, Regimes and States in the Post-Hegemonic Era*, (Brookfield, VT: Edward Elgar).

COHEN, B. J. (1996). 'Phoenix Risen: The Resurrection of Global Finance', *World Politics* 48: 268–96.

CORBETT, J. and JENKINSON, T. (1994). 'The Financing of Industry, 1970–89: An International Comparison', London: CEPR Discussion Paper No. 948.

CROTTY, J. (2006). 'The Neoliberal Paradox: The Impact of Destructive Product Market Competition and "Modern" Financial Markets on Nonfinancial Corporation Performance in the Neoliberal Era', in G. A. Epstein (ed.), *Financialization and the World Economy*, (Northampton, MA: Edward Elgar).

CULPEPPER, P. (2005). 'Institutional Change in Contemporary Capitalism: Coordinated Financial Systems since 1990', *World Politics* 57: 173–99.

DEEG, R. (2009). 'The Rise of Internal Capitalist Diversity: Changing Patterns of Finance and Corporate Governance in Europe', *Economy and Society*, 38/4: 577–604.

——and M. O'SULLIVAN (2006). 'The Financialization of Europe: The Evolution of Finance Capital in Britain, France, Germany and Italy'. Prepared for delivery at the 2006 Annual Meeting of the American Political Science Association, Philadelphia, Aug. 30–Sep. 3.

————(2009). 'The Political Economy of Global Finance Capital', *World Politics*, 61/4: 731–763.

DJELIC, M. and S. QUACK (eds.) (2003). *Globalization and Institutions*, (Cheltenham, UK: Edward Elgar).

——and K. SAHLIN-ANDERSSON (eds.) (2006). *Transnational Governance: Institutional Dynamics of Regulation*, (Cambridge: Cambridge University Press).

DUMÉNIL, G. and D. LÉVY (2004). *Capital Resurgent: The Roots of the Neoliberal Revolution*, (Cambridge, MA: Harvard University Press.)

Economist (2008). 'What went wrong', *The Economist*, (Mar. 22).

EICHENGREEN, B. (2006). *The European Economy since 1945: Coordinated Capitalism and Beyond*, (Princeton, NJ: Princeton University Press).

EPSTEIN, G. A. and JAYADEV, A. (2006). 'The Rise of Rentier Incomes in OECD Countries: Financialization, Central Bank Policy and Labor Solidarity', in G. A. Epstein (ed.), *Financialization and the World Economy*, (Northampton, MA: Edward Elgar).

FARRELL, D. S. LUND, C. FÖLSTER, R. BICK, M. PIERCE, and C. ATKINS (2008). *Mapping Global Capital Markets—Fourth Annual Report*, (San Francisco: McKinsey Global Institute), retrieved on Mar. 12, 2008 from http://www.mckinsey.com/mgi/publications/Mapping_Global/index.asp.

FISS, P. C. and E. ZAJAC (2004). 'The Diffusion of Ideas over Contested Terrain: The (Non) adoption of a Shareholder Value Orientation among German Firms', *Administrative Science Quarterly* 49: 501–34.

FLIGSTEIN, N. (1990). *The Transformation of Corporate Control*, (Cambridge, MA: Harvard University Press).

FRANKS, J. and C. MAYER (1990). 'Corporate Ownership and Control: A Study of France, Germany and the UK', *Economic Policy*, 10: 189–232.

FRIEDEN, J. A. (1991). 'Invested Interests: The Politics of National Economic Policies in a World of Global Finance', *International Organization* 45/4: 425–52.

FROUD, J. S. JOHAL, A. LEAVER, and K. WILLIAMS (2006). *Financialization and Strategy: Narrative and Numbers*, (London; Oxon: Routledge).

GERSCHENKRON, A. (1962). *Economic Backwardness in Historical Perspective*, (Cambridge, MA: Harvard University Press).

GOUREVITCH, P.A. and J. SHINN (2005). *Political Power and Corporate Control: The New Global Politics of Corporate Governance*, (Princeton, NJ: Princeton University Press).

GOYER, M. (2003). 'Corporate Governance, Employees, and the Focus on Core Competencies in France and Germany', In Curtis J. Milhaupt (ed.) *Global Markets, Domestic Institutions: Corporate Law and Governance in a New Era of Cross-Border Deals.* (New York: Columbia University Press), 183–213.

HACKETHAL, A. R. H. SCHMIDT, and M. TYRELL (2005). 'Banks and German Corporate Governance: On the Way to a Capital Market-Based System?', (Frankfort: Johann Wolfgang Goethe University). Working Paper No. 146.

HALL, P. A. and D. SOSKICE (2001). 'An Introduction to Varieties of Capitalism', in P. A. Hall and D. Soskice (eds.), *The Institutional Foundations of Comparative Advantage*, (Oxford: Oxford University Press), 1–70.

HELLEINER, E. (1994). *States and the Reemergence of Global Finance: From Bretton Woods to the 1990s*, (Ithaca, NY: Cornell University Press).

HERRING, R. J. and R. E. LITAN (1994). *Financial Regulation in the Global Economy*, (Washington, DC: Brookings Institute).

IFSL (International Financial Services London) (2008). *International Financial Markets in the UK*, (London: IFSL) (downloaded from www.ifsl.org.uk/research).

JABKO, N. (2006). *Playing the Market: A Political Strategy for Uniting Europe, 1985–2005*, (Ithaca, NY: Cornell University Press).

JACKSON, G. and R. DEEG (2008). 'From Comparing Capitalisms to the Politics of Change', *Review of International Political Economy* 15/4: 680–709.

KAPSTEIN, E. B. (1994). *Governing the Global Economy: International Finance and the State*, (Cambridge, MA: Harvard University Press).

KRIPPNER, G. (2005). 'The Financialization of the American Economy', *Socio-Economic Review* 3/2: 173–208.

LA PORTA, R., F. LOPEZ-DE-SILANES, and ANDREI SHLEIFER (2000). 'Investor Protecton and Corporate Governance', *Journal of Financial Economics* 58/3.

LÜTZ, S. (2004). 'Convergence within Diversity: The Regulatory State in Finance', *Journal of Public Policy*, 24/2: 169–97.

MACKENZIE, D. A. (2006). *An Engine, Not a Camera: How Financial Models Shape Markets*, (Cambridge, MA: MIT Press).

MCNAMARA, K. (1998). *The Currency of Ideas: Monetary Politics in the European Union*, (Ithaca, NY: Cornell University Press).

MENGOLI, S., F. PAZZAGLIA, and E. SAPIENZA (2007). 'Is it Still Pizza, Spaghetti and Mandolino—On the Evolution of Corporate Ownership in Italy'. Retrieved on June 12, 2007 from http://ssrn.com/abstract=966085.

MORAN, M. (1991). *The Politics of the Financial Services Revolution: The USA, UK and Japan*, (New York: St. Martin's Press).

MURINDE, V., J. AGUNG, and A. MULLINEUX (2004). 'Patterns of Corporate Financing and Financial System Convergence in Europe', *Review of International Economics* 12: 693–705.

NÖLKE, A. and J. PERRY (2007). 'The Power of Transnational Private Governance: Financialisation and the IASB', *Business and Politics*, 9/3: article 4. Retrieved on Feb. 8, 2007 from http://www.bepress.com/bap/vol9/iss3/art4.

OATLEY, T. H. (1997). *Monetary Politics: Exchange Rate Cooperation in the European Union*, (Ann Arbor, MI: University of Michigan Press).

O'BRIEN, R. (1992). *Global Financial Integration: The End of Geography*, (London: Pinter).

O'SULLIVAN, M. (2007). 'Acting Out Institutional Change: Understanding the Recent Transformation of the French Financial System', *Socio-Economic Review* 5: 389–436.

PAULY, L. (1997). *Who Elected the Bankers: Surveillance and Control in the World Economy*, (Ithaca, NY: Cornell University Press).

PEREZ, S. (1998). 'Systemic Explanations, Divergent Outcomes: The Politics of Financial Liberalization in France and Spain', *International Studies Quarterly* 42/4: 755–84.

POSNER, E. (2005). 'Sources of Institutional Change: The Supranational Origins of Europe's New Stock Markets'. *World Politics* 58: 1–40.

——(2009). 'Making Rules for Global Finance: Transatlantic Regulatory Cooperation at the Turn of the Millennium,' *International Organization*, 63: 655–99.

RAJAN, G. R. and L. ZINGALES (2003). 'Banks and Markets: The Changing Character of European Finance', London: CEPR Discussion Paper No. 3868.

RIVAUD-DANSET, D., E. DUBOCAGE, and R. SALAIS (1998). 'Comparison between the Financial Structure of SME versus Large Enterprise Using the Bach Database'. Centre National de la Recherche Scientifique, retrieved on May 15, 2007 from http://papers.ssrn.com/sol3/papers.cfm-abstract_id=141478.

ROE, M. (2003). *Political Determinants of Corporate Governance: Political Context, Corporate Impact*, (Oxford: Oxford University Press).

RUGGIE, J. (1982). 'International Regimes, Transactions, and Change: Embedded Liberalism in the Postwar Economic Order', *International Organization* 47/1: 139–74.

SCHMIDT, R. H., A. HACKETHAL, and M. TYRELL (2002). 'The Convergence of Financial Systems in Europe', *Schmalenhach Business Review*. Special Issue 1: 7–53.

SIMMONS, B. A. (2001). 'The International Politics of Harmonization: The Case of Capital Market Regulation', *International Organization*, 55/3: 589–620.

——F. DOBBIN, and G. GARRETT (2008). 'Introduction: The Diffusion of Liberalization,' in B. A. Simmons, F. Dobbin, and G. Garrett (eds.), *The Global Diffusion of Markets and Democracy*, (Cambridge: Cambridge University Press).

SINCLAIR, T. (2005). *The New Masters of Capital: American Bond Rating Agencies and the Politics of Creditworthiness*, (Ithaca, NY: Cornell University Press).

SOBEL, A. C. (1994). *Domestic Choices, International Markets: Dismantling National Barriers and Liberalizing Securities Markets*, (Ann Arbor, MI: University of Michigan Press).

STRANGE, S. (1996). *The Retreat of the State: The Diffusion of Power in the World Economy*, (Cambridge: Cambridge University Press).

UNDERHILL, G. R. D. (1991). 'Markets beyond Politics: The State and the Internationalisation of Financial Markets', *European Journal of Political Research*, 19/2, 3: 197–225.

VITOLS, S. (2004). 'Changes in Germany's Bank-Based Financial System: A Varieties of Capitalism Perspective', (Berlin: Wissenschaftszentrum Berlin). Discussion Paper SP II 2004–2003.

VITTAS, D., T. HINDLE, P. FRAZER and R. BROWN. (1978). 'Banking Systems Abroad: the role of large deposit banks in the financial systems of Germany, France, Italy, the Netherlands, Switzerland, Sweden, Japan and the United States'. London: Inter-Bank Research Organisation.

WHITLEY, R. (1986). 'The Rise of Modern Finance Theory: Its Characteristics as a Scientific Field and Connections to the Changing Structure of Capital Markets', *Research in the History of Economic Thought and Methodology*, 4: 147–78.

——(2008). *Business Systems and Organizational Capabilities*, (Oxford University Press).

ZYSMAN, J. (1983). *Governments, Markets, and Growth: Financial Systems and the Politics of Industrial Change*, (Ithaca, NY: Cornell University Press).

CHAPTER 12

....

THE COMPARATIVE INSTITUTIONAL ANALYSIS OF INNOVATION: FROM INDUSTRIAL POLICY TO THE KNOWLEDGE ECONOMY

....

STEVEN CASPER[1]

INTRODUCTION

....

This chapter surveys comparative institutional research from sociology and political science that seeks to explain patterns of innovation across the advanced industrial economies. The survey has two broad aims. Firstly, it reviews three scholarly

[1] I thank Glenn Morgan and Richard Whitley for their helpful comments on earlier drafts of this chapter.

literatures that link innovation to the orientation of national institutional models: political science research on industrial policy and competitiveness, sociological institutionalism, and the varieties of capitalism tradition. Surveying these research fields helps identify numerous empirical domains and theoretical mechanisms by which national institutions can plausibly impact innovation. Secondly, the chapter explores in more detail how national institutional differences across the advanced industrial economies impact innovation within the knowledge economy. Drawing on recent research linking sectoral systems of innovation and national institutional models, the article explores how financial, labour market, and corporate governance institutions across different types of economies impact the organization of 'radically innovative' companies in new technology often associated with Silicon Valley. The chapter ends with a discussion of future research directions.[2]

COMPETITIVENESS AND INDUSTRIAL POLICY

Much comparative institutional research on innovation has its origins in studies conducted during the 1970s and 1980s that linked the competitiveness of national economies to the orientation of government policy, and in particular industrial policy (see Hart, 1992; Zysman and Tyson, 1983; Katzenstein 1978). Research on industrial policy suggests that processes of industrial restructuring, prime determinants of international competitiveness, are shaped by the organization of state policies and institutions. While not specifically analysing innovation or knowledge production as explanatory variables, the focus on competitiveness led researchers to identify several aspects of industrial organization, such as the level or type of R & D investments made by firms, as key dependent variables. Moreover, through linking the structure of state institutions to patterns of industrial adjustment within the economy, research on industrial policy established the basic explanatory framework used in much comparative institutional research on innovation.

A key premise of the competitiveness approach is that differences in the institutional organization of the state affect the type of policy instruments governments have at their disposal for governing the economy (Katzenstein 1978; Hall, 1986). In an important study in this field, Zysman (1983) argues that differences in French and British industrial policy after the Second World War resulted from variations in the ability of the two countries to channel finance to key industries. Because the UK government had few policy instruments with which to manage the country's

---

[2] This chapter focuses primarily on commercial innovation. Recent research has begun to view the creation of public knowledge through similar comparative institutional frameworks. See, for example, Whitley (2003) for an analysis of how the institutional structuring of academic research systems shapes public knowledge creation.

decentralized, autonomous, and equity-based financial system, it was not able to manage the flow of most private investment after the war. On the other hand, because the French government was able to control key banks and other financial institutions, it could directly channel savings into a number of heavy manufacturing industries. The successful modernization of the French economy in the 1950s and 1960s, compared to Britain's long relative economic decline, can be viewed as the result of the development of state institutional capacities sustaining a more effective industrial policy. Zysman and a number of other scholars have applied a similar analysis to Japan, which for much of the post-war period also had a state-coordinated financial system (Zysman, 1983; Samuels 1987; Calder 1993; Schmidt 2002). Studies of Japan have also suggested that the Japanese Ministry of Trade and Industry (MITI) has played an important role over Japanese technology policy during the post-war reconstruction phase (Johnson 1979). It used control over standards, market access, and funds for technology promotion projects to shape the structure of many Japanese industries (Calder 1993).

While this literature does not explicitly examine innovation, the focus on competitiveness and industrial performance led scholars to examine closely how government policies have historically structured the organization of markets and the resources available to companies, both important determinants in how companies invest in research and development. In a classic study of the semiconductor industry, Borrus, Millstein, and Zysman (1981) traced the success of the Japanese memory chip market to a number of government policies that stabilized (and protected) the Japanese market such that large companies could invest in several generations of expensive R & D surrounding the design and manufacture of chips (see also Breznitz 2007). A number of scholars (Malerba 1985; Lécuyer 2006; Borrus, Millstein, and Zysman 1981) have explained the early success of the Silicon Valley semiconductor industry at least in part to large-scale federal government investments in electronics during the 1950s and 1960s in support of defence and space programmes. Borrus, Millstein, and Zysman (1981) link the decline of the US memory chip market during the 1970s to a decrease in government spending on electronics R & D, coupled with more liberal government policies that refused to protect markets or rationalize industrial structures along the Japanese model (see also Prestowitz 1993).

While governments continue to invest in new technology development, within most high technology industries the modalities by which governments can influence industrial structure have become more nuanced. In heavy industries such as steel, shipbuilding, or petrochemicals, success could in large part be determined by state policies (Hart 1992). Governments could develop an institutional capacity to provide investment, organize domestic markets, offer protection against foreign competition, and champion industry abroad. These policy instruments are especially effective in dealing with large, vertically integrated industries relying on mass production techniques. Large enterprises with hierarchical management structures could feasibly be created and supported by the state (Zysman 1977; Perrow 1984).

From the early 1980s onwards, however, innovation systems in many technologically intense industries have become more complex, dependent on relationships between large and small firms as well as diffuse networks of experts linking companies with universities and a variety of applied research institutions (Nelson, 1993; Kitschelt 1991). Moreover, much recent research has located the competitiveness of industries to the development of sophisticated organizational capabilities within companies (Teece and Pisano 1994; Milgrom and Roberts 1993; Miller 1992). Within this context, the viability of state-centred policy instruments used to manage the immediate post-Second World War economy has declined. Within a more decentralized economy, a central problem has become the management of complex forms of industrial organization within a market setting. Finance can no longer be managed by the state, in part because it has become increasingly difficult for governments to accurately 'pick winners' (Loriaux 1991; Vogel 1996). Instead of directing technology in the classic style used by Japan's MITI throughout the post-war period, most countries are today trying to provide sophisticated technology infrastructures that subsidize the cost of innovation and attempt to impact the flow of new technology to domestic industries, but do not attempt to direct its path.

Sociological Institutionalism

A second generation of comparative institutional research has focused on how a broader set of national institutional frameworks in a variety of areas impact firms, such as industrial relations, skill formation, and corporate governance. Within this research tradition the role of the state is usually viewed as more indirect (Weiss 1998 and in this volume). Instead of overtly governing the activities of firms within the economy, governments are seen as the forum in which key institutional frameworks are deliberated upon, legislated, and enforced upon the economy. Moreover, research began to focus more specifically on innovation and knowledge production as core outcomes to be explained.

There is a large body of sociologically informed research oriented towards the comparative institutional analysis of innovation and knowledge within the economy. This review discusses two specific schools of research, the historical institutionalism perspective from political science and neoinstitutional research from economic sociology. Both perspectives stress the constitutive role of institutions in structuring the organization of a range of market and non-market relationships within economies (DiMaggio and Powell 1983). The most direct descendant of the industrial policy literature is the historical institutionalism approach that emerged within the comparative politics sub-field of political science during the early 1990s (see Steinmo, Thelen, and Longstretch 1992). This body of research stresses the importance of national institutional frameworks in mediating the process by which governmental and societal actors negotiate processes of industrial adjustment. While the state has created legal frameworks facilitating such negotiations and sometimes intervenes as a third party, most important industrial adjustment processes lie outside formal state institutions. This shift—from a focus on state capacities to the orientation of national institutional frameworks—has become the starting point for much comparative institutional research on innovation and knowledge production within the economy.

Historical institutional scholars within political science have focused attention on the impact of institutional structures on distributive outcomes within economies, such as wage bargaining, and have generally avoided detailed studies of the impact of institutions on firms within the economy. Due to the interest of many comparative political economy scholars in the field of industrial relations, a large body of research has examined the impact of 'neo-corporatist' patterns of industrial adjustment in Europe. Research has examined the legal and historical traditions that have produced cohesive social actors in Germany, as well as the particular institutional frameworks in areas such as wage bargaining, vocational training, and the organization of employee representation within companies (see for overviews Katzenstein 1987, 1989; Thelen 1991; Turner, 1991). Comparative analysis has also been applied to countries in which the government directly bargains in more centralized institutional forums (corporatism in Sweden or Austria), or in which the social constitution of social actors is weak and institutional linkages are decentralized (the US and UK) (see Steinmo, Thelen, and Longstretch 1992).

Economic sociologists working within the comparative institutional tradition adopted a similar mode of analysis as political scientists, but began to directly explore the impact of institutions on innovation. Wolfgang Streeck has made especially important contributions to the institutional analysis of innovation. Streeck (1984, 1992) carefully examines a series of institutional constraints and incentives placed on workplace arrangements within German firms that, collectively, encouraged firms to specialize in what he calls 'diversified quality production' (DQP). Limits created by labour laws on the ability of German employers to easily hire and fire workers create a 'beneficial constraint' on firms within the economy (see Streeck 1997). Streeck argues that German employers are forced to treat workers as long-term or fixed assets within a company. Facing this constraint, German firms have an incentive to invest in the training of workers. Reconciled towards the expectation of long-term employment, employers also create what Streeck calls 'productivity coalitions' with workers, achieved by many large industrial firms through using legally mandated works councils as joint-management forums. Moreover, because labour must be treated as a long-term asset, German firms also have an incentive to invest in a range of what Katzenstein calls 'para-public' institutions, such as the country's industry-focused vocational training system (Offe, 1981; Schmitter, 1981; Katzenstein, 1987, 1989).

Streeck's research pushed comparative institutional analysis in the direction of linking national institutional frameworks to distinct types of industrial outputs. Diversified quality production became linked to a variety of 'medium technology' industries focused on incremental process improvements within established technologies. Much of Germany's long-term competitiveness in machine tools, car manufacturing, speciality chemicals, and a range of other engineering industries is consistent with the DQP explanation (see Katzenstein 1989). More recent research associated with the 'varieties of capitalism' approach, discussed below, adopts Streeck's analysis of institutional preconditions of diversified quality as the centrepiece of a broader argument associating Germany and other 'organized' economies with the development of institutions encouraging incremental innovation.

Streeck's research became the cornerstone of a large comparative institutional literature mapping out the architecture of institutional frameworks across the advanced industrial economies and then linking these institutions to distinct patterns of industrial organization. One of the most comprehensive projects designed to compare and contrast different models of capitalism is the 'social systems of production' approach led by J. Rogers Hollingsworth (Hollingsworth and Boyer 1997; Hollingsworth 1997). Synthesizing a great deal of earlier nation-specific research, Hollingsworth and his collaborators compared the architecture of key institutions in the areas of finance and corporate governance, industrial relations, and other areas across a number of economies, and then linked variations to distinct 'systems of production' within each economy.

Through cataloguing institutional similarities and differences, across the advanced industrial economies and then linking institutional complexes to patterns of production within the economy, the social systems of production approach helped solidify the comparative institutional analysis of economies as a legitimate field, particularly within economic sociology. The social systems of production approach also edged the field closer to an explicit focus on innovation and knowledge production as a dependent variable. Thus, in analysing Japan, the social systems of production approach shifted analysis away from the state and stressed how unique Japanese institutions, such as the main bank system, the pattern of *keiretsu* industry organization, and the employment system conduced towards a flexible mass production strategy. A similar shift surrounds analysis of more liberal market oriented economies, such as the United States. In explaining the preponderance of many US firms to focus on more straightforward 'Fordist' production strategies drawing on scale economies, Hollingsworth draws attention away from the 'weak state' explanation associated with the industrial policy literature and towards a national institutional approach focused on an analysis of incentives created for companies through labour markets, industrial relations, and financial institutions in the United States. The United States is associated primarily with 'Fordism', though the emergence of Silicon Valley as centre of new technology development has shifted attention to how institutions in the US also encouraged more radical forms of innovation (see Crouch 2005 and Whitley in this volume).

While sociological institutionalism helped establish the basic parameters of cross-national research linked to innovation, the approach has important weaknesses. To drive outcomes, historical institutionalism and many sociologically oriented studies, such as the social systems of production approach, adopt a strong concept of sociological embeddedness (Granovetter, 1973). Drawing on neoinstitutional theory (DiMaggio and Powell 1983), the strategies of actors within the economy are assumed to be isomorphic to, or structured by, the logic of institutions within which they are embedded. In a sense, outcomes are 'read off' from institutional architectures. Moreover, as prominent contributors to sociological institutionalism have begun to emphasize, the approach makes it difficult to explore change (Thelen, 2004; Pierson 2004; Crouch 2005). Strongly socialized versions of institutional theory, through minimizing the agency of actors, are especially prone to create a static analysis.

Placing limits on the role of agency makes it difficult to explore how actors within the economy strategize within institutional frameworks to compete. To discuss a well-known example linked to the earlier discussion of institutions surrounding diversified quality production in Germany, Streeck (1984) and a number of other scholars have examined the importance of German co-determination law in structuring workplace relations within German manufacturing companies (Thelen 1991; Turner 1991; see also Kristensen and Zeitlin 2005). As an institution, co-determination law gives a right to employees in most companies to establish work councils that have consultation rights with management over a number of personnel issues. As the West German model of workplace relations developed, companies used works councils as institutions in which bargaining between management and workers takes place over work organization issues. Within the manufacturing sector, members of Germany's strong industrial unions usually dominate West German works councils. Works councils have traditionally given unions a direct voice in shaping work organization issues (Thelen 1991). When negotiating solutions to new forms of work organization, such as group work, industrial unions have developed coordinated strategies to introduce similar agendas through works councils across their industry (Turner 1991). Solutions adopted in Volkswagen and a few other highly visible companies served as blueprints for companies elsewhere within similar sectors.

Industry-wide patterns of 'negotiated adjustment' (Thelen 1991) became so dominant in the West German industrial economy during the 1970s and 1980s that these patterns were seen as a basic feature of the German institutional model. It came as a major surprise when, after German unification, companies in the new Eastern states began engaging works councils very differently than in the West. During the 1990s, union membership was high in most East German manufacturing firms and union members usually staffed works councils, but co-determination within the workplace developed differently. Unions have played their traditional collective wage bargaining role across East Germany, but have seen their influence within companies wane (see Turner 1997; Thelen 2004). Instead, many works councils have formed much closer bonds with company management (often in efforts to preserve jobs) and have adopted many flexible work organization practices that have long been taboo, and in some cases illegal, in West Germany (for a review see Hassel 2007).

Co-determination law is an institution that management and workers within an enterprise can easily engage to foster the patterns of workplace cooperation associated with diversified quality production. But the form of cooperation can vary.

Because sociological institutionalism, as an explanatory framework, does not have an adequate theory of how micro-level actors (firms, their managers, their employees) engage institutions, an institutional outcome (pattern bargaining on work organization issues through union control of work councils) has become confused with the institution itself (German co-determination law). Given the dire economic situation in East Germany during the 1990s and the different socialization of East German workers and managers, it is no surprise that works councils would function differently in East Germany (Turner 1997).

The problem of dealing with micro-level strategies of institutional engagement becomes more acute when studying smaller companies, particularly entrepreneurial technology firms. This is in part because firms with different innovation strategies engage institutional frameworks very differently, and at times, selectively. It is important to understand these variations in institutional engagement in order to examine how effective laws may be developed. Because companies play a major role in driving change, we need a theory in which preferences, or strategies for action, are not entirely determined by the institutions within which they are embedded. Recent research focused broadly on models of capitalism retains the central institutionalist insight, but uses micro-foundations borrowed from the economics of organization and contingency theories within sociology, to better explore the link between institutions and the innovation strategies of firms.

MODELS OF CAPITALISM

The comparative analysis of competing capitalisms (Hall and Soskice 2001; Amable 2003; Whitley 1999; 2003) facilitates a more sophisticated understanding of the relationship between company strategy and patterns of institutional engagement. This is achieved through a more subtle analysis of embeddedness compared with the strongly sociological conception employed within most neoinstitutional approaches. Drawing on ideas from the economics of organization and contingency theory, varieties of capitalism theory attempts to develop micro-foundations that can be used to better understand the link between institutional frameworks, innovation patterns adopted by firms, and resulting patterns of national competitive advantage.

Varieties of capitalism research uses a mode of analysis similar to that used within contingency theories developed in the fields of industrial organization (Woodward 1965) and sociology (see Perrow 1984). Contingency theorists argue that in order to achieve satisfactory organizational performance within a given field of activity, technological characteristics of that field of activity require, in a functional sense, the development of an associated pattern of organization. Performance becomes dependent on achieving an organizational alignment with technology. This argument was taken up by Zysman (1977) in an important study of French industrial policy towards the computer industry. Zysman argues that the French government policy of creating national champions, organized in a hierarchical manner long associated with French bureaucracies, created strong barriers to successfully managing innovation within the computer industry, which typically relies upon more decentralized and market-oriented patterns of industrial organization. While much comparative institutional research during the 1980s and early 1990s proceeded to adopt a strongly sociological theoretical approach, as discussed above, the idea of creating actor-level micro-foundations surrounding particular forms of industrial organization—and innovation—became a central component of the varieties of capitalism approach (see also Aoki 2002 for a similar approach).

To create micro-foundations, Hall and Soskice (2001) adopt a theoretical approach more closely aligned with rational choice theories of agency, and then draw on ideas from the field of institutional economics to identify a series of organizational dilemmas facing firms (see Milgrom and Roberts, 1993 and Miller, 1992 for overviews). This approach views each aspect of company organization as a strategic response to a bundle of technical and relational problems specific to a given industry. The orientation of institutional frameworks, according to Hall and Soskice, impacts the governance costs of supporting particular product market strategies. Moreover, these product market strategies have been characterized primarily through focusing on different types of innovation.

Hall and Soskice argue that particular innovation strategies require different forms of coordination across actors within the economy. Simplifying their argument a great deal, they argue that 'radical' forms of innovation, such as those associated with new technology industries such as biotechnology or software, draw on largely market-oriented patterns of industrial organization. On the other hand, more 'incremental' forms of innovation, such as those found within the machine-tool industry and other 'diversified quality production' type industries, require that actors overcome a series of incomplete contract dilemmas. National institutional frameworks create patterns of incentives and constraints within economies that encourage certain forms of coordination across firms and discourage others. 'Liberal market economies', such as the United States and the United Kingdom, contain institutions that facilitate the type of primarily market coordination associated with radical innovation. Germany, Japan, and other 'coordinated market economies,' on the other hand, have developed institutions that facilitate non-market forms of organization that allow incomplete contracts to be adequately resolved and, through so doing, encourage incremental innovation. In this respect, a key premise of the varieties of capitalism approach is that national institutional frameworks tend to promote certain forms of economic organization—and hence innovation—while constraining others. This leads to the argument that countries develop comparative institutional advantages in the economic governance of certain forms of innovation.

The idea of comparative institutional advantage helps explain why distinct models of capitalism endure. Numerous scholars have suggested that increased patterns of globalization will lead to a levelling or harmonization of economies and the creation of global markets (Ohmae 1990, Castells 1996). While the comparative capitalism tradition has long noted the historical persistence of national institutional models, much of this research lacked a convincing explanation, outside of path dependency, of why this is the case. The theory of comparative institutional advantage creates a more positive theory of why distinct national models persist—they create enduring competitive advantage for firms in managing commercial innovation.

Proponents of the models of capitalism approach have created an elaborate theoretical argument suggesting that comparative institutional advantages should explain innovation patterns across the advanced industrial economies. Does empirical evidence support this claim? On this point a lively debate has emerged. On one hand, a number of studies, designed primarily by advocates of the national institutional approach, show that at an aggregate level relatively clear patterns of industry specialization exist within different types of technology intensive industries. This includes research on macro-level technological specialization across numerous liberal and coordinated market economies using patent data (Hall and Soskice 2001; Allen 2006) and several studies exploring the performance of new technology industries such as biotechnology and software (see Casper and Whitley 2004; Casper 2007).

Other studies, however, have cast doubt on these claims. A key point made by more critical studies is that much research within the models of capitalism field, and particularly studies motivated by Hall and Soskice's framework, focus on a narrow pool of countries that best conform to ideal-typical liberal and coordinated market economies. The US, UK, Ireland, Canada, and Australia are typically identified as liberal market economies, while Germany, Japan, Sweden, and Austria are usually labelled 'organized' or coordinated market economies. Seemingly important economies, such as Italy or France, don't easily fit into Hall and Soskice's dichotomy (see Locke 1995 for Italy and Hancké 2002 for France). This has led some researchers to call for broader typologies (see Amable 2004; Crouch 2005). Empirical research that includes countries such as Italy or France typically generate findings that run contrary to Hall and Soskice's predictions surrounding comparative institutional advantage. A study of the European pharmaceutical industry by Herrmann (2008a), for example, finds evidence supporting the claim that national institutional frameworks impact patterns of industry specialization for the UK and Germany, but not for Italy. More broadly, a study by Taylor (2004) finds that Hall and Soskice's research linking patenting to patterns of technological innovation is not confirmed for a larger sample of countries within the OECD. Combined, these studies suggest that a more nuanced comparative institutional approach is needed to capture important country variations.

A second stream of criticism surrounds a key assumption across most models of capitalism research, that institutions structuring innovation are primarily national and economy-wide in scope. According to this logic, a country can only sustain one financial system, one labour market system, and so forth. Critics have challenged the historical existence of coherent national models, arguing that institutional heterogeneity often exists within economies. Schneiberg (2007), for example, has shown that over its history important sources of institutional diversity existed within the US economy. Lange (2009) has taken up this argument to explain the persistence of radically innovative biotechnology firms in Germany, arguing that sector-specific institutions have emerged to help support radically innovative companies. During the 1995–2001 period, a time during which Germany experienced a dramatic upswing in entrepreneurial activity, these institutional arrangements included the creation of a specialized stock-market focused on technology firms, the *Neuer Markt*, and a variety of government supported programmes designed to encourage venture capital and university technology-transfer activities (see Lange 2009 and Casper 2007, ch. 4). While the *Neuer Markt* subsequently failed, the continued existence of a small venture capital industry in Germany gives credence to the idea that a plurality of institutional arrangements might coexist within a national economy.

The idea of institutional heterogeneity strongly resonates with recent public policy research in the area of competitiveness. This research draws on the industrial policy tradition of the 1970s and 1980s, but with a stronger emphasis on the sustaining role of institutions. Recent scholarship has emphasized the importance of government policy in creating 'sectoral support systems' (Mowery and Nelson 1999) needed to elevate the performance of firms within particular sectors. Governments, according to the sectoral system approach, should search for obstacles blocking innovation processes within particular sectors and then introduce policies orchestrating the coordination of the necessary linkages within the innovation chain (see Lehrer 2000). Much public policy towards biotechnology and other new economy industries, particularly within coordinated market economies, follows the sectoral support system approach. Policies typically mix resource provision, such as financial subsidies to newly launched companies and support for technology parks and other support infrastructure, with the creation of sector-specific rules and regulation. Examples of sector-specific rules and regulation include tax incentives, regulatory support for investment banking activities needed to support the initial public offerings of start-up companies, and new or revised rules aimed at creating stronger incentives for universities to commercialize science.

If institutional heterogeneity could exist within economies, then governments could potentially craft institutional complexes needed to support innovation within a variety of industries. Moreover, the central idea from varieties of capitalism research that comparative institutional advantages exist would be undermined.

To support the claim that coherent national models exist, Hall and Soskice (2001) have developed a theoretical argument linking comparative institutional advantage to the existence of institutional complementarities (see Milgrom and Roberts 1995). According to this argument, if institutions structuring different aspects of economic activity (say wage bargaining and vocational training) are organized along a similar logic of coordination, then the effectiveness or efficiency of both institutions will increase compared to a situation in which these two institutions ran along different logics of coordination. This idea implies that companies face increasing returns in performance from the correct alignment of institutions and, conversely, face obstacles to effective performance when institutions support contradictory patterns of business coordination within an economy.

The existence of institutional complementarities has not been rigorously tested empirically, creating an interesting pasture for future research (though see Deeg and Jackson 2007; Gingerich and Hall 2006). If institutional complementarities are indeed strong, then it is unlikely that policies aimed at designing sector-specific institutional arrangements within key areas of the economy, such as finance, could succeed. For example, in Germany from the late 1990s onwards there has been ongoing discussion about moving the country's financial system from a primarily bank-based system with concentrated ownership towards a capital-market system focused more on dispersed corporate ownership and shareholder value norms of governance (Vitols 2001). These changes would however be enacted with little or no change to the German institutions structuring company law, industry-led skill formation, or industrial relations. As German new technology start-ups are strongly impacted by the structure of financial markets, but at least in the start-up phase do not participate in the apprenticeship system and are not unionized, they might benefit from the development of a mixed set of institutions.

From the varieties of capitalism perspective, however, it seems unlikely that this shift would succeed in dramatically changing the performance of most companies, so long as company law continues to promote the stakeholder system of company governance and industrial relations patterns continue to conduce towards long-term employment of most skilled employees and managers. According to the logic of institutional complementarities such a change could disrupt the performance of 'normal' German companies embedded within sectors focused on incremental innovation, for example, through impacting the ability of firms to obtain long-term 'patient' finance. If the logic of institutional complementarities is indeed strong, one would also expect the performance of more radically innovative firms to continue to suffer, for example in terms of the ability of companies to employ flexible human resource policies.

MODELS OF CAPITALISM AND INNOVATION WITHIN THE KNOWLEDGE ECONOMY

Through the 1990s and early 2000s a strength of the United States economy has been its ability to foster large numbers of entrepreneurial technology companies, a few of which have grown to dominate new industries, such as Microsoft in software, Genentech in biotechnology, or Google on the Internet. US technology clusters such as Silicon Valley have become engines of innovation and wealth creation, and the envy of governments around the world. Recent studies within the models of capitalism tradition have drawn on research by institutional economists stressing the importance of 'sectoral systems of innovation' (Breschi and Malerba 1997; Malerba and Orsenigo 1993). Through developing a clearer analysis of technological and market characteristics of different types of high-technology sectors, comparative institutional researches can more carefully explore the link between national institutional frameworks and innovation within high-technology industries (see Casper and Whitley 2004; Casper 2007). In addition to helping to explain why the US and other liberal market economies have succeeded in radical innovation, linking models of capitalism and sectoral systems of innovation research can help explain the difficulties many of the more organized economies have experienced in competing in biotechnology, software, and other new economy industries (see Casper 2007).

The sectoral systems of innovation approaches argues that sectors are characterized by enduring 'technological regimes' comprising of a number of knowledge, technology, and market characteristics (Breschi and Malerba 1997; Malerba and Orsenigo 1993). Sectoral systems of innovation theorists have demonstrated empirically that industries differ widely in their particular constellation of these and other technology regime attributes (Malerba 2004). This version of contingency theory is particularly useful in helping to distinguish between radically innovative and incrementally innovative industries. Following this logic, firm-level organizational capabilities needed to innovate will differ strongly across sectoral technology regimes. Later, when introducing institutional arguments, this leads to predictions linking the orientation of institutional frameworks to firm-level advantages in governing managerial risks associated with particular competencies.

It is useful to survey the explanatory structure of this argument with regards to 'new economy' industries such as biotechnology or software. The following discusses how, in terms of their underlying technological regime, radically innovative industries pose distinct organizational and financing dilemmas for companies, and then explores how institutional frameworks within coordinated and liberal market economies effects their governance.

Radically innovative new technology firms represent stereotypical Silicon Valley type start-up firms attempting to pioneer new fields.[3] Sectors with radically innovative technology regimes share several features. A defining characteristic of such industries is attractive opportunity conditions, in the sense that firms compete to create important innovations in markets where winners of innovation races can plausibly capture a large share of an emerging market (Breschi and Malerba 1997). Moreover, firms within most radically innovative industries can realistically capture the profits from their innovations; what economists call appropriability regimes (Teece 1986) are strong. When risks of expropriation are low, and particularly when standard forms of intellectual property protection are sufficient to guard technical innovations from being copied, then companies can readily embark in R&D programs confident that innovation will capture their market value.

Radically innovative industries offer large, defensible markets for companies that successfully develop innovative competencies. However, such industries share two additional characteristics, both of which often create organizational dilemmas for

---

[3] This section draws on Casper 2007, ch. 2.

firms. First, levels of technological volatility are high within radically innovative industries, what economists label as low levels of cumulativeness (Breschi and Malerba 1997). Low cumulativeness suggests that a variety of technological approaches may be available to solve a particular innovative challenge, though few if any might eventually succeed. While technological uncertainty is a determinant of high failure rates of particular projects, it is also increased by racing activity across many firms to develop or establish new technologies within 'winner takes all' markets.

A final technology regime characteristic shared by radically innovative firms surrounds knowledge properties of inventions (Winter 1987). Knowledge differs in the extent it can be easily written down and communicated to third parties. Firms operating in radically innovative segments, such as biotechnology or software, typically focus their innovative activities on knowledge that can be codified. Codification allows companies to obtain intellectual property surrounding key inventions. Moreover, codified intellectual property can often be leveraged as a development milestone used to obtain financing or transferred to other firms through partnerships. Within organizations, however, there is a risk that key employees responsible for inventions may decide not to codify such knowledge and transfer it to the owners of firms. Employees may use such knowledge as leverage to demand more salary. However, a more common occurrence, as witnessed repeatedly in the history of Silicon Valley (Lécuyer 2006), is for employees to leave the firm, using uncodified knowledge as the founding idea for a new start-up.

How do the owners and managers of companies develop competences to manage these dilemmas? Most firms in new technology sectors attempt to develop organizational and financing models commonly associated with companies located in Silicon Valley and other US technology clusters (see, for overviews of Silicon Valley, Saxenian 1994; Kenney, 2000). The organization of technology start-ups is associated with the development of three key competencies, each of which helps manage technology regime risks associated with radically innovative technologies.

Managing high-risk finance

Successful technology start-ups often create enormous financial returns. Leading US biotechnology firms, such as Amgen and Genentech, for example, have successfully launched pharmaceuticals capable of earning over a billion dollar revenues per year. However, high technological volatility, reliance on often unproven business models, and appropriability risks created by low entry barriers can produce substantial financial risks (Teece 1986). Technology oriented new ventures generally have high research and development costs, coupled with low profitability in start-up and expansion phases. To obtain investment funds most new technology firms employ equity based financing schemes—trading equity within the firm for finance at different periods in its development (Zider 1998). At early stages, equity deals are made with venture capitalists and then later through the investment banking community and third party investors through stock offerings. From the perspective of venture capitalists, the viability of attractive 'exits' for their investments, particularly through initial public offerings on stock exchanges, affects their willingness to invest. (see Lerner and Gompers 2001).

Developing human resources within a 'competence destroying' environment

Attracting and retaining staff and managers to work in the risky and dynamic environments of technology start-ups is a second challenge facing most biotechnology start-ups. High employee turnover is routine at many technology start-ups (Almeida and Kogut 1999; Saxenian 1994). A large number of projects fail on technological grounds, are cut for commercial reasons (due to the failure of surrounding business models), or change focus over time. When competence destruction is high, managing human resources becomes an important organizational problem (Bahrami and Evans 1995). To achieve flexibility, managers of technology firms benefit from the ability to develop quickly new research and development trajectories while cutting others. To achieve this goal, firms typically draw on a pool of scientists, technicians, and other specialists with known reputations in particular areas that can quickly be recruited to work on projects. If labour markets' flexibility is limited or if there is a cultural stigma attached to failing or changing jobs regularly, then engineers and managers may choose not to commit to firms with high-risk research projects, for fear that if the project fails the value of his or her engineering and/or management experiences could significantly decline.

Organizing high-powered motivational incentives for personnel

To succeed, managers of new technology companies must motivate staff to commit to what are often demanding, competitive, and time-intensive work environments. Firms often employ performance-based incentive schemes to induce employees to commit to intense work environments. The prospect of large financial rewards helps align the private incentives of engineers and scientists with those of commercial managers (see generally Miller 1992). In addition to salary increases and performance-related pay, over the last decade companies have primarily used share-options packages, made attractive by the expectation that share-value will multiply many times if the company goes public or is sold at a high valuation to another firm.

How do institutional frameworks affect the viability of these organizational arrangements? Scholars working within the models of capitalism tradition argue that the market-oriented orientation of institutions within liberal market economies facilitates success in organizing each element of the Silicon Valley model, and that national institutional frameworks within coordinated markets constrain the effective governance of this model.

Within liberal market economies such as the United States or United Kingdom the property rights structure of firms is primarily financial in nature (see generally Roe 1994). Owners, or their representatives on company boards, enjoy a high amount of autonomy in governing the firm. Few, if any, legally stipulated rights of board representation for employees or other stakeholders exist (see Goyer, this volume, and Morck 2005). This allows company boards to create a series of high-powered incentive structures for top management (i.e. very high salaries often paid in company shares or share-options), who are then given large discretion in shaping organizational structures within the firm. Such shareholder-dominated systems also allow boards to quickly remove top managers who are viewed as underperforming.

Shareholder dominated corporate governance within liberal market economies is complemented by the existence of large capital markets that companies can draw upon for finance. Such financing tends to be short-term in nature, meaning that the value of company shares will rapidly decline if firms fail to meet growth or profitability goals or if products fail to live up to expectations in the marketplace. This system is reinforced by an active marketplace for corporate control, suggesting that controlling shareholdings in failing firms can be easily bought by new ownership groups, who can then engage in restructuring of public companies including the hiring and firing of senior management. However, companies that do meet growth or profitability expectations can leverage high market valuations into a mechanism to raise substantial new funds through additional stock offerings or can use their shares as a currency for acquisitions.

Labour markets are often deregulated within liberal market economies. To preserve flexibility, the top management of most firms offer limited employment contracts to managers and skilled personnel. A corporate governance system focused on short-term incentive contracts reinforce this system. Extensive career mobility also permeates the ranks of middle management and skilled personnel. Laws restricting the mobility of skilled personnel within a given industry are weak. Courts in some states refuse to enforce 'competition clauses' inserted into employment contracts to prevent the movement of personnel to competitors (see Hyde 1998). As a result, poaching of personnel is widespread and within most liberal market economies a headhunting industry exists to assist firms in recruiting management. While firms can ask employees to sign non-disclosure agreements covering specific technologies, scientists and managers are generally free to move from firm to firm as they see fit, while managers can shed assets through hiring and firing as circumstances within the firm develop.

Within this ideal-typical description of a liberal market economy, patterns of financing, corporate governance, and labour market organization create a comparative institutional advantage towards the orchestration of radically innovative competencies. Each of the three characteristics associated with the Silicon Valley model of organizing entrepreneurial companies is supported by the LME model. Large and liquid capital markets generate support for initial public offerings for venture financed companies, while enabling corporate governance facilitate risk reduction strategies used by venture capitalists (see Tylecote and Visintin 2008).

Deregulated labour markets and the organization of career paths within firms based on the assumption of frequent employee turnover create active labour markets for managers and technical professionals. Finally, managers of high-technology start-ups within liberal market economies face few restrictions on the organization of remuneration and performance incentives. Patterns of large company organization focused on merit-based pay and promotion legitimate the use of high-powered incentive instruments within start-up firms.

While institutional frameworks within coordinated market economies (CMEs) favour the development of managerial commitments needed to support more cumulative or incremental innovation strategies, they create obstacles to the governance of organizational dilemmas facing radically innovative firms. Within CMEs labour market regulation and a stake-holder system of corporate governance promote long-term employment. Although there are important country variations in industrial relations and corporate governance laws that generate long-term employment equilibriums, within Northern European economies—such as Germany, the Netherlands, and Sweden—organized labour has used its power on supervisory boards as well as its formal consultative rights under co-determination laws over training, work organization, and hiring to obtain unlimited employment contracts (see Streeck 1984). Once the long-term employment norm for skilled workers was established, it spread to virtually all mid-level managers and technical employees. Overall, the active labour market for mid-career scientists and technicians is typically limited within CMEs.

Ownership and financial relationships within CMEs are strongly influenced by particular corporate governance rules. These economies are characterized by bank- or credit-based financial systems (Zysman 1983, Deeg 1999; Vitols 2001). Banks and other large financial actors such as insurance companies have historically had a strong oversight role on firms through seats on supervisory boards and through continuing ownership or proxy-voting ties linking large public companies (Edwards and Fischer 1994). Companies can obtain bank loans for long-term investments for assets that can be easily secured, such as land, capital investments, and merger and acquisition activity. Banks within CMEs can adopt a longer-term focus in part because they know that firms are able to offer long-term commitments to employees and other stakeholders to the firm, and can often closely monitor the status of their investments through seats on the supervisory board or other direct contacts. However, funding for riskier investments, such as human capital intensive research and development is more limited. For such investments companies within CMEs typically rely on retained earnings, limiting rapid investment into new technology areas.

Long-term employment and the stakeholder model of corporate governance have important repercussions for patterns of company organization (Charkham 1995). Managers have an incentive to create a broad consensus across the firm when major decisions will be made. As unilateral decision-making is limited, it is difficult for senior managers to create strong performance incentives for individual employees. Performance rewards are targeted at groups rather than individuals within companies located within CMEs, and individual performance assessments and bonus schemes are limited. Another implication of this system is that career structures become well defined and primarily based on broad education and experience within the firm rather than on short-term performance. Promotion tends to be based primarily on seniority within the firm and educational credentials rather than short-term individual performance.

Predominately non-market patterns of economic coordination create a series of disincentives towards the successful governance of each of the competency associated with the Silicon Valley model of organizing technology start-ups. The orientation of financial systems towards bank-based financing limits the viability of initial public offerings for new technology companies, particularly during their formative years. Long-term employment strategies used by large firms within CMEs limit the ability of start-ups with substantial failure risks to recruit experienced managers and skilled personnel, and also limit the viability of 'hire and fire' strategies used to manage technological volatility. Moreover, long-term employment patterns by large companies severely limit the size of labour markets for skilled personnel and, by so doing, inflate the career risk of leaving a 'safe' job to move to a failure-prone new technology venture. Finally, the collectivist orientation of decision-making and performance reviews within large companies weakens the credibility of high-powered performance incentives.

Does empirical evidence support the claim that LMEs enjoy a comparative institutional advantage over CMEs within radically innovative industries? While evidence does show variation in the success of radically innovative firms across liberal and coordinated market economies, some disconfirming evidence also exists. A study of patterns of industry specialization across software and biotechnology firms using data from stock market listings broadly showed that the UK had fostered many more publicly listed companies than Germany or Sweden (Casper and Whitley 2004). This study also found that a large majority of German companies within the software industry (fifty-four of sixty publicly listed firms) had avoided radically innovative strategies, having instead developed more 'incrementally innovative' strategies associated with enterprise software. Research has also compared the performance of the German, UK, and US biotechnology industries (Casper 2007; Casper and Kettler 2001; Casper 2000). These studies show that at an aggregate level the US and UK industries have outperformed the German industry, despite the German government's investment of some $3 billion in technology policies aimed at this industry during the 1995–2003 period. Moreover, key institutional reforms in Germany designed to better support Silicon-Valley-inspired organizational and financial models, such as the creation of a technology oriented stock market, have failed (see Vitols and Engelhardt 2005).

On the other hand, critics point towards the existence of a modest number of internationally competitive new technology firms within coordinated market economies, and particularly within the German biotechnology sector, as evidence that the varieties of capitalism approach is flawed (see e.g. Herrmann 2008a, b; Lange 2009). For example, while evidence suggests that at a more macro-level most German biotechnology firms are performing poorly (see Casper 2007, ch. 4), as of 2007 some thirty-five internationally competitive firms emerged, most of which are engaged in radically innovative therapeutic discovery research (Lange 2009). Clusters of radically innovative firms have appeared in other coordinated market economies, such as a cluster of highly innovative networking technology firms in Stockholm, Sweden (Glimstedt and Zander 2003).

Evidence that at least some firms within coordinated market economies have successfully developed radically innovative firms highlights an important theoretical issue within models of capitalism research, particularly versions of the approach drawing on institutional economics to establish micro-foundations. While drawing upon sectoral systems of innovation theory to help differentiate the characteristics of technology sectors is useful, the approach is functionalist at heart, minimizing the agency of firms and other activities within the economy. While the theory may have stronger micro-foundations linking institutional frameworks to actor-level organizational structure, in practice varieties of capitalism scholarship employs a similar explanatory logic as more sociologically informed studies: innovative outcomes are 'read off' from institutional logics.

Put differently, an implicit assumption within most comparative institutional theory is that micro-levels are cognitively aware of their institutional environment. This assumption is central within both sociological and rational-actor versions of institutional theory (see e.g. DiMaggio and Powell 1983). However, there is evidence that many actors, and especially entrepreneurs, do not chose their innovation strategy or corresponding organizational structures primarily in response to national institutional incentives and constraints within which they are embedded. Surveys of German biotechnology firms taken during the height of the country's technology boom, in 2001, showed that 65 per cent, or 240 biotechnology firms, had adopted therapeutics discovery as their primary strategy (Ernst and Young 2002). German entrepreneurs appear to have been far more responsive to international trends in the organization and strategy of biotechnology companies than to local institutional framework conditions. Comparative institutional research should not assume that firms or other actors are reflexive to the national institutions within which they are embedded.

In explaining the emergence of radically innovative biotechnology firms within coordinated market economies Herrmann (2008b) argues that these firms succeed, in part, through 'defecting' from their national model. This strategy is often plausible, as small innovative companies within coordinated market economies may not be legally obligated to follow regulative institutions, such as wage bargaining and industrial relations institutions that are structured around large companies within well-established industries (see Herrmann 2008b). Moreover, as discussed in more detail below in relation to globalization, companies may be able to develop effective work-arounds to create needed competencies.

While entrepreneurial start-ups with coordinated market economies may enjoy relative autonomy from institutions, this does not mean that national institutional frameworks do not strongly affect the performance of companies. In the German biotechnology case, for example, most firms have had severe trouble recruiting scientific managers. A comparative study of US, UK, and German firms showed that only 11 per cent of senior managers employed within German biotechnology firms had previous industry experience, compared to 88 per cent employed within the San Diego area within the US and 67 per cent in the Cambridge region of the UK (Casper 2007, ch. 4–5). In this case, labour market institutions, coupled with different employment practices within large pharmaceutical companies, created dramatically different markets for competencies across these countries, to the detriment of German biotechnology companies. Moreover, during the 2000s most German start-up companies faced severe challenges in raising finance, as over 80 per cent of German venture capital companies collapsed in the post-2001 period following the bursting of the Internet bubble in the United States.

Through structuring markets for competencies, institutional frameworks can strongly affect the competitive viability of firms with different innovation strategies. While over 200 German biotechnology companies initially selected radically innovative therapeutics research, as of 2008 no German biotechnology firm had successfully commercialized a drug discovered in its labs and the drug development pipeline of German firms contains about 50 per cent fewer candidate drugs than that for UK firms (Casper 2007, ch. 5; see also Lange 2009). Moreover, while the majority of German firms initially chose radically innovative strategies, most of the successful firms have adopted the more incrementally innovative platform technology strategy. During the height of the German biotechnology boom, in 2001, thirteen of sixteen German firms listed on the stock market had specialized in a variety of platform technologies in areas such as laboratory automation (Casper and Whitley 2004). In terms underlying technological characteristics, platform technologies share much in common with the machine tool industry, long an industry in which Germany has developed a strong competitive advantage.

An interesting avenue for future comparative institutional research is exploring more closely these and other mechanisms by which institutional frameworks impact companies. Research on subsequent waves or generations of entrepreneurial technology firms launched within Germany, and other coordinated market economies, might provide interesting insights into logics by which institutions impact and how actors strategize within the economy. Will founders of second generation technology start-ups in new industries such as biotechnology be more reflexive to institutions?

FUTURE RESEARCH DIRECTIONS

This survey set out to explore the rich terrain of research linking commercial innovation outcomes to comparative institutional research. While most comparative institutional research on innovation privileges the national level of analysis, a key agenda for future research is to more carefully understand how national institutions interact with variables and the local and international levels. This survey ends with a discussion of how recent research in the areas of regional economies and internationalization can be leveraged into the broad literature linking models of capitalism to innovation.

Alternative forms of coordination within regional economies

An important area for future research is reconciling the large literature from economic geography and regional studies more generally with the models of capitalism perspective. The emergence of regional economies creates challenges for the comparative institutional analysis of innovation. In particular, why does there exist so much regional heterogeneity surrounding the performance of high-technology industries, particularly within liberal market economies? Within the biotechnology sector, for example, the existence of regional clusters can be explained through the importance of local universities as a scientific hub that companies draw upon for technology and a scientific labour market. However, there are only three well-performing regional clusters within the United States, located in San Francisco, San Diego, and Boston. Most regions that have promising starting conditions for biotechnology have not developed successful regional clusters. A study by Romanelli and Feldman (2006) found that the majority of US regions that had established biotechnology companies during the launch of the industry, prior to 1980, did not develop successful clusters. Moreover, several US cities with prominent universities and medical schools, such as New York, Los Angeles, and Chicago, have not developed biotechnology clusters.

Patterns of coordination, particularly within the labour market, may be a key to explaining why some technology clusters within liberal market economies have achieved superior performance (see Christopherson and Storper 1987). Saxenian's (1994) well-known comparison of the Silicon Valley and Boston/Route 128 computer industries can help shed light on this problem. Saxenian argues that Silicon Valley's success is linked to the development of a social structure encouraging the development of numerous informal links across the region's scientists, engineers, and managers. These links raised the innovative capacity of Silicon Valley's firms through diffusing technological and market intelligence. Drawing on Granovetter's (1973) research on referral networks within labour markets, Saxenian argues that social networks within Silicon Valley increased labour mobility across firms and by so doing created an additional mechanism of knowledge diffusion. The declining fortunes of Route 128's computer and semiconductor industry, on the other hand, was influenced by autarkic practices of long-term employment within its companies that hindered the creation of flexible labour markets, coupled with very limited informal sharing across firms through social networks (see also Almeida and Kogut 1999).

Saxenian's approach shares a similar emphasis on coordination, though from a regional perspective, as the varieties of capitalism approach. From the point of view of individuals, there is a strong rationale for choosing to work only within start-up companies embedded within an agglomeration in which social ties promoting mobility are strong. Doing so can dramatically lower the career risk for founding teams and R & D staffs by creating numerous alternative employment options should a given venture fail, undergo managerial shake-ups at the behest of investors, or need to change its competency structure due to technological volatility. This helps explain why successful and presumably risk averse scientists and managers would give up prestigious careers in established companies or university labs to work within lucrative but highly risky start-ups: within successful clusters the embeddedness of individuals within social networks makes it 'safe' to do so. While focusing attention on explaining successful cases, and especially Silicon Valley, the career mobility approach also contains an explanation of why most regional economies fail. Most clusters, even if they reach sufficient size, do not develop the social networks or norms of high labour market flexibility needed to create the 'regional advantage' associated with Silicon Valley.

An important area for future research is to integrate findings from a regional level within a broader national institutional approach. The regional studies perspective implicitly assumes that patterns of coordination within regions may develop autonomously from the more overarching national patterns stressed by most models of capitalism research. The US, UK, and other liberal market economies have been leaders in developing regional clusters of radically innovative companies because national institutions structuring corporate governance rules, labour markets, and financial systems all conduce towards the creation of competencies along the Silicon Valley model. It is likely, however, that a regional level of coordination is missing from the broad varieties of capitalism approach.

The finding that there is a regional component to the successful creation of Silicon Valley-type technology clusters within LMEs opens the question of whether regional mechanisms could also emerge in CMEs to achieve patterns of economic coordination needed to support radically innovative companies. While studies of large coordinated market economies such as Germany lend support to the varieties of capitalism approach, research has identified cases of this type. Glimstedt and Zander (2003), for example, have argued that in the Stockholm region of Sweden, the local telecommunications giant Ericsson has used its leadership in a number of wireless technologies as a mechanism to promote entrepreneurship in the region, helping to create a cluster of radically innovative software companies (see also Casper and Whitley 2004).

The emphasis on mechanisms exposes a weakness of some institutional theory, a difficulty in examining the role of agency in developing mechanisms of change. The Stockholm case suggests that large companies may be catalysts. Studies have begun using social network analysis to examine processes by which coordination occurs within the economy. This research emphasizes the role of companies and entrepreneurs in forming the 'backbone' of social networks that can seed regional development (see Powell et al. 2005; Casper 2007). As well-performing technology clusters are rare, even within liberal market economies, gaining an understanding of the catalysts that help create necessary patterns of regional coordination is an important area for future research.

The impact of internationalization

A second area for future research is to integrate insights from the large literature on globalization into the comparative institutional analysis of innovation. As a complement to the assertion that entrepreneurial companies can, at times, defect from domestic institutions, several recent studies stress the importance of internationalization in creating new opportunities for firms located within inappropriate national institutional environments (Lange 2009; Herrmann 2008a; Jong 2006). Support for this theory is clearest in the case of venture capital. While most early or seed financing within German biotechnology companies has come from local investors, both public and private, there are numerous cases of German companies successfully recruiting UK venture capitalists to join syndicates for follow-on financing rounds. Moreover, the largest UK venture capital firms have set up offices in Munich, Germany's major biotechnology hub (Lange 2009). Venture capital has evolved into a cross-national industry, particularly in Europe, helping to lessen the dependence for at least some companies on domestic financial markets (see De Paauw 2008).

New technology companies can also shop globally for talent. An interesting study by Jong (2006), for example, finds that half the CEOs of Munich biotechnology firms are of international origin. Earlier research on the Munich cluster corroborates this finding; many of the senior executives of these firms are German returnees with valuable experience earned from working within the US biotechnology sector. German firms have also routinely tapped into international networks to recruit members to scientific advisory boards. In 2003, foreigners comprised 59 per cent of the scientific advisers of Munich biotechnology firms (Casper and Murray 2003: 339).

Clearly, the internationalization of some elements of the market for venture capital, combined with the creation of global labour markets, particularly for high-level managers, can lessen the impact of unfavourable domestic institutions. It makes sense, particularly within the tightly knit European economies, that companies can shop around for needed competencies. Less research exists on whether this is a common phenomenon outside Europe, and especially in the Asian economies.

Research on the globalization of markets within the context of varieties of capitalism needs to establish a theoretical terrain on the types of activities that are most likely to become impacted by globalization. Here the commonly used distinction found within strategic management theory between resources and capabilities may be important (see, e.g. Walker 2003, ch. 2). Most of the examples provided by

Herrmann, Jong, and Lange in their studies of German biotechnology concern resources: finance, individual employees, or advisers. It seems less likely that a similar market exists for organizational capabilities, for example, a research or development unit that has developed organizational routines needed to innovate within a complex technology area. It seems far more likely that companies will engage in foreign direct investment to acquire access to such competencies. At least three prominent German biotechnology companies, for example, have acquired competitors located in the Cambridge UK, Boston, and San Diego technology clusters in order to augment their drug discovery capabilities (see Casper 2007 ch. 4). Japanese pharmaceutical companies have pursued a similar strategy (Kneller 2007). This form of institutional arbitrage is likely to reinforce national institutional models rather than erode them (see Hall and Soskice 2001).

REFERENCES

ALLEN, M. (2004). 'The Varieties of Capitalism Paradigm: Not Enough Variety?', *Socio-Economic Review* 2, 87–108.

——(2006). 'Can Variation in Public Policies Account for Differences in Comparative Advantage?', *Journal of Public Policy* 26: 1–19.

ALMEIDA, P. and B. KOGUT (1999). 'Localization of Knowledge and the Mobility of Engineers in Regional Networks', *Management Science* 45(7): 905–17.

AMABLE, B. (2004). *The Diversity of Modern Capitalism*, (Oxford: Oxford University Press).

AOKI, M. (2002). *Toward a Comparative Institutional Analysis*, (Cambridge, MA: MIT Press).

BAHRAMI, H. and S. EVANS (1995). 'Flexible Re-cycling and High-Technology Entrepreneurship', *California Management Review* 37(3) (Spring): 62–88.

BORRUS, M., J. MILLSTEIN, and J. ZYSMAN (1981). 'Trade and Development in Semiconductors: Japanese Challenge and American Response', in J. Zysman and L. Tyson (eds.), *American Industry in International Competition*, (Ithaca, NY: Cornell University Press).

BRESCHI, S. and F. MALERBA (1997). 'Sectoral Innovation Systems: Technological Regimes, Schumpeterian Dynamics, and Spatial Boundaries', in C. Edquist (ed.), *Systems of Innovation: Technologies, Institutions and Organizations*, (London: Pinter), 130–55.

BREZNITZ, D. (2007). *Innovation and the State: Political Choice and Strategies for Choice in Israel, Taiwan, and Ireland*, (New Haven: Yale University Press).

CALDER, K. (1993). *Strategic Capitalism*, (Princeton, NJ: Princeton University Press).

CASPER, S. (2000). 'Institutional Adaptiveness, Technology Policy, and the Diffusion of New Business Models: The Case of German Biotechnology', *Organization Studies* 21: 887–914.

——(2007). *Creating Silicon Valley in Europe: Public Policy Towards New Technology Industries*, (Oxford: Oxford University Press).

——and H. KETTLER (2001). 'National Institutional Frameworks and the Hybridization of Entrepreneurial Business Models: The German and UK Biotechnology Sectors', *Industry and Innovation* vol. 8.

——and F. MURRAY (2003). 'Examining the Marketplace for Ideas: How Local are European Biotechnology Clusters', in Maureen McKelvey and Jens Hageman (eds.), *Industrial Dynamics in European Biotechnology*, (London: Edward Elgar).

——and D. Soskice (2004). 'Sectoral Systems of Innovation and Varieties of Capitalism: Explaining the Development of High-Technology Entrepreneurship in Europe', in F. Malerba (ed.), *Sectoral Systems of Innovation*, (Cambridge: Cambridge University Press), 348–87.

——and R. Whitley (2004). 'Managing Competences in Entrepreneurial Technology Firms: A Comparative Institutional Analysis of Germany, Sweden and the UK', *Research Policy* 33 (1): 89–106.

——M. Lehrer, and D. Soskice (1999). 'Can High-technology Industries Prosper in Germany: Institutional Frameworks and the Evolution of the German Software and Biotechnology Industries', *Industry and Innovation* 6: 6–23.

Castells, M. (1996). *The Rise of the Network Society*, (Oxford: Blackwell).

Charkham, J. (1995). *Keeping Good Company: A Study of Corporate Governance in Five Countries*, (Oxford: Oxford University Press).

Christopherson, S. and M. Storper (1987). 'Flexible Specialization and Regional Industrial Agglomeration: The Case of the US Motion Picture Industry', *Annals of the Association of American Geographers* 77: 104–17.

Crouch, C. (2005). *Capitalist Diversity and Change*, (Oxford: Oxford University Press).

De Paauw, L. (2008). 'Institutional Recombination and Change in Organizational Strategy: The Case of the Biotech Hybrid'. Working paper, Manchester Business School.

Deeg, R. (1999). *Finance Capitalism Unveiled: Banks and the German Political Economy*, (Ann Arbor: University of Michigan Press).

——and G. Jackson (2007). 'Towards a More Dynamic Theory of Capitalist Variety', *Socio-Economic Review* 5: 149–79.

DiMaggio, P. J. (1988). 'Interest and Agency in Institutional Theory', *Institutional Patterns and Organisations*, (Cambridge, MA: Ballinger).

——and W. Powell (1983). 'The Iron Cage Revisited: Institutional Isomorphism and Collective Rationality in Organizational Fields', *American Sociological Review* 48: 147–60.

Edwards, J. and K. Fischer (1994). *Banks, Finance and Investment in Germany*, (Cambridge: Cambridge University Press).

Ernst and Young (2002). 'Neue Chancen: Deutscher Biotechnologie Report 2002', Mannheim: Ernst and Young.

Gingerich, D. and P. Hall (2006). 'Varieties of Capitalism and Institutional Complementarities in the Macroeconomy: An Empirical Analysis'. MPIfG Discussion Paper 04/05.

Glimstedt, H. and U. Zander (2003). 'Sweden's Wireless Wonders: Defining the Swedish Internet Economy', in B. Kogut (ed.), *The Global Internet Economy*, (Cambridge, MA: MIT Press).

Granovetter, Mark (1973). 'The Strength of Weak Ties', *American Journal of Sociology*, 78(6) (May): 1360–80.

Hall, P. (1986). *Governing the Economy*, (Princeton, NJ: Princeton University Press).

——and David Soskice (2001). 'Introduction', in Peter Hall and David Soskice (eds.), *Varieties of Capitalism*, (Oxford: Oxford University Press), 1–70.

Hancké, R. (2002). *Large Firms and Institutional Change: Industrial Renewal and Economic Restructuring in France*, (Oxford: Oxford University Press).

Hart, J. (1992). *Rival Capitalists*, (Ithaca, NY: Cornell University Press).

Hassel, A. (2007). 'The Curse of Institutional Security: The Erosion of German Trade Unionism', *Industrielle Beziehungen* 14: 176–91.

Herrigel, G. (1993). 'Large Firms, Small Firms, and the Governance of Flexible Specialization: The Case of Baden Württemberg and Socialized Risk', in Bruce Kogut (ed.), *Country Competitiveness*, (New York: Oxford University Press).

HERRMANN, A. (2008a). *One Political Economy, One Competitive Strategy?*, (Oxford: Oxford University Press).

——(2008b). 'Rethinking the Link between Labor Market Flexibility and Corporate Competitiveness: A Critique of the Institutionalist Literature', *Socio-Economic Review* 6: 237–669.

HOLLINGSWORTH, R. (1997). 'Continuities and Changes in Social Systems of Production: The Cases of Germany, Japan, and the United States', in R. Hollingsworth and R. Boyer (eds.), *Contemporary Capitalism*, (Cambridge: Cambridge University Press), 265–310.

——and R. BOYER (eds.) (1997). *Contemporary Capitalism*, (Cambridge: Cambridge University Press).

HYDE, A. (1998). 'Employment Law after the Death of Employment', *University of Pennsyvania Journal of Labor Law* 1: 105–20.

JONG, S. (2006). 'The Development of Munich and Cambridge Therapeutic Biotech Firms: A Case Study of Institutional Adaption', EUI Working Paper, SPS no. 2006/10.

KATZENSTEIN, P. (1978). 'Conclusion: Domestic Structures and Strategies of Foreign Economic Policy', in P. Katzenstein (ed.), *Between Power and Plenty*, (Madison: University of Wisconsin Press).

——(1987). *Policy and Politics in West Germany: Towards the Growth of a Semi-Sovereign State*, (Philadelphia: Temple University Press).

——(1989). 'Stability and Change in the Emerging Third Republic', in P. Katzenstein (ed.), *Industry and Politics in West Germany*, (Ithaca, NY: Cornell University Press).

KENNEY, M. (ed.) (2000). *Understanding Silicon Valley: The Anatomy of an Entrepreneurial Region*, (Palo Alto: Stanford University Press).

KITSCHELT, H. (1991). 'Industrial Governance, Innovation Strategies, and the Case of Japan: Sectoral Governance or Cross-national Comparative Analysis?', *International Organization* 45: 453–93.

KNELLER, R. (2007). *Bridging Islands: Venture Companies and the Future of American and Japanese Industry*, (Oxford: Oxford University Press).

KRISTENSEN, P. H. and J. ZEITLIN (2005). *Local Players in Global Games: The Strategic Constitution of a Multinational Corporation*, (Oxford: Oxford University Press).

LANGE, K. (2009). 'Institutional Embeddedness and the Strategic Leeway of Actors: The Case of the German Therapeutic Biotech Industry', *Socio-Economic Review* 7.

LÉCUYER, C. (2006). *Making Silicon Valley: Innovation and the Growth of High Tech, 1930–1970*, (Cambridge, MA.: MIT Press).

LEHRER, MARK (2000). 'Has Germany Finally Solved Its High-Tech Problem? The Recent Boom in German Technolology-based Entrepreneurism', *California Management Review* 42: 89–107.

LERNER, J. and P. GOMPERS (2001). *The Money of Invention: How Venture Capital Creates New Wealth*, (Cambridge, MA: Harvard Business School Press).

LOCKE, R. (1995). *Remaking the Italian Economy*, (Ithaca, NY: Cornell University Press).

LORIAUX, M. (1991). *France After Hegemony*, (Ithaca, NY: Cornell University Press).

MALERBA, F. (1985). *The Semiconductor Business: The Economics of Rapid Growth and Decline*, (Madison: University of Wisconsin Press).

——(2004). *Sectoral Systems of Innovation*, (Cambridge: Cambridge University Press).

——and L. ORSENIGO (1993). 'Technological Regimes and Firm Behavior', *Industrial and Corporate Change* 2, 45–71.

MILGROM, P. and J. ROBERTS, (1993). *Economics, Organization, and Management*, (Eaglewood Cliffs: Prentice Hill).

————(1995). 'Complementarities: Industrial Strategy, Structure, and Change in Manufacturing', *Journal of Accounting and Economics* 19: 179–208.

MILLER, GARY (1992). *Managerial Dilemmas*, (Cambridge: Cambridge University Press).

MORCK, R. (ed.) (2005). *History of Corporate Governance around the World*, (Chicago: University of Chicago Press).

MOWERY, D. and R. NELSON (1999). *Sources of Industrial Leadership*, (Cambridge: Cambridge University Press).

NELSON, R. (1993). *National Innovation Systems*, (Oxford: Oxford University Press).

OHMAE, K. (1990). *The Borderless World*, (New York: Harper Collins).

PERROW, C. (1984). *Normal Accidents: Living with High-Risk Technologies*, (New York: Basic Books).

PIERSON, P. (2004). *Politics in Time: History, Institutions, and Social Analysis*, (Princeton, NJ: Princeton University Press).

PORTER, M. (1985). *Competitive Advantage*, (New York: Free Press).

POWELL, W., D. WHITE, K. KOPUT, and J. OWEN-SMITH (2005). 'Network Dynamics and Field Evolution: The Growth of Inter-organizational Collaboration in the Life Sciences', *American Journal of Sociology* 110: 1132–1205.

PRESTOWITZ, C. (1993). *Trading Places*, (New York: Basic Books).

ROE, M. (1994). *Strong Managers, Weak Owners: The Political Roots of American Corporate Finance*, (Princeton, NJ: Princeton University Press).

ROMANELLI, E. and M. FELDMAN (2006). 'Anatomy of Cluster Development: The Case of U.S. Human Biotherapeutics, 1976–2003', in P. Braunerhjelm and M. Feldman (eds.), *Cluster Genesis: The Origins and Emergence of Technology-based Economic Development*, (Oxford: Oxford University Press).

SAMUELS, R. (1987). *The Business of the Japanese State: Energy Markets in Comparative and Historical Perspective*, (Ithaca, NY: Cornell University Press).

SAXENIAN, A. (1994). *Regional Advantage*, (Cambridge MA: Harvard University Press).

SCHMIDT, V. (2002). *The Futures of European Capitalism*, (Oxford: Oxford University Press).

SCHMITTER, P. (1981). 'Interest Intermediation and Regime Governability in Contemporary Western Europe and North America', in S. Berger (ed.), *Organizing Interests in Western Europe*, (Cambridge: Cambridge University Press).

SCHNEIBERG, M. (2007). 'What's on the Path? Path Dependence, Organizational Diversity and the Problem of Institutional Change in the US Economy, 1900–1950', *Socio-Economic Review* 5, 47–80.

STEINMO, S., K. THELEN, and F. LONGSTRETCH (eds.) (1992). *Structuring Politics: Historical Instituitonalism in Comparative Analysis*, (Cambridge, UK: Cambridge University Press).

STREECK, W. (1984). *Industrial Relations in West Germany: A Case Study of the Car Industry*, (New York: St. Martin's Press).

————(1992). 'On the Institutional Preconditions of Diversified Quality Production', in W. Streeck (ed.), *Social Institutions and Economic Performance*, (London and Newberry Park: Sage).

————(1997). 'Beneficial Constraints: On the Economic Limits of Rational Voluntarism', in Hollingsworth and Boyer, (eds.), *Contemporary Capitalism*, (Cambridge: Cambridge University Press).

TAYLOR, M. (2004). 'Empirical Evidence Against Variety of Capitalism's Theory of Technological Innovation', *International Organization* 58: 601–31.

TEECE, D. (1986). 'Profiting from Technological Innovation: Implications for Integration, Collaboration, Licensing, and Public Policy', *Research Policy* 15: 285–305.

TEECE, D. and G. PISANO (1994). 'Dynamic Capabilities and the Firm: An Introduction', *Industrial and Corporate Change* 3: 537–56.

THELEN, K. (1991). *Union of Parts*, (Ithaca, NY: Cornell University Press).

——(2004). *How Institutions Evolve: The Political Economy of Skills in Germany, Britain, Japan and the United States*, (Cambridge: Cambridge University Press).

TURNER, L. (1991). *Democracy at Work: Changing World Markets and the Future of Labor Unions*, (Ithaca, NY: Cornell University Press).

——(1997). *The Remarkable Success of German Unification: Testing the Limits of Social Partnership*, (Ithaca, NY: Cornell University Press).

TYLECOTE, A. and F. VISINTIN (2008). *Corporate Governance, Finance and the Technological Advantage of Nations*, (London: Routledge).

VITOLS, S. (2001). 'Varieties of Corporate Governance: Comparing Germany and the UK', in P. Hall and D. Soskice (eds.), *Varieties of Capitalism: The Institutional Foundations of Comparative Advantage*, (Oxford: Oxford University Press), 337–60.

——and L. ENGELHARDT (2005). 'National Institutions and High Tech Industries: A Varieties of Capitalism Perspective on the Failure of Germany's "Neuer Markt"'. WZB Discussion Paper SP II 2005–03, Berlin: WZB Feb. 2005.

——STEVEN CASPER, DAVID SOSKICE, and STEPHEN WOLCOCK (1997). *Corporate Governance in Large British and German Companies*, (London: Anglo-German Foundation).

VOGEL, S. (1996). *Freer Markets, More Rules*, (Ithaca, NY: Cornell University Press).

WALKER, G. (2003). *Modern Competitive Strategy*, (New York: McGraw-Hill).

WEISS, L. (1998). *The Myth of the Powerless State*, (Ithaca, NY: Cornell University Press).

WHITLEY, R. (1999). *Divergent Capitalisms: The Social Structuring and Change of Business Systems*, (Oxford: Oxford University Press).

——(2003). 'Competition and Pluralism in the Public Sciences: The Impact of Institutional Frameworks on the Organization of Academic Science', *Research Policy* 32: 1015–29.

WINTER, S. (1987). 'Knowledge and Competence as Strategic Assets', in D. J. Teece (ed.), *The Competitive Challenge: Strategies for Industrial Innovation and Renewal*, (Cambridge, MA: Ballinger).

WOODWARD, J. (1965). *Industrial Organization: Theory and Practice*, (Oxford: Oxford University Press).

ZIDER, B. (1998). 'How Venture Capital Works', *Harvard Business Review* 76(6): 131–39.

ZYSMAN, J. (1977). *Political Strategies for Industrial Order: State, Market, and Industry in France.* (Berkeley: University of California Press).

——(1983). *Governments, Markets, and Growth: Finance and the Politics of Industrial Change*, (Cornell: Cornell University Press).

——and L. TYSON (1983). *American Industry in International Competition*, (Ithaca, NY: Cornell University Press).

CHAPTER 13

....

CHANGING COMPETITION MODELS IN MARKET ECONOMIES: THE EFFECTS OF INTER-NATIONALIZATION, TECHNOLOGICAL INNOVATIONS, AND ACADEMIC EXPANSION ON THE CONDITIONS SUPPORTING DOMINANT ECONOMIC LOGICS[1]

....

RICHARD WHITLEY

[1] Earlier versions of this chapter were presented to the final workshop of the Translearn project—*Transnational Learning through Local Experimenting*—held at Sannas Manor, Porvoo, Finland, 18–19 March, 2009 and to an ERIM workshop held at the Erasmus University, Rotterdam on 3 April, 2009. Comments and suggestions made on these occasions, and by Glenn Morgan and John L. Campbell, have been helpful in improving the argument and its presentation.

INTRODUCTION

Comparative analyses of economic organization and development have identified a number of distinctive complexes of dominant institutions, types of leading firms, and economic coordination processes that became established in different kinds of market economies (e.g. Amable 2003; Hall and Soskice 2001; Hollingsworth and Boyer 1997b). These models of social systems of production or varieties of capitalism typically linked particular institutional arrangements governing economic activities with particular kinds of firms and competition models to constitute relatively coherent systems that dominated certain economies in specific historical periods or, in some accounts, entire epochs of capitalism.

A central concern of these analyses of competing capitalisms has been to show how the dominant institutions governing private property rights, access to capital, the development and use of labour power, competitive behaviour, and other economic activities vary significantly across capitalist economies in ways that structure the nature, direction, and actions of firms and other significant economic actors (Casper and Whitley 2004; Morgan et al. 2005; Whitley 1999, 2007). In particular, the business strategies and competitive capabilities of leading firms were seen as being heavily influenced by the kinds of institutions that structured capital, labour, and product markets in different market economies such that their relative success varied between industries and markets. Constraints on short-term opportunism in West Germany, for instance, have been seen to encourage companies to pursue diversified quality production strategies rather than to focus on cutting costs and competing on price (Streeck 1992).

In practice, if not always in theory, many such configurations of institutional arrangements and dominant firm types and strategies have tended to be identified with particular post-Second World War nation-states. The United States, for example, is often taken to exemplify a liberal market economy, while post-war West Germany manifests many features of coordinated market economies (Soskice 1999). However, the extent to which the key institutions in any nation-state are mutually supportive in their implications for economic action varies greatly between countries and historical periods, as does their standardization of economic logics across sectors and sub-national regions (Whitley 2007: 46–55).

Furthermore, in considering how and why particular competitive priorities become dominant in differently organized market economies, it is important to distinguish between the conditions encouraging leading firms to pursue particular kinds of strategies, on the one hand, and the varied institutional arrangements that contribute to fulfilling these conditions, on the other. As Boyer (1988) has emphasized, different institutions can have similar consequences for firm behaviour in different economies, and similar kinds of institutional change can have different effects in contrasting circumstances, as the so-called 'big bang' financial deregulation efforts did in London and Tokyo (Laurence 2001).

Equally, changing conditions can render once dominant competitive strategies less effective in certain economies. If, for instance, the pursuit of low-cost production and price-based competition in the Fordist model depends on a particular kind of regulatory regime that stabilizes demand levels, as Hirst and Zeitlin (1997) among others have suggested, then changes in the business environment that threaten such regimes can be expected to reduce its success. Similarly, removing barriers to entry by large firms and reducing trust between small firms in coordinated industrial districts will probably weaken some of the key conditions supporting the effectiveness of quality focused competition models and could destroy their economic viability (Crouch et al. 2001; 2004; Friedman 1988). In general, changes in particular institutions and other features of the business environment are likely to affect the key supporting, or inhibiting, conditions for different competition models, differently in contrasting situations and so have varied outcomes across market economies (Rule 1997).

In so far as distinctive forms of capitalism in which leading firms followed particular kinds of competition model did become institutionalized in differently organized market economies during the first three decades after 1945, then, we would expect these to have been affected by subsequent changes in national and international institutions, geo-political shifts such as the collapse of the Soviet Union, and other changes in the international business environment. In particular, changes in state policies and dominant socio-political coalitions in OECD countries that have encouraged greater economic internationalization can be expected to result in a reduction of the national specificity of dominant competition models based on different levels of flexibility in responding to change, customization, and price in gaining market share and profitability.

To understand how the post-war forms of capitalism and prevalent competition models are likely to have altered as a result of changes in national and international business environments, then, it is important to examine these connections between different kinds of competition models and institutional regimes in the context of shifting markets, technologies, and institutions in more detail. To do this, we need to specify: a) the main ways in which dominant competition models have varied in the post-war period, b) the key socio-economic conditions encouraging leading firms to follow such models, and c) the likely impact of recent institutional, market, and technological changes on these conditions (Boyer 2004). Accordingly, in this chapter, I distinguish between the major competitive approaches adopted by leading firms in the OECD economies in the post-war period and outline a framework for analysing how some of the key changes in the business environment since the collapse of the Bretton Woods system have affected the conditions encouraging companies to pursue these in different contexts.

First, I present a taxonomy of seven ideal types of competition models that resemble many of the dominant business strategies identified in comparative studies of twentieth-century capitalisms, such as Fordism, Diversified Quality Production (DQP), and radical, discontinuous innovation. These models reflect the different priorities that firms adopt in deciding how to compete in different markets and how they adapt to changing patterns of demand. In the following section, I suggest how different kinds of conditions seem likely to encourage firms to follow particular types. Next, I summarize the major changes that have taken place in, and between, many market economies since the 1960s that have often been cited as important factors influencing institutional and business system restructuring, and indicate how they can be expected to alter these conditions, and so affect dominant competition models in different economies.

TYPES OF COMPETITION MODELS

Competition models are here understood as idealized combinations of particular kinds of trade-offs that firms are encouraged by the dominant institutions governing economic activities to make when competing in market economies. The rise of the mass production–mass consumption 'paradigm' (Freeman and Louca 2001: 273–7) in some twentieth-century societies, for instance, was greatly facilitated by the absence of strong constraints on market entry and exit, predatory pricing, and rapid hiring and firing of employees at managerial behest (Hollingsworth 1991). Additionally, since this kind of mass production involves substantial investment in dedicated technologies and routines for manufacturing highly standardized products using predominantly unskilled labour, it depends on market demand being reliably large, and so the Fordist economic logic typically incorporates mass markets dominated by large oligopolistic enterprises as well as mass production. Such sustained and pre-dictable patterns of demand have been supported by the development of the welfare state in many countries in the post-war period (Hirst and Zeitlin 1997).

In many of the discussions of the different kinds of competition models current in the twentieth century, Fordism has been contrasted with what came to be described as flexible specialization (e.g. Hirst and Zeitlin 1991; Piore and Sabel 1984), although the term has been used in many different senses. This model typically includes small batch production of largely customized goods made with flexible general-purpose machinery by skilled workers. Competitive strategies are here focused more on the quality of goods and services and their customization for different kinds of demand than on price, and rely on the existence of consumers able and willing to pay more for distinctive, high-quality outputs.

Extending this contrast between Fordism and flexible specialization, Hollings-worth and Boyer (1997a) suggest that three key dimensions for comparing different social systems of production are the volume of production, the basis of competition, and the flexibility or speed of adjustment to market and technical changes. These involve trade-offs between: a) realizing economies of scale in producing large vol-umes of standard products versus meeting the needs of different customers through shorter and more customer-specific production runs, b) gaining and keeping business through low prices versus high quality and functionality, and c) responding rapidly and radically to changing demand and technologies versus reducing costs by limiting changes to production processes and products. While firms often try to combine these features of competition models, by, for instance, standardizing components while differentiating final products or improving quality while keeping prices down through outsourcing some parts of the production chain, at some point on these dimensions trade-offs between them are involved and reflect variations in market conditions, technologies, and dominant institutions.

On the basis of these three dimensions, four distinct alternative social systems of production to Fordist mass production were identified by Hollingsworth and Boyer: Adaptive production, flexible diversified quality production, customized production, and diversified quality mass production (see, also, Rubery and Grimshaw 2003: 56–70). Most of these emphasize quality-based competition as opposed to the Fordist focus on price, but vary in their speed of response to environmental changes. Examples of these four types of social systems of production at the end of the twentieth century are claimed to be found in the pharmaceutical and software sectors, the consumer electronics industry, consumer fashion goods industries, and the car industry, respectively.

These examples highlight the variety of different kinds of competition models to be found in late twentieth-century capitalism and the need to go beyond simple dichotomies if we are to understand how established systems of economic coordination and control are changing. By combining the three main dimensions of volume, competitive basis, and flexibility used by Boyer and Hollingsworth, we can identify eight possible types of competition models as shown in Table 13.1. These dimensions are particularly important in contrasting competition models because they deal with the major trade-offs that firms make in deciding how to compete and develop organization-specific competitive advantages. Although much of the literature concerned with these features focuses on manufacturing sectors, most of the trade-offs involved are equally applicable to service sector businesses.

In this table, I have dichotomized the three dimensions between 'low' and 'medium to high production volumes' of standardized goods and services, competition based primarily on 'cost and price' reductions or on 'improving quality and functionality', and 'low to medium flexibility' versus 'high levels of fast responsiveness' to changing conditions. Low production volumes are differentiated from medium to high levels because the key decision here is whether to seek economies of scale through substantial batch sizes or contrarily focus on satisfying customer needs by tailoring outputs to suit them. Similarly, the key distinction with respect to organizational flexibility concerns the rapidity and wide ranging nature of firms' responsiveness to changing environments, particularly the speed with which, and extent to which, product ranges and work processes are modified as patterns of demand and technologies alter, rather than incremental, competence enhancing improvements.

Two of these ideal types of competition models, *Fordism* and *opportunism*, focus on high volume, price-based competition but differ greatly in their flexibility and

Table 13.1: Ideal types of competition models

Dominant Basis of Competition					
		Reducing costs and prices	Improving quality and functions		
Volumes of standardized outputs	Low	Low cost, small batch production with cheap labour that becomes uncompetitive once large volume factory production develops	Craft and traditional professional production	Low to medium	Flexibility and speed of response to market and technical change
			Flexible customized production of goods and services	High	
	Medium to high	Fordism	Diversified quality production	Low to medium	
		Opportunism	Flexible mass production of differentiated goods and services	High	
		Discontinuous innovation			

speed or responsiveness to changes in demand. Fordism focuses on the large-scale production of homogenous goods with dedicated machinery and highly routinized work procedures for mass, largely undifferentiated consumer markets. As Chandler (1977, 1990) has emphasized, it was the integration of rationalized production processes, with extensive advertising and mass marketing techniques through large managerial hierarchies in the USA that enabled many large companies to reap substantial economies of scale and scope throughout much of the twentieth century in that very large consumer market. The Fordist competition model therefore involves more than the pursuit of low costs and prices through standardization and routinization of production. It additionally incorporates the control—or at least rendering predictable—of large markets for the volume of outputs and the systematic coordination of production with marketing and sales activities through managerial routines.

Key to its success has been the ability of engineers and managers to design and control production processes to achieve high throughput levels, reduce costs continually, and ensure market dominance through low prices. Fordist firms therefore had to develop strong coordinating capabilities to realize economies of scale through the establishment of a powerful technostructure (Mintzberg 1983: 15–16) to specify, control, and integrate work routines and activities. By routinizing work procedures and dividing tasks into their simplest components, firms were able to rely on unskilled or semi-skilled workers who could easily be replaced when business conditions changed. Flexibility of outputs was therefore achieved by changing the volume of goods produced, not their characteristics or the ways they were produced. As Boyer and Durand (1997) have emphasized, Fordism is essentially a producer driven production system, in which consumers are sold what companies produce rather than firms producing what consumer tastes demand.

Such an elaborate and large-scale system focused on the low-cost production and sale of standardized goods was expensive to establish and difficult to change quickly to accommodate market shifts. It therefore required control over critical inputs to ensure continuous throughput and use of the costly specialized machinery. Particularly in the USA since the implementation of anti-trust legislation, this encouraged substantial vertical integration to ensure continuity of supply and, in some sectors, control over distribution channels and after-sales service (Hirst and Zeitlin 1997; Hollingsworth 1991; Langlois 2003). The most obvious example of the Fordist competition model is the twentieth-century US car industry, but it also has been followed in many consumer durable sectors in the USA, as well as in parts of the food industry (Chandler 1977). More recently, a number of service sector firms have developed Fordist characteristics, as in the fast food restaurant business and retail banking, in order to realize economies of scale by standardizing work processes, outputs, and customer contacts.

While opportunistic production shares many of these characteristics, it is distinguished from Fordism by its ability to shift production between product lines such as wigs, plastic flowers, and toys relatively quickly and adapt rapidly to changing market demands. Exemplified by the 'hustle' economy of Hong Kong, as well as some other Asian Pacific Asian economies in the 1970s and 1980s (Enright et al. 1997: 45–8; Redding 1990), which switched its major industries with impressive speed, this kind of production system competes both on price and fast responsiveness to changes in customer needs in its major markets that are often some distance away. In many East Asian economies, the rapid growth of this competition model was tied to the restructuring of the US retail sector and the rise of large retail chains such as Wal-Mart, as well as, of course, reductions in transport and information transmission costs (Hamilton 2006: 156–78).

In contrast to Fordism, this flexibility is based on relatively low investment in capital intensive, dedicated machinery, limited development of managerial routines, and formal procedures. Instead of realizing large economies of scale through high levels of formal standardization of work processes and coordination routines, the key competences here are entrepreneurial; especially the ability of the owner manager to seize new opportunities rapidly by changing products, processes, and industries, together with an ability to reorganize work processes and direct semi-skilled labour. They do not, though, involve the development of radically new products and processes that restructure markets. Responsiveness is here more reactive to changing demand patterns than proactively reshaping them.

The remaining two possible price-based with low volumes types of competition model are unlikely to be stable because high volume production strategies can usually dominate small-scale producers unless the latter are institutionally protected from predatory pricing by large firms. While small-scale production of cheap goods with poorly paid labour is of course not uncommon in the history of capitalism, it is difficult to see how it can compete on price against large volume factory-based competition. This has especially become the case since declining communication and transport costs coupled with the internationalization of competition have intensified competitive pressures from large volume producers across the world and helped to create mass international markets that encourage investment in high volume production facilities.

The four types of quality-based competition models differ in their standardization of outputs and batch volume sizes, on the one hand, and in their flexibility and speed of responsiveness on the other. Craft production combines small-batch production by highly skilled workers with considerable customization and an ability to respond to incremental demand changes. However, the formal development and certification of such skills can limit the speed of adjustment to radical technical and market shifts, particularly where these devalue current competences and threaten social identities. Cooperation between specialist producers can facilitate learning and incremental innovation in craft-based industrial districts so that firms can continue to adapt effectively to such shifts, but their dependence on institutionalized and slow chang- ing forms of expertise limits the degree of work restructuring that can be achieved in the short term. The stability of craft skills here resembles that of the traditional professions where practitioner elites control training, certification, and labour mar- ket entry and some project-based firms in the feature film industry (Christopherson 2002; Whitley 2006).

Flexible customized production, however, combines limited volume production of quite customized goods and services and quality-based competition with faster rates of market responsiveness and flexibility. It is perhaps particularly noticeable in many business service industries where highly skilled staff work together to produce specialized services for a wide range of customers. Innovation in developing new services is here key to firm growth and personal careers, as Anand et al. (2007) have shown in their study of new practice development in management consultancy and related fields. Similarly in advertising, originality and 'freshness' seem to be a competitive advantage (Grabher 2002), and so employers and employees frequently change the kinds of services and skills they offer. Here, firms are able to organize product development and delivery teams in a variety of ways for different customers and can acquire—or coordinate through subcontracting and various forms of col- laboration—new knowledge and skills relatively easily. While depending greatly on the skills of staff to provide high quality services, their expertise is organized and directed to deal with a range of complex and novel problems in this model.

Whereas traditional professional and craft production systems typically segment tasks and problems around established skills, as in Mintzberg's (1983: 190–210) characterization of professional bureaucracies, in this competition model they are dealt with by collectively coordinated teams of experts that have to work together in novel ways and generate new knowledge and expertise in tackling unusual problems. Work roles and the division of labour are more flexible and responsive to changing customer demands in this model. Solutions and outputs are correspondingly varied and not so bounded by certified skills. It follows that a key managerial competence here concerns the ability to acquire, coordinate, and motivate teams of diversely skilled people to work together in solving customers' problems in ways that develop collective capabilities as much as individual skills. Many business service firms employing professionally trained staff to solve complex and novel customer problems pursue this kind of competition model.

Diversified quality production (DQP) combines relatively large volume production of differentiated goods and services with a competitive focus on high quality and responding to changing customer needs. According to Streeck (1992: 5–7), technological changes in the 1970s, particularly the growing use of micro-electronic control devices, enabled many German firms to lower the breakeven point of mass production and customize production of high quality goods to a much greater extent than before. In the institutionally rich society of West Germany, where market relationships were embedded in an array of cooperative institutions and a highly skilled labour force was used to engaging in joint problem solving, such new technologies led many firms in the broad engineering sector to focus on customized quality production in which small-batch production of customer-specific goods was combined with large-batch production of basic components.

Flexible mass production of differentiated goods and services (Flexible MPDG) is differentiated from the DQP model by its much faster responsiveness to technological and market changes. While both of these models are more flexible than Fordism in adapting their product lines for changing consumer tastes as well as improving production processes, flexible MPDG is more able to restructure production and incorporate technical changes into the development of new product ranges speedily. In particular, firms pursuing flexible MPDG strategies focus on the rapid development and commercialization of new products on a continuing basis by investing considerable resources in R & D and using their technological competences to diversify into related fields and markets. A key competitive capability for such firms is their ability to absorb, develop, and adapt new knowledge quickly for product development and marketing, and so integrating research, design, manufacturing, and marketing activities through cross-functional project teams is often a core competence, as seems to be the case in the Japanese consumer electronics industry (Berggren and Nomura 1997; Sturgeon 2007). DQP strategies, in contrast, are less concerned with the rapid introduction of new products to large markets as opposed to continuing incremental improvements of more customized outputs within particular technological trajectories.

In addition to these eight ideal types of competitive models, the success of radical innovation strategies in some emerging industries, such as biotechnology and parts of the ICT sector, suggest a need to distinguish further between forms of responsiveness to change, as do Boyer and Hollingsworth (1997) in their separation of adaptive production from flexible DQP. In particular, recent work on what Teece (2000: 54–9) has termed high-flex Silicon Valley type firms and networks and their reconfigurational dynamic organizational capabilities has highlighted the growing significance of *discontinuous innovation* strategies in which current competences become superseded by quite different ones (Casper 2007; Teece et al. 1997). Such competitive models focus on generating and commercializing disruptive technologies that radically change markets and threaten the leading position of dominant firms in them (Christensen 1997).

Whereas the flexible MPDG logic focuses on extending and enhancing current organizational capabilities and competitive competences to produce new products and services, firms pursuing discontinuous innovation models are more concerned to develop new kinds of knowledge and skills that are qualitatively distinct from those currently dominating markets and effectively destroy their competitive advantage. In highly technologically dynamic industries, such competence destructive strategies often involve the rapid acquisition and use of new scientific and technological knowledge, much of which is produced by researchers in public science systems as well as by private companies' R & D laboratories.

These innovations qualitatively alter processes and products so much that many current organizational capabilities become uncompetitive, either by reducing costs considerably or by radically improving the functionality or quality of products, as in the hard disk drive industry (Christensen 1997; McKendrick et al. 2000). They therefore can compete on price or quality, and often both. In industries dominated by this model, fast responsiveness to new scientific and technological knowledge and market opportunities is *a*, if not *the*, crucial competence, which includes the ability to invent, develop, and manufacture new products faster than competitors in ways that enable the winning firm to dominate existing markets or create new ones, as in the case of FrontPage (Ferguson 1999).

While the overall economic significance of this kind of competitive model may have been overstated by some enthusiasts of the knowledge-based economy, its importance in some emerging and fast growing industries suggests that it is worthwhile to distinguish flexible competitive models that build on and enhance existing knowledge, skills, and collective capabilities from those that imply a much greater and more radical reshaping of organizational competences, often through the acquisition of new staff and/or companies. Additionally, since much of the literature of Silicon Valley and similarly innovative regions emphasizes the distinctiveness of the business environment and supporting institutional arrangements, it is important to separate this kind of ideal type from flexible MPDG if we are to understand how different conditions and contingencies encourage or discourage the dominant role of different competition models in different contexts.

CONDITIONS SUPPORTING DIFFERENT
COMPETITION MODELS

....

These different kinds of competition models are likely to become established as dominant economic logics in particular kinds of sectors, regions, and countries with distinctive technological regimes, market conditions, and institutional contexts. Fordist strategies focusing on very high volumes of standardized goods, for instance, depend on access to mass markets for relatively undifferentiated products where demand is predictable enough to justify the considerable investment in dedicated machinery and managerial coordination. In capital-intensive sectors, they also depend on a ready supply of technical specialists and managers to design, coordinate, and manage the integration of mass production with mass marketing. Price-based competition additionally relies on a large supply of unskilled and semi-skilled labour constrained to work on routinized, standardized tasks under the control of employers' agents.

More quality-based competitive strategies, on the other hand, depend on firms continually improving products and processes and adapting to customers' needs. Developing these competences usually requires considerable restriction of short-term opportunistic behaviour to encourage firms and employees to invest in collective firm-specific capabilities to develop and produce high-quality goods and services (Hirst and Zeitlin 1997; Streeck 1992). They additionally rely on firms being able to sell their outputs to differentiated markets where consumers are willing and able to pay for better quality and distinctive products and services.

Fast responsiveness to market and technical changes requires considerable organizational flexibility and an ability to develop and adapt to new knowledge. While this can be achieved through numerical flexibility in less complex production processes where quality is not central to competitive success, it usually depends on employees being willing and able to learn new skills and develop novel work processes to meet changing customer demands. Rapid adjustment to changing conditions is additionally supported by modular production processes where the design and manufacturing of particular components in value chains can be changed without having to alter the whole system (Gereffi et al. 2005; Sturgeon 2002). Much more radical and competence destructive strategies depend on greater flexibility in generating and using new knowledge and skills, as well as ready access to risk capital and highly skilled technical specialists. Again, modularity helps to limit the amount of capital at risk in developing and commercializing any one such innovation by restricting the investment needed to only one part of the system.

The key conditions supporting these seven distinct types of competition models include, then, market characteristics, institutional frameworks, and technical capacities. Simplifying considerably, they can be summarized as six dimensions. First, the size of product markets and their differentiation by taste, income levels, and preferences for high quality goods and services. Second, the level of institutional constraints *on short-term economic opportunism* that restrict rapid entry to, and exit from, business relationships, including employment, and the unilateral exercise of market power. These institutional arrangements include strong employer and trade associations that limit free riding strategies, as well as rules governing competitive behaviour that limit predatory pricing and taking advantage of short-term difficulties to squeeze suppliers. Third, the widespread *availability of knowledgeable risk capital* in the form of a sophisticated venture capital industry that provides funding for high-risk activities. Fourth, access to a large *supply of high-skilled technical specialists* and professional staff whose skills are reliably certified. Fifth, rapid access to the growing amount of *new scientific and technical knowledge*. Sixth, the ease of *modularizing* the value chain and disintegrating production processes.

Some of these conditions are most relevant to only a few of the seven competition models and overlap in their implications. Many also complement each other to a considerable degree in their impact on the establishment of particular economic logics. In Table 13.2, I suggest how different levels of these six conditions support their institutionalization, distinguishing between low, medium, and high degrees, and will now discuss these interconnections further.

In the case of Fordism, ready access to mass markets that are largely undifferentiated by regional or cultural tastes is a crucial condition for it to dominate a particular market economy (Piore and Sabel 1984). Its focus on maintaining optimal use of dedicated machinery and other capital equipment also implies that flexibility in responding to market shifts is mostly achieved through changing input volumes and labour utilization. Such changes are greatly facilitated by a business environment in which there are few constraints on opportunistic behaviour, especially in labour markets where there are few legal restrictions on employers hiring and firing staff at short notice, and few strong labour unions capable of resisting such managerial actions. They are also made easier by making most jobs highly routinized and tasks easily carried out by semi-skilled workers who can be trained in a few hours. Such staff are usually thought to have few, if any, firm-specific skills and knowledge that add substantially to their employers' competitive competences, and so can readily be dismissed without serious effects on their future growth.

The dominance of price-based competition additionally encourages such companies to develop adversarial and arm's length relationships with their suppliers and take advantage of their size in negotiating low prices, rather than engaging in more collaborative and longer term partnerships in which both firms benefit from joint development of product and process improvements and skills. Economies in which firms can become very large, through acquisitions for instance, and there are few restrictions on exercising market power, are therefore more likely to encourage Fordist strategies than those in which companies are limited in their freedom to dominate industry partners.

Finally, it is important to note the crucial role of technical specialists and managers in establishing and running such large and complex organizations coordinating mass production with mass marketing activities. As Chandler (1977; 1990) claimed in the case of large US firms in the twentieth century, it was these middle and senior

Table 13.2: Conditions supporting the dominance of competitive models

Conditions		Competition Models					
	Fordism	Opportunistic	Craft production	Flexible customized production	Diversified quality production	Flexible MPDG	Discontinuous innovation
Product market size and differentiation	Mass, undifferentiated	Large, price/ fashion focused	Niche, quality focused	Niche, quality focused	Large, differentiated and quality focused	Large, differentiated and quality focused	Large, price and/or quality focused
Constraints on short term opportunism	Low	Low	High	Medium	High	High	Low
Availability of knowledgeable risk capital	Low	Low	Low	Low	Low	Low	High
Supply of technical specialists	High	Low	Low	High	High	High	High
Availability of new technical knowledge	Low	Low	Low	Medium	Medium	High	High
Modularization	Medium	High	Low	Medium	Low	High	High

managerial employees who effectively constructed the key coordination and control mechanisms that generated economies of scale and scope in capital-intensive sectors. Such staff are also important in constructing service factories in which standardized outputs are generated through formalized work processes for a large number of undifferentiated customers, as in many forms of retailing, including banking. A necessary condition for the dominance of Fordist models, then, is a ready supply of competent staff to design and implement such mechanisms, who are committed to their employers' success and develop firm-specific skills and knowledge.

In sum, for Fordism to develop and become established as the major competitive model in a market economy, owners and managers have to be able to construct large and complex organizations for producing standardized goods and services for mass markets with few institutional constraints on how they do so. Weakly organized skilled workers, as well as easy access to specialized production machinery are also important conditions. In addition, few formal and informal regulatory constraints on predatory pricing or on changing business partners at short notice are necessary to enable dominant firms to be responsive to changing circumstances (Hollingsworth 1991).

Many of these conditions are also important for opportunistic competition models to develop, especially weak constraints on short-term economic opportunism and easy access to mass markets. The major difference from Fordism concerns the speed of responsiveness to market changes and the ability to seize new commercial opportunities when they arise. This effectively means that firms do not invest in the creation of large and complex organizations dedicated to the mass production of homogenous outputs with capital-intensive facilities.

Rather, they focus on low-cost production of relatively simple products for large consumer markets with facilities that can be amortized and changed over much less time than Fordist ones. In some cases, product specific machinery is provided by customers in buyer-driven commodity chains and opportunistic firms concentrate on managing work processes directly rather than investing in elaborate managerial hierarchies. Since key competitive advantages for such firms are access to, and efficient management of, easily trained and low-cost labour that can be changed rapidly to suit changing market needs, both low-cost communication technologies and the ability to codify knowledge easily in design and production activities are important enabling conditions. These factors have also facilitated the development of some routine service activities in emerging economies, such as call centres.

Competitive models that focus more on quality than price tend to rely much more on the knowledge and commitment of skilled production workers to improve products and processes continuously and to respond flexibly to changing conditions. In the case of craft production, for instance, the emphasis is on meeting the demands of customers for high quality and specific goods and services with flexible, multi-purpose machinery operated by highly skilled staff. Responsiveness to customers' needs and incremental improvements in performance are more important competences here than are reducing unit costs and realizing economies of scale through standardized work processes.

To remain competitive with low price, high-volume Fordist strategies, such models depend on there being effective barriers to short-term opportunism that prevent large firms from undercutting craft producers with predatory pricing and taking over successful SMEs with their skilled workers. In the case of the traditional professions, of course, practitioner elites control access to their services and the certification of those able to provide these. In many industrial districts, these kinds of competition models have been supported by local institutions providing what Crouch et al. (2001; 2004) have termed collective competition goods.

For example, in the 1980s small- and medium-sized Japanese machine tool firms in Sakaki township were supported by the local provision of substantial collective competition goods by the Chamber of Commerce, local government, and strong regional identity of workers and owners that encouraged equipment sharing, facilitated product diversification, and prevented price and wage squeezing by large customers. According to Friedman (1988), this collective commitment to high-quality products made with highly skilled workers depended on, and was reproduced by, continuous training and upgrading of machinery and competences to attract the best staff. Similar commitments to high-quality outputs and continuing technical improvements with extensive training for skilled and less skilled staff that limit both customers' ability to enforce lower prices and competitors' competences in mass producing similar products have been found in Denmark and some other parts of continental Europe (Crouch et al. 2001; Kristensen 1992).

Because firms' competitiveness depends so much here on the flexibility, technical abilities and commitment to learning of employees, companies have to maintain high wages, offer jobs with considerable technical interest and challenges and provide access to training if they are to retain key staff. This tends to restrict them from competing for large orders at low prices that threaten to routinize major parts of the production process. Work intensity, however, remains quite high in such models, together with job satisfaction (Kristensen et al. 2009; Kyotani 1996).

The main differences between craft production and flexible customized production concern the ability to respond quickly to changing market conditions and technical innovation through restructuring work processes and teams to generate new solutions to complex problems for relatively sophisticated customers. This involves combining and enhancing skills and expert knowledge in novel ways that not only extend current competences, but also create new ones that enable firms to enter new markets such as those leading to the establishment of new professional practices in some business services (Anand et al. 2007). Greater levels of organizational flexibility are therefore an important requirement for flexible customized competition models, which depend on considerable employee commitment to meeting, and adapting to, customers' needs. A willingness to develop innovative work processes and collaborate in dealing with novel and complex problems is therefore important for firms pursuing this kind of competitive strategy, and so constraints on changes to personnel and business partners cannot be very strong.

While strong skilled labour unions support craft-based strategies, then, they may well limit such skill enhancement and restructuring, especially where job territories are tied to narrowly defined and inflexible skills (Marsden 1999: 42–4), thus inhibiting the generation of new knowledge in project teams. Since the coordination and organization of highly skilled teams is more critical to a firm's success in this approach, it follows that an ample supply of competent project managers is also more important in this case than it is for craft production strategies. A large supply of certified technical and professional specialists is also required, together with access to new technical knowledge that can be used to develop new products and services.

In the case of DQP, cooperative relationships between firms and between employer and employees depend greatly on institutions encouraging investment in broad skills and wide-ranging collective capabilities and restricting short-term opportunistic behaviour, such as free-riding on competitors' training provision. It 'requires', as Streeck (1992: 4) puts it: 'a congenial organisational ecology, the presence of redundant capacities and a rich supply of collective production inputs', which in turn rely on effective formal and informal institutional constraints on highly short-term market rationality and support the collective provision of key inputs.

These include training systems that encourage both employers and workers to invest in the development of broad skills and abilities to learn new knowledge, wage setting arrangements that prevent poaching of skilled staff, and collective institutions that encourage companies to share knowledge about technologies and markets and some investment risks. Strong trade associations that advance the interests of their members effectively and are able to sanction opportunistic behaviour, which could harm collective capabilities, are often key features of market economies in which DQP becomes established.

Key to such developments are institutions that encourage trust and commitment between the major groups involved, whether these are formal and legally constituted constraints on opportunistic behaviour or more informal collective commitments as found in some Asian countries, that extend beyond single contractual exchanges and incorporate both skill and knowledge sharing and collective investments. Such collaboration depends on legal regimes that permit some inter-firm cooperation and restrict the exclusivity of private property rights. It therefore is inhibited by strong and effective anti-trust legislation such as that developed in the USA in much of the twentieth century (Campbell and Lindberg 1991).

Diversified quality production of larger quantities than those typical of craft production—often incorporating standardized components—additionally implies the existence of a customer base that has sufficient disposable income and varied tastes to pay for differentiated high-quality products. The expansion of consumer markets during the 'trente glorieuses' after 1945 in many OECD economies helped to create such a pattern of demand, especially in societies where cultural distinctions remained significant and were reflected in consumer preferences. Relatively large markets for distinctive products thus helped to support the replacement of Fordism by DQP in many of the richer market economies during the last third or so of the twentieth century.

As the contrast of post-war Germany with Japan highlights, many aspects of DQP can be achieved in different ways. In particular, strong unions, sector-wide wage determination through formal procedures and organizations, and national training systems coordinated by the state, unions, and employer groups do not seem to be necessary institutions for DQP. However, strong trade associations, employer agreements on wage policies, poaching, and similar issues, effective diffusion oriented technology policy (Morris-Suzuki 1994), and the provision of many collective competition goods at local, regional, and national levels, in conjunction with limited restrictions on inter-firm cooperation, do appear to be important factors in the development of DQP as a major competition model.

The critical feature of such business environments is their encouragement of employer and employee investment in developing broadly based competences and knowledge that enable them to adapt to, and anticipate, changing circumstances through joint problem-solving and collective commitment to organizational success. This implies the discouragement of owners and managers taking advantage of business partners' short-term difficulties, whether employees, suppliers, customers, or investors, at the expense of longer term collective advantages.

More flexible and rapidly responsive mass production of differentiated goods implies a faster rate of product innovation, often linked to new scientific and technological knowledge. Key competences here include the ability to translate new knowledge into new products and services and reach consumer markets quickly. This typically requires extensive investment in engineers and managers, easy access to new formal knowledge, and a strong capability to integrate development, production, and distribution effectively.

It also relies on high levels of organizational commitment and cross-functional collaboration in project teams such that skilled staff focuses on contributing to firm-specific competences, even at the possible expense of developing their own specialist skills. In turn, long-term employer–employee commitment and organization-specific career paths encourage such collective cooperation and are supported by relatively weak external labour markets. Weak occupational identities, as Cawson (1994) suggests, was key to Japanese electronics firms' success in the 1980s. High levels of flexibility are also enhanced by the modularization of production and distribution processes that enables part of technological systems to be altered without having to make systemic changes to the whole

Considering finally the conditions supporting the establishment of the discontinuous innovation competition model, a considerable number of factors have been suggested in the literature on Silicon Valley and similarly innovative regions (see, e.g. Bahrami and Evans 1995; Casper 2007; Kenney 2000; Lee et al. 2000). Among these are: flexible labour markets, strong and knowledgeable venture capital companies coupled with liquid stock markets that enable such firms to exit from successful start-ups and so adopt a portfolio approach to investing in highly risky new ventures, a supply of highly educated scientists and technologists as well as experienced managers of such companies, close connections between leading research universities and innovative firms, including effective mechanisms for transferring new knowledge and skills between them, and a generally supportive environment for developing innovative technologies and markets with a wide range of business services and skills for facilitating new firm formation (Suchman 2000).

The key requirements for this model concern: a) incentives to make the high risks involved worth undertaking, b) means of limiting these through diversifying commitments and/or easily shifting resources to new activities and obtaining alternative employment, c) institutions that enable firms to deal with market and technical failure by acquiring new kinds of knowledge and skills at relatively low cost, and d) a ready supply of business services that support entrepreneurs in seizing opportunities quickly. Among the major incentives are winner-takes-all markets in which successful new ventures are able to dominate large markets and reap the concomitant rewards. Allied to this is the ability to restrict appropriability risks through patenting or similar intellectual property protections and the existence of visible milestones of progress towards product development and manufacture that enable investors to assess technical progress at frequent intervals (Tylecote and Visintin 2008).

Investors are more able to manage the high failure risks involved in such innovatory activities when they are well informed about the technologies and markets involved, can offset frequent setbacks, and project collapses with less common— but highly lucrative—successes in diversified investment portfolios, and are able to realize their profits through trade sales or initial public offerings on large and liquid stock markets. These kinds of competition models are therefore more likely to become established when financial systems encourage the development of large groups of knowledgeable venture capitalists, and serial business angels who are able to raise large funds from institutional and private investors, and can sell stakes in successful companies in a well-established market for corporate ownership.

Risks can also be mitigated by focusing on products that function as parts of technological systems rather than attempting to create an entire system from scratch. Modularity and the ability to concentrate on part of the invention, development, manufacture, and distribution process, and thus restrict the amount of capital required, are therefore common features of industries where this kind of competition model predominates.

From the point of view of employees, failure risks are easier to deal with when companies are located in regions where there is an agglomeration of similar firms that can offer employment to staff of failed enterprises. As Casper (2007) has emphasized, the existence of such potential employers encourages professionals to contemplate investing their energy and skills in risky endeavours, just as many industrial districts provide some safety cushions for skilled staff wanting to set up their own businesses.

Where innovations are, in addition, closely dependent on new formal knowledge about physical and biological processes, and on research skills for producing it, fluid labour markets for research scientists and engineers and for technically competent managers, are also important supportive factors. This is especially so if they encourage movement between research organizations such as universities and private firms. This both facilitates the transfer of knowledge and expertise and provides some possibility of re-employment for researchers who join companies that fail or are taken over. If business employment is seen as a sign of intellectual weakness and universities are segmented from commercial goals and interests, on the other hand, then the establishment of radically responsive, discontinuous innovation models is less likely.

THE IMPACT OF CHANGES IN THE BUSINESS ENVIRONMENT ON THE CONDITIONS SUPPORTING DIFFERENT COMPETITION MODELS

Many of these conditions supporting the establishment of particular competition models have been affected by significant changes in the institutional, technological, and macroeconomic contexts of business activities since the collapse of the Bretton Woods system. These can be summarized in terms of five main sets of changes that have resulted from, and in many cases reinforced, changing interest group coalitions in some of the major OECD economies and a widespread tendency for many states to reduce formal controls over competitive behaviour in, and entry to, many markets, especially financial ones. First, the internationalization of product markets, capital markets, and managerial coordination of economic activities through MNCs and various forms of quasi-organizational integration. While the extent and significance of these changes remain hotly debated, they have certainly altered many features of the environment in which such conditions became established.

Second, the geo-political changes associated with the collapse of the Soviet Union and economic reforms in China and other state socialist regimes have had major consequences for many of the conditions supporting or inhibiting competition models. Third, the dramatic changes in information and communication technologies, including the digitalization of much codified knowledge, have sharply reduced communication costs and greatly facilitated the coordination of activities over large distances, thus of course aiding the international coordination of production and exchange. Whether they amount to a radically new techno-economic 'paradigm', as some have suggested (Freeman and Louca 2001; Tylecote and Visintin 2008), is debatable, but they can be expected to affect organization structures and integration processes.

Fourth, the extensive periods of economic growth in most OECD countries since 1945 have greatly increased consumers' disposable income as well as enabling the expansion of state welfare services and social protection. Together with market saturation in many consumer goods industries, this has reinforced shifts in patterns of demand. Finally, fifth, most national governments have invested in the expansion of state education systems, particularly higher education, and of support for public scientific research, albeit in different ways in different countries. Many have also developed science and technology policies aimed to improve national economic competitiveness through encouraging technical change and innovation.

These varied changes in national and international business environments are having different kinds of consequences for the conditions listed in Table 13.2, both separately and in conjunction with each other. Furthermore, how they affect established competition models and business systems, in particular socio-economic contexts, depends greatly on dominant institutional regimes and interest group coalitions (Amable 2003; Whitley 2007). In Table 13.3, I summarize the major kinds of effects these five sets of changes can be expected to have on the critical conditions supporting or inhibiting the seven types of competition models identified in Table 13.1. As can be seen from the blank spaces, many of these changes are likely to affect only some of the six conditions discussed above.

In very broad terms, all three aspects of economic internationalization can be expected to reduce national institutional constraints on economic opportunism and the cohesion of national interest groups supporting these. Beginning with the opening of national product markets to foreign companies and extension of most favoured nation principles to firms from most countries in the world trading system (Braithwaite and Drahos 2000), this has facilitated the expansion of markets for standardized goods, lowered entry barriers, and intensified competition. It also weakens the ability of domestic firms and their employees to limit price competition and collaborate in preventing free-riding.

However, it does create opportunities for firms pursuing quality based competitive strategies to sell to foreign markets and, when coupled with reduced communication and coordination costs, integrate supply chains across different market economies. In societies with a large supply of skilled labour and strong domestic labour unions, these opportunities may encourage such companies to continue to follow DQP logics by combining lower costs with larger markets for their higher quality products, as has perhaps happened in Denmark since 1990 (Kristensen et al. 2009).

For quality-focused firms under pressure from lower cost foreign producers, these opportunities enable them to reduce domestic diversification and focus more on delivering specialized outputs for international customers, as Meyer (2006) found in the case of some large Danish firms. Such strategies are of course facilitated by ICT innovations, which speed up feedback from distant markets and encourage flexibility. The general opening up of foreign product markets can therefore increase the volume of demand for both standardized and more differentiated products and services as well as supporting both price and quality focused competition models. It additionally supports the development of radical innovations by enlarging the potential market for new products and services, thus increasing the possible pay-offs from risky innovations.

The internationalization of capital markets has likewise reduced the ability of financial and business elites to coordinate their activities and limit opportunism within national borders, especially when combined with the growth of institutional fund management, declining state regulation of financial markets, and the removal of barriers between different financial services businesses. Pressures for increasing

Table 13.3: Effects of the changing business environment on conditions affecting competition models

Conditions	Changing features of the business environment						
	Product market internationalization	Capital market internationalization	Internationalization of organizational integration	Collapse of state socialism	ICT innovations	Increasing consumer incomes	Expansion of higher education and public science systems
Product markets	Increased in size			Increased in size	Increased access	Increased differentiation of demand	
Constraints on opportunism	Reduced	Reduced by high levels of foreign portfolio investment	Reduced, except where strategic assets are dependent on longer-term commitments		Reduced when they facilitate access to foreign locations		
Availability of risk capital		Increased					Increased supply of knowledgeable venture capitalists
Supply of technical specialists			Increased	Increased in industrialized societies	Increased access to them		Increased
Availability of new technical knowledge			Increased		Increased access		Increased
Modularization					Increased, except where product architectures are integrated		Increased where new knowledge increases digitalization

financial returns are being intensified as foreign investors seek to improve investment fund performance across national markets and limit the ability of labour unions to maintain their share of national income. As fund managers are increasingly subject to short-term performance measures, such pressures are likely to inhibit the ability and willingness of firms to invest in medium- to long-term commitments to business partners and employees at the possible expense of shorter-term financial returns.

Again, though, these pressures can be mitigated, or even negated, by national restrictions on shareholder powers, variations in shareholders' voting rights, limitations on hostile takeovers, and the capacity of national political and economic elites to mobilize opposition to foreign investors' short-term interests, as many European states have shown in recent years (Morck 2007). Additionally, the growth of cross-border capital flows can facilitate access to well-informed venture capital, thus enabling new firms in emerging industries to overcome national resistance to providing risk capital for radically new technologies, as seems to have happened in some Dutch and German biotechnology companies (Lange 2009; Paauw 2009).

While, then, the internationalization of the shareholder base of large firms pursuing DQP and similar strategies may reduce employer–employee commitment, investment in training, and continuing product and process upgrading domestically, this effect varies between industries and also depends greatly on the market for corporate control. Where this is quite restricted and managers need not be so concerned about share prices as they have become in some capital market-based financial systems, the impact of investor internationalization on these kinds of dominant competition models is likely to be limited.

The growth of managerial coordination and control of economic activities across national borders has also enhanced many of the conditions supporting Fordist strategies. While this is partly because multi-national corporations (MNCs) are able to access low cost labour and other resources in different market economies, it also reflects their variable, and often limited, integration with particular national and regional governance arrangements. As firms with facilities in different economies, MNCs are more able to opt out, or at least distance themselves from, local associations, collective agreements, and other nationally specific coordination processes that restrain short-term economic opportunism. Increasing cross-national economic integration through organizational routines is likely, then, to reduce the ability of national trade associations and similar bodies to organize markets collectively and sanction free-riding behaviour, thus limiting longer term collaboration between companies and support for investment in collective competition goods.

Such international integration does also, though, enable firms to acquire and manage directly strategic assets located in different parts of the world, particularly highly skilled technologists and researchers, and where these are highly interdependent with local governance arrangements, foreign MNCS are likely to follow them. The more they invest abroad in order to acquire and/or control such assets, as distinct from gaining market access or reducing input costs, the more they can be expected to become embedded in national and regional coordination mechanisms and cooperate with business partners where this is institutionalized.

Additionally, of course, if host economies are large, rich and highly significant for MNCs, and their dominant institutional arrangements are both mutually supportive and strongly entrenched in dominant political-economic coalitions, the ability of foreign firms to change established patterns of collective organization will be quite limited, as many MNCs have found in post-war Japan. In general, the more MNCs seek to integrated strategic assets in economies where those assets gain much of their value from particular governance patterns and institutions, the more they are likely to adapt to, and perhaps reinforce, those patterns.

While, then, the internationalization of many economic activities may have reduced the cohesion and effectiveness of regional and national institutions supporting incremental quality improvements through employer–employee commitment, it has also created more possibilities for firms to reach larger markets, reduce costs, and respond more flexibly to demand changes while maintaining some collaborative relations with domestic business partners and cooperating with foreign ones. To an extent, the loosening of domestic commitments seems to be partially compensated by their extension abroad and greater flexibility to alter suppliers while improving their capabilities.

The collapse of the Soviet Union and opening of many state socialist economies to foreign firms, both as exporters and as strategic investors, have greatly enlarged markets for many goods and services, although these vary in their segmentation by taste, income, and education. In the case of industrializing economies, they have also greatly increased the availability of unskilled and low-cost labour for MNCs, as well as facilitating access to more highly skilled labour in Russia and the other more industrialized state socialist societies. Since there are few institutional constraints on short-term opportunistic behaviour in many of these developing market economies, price-based competition is dominant and the large supply of unskilled labour in those still industrializing facilitates rapid adjustment to demand changes through numerical flexibility. To some extent, this has probably weakened the power of labour unions organizing lower skilled workers in many OECD countries, but, as the examples of Denmark and other Nordic countries indicate, it need not always lead to a decline in the effectiveness of corporatist institutions or an increase in managers' control of work processes (Kristensen 2009).

Many of these changes and their likely effects have been facilitated by the large number of innovations in information and communication technologies that have been introduced and widely diffused since the end of the Second World War. As well as greatly reducing the cost of communicating over large distances, these have enhanced the codification of knowledge and data such that they can be circulated at high speed to large numbers of people and so enable the cheap and fast coordination of activities in a wide range of locations.

As Tylecote and Visintin (2008: 228–33) have suggested, the new ICT paradigm is helping to drive international economic integration by facilitating the coordination of activities in capital and labour markets around the world. In particular, the increasing digitalization of information and codification of knowledge enables firms to communicate more effectively with suppliers and customers across large distances, and so be able to access a wider range of business partners at low cost through electronic data interchange (EDI) and similar technologies.

In so far as this means that they can standardize their requirements and formalize their contracting procedures, it may facilitate the fast switching of suppliers, and so encourage more arm's length contracting across the world and modularization of production processes, as in many buyer dominated commodity chains (Bair 2005; Gereffi and Korzeniewicz 1994) and some service sectors such as banking, IT problem solving, and legal contracting. As well, then, as enabling firms to reach mass international markets by reducing coordination costs, ICT innovations can facilitate rapid adjustments to changing markets through reorganizing supply chains, as we have seen in the electronics industry in Pacific Asia (Ernst 2006; Sturgeon 2002).

However, such technologies can also increase the mutual dependence and integration of customers and suppliers, especially in industries where integrated product architectures limit the degree of modularization of production chains that is feasible (Chesbrough 2003). Especially where quality improvements are dependent on both continually upgrading complex assembly processes and integrating these with component supplies, as in much of the car industry, arm's length contracting for key inputs has become less feasible and many firms are using the new technologies to achieve closer integration with their major suppliers around the world (Herrigel and Zeitlin in this Handbook; MacDuffie and Helper 2006).

Indeed, the ability of new ICT to reduce coordination costs and integrate economic activities carried out in different labour markets can facilitate international learning and innovation by SMEs, as Kristensen et al. (2009) have found in Denmark. Rather than simply using such technologies to reduce input costs and control suppliers' operations at a distance, as many US firms appear to do, some Danish companies are working with their business partners in low-cost economies to improve performance and seize opportunities jointly. In some cases, this involves skilled workers and technicians from Denmark helping to train and develop staff in their supplying firms. While this may be an unusual phenomenon deriving from the Danish institutionalization of training and continuous skill enhancement as the dominant means through which workers and firms compete in providing high-quality goods and services for specific customers, it does show how internationalization and the development of ICT can facilitate high-quality and flexible competition models rather than always supporting Fordist ones.

The extent to which such integration of key tasks leads to risk sharing and mutual trust more generally remains highly variable, though, as MacDuffie and Helper point out (2006: 428–56). Close collaboration and technology sharing between large assemblers and their suppliers on operational matters such as design and engineering can be quite high without necessarily implying that the purchasing regime is equally cooperative and mutually trusting. A similar distinction between operational collaboration and strategic or governance cooperation was found in a study of customer–supplier relations at a British airport where the airport authority, baggage handling companies, airlines, and air traffic control agencies were forced to work closely together on day-to-day tasks but were much more adversarial and antagonistic in their strategic dealings with each other (Lelievre-Finch 2008). It is a mistake, then, to assume that increasing international customer–supplier cooperation and information sharing on task matters automatically means closer trust on governance matters. These latter seem much more affected by institutional constraints and what MacDuffie and Helper (2006: 453) term 'legacy modes of exchange', i.e. effective practices that have largely been developed in firms' domestic environments.

Similarly, these technological changes can have a variety of different consequences for firms' internal structures and work systems. On the one hand, they can greatly improve the flow of codified knowledge throughout an organization, thus reducing the number of employees processing information and facilitating managerial control over work processes, the flow of materials and performance outcomes. Integrating computer-aided design with computer-aided manufacturing and other functions reduces coordination costs and can speed up product development and production. Additionally, micro-electronic control systems and similar innovations have increased the flexibility of production lines in many industries so that smaller batch volumes have become viable and product changeovers made cheaper and quicker.

On the other hand, they can also be used to enhance skilled workers' abilities and integrate planning and execution activities on the shop floor, which enables faster responses to market and technical changes and greater employee involvement in problem solving and business development activities (Kristensen 1992; 2009; Sorge 1991; Sorge and Warner 1986). This depends considerably, of course, on the availability and level of skills among employees and the strength of institutions encouraging collaboration between managers and workers and the adoption of quality focused competition models.

Turning, finally, to consider the impact of sustained economic growth and expansion of education and public science systems in most OECD economies since the end of the Second World War. These have tended to increase demand for higher quality, more differentiated goods and services and generated a more technically competent workforce, including those capable of contributing to formal scientific and technological knowledge (Boyer 2004; Boyer and Durand 1997). This workforce will find it easier to adapt to new technologies and work processes without needing detailed supervision and limit the degree of managerial direction of task performance.

The combination of growth in higher education and support for public scientific research expands the labour force capable of both producing new formal knowledge and understanding how this could be used for innovative purposes. In principle, then, these collective investments in most OECD countries should facilitate competitive strategies based on radical, discontinuous innovations. However, as the numerous studies of Silicon Valley and other regional innovation systems have shown, although such expansion may well be an important, if not necessary, condition for the success of these kinds of competition models, it is by no means sufficient. Its effectiveness in generating similar patterns of innovation is highly dependent on other contextual factors, such as the nature of dominant labour market institutions, the organization of public science systems, and the provision of other collective competition goods (Asheim and Gertler 2005; Casper 2007; Mowery and Sampat, 2005; Whitley 2003).

CHANGING COMPETITION MODELS

In the light of these expected connections between the increasing internationalization of economic activities, geo-political shifts, ICT innovations and the growth of incomes, higher education and the public sciences, and the conditions supporting different competition models, what can be concluded about the development of established competition models and dominant economic logics in differently organized economies? In Table 13.4, I summarize the likely consequences of these changes for the seven ideal types identified earlier, and will now consider these in more detail.

In the case of the two price-based strategies of Fordism and opportunism, these continue to be supported by the international expansion of mass markets for standardized goods and services and the increasing ease of coordinating development, production, and marketing across labour and product markets through ICT. This is especially so where much information and knowledge is readily codified and processes can be decomposed into modular components, as in many parts of the electronics industry. While Fordism may, then, have declined considerably as a nationally dominant economic logic in richer societies as markets become saturated and tastes change, it has grown in international significance and continues to constrain the pursuit of more quality-focused strategies by limiting price levels.

In many service sector activities, these changes have further encouraged the internationalization and standardization of service provision, especially where states have deregulated market entry and reduced legal constraints on competitive behaviour. Recently, such mass production of services has become extended to some of the established professions as well as knowledge intensive business services (Miozzo and Grimshaw 2006), and can be seen as the broadening of Fordist models to novel areas of economic activity.

Similarly, we would expect the increased internationalization of markets, use of ICT to reduce coordination costs and modularization of value chains to encourage opportunistic competition models in labour intensive sectors. However, the ease of entry to many buyer-driven commodity chains and focus on low prices mean that firms are always vulnerable to new competitors from lower cost economies. Additionally, when income levels rise and demand in the richer countries becomes saturated and differentiated, purely price-driven competition models may become less viable for those markets.

The combination of such international competition based on price and increasing flexibility of both quality-based large-batch production and more customized

Table 13.4: Expected effects of the changing business environment on established competition models

Changing business environment	Established Competition Models						
	Fordism	Opportunism	Craft production	Flexible customized production	DQP	Flexible MPDG	Discontinuous innovation
Internationalization	Supported by expansion of markets for standardised goods and supply of cheap labour	Supported by opening of product markets to low cost producers	Threatened by intensification of price competition, supported by access to low cost inputs, especially in collaborative institutional regimes	Supported by growth of niche markets and access to skilled labour, where training is available	Supported by growth of niche markets and access to reduced cost inputs in modularized sectors, but threatened by weakened constraints on opportunism, price competition from low cost economies, and demands for faster responsiveness		Supported by growth of markets for new products, internationalization of venture capital, and access to strategic assets
Collapse of state socialism							
ICT innovations	Supported by facilitating international integration		Supported by enabling outsourcing	Supported by modularization cross-national integration of activities	Supported by increasing production flexibility but threatened by ease of outsourcing	Supported by facilitation of organizational flexibility, internationalization, and modularization	Supported by modularization and ease of cross-national coordination
Income growth, expansion of higher education, and public sciences	Decline in wealthier markets	Limited to fashion goods	Supported by market growth for high quality, customized goods but threatened by new technologies	Supported by market growth for high quality, skilled labour and new technologies where labour markets are fluid	Supported by market growth for quality goods but threatened by new technologies	Supported by increase in technologists and market growth	Supported by market growth, production of new formal knowledge and technologies, and fluid labour markets.

outputs seems likely to put considerable pressure on traditional craft competition models, especially where these depended on highly paid skilled workers in markets that were relatively protected from foreign competition. As it becomes easier for large firms to reduce input costs through international sourcing, and to differentiate product ranges more in response to changing customer demands by using ICT to increase the flexibility of production processes, they can threaten smaller companies more reliant on local markets and incrementally upgraded skills. In some of the traditional professions, such as accountancy and law, these changes have encouraged the standardization and internationalization of some activities, as well as increasing cross-national coordination between organizations and, in some cases, mergers (Morgan and Quack 2005).

One way of dealing with such intensified competition in some Italian industrial districts has been for SMEs to move their more routine operations to low-cost countries such as China and/or buy in simpler components from there (Bellandi and Caloffi 2008), just as some Chinese firms are establishing units in Italy to be able to label their products as being 'Made in Italy'. The management of such international integration has been facilitated by institutionalized collaboration patterns and the local provision of collective competition goods in Germany and Italy (Herrigel and Zeitlin in this Handbook).

An additional response of SMEs reliant on highly paid, highly skilled workers to produce limited production runs of high-quality goods for demanding customers in this situation is to invest—or encourage employees to invest—considerable time and energy in further training and skill enhancement to the extent that they change the nature of their capabilities over time. According to Kristensen et al. (2009), this is what many Danish companies and workers have done to improve the products and services they provide continuously. By upgrading and extending their technical knowledge and skills, they become able to offer new kinds of competences to their customers and so adopt more of a flexible customized competition model than a craft one.

Rather than solving similar kinds of problems with relatively stable skills and knowledge, as in many established professions, such continuing training enables firms to extend their services to deal with new problems and concerns of their customers, as in many flexible project teams in organizations that resemble more Mintzberg's adhocracies (1983). This does, though, depend greatly on the wide availability of such training at low cost and, at least in the case of Denmark, has been supported by considerable levels of social protection that enable workers and firms to experiment with new ways of working (Kristensen 2009).

More generally, flexible customized competition models are encouraged by most of these changes to the business environment by enlarging the number of potential customers for specialized goods and services, expanding the supply of highly educated workers able to acquire new technical skills, and through using new ICT to coordinate skills and activities both within national boundaries and across them to respond quickly to changing demands. Internationalization of product markets enables providers of high-quality goods and services to increase their niches beyond national customers and operating internationally allows them to access staff from different labour markets. Cross-national project teams, for instance, are increasingly providing problem-solving services in consultancy and other knowledge intensive business services (Miozzo and Grimshaw 2006).

Similarly, while the domestic institutional context supporting DQP strategies in some economies may have been weakened by internationalization, the combination of expanding international product markets and increasing consumer education and income levels offers firms pursuing high-quality competition models a much larger market for their outputs. Additionally, by locating major production facilities in both their larger foreign markets and in lower labour cost countries, and coordinating these through managerial procedures with their domestic operations, such companies, can, at least in principle, combine DQP models with lower costs, especially where ICT innovations facilitate cross-national integration (Tylecote and Visintin 2008).

In so far as firms pursuing these strategies are able to maintain high levels of collective commitment to improving quality and adapting to changing patterns of demand in their domestic and some foreign facilities, while taking advantage of cheaper input costs in other foreign locations, they should benefit from such internationalization. Where product architectures are highly integrated so that modularization is difficult, and competitiveness depends greatly on the organizational integration of problem-solving and continuous improvement activities, firms facing increasing pressures to respond to foreign customers' demands, as in for example the Brazilian car industry, are investing in upgrading their suppliers' capabilities in lower-cost locations so that they can become more flexible in foreign markets (Herrigel and Zeitlin in this Handbook; Sako 2003).

While some MNCs may have originally intended to operate at arm's length from their new suppliers in low-cost economies and focus on price reductions, as local foreign markets become more important and differentiated, many are having to develop more collaborative and responsive capabilities in their foreign operations, especially where modularization is limited, thus in a sense extending the DQP model abroad. Flexible MPDG has, then, become more widespread, encouraged particularly by modularization and ICT innovations, while purely domestic DQP strategies have probably been weakened by the recent changes in the business environment. Flexible MPDG models have also been encouraged by the expansion of higher education and public science systems, especially where the growing number of scientists and technologists have strong incentives to work for leading companies and labour market institutions facilitate collaborative problem-solving activities in the development and commercialization of new products and technologies along current trajectories.

The combination of internationalizing product and capital markets, expanding higher education and public science systems and income growth, and ICT innovations has supported the development of discontinuous innovation competition models. Modularization, access to large markets for new goods, growth of new formal knowledge and capabilities for commercializing it, and the increasing ability of venture capitalists and other business services to support new, high risk innovations across national boundaries help to facilitate the development of new products and industries, especially where there are few barriers to restructuring project teams and ready access to a wide variety of technical specialists.

CONCLUDING REMARKS

This discussion of the likely relationships between different competition models, institutional arrangements, and changes in the political-economic and technological environment suggests a number of points that are worth mentioning in conclusion. First, most of the changes considered here vary in their expected impact on firms' priorities depending on their current competition models and institutional contexts. While some do threaten quality-based models, many also offer opportunities to extend and/or modify the ways in which they follow these. In the case of product market internationalization, for example, this both intensifies price-based competition for many companies in the richer economies, and enlarges the market for higher quality, more differentiated goods. Similarly, while the factors supporting the growth of MNCs can weaken constraints on opportunism and encourage more of a focus on price-based competitive strategies, they can also facilitate quality-focused firms obtaining low-cost inputs and increasing their organizational flexibility. It is therefore unlikely that any single change has the same and unequivocal implications for all the models discussed here.

Second, the identification of national institutional regimes with a single dominant economic logic such as Fordism or DQP—which in any case varies greatly between types of regimes (Whitley 2007)—is weakening with greater internationalization, and many competition models now involve cross-border coordination of economic activities. Both the complementarity of dominant institutions in encouraging particular patterns of behaviour and cohesion of the major post-war interest groups within nation-states is declining in many market economies, which decreases the national homogeneity of business system characteristics and economic logics. The scope for sectorally specific patterns of collaboration and competition has grown correspondingly, which is especially noticeable in the more corporatist societies as Lechevalier (2007) has highlighted in Japan.

Third, the combination of internationalization, increasingly differentiated patterns of demand, and increased rate of product innovation is encouraging many firms to respond more rapidly to changing circumstances. Adaptability in meeting customers' demands has become more important for many companies in recent decades, especially in the wealthier countries. This has intensified the need for organizational flexibility, updating skills, and incorporating new knowledge quickly into new products and services. Both traditional craft and DQP models are threatened by such pressures and many companies following these models are adapting to them by outsourcing some of their more routine activities to lower-cost economies as well as by investing in the improvement of their suppliers' knowledge and capabilities in such countries (Herrigel and Zeitlin in this Handbook; Kristensen et al. 2009).

Fourth, how firms respond to such pressures and opportunities still seems, though, to be strongly affected by their domestic environment and its conditioning of their priorities and capabilities. As Sturgeon (2007) has emphasized, while many US firms in the electronics industry embraced modularization and outsourcing enthusiastically, both in their home economy and abroad, most Japanese ones have preferred to maintain their central design, development, and manufacturing facilities in Japan, together with their established close ties to major suppliers. At least in the early 2000s, they took advantage of internationalization opportunities by outsourcing their more routine and old generation product development and production to lower cost economies, while retaining their established patterns of collaboration and competition at home. Similarly, Takeishi and Fujimoto (2003) found that Japanese car manufacturers were less willing to attempt modularization of their production systems than were US and some European ones.

In this large, rich, and distinctively organized market economy that encourages employers and employees to invest in the continued development and improvement of firm-specific competences, then, internationalization has not yet led to the radical change of established economic logics. While changing environments offer both opportunities and threats to established patterns of economic coordination and control, how leading firms respond to these remains strongly influenced by their established capabilities and the context in which they developed and continue to be reproduced.

REFERENCES

AMABLE, BRUNO (2003). *The Diversity of Modern Capitalism*, (Oxford: Oxford University Press).

ANAND, N., H. K. GARDNER, and T. MORRIS (2007). 'Knowledge-Based Innovation: Emergence and Embedding of New Practice Areas in Management Consulting Firms', *Academy of Management Journal* 50: 406–28.

ASHEIM, BJORN and MARIC GERTLER (2005). 'The Geography of Innovation: Regional Innovation Systems', in Jan Fagerberg, David Mowery, and Richard Nelson (eds.), *The Oxford Handbook of Innovation*, (Oxford: Oxford University Press), 291–317.

BAHRAMI, H. and S. EVANS (1995). 'Flexible Re-cycling and High Technology Entrepreneurship', *California Management Review* 37: 62–88.

BAIR, JENNIFER (2005). 'Global Capitalism and Commodity Chains: Looking Back, Going Forward', *Competition and Change* 9: 153–80.

BELLANDI, M. and A. CALOFFI (2008). 'District Internationalisation and Trans-local Development,' *Entrepreneurship and Regional Development* 20: 517–32.

BERGGREN, C. and M. NOMURA (1997). *The Resilience of Corporate Japan: New Competitive Strategies and Personnel Practices*, (London: Paul Chapman Publishing).

BOYER, ROBERT (1998). 'Hybridization and Models of Production: Geography, History and Theory', in R. Boyer, E. Charron, U. Jurgens, and S. Tolliday (eds.), *Between Imitation and Innovation: The Transfer and Hybridization of Productive Models in the International Automobile Industry*, (Oxford: Oxford University Press), 23–56.

——(2004). 'New Growth Regimes, but still Institutional Diversity', *Socio-Economic Review* 2: 1–32.

——and JEAN-PAUL DURAND (1997). *After Fordism*, (London: Macmillan).

——and J. ROGERS HOLLINGSWORTH (1997). 'From National Embeddedness to Spatial and Institutional Nestedness', in Hollingsworth and Boyer(eds.) (1997b), 433–84.

BRAITHWAITE, JOHN and PETER DRAHOS (2000). *Global Business Regulation*, (Cambridge: Cambridge University Press).

CAMPBELL, JOHN and LEON LINDBERG (1991). 'The Evolution of Governance Regimes', in J. L. Campbell, J. R. Hollingsworth, and L. N. Lindberg (eds.), *Governance of the American Economy*, (Cambridge: Cambridge University Press), 319–55.

CASPER, STEVEN (2007). *Creating Silicon Valley in Europe: Public Policy Towards New Technology Industries*, (Oxford: Oxford University Press).

——and R. WHITLEY (2004). 'Managing Competences in Entrepreneurial Technology Firms: A Comparative Institutional Analysis of Germany, Sweden and the UK', *Research Policy*, 33: 89–106.

CAWSON, ALAN (1994). 'Sectoral Governance in Consumer Electronics in Britain and France', in J. R. Hollingsworth, P. C. Schmitter, and W. Streeck (eds.), *Governing Capitalist Economies: Performance and Control of Economic Sectors*, (Oxford: Oxford University Press), 215–43.

CHANDLER, ALFRED (1977). *The Visible Hand*, (Cambridge, MA: Harvard University Press).

——(1990). *Scale and Scope*, (Cambridge, MA: Harvard University Press).

CHESBROUGH, H. (2003). 'Towards a Dynamics of Modularity', in A. Prencipe, A. Davies, and M. Hobday (eds.), *The Business of Systems Integration*, (Oxford, Oxford University Press), 174–98.

CHRISTENSEN, CLAYTON M. (1997). *The Innovator's Dilemma: When New Technologies Cause Great Firms to Fail*, (Boston: Harvard Business School Press).

CHRISTOPHERSON, SUSAN (2002). 'Project Work in Context: Regulatory Change and the New Geography of Media', *Environment and Planning A* 34: 2003–15.

CROUCH, COLIN, PATRICK LE GALES, CARLO TRIGILIA, and HELMUT VOELZKOW (2001). *Local Production Systems in Europe: Rise or Demise?*, (Oxford: Oxford University Press).

————————(2004). *Changing Governance of Local Economies: Responses of European Local Production Systems*, (Oxford: Oxford University Press).

DEEG, RICHARD and GREGORY JACKSON (2007). 'Towards a More Dynamic Theory of Capitalist Variety', *Socio-Economic Review* 5: 149–79.

EDQUIST, CHARLES (2005). 'Systems of Innovation: Perspectives and Challenges', in Jan Fagerberg, David C. Mowery, and Richard R. Nelson (eds.), *The Oxford Handbook of Innovation*, (Oxford: Oxford University Press), 181–208.

ENRIGHT, MICHAEL, EDITH SCOTT, and DAVID DODWELL (1997). *The Hong Kong Advantage*, (Hong Kong: Oxford University Press).

ERNST, DIETER (2006). 'Searching for a New Role in East Asian Regionalization: Japanese Production Networks in the Electronics Industry', in P. J. Katzenstein and T. Shiraishi (eds.), *Beyond Japan: The Dynamics of East Asian Regionalization*, (Ithaca, NY: Cornell University Press), 161–87.

FERGUSON, CHARLES (1999). *High Stakes, No Prisoners: A Winner's Tale of Greed and Glory in the Internet Wars*, (New York: Random House).

FREEMAN, CHRISTOPHER and FRANCISCO LOUCA (2001). *As Time Goes By: From the Industrial Revolution to the Information Revolutions*, (Oxford: Oxford University Press).

FRIEDMAN, DAVID (1988). *The Misunderstood Miracle*, (Ithaca, NY: Cornell University Press).

GEREFFI, G. and G. KORZENIEWICZ (eds.) (1994). *Commodity Chains and Global Capitalism: Studies in the Political Economy of the World System*, (Westport, CT: Greenwood Press).

——J. HUMPHREY, and T. J. STURGEON (2005). 'The Governance of Global Value Chains', *Review of International Political Economy* 12(1): 78–104.

GRABHER, GERNOT (2002). 'The Project Ecology of Advertising: Tasks, Talents and Teams', *Regional Studies* 36: 245–62.

HALL, PETER and DAVID SOSKICE (eds.) (2001). *Varieties of Capitalism: The Institutional Foundations of Comparative Advantage*, (Oxford: Oxford University Press).

HAMILTON, GARY (2006). *Commerce and Capitalism in Chinese Societies*, (Abingdon, UK: Routledge).

HERRIGEL, GARY and JONATHAN ZEITLIN (2010). 'Inter-Firm Relations in Global Manufacturing: Disintegrated Production and Its Globalization', in G. Morgan et al. (eds.), *Oxford Handbook of Comparative Institutional Analysis*, (Oxford: Oxford University Press).

HIRST, P. and J. ZEITLIN (1991). 'Flexible Specialization versus Post-Fordism: Theory, Evidence and Policy Implications', *Economy and Society* 20(1): 1–55.

————(1997). 'Flexible Specialization: Theory and Evidence in the Analysis of Industrial Change', in J. R. Hollingsworth and R. Boyer (eds.) (1997*b*), 220–39.

HOLLINGSWORTH, J. ROGERS (1991). 'The Logic of Coordinating American Manufacturing Sectors', in J. L. Campbell, J. R. Hollingsworth, and L. Lindberg (eds.), *Governance of the American Economy*, (Cambridge: Cambridge University Press), 35–73.

————and ROBERT BOYER (1997*a*). 'Coordination of Economic Actors and Social Systems of Production', in J. R. Hollingsworth and R. Boyer (eds.) (1997*b*), 1–47.

————(eds.) (1997*b*). *Contemporary Capitalism: The Embeddedness of Institutions*, (Cambridge: Cambridge University Press).

KENNEY, MARTIN (ed.) (2000). *Understanding Silicon Valley: The Anatomy of an Entrepreneurial Region*, (Stanford: Stanford University Press).

KRISTENSEN, PEER HULL (1992). 'Strategies against Structure: Institutions and Economic Organisation in Denmark', in R. Whitley (ed.), *European Business Systems*, (London: Sage), 17–36.

————(1996). 'On the Constitution of Economic Actors in Denmark: Interacting Skill Container and Project Coordinators', in R. Whitley and P. H. Kristensen (eds.), *The Changing European Firm: Limits to Convergence*, (London: Routledge), 118–58.

————(2009). 'Conclusion: Developing Comprehensive, Enabling Welfare States for Offensive Experimentalist Business', in P. H. Kristensen and K. Lilja (eds.), *New Modes of Globalizing: Experimental Forms of Economic Organization and Enabling Welfare Institutions*, (Helsinki: Helsinki School of Economics), 296–337.

————M. LOTZ, and R. ROCHA (2009). 'The Danish Case: Complementarities of Local and National Dynamics', in P. H. Kristensen and K. Lilja (eds.), *New Modes of Globalizing*, (Helsinki: Helsinki School of Economics), 97–150.

KYOTANI, EIJI (1996). 'Sociological Foundations of Inter-firm Cooperation: The Case of Sakaki Township in Japan', presented to the 14th International Labour Process Conference, Aston University, (Mar.).

LANGE, KNUT (2009). 'Institutional Embeddedness and the Strategic Leeway of Actors: The Case of the German Therapeutic Biotech Industry', *Socio-Economic Review*, 7: 181–207.

LANGLOIS, RICHARD (2003). 'The Vanishing Hand: The Changing Dynamics of Industrial Capitalism', *Industrial and Corporate Change* 12: 351–85.

LAURENCE, HENRY (2001). *Money Rules: The New Politics of Finance in Britain and Japan*, (Ithaca, NY: Cornell University Press).

LECHEVALIER, SEBASTIEN (2007). 'The Diversity of Capitalism and Heterogeneity of Firms— A Case Study of Japan During the Lost Decade', *Evolutionary and Institutional Economic Review* 4: 113–42.

LEE, CHONG-MOON, WILLIAM F. MILLER, MARGUERITE GONG HANCOCK, and HENRY S. ROWEN (eds.) (2000). *The Silicon Valley Edge: A Habitat for Innovation and Entrepreneurship*, (Stanford: Stanford University Press).

LELIEVRE-FINCH, DOMINIQUE (2008). *Changing Forms of Inter-firm Governance within Supply Chains and the Building of Firms' Capabilities*, unpublished PhD thesis, Manchester Business School, University of Manchester.

MACDUFFIE, JOHN PAUL and SUSAN HELPER (2006). 'Collaboration in Supply Chains: With and Without Trust', in C. Heckscher and P. Adler (eds.) *The Firm as a Collaborative Community*, (Oxford: Oxford University Press), 417–66.

MCKENDRICK, DAVID, RICHARD F. DONER, and STEPHAN HAGGARD (2000). *From Silicon Valley to Singapore: Location and Competitive Advantage in the Hard Disk Drive Industry*, (Stanford, CA: Stanford University Press).

MARSDEN, DAVID (1999). *A Theory of Employment Systems*, (Oxford: Oxford University Press).

MEYER, KLAUS (2006). 'Globalfocusing: From Domestic Conglomerate to Global Specialists', *Journal of Management Studies* 43: 1109–44.

MINTZBERG, HENRY (1983). *Structure in Fives: Designing Effective Organizations*, (Englewood Cliffs, NJ: Prentice-Hall).

MIOZZO, MARCELA and DAMIAN GRIMSHAW (eds.) (2006). *Knowledge Intensive Business Services: Organizational Forms and National Institutions*, (Cheltenham: Edward Elgar).

MORCK, RANDALL (ed.) (2007). *A History of Corporate Governance Around the World*, (Chicago: University of Chicago Press).

MORGAN, GLENN (2005). 'Institutional Complementarities, Path Dependency, and the Dynamics of Firms', in G. Morgan et al. (eds.), *Changing Capitalisms?*, 415–46.

——and SIGRID QUACK (2005). 'Internationalization and Capability Development in Professional Service Firms', in G. Morgan, R. Whitley, and E. Moen (eds.), *Changing Capitalisms?*, 277–311.

——RICHARD WHITLEY, and ELI MOEN (eds.) (2005). *Changing Capitalisms? Internationalization, Institutional Change, and Systems of Economic Organization*, (Oxford: Oxford University Press).

MORRIS-SUZUKI, TESSA (1994). *The Technological Transformation of Japan: From the Seventeenth to the Twenty-First Century*, (Cambridge: Cambridge University Press).

MOWERY, DAVID and BHAVEN SAMPAT (2005). 'Universities in National Innovation Systems', in J. Fagerberg, D. Mowery, and R. Nelson (eds.), *The Oxford Handbook of Innovation*, (Oxford: Oxford University Press), 209–39.

PAAUW, LORI DE (2009). *The Effects of Institutional Systems on Biotech Start-ups in Great Britain and the Netherlands*, unpublished PhD thesis, Manchester Business School, University of Manchester.

PIORE, M. and C. F. SABEL (1984). *The Second Industrial Divide*, (New York, Basic Books).

REDDING, S. G. (1990). *The Spirit of Chinese Capitalism*, (Berlin: de Gruyter).

RUBERY, JILL and DAMIAN GRIMSHAW (2003). *The Organization of Employment*, (Basingstoke: Palgrave Macmillan).

RULE, JAMES B (1997). *Theory and Progress in Social Science*, (Cambridge: Cambridge University Press).

SAKO, MARI (2003). 'Modularity and Outsourcing: The Nature of Co-evolution of Product Architecture and Organization Architecture of the Global Automobile Industry', in A. Prencipe, A. Davies, and M. Hobday (eds.), *The Business of Systems Integration*, (Oxford: Oxford University Press), 229–53.

SOSKICE, D. (1999). 'Divergent Production Regimes: Coordinated and uncoordinated market economies in the 1980s and 1990s,' pp. 101–134 in Kitschelt, H., P. Lange, G. Marks and J. Stephens (eds.) *Continuity and Change in Contemporary Capitalism*, (Cambridge: Cambridge University Press).

Sorge, Arndt (1991). 'Strategic Fit and the Societal Effect: Interpreting Cross-national Comparisons of Technology, Organization and Human Resources', *Organization Studies*, 12: 161–90.

——and Malcolm Warner (1986). *Comparative Factory Organisation: An Anglo-German Comparison of Management and Manpower in Manufacturing*, (Aldershot: Gower).

Streeck, Wolfgang (1992). *Social Institutions and Economic Performance: Studies of Industrial Relations in Advanced Capitalist Economies*, (London: Sage).

——and Kathleen Thelen (eds.) (2005). 'Institutional Change in Advanced Political Economies', in W. Streeck and K. Thelen (eds.), *Beyond Continuity*, (Oxford: Oxford University Press). 1–39.

Sturgeon, Timothy (2002). 'Modular Production Networks: A New American Model of Industrial Organization', *Industrial and Corporate Change* 11: 451–96.

——(2007). 'How Globalization Drives Institutional Diversity: The Japanese Electronics Industry's Response to Value Chain Modularity', *Journal of East Asian Studies* 7(1): 1–34.

Suchman, Mark (2000). 'Dealmakers and Counsellors: Law Firms as Intermediaries in the Development of Silicon Valley', in M. Kenney (ed.), *Understanding Silicon Valley*, 71–97.

Takeishi, Akira and Takahiro Fujimoto (2003). 'Modularization in the Car Industry: Interlinked Multiple Hierarchies of Product, Production, and Supplier systems', in A. Prencipe, A. Davies, and M. Hobday (eds.), *The Business of Systems Integration*, (Oxford: Oxford University Press), 254–78.

Teece, David (2000). *Managing Intellectual Capital*, (Oxford: Oxford University Press).

——G. Pisano and A. Shuen (1997). 'Dynamic Capabilities and Strategic Management', *Strategic Management Journal*, 18(7): 509–533.

Tylecote, Andrew and Francesca Visintin (2008). *Corporate Governance, Finance and the Technological Advantage of Nations*, (Abingdon, UK: Routledge).

Whitley, Richard (1999). *Divergent Capitalisms: The Social Structuring and Change of Business Systems*, (Oxford: Oxford University Press).

——(2003). 'Competition and Pluralism in the Public Sciences: The impact of Institutional Frameworks on the Organisation of Academic Science', *Research Policy* 32: 1015–29.

——(2006). 'Project-based Firms: New Organisational Form or Variations on a Theme?', *Industrial and Corporate Change* 15: 77–99.

——(2007). *Business Systems and Organizational Capabilities*, (Oxford: Oxford University Press).

Yamamura, Kozo and Wolfgang Streeck (eds.) (2003). *The End of Diversity? Prospects for German and Japanese Capitalism*, (Ithaca, NY: Cornell University Press).

CHAPTER 14

INSTITUTIONS, WEALTH, AND INEQUALITY

LANE KENWORTHY[1]

INTRODUCTION

Wealth and inequality are among the key macro-level outcomes studied by social scientists. They are of considerable interest not only to researchers but also to citizens and policymakers. This chapter reviews and assesses theories and empirical findings on the impact of institutions on national wealth and inequality. I focus on macro-comparative research on affluent countries.

National wealth typically is measured as gross domestic product (GDP) per capita. Prior to the 1970s, thinking about the determinants of national wealth was dominated by the approach used by mainstream economists. That approach focuses on capital, labour, and technology, and it assumes that poorer countries catch up with richer ones via factor equalization. In the 1950s and 1960s, patterns among the world's richest countries seemed to more or less conform to this expectation. But in the 1970s a number of these countries experienced sharp economic downturns. Moreover, their macroeconomic performance varied in ways not easily accounted for by the standard framework.

---

[1] A web appendix is available at www.u.arizona.edu/~lkenwor; it includes a list of data definitions and sources, figures referred to in the chapter but not shown here, and the data used in the analyses.

This generated interest in the impact of economic, social, and political institutions on national wealth. Such institutions range from the organization of workers and employers to policymakers' partisan orientations to non-market or extra-market relationships between firms. Since the 1970s a growing number of social scientists have theorized and empirically assessed the effects of these and other institutions on macroeconomic outcomes such as growth, unemployment, and inflation. I re-examine the leading hypotheses about the effect of institutions on national wealth. I find little or no support for most of them in accounting for differences across affluent countries in recent decades.

The impact of institutions on inequality has received somewhat less attention from comparative researchers. This is due in part to the fact that in many countries inequality appears to have changed very little in the 1950s, 1960s, and 1970s. Perhaps more importantly, until relatively recently comparative analysis was hindered by limited availability of cross-nationally comparable data on the distribution of earnings and income. Better data are now available, and research has blossomed in the past decade. The data indicate sizeable cross-country differences in the level of inequality in the rich nations as well as substantial changes since the 1970s in some of them. Recent comparative study suggests strong effects of institutions on inequality, though important questions are as yet unanswered.

Institutions and National Wealth

There is considerable variation in national wealth among the twenty affluent OECD countries on which comparative analysis has tended to focus. As of 2007, per capita GDP ranged from just under $40,000 in Norway to less than $20,000 in Portugal (in 2000 US dollars). Economic growth too has differed sharply: between 1973 and 2007 (both business cycle peak years), the average annual rate of growth ranged from 4 per cent in Ireland to 1 per cent in Switzerland.

How much of this variation, if any, is due to differences in institutions? I begin with a summary of existing theory and then turn to empirical assessment.

Theory

A variety of hypotheses suggest effects of institutions and institutional configurations on national wealth. I focus on eight prominent ones.

State guidance

Markets are good at allocating resources to productive use. But they are far from perfect in so doing. Private investors may have short-time horizons, emphasizing near-term profits over productivity, long-run returns, market share, or export competitiveness. They may have limited information. They may be unconcerned about spillover benefits from particular firms and industries. They may benefit from, and thereby accentuate, limits to competition. In these ways, market allocation of resources may be growth-inhibiting.

Governments can help to remedy this sort of market failure via proactive steering of capital toward particular firms or sectors (Shonfield 1965; Johnson 1982; Magaziner and Reich 1983; Zysman 1983; Hall 1986; Dore 1987; Amsden 1989; Stiglitz 1989; Rodrik 2007). Means of doing this include subsidies, favourable loan terms, assistance with coordination, export help, import protection, and public ownership. This type of state guidance sometimes is referred to as 'industrial policy'. Arguments suggesting that industrial policy boosts economic growth were particularly prominent in the 1980s and early 1990s. They often identified Japan and France as exemplars. Even the comparatively non-interventionist US government played a key role in the development of industries such as agriculture and commercial aircraft.

Sceptics of government steering of capital tend to focus on government failure (Friedman 1961; Krugman 1994). Governments too have limited information. They are subject to pressure from rent-seeking interest groups who aim for their own benefit rather than the most productive allocation of investment. While this type of government action might help in principle, say critics, in practice it tends not to.

Organization of interest groups

In democratic societies, individuals tend to organize in interest groups. These groups can contribute to well-being and happiness. But such groups also have an incentive to lobby government for special favours and impede market functioning, creating what Mancur Olson (1982) termed 'institutional sclerosis'. This tends to reduce economic growth. Olson argued that interest groups tend to accumulate over time, though wars may weaken or destroy them. The longer a country has experienced a period of uninterrupted democracy, therefore, the greater the sclerosis and the slower the rate of growth.

Olson noted that 'encompassing' interest groups—ones that represent a relatively large share of the population—have an incentive to act differently from smaller ones. Encompassing groups are more likely to internalize the costs of rent-seeking and thus to engage in behaviour that is good, rather than bad, for economic growth.

Olson (1982, 1996) thus offered two predictions about the impact of interest groups on national wealth. First, the number of years of uninterrupted democracy should be negatively related to economic growth. Second, the relationship between interest group encompassingness and economic growth should be U-shaped, with both low and high levels conducive to healthy performance.

Corporatist concertation

Regularized dialogue among organized interest groups and between interest groups and government may produce less conflictual behaviour and greater policy coherence (Katzenstein 1985; Wilensky and Turner 1987). Government policy choices should tend to be based on more and better information, to be better coordinated across policy areas, and to be less subject to dispute and resistance once implemented.

This type of arrangement, usually referred to as corporatism or corporatist concertation, has received perhaps more attention from comparative institutionalists than any other. Much of the theorizing and empirical assessment, however, has focused on employment performance (unemployment or employment rates and growth) rather than national wealth (see Kenworthy 2001 for citations).

Left government

Political parties can be expected to pursue policies that serve the real and/or perceived economic interests of their chief constituencies. For left parties this means the working class and the poor; for right parties it means owners of capital and higher-paid employees. Douglas Hibbs (1977) and others have argued that left parties are therefore likely to implement macroeconomic policy strategies that aim for low unemployment (and thus rapid economic growth), while right parties are more likely to favour low inflation (and thus slower growth).

Hibbs (1977, 1987) found support in a cross-country analysis and in an examination of the United States. Carles Boix (1999) found support in analyses of cross-country patterns, though he argued that the relevant policies are public investment and education rather than monetary and fiscal. Larry Bartels (2008) has recently updated the analysis of the US case, again finding strong support.

Interest group-government coherence

Following on the growing attention to government partisanship and corporatism in the 1970s and the early 1980s, Peter Lange and Geoffrey Garrett (1985) suggested a modification of the corporatism hypothesis that takes into account a potential interaction with government partisanship. They argued that when unions are centralized and strong, left governments tend to pursue expansionary fiscal and social policy, knowing that doing so will not lead to wage militancy. When unions are fragmented and weak, right governments are able to implement free-market policies. Each of these scenarios, they argued, is conducive to economic growth. In the other two possible configurations—strong unions with right government, weak unions with left government—incoherence between government action and union wage behaviour were predicted. This should produce slower growth. Their analyses of patterns of economic growth in affluent democracies in the 1970s and 1980s suggested support for the hypothesis (Lange and Garrett 1985; Alvarez, Garrett, and Lange 1991; Beck et al. 1993).

Cooperation-promoting institutions

Long-term relationships and formal organization promote cooperation within and between firms and between interest groups and the state (Zysman 1983; Dore 1987; Aoki 1988; Florida and Kenney 1990; Womack, Jones, and Roos 1990; Herrigel 1994). For example, long-term partnerships with suppliers potentially offer companies advantages relative to short-term, market-based supplier relationships or vertical integration. Such partnerships enable firms to reap the benefits of low fixed costs and supplier expertise while encouraging suppliers to invest in long-term improvements and to communicate extensively both with the purchaser and with other suppliers. Within the firm, functional specialization of the stages along the production chain—research, design, development, production, and so on— can render companies slow and ineffective at moving from creation to production. The process becomes disjointed, leading to less coherence, more delays, and higher costs as errors are discovered late in the process. Cross-functional project teams, whose members represent different departments and stay with a project as it moves through the various stages, can enhance coordination and continuity and thereby reduce the time and costs involved in bringing new products, or product improvements, to market.

Kenworthy (1995) and Hicks and Kenworthy (1998) identified cooperation-inducing institutions in nine spheres. Some apply to 'macro'-level actors (government, union confederations, employer confederations), some to the 'meso'-level (between firms), and some to the 'micro'-level (within firms). They are: (1) relations among firms across industries; (2) relations among unions; (3) relations between the state and interest groups; (4) relations among firms and investors; (5) relations among firms and suppliers; (6) relations among competing firms; (7) relations between labour and management; (8) relations among workers; (9) relations among functional departments within firms. Hicks and Kenworthy suggested that countries with greater prevalence of cooperation-inducing institutions are likely to grow more rapidly.

Institutional coherence

Peter Hall and David Soskice's (2001) 'varieties of capitalism' typology has been highly influential over the past decade. Hall and Soskice examined five economic 'spheres': (1) industrial relations (bargaining over wages and working conditions); (2) vocational training and education; (3) corporate governance (relations between firms and their investors); (4) inter-firm relations (between firms and their suppliers, clients, and competitors); (5) relations with employees (information-sharing, work effort incentives). Their core hypothesis is that political economies tend to be characterized by 'institutional complementarities', whereby the presence of one institution increases the efficiency of another. For instance,

long-term employment is more feasible where the financial system provides capital on terms that are not sensitive to current profitability. Conversely, fluid labor markets may be more effective at sustaining employment in the presence of financial markets that transfer resources readily among endeavors thereby maintaining a demand for labor. (Hall and Soskice 2001: 18)

Hall and Soskice found that institutional complementarities do indeed tend to be present in the affluent OECD economies, and they suggested that these economies fall into two groups. Coordination is market-based in six 'liberal market economies': Australia, Canada, Ireland, New Zealand, the United Kingdom, and the United States. Coordination is based largely on non-market or extra-market institutions in ten 'coordinated market economies': Austria, Belgium, Denmark, Finland, Germany, Japan, the Netherlands, Norway, Sweden, and Switzerland.

Hall and Soskice (2001) and Hall and Gingerich (2004) hypothesized that economic performance is a function of institutional coherence. Both non-market- and market-oriented institutions can work well provided they are coupled with complementary institutions in other spheres. Institutional configurations that more closely correspond to either of the two pure types tend to promote growth.

Ease of business start-up, hiring and firing, and reaping rewards from innovation

Since Adam Smith (1776), a stream of analysts and commentators have argued that the institutions most conducive to national wealth in a capitalist economy are those that facilitate the ability of economic actors to form companies, hire and fire employees, and reap the rewards of innovation (North 1990; Porter 1990; Sapir et al. 2004; Baumol, Litan, and Schramm 2007). Such institutions include strong and clear protection of property rights, effective anti-trust enforcement, limited protection of market position for firms and job security for employees, a financial system that provides capital at reasonable cost, stable and consistent macroeconomic policy, government support for research and development, and wide-reaching provision of high-quality education.

This is not the same thing as *laissez-faire*, as such a framework requires an active government and may well benefit from interest group organization and coordination. Nor does it presuppose minimal taxation and government spending. As we will see in the next section, the affluent countries rated as having the best institutional framework in this respect include some with comparatively high tax and spending levels and governments that actively intervene in certain aspects of the economy.

Empirical assessment

Though by no means immune to criticism, each of these eight hypotheses is theoretically sensible. The debate cannot be resolved on theoretical grounds; it can only be adjudicated empirically. An additional virtue of an empirical assessment is that most of these theories were initially tested over a particular and relatively short time period. To mention just one example, Katzenstein's (1985) influential book on corporatism and economic performance examined data for only the 1970s. Which of these hypotheses prove helpful when examined over a relatively lengthy set of years?

Data, measures, method

We need a measure of national wealth. As I noted earlier, the standard one is GDP per capita. GDP is a measure of economic output, and a per capita measure is an average. Both of these aspects are potentially problematic. Median household income more directly and accurately taps how the typical household is faring. However, available data suggest that across countries GDP per capita and median household income correlate quite closely (Kenworthy 2004, ch. 4). Given this, it makes sense to use GDP per capita, as it is available for more countries and years.

Should the focus be on variation in levels of per capita GDP or on variation in growth? I see no strong reason to prefer one or the other and so will include both.

What period should be covered? The post-war 'golden age' is widely viewed as having ended in 1973. I focus on the years since then.

In measuring economic growth, it is essential to adjust for 'catch-up' effects: countries that begin with a lower level of per capita GDP are able to grow more rapidly by borrowing technology from richer nations. I do so by regressing growth of per capita GDP on each country's level of per capita GDP in the initial year (1973). The residuals from this regression represent 'catch-up-adjusted' economic growth.

Most empirical analyses have examined growth over relatively short periods. Three considerations favour an empirical focus on the long run. First, long-term growth matters much more for countries than growth in particular periods. Second, among the countries of interest, long-run growth patterns have differed from period-specific growth patterns. Across these nations, correlations between (catch-up-adjusted) growth over 1973–2007 and over the business cycles of 1973–79, 1979–89, 1989–2000, and 2000–07 are mostly moderate in strength: .61, .32, .93, and .51, respectively. Third, many of the institutions identified in this literature change slowly, if at all, over time; hence the cross-country variation has remained relatively constant. For these reasons, I use a long-run measure. There are drawbacks: this will hide patterns that, due to variation over time in the institution or in its causal effects, are period-specific and some of these institutions are measured over only part of the 1973–2007 period. Nonetheless, in my view an assessment of long-run patterns is the preferable strategy.

As the first chart in Figure 14.1 indicates, levels of per capita GDP as of 2007 correlate quite closely with catch-up-adjusted growth rates of per capita GDP over 1973–2007: $r = .85$. I therefore combine the two into a single index. I rank the countries on each of the two measures, then average each country's ranking, then rescale the average rankings to vary between zero and one. The resulting measure is shown in the second chart in Figure 14.1. Higher scores indicate better national

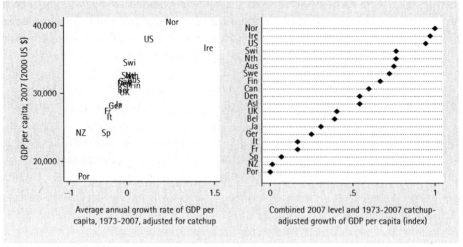

Figure 14.1: National wealth performance, 1973–2007
Note: The measure in the second chart is an index that combines the two indicators shown in the first chart. It is described in the text and in the web appendix.

wealth performance over the 1973–2007 period. I use this index as the dependent variable in the analyses to follow.

How do the institutional theories fare?

Most discussions of state guidance or industrial policy have not attempted a thorough comparative assessment of the hypothesis. Many single out Japan and France as the exemplary cases. Over the 1973–2007 period these two countries were not among the strongest performers. In the second chart in Figure 14.1, Japan ranks fourteenth and France seventeenth among the twenty countries. A dichotomous scoring in which Japan and France are coded as 'high' and all other countries 'low' correlates negatively with the national wealth performance measure. Harold Wilensky and Lowell Turner (1987: 32) attempted to rank-order eight of the countries on degree of industrial policy intervention, based on their reading of the secondary literature. This ranking too is negatively associated with the national wealth index (web appendix figure A1). Neither of these scorings, then, yields support for the government intervention hypothesis.

Two principal variables have been used to capture Mancur Olson's institutional sclerosis theory, which emphasizes the organization of interest groups. One is the number of years since a country became democratic. The hypothesis is that in the absence of major societal disruptions, such as war, interest groups grow in size and influence, which is bad for national wealth. For this measure the expectation is for a negative association. The second is unionization. Unions are viewed as the principal example of an interest group that may impede market functioning, both by influencing wages and employer behaviour and by lobbying government for special privileges. For this measure the expectation is for a U-shaped pattern, with countries that score low or high doing better than those at intermediate levels. Bivariate patterns do not support the Olson hypothesis (web appendix figure A2).

Corporatism has been measured in a variety of ways (Siaroff 1999; Kenworthy 2003). Some focus on the degree or centralization of union and/or employer organization. Others concentrate on the degree or type of input organized interest groups have in policy-making. The latter is the focus of the hypotheses of Katzenstein, Wilensky, and Turner, and others who argue that corporatist concertation contributes to national wealth. I consider two measures here. One, created by Siaroff (1999), is a composite index of 23 corporatism measures. The other, from Franz Traxler, Sabine Blaschke, and Bernhard Kittel (2001), aims to directly measure union participation in the policy-making process. The Siaroff corporatism index is positively correlated with the national wealth performance index, though the association is modest in magnitude ($r = .37$). There is no bivariate association between union participation in policy-making and national wealth (web appendix figure A3).

The most common indicator of left government is the share of cabinet seats held by parties of the left. An alternative measure, devised and scored by Thomas Cusack (2002), assesses the political centre of gravity of the legislature, with higher scores indicating a stronger left presence. Unfortunately, these centre of gravity scores are available only through 1997. These two partisanship measures correlate at .62, suggesting similarity but far from perfect overlap. Neither is positively correlated with national wealth at the bivariate level (web appendix figure A4).

Lange and Garrett analyse the impact of interest group–government coherence using an interaction. I use an alternative measure. First, I use their 'labour organization index' (Alvarez, Garrett, and Lange 1991: 553) to create the union encompassingness component. Countries that score high on the index are Sweden, Norway, Austria, Denmark, Finland, and Belgium. Countries that score low are Japan, France, the United States, and Canada. New Zealand and Switzerland were not included in their scores; I add them to this low-scoring group (see Kenworthy 2003 for justification). For countries with high union encompassingness, I calculate the number of years from 1973 to 2002 (the latest year for which data are available) in which left party cabinet share was 50 per cent or more. For countries with low encompassingness, I calculate the number of years in which right party cabinet share exceeded 50 per cent. In other words, the measure is a count of the number of years in a country in which there were strong unions with left government or weak unions with right government. Higher scores reflect more interest group–government coherence. There is no indication of the expected positive association between this measure and national wealth performance; the bivariate correlation is nil (web appendix figure A5).

In testing the hypothesis that cooperation-promoting institutions boost national wealth, Kenworthy (1995) and Hicks and Kenworthy (1998) used composite measures. In the latter study, each country was scored on the prevalence (low, medium, or high) of cooperation-inducing institutions in each of nine economic spheres.

A factor analysis suggested two dimensions of cooperation: 'firm-level cooperation' and 'neocorporatism'. The former was positively associated with economic growth in pooled regressions covering eighteen countries and four business-cycle periods. But the average scores for this firm-level cooperation index over 1973–94 (the most recent years available) do not correlate positively with the national wealth index. Nor do the average cooperation scores for all nine economic spheres (web appendix figure A6).

Hall and Soskice did not attempt an empirical assessment of their hypothesis that institutional coherence contributes to national wealth, but Hall and Daniel Gingerich (2004) have done so. They develop a 'coordination index' that aims to gauge the degree to which countries rely on non-market economic institutions. The index is created via factor analysis of six indicators, each measured as of the early- or mid-1990s: (1) shareholder power; (2) dispersion of control; (3) size of the stock market; (4) level of wage coordination; (5) degree of wage coordination; (6) labour turnover. The factor analysis yielded a single factor, which is highly correlated with each of these six indicators. I have rescored the Hall-Gingerich factor scores to create a variable in which more institutional coherence is scored high and less coherence is scored low. Additionally, in a re-examination of the Hall-Gingerich analysis I created an alternative measure of institutional coherence (Kenworthy 2006). It is a three-category ranking. The bivariate association between each of these two institutional coherence measures and the national wealth index is very close to zero (web appendix figure A7).

Baumol, Litan, and Schramm (2007) suggest that a useful measure of the ease of starting a business, hiring and firing employees, and reaping the rewards of innovation is an 'ease of doing business' index created by the World Bank. Each country is scored in five areas: (1) the cost of starting a business (percentage of income per capita); (2) the cost of registering property; (3) the difficulty of hiring employees (index); (4) the difficulty of firing employees (index); (5) the cost of enforcing contracts (percentage of debt). These scores are aggregated to form an index, which is rescaled to vary from zero to one. A key limitation of the ease of doing business index is that it is available only beginning in the mid-2000s, which is the end of the period over which national wealth performance is measured. An alternative is an index of product market regulations. Such regulations include barriers to entry, barriers to trade, price controls, government involvement in business operations, public ownership, and market concentration. The OECD (2002a) has created a summary indicator—an index ranging from zero to six—based on product market regulations in seven industries. I use an updated version of these data from Bassanini and Duval (2006); it covers the period from 1982 to 2003. For both of these indicators, the bivariate association with the national wealth measure is in the hypothesized direction, and the correlation coefficients are of moderate magnitude ($r = .37, -.30$; see web appendix figure A8).

Among these eight hypothesized institutional determinants of national wealth, then, the bivariate patterns suggest support for only two: corporatist concertation and the ease of doing business.

Figure 14.2 shows the results of multivariate regression analyses. The regressions are ordinary least squares. The dependent variable is the national wealth performance

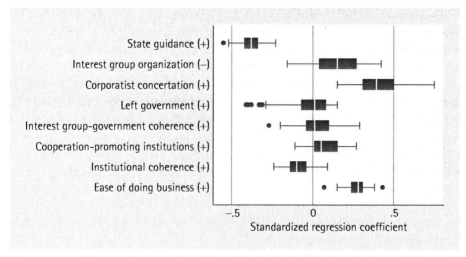

Figure 14.2: Regression results: hypothesized institutional determinants of national wealth

Note: Standardized coefficients from ordinary least squares (OLS) regressions using all possible combinations of three or fewer of the independent variables. The independent variables include the eight listed in the figure plus imports and real long-term interest rates. The expected coefficient signs are shown in parentheses. The sign for interest group organization is expected to be negative because the indicator is the number of years of uninterrupted democracy. Dependent variable: national wealth performance, 1973–2007 (see Figure 14.1). Portugal and Spain are not included due to missing data. The 'whiskers' represent the minimum and maximum coefficients. The edges of the box indicate the 25th- and 75th-percentile coefficients. The vertical white line is the median coefficient. Separate dots indicate 'outliers'—coefficients that are substantially larger or smaller than the others for that variable. The number of regressions for each independent variable ranges from 37 to 45. For data definitions and sources, see the web appendix.

index (Figure 14.1). There are eighteen observations: the twenty countries minus Portugal and Spain, which are missing for too many of the measures to be included. Each institutional hypothesis is represented by one indicator. In all but one instance I use the one for which the evidence from the bivariate analyses is most supportive. The exception is the institutional coherence hypothesis; I use the Hall-Gingerich index because the other measure was created largely for purposes of sensitivity testing. To the eight institutional variables I add two controls: (1) imports as a share of GDP averaged over 1973 to 2007, to account for impact of globalization; (2) real long-term interest rates, also averaged over 1973–2007, to control for monetary policy choices that often are outside the influence of interest groups and political parties.

I estimate a series of regressions that include all possible combinations of three or fewer of the independent variables. This amounts to approximately forty regressions for each institutional variable. Figure 14.2 reports the results for each variable in a 'box-and-whisker' plot (boxplot). To enable comparison of their magnitude, the coefficients are standardized. No estimates of statistical significance are reported, as this group amounts to more or less the full population of rich countries over the past several decades rather than a representative sample.

The multivariate results are largely consistent with the bivariate patterns. Six of the eight institutional hypotheses receive little or no support. The coefficients for state guidance, interest group organization, and institutional coherence tend to be notably different from zero, but they have the wrong sign. The state guidance and institutional coherence coefficients are expected to be positively signed, but they are almost always negative. Olson's interest group organization hypothesis is operationalized as a country's number of years of uninterrupted democracy; its coefficient is expected to be negatively signed but instead is nearly always positive. Left government, interest group-government coherence, and cooperation-promoting institutions are expected to have positively signed coefficients. Each does tend to be positive, but most of the coefficients are close to zero.

Corporatist concertation is hypothesized to have a positive effect on national wealth. Its coefficients are always positive in the regressions, and their median size is .39. Norway is a key supportive case—high corporatism, strong national wealth performance (see web appendix figure A3)—and Norway's position on the national wealth measure must be tempered by recognition of the role North Sea oil has played in raising the country's gross domestic product. If Norway is omitted from the regressions, the median coefficient drops to .29; but the smallest remains well above zero, at .15.

The 'ease of doing business' coefficient is consistently positive in the regressions. The median coefficient is .28. This result is somewhat sensitive to the countries included. If Norway or the United States is omitted, the association remains consistently positive but the median coefficient shrinks to .18 and .17, respectively. On the other hand, with New Zealand excluded the median coefficient jumps to .50. As noted earlier, it bears emphasizing that the 'ease of doing business' does not require low taxes or a minimal welfare state. All of the Nordic countries feature comparatively heavy taxation and government spending, yet Norway and Denmark rank among the top five on the 'ease of doing business' index and Sweden and Finland are among the top ten (web appendix figure A8). Nor are any of these countries on the high end in strictness of product market regulations.

Summary: Institutions and national wealth

We have a number of plausible theories about the impact of institutions on national wealth. But the empirical record of the past generation offers little evidence of strong institutional effects. Six of the eight hypotheses examined here receive no support at all. And a regression that includes the only two that are robustly associated with national wealth performance in the expected direction—corporatist concertation and the 'ease of doing business'—accounts for a relatively small amount of the cross-country variation ($R^2 = .24$).

The lack of association between most of the institutional factors and national wealth does not necessarily mean these theories are wrong. One or more may apply to a subset of the countries but not to others. And some may hold only for certain time periods. Also, some may work only under particular conditions; that is, they may be observable only via interactions that I have not considered here. An additional possibility is that measurement problems have prevented true associations from being revealed.

Still, this look at the data, across a larger number of countries and a longer period of time than in previous research, suggests reasons for a healthy dose of scepticism about most of these institutional hypotheses.

INSTITUTIONS AND INEQUALITY

In this section, I explore the impact of institutions on cross-country and over-time variation in inequality. There are numerous aspects of inequality. Reliable comparative data are available mainly for earnings and income, so that will be my focus here. The distribution of posttransfer-posttax ('disposable') income among households is what researchers and policymakers should, ultimately, be most interested in understanding (Kenworthy 2008). This is influenced primarily by the distribution of earnings among employed individuals, by the distribution of employment and earnings among households, and by government redistribution (Kenworthy 2004, 2008). I consider each of these three here. The comparative evidence suggests strong effects of institutions on inequality.

Inequality of earnings across employed individuals

Earnings inequality refers to the distribution of earnings among individuals who are employed. The best available comparative data, compiled by the OECD, include only people employed full-time (30 hours or more per week). This is sensible, as those employed part-time tend to earn less not only on a per hour basis but also because they work fewer hours.

The most common framework for explaining earnings inequality among employed individuals focuses on supply and demand factors. These include the distribution of skills across individuals, employer demand for different skills, the distribution of employment across sectors and firms, the degree of trade and foreign investment, and the gender and immigrant share in employment, among others (Katz and Autor 1999; Morris and Western 1999; Gottschalk and Danziger 2005; Mishel, Bernstein, and Shierholz 2009).

Earnings inequality is closely correlated across countries with the distribution of skills, if the latter is measured using literacy. But there is reason to doubt that this correlation indicates a strong causal relationship. Dan Devroye and Richard Freeman (2002) decompose the variation in earnings inequality across four countries: Germany, the Netherlands, Sweden, and the United States. They find that literacy inequality accounts for only 7 per cent of the variation. A much larger portion of the variation, 36 per cent, owes to the larger skill premium in the United States than in the other three countries. In other words, the variation in earnings inequality across these four countries is more a product of the degree to which skills differences translate into earnings differences than of the degree of skills differences per se. Devroye and Freeman then examine earnings inequality among Americans within relatively narrow bands of skills and find that earnings inequality within such groups tends to exceed earnings inequality among *all* employed individuals in the other three countries. Francine Blau and Lawrence Kahn (2002b) have used the International Adult Literacy Survey (IALS) data to examine men and women separately and native-born and immigrant Americans separately, and they reach a similar conclusion.

Institutional factors that have been highlighted include the level of unionization, the centralization of wage bargaining, government-established minimum wages, the share of employment that is in the public sector, and the types of pay schemes used by firms (skill-based, seniority-based, performance-based). Among the rich nations, a sizable amount of the cross-country variation in earnings inequality can be explained by two of these institutional factors: the degree of unionization and the degree of centralization of wage bargaining (web appendix figure A9; Wallerstein 1999; Rueda and Pontusson 2000; Blau and Kahn 2002b; Devroye and Freeman 2002; Card, Lemieux, and Riddell 2003; DiPrete 2005; Koeniger, Leonardi, and Nunziata 2007; Baccaro 2008; Kenworthy 2008).

What are the causal mechanisms linking unionization and wage centralization to low earnings inequality? Unions tend to be committed to some degree of wage compression, for ideological reasons and as a strategy for helping their least advantaged members (Freeman and Medoff 1984; Swenson 1989; Wallerstein 1999). They have greater leverage in wage bargaining than do individual employees, and hence are to some degree able to implement this preference. Centralization of wage bargaining across firms and sectors magnifies both the incentive and power effects.

Does one of these two institutional factors matter more than the other? Cross-sectional analysis cannot help, because unionization and wage centralization are too closely correlated across nations. We might, therefore, turn to over-time developments within countries since the early 1970s (see web appendix figure A10). Unfortunately, this too yields no definitive answer. In the United States earnings inequality has risen sharply. Unionization declined through most of this period, whereas wage centralization began minimal and remained so. This suggests a key role for unionization. In Sweden, by contrast, earnings inequality increased in the 1980s (though far less than in the US) despite rising union density. This rise seems much more likely to have been influenced by the decline in bargaining centralization that occurred in the early 1980s. In the United Kingdom, rising earnings inequality in the 1980s coincided with 'both' falling unionization and a decline in wage centralization.

In a recent analysis of cross-country variation in change in earnings inequality, Oskarsson (2005) suggests that the level of wage centralization mediates the impact of factors such as trade and unionization (see also Kenworthy 2007). In a decentralized bargaining context, increased trade with less developed countries and/or declining unionization yield rising earnings inequality. Where bargaining is centralized, they do not.

The theories and data I have discussed thus far apply to inequality of earnings among the bulk of those with paying jobs. But surveys, which are the basis of data on earnings for most countries, have a difficult time capturing the earnings and incomes of those at the very top of the distribution; to ensure participation of the highest earners in such surveys, high earnings often are 'top coded'. In recent years several analysts have examined tax data in order to get better information about top earnings and incomes (Atkinson and Piketty 2007a, 2007b; Leigh 2007).

In most of the countries for which data are available, the top 1 per cent's share declined from 1950 through the 1970s (web appendix figure A11). Around 1980 the trend began to diverge sharply. In five English-speaking countries—Australia, Canada, New Zealand, the United Kingdom, and the United States—the top 1 per cent's share has risen rapidly. In five other nations—France, Germany, Japan, the Netherlands, and Sweden—it has either held constant or risen only slightly. These data are for incomes rather than earnings; but they exclude capital gains, so changes over time are likely to reflect changes in earnings rather than in investment income. Thomas Piketty and Emmanuel Saez (2006: 204) conclude that in the English-speaking countries 'This rise in top income shares is not due to the revival of top capital incomes, but rather to the very large increases in top wages (especially executive compensation).'

What accounts for the cross-country variation? Hypotheses include market competition, labour power, government partisanship, tax systems, corporate governance practices, the demand for entertainment, athletic, and English-speaking executive talent ('winner-takes-all' markets), and norms (Piketty and Saez 2006; Atkinson and Leigh 2007; Gordon and Dew-Becker 2007; Krugman 2007; Levy and Temin 2007; Reich 2007; Roine, Vlachos, and Waldenström 2007; Scheve and Stasavage 2007; Leigh 2009). Because the data have become available only recently, however, there has been limited systematic analysis as of yet.

Inequality of employment across households

Earnings vary across individuals, but that is not the only determinant of market (pretransfer-pretax) income differences across households. Also relevant is the distribution of employment across households. Households differ in the number of adults they have, and those with the same number of adults differ in employment. Some households therefore have zero jobs, some have half a job (one part-time job), some one job, some one and a half, some two, and a few more than two.

Differences in individual earnings inequality account for more of the cross-country variation in levels of pretransfer-pretax household income inequality than do various measures that tap employment variation among households (Kenworthy 2008, ch. 3). However, that is due in part to the lack of data on between-household inequality in total hours worked, which is the most appropriate indicator.

Kenworthy (2004, ch. 3) and Kenworthy and Pontusson (2005) find that cross-country variation in changes in pretransfer-pretax household income inequality in the 1980s and 1990s were heavily influenced by differences in employment growth. In countries with rapidly growing employment rates, such as the Netherlands, households that previously had no earners or one earner tended to experience a greater increase in employment than did households that began with more employed members. As a result, market income inequality across households decreased. In countries that experienced employment rate declines, such as Sweden, households beginning with fewer employed members suffered disproportionately, producing a rise in inter-household inequality.

Have institutions affected cross-country variation in employment change? There is an extensive body of research on the impact of institutions such as pay compression, employment protection regulations, government benefit generosity, and taxes on employment performance. Much of it has focused on levels of unemployment or employment (OECD 1994; Nickell and Layard 1999; Scharpf 2000; Blau and Kahn 2002a; Baker et al. 2005; Baccaro and Rei 2007; Bradley and Stephens 2007). Fewer studies have examined changes in employment rates (Iversen and Wren 1998; Esping-Andersen 2000; Kenworthy 2004, 2008; Bassanini and Duval 2006; OECD 2006). The latter have tended to find a negative association across countries between these institutions and employment growth, but one that may be modest in magnitude.

Redistribution

The third major determinant of the posttransfer-posttax distribution of income is government redistribution. Here too there is clear evidence that institutions have mattered.

A long line of research has demonstrated an association across rich nations between left government and the generosity of welfare states (Korpi 1983; Esping-Andersen 1985; Hicks 1999; Huber and Stephens 2001; Swank 2002; Kwon and Pontusson 2010). For ideological reasons and to better serve the material interests of key constituencies—the working class and the poor—left parties tend to favour more extensive government supports and transfers. Other studies have found a similarly-strong association between corporatist concertation and social policy generosity (Hicks and Swank 1992; Hicks and Kenworthy 1998; Hicks 1999). Corporatist arrangements provide worker organizations with direct input into the policymaking process and are thus likely to yield policy outputs that better reflect those organizations' preferences for generous social programmes. Over recent decades both left government and corporatism are strongly associated with social policy generosity (web appendix figure A12).

While there is considerable agreement that left government and corporatism have contributed to redistributive generosity, researchers disagree about their relative importance. The two are too closely correlated with one another to include together in cross-country regression analyses (Huber and Stephens 2001). An alternative strategy is to examine over-time patterns. Unfortunately, this offers little help. Consider three countries in which at least one of these two institutions has varied notably over time since the early 1970s: the United Kingdom, Sweden, and Italy (web appendix figure A13). In the United Kingdom cumulative left government increased in the late 1970s and then held constant for most of the 1980s and 1990s, while corporatist concertation declined sharply between 1979 and the early 1990s. The trend in the redistribution measure followed that of cumulative left government. In Sweden, by contrast, the trend in redistribution followed that of corporatist concertation, particularly in the 1990s. In Italy both cumulative left government and corporatist concertation rose slowly over time, and so too did redistributive generosity.

After increasing steadily for several decades, in the 1980s or 1990s redistributive generosity levelled off or began to decrease in a number of countries. How useful are government partisanship and corporatism in explaining cross-country variation in the timing and degree of this retrenchment process? Studies have focused on the impact of partisanship, with some suggesting a continuing role and others finding little evidence of such an impact (Hicks 1999; Huber and Stephens 2001; Pierson 2001; Swank 2002; Korpi and Palme 2003; Allan and Scruggs 2004; Hicks and Zorn 2005; Kwon and Pontusson 2010).

Summary: Institutions and inequality

Posttransfer-posttax household income inequality is influenced by the distribution of earnings across employed individuals, the distribution of employment across households, and government redistribution. Institutions appear to play a role in accounting for cross-country variation in each of these.

There are two key issues with respect to earnings inequality: the gap among the bulk of the population (often measured with the P90/P10 ratio) and the earnings of those at the very top. Wage bargaining arrangements clearly matter in understanding cross-country differences in the former. Because comparative data on the latter have become available so recently, we have far less understanding of it.

High low-end wages, strong employment protection regulations, generous government benefits, and high payroll and consumption taxes help to reduce inequality in some respects. But by impeding employment growth, they may hinder reduction of inequality of employment across households.

Cross-national differences in redistribution have been heavily influenced by government partisanship and corporatist concertation, though researchers disagree about the relative importance of each and about their continuing relevance.

CONCLUSION

We have extensive theorizing about the influence of institutions and institutional configurations on national wealth, but little empirical support. There has been less theorization of the effect of institutions on inequality, but the empirical record offers much more support for the hypothesized effects. That does not end the story, of course. Empirical analyses, including those in this chapter, may have missed something; and patterns in coming years may differ from those of the past several decades. But that is my take on where we stand at the moment.

REFERENCES

ALLAN, JAMES P. and LYLE SCRUGGS (2004). 'Political Partisanship and Welfare State Reform in Advanced Industrial Societies', *American Journal of Political Science* 48: 496–512.

ALVAREZ, R. MICHAEL, GEOFFREY GARRETT, and PETER LANGE (1991). 'Government Partisanship, Labor Organization, and Macroeconomic Performance', *American Political Science Review* 85: 539–56.

AMSDEN, ALICE (1989). *Asia's Next Giant: South Korea and Late Industrialization*, (Oxford: Oxford University Press).

AOKI, MASAHIKO (1988). *Information, Incentives, and Bargaining in the Japanese Economy*, (Cambridge: Cambridge University Press).

ATKINSON, ANTHONY B. and ANDREW LEIGH (2007). 'The Distribution of Top Incomes in Five Anglo-Saxon Countries Over the Twentieth Century'. Unpublished.

——and THOMAS PIKETTY (eds.) (2007a). *Top Incomes over the Twentieth Century*, (Oxford: Oxford University Press).

——(2007b). 'Towards a Unified Data Set on Top Incomes', in *Top Incomes over the Twentieth Century*, eds. Anthony B. Atkinson and Thomas Piketty, (Oxford: Oxford University Press), 531–65.

BACCARO, LUCIO (2008). 'Labour Institutions, Globalization, and Inequality'. International Labour Organization.

——and DIEGO REI (2007). 'Institutional Determinants of Unemployment in OECD Countries: Does the Deregulatory View Hold Water?', *International Organization* 61: 527–69.

BAKER, DEAN, ANDREW GLYN, DAVID R. HOWELL, and JOHN SCHMITT (2005). 'Labor Market Institutions and Unemployment: Assessment of the Cross-Country Evidence', in *Fighting*

Unemployment: The Limits of Free Market Orthodoxy, ed. David R. Howell, (Oxford: Oxford University Press), 72–118.

BARTELS, LARRY (2008). *Unequal Democracy*, (New York and Princeton, NJ: Russell Sage Foundation and Princeton University Press).

BASSANINI, ANDREA and ROMAIN DUVAL (2006). 'Employment Patterns in OECD Countries: Reassessing the Role of Policies and Institutions', OECD Social, Employment, and Migration Working Paper 35. Organization for Economic Cooperation and Development. Available at www.oecd.org.

BAUMOL, WILLIAM J., ROBERT E. LITAN, and CARL J. SCHRAMM (2007). *Good Capitalism, Bad Capitalism, and the Economics of Growth and Prosperity*, (New Haven, CT: Yale University Press).

BECK, NATHANIEL, JONATHAN N. KATZ, R. MICHAEL ALVAREZ, GEOFFREY GARRETT, and PETER LANGE (1993). 'Government Partisanship, Labor Organization, and Macroeconomic Performance: A Corrigendum', *American Political Science Review* 87: 945–48.

BLAU, FRANCINE D. and LAWRENCE M. KAHN (2002a). *At Home and Abroad: U.S. Labor Market Performance in International Perspective*, (New York: Russell Sage Foundation).

——(2002b). 'Do Cognitive Test Scores Explain Higher U.S. Wage Inequality?' unpublished, Department of Economics, Cornell University.

BOIX, CARLES (1999). *Political Parties, Growth, and Equality*, (Cambridge: Cambridge University Press).

BRADLEY, DAVID and JOHN STEPHENS (2007). 'Employment Performance in OECD Countries', *Comparative Political Studies* 40: 1486–1510.

CARD, DAVID, THOMAS LEMIEUX, and W. CRAIG RIDDELL (2003). 'Unionization and Wage Inequality: A Comparative Study of the U.S., the U.K., and Canada'. Working Paper 9473. National Bureau of Economic Research. Available at www.nber.org.

CUSACK, THOMAS (2002). 'Center of Political Gravity Data Set'. Available at www.wzb.eu/alt/ism/people/misc/cusack/d_sets.en.htm.

DEVROYE, DAN and RICHARD FREEMAN (2002). 'Does Inequality in Skills Explain Inequality of Earnings Across Advanced Countries?' CEP Discussion Paper 0552. Centre for Economic Performance.

DIPRETE, THOMAS A. (2005). 'Labor Markets, Inequality, and Change', *Work and Occupations* 32: 119–139.

DORE, RONALD (1987). *Taking Japan Seriously*, (Stanford: Stanford University Press).

ESPING-ANDERSEN, Gøsta (1985). *Politics against Markets*, (Princeton, NJ: Princeton University Press).

——(1990). *The Three Worlds of Welfare Capitalism*, (Princeton, NJ: Princeton University Press).

——(2000). 'Regulation and Context: Reconsidering the Correlates of Unemployment', in *Why Deregulate Labour Markets?* eds. Gøsta Esping-Andersen and Marino Regini, (Oxford: Oxford University Press), 99–112.

FLORIDA, RICHARD and MARTIN KENNEY (1990). *The Breakthrough Illusion: Corporate America's Failure to Move from Innovation to Mass Production*, (New York: Basic Books).

FREEMAN, RICHARD B. and JAMES L. MEDOFF (1984). *What Do Unions Do?*, (New York: Basic Books).

FRIEDMAN, MILTON (1961). *Capitalism and Freedom*, (Chicago: University of Chicago Press).

GORDON, ROBERT J. and IAN DEW-BECKER (2007). 'Unresolved Issues in the Rise of American Inequality'. Paper presented at the Brookings Panel on Economic Activity.

GOTTSCHALK, PETER and SHELDON DANZIGER (2005). 'Inequality of Wage Rates, Earnings, and Family Income in the United States, 1975–2002', *Review of Income and Wealth* 51: 231–54.

HALL, PETER A. (1986). *Governing the Economy,* (Oxford: Oxford University Press).

——and DANIEL W. GINGERICH (2004). 'Varieties of Capitalism and Institutional Complementarities in the Macroeconomy: An Empirical Analysis'. Discussion Paper 04/5. Max Planck Institute for the Study of Societies. Cologne, Germany. Available at www.mpi-fg-koeln.mpg.de.

——and DAVID SOSKICE (2001). 'An Introduction to Varieties of Capitalism', in *Varieties of Capitalism,* eds. Peter A. Hall and David Soskice, (Oxford: Oxford University Press), 1–68.

HERRIGEL, GARY (1994). 'Industry as a Form of Order: A Comparison of the Historical Development of the Machine Tool Industries in the United States and Germany', in *Governing Capitalist Economies: Performance and Control of Economic Sectors,* eds. J. Rogers Hollingsworth, Philippe C. Schmitter, and Wolfgang Streeck, (Oxford: Oxford University Press).

HIBBS, JR., DOUGLAS A. (1977). 'Political Parties and Macroeconomic Policy', *American Political Science Review* 71: 1467–87.

——(1987). *The American Political Economy: Macroeconomics and Electoral Politics,* (Cambridge, MA: Harvard University Press).

HICKS, ALEXANDER (1999). *Social Democracy and Welfare Capitalism,* (Ithaca, NY: Cornell University Press).

——and LANE KENWORTHY (1998). 'Cooperation and Political Economic Performance in Affluent Democratic Capitalism', *American Journal of Sociology* 103: 1631–72.

——and DUANE SWANK (1992). 'Politics, Institutions, and Welfare Spending in Industrialized Democracies, 1960–1982', *American Political Science Review* 86: 658–74.

——and CHRISTOPHER ZORN (2005). 'Economic Globalization, the Macro Economy, and Reversals of Welfare: Expansion in Affluent Democracies, 1978–94', *International Organization* 59: 631–62.

HUBER, EVELYNE and JOHN D. STEPHENS (2001). *Development and Crisis of the Welfare State,* (Chicago: University of Chicago Press).

IMF (International Monetary Fund) (n.d.). International Financial Statistics database. Available at www. imfstatistics.org.

IVERSEN, TORBEN and ANNE WREN (1998). 'Equality, Employment, and Budgetary Restraint: The Trilemma of the Service Economy', *World Politics* 50: 507–546.

JOHNSON, CHALMERS (1982). *MITI and the Japanese Miracle,* (Stanford: Stanford University Press).

KATZ, LAWRENCE F. and DAVID AUTOR (1999). 'Changes in the Wage Structure and Earnings Inequality', in *Handbook of Labor Economics,* vol. 3A, eds. Orley Ashenfelter and David Card, (Amsterdam: Elsevier).

KATZENSTEIN, PETER J. (1985). *Small States in World Markets,* (Ithaca, NY: Cornell University Press).

KENWORTHY, LANE. (1995). *In Search of National Economic Success: Balancing Competition and Cooperation.* (Thousand Oaks, CA: Sage).

——(2001). 'Wage-Setting Measures: A Survey and Assessment', *World Politics* 54: 57–98.

——(2003). 'Quantitative Indicators of Corporatism', *International Journal of Sociology* 33(3): 10–44.

——(2004). *Egalitarian Capitalism,* (New York: Russell Sage Foundation).

——(2006). 'Institutional Coherence and Macroeconomic Performance', *Socio-Economic Review* 4: 69–91.

——(2007). 'Inequality and Sociology', *American Behavioral Scientist* 50: 584–602.

——(2008). *Jobs with Equality,* (Oxford: Oxford University Press).

——and JONAS PONTUSSON (2005). 'Rising Inequality and the Politics of Redistribution in Affluent Countries', *Perspectives on Politics* 3: 449–71.

KOENIGER, WINFRIED, MARCO LEONARDI, and LUCA NUNZIATA (2007). 'Labor Market Institutions and Wage Inequality', *Industrial and Labor Relations Review* 60: 340–56.

KORPI, WALTER (1983). *The Democratic Class Struggle*, (London: Routledge & Kegan Paul).

——and JOAKIM PALME (2003). 'New Politics and Class Politics in the Context of Austerity and Globalization: Welfare State Regress in 18 Countries, 1975–95', *American Political Science Review* 97: 425–46.

KRUGMAN, PAUL (1994). *Peddling Prosperity*, (New York: W. W. Norton).

——(2007). *The Conscience of a Liberal*, (New York: W. W. Norton).

KWON, HYEOK and JONAS PONTUSSON (2010 forthcoming). 'Globalization, Labor Power, and Partisan Politics Revisited?', *Socio-Economic Review*.

LANGE, PETER and GEOFFREY GARRETT (1985). 'The Politics of Growth', *Journal of Politics* 47: 794–809.

LEIGH, ANDREW (2007). Data set for 'How Closely Do Top Income Shares Track Other Measures of Inequality?' Available at econrsss.anu.edu.au/~aleigh.

——(2009). 'Top Incomes', in *The Oxford Handbook of Economic Inequality*, eds. Wiemar Salverda, Brian Nolan, and Timothy Smeeding, (Oxford: Oxford University Press), 150–76.

LEVY, FRANK and PETER TEMIN (2007). 'Inequality and Institutions in 20th Century America'. Working Paper 13106. National Bureau of Economic Research. Available at www.nber.org.

MAGAZINER, IRA C. and ROBERT B. REICH (1983). *Minding America's Business*, (New York: Vintage).

MISHEL, LAWRENCE, JARED BERNSTEIN, and HEIDI SHIERHOLZ (2009). *The State of Working America, 2008–09*. An Economic Policy Institute book, (Ithaca, NY: Cornell University Press).

MORRIS, MARTINA and BRUCE WESTERN (1999). 'Inequality in Earnings at the Close of the Twentieth Century', *Annual Review of Sociology* 25: 623–57.

NICKELL, STEPHEN and RICHARD LAYARD (1999). 'Labor Market Institutions and Economic Performance', in *Handbook of Labor Economics*, vol. 3C, eds. Orley Ashenfelter and David Card, (Amsterdam: Elsevier), 3029–84.

NORTH, DOUGLASS C. (1990). *Institutions, Institutional Change, and Economic Performance*, (Cambridge: Cambridge University Press).

OECD (Organization for Economic Cooperation and Development) (1994). *The OECD Jobs Study*, (Paris: OECD).

——(2006). *OECD Employment Outlook: Boosting Jobs and Incomes*, (Paris: OECD).

——(2009). OECD. Stat. Database available at www.oecd.org.

OLSON, MANCUR (1982). *The Rise and Decline of Nations*, (New Haven, CT: Yale University Press).

——(1996). 'The Varieties of Eurosclerosis: The Rise and Decline of Nations since 1982', in *Economic Growth in Europe since 1945*, eds. N. Crafts and G. Toniolo, (Cambridge: Cambridge University Press) 73–94.

OSKARSSON, SVEN (2005). 'Divergent Trends and Different Causal Logics: The Importance of Bargaining Centralization When Explaining Earnings Inequality across Advanced Democratic Societies', *Politics and Society* 33: 359–85.

PIERSON, PAUL (ed.) (2001). *The New Politics of the Welfare State*, (Oxford: Oxford University Press).

PIKETTY, THOMAS and EMMANUEL SAEZ (2006). 'The Evolution of Top Incomes: A Historical and International Perspective', *American Economic Review* 96, (Papers and Proceedings): 200–5.

PORTER, MICHAEL (1990). *The Competitive Advantage of Nations*, (New York: Free Press).

REICH, ROBERT (2007). *Supercapitalism*, (New York: Knopf).

RODRIK, DANI (2007). *One Economics, Many Recipes*, (Princeton, NJ: Princeton University Press).

ROINE, JESPER, JONAS VLACHOS, and DANIEL WALDENSTRÖM (2007). 'What Determines Top Income Shares? Evidence from the Twentieth Century'. IFN Working Paper 721. Research Institute of Industrial Economics. Available at www.ifn.se/web/721_1.aspx.

RUEDA, DAVID and JONAS PONTUSSON (2000). 'Wage Inequality and Varieties of Capitalism', *World Politics* 52: 350–83.

SAPIR, ANDRÉ, PHILIPPE AGHION, GUISEPPE BERTOLA, MARTIN HELLWIG, JEAN PISANNI-FERRY, DARIUSZ ROSATI, JOSE VIÑALS, and HELEN WALLACE, with MARCO BUTI, MARIO NAVA, and PETER M. SMITH (2004). *An Agenda for a Growing Europe: The Sapir Report*, (Oxford: Oxford University Press).

SCHARPF, FRITZ W. (2000). 'Economic Changes, Vulnerabilities, and Institutional Capabilities', in *Welfare and Work in the Open Economy*. Volume 1: *From Vulnerability to Competitiveness*, eds. Fritz W. Scharpf and Vivien A. Schmidt, (Oxford: Oxford University Press), 21–124.

SCHEVE, KENNETH and DAVID STASAVAGE (2007). 'Institutions, Partisanship, and Inequality in the Long Run', unpublished.

SCRUGGS, LYLE (2005). 'Revised Decommodification Scores'. Data set, unpublished. Department of Political Science, University of Connecticut.

SHONFIELD, ANDREW (1965). *Modern Capitalism*, (Oxford: Oxford University Press).

SIAROFF, ALAN (1999). 'Corporatism in 24 Industrial Democracies: Meaning and Measurement', *European Journal of Political Research* 36: 175–205.

SMITH, ADAM ([1776] 1937). *The Wealth of Nations*, (New York: Random House).

STIGLITZ, JOSEPH E. (1989). 'On the Economic Role of the State', in *The Economic Role of the State*, ed. Arnold Heertje, (London: Basil Blackwell).

SWANK, DUANE (2002). *Global Capital, Political Institutions, and Policy Change in Developed Welfare States*, (Cambridge: Cambridge University Press).

——(2008). 'Comparative Parties Data Set'. Available at www.marquette.edu/polisci/Swank.htm.

SWENSON, PETER (1989). *Fair Shares: Unions, Pay, and Politics in Sweden and West Germany*, (Ithaca, NY: Cornell University Press).

TRAXLER, FRANZ, SABINE BLASCHKE, and BERNHARD KITTEL (2001). *National Labour Relations in Internationalized Markets*, (Oxford: Oxford University Press).

VISSER, JELLE. (2008). 'Institutional Characteristics of Trade Unions, Wage Setting, State Intervention and Social Pacts (ICTWSS)'. Database. Amsterdam Institute for Advanced Labour Studies (AIAS). Available at www.uva-aias.net.

WALLERSTEIN, MICHAEL (1999). 'Wage-Setting Institutions and Pay Inequality in Advanced Industrial Societies', *American Journal of Political Science* 43: 649–80.

WILENSKY, HAROLD L. and LOWELL TURNER (1987). *Democratic Corporatism and Policy Linkages*, (Berkeley: Institute of International Studies).

WOMACK, JAMES P., DANIEL T. JONES, and DANIEL ROOS (1990). *The Machine That Changed the World*, (New York: Rawson Associates).

WORLD BANK (2008). 'Ease of Doing Business: Economy Rankings'. Available at www.doing-business.org/economyrankings.

ZYSMAN, JOHN (1983). *Governments, Markets, and Growth*, (Ithaca, NY: Cornell University Press).

PART III

THE ORGANIZATION OF ECONOMIC ACTORS

CHAPTER 15

CORPORATE GOVERNANCE

MICHEL GOYER[1]

INTRODUCTION

How do institutional arrangements affect corporate governance outcomes? Institutional analyses of comparative corporate governance raise many issues also found in other areas of the social sciences. The focus of many corporate governance inquiries might be specific to particular subfields—determinants of ownership structures, legal protection of minority shareholders, impact of the market for corporate control, and many others—but questions and insights about the role of institutions are present across disciplinary boundaries. Three key debates stand prominently in social science discussions.

The first one concerns the extent to which scholars assign analytical primacy to institutions. This debate often pits institutionally based versus interest-oriented theoretical perspectives. The first group highlights the ways in which differences in national institutional arrangements result in different trajectories regarding patterns of policy-making, economic performance, and clusters of innovative specialization (Hall and Soskice 2001; Whitley 1999). Institutions matter because they independently shape the distribution of power among social actors (Berger 1981; Hall 1986). The second group, in contrast, emphasizes how institutions reflect something deeper in society—the usual suspects being the underlying distribution of power between groups (Howell 2003; Pontusson 1995) and a set of functional requirements

[1] I thank Peter Gourevitch and Richard Whitley for their comments on this chapter. The usual disclaimer applies.

associated with the operation of capitalist economies (Boyer 1986). These critiques of institutional perspectives point to two alternative scenarios that lessen the importance of institutions: coalitional and policy realignments can take place within stable institutions; and institutions themselves become the objects of struggle if they are so influential over outcomes.

A second debate concerns the nature of interaction of institutions with other features. Scholars working with an institutional perspective rarely advance the notion that only institutions matter for outcomes. For some, institutions are mid-level variables (as distinct from macro-structures) that act as a mid-range theory (Thelen and Steinmo 1992). For instance, Katzenstein (1977) analyses how variations in institutional frameworks provided for divergent political responses to the changes in the world economy in the 1970s—but does not seek to account for these important macro changes. Institutions are highly important at a given analytical level. For others, institutions are part of a phenomenon of complex causation whereby an outcome results from potentially different combinations of conditions (Mahoney 2004; Ragin 1987; Skocpol 1979).[2] Institutions might be necessary to generate a specific event, but they are rarely sufficient.

A third source of debate is methodological and takes two forms. First, the dichotomy between institutional-based and interest-oriented theoretical perspectives often entails specific research design choices that mirror the other perspective's approach. Institutionally oriented researchers hold preferences constant with the aim of showing how changing institutions produce different outcomes. Interest-driven scholars, on the other hand, hold institutions constant to show how changing interests lead to different results. A problem with this often necessary but incomplete ploy is that both institutions and interests can be changing—i.e. nothing is constant (Gourevitch 1999).

Second, the presence of change or stability of institutional frameworks is riddled with problems of assessment. For instance, the occurrence of institutional change is not always interpreted as leading to behavioural change. Comparative political economy scholars increasingly distinguish between institutional change that does not affect the process by which firms coordinate their activities versus institutional transformation that imply a transformation of coordination (Culpepper 2005; Goyer 2006; Hall 2007; see also Sorge 2005: 142–183). Distinguishing between radical and incremental institutional change becomes crucial (see e.g. Campbell 2004). On the other hand, the presence of institutional stability can be associated with substantial modifications in the behaviour of actors. The occurrence of functional conversion—whereby institutions are redirected to new purposes in the presence of formal institutional stability—complicates analytical inquiries (Gilson 2001; Thelen 2003 and 2004). The practice associated with an institution can change without a corresponding transformation in its formal structure.

---

[2] See Kogut and Ragin (2006) for an analysis of complex causation for issues of comparative corporate governance.

The above overview of the debates surrounding institutional analyses in contemporary capitalism points to the difficulties in assessing whether institutions matter for corporate governance outcomes. Should one attempt to account for institutional variation across national systems of corporate governance? Or, in contrast, should the analytical focus revolve around differences in corporate governance outcomes between advanced capitalist economies? The nature and role of institutions do not lend themselves to a single viewpoint. An inquiry based on either of these two questions implies that institutions matter while at the same time avoiding inferring a mechanical relationship between institutional stability/change and outcomes. To overcome these conceptual and methodological issues, this chapter is structured around the three most prominent theoretical perspectives in the analysis of comparative corporate governance: law and economics, sociology, and politics. I proceed to review their contributions to the analysis of diversity in both institutional arrangements and outcomes across national systems of corporate governance. These approaches are also characterized by substantial internal diversity on the role of institutions—thereby increasing the analytical variety of inquiries. I conclude the chapter with a section that deals with the place of economic incentives and rationality in the joint interaction between institutions and interests for these three theoretical perspectives.

Institutional Arrangements of Corporate Governance: The Law and Economics Perspective

Early studies of corporate governance focused on the divergence of interests between the principal and the agent (Berle and Means 1932; Jensen and Meckling 1976). The key idea is that unmonitored managers will pursue goals that are not in the interests of shareholders—ranging from actions that allow them to profit personally (embezzlement, misappropriations) to empire building.[3] The presence of dispersed shareholders implies a free-rider problem since the gains associated with managers being monitored are shared pro rata among owners. Why would a shareholder owning a small amount of stocks proceed to monitor corporate executives? Moreover, the impossibility of predicting all future contingencies results in the inability of dispersed shareholders to write complete contracts that would cover every scenario where important corporate decisions have to be taken (Grossman and Hart 1981). Management remains in control under most circumstances.

---

[3] See Pollard (1965) for an historical analysis of these problems in early British management structures.

The focus of the early law and economics studies was organized around a puzzle—namely, why would minority investors provide funding to companies run by unaccountable, dominant managers. The argument presented was that inefficient firms would be punished on financial and product markets—thereby providing incentives for management to pursue strategies of enhancing shareholder value. Working backwards from this assumption, early law and economic studies on corporate governance interpreted institutions as the functional response designed to reduce the costs associated with taming managers acting in their own interests (for a critical analysis, see Davis 2005).

These early law and economics analyses of corporate governance, however, are plagued by a fundamental shortcoming despite their influence over the intellectual development of the discipline. The main point of contention is that ownership dispersion is only characteristic of a few countries, essentially Anglo-Saxon economies. The analytical foundations of these early studies of corporate governance lacked a comparative focus. In ownership concentrated systems, the separation of ownership from control is largely non-existent since the dominant shareholder has both the incentive and the power to discipline management (Morck, Shleifer, and Vishny 1988). Instead, the main issue in such systems of corporate governance is the divergence of interests between the controlling shareholder and minority investors. The concentration of ownership, with its associated control over corporate policies, is valuable since the controlling shareholder is able to transfer value from the firm at the expense of minority shareholders—i.e. the private benefits of control (Zingales 1998). The result is the creation of a wedge between the value of the company for the controlling shareholder and the other (minority) investors.

A second wave of law and economics studies emerged in the early 1990s with the aim of accounting for diversity in ownership structures across national systems of corporate governance. The fundamental argument that accounts for the extensively documented differences in ownership structures focuses on the extent to which minority investors are protected by law from expropriation by managers or controlling shareholders (La Porta et al. 2000).[4] The role of institutional arrangements and rules, as well as their enforcement, is critical in this process. The investigative starting point is that minority shareholders need assurance that they will get a return on their investment (Shleifer and Vishny 1997). A combination of standard tort law and private bonding is not sufficient to provide adequate guarantees to outside shareholders (Glaeser et al. 2001). Specific institutions and rules in the areas of stock exchange regulations, accounting standards and financial transparency, corporate law, and takeover regulation protect minority investors better (Coffee 2006; La Porta et al. 2000).

Some of these key institution arrangements concern the fiduciary duties of directors, the mandatory rules to disclose extensive financial information on a continual basis, the respect of the one-share-one-vote rule, the equal treatment of

---

[4] For analytical treatments of the importance of the institutions of the legal system in other areas, see also the chapters by Quack and Whitley in this handbook.

minority shareholders during takeover bids, and an efficient and uncorrupted judicial system. Moreover, institutions that protect the rights of minority shareholders tend to be found in common law systems rather than in their civil law counterparts (Coffee 1999; Johnson et al. 2000). Legal rules in systems of common law are made by judges, are based on precedents, and are inspired by general principles such as fiduciary duty. These general principles are applicable in new situations even when specific conduct that would violate the rights of minority shareholders has not yet been described or prohibited in the statutes.

The theoretical implication flowing from the presence of different ownership structures for the law and economics perspective is that the nature of agency costs differs across national systems of corporate governance. There are many varieties of agency costs—which all contribute to destroy shareholder value—but for which different institutional solutions should prevail (for a critical overview, see Roe 2005). A first type of agency costs is diversion by managers—stealing, embezzling, and shirking. A second variety of agency costs comes in the form of managerial mistakes—executives not being up to running the firm because of changed circumstances. Institutions that work well in solving the first type of agency costs might not be as effective in dealing with its second variety.

The policy implication from the above discussion, in turn, is that institutional responses to potential violation of the rights of minority shareholders should differ according to the specificity of the agency costs found across national settings. For instance, the bulk of financial scandals in the United States in the 1990s dealt with corporate managers engaged in earnings manipulation and accounting irregularities to inflate stock price; distortion of shareholder value in continental Western Europe and in formerly communist countries of central Europe involved self-dealing by controlling shareholders (Coffee, 2005). The effectiveness of institutions in corporate governance in this context is contingent upon its match with the prevailingly dominant ownership structure of a given economy. The current wave of legislative reforms in the three largest continental European countries (France, Germany, and Italy) should be viewed with suspicion since they are dealing essentially with improving the exercise of voting rights, not with reducing the ability of the controlling owner to engage in self-dealing manoeuvres (Enriques and Volpin 2007).

The law and economics perspective has generated impressive empirical results. Legal-institutional arrangements are associated with differences in regard to ownership structures, size and depth of securities markets, number of listed firms, dividend payments, and rates of IPO (La Porta et al. 2000). If prospective minority shareholders feel uncertain about whether their rights will be protected once they provide equity capital to the firm, then they are less likely to invest on stock markets. However, correlation is not causation and this approach has been criticized on both empirical and intellectual grounds.

First, the overall stability of legal systems contrasts with changes in ownership structures in several advanced capitalist economies in the twentieth century—thereby making it difficult to explain variation with a constant (Gourevitch and

Shinn 2005: 4–10; Herrigel 2008: 479–88; Rajan and Zingales 2003).[5] The case of the United Kingdom, on the other hand, highlights the emergence of ownership diffusion and vibrant securities markets despite a legal environment apparently conducive to private benefits of control (Cheffins 2001; Franks, Mayer and Rossi, 2005).

Second, the argument that institutional arrangements of corporate governance are better suited to solve different type of agency costs raises problems of functionalism. For one thing, the introduction of institutional arrangements of corporate governance is not driven exclusively by concerns related to agency costs. A myriad of political and societal concerns also stand prominently in accounting for institutional diversity across national systems of corporate governance (Gourevitch and Shinn 2005; Roe 1998 and 2003).[6] Moreover, legal arrangements do not cover every instance where corporate executives can destroy firm value—thereby highlighting the insufficient character of corporate law to account for the presence of ownership dispersion. A prominent application of this insight concerns the limits of American/British system of corporate law, which are comparatively highly protective of the rights of minority shareholders, in accounting for the presence of ownership dispersion. Corporate law is generally, although not always, effective at dealing with agency costs that take the form of diversion of value by executives (stealing, embezzling, and shirking)—but is largely unconnected to a second type of agency costs related to value destruction in the form of managerial mistakes (Roe 2002). The issue is not one of a misfit between institutions and the type of agency costs faced by firms—but the limits on the extent to which legal arrangements can cover every instance of shareholder value destruction in either concentrated or dispersed ownership settings.

Third, the effectiveness of institutional legal arrangements is contingent upon the context in which they are embedded with the implication that there is no universal link between institutions of corporate governance and outcomes. The second wave of law and economics studies correctly recognizes the presence of institutional diversity across national systems of corporate governance, but interprets the absence of convergence as deviations from best practices. The assumptions of the law and economics perspective are that development of economic activities and the provision of capital require the protection of investors through legal arrangements; the Anglo-American systems of corporate governance generate higher rates of economic growth and securities market development precisely because of their relatively high degrees of protection for minority shareholders; and that legal reforms in non-common law countries is largely a technocratic endeavour where the main task of policymakers is to transplant the institutional legal features of Anglo-American economies (La Porta et al. 2000 and 2006).

---

[5] See the contributions in Morck (2005) for historical analyses of the evolution of national systems of corporate governance in a number of specific countries.

[6] For instance, the construction of institutional arrangements that protect minority shareholders is not 'rocket science'—the reason why non-common law advanced capitalist economies have refrained for a long time to build them is better accounted for by their reluctance to embrace principles of shareholder value (Roe 2003).

There are two problems with these assumptions. The first issue is that the impact of institutional arrangements is contingent upon the context in which they are embedded (Hall and Soskice 2001; Milhaupt and Pistor 2008; Whitley 1999). The presence of interdependencies between legal arrangements and other institutions shape the effectiveness of the former on various outcomes.[7] The second issue is that the law and economic perspectives conceptualize institutional arrangements— essentially Anglo-American legal features—as fixed endowments that are both necessary for economic activities to occur and that, once in place, are themselves immune to change. The irony of the legal perspective is that politics and conflict matter in the origins of legal arrangements, but completely disappear after their enactment (see e.g. Mahoney 2001). By contrast, Milhaupt and Pistor (2008) highlight the continuous interactive process between legal arrangements and markets that results from three features: the extent to which legal systems are centralized/decentralized in relation to law-making and enforcement processes; the presence of multiple functions performed by the legal system in supporting economic activities beside that of shareholder protection, and the contested nature of legal institutions that follows from their asymmetric distribution of gains for political and social actors.[8]

Fourth, the consequences of the strategic position of the controlling shareholder are also contingent upon the specificities of the context. The presence of a shareholder with a substantial equity stake in the company eliminates problems inherent in the separation of ownership and control—such as issues of collective action in the monitoring of managers. On the other hand, an unconstrained, controlling owner is likely to seek to secure private benefits of control at the expense of shareholder value-oriented strategic moves that would benefit every category of investors. The presence of a controlling shareholder is interpreted as the consequence of the failure of corporate law to protect minority shareholders (La Porta et al. 1999).

However, recent studies have raised doubts about the overwhelming focus on controlling shareholders as value destroying actors in concentrated ownership systems of corporate governance. The argument is that some private benefits of control are necessary for inducing the controlling shareholder to exercise a monitoring function (Gilson 2006; Mayer 2001). There is a potential trade-off where the presence of a controlling shareholder reduces managerial agency problem, but at the costs of the problems of the private benefits of control. Institutional reforms constitute a balancing act whereby the actions by the controlling shareholder that lead to the

---

[7] See Aguilera et al. (2008) for an extensive analytical overview of the context specific effectiveness of institutions of corporate governance.

[8] The argument about legal arrangements constantly interacting with market developments is further supported by the analysis of Kogut and Ragin (2006) on the institutional determinants of financial markets. Using the methodology of Qualitative Comparative Analysis (Ragin 1987), they highlight how common law regimes are uniformly associated with extensively developed capital markets—but only in the joint presence of judicial efficiency (enforcement, rule of law, contract respect) and indigenous law. In other words, the transplant of common law regimes does not causally lead to bigger securities markets since the above combination of conditions captures only a small number of countries. The implication is that the transplant of legal arrangements is mediated by existing institutional configurations.

capture of private benefits of control do not impinge on his ability to monitor corporate executives. The need to secure activism from the controlling shareholder is made particularly crucial in countries with both inadequate corporate law and poor commercial law (Gilson 2007).

Fifth, the differences between the two legal families have experienced an erosion in recent years since both systems regulate and codify; and recent legislation has generated opposite results than would have been predicted by the law and economics perspective—the quite directive Sarbanes-Oxley act in the United States as compared to the market-preferring, transparency-enhancing Kontrag law in Germany (Roe 2006: 468–82). Moreover, and more importantly, the point is not that institutional differences between legal families do not matter—but that current differences between national systems of corporate governance are probably better accounted for by more recent political decisions that lead some countries to embrace/denigrate principles of shareholder value than institutional-legal variables introduced some centuries ago (Roe 2007; see also below the discussion of the political perspectives on corporate governance).

Finally, the law and economics perspective overlooks a key first-order condition for financial markets to develop and ownership to become dispersed—namely, the political legitimacy of capitalist economic arrangements (Roe 1998). Political stability is necessary for production to take place since more efficient but politically and socially illegitimate economic arrangements could be challenged. The importance of legal-institutional arrangements becomes important only in a polity that is market friendly. The specification of the impact of legal-institutional arrangements is critical since other indicators also strongly correlate with differences in ownership structures, most notably the regulation of employment protection and the Gini measures of economic inequalities.

SOCIOLOGY AND INSTITUTIONAL DIVERSITY IN CORPORATE GOVERNANCE

The above criticisms of the law and economics perspective point to the foundations of the sociological (and political) perspectives on corporate governance. The law and economics perspective interpret institutions through a backward inference. The diversity of institutional frameworks is analysed through the functions they ultimately serve. The sociological (and political) perspectives on corporate governance provide far richer analyses of institutional origins and evolution.

The overall argument of institutionally oriented economic sociologists is that firms are embedded in a system of social norms, practices, and relationships that shape the range of actions that are possible and permitted. The influence of institutions over the behaviour of actors stems from their ability to provide cognitive scripts and taken for granted practices that able them to interpret the world around them (Meyer and Rowan 1977; DiMaggio and Powell 1991). The institutional arrangements and practices found in national economies specify the very terms through which the interpretation of events is constructed and, as a result, should be seen as culturally and context-specific. The presence of institutional diversity reflects institutional constraints stemming from 'context-specific scripts' on the appropriate standards by which firms should be run—rather than constituting a functional response to a given set of problems (Aguilera and Jackson 2003; Scott 2001). The point is not that actors are irrational and institutional arrangements inherently inefficient—but that their actions are socially constructed (Hall and Taylor 1996: 946–50).

The notion of institutions as reflecting context-specific systems of social norms shapes the range of potential actions of actors and, in turn, implies diversity of causal mechanisms across economies. For instance, studies on the spread of shareholder value in Germany—an advanced capitalist economy institutionally organized at the antipode of its American counterpart—highlight the importance of the context-specific institutional arrangements (see Fiss and Zajac 2004). The concept of embeddedness for the study of German corporate governance illustrates the importance of the specific characteristics of the educational background and career patterns of corporate executives. These variables affect the normative expectations of executives of what are considered legitimate strategies and act as a focal point in the process by which changes are introduced. German managers have been praised for their high level of technical expertise that results from their productionist, engineering-oriented focus—in contrast to the finance background of top American executives (Herrigel 1996; Whitley 2003). Therefore, it does not come as a surprise to learn that the most important factor accounting for CEO compensation—one important indicator of shareholder value—is the extent to which board chairs and CEOs have a similar educational background (Fiss 2006).

Discussions about the role of the board of directors in the promotion of shareholder value in Germany make considerably less sense. For one thing, employees occupy half of the seats with the implication that an empowered board with independent directors might well be oriented around the protection of workers rather than promoting the interests of minority shareholders (Roe 1999). Moreover, German corporate law requires a legal split between two boards—management and supervisory—whereby members of one board cannot sit on the other. The positions of CEO (management board) and chair (supervisory board) are occupied by a different person. Institutional arrangements—that reflect legitimacy concerns about the role of employees inside companies—prevent German CEOs from controlling the board through their influence over the selection of directors—in sharp contrast to the situation that prevails in the United States (Roe 2003).[9]

---

[9] See Westphal and Zajac (1995) for an analysis of the influence of CEOs in the appointment of directors at large American companies.

An important subset of analytical inquiries in economic sociology inspired by the concept of embeddedness is that of networks. The underlying assumption of these studies is that behaviour is socially embedded in the sense that an actor's ability to further its ends is contingent on the behaviour of other participants. The relations between actors are embedded in social networks and are not simply epiphenomena of market and other forms of interaction. Networks are communities of practices with their own shared ideologies, scripts, and norms that contribute to link individual's behaviour with their position in them (Granovetter 1985). The (economic/social) networks in which actors are embedded significantly shape their identity and behaviour. They contribute to the maintenance of the meaning that actors give to institutions by constraining the range of behavioural actions deemed legitimate—particularly through the enforcement of norms via informal sanctions. They influence one's understanding of how other actors in similar/different roles should behave—thereby rewarding what is perceived as legitimate behaviour and punishing norm deviant actions.

One strand of network analysis highlights the importance of their structural characteristics—i.e. the density of ties among individual members (see e.g. Kogut and Walker 2001). The process of institutional change reflects the presence of two sequential features: the formal adoption of a new institution by an actor and the speed by which it spreads within a network. First, institutions whose content is viewed as being comprised of normatively appropriate practices that already fit with social norms are more likely to be adopted (Burt 1982; Strang and Macy 2001). The connectivity of an institution with prevailing cognitive schemas that enable actors to make sense of the world constitutes a necessary condition for its adoption (DiMaggio and Powell 1983; Meyer and Rowan 1977). The ability of actors to frame the adoption of these new institutions as fitting with established norms of legitimacy increases their successful introduction, since practices often have multiple meanings that can be interpreted in different ways. Second, the spreading speed of the newly adopted institutions, on the other hand, is about the density of ties within an existing network (Burt 1982; Haveman 1993; Watts 1999). Density of network ties matter in two ways: the adoption of new institutions tend to spread more rapidly in *dense* as compared to *thin* networks since participants possess greater degrees of connectivity among themselves; and the adoption of new institutional practices by a centrally located and legitimately perceived actor increases its spreading speed since it enables other participants to justify their actions.

The institution of the board of directors in American corporate governance illustrates quite well the importance of networks via their influence on social norms and practices on the behaviour of actors. For law and economics scholars, effective institutional arrangements result in directors serving as the dutiful agents of their shareholder principals (Fama and Jensen 1983; Jensen and Meckling 1976). The sociological critique, in contrast, stresses the importance of directors being embedded in networks as the major source of influence on their actions (Mizruchi 1989). Several studies have highlighted the importance of embeddedness of board interlocks as a key mechanism that links the actions of firms and corporate governance outcomes.

First, the adoption of specific anti-takeover instruments—namely poison pills and/or golden parachutes—by American firms in the 1980s was shaped by the density of network ties and by the extent to which they shared directors with companies that had previously done so (Davis 1991; Davis and Greve 1997). Network centrality serves as a provider of information through the network while the previous adoption of anti-takeover devices increases the legitimacy for their subsequent adoption by other actors. Second, another stream of research has focused on the role of boards in accounting for executive compensation. In their analysis of CEO remuneration packages in large American firms, Zajac and Westphal (1995) moved beyond the dichotomy between empowered boards setting an ideally constructed compensation contract versus overcompensated CEOs and weak boards. Their argument highlights the importance of symbolic considerations whereby firms justify their actions in an attempt to reflect prevailing beliefs about the socially legitimate purpose of executive remuneration. The behaviour of directors is embedded in a context where CEO compensation practices must be justifiable in the eyes of outside parties. Directors with interlocking ties are more than willing to engage in legitimizing exercises—as opposed to advocate the implementation of substantial corporate changes that would limit managerial autonomy—if they seek to escape informal social sanctioning from the other members of the network in which they are embedded (Westphal and Khanna 2003).

The notion of embeddedness and its network analytical subset significantly contribute to our understanding of institutional diversity across systems of corporate governance. Sociologists—especially within the field of organizational theory—provide an alternative to efficiency-oriented explanations that solely focus on the agency problem. The importance assigned to norms and practices that shape the range of actions, significantly enrich our knowledge of the fundamental determinants of the behaviour of actors. This sociological variant provides for a clear understanding of how preferences and identities are socially constructed through an embedded position in an institutional setting.

However, an important issue remains unresolved for the sociological notion of embeddedness and its network subset. 'The focus on social norms and taken for granted practices often leads to a neglect on power-distributional elements'—what Hall and Taylor (1996: 954) refer to as sociology having a curiously bloodless perspective on political and social life (see also Thelen 2004: 31–7 for an overview). The search for legitimacy obscures how institutional arrangements of corporate governance reflect the outcome of political, social, and economic struggles in a historically and contextually specific setting.

The legitimating and taken for granted dimensions of institutional arrangements can reduce the richness of the explanatory power of institutions. The embeddedness of institutions implies a corresponding match between structure and norms that, in turn, make it difficult for sociological explanations to accommodate gaps between preferences and institutional frameworks. The importance of path dependent phenomena becomes more difficult to conceptualize for the sociological perspective since legitimately perceived courses of action might become unavailable as the result of previous choices in a particular direction that, in turn, encourage further development along the same path (Bebchuk and Roe 1999; Mahoney 2000). The concept of path dependence is associated with three central notions: particular courses of action can be extremely difficult to reverse because of switching costs and increasing returns associated with them; timing and sequencing of developments matter as much as their specific content; and a wide range of outcomes are possible across settings even if starting from similar institutional environments (Pierson 2000). The implication is that institutional frameworks can outlive the constellations of interests that initially created them, therefore mediating the translation into actions of legitimately induced preferences from socially-embedded positioning in networks (Thelen 2004). The issue becomes one of identifying the path dependent effects of institutions—in the circumstances in which national systems of corporate governance are experiencing evolutionary or radical institutional change (Deeg 2001). Moreover, the notion of socially-embedded institutions implies institutional plasticity whereby the process of structural change is unproblematic given the primacy of social norms. The lock-in effects of institutions become relatively marginalized.[10]

By contrast, a second variant of the sociological perspective on the importance of embeddedness precisely emphasizes the centrality of political and social conflicts as the basis for the presence of institutional diversity across national systems of corporate governance (Fligstein 1990; Morgan 2005; Roy 1997; Streeck 1997). This variant builds on the works of sociologists using comparative historical methods in the provision of qualitatively oriented causal inferences about important large-scale outcomes (Mahoney 2004; Ragin 1987; Rueschemeyer et al. 1992; Skocpol 1979). This variant assigns a greater importance to process analysis (Lieberson 1991), sequencing (Abbott 2001; Tilly 1984), historical legacies (Dobbin 1994), and institutional openness to policy innovations (Weir and Skocpol 1985).

The work of Fligstein (1990) on the governance of large American corporations embodies quite well the importance of struggles and contingencies in institutional arrangements of corporate governance. The focus of his analysis deals with the factors that account for the rise and decline of the conglomerate firm. The strategy of large American corporations in the last 120 years or so has witnessed major transformations—from large industrial monopolies to diversified conglomerates to core competencies organizations. For Chandler (1977 and 1990), the dean of business historians, the change in strategy of large firms constitutes a natural progression toward economic efficiency.

Fligstein, in contrast, highlights the ability by which different groups—production managers, marketing executives, finance officers, and institutional investors—have seized upon the opportunities presented by changes in the external environment to advance their position within the firm. For instance, finance managers have seized upon the opportunity presented by the 1950 Celler-Kefauver act—that made it highly difficult for companies to acquire others in related fields—to provide a new strategic

---

[10] See also Liebowitz and Margolis (1995) for a discussion of lock-in institutional effects.

model whereby the activities are managed in the same fashion as a diversified portfolio. The outcome was the growth of large conglomerates involved in unrelated business activities and the central position of the finance office in the development of the diversification strategy. Activist institutional investors, financial analysts, and takeover raiders, in contrast, have used the relaxed attitude of the Reagan administration towards economic concentration on forcing firms to dismantle the conglomerate structure and to focus on core competencies.[11] The newly adopted specialization focus promoted the rise of shareholder value as the central governing tenet of the firm. Governance struggles between groups to impose their preferences—and to benefit from the new strategy—provide a more compelling account for the changes in strategic directions of large American corporations.

The specifics of the American case are also highlighted by the contrasting experiences of European economies that point to sharply different historical processes in the development and consolidation of conglomerates—with different implications regarding its evolution (Whittington and Mayer 2000). For instance, the strategy of diversification of large German conglomerates such as Siemens is not based on a financial logic of portfolio diversification, but reflects the quality differentiation of its products that requires broad skills and technological competences building on the cumulative learning of highly skilled blue-collar employees (see Boersch 2007: 74–101).

The incorporation of conflict and power substantially strengthens the analysis of institutional diversity in corporate governance. The concept of path dependence—where institutions with asymmetric distribution of power remain operational despite changes in the external environment—is better accommodated by this sociological variant. Something as important as the control over the cash flows rights of the firm is certainly worth fighting about. Moreover, this variant of the sociological perspective also uses a broader definition of the concept of institutions than law and economics scholars, focusing on 'efficient' solutions to the different agency problems. Institutional frameworks represent compromises between actors—not a search for an optimal solution to a coordination problem—with significant consequences for the distribution of power in the economy.

An issue of contention with this sociological variant, however, is that it neglects the discrete charm (and influence) of networks. Major political cleavages and social upheavals do not always translate into significant institutional transformations. Societal pressures are mediated by networks. The previously mentioned case of executive compensation in American corporate governance illustrates well the

---

[11] However, it must be noted that Chandler does not analyse the latest strategic orientation of American corporations—namely the dismantling of the conglomerate firm and the return to a focus on economic specialization. A full comparison with the analysis of Fligstein is not therefore possible. On the other hand, the increase in vertical specialization of the focused firm has been interpreted as a challenge to Chandler's vision of the multi-unit managerial enterprise coordinating the multiple stages of production within a corporate framework. The M-firm might have constituted a response to the environmental conditions of a specific historical episode in American capitalism rather than representing the inevitable result of efficiency searching (see Langlois 2003).

potential disconnection between power and outcomes. The meteoric rise of pay in executive compensation in the last fifteen years has attracted much attention and generated intense public criticism from many quarters—but legislative intervention has been rather limited (see Bebchuk 2006). What accounts for this discrepancy? The standard law and economics defence of executive compensation stresses the importance of autonomous and independent boards designing executive compensation packages, which are designed to increase shareholder value—with deviant cases of CEOs exercising substantial influence over the process as being examples of 'rotten apples'. The network-oriented sociological perspective, in contrast, highlights the symbolically oriented actions of CEOs and boards of directors (Zajac and Westphal 1995). The actions of these two groups of actors are driven by a desire to limit 'outrage' costs (Bebchuk and Fried 2004). The central preoccupation of CEOs and directors in the designing of executive compensation packages is the extent to which they will be perceived negatively by important outsiders. This desire to limit 'outrage' costs, in turn, leads firms to engage in decoupling—i.e. announced reforms not being implemented (Westphal and Zajac 1994; see also Fiss and Zajac 2004). The second variant of the sociological perspective is ill suited to capture phenomena of decoupling.

This review of these variants of the sociological perspective on corporate governance highlights their complementary nature. While they move beyond the purely efficiency driven explanations of most law and economics accounts, their contributions and shortcomings mirror each other. This symmetry suggests a need for greater integration (Dobbin 2004). Holding constant one variant while highlighting how variation of another variant affects outcomes is often a necessary methodological ploy, but such piecemeal analytical focus runs the risks of confusing a necessary condition for a sufficient one. The process of institutional change is shaped by both networks and power considerations—with the ability of actors to present new institutional proposals in a cognitive framing that fits with existing conceptions of legitimacy.[12]

POLITICS AND INSTITUTIONAL DIVERSITY IN CORPORATE GOVERNANCE

The political perspective on corporate governance comes into two variants. The central feature of the first variant is that differences in ownership structures reflect the extent to which the political climate and orientation of a polity is conducive to the pursuit of market-oriented policies (Roe 2003). The diversity of

---

[12] For instances of such integrated works, see Davis et al. (1994) and Dobbin and Dowd (2000).

institutional arrangements of corporate governance represents the out
political, social, and economic struggles in those countries and cannot b/
to efficiency considerations alone. Governments have traditionally er.,
distributional considerations that privileged employees over shareholders in
European social democracies and Japan from as early as the late 1940s in the
post-war period. The outcome is one whereby employees benefit from greater
degrees of protection from shareholder value enhancing measures that minority
stockholders (and managers) would like to implement such as proceeding to
important lay-offs. Social democracies make it harder for corporate executives
to pursue unbridled shareholder value strategies with the upshot that minority
shareholders shy away.

Thus, the reason why small investors are reluctant to invest in the stock market in
social democracies is not primarily driven by issues of managerial opportunism or
self-dealing by the controlling shareholder, but by an antecedent factor—namely, the
political environment that constrains the range of actions of corporate executives.
The pressures and social climate of social democracies induce managers to implement alternative strategies to pure shareholder value that, in turn, raise agency costs
since corporate executives (or controlling shareholders) end up with substantial
amounts of residual power.

This political variant emphasizes two elements of the relationship between institutions and corporate governance outcomes. First, institutions are secondary to
politics. The absence of institutional arrangements that would protect the rights and
promote the interests of minority shareholders in advanced capitalist economies
cannot be attributed to technological shortcomings or financial issues (Roe 2002).
For instance, the understaffing of stock market regulatory agencies in continental
Europe and Japan is not a problem of expertise or budgetary constraints, but rather a
politically conscious decision not to empower an institution whose goals would be
diverging from political norms of legitimate market operations. The political climate
in European social democracies and Japan militates against the introduction of
specific strategies of shareholder value whose distributional consequences would
negatively affect employees and other stakeholders. In developing economies, by
contrast, financial and technical issues—as well as politics—militate against such
institutional innovations in developing economies. Conversely, the presence of
shareholder value enhancing institutions in dispersed ownership economies reflects
the prior acceptance of market principles that privileges, or does not discriminate
against, the preferences of minority shareholders.

Second, the presence of institutional variation within families of corporate governance is not central to the argument (Roe 2003: 27–46). The politics of corporate
governance in Germany resulted in formal institutional arrangements, namely co-
determination. In France, political settlements provided for a strong role for the state
in the regulation of economic outcomes. In Japan, informal arrangements and social
norms protect core employees of large firms against market fluctuations post-1961.
Nonetheless, the presence of varieties in institutional arrangements in these three
countries should not mask the concentration of corporate ownership that results

from a political environment that deters minority shareholders from investing on the stock market.

The political perspective has substantially contributed to our understanding of major corporate governance outcomes. The institutional differences in the authority structure of firms result in important consequences for the allocation of resources in the economy. It is no wonder, then, that politics should be intimately linked to the study of corporate governance. Despite its theoretical elegance, however, two internal issues—as opposed to theoretical challenges that would seek to undermine the importance of politics itself—remain unanswered.

First, the political model of corporate governance elaborated by Roe is one where the coalition building process between interest groups takes the form of class conflict, namely workers against an alliance of managers and owners. The interests of employees prevail in European social democracies; the capitalist alliance of corporate executives and shareholders carries the day in liberal America and Britain. However, this coalition scenario represents one potential outcome—the other two coalition line-ups being sectoral conflict (managers and workers vs. owners) and property and voice conflict (owners and shareholders vs. managers) (Gourevitch 2003). In particular, the presence of cross-class coalitions in continental Europe was often critical in the development of welfare state policies and arrangements of labour market rigidities that, in turn, made it attractive for firms to develop strategies devoid of shareholder value orientation (Mares 2003; Swenson 2002).[13]

Second, the importance of political, social, and economic struggles in the implementation and removal of institutional arrangements of corporate governance constitutes too broad a category to capture the evolution of national systems of corporate governance. For Roe, the specific content of how settlements of conflict are negotiated and become the basis for the institutional diversity across national systems of corporate governance represents a second-order variable. The presence of institutional diversity of institutions is characterized by an element of functional equivalence. The importance of social democratic values in the first post-war decades translated into co-determination in Germany and into state activism (*dirigisme*) in France—with the ultimate outcomes being highly concentrated ownership and strategies of shareholder value shunned.

The impact of economic liberalization, trade integration, currency stability, and capital mobility across borders of France and Germany, for instance, however, has been uneven and reflects the specific content of their previous political settlements. In France, the advent of the above liberalizing measures has been associated with a specific pattern by which shareholder value was introduced—namely, through the one-sided unilateral imposition of managerial power over the implementation of flexibility and other strategic measures in the workplace (Goyer and Hancké 2005; Hancké 2002; Howell 2006). An unintended outcome of the ability of French top executives to restructure the firm in a quasi-unilateral fashion is the massive arrival of

---

[13] Sectors—such as export vs. public sector employees—constitute an increasingly important source of cleavages in continental Europe (see e.g. Pontusson and Swenson 1996).

short-term institutional investors, namely hedge funds and actively managed mutual funds (Goyer 2006 and 2007).

In Germany, in contrast, firm-level institutions impose numerous constraints on the ability of management to develop and implement strategies in a unilateral fashion (Muller-Jentsch 2003). Several legal obstacles stand in the way of a rapid and unilateral reorganization of the shop floor, so that the introduction of strategies of shareholder value has been the result of negotiation between management and employee representatives (Hoepner 2001; Sorge 2005; Vitols 2004). The differences in the introduction of shareholder value strategies in the two countries reflect the specific content by which settlements of conflict were negotiated in the two countries—and institutional arrangements of corporate governance were set up—in the high days of social democracy (see also Crouch 1993). The reliance on the state in France left firm-level unions ill-prepared with the advent of economic liberalization (Howell 1992); the strength of works councils in Germany, in contrast, is contingent on the combination of legal rights and on their contribution by which firms develop their innovative capabilities (O'Sullivan 2000; Thelen 1991; Whitley 2002).

A second variant of the political perspective on corporate governance precisely enlarges the coalitional possibilities (Gourevitch and Shinn 2005). This political variant is built around the interaction of economic preferences and political institutions. On the side of preferences, actors could choose different types of coalitions— class, sectoral, and property and voice coalitions—to pursue their objectives. Gourevitch and Shinn provide a three-actor coalitional model.[14] Shareholders prefer to minimize agency costs arising from managerial shirking that affect the competitive position of the firm—a shared preference with workers; but they also resent government legislation that prevent executives from pursuit shareholder value strategies— a shared preference with managers.[15]

Managers seek to preserve their autonomy against both intervention by shareholders regarding the processes by which they run the firm and against workers' claims over the control of the firms' cash flows rights. Workers care about their jobs and would view unfavourably attempts by shareholders to push for shareholder value policies that would threaten their job tenure; but they are also suspicious of situations of managerial entrenchment that would affect the value of their pension fund via its effects on the stock market capitalization of the firm in retirement systems based on capitalization. The preferences of actors are not monolithic—thereby enlarging the coalitional possibilities. Each group of actors can stress different objectives by making different coalitions with one of the other factions.

The process of preference formation is not contingent solely upon the dynamics of negotiation between these three actors. Something is missing from this

---

[14] For an excellent analysis of the importance of interest groups in the political process of building institutional complementarities in contemporary capitalism, see Amable (2003).

[15] Finer-grain differentiations would also highlight the differences between concentrated versus diffused patterns of ownership as well as shareholders with short-term versus long-term holding strategies (see e.g. Goyer 2006).

conceptualization—namely, institutions. The translation of preferences into policy outputs necessitates an analysis of prevailing institutional configurations (Garrett and Lange 1995). Which coalition forms (and triumphs) depends on institutional frameworks since they shape the range of possible outcomes by precluding certain trajectories of change as well as providing incentives for actors to learn to operate within them (Hancké and Goyer 2005). In other words, institutions shape the process of preference aggregation by increasing the odds of winning for specific coalitions (Berger 1981). On the side of political institutions, therefore, Gourevitch and Shinn distinguish between majoritarian/first-pass-the-post systems and consensus/ proportional representation systems. In majoritarian systems, the occurrence of small shifts of votes can translate into a substantial impact on public policy. A single party is more likely to be in control of the executive and legislative branches since single member districts are won by a plurality of the votes. In consensus systems, small shifts of vote have little impact on public policy. The electoral system rewards political parties in proportion of the votes they received—usually with a threshold of 5 per cent.

The interaction between political institutions and preference aggregation via coalition making, in turn, encourages the formation of different institutional varieties of capitalisms in the areas of corporate governance, employment relations, skill formation, and inter-firm relations. Firms coordinate their activities in different ways (Berger 2006; Hall and Soskice 2001). The nature of firm coordination is shaped by the institutions found in the four above mentioned spheres—which are themselves the product of politics—i.e. the interaction between political institutions and preference aggregation via coalition making.[16]

The importance of the different institutions of political systems lies in their impact on the ability of actors to issue credible commitments. Consensus political systems enable actors to make credible commitment to each other since they know that public policy outcomes are unlikely to change dramatically. The ability to issue credible commitments is essential for the sustainability of institutional arrangements in coordinated market economies whereby the coordination of firm activities rests on a high degree of interdependence among various actors (Hall and Soskice 2001). Extensive spillovers in specific innovation niches require the inclusion of stakeholders in the development of the innovative capabilities of firms (Tylecote and Visintin 2008; see also O'Sullivan 2000). The possibility of developing a long-term, interactive relationship with other actors in the firm constitutes a necessary condition for employer and employee investment in the long-term development of firm/ sector specific skills (Culpepper 2003; Estevez-Abe, Iversen, and Soskice 2001). Majoritarian political systems, in contrast, encourage the formation of institutional frameworks in liberal market economies that reward actors that can adjust quickly to take advantage of market shifts. The presence of a majoritarian political system

---

[16] In other words, institutional arrangements of corporate governance are shaped by the interaction between political institutions and preference formation via coalition formation and constitute one set of institutional variables that affect firm coordination.

makes it risky for actors to invest in specific skills and, therefore, contributes to the prominence of transferable skills (Hall and Soskice 2001; see also Deakin et al. 2002).

The final element in the Gourevitch-Shinn political variant is that the differences in the varieties of capitalism among advanced capitalist economies, in turn, translate into different ownership structures. The major institutional features of liberal market economies enable firms to take risks and to adjust quickly to shifts in demand through market-based mechanisms of coordination and, as a result, are also congruent with an exclusive focus on the interests of minority shareholders. In coordinated market economies, the institutional features of firm coordination build on the incorporation of the skills of the bulk of employees. The importance of issuing credible commitments to stakeholders implies different types of adjustment to shifts in market conditions compared to those in liberal market economies. The interests of minority shareholders do not occupy a privileged status with the consequence that investments in equity markets do not constitute as attractive a proposition as in liberal market economies.

Therefore, the Gourevitch-Shinn variant predicts the formation of two 'packages' of corporate governance: (1) consensus political systems, coordinated market institutions, and concentrated ownership; and (2) majoritarian political systems, liberal market institutions, and dispersed ownership. This approach is based on three analytical stages. The independent variable is the interaction between political institutions and the preferences of actors embedded in specific coalitions. The intervening variable is the types of institutional varieties from which firms coordinate their activities. The dependent variable is the structure of ownership of listed companies.

This second variant of the political perspective significantly contributes to the study of institutional analysis in comparative corporate governance. In addition to stressing the importance of power and conflict in politics, the analysis of Gourevitch-Shinn presents a sophisticated differentiation between and within categories of actors. The upshot of this finer-grained analysis is the enlargement of coalitional possibilities and the undetermined nature of preferences as actors can stress different objectives by making bargains with different partners. Moreover, it extends the range of institutional variables that affect ownership structures and other important features of corporate governance. The importance of the legal arrangements of minority shareholder protections are indeed important, but must be also complemented by the institutional arrangements in other sub-spheres of the economy (see also Milhaupt and Pistor 2008). This political variant highlights the importance of disentangling the effects associated with institutional frameworks. The impact of institutions is mediated by the wider framework in which they are embedded, thereby resulting in a contingent analysis according to nationally and historically specific contexts.

Nonetheless, two issues remain unsolved regarding the explanatory power of the second political variant. First, the direction of causality has been challenged by advocates of the varieties of capitalism perspective. The presence of institutional complementarities can constitute an important—albeit not the only—determinant for processes of institutional creation and change (Hall 2005 and 2007). The institutional arrangements of the varieties of capitalism type matter in the process of adjustment, as actors often seek institutional and functional equivalents to pre-existing forms of coordination. The implication is that a feedback loop can operate between the intervening variable (varieties of capitalism institutional types) and the independent variable (interaction between preferences and institutional arrangements of political systems) (see e.g. Pierson 1993).

Second, the presence of change in national systems of corporate governance requires expanding beyond the concept of political institutions. The occurrence of change in this second political variant can happen either from the transformation of political institutions or as a result of a shift in the preferences being stressed by actors. Since electoral and political systems—at least in advanced capitalist economies—have been relatively stable, then change is more likely to occur when preferences shift. This observation leads to three potential scenarios. The first one is that political institutions constitute a necessary, but a trivially necessary, condition for the study of diversity in corporate governance. The concept of triviality refers to the degree of importance of a necessary condition to account for the values taken by the dependent variable.[17] For the specific case of comparative corporate governance, stable political institutions are present in all cases in the universe of analysis of the dependent variable.

The second scenario is that the origins of electoral systems are endogenous—i.e. determined by the institutional arrangements found in other spheres. For instance, Cusack et al. (2007) highlight how the adoption of an electoral system in advanced capitalist economies has been shaped to a substantial extent by the adversarial nature of the system of industrial relations—proportional representation when consensual regulatory frameworks for the development of co-specific investments already existed; majoritarian in the case of adversarial industrial relations.

The third scenario is that each set of political institutions is not associated with a single outcome—how actors operate in particular institutional frameworks matters for their effect. The case of international trade negotiation in the institutional setting of the American system illustrates this dynamic—the use of fast track being associated with a desire to avoid pork barrel politics inherent in the two-chamber, single-member district system of the US Congress (Haggard 1988).

INTERESTS AND INSTITUTIONS IN COMPARATIVE CORPORATE GOVERNANCE

This section of the chapter deals with the place of economic incentives and rationality in the joint interaction between institutions and interests. Analyses of the role of

---

[17] See Braumoeller and Goertz (2000) for an analysis of the concept of trivially necessary condition.

strategic choice in social sciences are often accompanied by a dichotomy between the relative influence of institutions versus interests on the motivations of actors (see Hall 1997 and Whittington 1988 for overviews). The preference formation process—by which actors decide what they want and what to pursue—must distinguish between the respective or joint influence of institutions and interests on the behaviour of actors. What are the contributions of the three theoretical perspectives regarding the role of interests and institutions in the analysis of corporate governance?

The major difference on this question concerns the role of economic incentives on the motivation of actors. Both the law/economics and political perspectives assign great importance to rationalist considerations, but disagree on which types of institutions are important (see Gourevitch 2007). These two perspectives share a similar assumption on the motivation of actors—namely, that of 'a strategy of optimizing their utility function for the control of the firm's cash flow' (ibid: 30). However, they differ on the source of these incentives. For the law and economics perspective, the primacy issue is whether institutions adequately protect the rights of minority shareholders. The institutional arrangements of corporate governance are designed to resolve agency costs and to insure that minority shareholders get a return on their investment.

From the political perspective, institutions of corporate governance constitute the outcomes of struggles between actors seeking to advance their aims. The institutional arrangements related to the protection of minority shareholders are not sufficient to explain diversity of corporate governance. The presence of legal arrangements protective of minority shareholders sometimes result in ownership dispersion, but not in all countries (Roe 2002). In fact, Gourevitch and Shinn (2005) found a stronger correlation between ownership structures and the institutions of varieties of capitalism[18] than between ownership structures and legal protections for minority shareholders (see also Culpepper 2005).

The agreement between the law/economics and political perspectives on the importance of rationality and economic incentives—but with different viewpoints on which incentives are important—stand in contrast to the different strands in economic sociology. The prominence of economic incentives is significantly reduced. The comparison between two finer-grained differentiation of actors illustrated quite well this difference. For Gourevitch and Shinn (2005), the elaboration of a model of corporate governance of three actors with non-monolithic preferences serves to highlight the role of strategic interaction in the process of coalition formation. For Aguilera and Jackson (2003), in contrast, the presentation of the non-monolithic preferences of managers, shareholders, and workers is designed to illustrate how interests are socially constructed and result in variation in the identities of groups across national settings. The issue is not one of actors behaving

---

[18] Of which legal arrangements to protect the rights of minority shareholders only constitute one institutional subset.

irrationally, but having socially constructed sets of incentives that are embedded in a specific social context.

The distinct positioning of these perspectives on the question of the relative influence of interests and institutions implies important methodological considerations. The strategy for institutionally oriented researchers is to hold preferences constant which, in turn, reveals how changing institutions produce different outcomes across contexts. Similarly, interest-driven scholars hold institutions constant in order to show how changing interests lead to different results. This methodological trick gives rise to different problems for the political and sociological perspectives. For the political perspective, the concern with this strategy is that institutions might become the objects of struggle if they are so important (Gourevitch 1999). Existing institutions give more power to some actors over others. Actors understanding the asymmetry distribution of benefits flowing from institutional frameworks will seek to change them. In other words, institutional analysis suffers from an endogeneity problem. Moreover, what happens when nothing is constant—i.e. when both institutions and interests are evolving?

For the sociological perspective, in contrast, the challenge is to specify how interests result from a process of preference formation that is distinct from that of the strategic setting—i.e. the way actors go about obtaining their predefined goals (Frieden 1999). The sociological perspective emphasizes two attributes: how social contexts shape the identities of actors, and then how actors implement a strategy to achieve their preferred goals. However, preferences must be kept constant for at least two interactive analytical rounds if we are to distinguish between the interests of actors and the strategy designed to pursue these interests.

CONCLUSION

The comparative institutional analysis of corporate governance presented in this chapter made it clear that it would be a futile exercise to try to reconcile different perspectives around a single institutional viewpoint. Nonetheless, this chapter has highlighted the different mechanisms that help to understand variations across and changes within national systems of corporate governance. The three theoretical perspectives embody specific assumptions on the origins of institutions, processes by which institutional stasis prevails, and mechanism of change.

Methodological contributions could provide significant insights for the study of comparative corporate governance. The assessment of the impact of institutions on major issues requires the operationalization and specification of the nature of illusory differences (see Ragin 1987: 44–9). First, the illusion of change characterizes situations whereby processes of institutional change do not entail a modification in the behaviour of actors (Culpepper 2005; Goyer 2010; Hall 2007). The task consists in distinguishing between radical and incremental institutional change. Second, the illusion of similarity refers to the occurrence of functional conversion—namely, the change in the practices of an institution without a corresponding transformation in its formal structure (Gilson 2001; Thelen 2003 and 2004). The issue becomes one of identifying when an existing institution is serving new functions (see e.g. Deeg 2001).

REFERENCES

ABBOTT, ANDREW (2001). *Time Matters: On Theory and Method*, (Chicago: University of Chicago Press).

AGUILERA, RUTH and GREGORY JACKSON (2003). 'The Cross-national Diversity of Corporate Governance: Dimensions and Determinants', *Academy of Management Review* 28: 447–65.

——IGOR FILATOTCHEV, HOWARD GOSPEL, and GREGORY JACKSON (2008). 'An Organizational Approach to Comparative Corporate Governance: Costs, Contingences, and Complementarities', *Organization Science* 19: 475–92.

AMABLE, BRUNO (2003). *The Diversity of Modern Capitalism*, (Oxford: Oxford University Press).

BEBCHUK, LUCIAN (2006). 'Letting Shareholders Set the rules', *Harvard Law Review* 119: 1784–1813.

——and JESSE FRIED (2004). *Pay without Performance: The Unfulfilled Promise of Executive Compensation*, (Cambridge, MA: Harvard University Press).

——and MARK ROE (1999). 'A Theory of path Dependence in Corporate Ownership and Governance', *Harvard Law Review* 52: 127–70.

BERGER, SUZANNE (1981). 'Introduction', in ibid, (ed.), *Organizing Interests in Western Europe*, (New York: Cambridge University Press).

——(2006). *How We Compete: What Companies Around the World are Doing to Make it in Today's Global Economy*, (New York: Doubleday).

BERLE, ADOLF and GARDINER MEANS (1932). *The Modern Corporation and Private Property*, (New York: Harcourt, Brace & World).

BOERSCH, ALEXANDER (2007). *Global Pressure, National System: How German Corporate Governance is Changing*, (Ithaca, NY: Cornell University Press).

BOYER, ROBERT (1986). *La Théorie de la Régulation: Une Analyse Critique*, (Paris: Editions de la Découverte).

BRAUMOELLER, BEAR and GARY GOERTZ (2000). 'The Methodology of Necessary Conditions', *American Journal of Political Science* 44: 844–58.

BURT, RONALD (1982). *Toward a Structural Theory of Action: Network Models of Social Structure, Perception, and Action*, (New York: Academic Press).

CAMPBELL, JOHN (2004). *Institutional Change and Globalization*, (Princeton, NY: Princeton University Press).

CHANDLER, ALFRED (1977). *The Visible Hand: The Managerial Revolution in American Business*, (Cambridge, MA: Harvard University Press).

——(1990). *Scale and Scope: The Dynamics of Industrial Capitalism*, (Cambridge, MA: Harvard University Press).

CHEFFINS, BRIAN (2001). 'Does Law Matter? The Separation of Ownership and Control in the United Kingdom', *Journal of Legal Studies* 30: 459–84.

COFFEE, JOHN (1999). 'Privatization and Corporate Governance: The Lessons from Securities Market Failure', *The Journal of Corporation Law* 25: 1–39.

——(2005). 'A Theory of Corporate Scandals: Why the USA and Europe Differ', *Oxford Review of Economic Policy* 21: 198–211.

——(2006). *Gatekeepers: The Professions and Corporate Governance*, (New York: Oxford University Press).

CROUCH, COLIN (1993). *Industrial Relations and European State Traditions*, (Oxford: Clarendon Press).

CULPEPPER, PEPPER (2003). *Creating Cooperation: How States Develop Human Capital in Europe*, (Ithaca, NY: Cornell University Press).

——(2005). 'Institutional Change in Contemporary Capitalism: Coordinated Financial Systems since 1990', *World Politics* 57: 173–99.

CUSACK, THOMAS, TORBEN IVERSEN, and DAVID SOSKICE (2007). 'Economic Interests and the Origins of Electoral Systems', *American Political Science Review* 101: 373–91.

DAVIS, GERALD (1991). 'Agents without Principles? The Spread of the Poison Pill through the Intercorporate Networks', *Administrative Science Quarterly* 36: 583–613.

——(2005). 'New Directions in Corporate Governance', *Annual Review of Sociology* 31: 143–62.

——and HENRICH GREVE (1997). 'Corporate Elite Networks and Governance Changes in the 1980s', *American Journal of Sociology* 103: 1–37.

——KRISTINA DIEKMANN, and CATHERINE TINSLEY (1994). 'The Decline and Fall of the Conglomerate Firm in the 1980s: The Deinstitutionalization of an Organizational Firm', *American Sociological Review* 48: 147–60.

DEAKIN, SIMON, RICHARD HOBBS, DAVID NASH, and GILES SINGER (2002). 'Implicit Contracts, Takeovers, and Corporate Governance: In the Shadow of the City Code'. ESRC Centre for Business Research, University of Cambridge. Working paper 254.

DEEG, RICHARD (2001). 'Institutional Changes and the Uses and Limits of Path Dependency: The Case of German Finance', Discussion paper #01/6. (Cologne: Max Planck Institute).

DIMAGGIO, PAUL and WALTER POWELL (1983). 'The Iron Cage Revisited: Institutional Isomorphism and Collective Rationality in Organizational Fields', *American Sociological Review* 48: 147–60.

————(1991). 'Introduction', in Walter Powell and Paul J. DiMaggio (eds.), *The New Institutionalism in Organizational Analysis*, (Chicago: University of Chicago Press).

DOBBIN, FRANK (1994). *Forging Industrial Policy: The United States, Britain, and France in the Railway Age*, (New York: Cambridge University Press).

——(2004). 'The Sociology World of the Economy', in ibid., (ed.), *The New Economic Sociology: A Reader*, (Princeton, NJ: Princeton University Press).

——and TIMOTHY DOWD (2000). 'The Market that Antitrust Built: Public Policy, Private Coercion, and Railroad Acquisitions, 1825–1922', *American Sociological Review* 65: 635–57.

ENRIQUES, LUCA and PAOLO VOLPIN (2007). 'Corporate Governance Reforms in Continental Europe', *Journal of Economic Perspectives* 21: 117–40.

ESTEVEZ-ABE, MARGARITA, TORBEN IVERSEN, and DAVID SOSKICE (2001). 'Social Protection and the Formation of Skills: A Reinterpretation of the Welfare State', in Peter Hall and David Soskice (eds.), *Varieties of Capitalism: The Institutional Foundations of Comparative Advantage*, (New York: Oxford University Press).

FAMA, EUGENE and MICHAEL JENSEN (1983). 'The Separation of Ownership and Control', *Journal of Law and Economics* 26: 301–25.

FISS, PEER (2006). 'Social Influence Effects and Managerial Compensation Evidence From Germany', *Strategic Management Journal* 27: 1013–31.

——and EDWARD ZAJAC (2004). 'The Diffusion of Ideas Over Contested Terrain: The (non) Adoption of a Shareholder Value Orientation among German Firms', *Administrative Sciences Quarterly* 49: 501–34.

FLIGSTEIN, NEIL (1990). *The Transformation of Corporate Control*, (Cambridge, MA: Harvard University Press).

FRANKS, JULIAN, COLIN MAYER, and STEFANO ROSSI (2005). 'Spending Less Time with the Family: The Decline of Family Ownership in the United Kingdom', in Randall Morck (ed.), *A History of Corporate Governance around the World: Family Business Groups to Professional Managers*, (Chicago: University of Chicago Press).

FRIEDEN, JEFFRY (1999). 'Actors and Preferences in International Relations', in David Lake and Robert Powell (eds.), *Strategic Choice and International Relations*, (Princeton, NJ: Princeton University Press).

GARRETT, GEOFFREY and PETER LANGE (1995). 'Internationalization, Institutions, and Political Change', *International Organization* 49: 627–55.

GILSON, RONALD (2001). 'Globalizing Corporate Governance: Convergence of Form or Function?', *American Journal of Comparative Law* 49: 329–57.

——(2006). 'Controlling Shareholders and Corporate Governance: Complicating the Comparative Taxonomy', *Harvard Law Review* 119: 1641–79.

——(2007). 'Controlling Family Shareholders in Developing Countries: Anchoring Relational Exchange', *Stanford Law Review* 60: 633–55.

GLAESER, EDWARD, SIMON JOHNSON, and ANDREI SHLEIFER (2001). 'Coase vs. the Coasians', *Quarterly Journal of Economics* 116: 853–99.

GOUREVITCH, PETER (1999). 'The Governance Problem in International Relations', in David Lake and Robert Powell (eds.), *Strategic Choice and International Relations*, (Princeton, NJ: Princeton University Press).

——(2003). 'The Politics of Corporate Governance Regulation', *Yale Law Journal* 112: 1829–80.

——(2007). 'Explaining Corporate Governance Systems: Alternative Approaches', in Henk Overbeek, Bastian van Apeldoorn, and Andreas Nolke (eds.), *The Transnational Politics of Corporate Governance Regulation*, (London: Routledge).

——and JAMES SHINN (2005). *Political Power and Corporate Control: The New Global Politics of Corporate Governance*, (Princeton, NJ: Princeton University Press).

GOYER, MICHEL (2006). 'Varieties of Institutional Investors and National Models of Capitalism: The Transformation of Corporate Governance in France and Germany', *Politics and Society* 34: 399–430.

——(2007). 'Institutional Investors in French and German Corporate Governance: The Transformation of Corporate Governance and the Stability of Coordination'. Programme for the study of Germany and Europe. Working paper 07.2, (Center for European Studies: Harvard University).

——(2010). *Contingent Capital: The Evolution of Corporate Govenance in France and Germany*, (Oxford: Oxford University Press).

——and BOB HANCKÉ (2005). 'Labour in French Corporate Governance: The Missing Link', in Howard Gospel and Andrew Pendleton (eds.), *Corporate Governance and Labour Management: An International Comparison*, (New York: Oxford University Press).

GRANOVETTER, MARK (1985). 'Economic Action and Social structure: The Problem of Embeddedness', *American Journal of Sociology* 91: 481–510.

GROSSMAN, SANFORD and OLIVIER HART (1981). 'Implicit Contracts, moral Hazard, and Unemployment', *American Economic Review* 71: 301–7.

HAGGARD, STEPHAN (1988). 'The Institutional Foundations of Hegemony: Explaining the Reciprocal Agreement Act of 1934', *International Organization* 42: 91–119.

HALL, PETER (1986). *Governing the Economy: The Politics of State Intervention in Britain and France*, (New York: Oxford University Press).

——(1997). 'The Role of Interests, Institutions, and Ideas in the Comparative Political Economy of the Industrialized Nations', in Mark Irving Lichbach and Alan Zuckerman (eds.), *Comparative Politics: Rationality, Culture, and Structure*, (New York: Cambridge University Press).

——(2005). 'Institutional Complementarity: Causes and Effects', *Socio-Economic Review* 3: 373–77.

——(2007). 'The Evolution of Varieties of Capitalism in Europe', in Bob Hancké, Martin Rhodes, and Mark Thatcher (eds.), *Beyond Varieties of Capitalism: Conflict, Contradictions, and Complementarities in the European Economy*, (Oxford: Oxford University Press).

——and DAVID SOSKICE (2001). 'An Introduction to Varieties of Capitalism', in ibid., (eds.), *Varieties of Capitalism: The Institutional Foundations of Comparative Advantage*, (New York: Oxford University Press).

——and ROSEMARY TAYLOR (1996). 'Political Science and the Three New Institutionalisms', *Political Studies* 44: 936–57.

HANCKÉ, BOB (2002). *Large Firms and Institutional Change: Industrial Renewal and Economic Restructuring in France*, (New York: Oxford University Press).

——and MICHEL GOYER (2005). 'Degrees of Freedom: Rethinking the Institutional Analysis for Economic Change', in Glenn Morgan, Richard Whitley, and Eli Moen (eds.), *Changing Capitalisms? Internationalization, Institutional Change, and Systems of Economic Organization*, (New York: Oxford University Press).

HAVEMAN, HEATHER (1993). 'Follow the Leader: Mimetic Isomorphism and Entry into New Markets', *Administrative Sciences Quarterly* 38: 593–627.

HERRIGEL, GARY (1996). *Industrial Constructions: The Sources of German Industrial Power*, (New York: Cambridge University Press).

——(2008). 'Corporate Governance: History without Historians', in Geoffrey Jones and Jonathan Zeitlin (eds.), *The Oxford Handbook of Business History*, (New York: Oxford University Press).

HÖPNER, MARTIN (2001). 'Corporate Governance in Transition: Ten Empirical Findings on Shareholder Value and Industrial Relations in Germany', Discussion paper #01/5, (Cologne: Max Planck Institute).

HOWELL, CHRIS (1992). *Regulating Labor: The State and Industrial Relations Reform in Postwar France*, (Princeton, NJ: Princeton University Press).

——(2003). 'Varieties of Capitalism: And Then There Was One?', *Comparative Politics* 36: 103–24.

——(2006). 'The State and the Reconstruction of Industrial relations Institutions after Fordism: Britain and France Compared', in Jonah Levy (ed.), *The State after Statism: New State Activities in the Age of Liberalization*, (Cambridge, MA: Harvard University Press).

JENSEN, MICHAEL and WILLIAM MECKLING (1976). 'Theory of the Firm: Managerial Behavior, Agency Costs, and Ownership Structure', *Journal of Financial Economics* 3: 305–60.

JOHNSON, SIMON, RAFAEL LA PORTA, FLORENCIO LOPEZ-DE-SILANES, and ANDREI SHLEIFER (2000). 'Tunneling', *American Economic Review* 90: 22–7.

KATZENSTEIN, PETER (1977). 'Introduction: Domestic and International Forces and Strategies of Foreign Economic Policy', *International Organization* 31: 587–606.

KOGUT, BRUCE and GORDON WALKER (2001). 'The Small World of Germany and the Durability of National Networks', *American Sociological Review* 66: 317–35.

——and CHARLES RAGIN (2006). 'Exploring Complexity when Diversity is Limited: Institutional Complementarity in Theories of Rule of Law and National Systems Revisited', *European Management Review* 3: 44–59.

LANGLOIS, RICHARD (2003). 'The Vanishing Hand: The Changing Dynamics of Industrial Capitalism', *Industrial and Corporate Change* 12: 351–85.

LA PORTA, RAFAEL, FLORENCIO LOPEZ-DE-SILANES, and ANDREI SHLEIFER (1999). 'Corporate Ownership Around the World', *Journal of Finance* 54: 471–517.

————(2006). 'What Works in Securities Laws?', *Journal of Finance* 61: 1–32.

————and ROBERT VISHNY (2000). 'Investor Protection and Corporate Governance', *Journal of Financial Economics* 58: 3–27.

LIEBERSON, STANLEY (1991). 'Small N's and Big Conclusions: An Examination of the Reasoning in Comparative Studies Based on a Small Number of Cases', *Social Forces* 70: 307–20.

LIEBOWITZ, STANLEY and STEPEHEN MARGOLIS (1995). 'Path Dependence, Lock-in, and History', *Journal of Law, Economics, and Organization* 11: 205–26.

MAHONEY, JAMES (2000). 'Path Dependence in Historical Sociology', *Theory and Society* 29: 507–48.

——(2004). 'Comparative-historical Sociology', *Annual Review of Sociology* 30: 81–101.

MAHONEY, PAUL (2001). 'The Common Law and Economic Growth: Hayek Might be Right', *Journal of Legal Studies* 30: 503–25.

MARES, ISABELA (2003). *The Politics of Social Risk: Business and Welfare State Development*, (New York: Cambridge University Press).

MAYER, COLIN (2001). 'Firm Control', in Joachim Schwalbach (ed.). *Corporate Governance: Essays in Honor of Horst Albach*, (Berlin: Springer-Verlag).

MEYER, JOHN and BRIAN ROWAN (1977). 'Institutionalized Organizations: Formal Structure as Myth and Ceremony', *American Journal of Sociology* 83: 144–81.

MILHAUPT, CURTIS and KATHARINA PISTOR (2008). *Law and Capitalism: What Corporate Crises Reveal about Legal Systems and Economic Development around the World*, (Chicago: Chicago University Press).

MIZRUCHI, MARK (1989). 'Similarity of Political Behavior among Large American Corporations', *American Journal of Sociology* 95: 401–24.

MORCK, RANDALL (2005). *A History of Corporate Governance around the World: Family Business Groups to Professional Managers*, (Chicago: University of Chicago Press).

——ANDREI SHLEIFER, and ROBERT VISHNY (1988). 'Management Ownership and Market Valuation: An Empirical Analysis', *Journal of Financial Economics* 20: 293–315.

MORGAN, GLENN (2005). 'Institutional Complementarities, Path Dependency, and the Dynamics of firms', in Glenn Morgan, Richard Whitley, and Eli Moen (eds.), *Changing Capitalisms? Internationalization, Institutional Change, and Systems of Economic Organization*, (New York: Oxford University Press).

MULLER-JENTSCH, WALTER (2003). 'Re-assessing Co-determination', in Walter Muller-Jentsch and Hansjorg Weitbrecht (eds.), *The Changing Contours of German Industrial Relations*, (Munich: Rainer Hampp Verlag).

O'SULLIVAN, MARY (2000). *Contests for Corporate Control: Corporate Governance and Economic Performance in the United States and Germany*, (Oxford: Oxford University Press).

PIERSON, PAUL (1993). 'When Effects become Causes: Policy Feedback and Policy change', *World Politics* 45: 595–628.

——(2000). 'Increasing Returns, Path Dependence, and the Study of Politics', *American Political Science Review* 94: 251–67.

POLLARD, SIDNEY (1965). *The Genesis of Modern Management: A Study of the Industrial Revolution in Great Britain*, (Cambridge, MA: Harvard University Press).

PONTUSSON, JONAS (1995). 'From Comparative Public Policy to Political Economy: Putting Political Institutions in their Place and Taking Interests Seriously', *Comparative Political Studies* 28: 117–47.

PONTUSSON, JONAS and PETER SWENSON (1996). 'Labor Markets, Production Strategies, and Wage Bargaining Institutions: The Swedish Employer Offensive In Comparative Perspective', *Comparative Political Studies* 29: 223–50.

RAGIN, CHARLES (1987). *The Comparative Method: Moving beyond Qualitative and Quantitative Strategies*, (Berkeley: University of California Press).

RAJAN, RAGHURAM and LUIGI ZINGALES (2003). 'The Great Reversals: The Politics of Financial Development in the Twentieth Century', *Journal of Financial Economics* 69: 5–50.

ROE, MARK (1998). 'Backlash', *Columbia Law Review* 98: 217–41.

——(1999). 'Codetermination and German Securities Markets', in Margaret Blair and Mark Roe (eds.), *Employees and Corporate Governance*, (Washington, DC: Brookings Institution Press).

——(2002). 'Corporate Law's Limits', *Journal of Legal Studies* 31: 233–71.

——(2003). *Political Determinants of Corporate Governance: Political Context, Corporate Impact*, (New York: Oxford University Press).

——(2005). 'The Institutions of Corporate Governance', in Claude Menard and Mary Shirley (eds.), *Handbook of New Institutional Economics*, (New York: Springer).

——(2006). 'Legal Origins, Politics, and Stock Markets', *Harvard Law Review* 120: 462–527.

——(2007). 'Juries and the Political Economy of Legal Origins', *Journal of Comparative Economics* 35: 294–308.

ROY, WILLIAM (1997). *Socializing Capital: The Rise of the Large Industrial Corporation in America*, (Princeton, NJ: Princeton University Press).

RUESCHEMEYER, DIETRICH, EVELYNE HUBER STEPHENS, and JOHN STEPHENS (1992). *Capitalist Development and Democracy*, (Chicago: University of Chicago Press).

SCOTT, RICHARD (2001). *Institutions and Organizations*, 2nd edn., (Thousand Oaks, CA: Sage).

SHLEIFER, ANDREI and ROBERT VISHNY (1997). 'A Survey of Corporate Governance', *Journal of Finance* 52: 737–82.

SKOCPOL, THEDA (1979). *States and Social Revolutions: A Comparative Analysis of France, Russia and China*, (New York: Cambridge University Press).

SORGE, ARNDT (2005). *The Global and the Local: Understanding the Dialectics of Business Systems*, (New York: Oxford University Press).

STRANG, DAVID and MICHAEL MACY (2001). 'In Search of Excellence: Fads, Success Stories, and Adaptive Emulation', *American Journal of Sociology* 107: 147–82.

STREECK, WOLFGANG (1997). 'Beneficial Constraints: On the Economic Limits of Rational Voluntarism', in J. Rogers Hollingsworth and Robert Boyer (eds.), *Contemporary Capitalism: The Embeddedness of Institutions*, (New York: Cambridge University Press).

SWENSON, PETER (2002). *Capitalists Against Markets: The Making of Labor Markets and Welfare States in the United States and Sweden*, (New York: Oxford University Press).

THELEN, KATHLEEN (1991). *Union of Parts: Labor Politics in Postwar Germany*, (Ithaca, NY: Cornell University Press).

——(2003). 'How Institutions Evolve: Insights from Comparative Historical Analysis', in James Mahoney and Dietrich Rueschemeyer (eds.), *Comparative Historical Analysis in the Social Sciences*, (New York: Cambridge University Press).

——(2004). *How Institutions Evolve: The Political Economy of Skills in Germany, Britain, and Japan*, (New York: Cambridge University Press).

——and SVEN STEINMO (1992). 'Historical Institutionalism in Comparative Politics', in Sven Steinmo, Kathleen Thelen, and Frank Longstreth (eds.), *Structuring Politics: Historical Institutionalism in Comparative Analysis*, (New York: Cambridge University Press).

TILLY, CHARLES (1984). *Big Structures, Large Processes, Huge Comparisons*, (Sage: New York).

TYLECOTE, ANDREW and FRANCESCA VISINTIN (2008). *Corporate Governance, Finance and the Technological Advantage of Nations*, (London: Routledge).

VITOLS, SIGURT (2004). 'Negotiated Shareholder Value: The German Varient of an Anglo-American Practice', *Competition and Change* 8: 357–94.

WATTS, DUNCAN (1999). *Small Worlds: The Dynamics of Networks between Order and Randomness*, (Princeton, NJ: Princeton University Press).

WEIR, MARGARET and THEDA SKOCPOL (1985). 'State Structures and the Possibilities for "Keynesian" Responses to the Great Depression in Sweden, Britain, and the United States', in Peter, Evans, Dietrich Rueschemeyer, and Theda Skocpol (eds.), *Bringing the State Back In*, (New York: Cambridge University Press).

WESTPHAL, JAMES and POONAM KHANNA (2003). 'Keeping Directors in Line: Social Distancing as a Control Mechanism in the Corporate Elite', *Administrative Sciences Quarterly* 48: 361–98.

——and EDWARD ZAJAC (1994). 'Substance and Symbolism in CEOs' Long-term Incentive Plans', *Administrative Sciences Quarterly* 39: 367–90.

————(1995). 'Who shall Govern? CEO/Board Power, Demographic Similarity, and the New Director Selection', *Administrative Sciences Quarterly* 40: 60–83.

WHITLEY, RICHARD (1999). *Divergent Capitalisms: The Social Structuring and Change of Business Systems*, (New York: Oxford University Press).

——(2002). 'Developing Innovative Competences: The Role of Institutional Frameworks', *Industrial and Corporate Change* 11: 497–528.

——(2003). 'The Institutional Restructuring of Organizational Capabilities: The Role of Authority Sharing and Organizational Careers', *Organization Studies* 24: 667–95.

WHITTINGTON, RICHARD (1988). 'Environmental Structure and Theories of Strategic Choice', *Journal of Management Studies* 25: 521–36.

——and MICHAEL MAYER (2000). *The European Corporation: Strategy, Structure, and Social Science*, (New York: Oxford University Press).

ZAJAC, EDWARD and JAMES WESTPHAL (1995). 'Accounting for the Explanations of CEO Compensation: Substance and Symbolism', *Administrative Sciences Quarterly* 40: 283–308.

ZINGALES, LUIGI (1998). 'Why it's Worth being in Control', in George Bickerstaffe (ed.), *Mastering Finance*, (London; Pearson Education).

CHAPTER 16

....

THE INSTITUTIONAL CONSTRUCTION OF FIRMS

....

RICHARD WHITLEY

INTRODUCTION

....

A major feature of post-Second World War capitalism has been the successful establishment of different systems of economic organization in the industrialized market economies. The prevalent ways in which economic activities are coordinated and governed in, for example, France, Germany, and Japan, continue to differ greatly from those dominant in the USA and UK, as well as varying considerably between themselves (Amable 2003; Hollingsworth 1991; Lincoln and Gerlach 2004; Schmidt 2002). It also seems likely that whatever forms of market economy eventually become established in China, they will both differ significantly from those institutionalized elsewhere and also vary in significant respects between different localities within the country (King and Szelenyi 2005; Krug and Hendrischke 2007; Wank 1999).

Despite the claims of some globalization enthusiasts, these differences are no more likely to converge to a single type of market economy in the twenty-first century than similarly varied forms of capitalism did in the internationalized world economy of the late nineteenth century (Hirst and Thompson 1996; Kenworthy 1997; 2005; Koechlin 1995; Wade 1996). In particular, the idea that the prevalent American variety of capitalism will come to dominate the world economy by virtue of its superior efficiency, which was widely held in the heyday of Fordism, is as flawed as the notion that Japanese capitalism would sweep all before it, as was popularly thought in the 1980s (Boyer and Durand 1997; Djelic 1998; Vogel 1988).

These continued differences in systems of economic organization are reflected in significant variations in the nature of leading firms in differently organized market economies. The powers, duties, and socio-economic functions of private companies continue to vary considerably between national jurisdictions and over time, as many scholars have shown (see, e.g. Milhaupt 2003; Roy 1997). In particular, the extent to which corporate entities combine legal personality, unified authority, limited liability, investor ownership, and easy transfer of private property rights—which Kraakman (2001) has suggested were key features of the late twentieth-century US corporation—is highly variable between differently organized market economies and subject to change as circumstances alter.

This is especially the case for the strategic role of the legally constituted firm, which is by no means always the key unit of private economic decision-making in market economies (see, e.g. Bauer and Cohen 1981; Hamilton and Kao 1990; Redding 1990; Westney 2001). These variations in the nature and role of firms reflect the contested nature of the dominant corporate form, as well as major differences in the key institutions governing economic activities in different nation-states (Dobbin 1994; Gourevitch and Shinn 2005; Goyer in this Handbook; Roy 1997). As a result, the nature, behaviour and role of firms in socio-economic development differ considerably between market economies, and cannot be assumed to converge on a single most efficient type of company.

The recognition that firms vary in their economic role, governance, and growth strategies across institutional environments implies: a) that the functions of legally established firms differ between market economies and can change over time, b) that their governing interests and dominant logics of action cannot be assumed to be reduced to a single slogan, such as maximizing shareholder value, which means the same in all societies, and c) that how leading firms compete effectively varies according to institutional regimes. These points emphasize the contingent nature of firms as economic actors and the need for comparative institutional analysis of their governance, structure, and capabilities in different societies. Such an analysis raises the question of how firms should be conceptualized and understood as collective economic actors.

Firms are commonly understood to be critical economic actors in capitalist societies because they combine financial accountability and control through ownership rights with authority over the direction and use of human and material resources that enables them to develop distinctive knowledge and capabilities (e.g. Kogut and Zander 1992; Teece et al. 2000). They constitute the key collective entities through which private property rights owners and their delegated agents and managers coordinate economic activities to create and appropriate value. It is this combination of authoritative integration and direction of resources through collective routines and procedures, which can be both formal and informal, with private ownership and strategic choices that makes firms crucial actors in market economies (Penrose 1959; Richardson 1998). Together with other organizations and associations such as labour unions, inter-firm networks, state and quasi-state agencies, and socio-political coalitions, their decisions and activities collectively affect market outcomes and economic development (Whitley 2007).

This view of firms as privately owned authoritative coordinators and directors of human and material resources suggests a number of dimensions for analysing how they vary between institutional environments. These can be combined into two major sets of characteristics that can be used to distinguish between the kinds of leading firms that become established and dominant in differently organized market economies. First, those dealing with issues of ownership, control, and direction, commonly referred to as governance concerns. These distinguish between the varied kinds of groups and interests that dominate firm decision-making and set strategic priorities. The second set of characteristics deal with the processes involved in coordinating and managing resources to create and maintain distinctive organizational capabilities that provide each firm with competitive advantages.

The comparative institutional analysis of firms studies how these characteristics vary between dominant companies in market economies that are governed by different kinds of institutional arrangements. These include the institutions concerned with: a) authority and trust relations, b) the organization and policies of the state and related political structures, including the legal framework within which firms are constituted and regulated, c) access to capital, and d) the development and use of skilled labour.

In the next section of this chapter, I shall describe these characteristics of leading firms in more detail, and then suggest how they could be used to identify five distinct ideal types of firms that have been prominent in a number of major industrialized economies since the Second World War. Subsequently, I shall describe the major features of dominant institutions that influence how firm governance and capabilities can be expected to vary between differently organized economies, and then suggest how they do so. In the final section I shall consider how the increasing managerial coordination of economic activities in different countries and institutional contexts through multinational companies are affecting these connections and can lead to the creation of novel kinds of transnational firms.

Key Characteristics of Firms in Market Economies

Firm governance

It is common in the Anglophone literature on corporate governance to focus on the relationship between shareholders and top managers, and the way that the growth of managerial autonomy resulting from increasingly dispersed shareownership in the largest companies has led to a disjunction between owners' interests and those of salaried managers (Berle and Means 1932; Blair 1995; Marris 1964). As shareholdings in some of the leading firms in the stock market dominated economies of the UK, USA, and similar societies have become more fragmented in terms of the proportion owned by individuals and families over the twentieth century, the connections between ownership and control of private firms have frayed to the point of invisibility and the strategic direction of these companies is more and more in the hands of its senior salaried employees.

This view was very much the product of the US corporate economy in the mid-twentieth century, where senior managerial autonomy and tenure were greater than they subsequently became, and hostile takeovers more difficult to accomplish (Lazonick and O'Sullivan 1996; O'Sullivan 2000), and is not fully supported by recent studies (Becht and DeLong 2007; Gadhoum et al. 2005). However, the conflict between the priorities of outside investors and managers dominates most analyses of corporate governance in economies with these kinds of financial systems (Gugler et al. 2004; Goyer in this volume).

This concentration on agency problems between investors as principals and managers as agents tends to ignore the broader context of corporate governance, especially the role of political conflicts and interests in structuring the legal and financial framework governing corporate forms and preferred growth strategies (Dobbin 1994; Fligstein and Choo 2005; Roe 2003; Roy 1997). It also neglects 'the governance of the process through which resources are developed as well as utilised in the economy' (O'Sullivan 2000: 58) and fails to consider the numerous industrialized economies in which control of large private firms is substantially concentrated in the hands of a small number of owners, banks, and other groups, such as many in Europe and Asia (Barca and Becht 2001; Gadhoum et al. 2005; Gugler et al. 2004; Morck 2007). In such economies, a key governance issue concerns the rights of minority shareholders in the face of controlling owners' manipulations rather than managerial autonomy from owners' interests.

More generally, the governance of private firms in market economies involves a much wider range of interests and issues than shareholder control, including 'the whole set of legal, cultural and institutional arrangements that determine what publicly traded corporations can do, who controls them, how that control is exercised, and how the risks and returns from the activities they undertake are allocated' (Blair 1995: 3). In particular, the comparative study of the governance of firms needs to consider how dominant interest groups and institutions influence the construction, direction, and development of major companies in different jurisdictions in such ways that their behaviour and economic consequences vary (Gourevitch and Shinn 2005). While this clearly involves issues of ownership and control, it also includes the impact of various kinds of employees, suppliers, customers, competitors, and other business associates on firm management and behaviour.

The relative influence of these groups, and how it is exercised in the pursuit of different purposes, varies between differently organized market economies, as well as changing over time, in ways that affect how leading firms develop distinctive competitive competences, as is exemplified by the twentieth-century histories of German and Japanese companies (see, e.g. Aoki and Dore 1994; Morck and Nakamura 2007; Odagiri 1994; Streeck and Yamamura 2001; Sorge 2005). A useful way of comparing patterns of firm governance, then, is to contrast the relative impact that different interest groups and institutionalized structures such as capital markets are able to exert on the strategic priorities and decisions of dominant firms in different kinds of society.

Beginning with the degree and type of ownership influence on strategic managers, at least four separate situations can be distinguished in terms of the relative directness of owner involvement in firm direction and management, and strategic managers' autonomy in determining priorities and growth strategies. First there is the archetypal owner-controlled firm in which majority owners directly control the day-to-day operations of the business and those that work for it. In this situation of direct owner control, salaried managers are clearly highly constrained by owners and their interests dominate.

Second, ownership—or at least control over major blocks of shareholders' votes—may be more remote from everyday managerial decision-making, yet still concentrated enough to influence greatly overall strategic priorities and the selection of top managers. Such concentrations of shareownership blocks are usually large enough to lock dominant investors into the fate of individual companies, so that they cannot exit easily and are necessarily 'committed' owners. Where banks and other financial organizations control large blocks of shares, as in much of post-war Germany, they too can function as committed owners in this sense, although their preferences may be more oriented to growth goals than some family owners. Managers are here often able to exert considerable autonomy in day-to-day decision-making but can become quite constrained when major strategic issues arise, such as those involving mergers and acquisitions and major restructuring of corporate units.

Third, market based forms of owner control refer to a situation of fragmented beneficial shareholdings where each individual investor controls a diversified portfolio of shares in different companies and focuses more on the overall performance of such portfolios than on the fate of any single firm. In principle, this dispersion of shareownership should grant managers considerable freedom of action, as discussed in the managerial revolution literature. However, where short-term control over the management of shares has become concentrated in the hands of a few fund managers and their advisers who are regularly evaluated in terms of their short-term financial performance, and capital markets are relatively deregulated and large and liquid enough to support strong markets for corporate control, capital market constraints on managerial actions can be considerable. It is therefore useful to distinguish between strong and weak varieties of capital market constraint on managerial strategies.

Turning next to consider the relative influence of other groups on firm direction and strategic choices, two major ones can be distinguished: employees and business associates. In this context, the constraining effects of employee interests go beyond the legal requirements of consultation and co-decision-making that have become established in some European countries, to include the more general influence that results from strong labour unions and institutionalized patterns of cooperation with employees (Jackson et al. 2005). Such cooperation is especially important when firms depend on highly knowledgeable and skilled staff to improve their products and services continuously, to anticipate customer needs, and invest in the development of new competences. The more dominant institutions in a society encourage this dependence, the more employee interests—or at least those of the key staff—constrain what strategic managers can do and how they do it.

The third set of constraints on managerial autonomy in setting strategic priorities and directing activities arise from membership of different kinds of business associations and other organizations. Companies are often encouraged to join powerful trade associations and employers' groups that restrict their ability to pursue independent strategies, especially in the more corporatist societies of continental Europe and Japan (Crouch 1999; Sorge 2005; Streeck and Schmitter 1985). In the past, some of these have organized cartels that have been supported by the legal system (Herrigel 1996) and many continue to play a substantial role in standardizing contracts and organizing inter-firm relationships (Casper 2001). As Hall and Soskice (2001) emphasize in their dichotomization of liberal and coordinated market economies, such strong business and employers' associations are important features of the latter type that restrict firms' short-term opportunism.

In broad terms, these two sets of constraints on top managers' freedom of action can be expected to encourage corporate growth at the expense of short-term profitability goals. Both employees, including most managerial ones, and business partners benefit from expansion of the existing business, and are more likely to support and be actively committed to incremental innovation that builds on existing competences than to radical discontinuous change that threatens existing skills. Competence enhancing diversification will be preferred to competence destructive strategic shifts when such constraints are strong.

A fourth set of influences on firm behaviour stem from state support of favoured industries and companies, as well as the pursuit of specific public policy goals in sectors such as defence and health through what Ergas (1987, see also Doremus et al. 1998) termed mission-oriented technology policies. However, these are more conveniently regarded as instances of political and public bureaucratic steering and encouragement of particular strategies in specific national and/or regional jurisdictions rather than as integral parts of firm governance, although clearly the role of the state more generally is a key factor in determining the constitution and behaviour of leading companies in a political economy. Since the structure, policies, and practices of different states incorporate the legal definition of property rights and their enforcement, the rules governing market boundaries and behaviour, and distributional regulation, are better considered as part of the business environment that strongly affects firm development and actions.

While these three aspects of firm governance can be combined in many different ways that are affected by broader features of the business environment, some combinations seem more likely than others. In particular, extensive employee and business partner constraint seems more likely to occur with committed ownership than where there is a strong market for corporate control and fragmented share-ownership because hostile takeovers and associated pressures for short-term financial returns in the latter situation will limit the influence of employees and business partners and their willingness to invest in developing firm-specific competences.

Developing organizational capabilities

In considering how firms develop different kinds of competitive capabilities in different market economies, a major variable concerns owners' and managers' use of authority to integrate and direct economic activities. As many discussions have emphasized, the authoritative direction and integration of economic activities is a key feature of firms. Hamilton and Feenstra (1997: 56), for instance, claim that firms, and economic organizations in general, are 'above all authoritative organisations that structure relationships according to established rules of conduct' in which participants recognize that they are bound to the authoritative norms of the organization, and there are coercive means to enforce collective rules.

The ability to direct employees to undertake specific tasks through delegated authority from private property rights holders is central to the organizational development of distinctive collective competences, not least because the flexibility that employment agreements provide enables managers to organize economic activities in different ways for varied purposes, and to change these to suit altered circumstances (Richardson, 1998; Rubery in this Handbook). This flexibility facilitates the management of increasingly complex and uncertain activities, particularly innovation. As Lazonick (1991; Lazonick and West 1998) and others have suggested, the planned coordination of a specialized division of labour has enabled firms to build distinctive organizational capabilities for developing process and product innovations on a continuing basis.

The systematic organization and control of activities through employment agreements encourages the production of common knowledge and skills that are specific to each company. By working together in organized ways, employees develop distinctive routines, understandings, and collective abilities that enable the firm as an organization to generate novel kinds of capabilities that provide distinctive competitive competences (Metcalfe and James 2000). It is perhaps worth pointing out that such authoritative direction need not always be imposed by a managerial hierarchy, but can be achieved through delegated powers from workers as in some professional service firms and employee owned companies.

However, the extent to which such authoritative integration and direction does in fact generate distinctive collective knowledge and competences varies greatly between firms and institutional contexts. In particular, they differ in how much employees and others involved in the firm's affairs, such as suppliers and customers, contribute to problem-solving and improving performance, as many comparisons of German, Japanese, and US companies have indicated (Aoki 2001; Casper 2000; Cole and

Whittaker 2006; Soskice 1999). Such contributions depend both on managers seeking them and on employees being committed to developing firms' distinctive capabilities, sometimes at the expense of improving their own individual skills. Two important ways in which owners and managers can elicit high levels of employee involvement in joint problem solving activities, and commitment to the improvement of firms' collective capacity to deal with complex issues, are to share substantial amounts of authority with them and to provide long-term organizational careers.

Authority sharing here involves property rights holders and their agents delegating considerable discretion over task performance—and sometimes task organization—to skilled employees, and encouraging them to contribute to product and process improvements. It varies in the degree of such delegation, i.e. the amount of discretion exercised by subordinates, and its scope, that is, the range of activities and decisions over which discretion is exercised. While these aspects are often positively correlated, it is clearly possible for managers to delegate high levels of discretion over specific, narrowly defined, tasks without extending it to more general features of the work.

Where the scope of authority sharing is low, the span of discretion is quite restricted to limited aspects of how tasks should be performed, while greater levels of authority sharing mean that employees are often involved in the selection, organization, and allocation of tasks as well as having considerable discretion over how they are conducted. In such cases, they may also be expected to contribute to departmental and wider problem-solving, often being assessed in terms of their contribution to overall firm performance.

Such intra-organizational delegation of discretion to employees is sometimes complemented by external authority sharing with suppliers, customers, and competitors in varied inter-firm networks, especially when there are strong institutional constraints on short-term opportunism. In both instances, firms are thereby enabled, in principle, to learn from the knowledge and experiences of their employees and business partners. On the whole, then, the greater the degree and scope of such authority sharing, the more firms should be able to integrate different kinds of activities and types of knowledge in dealing with complex problems, and to develop new routines and knowledge.

Long-term commitment to a firm's success through contributing to its specific knowledge and capabilities is additionally encouraged by offering organizational careers for those who demonstrably make such contributions on a continuing basis. By tying personal futures to the growth of the employing organization, and making credible commitments to maintain employment across the business cycle, such careers intensify employee commitment to the improvement of collective competences, even if that limits their visibility on external labour markets. Where, on the other hand, employment is seen as being vulnerable to market and technological shifts, as well as to changes in ownership, skilled workers will be more concerned to improve their position on external labour markets by enhancing their own personal knowledge, reputation, and skills than on sharing knowledge and opportunities with short-term colleagues.

Authority sharing and organizational careers are interrelated in the sense that providing the latter for some employees involves a considerable amount of the former. It seems most unlikely that owners would offer relatively long-term commitments for managers and skilled workers if they were not prepared to delegate substantial levels of task autonomy to them. While, then, firms that do not provide long-term careers for employees can vary in the degree of authority sharing they implement, between for instance owner controlled firms in many developing economies and project based firms in Silicon Valley (Bahrami and Evans 1995; Whitley 2007), those that do offer organizational careers for at least some groups of staff are also likely to delegate considerable task autonomy to them.

Considering next the different kinds of collective capabilities that firms develop through the authoritative coordination and direction of resources and activities, useful distinctions can be drawn between three major kinds: coordinating, learning, and reconfigurational (Teece et al. 2000; Dosi et al. 2000). Coordinating capabilities refer to the ability of companies to integrate different activities and knowledge through organizational procedures and thereby realize economies of scale and scope. While all firms integrate economic activities through unified authority structures to some extent, their capacity to achieve such economies varies considerably as Chandler (1990) among others has emphasized. In particular, the ability to coordinate new developments across departments and divisions can differ greatly between companies.

Such capabilities are often developed by strong managerial hierarchies that systematically control and direct a range of activities through formal rules and personal supervision. However, effective integration should be greater when key employees are both knowledgeable about the work and competences of colleagues in different departments and divisions and are committed to working with them to achieve overall organizational objectives. Accordingly, long-term organizational membership and experience of working in different parts of the firm seem likely to improve such integrating capabilities, especially when these are characteristic of a wide range of employees as in many large post-war Japanese companies (Aoki 1988; Koike 1987).

Organizational learning refers to the ability of a firm to develop new knowledge of its processes, products, and markets, and incorporate that knowledge into its practices and strategies. It involves the codification, diffusion, and application of new understandings developed by individuals and groups throughout the organization, so that routines and procedures are continuously being updated in a process of cumulative improvement (Nonaka and Takeuchi 1995). The critical feature of this capability is its organizational nature by which firms continuously develop new knowledge collectively and adapt to changing circumstances by incremental, competence enhancing innovations.

This again depends on encouraging employees and others associated with the operations of the firm to develop and share their knowledge with colleagues, and the development of systematic routines to ensure that valuable knowledge is incorporated into new processes, products, and services. On the whole, the more owners and managers share their authority with a wide range of skilled workers and

Japanese organisational learning.

reward their contributions to improving firm performance, the more effective such organizational learning is likely to be. Thus, where long-term membership of the firm is largely restricted to managerial employees, as in the dominant US corporation described by Chandler (1977; 1990) and others (O'Sullivan 2000), such organizational learning is likely to be less widespread and effective than in their Japanese equivalents that extended such commitments to many male manual workers (Fujimoto 2000).

Reconfigurational capabilities also involve innovation, but in a more radical, rapid, and discontinuous way, such that core competences and skills become transformed, as when pharmaceutical companies developed new drug discovery methods that incorporated the knowledge and skills of biologists (Casper and Matraves 2003; Gambardella 1995), IBM turned itself into an IT services firm, and Corning Glass became a fibre optics company. Of course, in the extreme case of such changes, the whole firm becomes so transformed that it may be doubted whether it is still the 'same' company, but most reconfigurations involve the restructuring of resources and redirection of activities into new technologies and markets, often with new skills and knowledge bases, rather than the wholesale destruction of existing organizational competences and administrative routines.

The ability to undertake such reshaping of a firm's activities and resources implies a capacity to recognize significant changes in its environment and alter what it does and how it does it accordingly, even if this means dropping significant lines of business and entering quite new ones that are known to be risky. The main contrast with organizational learning capabilities concerns the more rapid and radically discontinuous nature of reconfigurational ones, which are typically more competence destructive than enhancing.

IDEAL TYPES OF FIRMS

While these characteristics of firm governance and organizational capabilities can be combined in a number of different ways, some patterns seem more likely to be empirically common and stable than others. For example, employers' commitment to long-term organizational careers is unlikely to be highly credible when firms are liable to be taken over and restricted, or when authority is concentrated in the hands of the owner-manager and his or her immediate family. Equally, family controlled firms are unlikely to develop strong coordinating capabilities unless they delegate some authority to salaried managers and are able to make credible commitments to providing organizational careers for them. In considering the distinctive kinds of organizational capabilities developed by firms that have dominated many industrialized economies since the end of the Second World War, we can distinguish at least five ideal types that combine different patterns of governance and authority sharing to generate contrasting capabilities. These are summarized in Table 16.1 and will now be discussed.

Table 16.1: Ideal types of firms and their organizational capabilities

Characteristics	Type of firm				
	Opportunistic	Specialized network	Isolated hierarchy	Centralized hierarchy	Collaborative hierarchy
Owner control type	Direct	Direct/ Market	Market	Direct	Committed
Employee constraint	Low	Considerable	Limited to managers	Limited to top managers	Considerable
Business partner constraint	Low	Some in industrial districts	Limited	Limited	Considerable
Degree of authority sharing	Low	Considerable	Some	Limited	Considerable
Scope of authority sharing	Low	Considerable	Limited to managers	Limited	Considerable
Longevity and scope of organizational careers	Low	Low	Some for managers	Limited	Considerable
Strength of coordinating capabilities	Restricted to personal control	Restricted to specialized firms and limited in scope	Consider-able	Consider-able	High
Strength of organizational learning capabilities	Limited	Limited to teams	Limited to managers	Limited to top managers	Consider-able
Strength of reconfigurational capabilities	High for entrepreneurs	Limited in industrial districts, high in professional networks	Consider-able	Consider-able	Limited

Opportunistic firms represent the classic entrepreneurial enterprise built around the knowledge and skills of its owner-manager with few commitments to employees or business partners. Such firms tend to be highly responsive to short-term business opportunities, often changing their processes, products, and customers rapidly as circumstances alter. The archetypal Chinese family business in Hong Kong and other parts of Pacific-Asia exemplify this kind of company, whose key resource is the capacity of the owner to seize opportunities as they arise, maximizing flexibility and minimizing commitments to particular personnel, suppliers, or capital machinery (Enright et al. 1997; Redding 1990).

Integrating routines and systematic procedures coordinating different activities are rarely highly institutionalized in such firms, and so their capacity for realizing economies of scale and scope in the Chandlerian manner is limited. Similarly, organizational learning through continual incremental improvement of such routines and patterns of behaviour will be restricted where it threatens entrepreneurial initiatives. Reconfigurational capabilities, on the other hand, could be considerable in the sense of being able to rapidly change products, markets, and technologies—albeit not those involving complex and expensive capital resources. However, given the limited organizational specificity of such firms' capabilities—as distinct from those of the owner-manager—such abilities are more individual than collective.

Specialized network firms also have limited managerial coordinating capabilities and are often run by their owners, but depend much more on the knowledge and skills of their employees, sharing considerable authority with them. They are additionally more likely to engage in common activities with business partners in collaborative networks and cooperate with a wide range of external agencies. Coordinating capabilities are here restricted by most firms' relatively small size and specialized focus. However, learning within the enterprise should be greater as staff are encouraged to work together for common purposes, often with high-powered incentives such as stock options. Such learning may well involve external partners and knowledge producers as well, when labour markets are fluid and access to specialized skills relatively easy.

Reconfigurational capabilities will also be facilitated by active external labour markets and low levels of commitment to staff when market and technical uncertainty are high. However, in more established and stable labour markets, where knowledge and skill development changes at a slower rate, they will be more restricted, as in many industrial districts that specialize in particular industries.

Larger firms with more systematic and formal procedures for coordinating different activities and an administrative structure for planning them can be distinguished in terms of their prevalent pattern of ownership and control, on the one hand, and their willingness to share authority and gain employee commitment on the other. The combination of market owner-control and limited employer–employee commitment is exemplified by the dominant US corporation for much of the twentieth century, according to Chandler (1990) and others (e.g. O'Sullivan 2000). Many of these companies had a fragmented shareholder base and developed a large managerial infrastructure for coordinating different activities through formal routines that generated considerable economies of scale and scope under particular conditions (Langlois 2003).

While remote owners delegated considerable authority to salaried managers, these latter usually did not expect the bulk of the other employees to contribute to problem solving or the improvement of organizational capabilities. Organizational careers similarly tended to be restricted to the managerial ranks. This type of firm can be characterized as an isolated hierarchy since most authority was vested in the managerial hierarchy and they operated as integrated administrative structures amidst predominantly arm's length market relationships.

However, the extent of strategic managerial autonomy from capital market and other pressures varies in such firms. As O'Sullivan (2000) has emphasized, changes in the structure of household finances, the rise of institutional shareholdings, and macro-economic shifts in the 1970s encouraged both a concentration of fund management in the USA and some other stock market dominated financial systems, and demands for greater returns on equity shareholdings (see also Blair 1995; Lazonick and O'Sullivan 1996). In the last quarter of the twentieth century, these pressures intensified the market for corporate control in such economies and restricted the ability of top managers to implement long-term development plans. They also reduced the longevity of organizational careers for many managers and the overall level of employer–employee commitment in such companies.

The investment in managerial integration of activities characteristic of these types of firms means that they should have considerable coordinating capabilities, although the limited scope of authority sharing and careers can be expected to restrict the willingness of most staff to invest in the improvement of cross-functional and cross-divisional linkages at the expense of enhancing their own specialist skills. Similarly, while managers may be keen to improve performance through incremental innovation and learning, other employees of isolated hierarchies have fewer incentives to do so and the high level of job insecurity can be expected to inhibit their enthusiasm for changing technologies and work routines. In terms of commitment to, and identification with, the company, then, medium- to long-term membership tends to be limited to the managerial hierarchy in such firms, as are firm-specific knowledge and competences.

On the other hand, the relative weakness of authority sharing and employer–employee commitment should enable senior managers to carry out quite radical transformations of their activities and resources and so enhance their reconfigurational capabilities. Such unilateral decision-making also, of course, allows the managerial elite to ignore conflicting information and signals from the changing environment, as seems to have happened in the cases of Rubbermaid and Quaker Oats in the 1990s (Helfat et al. 2007).

More committed forms of ownership and control include those where shareholdings—or more often perhaps control over votes—are concentrated in the hands of an individual, family, or trust, and/or where firms are effectively constrained by banks, insurance companies, and similar providers of 'patient' capital in relatively illiquid capital markets. While these controllers may well have varied strategic priorities and preferences regarding authority sharing, they are all locked-in to the fate of individual companies, at least in the short term, and cannot easily trade their property rights. This means that they can make credible commitments to organizational careers for some employees over the medium term and build strong firm-specific capabilities through high levels of employer–employee interdependence.

Variations in the degree and scope of employer–employee commitment enable us to distinguish between two types of such firms: centralized hierarchies and collaborative hierarchies. In the first, authority is concentrated in the hands of the dominant share or vote controller and his or her closest colleagues who are often family members, with little delegation to other employees, or to external business partners. Rather authoritarian management styles are here often combined with paternalistic commitments to long-term employment for many white-collar workers that are made more credible by high levels of state support, particularly through subsidized credit for rapid expansion. Many of the South Korean *chaebol* have exemplified this kind of firm in the post-war period (see, e.g. Amsden 1989; Bae 1987; Kim 1992; Janelli 1993).

In the second kind of committed owner-controlled firm, authority and career commitments are much more widely shared, both with a wide range of employees and with external business partners and agencies. As a result, commitment to the continuous improvement of firm-specific knowledge and capabilities is much more likely to be widespread, as in many large Japanese firms in the post-war period (see, e.g. Aoki 1988; Fruin 1992; Fujimoto 2000).

Centralized hierarchies should be able to develop considerable coordinating cap-abilities through the central direction of activities and people by the top manage-ment, often aided by a powerful planning and control office that integrates operations and new developments across divisions through highly formalized pro-cedures and intensive personnel management (Amsden 1989). However, this degree of central control means that most organizational learning will be accomplished by the managerial elite of such firms. Little initiative and contribution to organizational problem-solving is expected of other employees, and it is rarely rewarded when it does occur.

Reconfigurational abilities, on the other hand, should be considerable, with few constraints on top managements' powers to restructure firms' resources and opera-tions, as is illustrated by the *chaebols*' rapid movement into new industries at the behest of the state during Korea's post-war industrialization (Amsden 1989; Fields 1995; Kim 1997; Woo 1991). However, as in the case of isolated hierarchies, such unilateral decision-making also enables large-scale mistakes to be made, as became more evident in Korea in the 1990s when state constraints were loosened and the level of support reduced. In general, it is arguable that the combination of highly perso-nalized and centralized authority with an extensive highly educated white-collar labour force characteristic of many centralized hierarchies is unsustainable in the long term, especially without domestic market protection and other forms of state support.

Collaborative hierarchies, in contrast, are more constrained by employee groups and external business partners, including business associations. This encourages strong growth goals and employee investment in ensuring effective coordination of the firm's operations and new developments. Because many staff have long-term commitments to the firm's expansion, they should be more willing to develop firm-specific knowledge and skills by, for instance, accepting inter-functional and cross-divisional transfers than would those in less collaborative companies. As a result, the integrative capabilities of these kinds of firms can be expected to be considerable. The widespread practice of moving general employees between departments and divisions in many large Japanese companies at the behest of the central personnel department, which typically assumes responsibility for managing their careers for the long-term health of the firm, exemplifies such commitment (Graham 2003; Jacoby 2005). For similar reasons, the organizational learning capabilities of this kind of firm should be considerable as staff have every incentive to contribute to the growth of the company (Aoki 1988; Clark 1979; Dore 1986).

However, radical reconfigurational capabilities are likely to be constrained by these commitments, especially when they threaten to become competence destructive. Growth strategies will be based more on developing current knowledge and skills than on acquiring quite different ones. This is not to say that over time such firms cannot transform themselves by moving into new technologies and markets, as did many Japanese cotton manufacturers in the early twentieth century, but this will be achieved more through related diversification into, for instance, artificial fibres, than by major disposals and acquisitions of quite different resources (Nishida and Redding 1992). The relatively slow adoption of biology-based methods of drug discovery by many Japanese pharmaceutical companies compared to their major UK and US competitors can in part be attributed to the greater level of employer–employee commitment in the former firms, as well as to differences in national scientific and regulatory systems (Kneller 1999; 2003; 2007; Thomas 2001).

THE INSTITUTIONAL STRUCTURING OF FIRM CHARACTERISTICS

Key institutional features

These kinds of differences in the governance characteristics and development of organizational capabilities of leading firms in differently organized market economies reflect variations in their dominant institutions. In this section, I summarize the key features of these institutions that affect the kinds of firms that become dominant and how they can be expected to do so. While their strength depends, *inter alia*, on the continued support and cohesion of major socio-political coalitions (Amable 2003), including the owners and managers of key industries, and so can change over time, most features of the institutional environment of firms in the established industrial capitalist societies are relatively stable and cannot easily be altered by any single interest group or firm in the short to medium term.

This is especially so for the more general institutions such as the overall predictability and reliability of the legal system and its protection of various kinds of private property rights, norms governing authority relationships, and the nature of the financial and labour systems (Whitley 1999; 2007). These institutional arrangements impinge upon, if not indeed actually structure, relationships between: a) investors and managers, b) employers and employees, and c) competitors, suppliers, and customers.

The key features of dominant institutions that affect the nature of behaviour of firms can be summarized under four main headings: a) the norms governing trust and authority relationships in a society, b) the nature and policies of the state in constituting, regulating, and supporting economic actors, c) the conventions and rules governing access to, and the use of, financial capital, and d) the nature of the skill formation system and of the regulations and norms governing the employment and management of people. There are eight major features of these institutions and agencies that are particularly important influences on firm governance and the development of capabilities, which are listed in Table 16.2.

Considering first the institutions governing trust relationships between economic actors, these are crucial to the establishment of industrial capitalist economies, especially the extent to which the formal procedures and structures organizing transactions, and economic activities more generally, are regarded as reliable and trustworthy. Where trust in formal institutions is so low that owners feel unable to rely on the legal system, accounting conventions, and formal mechanisms to control the behaviour of customers, suppliers, and employees in predictable ways, they will be reluctant to develop substantial commitments to people with whom they do not have strong personal bonds of loyalty and reciprocity.

Such low levels of trust are often associated with predatory states and unpredictable financial systems. In states where political elites are unwilling to allow the growth of large concentrations of privately controlled capital and/or seek to extract substantial amounts of surplus for their own benefit, owners are faced with a highly uncertain political and economic context in which personal connections are often the only reliable means of ensuring trust and predictable behaviour (Goetzman and Koell 2007; Hamilton 2006). The legal system in such countries is either very limited in its ability to resolve disputes, or liable to render capricious and unpredictable judgements.

Table 16.2: Institutional features affecting firm characteristics

Norms governing trust and authority relationships
a) Trust in formal institutions
b) Paternalist/Contractarian/Communitarian justifications of authority

State structures and policies
c) Dominance and directive role of the state
d) State encouragement of intermediary organizations in developing and implementing economic policies
e) State segmentation of markets

Financial system
f) Size, liquidity and significance of capital markets and ease of mounting hostile takeovers

Labour system
g) Effectiveness of public skill formation system
h) Strength of employer and labour federations and their role in coordinating bargaining

Many industrializing countries, and those undergoing radical institutional change such as the former state socialist societies of Eastern Europe in the early 1990s, exemplify this kind of institutional context (Fafchamps 1996; Humphrey and Schmitz 1998; Menkhoff 1992; Whitley and Czaban 1998; Whitley et al. 1996). When business owners do develop alliances and partnerships in such economies, these are usually based on personal ties, and are family-like if not actually based on close kinship links, as in Taiwan and other Pacific-Asian societies (Gates 1996; Hamilton 1997; Hamilton and Kao 1990). They also tend to be quite limited in scope, so that owner-managers are not exposed to high levels of risk by such shared commitments.

Authority relationships in these kinds of particularistic societies are often *paternalistic* in the sense that political and other leaders typically justify their superiors' positions in terms of their greater wisdom and ability to look after the best interests of their subordinates, analogously to parental roles in families (Beetham 1991). Generally, such paternalist ideologies encourage strong central control and low levels of delegation.

Alternatively, authority may be justified in terms of more formal and procedural norms governing the selection of leaders and how they exercise discretion over subordinates' activities (Eckstein and Gurr 1975). Such formal justifications of subordination can be further divided into two types: *contractarian* and *communitarian*. This distinction focuses on the extent to which authority rests upon widespread and diffuse appeals to common interests as opposed to highly specific and narrow agreements between discrete and separate contractors. Communitarian forms of authority imply relatively high levels of mutual trust and commitment, with shared understandings of priorities and interests, and often rely on expertise as a key quality of superordinates, while contractarian authority tends to presume more adversarial relationships and a dominant pursuit of self-interest. The former seems to have become institutionalized in some Scandinavian and continental European countries, while the latter is found more in Anglophone societies (Lodge and Vogel 1987).

The role of nation-states in organizing market economies has, of course, been extensively analysed in many comparative studies (see, e.g. Amable 2003; Crouch and Streeck 1997; Schmidt 2002; Weiss 2003). From the point of view of explaining variations in forms of firm governance and prevalent ways of developing organizational capabilities, three features of this role seem particularly important.

First, there is the extent to which the state is able and willing to play an active role in coordinating economic development and supporting particular industries and firms. Active promotional states (Evans 1994) vary in how much they dominate and direct firms' strategies, and reward or sanction their outcomes, in ways that affect dominant firm behaviour. In *dominant developmental states*, businesses are highly dependent on state policies and actions, to the extent that political risks often outweigh market ones. Less directive states, like perhaps the post-1950s Japanese one, pursue developmental policies in a more collaborative way through policies of what Samuels (1987: 8–9) has termed reciprocal consent. Others, such as many Anglophone states, have neither the wish to, nor the capability for, actively coordinating economic processes but focus on a more regulatory approach to managing economic development.

Second, states differ in their toleration of, and support for, intermediary groups and associations between individuals, firms, and the state that play a significant role in coordinating economic developments. These groupings include trade associations, employers' groups, and labour unions. This feature can be summarized as the degree of *state support for intermediary organizations*. Some European states, for instance, appear unable to tolerate such groupings while others, like the German and Austrian, seem to positively encourage their formation and to develop quite strong corporatist forms of intra-and inter-sectoral organization (Schmidt 2002). Clearly, inter-firm cooperation, alliances, and cartelization will be easier in the latter sets of states than in the former.

Third, there are significant differences in the extent to which states directly or indirectly regulate market boundaries and entry and exit, in addition to setting constraints on the short-term opportunism of economic actors. They are here termed the extent of *formal segmentation of markets*. In many countries, for instance, states regulate which sorts of organizations can offer financial services and how they can sell them, as well as where they can do so. Similarly, licences to undertake certain trades are often only issued by national and local state agencies when appropriate skill certificates have been acquired. In other countries, such powers are sometimes delegated to industry associations and quasi-statutory bodies. This affects the intensity of competition, mobility of resources between markets, and flexibility of firms.

The key feature of financial systems for firm governance and the development of organizational capabilities concerns the market for corporate control. The combination of liquid capital markets, legal and other restrictions on managers' ability to develop strong defensive measures against hostile takeovers, and fragmented shareholdings in outsider-based financial systems can result in a strong market for corporate control that limits investor-manager commitments and reduces the credibility of long-term career incentives (O'Sullivan 2000; Tylecote and Visintin 2008). Where capital is impatient and volatile it is difficult to convince skilled employees to become committed to the long-term development of a particular firm's organizational capabilities.

In contrast, credit-based financial systems are characterized by relatively small and illiquid capital markets and much greater concentrations of shareholder control over large companies. Here it is much more difficult to transfer ownership and change direction radically, especially if significant proportions of firms' shares are held by strategic investors and/or are effectively controlled by top managers, as is the case in many European countries (Barca and Becht 2001) and Japan (Sheard 1994).

Lastly, the skill formation systems of market economies vary considerably in ways that, together with labour market institutions, affect the kinds of skills developed, managerial policies, and organizational commitments. In particular, the *effectiveness of the public skill formation system* in training large numbers of workers in practical skills that are valued by employers, usually because they have been closely involved in providing training and setting standards as in the 'German Skills Machine'

(Culpepper and Finegold 1999), influences both internal organizational structures and marker strategies (Maurice et al. 1986; 1990; Soskice 1999).

The impact of the public training system on firm structures and behaviour is greatly enhanced when combined with certain features of the institutions governing labour markets and employment policies (Thelen 2004). Particularly important in this respect are the relative strength of sectoral and/or national employers and labour union groups and their coordination of bargaining over employment conditions. Where there are *strong employer and labour union federations with centralized bargaining*, firms tend to become accustomed to working together and with unions in relatively stable relationships that inhibit highly opportunistic behaviour, as in many continental European states (Jackson et al. 2005; Jurgens 2003; Thelen and Kume 2003).

Many of these features of dominant institutions are interrelated (Amable 2003; Schmidt 2002; Whitley 1994). For example, societies in which strong states play the dominant role in coordinating economic development and share risks with the private sector tend not to develop strong intermediary associations. Employers' associations and labour unions are, then, usually weak in such countries. Market segmentation, on the other hand, is often considerable since this is a major way in which state agencies coordinate development. These kinds of states also tend to be associated with bank credit-based rather than capital market-based financial systems for two reasons. First, because they are typical of late industrializing economies where capital is scarce and more readily mobilized through the banking system, and, second, because it is easier for the state to influence economic development through the financial system when it is dominated by banks rather than capital markets (Zysman 1983).

Conversely, low levels of state risk sharing and economic coordination are often combined with capital market-based financial systems in what might be termed *arm's-length* or differentiated business environments. In these contexts, institutional arenas and elites are organized quite separately from each other according to their own particular logics. Social relationships tend to be regulated by formal rules and procedures that treat actors as discrete individuals pursuing their separate interests, as exemplified by classical contracting. Authority and trust relations are here governed by formal institutions that limit mutual obligations to contractually specified duties. Collaboration between employers, unions, and other groups is difficult to establish in such societies because collective actors are typically adversarial in their relations with each other.

On the other hand, where strong intermediary associations have developed with state support, they tend to be involved in regulating market entry and exit. They are often engaged in negotiation with each other on a continuing basis with strongly institutionalized procedures limiting opportunistic behaviour. Such procedures depend on considerable trust between social partners and widespread beliefs in their joint dependence on cooperation for gaining group objectives. Commitment to relatively impersonal associations and an institutionalized ability to mobilize loyalties to collective goals beyond purely personal ones are important features of these kinds of societies. When combined with strong public training systems, as in many Continental European countries, these institutional features are conducive to collaboration between economic actors and so can be termed *collaborative* forms of institutional environments.

Finally, cultures where trust in formal institutions is low and loyalties are focused on the immediate family rather than more impersonal collectivities limit the growth of intermediary associations and the development of exchange relationships governed by formal procedures. Capital markets are unlikely to be significant sources of investment funds in such societies and the largely personal nature of authority relationships will restrict the development of strong labour unions. Social relationships in these cultures tend to be highly personal and particularistic, and so can be described as *particularistic* business environments.

The impact of institutional features on firm characteristics

Before continuing to outline the particular ways in which these eight features of dominant institutions can be expect to affect firm characteristics, it is important to bear in mind two points. First, the most direct connections between institutional features and characteristics of leading firms in a market economy often occur when institutions display particularly strong features at the extremes of the dimensions being considered. Relatedly, the connections are often not reversible in the sense that the negative relationship may not hold to the same extent. Second, interdependences between single institutional features and firm characteristics are tendencies that, in practice, are modified by other aspects of dominant institutions and by a variety of historical contingencies.

The effects of particular political, financial, labour, and cultural institutions on firms are often most marked when the strength of a particular feature is very high or low. For example, the link between a strong, developmentalist state and the prevalence of growth goals is not a linear, continuous one but rather is particularly significant—and dominates other factors—when the level of business dependence on the state is especially high, as in post-war Korea (Amsden 1989; Fields 1995; Whitley 1992; Woo 1991). Similarly, the effect of weak institutions governing trust relations on inter-firm alliances and sector organizations is most evident when formal institutions are widely regarded as unreliable, as in many expatriate Chinese dominated economies (Redding 1990; Silin 1976).

Additionally, these direct connections between particular institutional features and firm characteristics often do not apply in reverse. Where, for instance, the state is relatively weak and/or does not pursue developmentalist policies, firms' strategies may or may not follow growth goals. Although, then, the strong, developmental French state in much of the post-war period has, amongst other factors, encouraged large firms to pursue growth goals, the less *dirigiste* post-war federal

German state has not led German companies to pursue profit maximization priorities (Schmidt 2002). This is because of other institutional features, such as the financial system and strong intermediary organizations, which encourage growth goals (Lane 1992). Similarly, the existence of an effective legal system governing contractual trust does not necessarily lead to extensive delegation of control to salaried managers by owners, although the lack of such formal institutions is likely to encourage strong owner-control.

This point highlights the interdependence of these institutional features in structuring dominant firms. In any particular market economy, the prevalent type of firm will reflect the influence of all dominant institutions as they have developed in conjunction with each other during and after industrialization. The linkages between institutions and firm characteristics discussed in the following pages are, then, tendencies that are most likely to occur when institutional features are particularly distinctive and other features reinforce, rather than conflict with, them (Deeg 2005).

Bearing these points in mind, in Table 16.3 I summarize the expected relationships between particular features of dominant institutions in a market economy and prevalent patterns of firm governance and capability development in those environments. As can be seen, direct connections are not always unequivocal since the impact of particular features usually depends on the nature of other institutions. A very rough attempt at distinguishing the degree of influence has been made by using a five-point scale of low, limited, some, considerable, and high.

Considering first the connections between institutional features and forms of owner-control, direct owner-control is strongly encouraged in societies where trust in formal institutions governing relationships is low and authority is predominantly paternalist in nature. Without strong mechanisms ensuring that owners can rely on managers to carry out their instructions and act in their interests, it is unlikely that they will readily delegate control over their property to salaried employees. Similarly, if authority in a society is more personal and direct than formal and procedural, owners will be expected to exercise direct control over employees.

A high level of business dependence on the state in dominant developmentalist states also encourages direct control because owners typically manage political risks directly with decision-makers and would find it difficult to implement agreements through third parties. Since state coordination and direction are often not transparent and public, remote owners would be disadvantaged if they left political negotiations to managers, and so they have to become directly involved.

Conversely, market based forms of owner-control are only feasible when trust in formal procedures is high and authority predominantly procedural. They are less likely in credit-based financial systems because these typically lead to considerable interdependence and lock-in between the owners/controllers of financial assets and managers of enterprises. They are, though, strongly linked to the existence of liquid capital markets in which assets can be easily traded and managed as items in a portfolio. The stronger the market for corporate control in such financial systems, the more difficult it will be for firms to coordinate policies and work together in business associations and employers' groups since ownership and corporate

Table 16.3: Expected connections between institutional features and characteristics of leading firms

Features of dominant institutions	Characteristics of Leading Firms							
	Prevalent owner control type	Employee constraint	Business partner constraint	Authority sharing	Organizational careers	Coordination capabilities	Learning capabilities	Reconfigurational capabilities
Low trust in formal institutions	Direct	Low	Low	Low	Low	Limited	Limited	Some
Paternalist authority	Direct	Low	Limited	Limited	Limited	Some	Some	Varies
Communitarian authority	Direct or committed	Considerable	Varies	Considerable	Varies	High	High	Limited in short term
Dominant development state	Direct	Limited	Low	Low	Limited	Varies	Limited	High
Strong state encouragement of intermediaries and economic coordination	Direct or committed	Some	High	Considerable	Some	High	High	Limited in short term
Segmented markets	Direct or committed	Varies	Considerable	Some	Some	High	Considerable	Limited
Liquid capital markets and strong market for corporate control	Market	Limited	Low	Limited	Low	Varies	Limited	High
Effective public skill formation system	Varies	Considerable	Varies	Some	Varies	Some	Some	Varies
Strong employer and labour federations and centralized bargaining	Direct or committed	High	Considerable	Considerable	Some	Some	Some	Limited

strategies are liable to change rapidly. Highly capital market constrained governance relationships are unlikely, then, to occur in market economies with strong intermediary associations and coordinated employer–union bargaining practices.

Employee interests are unlikely to be significant influences on firms' strategies and actions when state dominance is high and trust in formal institutions is low. Major political risks focus attention on state interests and priorities so that other groups are subsidiary, except perhaps for a small cadre of senior managers. Equally, a culture in which trust in strangers is difficult to establish and maintain except on a personal basis is not likely to encourage reliance on employee skills and commitment to the organization as distinct from the individual owner-manager. Firms in this situation will not be greatly influenced by the needs of employees as a whole in making decisions. Employers will additionally be discouraged from giving weight to the interests of the bulk of employees, where there is a strong market for corporate control, since the threat of hostile takeovers focuses managers' attention on financial rates of return in the relatively short term.

Conversely, effective public training systems, centralized bargaining, and powerful employers and union federations, together with communitarian authority relationships encourage more concern with employee interests. Where unions have strong legal and/or labour market powers, they are obviously in a position to insist on worker interests being taken into account when strategies are being developed and implemented. Equally, a strong training system produces high-level skills that employers can rely upon since they are usually involved in developing them. Furthermore, where managerial authority rests largely—or even partly—on perceptions that employers and employees share a common destiny, and are jointly responsible for the future of the organization as a whole, the significance of employee interests is likely to be considerable relative to economies where authority is more contractarian.

Business partner constraints on strategic decision-making are likewise inhibited by dominant states, capital market financial systems, and low trust in formal institutions. High levels of business dependence on the state combined with considerable antagonism to intermediaries between the family, firms, and the central state in dominant developmental states, ensure that firms concentrate on developing close links with state agencies and compete with each other for state support, within and across industries. In such economies, it is clearly difficult for them to develop substantial and stable linkages with each other. Strong markets for corporate control in capital market financial systems also inhibit alliances and networks since ownership can change quickly in such markets, as can strategic choices and elite managerial personnel. For similar reasons to those mentioned above, an inability to rely on formal institutions for ensuring trust between firms limits the extent and stability of inter-firm networks since alliances are based on personal connections and risks are difficult to share in such societies.

Conversely, where: a) the state encourages regulation of markets, either directly or indirectly, b) banks and other financial intermediaries are locked-in to firms' destinies, and c) employers collaborate with the unions in managing the training system and with each other in centralized bargaining systems, firms will be encouraged to develop links with each other that are relatively wide-ranging and stable. All of these institutional features restrict the freedom of economic actors to change direction and act as short-term opportunists in terms of their immediate interests. They thus reduce the risks associated with making commitments to business partners, whether suppliers, customers, competitors, or employees, and enhance the likelihood of benefits accruing from them.

Turning now to consider how institutional features are related to the ways that firms develop different kinds of capabilities, both authority sharing and the provision of organizational careers, are likely to be limited to those with whom owners have strong personal relationships in societies where there is low trust in formal institutions and authority is justified in paternalistic terms. Building organizational capabilities around the contribution of most employees on a long-term basis will be difficult in large firms, and highly focused on individuals' skills—as distinct from collective ones—in small ones in such circumstances. Coordinating and learning capabilities are accordingly likely to be restricted to a relatively small group of elite managers in these kinds of particularistic business environments.

Similarly, in societies dominated by strong developmentalist states, most risks and opportunities for leading companies arise from state actions and support, and so firms are more likely to invest time and effort in meeting state demands and negotiating with officials than in investing in developing employee skills and commitment. When combined with paternalist ideologies justifying elite authority over subordinates, authority sharing within companies tends to be rather limited, and careers in the larger firms restricted to those demonstrating high levels of loyalty. The development of organizational capabilities will tend to be restricted to the senior managerial hierarchy in these kinds of situations, with little involvement by most employees.

Strong markets for corporate control are also likely to restrict authority sharing and organizational careers for most employees because changes in ownership and control are relatively easy in such economies. Managerial hierarchies may develop effective coordinating capabilities when market conditions allow firms to make credible commitments of organizational careers for managers, but pressures for continued high levels of investor returns from fund managers will limit these. On the other hand, highly liquid capital markets facilitate the rapid reallocation of resources and can provide venture capitalists with easy exit opportunities. In turn, this enables them to invest in a number of start-up enterprises on a portfolio basis, as well as supporting organizational restructurings.

Conversely, strong intermediaries, segmentation of product markets, and communitarian patterns of authority all encourage greater levels of authority sharing, both internally and externally, and enable firms to offer relatively long-term careers to many of their skilled workers. In turn, these facilitate the development of strong employer–employee commitment to the development of firm-specific coordinating and learning capabilities, although not all firms necessarily manage to do so successfully.

Such commitments are further encouraged by effective public training systems and extensive collaboration between firms that restrict poaching of skilled workers and opportunistic free-riding on others' investments. The combination of national and local state economic coordination of economic development, strong business associations, and centralized bargaining in the more coordinated economies of many continental European countries and Japan has encouraged widespread involvement in the enhancement of firm-specific capabilities and knowledge (Soskice 1999), while often limiting the ability of firms to undertake rapid and radical reconfigurations of their resources.

These relationships between institutional features and firm characteristics suggest how different kinds of firms are likely to become established as leading companies in differently organized market economies. The five ideal types identified earlier will be encouraged by some of these features and discouraged by others, as summarized in Table 16.4. In particular, opportunistic firms are most likely to be dominant in economies with low trust in formal institutions, where the state is predatory rather than developmental, and authority is primarily justified in paternalistic terms. They are less likely to be prevalent in societies where the financial system is largely autonomous from the state and operates according to its own, relatively impersonal and formal, rules, and the labour system is likewise governed by strong, separate institutions and federations.

Specialized network firms, in contrast, rely on more stable and reliable institutions to coordinate their activities through market contracting, and usually become established in cultures where authority is justified in contractarian or communitarian terms. They additionally tend to be significant economic actors in economies with relatively flexible labour markets and effective training systems that ensure both a supply of highly skilled workers and a means of matching skills to jobs. Given their specialist nature, such firms additionally need to be able to call upon a variety of complementary services and knowledge, whether these are primarily publicly or privately provided. Intermediary organizations and institutions that restrict predatory pricing and other means of large firm dominance are additionally important in establishing such firms.

Isolated hierarchies also rely on effective formal institutions governing economic relationships and limited state domination of the economy. In addition, though, they flourish where capital markets are firmly established and there are few restrictions on market entry and exit, including mergers and takeovers. Authority tends to be justified in terms of contractual relationships and skill formation is primarily a matter of individual initiative rather than being systematically coordinated through intermediary organizations. In general, they dominate in societies characterized by arm's length institutional environments that provide few constraints on short-term economic opportunism and relatively few collective competition goods.

Centralized hierarchies, in contrast, are most likely to be dominant where the state plays a strong developmental role and authority is largely paternalistic. The financial system is usually subservient to developmental goals and enables families to retain control of large and fast growing firms through cheap credit, often guaranteed by the state. The public training system tends to be weak in societies dominated by these kinds of companies, as are employer and employee unions.

Table 16.4: Institutional features associated with different ideal types of firms

Institutional features	Ideal types of firms				
	Opportunistic	Specialized network	Isolated hierarchy	Centralized hierarchy	Collaborative hierarchy
Low trust in formal institutions	+	−	−	varies	−
Paternalistic authority	+	−	−	+	−
Communitarian authority	+	Some in industrial districts, low in professional networks	−	−	+
Dominant developmental state	−	−	−	+	−
Encouragement of intermediaries	−	+	−	−	+
Segmented markets	−	Varies	−	Varies	+
Strong market for corporate control	−	Varies	+	−	−
Effective public skill formation system	−	+	−	−	+
Strong employer and union federations and centralized bargaining	−	Some in industrial districts, low in professional networks	−	−	+

Collaborative hierarchies, on the other hand, develop in much more coordinated institutional environments that combine communitarian patterns of authority with strong intermediary organizations, effective training systems, and coordinated bargaining between powerful employer and labour groups. The financial system is less separate from the rest of the economy than in arm's-length institutional systems, and the conventions governing capital markets are typically not supportive of hostile takeovers.

While these connections between institutions and dominant firm types have often been most apparent within nation-states, especially in the post-Second World War period dominated by the Bretton Woods system for managing international capital flows and exchange rates, they are by no means necessarily national in nature (Whitley 2005). Rather, the national specificity of institutional regimes and dominant firms is an empirical matter and the homogeneity of the national institutional environments faced by firms varies between countries and over time.

For example, many aspects of corporate governance, including the rights of shareholders, in the USA vary between states and changed over the course of the nineteenth and twentieth centuries (see, e.g. Becht and DeLong 2007; O'Sullivan 2000; Roy 1997; Tylecote and Visintin 2008). Other institutions affecting labour markets and property rights can also differ between regions in ways that affect inter-firm relations and growth strategies, as Saxenian (1994) has emphasized in her contrast of Route 128 firms in Massachusetts and Silicon Valley. Additionally, institutional regimes vary in the extent to which they standardize many characteristics of leading companies. Arm's-length regimes, for example, typically leave the organization of employment relationships much more to the discretion of individual firms than do more corporatist ones (Soskice 1999; Whitley 2005).

THE EFFECTS OF INCREASING INTERNATIONALIZATION ON FIRM CHARACTERISTICS

Such varying homogeneity and complementarity of the dominant institutions governing economic activities in different countries mean that the governance and capabilities of leading companies can vary between regions and sectors, as well as changing over time. The growing internationalization of many firms in the post-war period has additionally increased the heterogeneity of institutional environments that they have to deal with, and can weaken the influence of domestic institutions. By locating major facilities in quite differently organized market economies, some firms may be able to develop distinctive kinds of transnational competitive competences that are not tied to particular institutional environments (Bartlett and Ghoshal 1989; Ghoshal and Westney 1993). It is worthwhile, then, considering how the expansion of foreign direct investment (FDI) since the 1950s can be expected to affect the key characteristics of different kinds of firms operating in different institutional contexts, and in particular whether it has enabled them to become significantly different kinds of companies.

It is first important to note that any effects of internationalization on firm governance and capabilities are only likely to be significant when companies commit major resources and managerial attention to foreign locations, and are willing to adjust their domestically developed routines as a result of adapting to different environments. In general terms, multinational companies (MNCs) are most likely to become distinctive kinds of organization when they locate major proportions of key assets and activities in quite different kinds of institutional regimes, allow foreign subsidiaries to adapt to local conventions, and 'learn' from these novel develop-ments by adapting and integrating them with routines and procedures used elsewhere in the organization, especially in their domestic operations. It is the organizational integration of different ways of doing things in different kinds of business environments that makes MNCs potentially significant different kinds of strategic economic actors.

However, MNCs vary in the extent to which they allow their foreign subsidiaries to adapt to local conventions and innovate in their procedures, products, and services. Some, like Ford in England in the 1920s and 1930s, insist on their overseas units following domestic policies and practices (Tolliday 2000), while others permit more diverse responses to different markets and patterns of economic organization, and a few actively encourage subsidiaries to experiment with new approaches, as perhaps is the case with some German MNCs in the Americas and central Europe in recent years (Lane 2001; Meardi and Toth 2006). MNCs that simply export their domestic practices to foreign locations are unlikely to develop new knowledge and skills as a result of operating internationally, and therefore are more national companies with foreign operations (Hu 1992) than transnational enterprises, whereas those that allow foreign units to innovate could do so. Such innovation is more likely to happen when subsidiaries are forced to adapt to quite different environments that have strongly established patterns of business behaviour, reproduced through powerful and com-plementary institutions, as in post-war Japan.

Local innovations may not, though, lead to MNCs developing new kinds of transnational organizational capabilities if the parent company does not use them to change procedures and practices elsewhere. For such firms to become distinctive kinds of economic actors as a result of operating across national borders, they have to 'learn from abroad' in the sense of incorporating novel ideas, skills, and technologies from innovating subsidiaries in other parts of the organization. If they simply allow such units to continue to adapt to their particular situation without integrating any new approaches into the rest of the company, MNCs will not develop distinctively new kinds of collective competences.

It follows from this characterization of MNCs that only some of them are likely to develop distinctive kinds of transnational organizational capabilities (Whitley 1998; 2001). Firm specific organizational capabilities take time to build and usually involve relatively 'low powered' incentives to encourage employees to work together to deal with technical and organizational problems and to contribute to the improvement of organizational knowledge. For a MNC to learn systematically from its operations in quite different environments in such a way that it generates novel transnational competences, it has to encourage its employees and business partners in those environments to become committed to developing and enhancing its cross-national capabilities.

Developing such transnational commitment involves authority sharing with employees in different locations and some provision of organizational careers for those that contribute most to the development of MNC capabilities and knowledge. Since the willingness of owners and managers to share authority and offer organizational careers is strongly influenced by dominant institutions in each society, this means that MNCs with major facilities in different kinds of institutional regimes are likely to develop varying forms of authority sharing and careers in different locations. As a result, the kinds of collective capabilities they develop in different national subsidiaries can differ greatly, and may well conflict in their basic principles, as highlighted by Kristensen and Zeitlin (2005) in their study of APV.

The extent of transnational authority sharing and careers will also be affected by the nature and strength of the international institutions governing business behaviour and property rights across national boundaries. However, while transnational governance organizations have become more significant in recent years, few are powerful enough to override the wishes of major nation-states, such as the USA, and most have less ability to determine their own policies, select senior personnel, and sanction deviance than do national regulatory authorities (Braithwaite and Drahos 2000; McNicol and Bensedrine 2003; Lehmkuhl 2003). Furthermore, most of these have been concerned to establish common rules of the competitive game for cross-border trade and investment, and so internationalize markets for most products and services (Braithwaite and Drahos 2000; Majone 2005).

Driven by the interests of outside investors, investment banks, and multinational companies seeking large, liquid, and transparent capital markets, this focus on transparent and formalized regulatory procedures exemplifies central features of outsider dominated financial markets and arm's length capitalism (Laurence 2001; Lutz 2004). Few, if any, international institutions encourage investment in cross-national employer–employee commitment on a long-term basis. Constraints on both employer and employee opportunism are typically lower across national borders than within most OECD countries, and hence the extent and longevity of employee commitments to MNC corporate goals and success are likely to be less than those to national employers, especially amongst middle managers and professionals.

Pressures from international institutions, then, are unlikely to lead many MNCs to engage in the sorts of extensive authority sharing with, and long-term career commitments to, foreign employees that firms in collaborative market economies often develop with their domestic staff. As British employees of Japanese banks found out in the 1990s, the norm of long-term employment for male Japanese staff did not apply to them (Sakai 2000; Whitley et al. 2003). In general, then, the lack of strong international institutions encouraging long-term loyalties between business partners suggests that the degree and scope of cross-national authority sharing and organizational careers within MNCs will not be particularly high, and usually less than occurs in their home organizations.

There remain, however, considerable variations in patterns of authority sharing and career commitments across national borders. These result mostly from domestic and host economy institutional differences, as the large literature on Japanese and US MNCs illustrates (see, e.g. Almond and Ferner 2006; Beechler and Bird 1999; Kogut and Parkinson 1993; Tolliday 2000). In particular, the circumstances in which companies become established and develop distinctive competences are likely to have substantial influence on when and how they internationalize their operations and manage foreign subsidiaries. As Kogut (1993: 137) has suggested: 'Even as the firm internationalises, it remains imprinted by its early developmental history and domestic environment', especially how it learns and innovates (cf. Doremus et al. 1998).

We can explore how firms from different institutional regimes are likely to encourage varying degrees of employee commitment in foreign subsidiaries, and so their probable development of distinctive firm-specific international organizational capabilities, by comparing the probable patterns of international authority sharing and careers of firms from the three ideal types of business regime distinguished above: particularistic, arm's-length, and collaborative. These expectations are summarized in Table 16.5.

Beginning with firms based in particularistic institutional regimes, since owners in these kinds of market economies remain reluctant to share authority with employees in their domestic location because of unreliable formal institutions and an unpredictable political environment, they seem unlikely to trust foreign employees a great deal, and so delegate much discretion to them. The combination of a low trust home economy with weak transnational institutions is unlikely to encourage much authority sharing with foreign managers and staff.

Equally, the common restriction of long-term career opportunities to relatives and others with whom family-like relationships have been developed in these frameworks suggests that few firms will offer organizational careers to foreign employees. As a result, hardly any subsidiary staff are likely to become so committed to the parent company that they will invest their energies in improving firm-specific knowledge and skills on a medium- to long-term basis. This means that enterprises from such environments are unlikely to develop strong international organizational

---

Table 16.5: International authority sharing and careers in MNCs from different institutional regimes

International authority sharing and organizational careers	Home economy institutional regime		
	Particularistic	Arm's length	Collaborative
Extent of cross-border authority sharing	Low	Varies, but rarely extended beyond managers and experts with codified skills	Limited usually, but may be considerable when seeking specialist knowledge
Longevity and scope of cross-national organizational careers	Low	Varies, but long-term career opportunities rarely extended beyond managers in most MNCs	Low

capabilities, as distinct from those based on predominantly individual relationships and qualities. In particular, systematic cross-national organizational learning seems likely to be rather restricted, and coordinating capabilities limited to those tied to personal relationships.

In contrast, owners of firms from market economies dominated by arm's-length institutional regimes that share authority with, and develop organizational careers for, senior managers and some professional staff domestically could be expected to delegate rather more discretion to those in charge of foreign subsidiaries where formal institutions are considered reliable. They may also involve foreign managers and professional staff in cross-national problem-solving teams when their specialist expertise is highly valued. This is especially likely when dealing with complex problems that require knowledge of different business environments, as in many professional service companies such as those discussed by Morgan and Quack (2005).

Authority sharing with foreign professionals will here depend on the knowledge that managers of these MNCs have of their expertise and the reputation of national skill formation systems. Given the importance of technical knowledge and specialist skills in dealing with complex and uncertain tasks, domestic managers of MNCs are unlikely to share much authority with foreigners unless they are convinced that they are highly skilled and able to help with solving current problems. This will be greatly facilitated by skills being standardized through professional associations that operate in similar ways in different countries, and so is more straightforward between arm's-length economies that have flexible labour markets and similar institutional arrangements for developing high-level expertise.

In general, though, any such authority sharing by firms from arm's-length economies is unlikely to extend much beyond professional staff and managers, given similar limitations at home and the lack of strong international institutions that might restrain employer and employee opportunism. While their subsidiaries located in economies with strong collaborative institutions may develop greater levels of authority sharing with skilled workers, this seems likely to be limited to local operations given the arm's-length nature of the parent MNC's domestic business environment.

Similarly, few firms from these kinds of institutional frameworks are likely to make long-term career commitments to foreign employees, especially at the international level. Since commitments in general are short term in such economies, most employers will not feel able to offer cross-national organizational careers to more than a few senior foreign managers, nor would such offerings be viewed as highly credible. Again, where host economy institutions encourage high levels of employer–employee commitment and firms have to offer organizational careers to skilled staff in order to attract the most capable, MNCs may well enter into long-term employer–employee commitments at the local level, as do many foreign firms in Japan, but such commitments are unlikely to be extended internationally.

Coordination capabilities across national boundaries may be quite strong in such companies where they have established integrated transnational managerial hierarchies, and are able to provide credible organizational careers for their senior managers, as in, perhaps, some of the largest oil companies. However, their trans-national learning capabilities are likely to be restricted to project teams and similarly short-term collaborations, together with those developed through managerial transfers. As in more nationally specific companies, reconfigurational capabilities may be greater than in collaborative firms, but will be limited by strongly entrenched managerial routines and rules governing coordination practices.

Overall, then, we would not expect long-term commitment to building and improving cross-national problem-solving capabilities and skills, as opposed to extending domestic ones, to be high in most foreign subsidiaries of MNCs from arm's-length economies. Loyalty to the parent company and investment in the enhancement of its knowledge and capabilities will be no more extensive than in its domestic operations, and so continuing organizational learning at the international level will probably be restricted to senior managerial levels.

Conversely, MNCs based in more collaborative home economies are embedded in a number of relatively long-term obligations with particular business partners, including skilled employees. However, few of the institutions leading to such commitments transcend national boundaries and so foreign employees are not as locked into the fate of MNCs from these kinds of societies as are many domestic ones. This means that both employer and employee opportunism is likely to be less constrained across borders than within such economies. As a result, long-term employee willingness to invest in enhancing the capabilities of the MNC will probably be lower in foreign subsidiaries than in the domestic organization.

Furthermore, where such firms consider that their core capabilities are substantially derived from these long-term commitments and are highly specific to their home business environment, they will be reluctant to invest much in authority sharing with foreign staff. The more MNCs see their distinctive competences as being generated by their domestic organization and its particular pattern of employment relations, the less they are likely to involve foreign staff from quite different environments in substantial international problem solving activities. This seems to be the case for many Japanese MNCs (see, e.g. Ernst 2006; Kopp 1999; Pucik 1999).

However, some companies from collaborative institutional frameworks have become more willing to delegate considerable discretion to foreign managers and professionals in some subsidiaries, and to involve them extensively in international problem-solving teams as they seek to acquire new kinds of capabilities that their domestic business system appears unable to provide. In situations where the lock-ins encouraged by home economy institutions are seen to be inhibiting radical innovation and limiting growth, such MNCs may deliberately use foreign subsidiaries to try novel practices with the different kinds of approaches and skills developed in societies with contrasting institutional frameworks, such as Japanese investments in UK and US biotechnology facilities (Kneller 2003; Lam 2003). Some German companies seem to have tried to do this in the 1990s, although such plans have not always been realized in practice, particularly in the car industry (Fleury and Salerno 1998; Herrigel and Zeitlin in this volume: Jurgens 1998; Lane 2001).

These points suggest that, while developing coordinating capabilities through managerial hierarchies may be quite feasible in these kinds of firms, ensuring systematic organizational learning will be more difficult, especially if it involves radical changes to domestic operations. Equally, while establishing major facilities abroad may increase organizational flexibility, and enable firms to develop novel kinds of routines and ways of working in their foreign subsidiaries, their domestic institutional environment will restrict their reconfigurational capabilities, at least in the short to medium term.

This analysis of the organizational capabilities of MNCs in the light of differences in their home economy institutional frameworks suggests a number of conclusions about their development of transnational competences. First, while many companies with major facilities in different countries may develop distinctive collective capabilities at the national and regional levels, by no means all of them do so internationally. Because of a) the relative weakness of international institutions governing employer and employee opportunism, b) belief in the superiority of domestically developed competences, and c) variable nature of institutional frameworks across market economies, many companies are often reluctant to share authority with many foreign managers and professionals, or to offer them long-term organizational commitments. This means that their organizational capabilities as MNCs are little different from those of their domestic organization, together perhaps with those generated separately by some subsidiaries. The coordination of economic activities in different countries does not, then, necessarily produce distinctive cross-national collective capabilities, and so MNCs as such do not constitute a distinctive kind of company from the point of view of the competence-based view of the firm.

Second, the impact of host economy institutions governing skill formation and labour markets can affect the development of cross-national capabilities by varying in their standardization and certification of practical expertise, as well as in their control over employer and employee opportunism. In general, the more fluid are external labour markets in an economy, and the more standardized are skills through educational and/or professional development and certification, the more difficult it becomes to develop long-term employee commitment at both national and international levels. While such institutional arrangements do facilitate employers' ability to hire and fire staff with varied kinds of skills, and so rapidly transform their knowledge and expertise base, they limit employees' willingness to invest in developing firm-specific capabilities on a continuing basis.

This suggests, third, that cross-national problem-solving and learning should be easier when skill boundaries, knowledge bases, and organizational structures in different countries overlap. When they do, careers in both internal and external labour markets are likely to reward comparable kinds of technically specialized contributions, and externally certified skills are sufficiently standardized across labour markets to provide common languages for joint problem-solving. Even when commitments to developing employer-specific knowledge and skills differ considerably between national subsidiaries, continuing communication and gaining the cooperation of specialists across borders on a long-term basis will be greatly facilitated by organizational career structures that reward expertise-based performance, as distinct from broader contributions to general organizational success. However, such specialist careers can, of course, inhibit cross-functional collaboration.

These kinds of expertise-based career structures are in turn encouraged by similar kinds of public skill formation and evaluation systems that generate social identities and loyalties around certified skills. For MNCs to develop distinctive cross-national learning capabilities that enable different kinds of knowledge production and problem-solving to be transferred between subsidiaries—as opposed to the codified results of such activities—careers and commitments have to overlap across organizational subunits.

Overall, the more varied are subsidiaries' environments and their organization of careers, especially the kinds of contributions and skills that they reward, the more difficult it is likely to be for MNCs to develop distinctive international learning capabilities, particularly for developing new knowledge that is not readily codified. Establishing a common cross-national career structure for some middle managers and professionals will contribute to the generation of these kinds of capabilities, but this requires the MNC to be able to offer credible commitments over business cycles and national differences.

Fourth, the few MNCs that do develop strong coordinating and learning capabilities across borders through long-term international employer–employee commitments are unlikely to be able to reconfigure their skills and competences radically to deal with rapidly changing circumstances. This is because of their dependence on current employees' skills and their establishment of transnational integrating routines. Building and maintaining long-term firm-specific organizational capabilities at the international level usually involves considerable investments in cross-national procedures, routines, and competences. These are unlikely to encourage rapid and radical transformation of key skills and technologies that would enable firms to move effectively into quite novel industries with discontinuous technological trajectories and markets.

Conclusion

This analysis of how societal institutions affect the constitution, direction, and growth strategies of leading firms in different market economies has highlighted a number of points that are worth emphasizing in conclusion. First, the extent to which the dominant corporate form in an economy does indeed combine limited liability, legal personality, unified authority, external investor ownership, and easy transfer of property rights varies considerably between institutional regimes and over time. Furthermore, there is no good theoretical or empirical reason to expect such varied corporate forms to converge on a single type, let alone the current US one, despite Kraakman's (2001) claim to the contrary.

This means that, second, legally constituted firms are by no means the only—or the dominant—strategic actor in all market economies. In many cases, these are subsidiary members of business groups or diversified family-controlled business that are centrally directed. On the other hand, some legally defined firms can function more as hollow corporations with few, if any, distinctive organizational capabilities of their own (Teece et al. 1994) Additionally, the variety of different kinds of strategic economic actors differs considerably between economies, from those dominated by the Chandlerian multi-divisional company to those with powerful trades associations, union federations, and dynamic inter-firm networks that are able to mobilize resources and act strategically. In the latter kind of economy, the legally bounded firm is only one of a number of different types of authoritative integrator and director of economic interests (Whitley 2007).

Third, particular combinations of firm governance characteristics and capability development are likely to dominate market economies with particular kinds of governing institutions, especially when these are complementary, or mutually reinforcing with respect to their implications for firm strategies and prevalent competitive norms. Such complementary institutional regimes vary in their national homogeneity and standardization of leading firm characteristics, with many post-war corporatist ones being more nationally-specific and wider ranging in their scope than arm's-length ones that tend to leave patterns of business and labour representation, and many features of employment policies, to the discretion of individual actors. As a result, the variety of firm types, and economic coordination and control forms more generally, tends to be greater across subnational regions and sectors in the latter kinds of society than in the former ones.

Finally, the national specificity of such regimes and dominant firm types is empirically variable and contingent upon the relative strength and coherence of key institutions at the national level. This can, and does, change, as the history of the USA in the nineteenth and twentieth centuries illustrates (Dobbin 1994; Roy 1997), not least because of shifts in dominant political-economic coalitions (Amable 2003; Deeg and Jackson 2007; Gourevitch and Shinn 2005). The recent growth of international capital markets, trade, and business regulation may have lessened the significance of national institutional regimes, but the impact of such changes varies between differently organized market economies and rarely amounts to a radical replacement of established systems of economic organization by some 'global' economic order (Whitley 2005; 2007).

Equally, the development of new kinds of international capabilities in MNCs has been rather slower and less significant than some enthusiasts for the transnational corporation claimed, as the recent study of APV highlighted (Kristensen and Zeitlin 2005). Indeed, the conditions for developing genuinely transnational organizational capabilities on a long-term basis are much more demanding than is commonly recognized, and may inhibit MNCs' flexibility and ability to respond to market and technological changes. While some MNCs may become more than national firms with foreign operations, how they do so, and with what results, requires systematic comparative analysis of different kinds of internationalizing companies, rather than the broad presumption that they are all similar simply by virtue of controlling facilities in different national jurisdictions.

REFERENCES

ALMOND, PHIL and ANTHONY FERNER (eds.) (2006). *American Multinationals in Europe: Managing Employment Relations across National Borders*, (Oxford: Oxford University Press).

AMABLE, BRUNO (2003). *The Diversity of Modern Capitalism*, (Oxford: Oxford University Press).

AMSDEN, A. H. (1989). *Asia's Next Giant*, (Oxford: Oxford University Press).

AOKI, M. (1988). *Information, Incentives, and Bargaining in the Japanese Economy*, (Cambridge: Cambridge University Press).

——(2001). *Toward a Comparative Institutional Analysis*, (Cambridge, Mass.: MIT Press).

——and R. P. DORE (eds.) (1994). *The Japanese Firm: The Sources of Competitive Strength*, (Oxford: Oxford University Press).

BAE, K. (1987). *Automobile Workers in Korea*, (Seoul: Seoul National University Press).

BAHRAMI, H. and S. EVANS (1995). 'Flexible Re-cycling and High Technology Entrepreneurship', *California Management Review* 37: 62–88.

BARCA, FABRIZIO and MARCO BECHT (eds.) (2001). *The Control of Corporate Europe*, (Oxford: Oxford University Press).

BARTLETT, C. A. and S. GHOSHAL (1989). *Managing Across Borders: The Transnational Solution*, (London: Hutchinson Business Books).

BAUER, MICHEL and ELIE COHEN (1981). *Qui gouverne les groupes industriels?* (Paris: Seuil).

BECHT, MARCO and J. BRADFORD DELONG (2007). 'Why Has There Been So Little Block Holding in America?' in R Morck (ed.), *A History of Corporate Governance Around the World*, (Chicago: University of Chicago Press), 613–60.

BEECHLER, S. L. and A. BIRD (EDS.) (1999). *Japanese Multinationals Abroad: Individual and Organizational Learning*, (Oxford: Oxford University Press).

BEETHAM, DAVID (1991). *The Legitimation of Power*, (London: Macmillan).

BERLE, A. and G. C. MEANS (1932). *The Modern Corporation and Private Property*, (New York: Macmillan), repub. Harcourt, Brace and World, 1967.

BLAIR, MARGARET (1995). *Ownership and Control*, (Washington, DC: Brookings Institution).

BOYER, ROBERT and J.-P. DURAND (1997). *After Fordism*, (London: Macmillan).

BRAITHWAITE, JOHN and PETER DRAHOS (2000). *Global Business Regulation*, (Cambridge: Cambridge University Press).

CASPER, STEVEN (2000). 'Institutional Adaptiveness, Technology Policy and the Diffusion of New Business Models: The Case of German Biotechnology', *Organization Studies* 21: 887–914.

——(2001). 'The Legal Framework for Corporate Governance: The Influence of Contract Law on Company Strategies in Germany and the United States', in P. Hall and D. Soskice (eds.), *Varieties of Capitalism*, (Oxford: Oxford University Press), 387–416.

——and CATHERINE MATRAVES (2003). 'Institutional Frameworks and Innovation in the German and UK Pharmaceutical Industry', *Research Policy* 32: 1865–79.

CHANDLER, ALFRED (1977). *The Visible Hand*, (Cambridge, MA: Harvard University Press).

——(1990). *Scale and Scope*, (Cambridge, MA: Harvard University Press).

CLARK, RODNEY (1979). *The Japanese Company*, (New Haven: Yale University Press).

COLE, ROBERT and HUGH WHITTAKER (2006). 'Introduction', in Hugh Whittaker and Robert Cole (eds.), *Recovering from Success: Innovation and Technology Management in Japan*, (Oxford: Oxford University Press), 1–28.

CROUCH, COLIN (1999). *Social Change in Western Europe*, (Oxford: Oxford University Press).

——(2005). *Capitalist Diversity and Change: Recombinant Governance and Institutional Entrepreneurs*, (Oxford: Oxford University Press).

——and WOLFGANG STREECK (eds.) (1997). *Political Economy of Modern Capitalism*, (London: Sage).

CULPEPPER, PEPPER and DAVID FINEGOLD (1999) (eds.), *The German Skills Machine: Sustaining Comparative Advantage in a Global Economy*, (New York: Berghahn Books).

DEEG, RICHARD (2005). 'Path Dependency, Institutional Complementarity, and Change in National Business Systems', in G. Morgan, R. Whitley, and E. Moen (eds.), *Changing Capitalisms?* (Oxford: Oxford University Press), 21–52.

——and GREGORY JACKSON (2007). 'Towards a More Dynamic Theory of Capitalist Variety', *Socio-Economic Review* 5: 149–179.

DJELIC, MARIE-LAURE (1998). *Exporting the American Model*, (Oxford: Oxford University Press).

DOBBIN, FRANK (1994). *Forging Industrial Policy: The United States, Britain, and France in the Railway Age*, (Cambridge: Cambridge University Press).

DORE, RONALD (1986). *Flexible Rigidities*, (Chicago: Stanford University Press).

DOREMUS, P. N., W. W. KELLER, L. W. PAULY, and S. REICH (1998). *The Myth of the Global Corporation*, (Princeton, NJ: Princeton University Press).

DOSI, GIOVANNI, RICHARD NELSON, and SIDNEY WINTER (eds.) (2000). *The Nature and Dynamics of Organizational Capabilities*, (Oxford: Oxford University Press).

ECKSTEIN, H. and T. R. GURR (1975). *Patterns of Authority: A Structural Basis for Political Inquiry*, (New York: J. Wiley).

ENRIGHT, MICHAEL, EDITH SCOTT, and DAVID DODWELL (1997). *The Hong Kong Advantage*, (Hong Kong: Oxford University Press).

ERGAS, HENRY (1987). 'Does Technology Policy Matter?', in Bruce R. Guile and Harvey Brooks (eds.), *Technology and Global Industry: Companies and Nations in the World Economy*, (Washington, DC: National Academy Press).

ERNST, DIETER (2006). 'Searching for a New Role in East Asian Regionalization—Japanese Production Networks in the Electronics Industry', in Peter Katzenstein and Takashi Shiraishi (eds.), *Beyond Japan: The Dynamics of East Asian Regionalization*, (Ithaca: Cornell University Press), 161–187.

EVANS, PETER (1994). *Embedded Autonomy: States and Industrial Transformation*, (Princeton, NJ: Princeton University Press).

FAFCHAMPS, MARCEL (1996). 'The Enforcement of Commercial Contracts in Ghana', *World Development* 24: 427–48.

FIELDS, KARL J. (1995). *Enterprise and the State in Korea and Taiwan*, (Ithaca, NY: Cornell University Press).

FLEURY, ALFONSO and MARIO SERGIO SALERNO (1998). 'The Transfer and Hybridization of New Models of Production in the Brazilian Automobile Industry', in Robert Boyer, Elsie Charron, Ulrich Jurgens, and Steven Tolliday (eds.), *Between Imitation and Innovation: The Transfer and Hybridization of Productive Models in the International Automobile Industry*, (Oxford: Oxford University Press), 278–94.

FLIGSTEIN, NEIL and JENNIFER CHOO (2005). 'Law and Corporate Governance', *Annual Review of Law and Social Science* 1: 61–84.

FRUIN, MARK (1992). *The Japanese Enterprise System*, (Oxford: Oxford University Press).

FUJIMOTO, T (2000). 'Evolution of Manufacturing Systems and *ex post* Dynamic Capabilities', in G. Dosi et al. (eds.), *The Nature and Dynamics of Organizational Capabilities*, 244–80. (Oxford: Oxford University Press).

GADHOUM, YOSER, LARRY LANG, and LESLIE YOUNG (2005). 'Who Controls US?', *European Financial Management* 11: 339–63.

GAMBARDELLA, ALFONSO (1995). *Science and Innovation: The US Pharmaceutical Industry During the 1980s*, (Cambridge: Cambridge University Press).

GATES, H. (1996). *China's Motor: A Thousand Years of Petty Capitalism*, (Ithaca NY: Cornell University Press).

GHOSHAL, S. and E. WESTNEY (1993). 'Introduction and Overview,' in S. Ghoshal, and E. Westney (eds.), *Organization Theory and the Multinational Corporation*, (London: Macmillan).

GOETZMANN, WILLIAM and ELISABETH KOELL (2007). 'The History of Corporate Governance in China: State Patronage, Company Legislation and the Issue of Control', in R Morck (ed.), *A History of Corporate Governance around the World*, (Chicago: University of Chicago Press), 149–84.

GOUREVITCH, PETER and JAMES SHINN (2005). *Political Power and Corporate Control: The New Global Politics of Corporate Governance*, (Princeton, NJ: Princeton University Press).

GRAHAM, FIONA (2003). *Inside the Japanese Company*, (London: RoutledgeCurzon).

GUGLER, KLAUS, DENNIS MUELLER, and B. BERCIN YURTOGLU (2004). 'Corporate Governance and Globalization', *Oxford Review of Economic Policy* 20: 129–56.

HALL, PETER and DAVID SOSKICE (2001). 'An Introduction to Varieties of Capitalism', in P. Hall and D. Soskice (eds.), *Varieties of Capitalism: The Institutional Foundations of Comparative Advantage*, (Oxford: Oxford University Press), 1–68.

HAMILTON, GARY (1997). 'Organization and Market Processes in Taiwan's Capitalist Economy', in Marco Orru, Nicole Woolsey Biggart, and Gary Hamilton (eds.), *The Economic Organization of East Asian Capitalism*, (Thousand Oaks, CA: Sage), 237–93.

——(2006). *Commerce and Capitalism in Chinese Societies*, (London: Routledge).

——and CHENG-SHU KAO (1990). 'The Institutional Foundation of Chinese Business: The Family Firm in Taiwan', *Comparative Social Research* 12: 95–112.

——and ROBERT C. FEENSTRA (1997). 'Varieties of Hierarchies and Markets: An Introduction', in Marco Orru, Nicole Woolsey Biggart, and Gary Hamilton (eds.), *The Economic Organisation of East Asian Capitalism*, (Thousand Oaks, CA: Sage).

HELFAT, CONSTANCE E., S. FINKELSTEIN, W. MITCHELL, M. PETERAF, H. SINGH, D. TEECE, and S. WINTER (2007). *Dynamic Capabilities: Understanding Strategic Change in Organizations*, (Oxford: Blackwell).

HERRIGEL, GARY (1994). 'Industry as a Form of Order', in R. Hollingsworth, P. Schmitter, and W. Streeck (eds.) (1994). *Governing Capitalist Economies*, (Oxford: Oxford University Press).

——(1996). *Industrial Constructions*, (Cambridge: Cambridge University Press).

HIRST, P. and G. THOMPSON (1996). *Globalisation in Question*, (Oxford: Polity Press).

HOLLINGSWORTH, R. (1991). 'The Logic of Coordinating American Manufacturing Sectors', in J. L. Campbell et al. (eds.), *Governance of the American Economy*, (Cambridge: Cambridge University Press).

HUMPHREY, JOHN, and HUBERT SCHMITZ (1998). 'Trust and Inter-firm Relations in Developing and Transition Economies', *Journal of Development Studies* 34: 32–61.

Hu, Y.-S. (1992). 'Global Firms are National Firms with International Operations', *California Management Review* 34: 107–26.

Jackson, Gregory, Martin Höpner, and Antje Kurdelbusch (2005). 'Corporate Governance and Employees in Germany: Changing Linkages, Complementarities, and Tensions', in H. Gospel and A. Pendleton (eds.), *Corporate Governance and Labour Management: An International Comparison*, (Oxford: Oxford University Press), 84–121.

Jacoby, Sanford (2005). *The Embedded Corporation: Corporate Governance and Employment Relations in Japan and the United States*, (Princeton, NJ: Princeton University Press).

Janelli, R. L. (1993). *Making Capitalism: The Social and Cultural Construction of a South Korean Conglomerate*, (Stanford: Stanford University Press).

Jürgens, Ulrich (1998). 'Implanting Change: The Role of "Indigenous Transplants" in Transforming the German Productive Model', in Robert Boyer et al. (eds.), *Between Imitation and Innovation*, (Oxford: Oxford University Press), 319–60.

——(2003). 'Transformation and Interaction: Japanese, U.S., and German Production Models in the 1990s', in K. Yamamura and W. Streeck (eds.), *The End of Diversity?*, (Ithaca, NY: Cornell University Press), 212–39.

Kenworthy, L. (1997). 'Globalization and Economic Convergence', *Competition and Change* 2: 1–64.

——(2005). 'Institutional Coherence and Macroeconomic Performance', *Socio-Economic Review* 4: 69–91.

Kim, C. S. (1992). *The Culture of Korean Industry*, (Tucson: University of Arizona Press).

Kim, Eun Mee (1997). *Big Business, Big State: Collusion and Conflict in South Korean Development, 1960–1990*, (Albany, New York: State University of New York Press).

King, Lawrence and Ivan Szelenyi (2005). 'Post-Communist Economic Systems', in Neil Smelser and Richard Swedberg (eds.), *The Handbook of Economic Sociology*, 2nd edn. (Princeton, NJ: Princeton University Press), 205–29.

Kneller, Robert (1999). 'University–Industry Cooperation in Biomedical R & D in Japan and the United States', in L. Branscomb, F. Kodama, and R. Florida (eds.), *Industrializing Knowledge: University–Industry Linkages in Japan and the United States*, (Cambridge, MA: MIT Press), 410–38.

——(2003). 'Autarkic Drug Discovery in Japanese Pharmaceutical Companies: Insights into National Differences in Industrial Innovation', *Research Policy* 32: 1805–27.

——(2007). *Bridging Islands: Venture Companies and the Future of Japanese and American Industry*, (Oxford: Oxford University Press).

Koechlin, T. (1995). 'The Globalization of Investment', *Contemporary Economic Policy* 13: 92–100.

Kogut, Bruce (1993). 'Learning, or the Importance of Being Inert: Country Imprinting and International Competition,' in, S. Ghoshal and E. Westney (eds.), *Organization Theory and the Multinational Corporation*, (London: Macmillan).

——and David Parkinson (1993). 'The Diffusion of American Organizing Principles to Europe', in B. Kogut (ed.), *Country Competitiveness: Technology and the Organizing of Work*, (New York: Oxford University Press), 179–202.

——and Udo Zander (1992). 'Knowledge of the Firm, Combinative Capabilities, and the Replication of Technology', *Organization Science* 3: 383–97.

Koike, K. (1987). 'Human Resource Development and Labour–Management Relations', in K. Yamamura and Y. Yasuba (eds.), *The Political Economy of Japan I.* (Stanford: Stanford University Press).

Kopp, R. (1999). 'The Rice-Paper Ceiling in Japanese Companies: Why It Exists and Persists', in S. L. Beechler and A. Bird (eds.), *Japanese Multinationals Abroad: Individual and Organizational Learning*, (New York: Oxford University Press), 107–28.

Kraakman, Reinier (2001). 'The Durability of the Corporate Firm', in Paul DiMaggio (ed.), *The Twenty-First-Century Firm*, (Princeton, NJ: Princeton University Press), 147–60.

Kristensen, Peer Hull and Jonathan Zeitlin (2005). *Local Players in Global Games: The Strategic Constitution of a Multinational Corporation*, (Oxford: Oxford University Press).

Krug, Barbara and Hans Hendrischke (eds.) (2007). *China's Economy in the 21st Century*, (Cheltenham: Edward Elgar).

Lam, Alice (2003). 'Organisational Learning in Multinationals: R & D Networks of Japanese and U.S. MNEs in the U.K', *Journal of Management Studies* 40: 673–704.

Lane, Christel (1992). 'European Business Systems: Britain and Germany Compared', in R. Whitley (ed.), *European Business Systems: Firms and Markets in their National Context*, (London: Sage).

——(1998). 'European Companies between Globalization and Localisation: A Comparison of Internationalisation Strategies of British and German MNCs', *Economy and Society* 27: 462–85.

——(2001). 'The Emergence of German Transnational Companies: A Theoretical Analysis and Empirical study of the Globalization Process', 69–96, in G. Morgan, P. H. Kristensen, and R. Whitley (eds.), *The Multinational Firm: Organizing Across Institutional and National Divides*, (Oxford: Oxford University Press).

Langlois, Richard (2003). 'The Vanishing Hand: The Changing Dynamics of Industrial Capitalism', *Industrial and Corporate Change* 12: 351–85.

Laurence, Henry (2001). *Money Rules: The New Politics of Finance in Britain and Japan*, (Ithaca, NY: Cornell University Press).

Lazonick, W. (1991). *Business Organization and the Myth of the Market Economy*, (Cambridge: Cambridge University Press).

——and Mary O'Sullivan (1996). 'Organization, Finance and International Competition', *Industrial Corporate Change* 5: 1–49.

——and Jonathan West (1998). 'Organizational Integration and Competitive Advantage', in G. Dosi, D. J. Teece, and J. Chytry (eds.), *Technology, Organization, and Competitiveness*, (Oxford: Oxford University Press).

Lehmkuhl, Dirk (2003). 'Structuring Dispute Resolution in Transnational Trade: Competition and Coevolution of Public and Private Institutions', in M.-L. Djelic and S. Quack (eds.), *Globalization and Institutions*, (Cheltenham: Edward Elgar), 278–301.

Lincoln, James and Michael Gerlach (2004). *Japan's Network Economy: Structure, Persistence and Change*, (Cambridge: Cambridge University Press).

Lodge, G. C. and E. F. Vogel (eds.) (1987). *Ideology and National Competitiveness*, (Boston, MA: Harvard Business School Press).

Lutz, Susanne (2004). 'Convergence within National Diversity: The Regulatory State in Finance', *Journal of Public Policy* 24: 169–97.

McNichol, James and Jabril Bensedrine (2003). 'Multilateral Rulemaking: Transatlantic Struggles around Genetically Modified Food', in M.-L. Djelic and S. Quack (eds.), *Globalization and Institutions* (Cheltenham: Edward Elgar), 220–44.

Majone, Giandomenico (2005). *Dilemmas of European Integration: The Ambiguities and Pitfalls of Integration by Stealth*, (Oxford: Oxford University Press).

Marris, Robin (1964). *The Economic Theory of Managerial Capitalism*, (London: Macmillan).

Maurice, M., F. Sellier, and J. J. Silvestre (1986). *The Social Foundations of Industrial Power*, (Cambridge, MA: MIT Press).

——A. SORGE, and M. WARNER, (1980). 'Societal Differences in Organising Manufacturing Units', *Organisation Studies*, 1: 59–86.

MEARDI, GUGLIELMO and ANDRAS TOTH (2006). 'Who is Hybridising What? Insights in MNCs' Employment Practices in Central Europe', in A. Ferner, J. Quintanilla, and C. Sanchez-Runde (eds.), *Multinational Institutions and the Construction of Transnational Practices*, (Basingstoke: Palgrave Macmillan). 155–83.

MENKHOFF, THOMAS (1992). 'Xinyong or How to Trust Trust? Chinese Non-Contractual Business Relations and Social Structure: The Singapore Case', *Internationales Asienforum* 23: 26–288.

METCALFE, J. STANLEY and ANDREW JAMES (2000). 'Knowledge and Capabilities: A New View of the Firm', in Nicolai Foss and Paul Robertson (eds.), *Resources, Technology and Strategy: Explorations in the Resource Based Perspective*, (London: Routledge), 31–52.

MILHAUPT, CURTIS J. (ed.) (2003). *Global Markets, Domestic Institutions: Corporate Law and Governance in a New Era of Cross-Border Deals*, (New York: Columbia University Press).

MORCK, RANDALL (ed.) (2007). *A History of Corporate Governance Around the World*, (Chicago: University of Chicago Press).

——and MASAO NAKAMURA (2007). 'A Frog in a Well Knows Nothing of the Ocean: A History of Corporate Governance in Japan', in R. Morck (ed.), *A History of Corporate Governance Around the World*, (Chicago: Chicago University Press), 367–465.

MORGAN, GLENN and SIGRID QUACK (2005). 'Internationalization and Capability Development in Professional Service Firms', in G. Morgan, R. Whitley, and E. Moen (eds.), *Changing Capitalisms?*, (Oxford: Oxford University Press), 277–311.

NISHIDA, JUDITH and GORDON REDDING (1992). 'Firm Development and Diversification Strategies as Products of Economic Culture: The Japanese and Hong Kong Textile Industries', in R. Whitley (ed.), *European Business Systems*, (London: Sage), 241–66.

NONAKA, IKUJIRO and HIROTAKA TAKEUCHI (1995). *The Knowledge-Creating Company: How Japanese Companies Create the Dynamics of Innovation*, (Oxford: Oxford University Press).

ODAGIRI, H. (1994). *Growth through Competition, Competition through Growth*. (Oxford: Oxford University Press).

ODAGIRI, HIROYUKI and AKIRA GOTO (1996). *Technology and Industrial Development in Japan: Building Capabilities by Learning, Innovation, and Public Policy*, (Oxford: Oxford University Press).

O'SULLIVAN, MARY (2000). *Contests for Corporate Control*, (Oxford: Oxford University Press).

PENROSE, EDITH (1959). *The Theory of the Growth of the Firm*, (Oxford: Blackwell).

PUCIK, VLADIMIR (1999). 'When Performance Does Not Matter: Human Resource Management in Japanese-owned US Affiliates', in S. L. Beechler and A. Bird (eds.), *Japanese Multinationals Abroad*, (Oxford: Oxford University Press), 169–88.

REDDING, S. GORDON (1990). *The Spirit of Chinese Capitalism*, (Berlin: de Gruyter).

RICHARDSON, GEORGE (1998). 'Some Principles of Economic Organisation', in N. Foss and B. Loasby (eds.), *Economic Organisation, Capabilities and Coordination*, (London: Routledge), 44–62.

ROE, MARK (2003). *Political Determinants of Corporate Governance*, (Oxford: Oxford University Press).

ROY, WILLIAM G. (1997). *Socializing Capital: The Rise of the Large Industrial Corporation in America*, (Princeton, NJ: Princeton University Press).

SAKAI, JUNKO (2000). *Japanese Bankers in the City of London*, (London: Routledge).

SAMUELS, R. J. (1987). *The Business of the Japanese State*, (Ithaca, NY: Cornell University Press).

SAXENIAN, ANNALEE (1994). *Regional Advantage: Culture and Competition in Silicon Valley and Route 128*, (Cambridge, MA: Harvard University Press).

SCHMIDT, VIVIEN A. (2002). *The Futures of European Capitalism*, (Oxford: Oxford University Press).

SHEARD, PAUL (1994). 'Interlocking Shareholdings and Corporate Governance in Japan', in M. Aoki and R. Dore (eds.), *The Japanese Firm: The Sources of Competitive Strength*, (Oxford: Oxford University Press), 310–49.

SILIN, R. H. (1976). *Leadership and Values: The Organisation of Large Scale Taiwanese Enterprises*, (Cambridge, MA: Harvard University Press).

SORGE, ARNDT (2005). *The Global and the Local*, (Oxford: Oxford University Press).

SOSKICE, D. (1999). 'Divergent Production Regimes: Coordinated and Uncoordinated Market Economies in the 1980s and 1990s', in H. Kitschelt, P. Lange, G. Marks, and J. Stephens (eds.), *Continuity and Change in Contemporary Capitalism*, (Cambridge: Cambridge University Press), 101–34.

STREECK, WOLFGANG and PHILIPPE SCHMITTER (eds.) (1985). *Private Interest Government: Beyond Market and State*, (London: Sage).

——and KOZO YAMAMURA (eds.) (2001). *The Origins of Nonliberal Capitalism*, (Ithaca, NY: Cornell University Press).

TEECE, DAVID, GARY PISANO, and AMY SHUEN (2000). 'Dynamic Capabilities and Strategic Management', in G. Dosi et al. (eds.), *The Nature and Dynamics of Organizational Capabilities*, (Oxford: Oxford University Press), 334–62.

——RICHARD RUMELT, GIOVANNI DOSI, SIDNEY WINTER (1994). 'Understanding Corporate Coherence: Theory and Evidence', *Journal of Economic Behavior and Organization* 23: 1–30.

THELEN, KATHLEEN (2004). *How Institutions Evolve: The Political Economy of Skills in Germany, Britain, the United States and Japan*, (Cambridge: Cambridge University Press).

——and IKUO KUME (2003). 'The Future of Nationally Embedded Capitalism: Industrial Relations in Germany and Japan', in K. Yamamura and W. Streeck (eds.), *The End of Diversity?*, (Ithaca, NY: Cornell University Press) 183–211.

THOMAS, L. G. III (2001). *The Japanese Pharmaceutical Industry: The New Drug Lag and the Failure of Industrial Policy*, (Cheltenham, UK: Edward Elgar).

TOLLIDAY, STEVEN (2000). 'Transplanting the American Model? US Automobile Companies and the Transfer of Technology and Management to Britain, France, and Germany, 1928–1962', in J. Zeitlin and G. Herrigel (eds.), *Americanization and its Limits: Reworking US Technology and Management in Post-War Europe and Japan*, (Oxford: Oxford University Press), 76–119.

TYLECOTE, ANDREW and FRANCESCA VISINTIN (2008). *Corporate Governance, Finance and the Technological Advantage of Nations*, (Abingdon, UK: Routledge).

VOGEL, EZRA (1988). *Japan As Number One*, (Cambridge, MA: Harvard University Press).

WADE, R. (1996). 'Globalisation and its Limits: Reports of the Death of the National Economy are Greatly Exaggerated', in S. Berger and R. Dore (eds.), *National Diversity and Global Capitalism*, (Ithaca, NY: Cornell University Press).

WANK, DAVID (1999). *Commodifying Communism, Business, Trust and Politics in a Chinese City*, (Cambridge: Cambridge University Press).

WEISS, LINDA (ed) (2003). *States in the Global Economy: Bringing Institutions Back In*, (Cambridge: Cambridge University Press).

WESTNEY, ELEANOR (2001). 'Japanese Enterprise Faces the Twenty-First Century,' in Paul DiMaggio (ed.), *The Twenty-First-Century Firm*, (Princeton, NJ: Princeton University Press), 105–43.

WHITLEY, RICHARD (1992). *Business Systems in East Asia: Firms, Markets and Societies*, (London: Sage).

——(1994). 'Dominant Forms of Economic Organization in Market Economies', *Organisation Studies* 15: 153–82.

——(1999). *Divergent Capitalisms: The Social Structuring and Change of Business Systems*, (Oxford: Oxford University Press).

——(2005). 'How National are Business Systems? The Role of States and Complementary Institutions in Standardizing Systems of Economic Coordination and Control at the National Level', in G. Morgan et al. (eds.), *Changing Capitalisms?* (Oxford: Oxford University Press), 190–231.

——(2007). *Business Systems and Organizational Capabilities: The Institutional Structuring of Competitive Competences*, (Oxford: Oxford University Press).

——and LASZLO CZABAN (1998). 'Institutional Transformation and Enterprise Change in an Emergent Capitalist Economy: The Case of Hungary', *Organization Studies* 19: 259–80.

——J. HENDERSON, L. CZABAN, and G. LENGYEL (1996). 'Trust and Contractual Relations in an Emerging Capitalist Economy', *Organization Studies* 17: 397–420.

——GLENN MORGAN, WILLIAM KELLY, and DIANA SHARPE (2003). 'The Changing Japanese MNC', *Journal of Management Studies* 40: 639–68.

WOO, JUNG-EN (1991). *Race to the Swift: State and Finance in Korean Industrialization*, (New York: Columbia University Press).

ZYSMAN, JOHN (1983). *Governments, Markets and Growth: Financial Systems and the Politics of Industrial Change*, (Ithaca, NY: Cornell University Press).

CHAPTER 17

INSTITUTIONALIZING THE EMPLOYMENT RELATIONSHIP

JILL RUBERY

INTRODUCTION

Although a relatively recent institution, the internalized employment relationship is *intra-direct* a common institutional feature of modern organizational capitalism. The definition *employment* of an internalized employment relationship hinges on the distinction between a *relationship* contract for services and a contract of service. Instead of selling outputs or products coordinated by the market or the price mechanism (Coase 1937, Simon 1991), a contract for services involves the selling of labour time and the acceptance of the authority of the employer or entrepreneur to control or coordinate the activities of labour within certain limits. The source of these limitations is located in a range of institutional mechanisms including the law, collective bargaining, and social norms.

While the employment relationship varies in its specific characteristics, the institution of an internalized employment relationship is recognized and widely utilized in all advanced capitalist economies.

The employment relationship is not simply a legal contractual institution but also one that operates through social norms and customary expectations with respect to the rights and obligations of employers, employees, and indeed the state. The employment relationship has a pivotal role in an economic system, with consequences that extend beyond the production system to social and family organization.

It shapes not only the terms under which labour power is supplied to and utilized within firms but also the pattern of social stratification and associated standards of living. With the emergence of welfare support for citizens not in employment, the employment relationship also became integrated into state welfare arrangements with entitlements to benefits often dependent upon accumulated time spent in an employment relationship.

The employment relationship has also been recognized as a core institution for understanding the macroeconomy. For Marxists the development of the internalized employment relationship can be linked to capital's desire to increase the rate of surplus value extracted (Marglin 1974), while for Keynes the fact that the employment contract is made in monetary rather than in real terms provided a basis for his critique of the presumption that the economy will adjust through price changes to full employment. The French *regulationist* school further integrated the employment relationship into long-run economic cycles through its concept of *rapport salarial*, which is best rendered in translation as the wage relationship (Boyer 1979). The rapport salarial is not only to be understood as a micro-level institution but as the key institution in the regime of accumulation. It is the wage relationship that links together not only production and social reproduction but also production and consumption. For example, in the Fordist era of mass manufacturing the rapport salarial provided for rising real wage levels and security of employment in return for acquiescence in the development of Fordist production systems. The rising real wages in turn generated the consumption needed to match the growing volume of output in a mass production manufacturing economy.

The *regulationist* school also focuses on the distributional aspects of the employment relationship, thereby emphasizing the fundamental political function of the institution. The main lines of distribution may be regarded as a macroeconomic characteristic where there is a relatively homogenized employment relationship established at national level—possibly through state intervention, as in France. Alternatively there may be strong intra-country variations in the employment relationship, reflecting the differential influence and power of sectional interest groups both among employers and workers that give rise to protected employment segments (Rubery 1978, Whitley 1999).

One consequence of the integration of the employment relationship into production, family, welfare, and political relations (Esping-Andersen 2002) is that the form that it takes is the outcome of a range of historical and current institutional influences that extend beyond the direct regulation of employment through the legal system and more voluntary forms of regulations such as collective bargaining (Deakin et al. 2007). Also important, if in a more indirect way, are the provisions for skill development embedded in education and training systems and the social arrangements for supporting the non-employed—through the family, employers, or the welfare system. These institutional arrangements not only vary among societies but also within societies, by sector and organization and by occupations or professions. The extent of this internal variation depends on the homogeneity and inclusiveness of societal institutions. To take one of the key dimensions of societal difference, that is the security attached to the employment relationship, research shows that not only are there significant differences between an employment at will culture in the US and a job for life culture in the Japanese large firm economy, but that these differences spill over into the pay systems, skill and training systems, employee voice, and representation (Brown et al. 1997). These societal differences can be considerable, even if within these two societies there are still both secure and insecure employees.

The employment relationship is in fact one of the main forces implicated in the *societal* *effects* creation and maintenance of interlocking sets of institutional arrangements that in turn give rise to what has been called societal effects (Maurice et al. 1986; Maurice and Sorge 2000) or the now more frequently used term, 'varieties of capitalism' (Hall and Soskice 2001; Whitley 1999). The notion of a societal effect, or indeed a variety of capitalism, is that it is not possible to appreciate the impact of an institutional arrangement in isolation but only as part of a set of interlocking arrangements. The consequence is that despite the apparent commonality of form, to comprehend differences in the form and function of the employment relationship, it is essential to analyse the employment relationship embedded in its societal environment. As Rose (1985) put it:

> ...while all paid employment embodies 'exploitation'—the right of the employer to utilize labour capacity to extract a surplus of value—the mediating structures delimiting the exercise of this right are of infinitely greater significance in practice than the right itself, as well as being of interest to the social analyst because of their variability. Moreover, each societally specific employment relationship can be legitimately compared only as a whole. (Rose 1985: 74)

It is through these interconnections that the employment relationship can also be considered a central institution in processes of restructuring and change. This follows from the fact that the form of the employment relationship reflects a social compromise between capital and labour. As Deakin and Wilkinson (2006: 109) summarize:

> It is precisely this 'linking' of capitalist work relations to the wider risk-sharing role of the welfare or social state which was embodied in the 'compromise' of mid-twentieth century social and economic policy, and coded, juridically, in the contract of employment.... Thus the argument for the contract of employment is, in the final analysis, an argument in favour of an integrative mechanism, or set of mechanisms, which makes it possible for a market economy and a social state to co-exist.

However, this integrative role of the employment relationship leaves it open to pressure for change from multiple directions, particularly as the social compromise begins to fall apart. Instead of interlocking institutions acting to constrain change (Streeck and Thelen 2005), there are possibilities of spillover effects from one sphere to another, potentially increasing the scope of change through ripple or domino effects. Thus change to the internalized employment relationship has implications for the survival of the welfare system or the traditional family form. Likewise the origins of pressures for change in the employment relationship may be found in changes in different spheres: for example in the switch from manufacturing to services, in the reshaping of family and gender relations as women aspire to new roles and in changes in the mode of financing the welfare system or in defining eligibility for benefits.

Pressures for change not only challenge the form of the internalized employment relationship but even call into question its long-term survival for both high and low skilled workers. The rise of the knowledge worker has been associated with the development of more 'boundaryless' careers, that are less tied to upward career trajectories within a specific organization and involving not only more inter-organizational mobility but also an increasing frequency of freelance or self-employment (Arthur and Rousseau 1996). In the lower skilled segments the diversification of the labour force and the spread of lean services that link labour deployment closely to client demand are associated with the spread of non-standard employment, involving both more casualized or spot contracting. More triangular employment relationships involving close relations with clients who take on some employer functions (Marchington et al. 2005) add new complexities to the internalized employment relationship. Furthermore, the spread of global production networks (Herrigel and Zeitlin this volume) has potential implications for both the diffusion and the viability of internalized employment. In principle, international value chains could promote high quality employment and production practices to developing countries, including formal internalized employment relationships. However, such an outcome is by no means guaranteed (ILO 2004); international sourcing practices may fuel short-term competition, promoting a greater use of informal employment in both developing countries and developed economies.

This chapter takes up three main issues that have been raised by this short overview of the significance of the internalized employment relationship. First, to understand the origins of this recent but now ubiquitous institution, we review competing theoretical accounts of its emergence and evolution. Second, we explore the scope of variations in the employment relationship and their embeddedness in interlocking societal institutions. Third, as the employment relationship is at the centre of processes of restructuring and change, we review the prospects for the survival of not only the distinctive forms of the internalized employment relationship but also the institution of internalized employment itself.

CONTRACT FOR SERVICES AND CONTRACT OF SERVICE: THE DEVELOPMENT OF THE INTERNALIZED EMPLOYMENT RELATIONSHIP

The origins and evolution of the employment relationship have attracted interest from different disciplines and political perspectives. The main dividing line between competing accounts lies, however, not so much in discipline or political orientation, but in whether the evolution is understood as driven by the functional needs of the capitalist system or as an outcome of a dynamic process of tension and struggle between competing interests. A variety of 'rational choice' or functionalist explanations for the rise of the internalized employment relationship have been offered; for theorists of the firm such as Coase (1937) it provides organizing authority; for neo-institutional economists, such as Williamson (1975), it emerged and survives as an institution because it economizes on transaction costs; for Marx and Marxists it is the basis for the extraction of surplus value, and the emergence of the integrated firm is explained as the means to obtain control over the labour process (Marglin 1974; Friedman 1977). The functionalism derives from the prevailing assumption that the institution emerges to meet an economic need and survives until it is no longer of economic use, or in the case of Marxists, until there is a change in the accumulation regime. Even the regulationist school theorists, despite their historical and broad approach, can be considered, certainly in their earliest formulations (Boyer 1979), to have embraced a rather functionalist perspective in hypothesizing a neat matching between the micro- and macro-needs of the regime of accumulation.

The main opposing stand is to view the rise of the internalized employment relationship as the outcome of wider and more complex processes than that of agents acting in line with economic efficiency imperatives, whether macro or micro in origin. Here the move from more spot contracting or putting out systems to more open-ended employment contracts, underpinned by guarantees of wages and working hours, can be regarded as the outcome of conflicts and subsequent compromises between capital and labour. In some cases these compromises, as in France, are mediated by the state (Supiot 2001). The employment relationship is by nature a contested institution that has evolved to achieve cooperation between capital and labour in productive activities through mediating their conflicting interests with respect both to control and distribution.

The historical study of industrial relations provides support for the notion that the institution of the standard employment relationship is the manifestation of a compromise between competing interests and logics. Its development provided workers with some security of both employment and income, a tendency that was reinforced by the greater opportunities for the development of collective representation within workplaces that were based on stable employment relationships than in spot markets and fragmented putting out systems. Thus it was through collective organization that the compromise was both effected and consolidated (Jacoby 1984, Rubery 1978). These benefits to labour are notwithstanding the scope it provided for greater direct managerial control over the labour process.

Not only has the institution emerged out of conflict but its evolution has varied among countries and legal systems. Work by Deakin and colleagues suggests that in the UK the rules of the formal employment relationship emerged after industrialization and in fact evolved out of 'the quasi-penal master servant model' that preceded internalized employment relationships (Deakin and Wilkinson 2005). In contrast, in France, private law codes were both introduced before widespread industrialization and were based on a concept of equality between worker and employer that was notably absent in the UK case, where priority was given to the ownership rights of employers (Deakin et al. 2007). These differences in legal approaches continue to influence the nature of the employment relationship, with stronger employment protection offered under the civil law codes than the common law system in the UK.

However, while the common law system, as prevails in the UK, allows for continuous and incremental change through case law in the definition of the employment relationship to meet changing conditions, recent work has pointed to considerable change and adaptability within the apparently more rigid civil law systems such as are found in continental Europe (Deakin et al. 2007). Differences in the employment relationship are not therefore only, or primarily, explained by the legal origins of different national models.

A further major influence on the evolution of the employment relationship is social policy. In the UK it was the formalizing of the welfare state that triggered in turn the formalization of a contractual continuous employment relationship (Deakin and Wilkinson 2005). In most welfare systems eligibility conditions for social protection and health benefits as well as taxation rules are linked in various ways to the form of the employment relationship, with the standard full-time employment relationship often privileged over other contracts. As Supiot explains:

the core feature of the (Fordist) model, present everywhere to some extent, is the crucial importance of standard full-time non-temporary wage contracts (particularly the adult men), centring around the trade-off between high levels of subordination and disciplinary control on the part of the employer and high levels of stability and welfare/insurance compensations and guarantees for the employee (extended to family members as a result of the high, homogeneous existence of stable forms of nuclear households).   (2001: 1)

The incidence of other contract forms, such as part-time work, will be influenced by whether eligibility and taxation rules distinguish between work on a part-time (or low income) basis and other forms of employment. Such distinctions serve to embed social relationships—such as the male breadwinner model of household organization—in both the organization of employment and the welfare system, thereby creating potential problems of adjustment to changing social relations, including household arrangements.

The evolution of the employment relationship as an institution is also linked to the development of the economic system and its associated institutional framework. The employment relationship itself is a dynamic relationship, subject to constant renewal and renegotiation. One reason for the use of an open-ended internalized contract is the difficulty of anticipating the changes that will be required, but which will inevitably occur. Not only is the agreed content of the work tasks subject to continuous evolution, with changes in products, technologies, and clients, but the implied contract with respect to reward for labour is also constantly under review. The terms of the exchange are subject to a range of internal and external influences; the cost of the contract to employers varies according to the product price, revealed productivity, and the opportunity cost of new hires, particularly for skilled workers. While the value of the contract to employees depends upon retail price inflation and, in contexts where labour is regarded as mobile,[1] on the relative change in earnings for other employees both within the organization and in other segments of the economy.

This evolution also establishes precedents and practices that may be used in future renewals of the employment relationship. For many economic theorists, the use of custom and practice in shaping the employment relationship has been viewed as a source of rigidity and evidence of lack of adaptation to change (Hicks 1932), but a more interesting conceptualization is found in the industrial relations literature, where appeal to custom and practice and precedent are part of the dynamic bargaining that takes place over a changing wage-effort relationship (Marsden 1986; Brown 1973).

The development of the open-ended employment relationship has also been identified as a means of resolving two key dilemmas for capital, namely that labour retains its own free will and that any investment in skills and knowledge remains under the control of labour, whoever funds the investment in the first place. For Marsden (1999) the internalized employment relationship provides benefits for both employees and employers by providing 'a very flexible form of coordination and a platform for investing in skills', thereby providing a basis for resolving both dilemmas. Employees accept control in return for the security offered by the employing organizations and the open-ended employment relationship provides a basis on which firms may at least share the costs of investment in skills, as they may be able both to recoup the investment through the higher productivity of the workforce and capture the knowledge developed within their own internalized routines, thereby creating the basis for firm-specific comparative advantage. These benefits apply particularly in the case of firm-specific skills. On this basis, Marsden views it as one of the two great innovations behind the rise of the modern enterprise.[2]

Significantly, for Marsden, it is not simply the internalized employment relationship but its elaboration into a set of work rules that provides the basis for the key institutions—which he labels an employment system. He shows that there are alternative methods of resolving the key control and skill development dilemmas, but that these choices are embedded in societal arrangements, thereby constraining choice at the organization level (see below for further details). Likewise Whitley (1999) provides a categorization of different dominant work systems linked to interest group formation. Societal variations in the dominant form of the employment relationship can thus be expected to reflect not only societal differences in social status systems and welfare benefit arrangements but also societal differences in education and training systems (Crouch et al. 1999) and in interest group formation including industrial relations (Whitley 1999) which in turn influence the form of work organization.

The multiple functions served by the employment relationship and its embedding in contested relationships allow considerable scope for the employment relationship

---

[1] See below for differences between societies where employment tends to be for life and those where some mobility between employing organizations is possible.

[2] The other being the notion of a limited corporation.

to vary both in content and meaning between 'varieties of capitalism'. Such variations may be in part unplanned and subject to happenchance in their origins but nevertheless become embedded in the complex interactions between the production systems, the welfare state system, and the family system. As such, the particular form of the employment relationship cannot be clearly separated from the other institutional arrangements that underpin the particular national business system or welfare state arrangement.

Variations in the Form of the Employment Relationship: The Impact of Different Institutional Contexts

The range of variation in the form of the employment relationship is explored in this section. Where the employment relationship as an institution is highly codified and places strong limits on the discretion of employers, particularly with respect to termination of employment, there may be incentives for the maintenance of non-standard employment or contracts for services, although these incentives may be offset by strong enforcement of regulation across all employment forms.[3] There will also be variation in the extent of standardization within countries—by sector, region, or employment status group.

To capture variation within as well as between societal systems we draw on the insights of both the varieties of capitalism/societal effect schools (Hall and Soskice 2001; Maurice et al. 1986, Maurice and Sorge 2000), and labour market segmentation theory (see Rubery 2007), thereby explicitly recognizing divisions by sector and firm, class, gender, etc. These divisions emerge not only out of the incentives and opportunities created by societal level institutional arrangements to remain outside standard employment relationships, but also out of the specific historical developments and logics within different types of sectors and employing organizations. Again interactions are present; for example, the more the formal employment system has evolved as an exclusive system, oriented towards the male worker as a prime breadwinner, the more likely it is that the excluded group will be engaged in more informal work such as homeworking.

To simplify the analysis, the issues of variations within and across countries will be explored with respect to four key dimensions to the internalized employment

---

[3] Non-standard employment may be brought within the regulatory net through action to control the organizations providing non-standard employment or formalization may work though social norms and welfare state arrangements that reduce the supply of people willing to work outside employment arrangements, within the social protection/legal regulation net.

relationship. The first is 'employment security' as the internalized contract is in principle open-ended, but with varying degrees of security attached. The second is 'working time' as the contract involves the exchange of labour time, normally consolidated into standard working days. The third is the 'degree of autonomy' afforded to employees and the consequent limits on employer control. The fourth is the 'reward for employment', not only the wage but also the link to social protection[4] received in return for participating in the contract. The discussion under each heading focuses both on the extent of diversity across countries and on recent experiences and practices of change that may be occurring through changes in the institution of the employment relationship itself, associated institutions such as legal frameworks, welfare systems, education and training provision, or in the composition of both job structures and labour supply groups.

Security of employment

The protection provided by law with respect to the security of the employment relationship has been adopted as the primary indicator for describing varieties of employment systems by international agencies and by market economists. The OECD has a well developed and sophisticated index of employment protection (see Table 17.1) which distinguishes between employment rights for those on open-ended contracts and the regulations surrounding the use of non-standard employment contracts, such as temporary and fixed term. The implied position of the OECD is that the 'employment at will' doctrine found in the US is the appropriate norm against which to measure the protection offered in more rigid—and by implication less efficient—employment systems. The index now includes three dimensions of employment security; protection against individual dismissals, regulation of temporary contracts, and regulation of collective dismissals. Although the general direction has been towards less employment protection, much of this has come from deregulation of temporary contracts and there remain significant differences between countries both in overall scores and in their rankings across the three dimensions to the index. Furthermore the countries normally regarded as liberal economies—particularly the US, UK, Canada, and New Zealand—have the lowest scores.

The high level of formal protection offered to those on open-ended contracts in countries such as Spain is used to explain both the high share of workers employed

---

[4] There are a range of dimensions that can be chosen. For the regulationist school—see Boyer (1986)—the rapport salarial relates to the organization of the productive process; the hierarchy of qualifications; the mobility of workers; the principles of wage formation (direct and indirect); and the utilization of wage income (1986: 18). These dimensions reflect the interest of Boyer and others in the periodization of capitalism—across regimes of accumulation. The dimensions chosen here perhaps reflect more varieties within a regime of accumulation and are less concerned with the micro/macro linkages through consumption and more concerned with both varieties of production systems and varieties of social relations and gender regimes.

Table 17.1: Index of employment protection legislation: summary scores

| | 1. Overall strictness of protection against (individual) dismissals | | | 2. Overall strictness of regulation on temporary employment | | | 3. Overall strictness of regulation on collective dismissals | | Overall EPL strictness | | | | |
| | | | | | | | | | Version 1 (based on scores 1 and 2) | | | Version 2 (based on scores 1,2,3) | |
	1990	1998	2003	1990	1998	2003	1998	2003	1990	1998	2003	1998	2003
Australia	1.0	1.5	1.5	0.9	0.9	0.9	2.9	2.9	0.9	1.2	1.2	1.5	1.5
Austria	2.9	2.9	2.4	1.5	1.5	1.5	3.3	3.3	2.2	2.2	1.9	2.4	2.2
Belgium	1.7	1.7	1.7	4.6	2.6	2.6	4.1	4.1	3.2	2.2	2.2	2.5	2.5
Canada	1.3	1.3	1.3	0.3	0.3	0.3	2.9	2.9	0.8	0.8	0.8	1.1	1.1
Czech Republic	–	3.3	3.3	–	0.5	0.5	2.1	2.1	–	1.9	1.9	1.9	1.9
Denmark	1.5	1.5	1.5	3.1	1.4	1.4	3.9	3.9	2.3	1.4	1.4	1.8	1.8
Finland	2.8	2.3	2.2	1.9	1.9	1.9	2.6	2.6	2.3	2.1	2.0	2.2	2.1
France	2.3	2.3	2.5	3.1	3.6	3.6	2.1	2.1	2.7	3.0	3.0	2.8	2.9
Germany	2.6	2.7	2.7	3.8	2.3	1.8	3.5	3.8	3.2	2.5	2.2	2.6	2.5
Greece	2.5	2.3	2.4	4.8	4.8	3.3	3.3	3.3	3.6	3.5	2.8	3.5	2.9
Hungary	–	1.9	1.9	–	0.6	1.1	2.9	2.9	–	1.3	1.5	1.5	1.7
Ireland	1.6	1.6	1.6	0.3	0.3	0.6	2.4	2.4	0.9	0.9	1.1	1.2	1.3

Italy	1.8	1.8	1.8	5.4	3.6	2.1	4.9	4.9	3.6	2.7	1.9	3.1	2.4
Japan	2.4	2.4	2.4	1.8	1.6	1.3	1.5	1.5	2.1	2.0	1.8	1.9	1.8
Korea	–	2.4	2.4	–	1.7	1.7	1.9	1.9	–	2.0	2.0	2.0	2.0
Mexico	–	2.3	2.3	–	4.0	4.0	3.8	3.8	–	3.1	3.1	3.2	3.2
Netherlands	3.1	3.1	3.1	2.4	1.2	1.2	3.0	3.0	2.7	2.1	2.1	2.3	2.3
New Zealand	–	1.4	1.7	–	0.4	1.3	0.4	0.4	–	0.9	1.5	0.8	1.3
Norway	2.3	2.3	2.3	3.5	3.1	2.9	2.9	2.9	2.9	2.7	2.6	2.7	2.6
Poland	–	2.2	2.2	–	0.8	1.3	4.1	4.1	–	1.5	1.7	1.9	2.1
Portugal	4.8	4.3	4.2	3.4	3.0	2.8	3.6	3.6	4.1	3.7	3.5	3.7	3.5
Slovak Republic	–	2.5	2.3	–	1.1	0.4	3.8	4.0	–	1.8	1.3	2.2	1.7
Spain	3.9	2.6	2.6	3.8	3.3	3.5	3.1	3.1	3.8	2.9	3.1	3.0	3.1
Sweden	2.9	2.9	2.9	4.1	1.6	1.6	4.5	4.5	3.5	2.2	2.2	2.6	2.6
Switzerland	1.2	1.2	1.2	1.1	1.1	1.1	3.9	3.9	1.1	1.1	1.1	1.6	1.6
Turkey	–	2.6	2.6	–	4.9	4.9	1.6	2.4	–	3.8	3.7	3.4	3.5
United Kingdom	0.9	0.9	1.1	0.3	0.3	0.4	2.9	2.9	0.6	0.6	0.7	1.0	1.1
United States	0.2	0.2	0.2	0.3	0.3	0.3	2.9	2.9	0.2	0.2	0.2	0.7	0.7

Source: OECD Employment Outlook 2004. Data for Slovak Republic have been revised since the publication.

on non-standard or temporary contracts and the low overall employment rate, as employers are apparently dissuaded from 'permanent' employment creation by the potential costs of lay-off. However, the index treats the degree of employment security within the institution of the employment relationship as a function primarily of legal regulations. It is, though, not only legal rules but how these are understood and implemented that matters. To take the example of Spain, the trend towards reduction in employment protection for those on standard employment contracts has only had a limited effect on the use of temporary contracts (Amuedo-Dorantes 2001). This suggests that the decision as to which contract to use depends not only on a strict economic calculation of costs and risks but is also influenced by social norms; whatever the legal rules and associated direct costs of termination, employees on open-ended contracts in Spain expect these contracts to be permanent. Similar arguments can be made to explain the tendency of the public sector in the UK to make greater use of temporary contracts than the private sector (Kersley et al. 2006); in practice the legal protection offered to employees is low and similar between both employment forms, but public sector employers are aware of social expectations that public sector employment should be permanent unless jobs are explicitly signalled as temporary.

Even in the US the security of employment tends to be higher than might be expected, given the employment at will legal system. Indeed over time there has been some modification made in legal protection at state level to reflect the practices by which employers tend to provide guarantees of employment security for those performing at adequate levels of productivity, and to use due process in the termination of employment (Muhl 2001). In the US the risk of individual litigation on issues of race and gender equality has also been a major factor prompting employers to adopt institutionalized procedures with respect to grievance and dismissal (Dobbin et al. 1993; Piore and Safford 2006).

Thus, the extent of variation in the employment protection can not simply be read off from directly-related legal rules. The need for employers to motivate labour and induce loyalty and commitment to the organization tends to provide for some degree of protection in practice, even where this protection is not vested in the law. Thus trends towards deregulation of employment protection may have less impact on practice in those countries and organizations where the social norm of permanent employment is deeply embedded such as in Japan. Likewise, weakening of social norms or changes in mechanisms of enforcement may result in changes in effective employment protection, independently of changes in legal rules. In Britain, for example, employment protection was effectively ensured through trade union action prior to 1971 when unfair dismissal legislation was first introduced, although of course limited to well-organized sectors. The weakening of this legal regulation in the 1980s took on greater importance because of the decline in trade union power and presence.

Differences between societies with respect to collective dismissals' protection may result in even greater variations in practice. Legislation is a key determinant both of the procedures through which dismissals have to be agreed and the compensation payable. However, there is still a major role played here by social norms and shared understandings. The so-called job for life system in Japan has been established and maintained by social convention rather than by legislation. Problems of excess capacity and/or reduced productivity of individual workers are still mainly coped with through transfers to subcontracting organizations and by reduced hiring (Kato 2001).

Institutional arrangements and mechanisms used for adjusting employment to demand are often strongly linked to other institutional characteristics of the employment system. The focus in Germany on consultation and co-determination puts the works council at the forefront of negotiations over possible redundancies, and options for redeployment are explored at the workplace level before redundancies are called for. In France it is the state that gets involved in the approval process for collective dismissals, thereby following the model of France as state-led capitalism (Bosch 1992; Schmidt 2002). The available support for dismissed workers also influences practice; where there are state subsidized periods of temporary lay-offs, organizations are more likely to resort to temporary lay-offs, even of staff whom they are anxious to retain in the long term owing to their skills and knowledge.

This system is taken to the extreme in Denmark where the state provides generous support for staff laid off by companies, many of whom are frequently rehired. The costs of insecurity are thereby shared by the society through taxation to support the so-called flexicurity system (Madsen 2004). Analysing the degree of employment protection offered thus requires an understanding both of the institutions that provide alternative modes of support and of the behaviour of employers with respect to re-employment of laid-off workers, and so cannot be limited simply to the issue of dismissals or labour turnover.

The codification of the open-ended or standard employment relationship and its associated level of employment protection has its counterpart in the definition of other forms of employment that may stand outside these legal and social norms. One of the objectives of recent European initiatives in the area of non-standard employment has been to encourage member states to reduce the gap in legal protection between standard and non-standard employment. Directives providing for non-discrimination compared to full-time or permanent employees have been passed for part-time workers and staff on fixed term contracts but a similar directive for agency workers is still blocked at European level. These attempts to 'normalize' and improve protection for flexible working have been introduced alongside a general policy to reduce the degree of legal protection afforded to those on full-time and open-ended contracts, thereby promoting harmonization of protection from above and below. However, the spread and extent of non-standard forms is not simply related to regulation of employment; also important are the form of the family and the welfare system and indeed the organization of the production model, as we discuss further below.

Time and the employment relationship

While the codification of security attached to the employment contract provides workers with protection against the cessation of work opportunities, the struggles around working time have been aimed both at ensuring that employers provided regular work in continuous working days and at reducing the risks of employees working long hours, according to the dictates of the contracting employer. That is, the development of an internalized employment relationship involved the agreement to work under the control of the employer for regular and predictable periods of time, with time limits, and regulations that needed to be observed by both employees and managers (Thompson 1967). Where management wished to breach the time limits—by requesting overtime or unsocial working hours—the cost was the payment not only of additional hourly wages but also a premium rate for extra or unsocial hours. Work that interfered with shared family and community leisure time—for example, Sunday work—has been particularly likely to be paid at premium rates.

Although the regulation of working time has been important in all capitalist societies, the particular emphasis placed on elements of working time norms and regulations have varied between societies and indeed among types of sectors, firms, and labour force groups. These variations may be attributed to both different institutional arrangements and differences in actors' orientations, even though separation of these effects is both empirically and theoretically complex (see Jackson this volume). There are major differences in the focus of union actions in, for example, Germany, France, and the UK. In the former two countries, the main orientation has been to reduce working hours to protect shared leisure time and to use working time reductions to alleviate unemployment. In the UK campaigns to reduce the standard working week have been used as much to change the wage-effort bargain and to improve the prospects for overtime working (Rubery 1998). These differences in orientation arise out of differences in opportunities for trade unions to influence the wage-effort bargain.

In the UK, campaigns to reduce working time have been used at the local level to increase earnings from overtime, but in France the main space for union action has been to influence the policy of national governments, including state regulation of working hours and there has therefore not been the same link back to pay bargaining. In Germany, the focus on shared leisure time is found not just in working time negotiations but also in regulations governing private activities—including restrictions on shopping time and mowing lawns on Sundays. Trade unions, in supporting these regulations, may be regarded as reflecting and reinforcing social norms. Differences in social norms with respect to leisure time and family life are also evident in the greater emphasis in most of Europe on extending paid holiday entitlements, in contrast to the US and Japan where short holidays, or working through holiday entitlement, is much more commonplace. However, up until the 1970s it was the US where working times were shorter and paid holidays longer, indicating the potential for changes in social norms and practices (Schettkat 2003).

Differences in social norms, regulation, and actors' orientations can also be found with respect to non-standard working time arrangements. Variations in the utilization of part-time work, for example, are first of all related to differences in the historical integration of women into the wage economy and the associated gender division of labour; Finland has few part-time workers compared to Germany as women were integrated directly from full-time work in agriculture to full-time work in industry and services (Pfau-Effinger 1998). Variations in incidence also reflect social protection regulations; many societies have traditionally linked access to social protection to employment status as full-time continuous employees, thereby reinforcing distinctions between standard and non-standard working time contracts. In the USA part-time workers are often excluded from health benefits, a practice that has not been found to be discriminatory, unlike similar exclusions in Europe which have fallen foul of European laws on equal treatment for women and men, which allow for indirect as well as direct discrimination. As a consequence part-time work is an employment form more confined to students and disadvantaged workers and a less common employment form of choice for prime age women in the US (Drago et al. 2007).

Actors' orientations have also been significant. In southern Europe in particular (Karamessini 2008), part-time and other forms of non-standard work have been regarded by trade unions as a threat to the standard employment relationship and the associated protection of employment and income, independent of the availability of work. The EU has pressed member states through legislation and through its soft law policies to reduce the barriers to part-time work that were set up in many member states where part-time was regarded as not only an unattractive model for the participant but an illegitimate form of employment relationship. While there is now some harmonization of employment and social protection legislation, there are still substantive differences among European countries in attitudes towards, and the employment conditions of, non-standard workers, in part associated as Supiot (2001: 223) points out, with whether the development of non-standard working has emerged from a process of collective bargaining as has been the case in, for example, the Netherlands.

Authority, work organization, and the employment relationship

The legal and social norms associated with the employment relationship both influence and are influenced by modes of skill development and utilization. The prime division is between internal labour market systems, which provide a basis for firm-specific skill development, and occupational labour markets, where employees develop skills and competences that are recognized as general skills by alternative employing organizations. Occupational labour markets are often supported by the formation of strong interest groups that operate outside of employing organizations (Whitley 1999), while internal labour markets are shaped by the employing organizations themselves. The institutional configurations associated with the development of either strong internal labour market systems or strong occupational labour markets are both demanding and specific, and many countries and even sectors or organizations in practice operate hybrid systems (Rubery and Grimshaw 2003). Internal labour market systems are based on institutional arrangements that minimize the risk of poaching and provide employees with long-term employment guarantees. Here the prime example is post-war Japan but the extended recession from 1990 and other factors have led to questioning of the survival of the job for life system even within the large employer segment.

Strong occupational labour markets require employers to recognize common qualifications and to organize their job structures to facilitate the transfer of labour between organizations. Again there are problems faced by the key exemplars of the occupational labour market systems—Germany and Austria—in maintaining employer commitment to training, but the close connection between job category and the training/qualification of the employee has been largely maintained (Gangl 2001). Attempts to transfer such pure systems to other institutional contexts have, however, proved very difficult due to the need to align not only systems of education and training with workforce expectations but also to ensure employer design of jobs and pay structures supports an occupational system (Marsden 1986).

The emergence of the different institutional arrangements for skill development has been interpreted through different lenses. Mainstream and transaction costs economists (Williamson 1975), and even some segmentation theorists (Doeringer and Piore 1971), attribute the emergence of internal labour markets to employers' rational search for mechanisms to protect investment in firm-specific skills. These explanations do not account for the use of different 'solutions' to the issue of skill development found across countries for similar sectors. Moreover, instead of the rational employer account, where internal labour markets were established by employers to protect their investments, an alternative interepretation is that these internal labour market systems emerged as a consequence of the success of trade unions in requiring employers to offer more continuous and protected employment to replace practices of spot market contracting (Jacoby 1984, Osterman 1994). Occupational labour markets tend to be reinforced by a system of licences to practice and thus may be dependent upon both legal regulations and the historical development of both training and accreditation systems. Where occupational labour markets are not reinforced by external accreditation tied into the vocational training and the education system but instead are reliant on trade union organization of the craft labour process—as in the UK—they have been the most open to erosion through employer strategies of work reorganization.

The form of skill development adopted by country and, indeed, sector is closely associated with and reinforced by other institutional dimensions to the employment relationship. Pay systems, collective bargaining arrangements, and trade union organization will all be influenced by whether the primary organizing concept is occupation and skill qualification, on the one hand, or organizational identity and seniority, on the other. Marsden's (1999) theory of employment systems seeks to demonstrate that different systems of skill development are linked to different systems of work organization and authority systems; thus the 'production' 'approach' more clearly related to internal labour markets tends to 'mould men to tasks', while under the 'training approach' linked to occupational labour markets, tasks are organized according to their similarities in training requirements.

Marsden also allows for differences within these two approaches; the more Taylorist task-centred production approach is associated with countries such as the US where internal labour markets are used but in a weak form and there is less scope for investment in skills (see Table 17.2 and Cappelli et al. 1997). A function-centred approach places emphasis on competences that develop idiosyncratically within a specific internal labour market but, nevertheless, both provide the employee with more scope for discretion and rely on the employee's longer term commitments to the organization—as found in Japan. The training centred approach also has both a weak form—the apprenticeship system in the UK that established job territories but limited skill development—and a strong form, labelled the qualification rule, that is associated with the German occupational training systems where recognized qualifications are the basis for a person-oriented division of responsibilities. Differences in the utilization of these work rules can be expected not only across countries but also across sectors, organizations, and types of workers.

These varieties of approaches to skill development and to work organization also provide for both differences in the scope for acquisition of tacit knowledge and for differences in the strategies of employers to harness tacit knowledge in the interests of the organization. This issue is discussed further below, where we address the implications for varieties of capitalism of these different institutional forms. Here we should note that the ways in which employees are managed and controlled are strongly associated with the system of skill development and work organization. Hierarchical internal labour market systems are more likely to draw on managerial expertise, including people management skills, while occupational labour market systems tend to develop task-continuous status hierarchies where supervisors' knowledge and competences match or exceed those of the supervisee (Maurice et al. 1986, Offe 1976).

Employee voice mechanisms constitute another dimension to the management control system (Dundon et al. 2004). One of the key differences between varieties of

Table 17.2: Marsden's varieties of employment systems

	Production approach	Training approach
Task-centred rules	Work post (e.g. France, US)	Job territory (e.g. Britain)
Function-centred rules	Competence rank (e.g. Japan)	Qualification rule (e.g. Germany)

Source: Based on Marsden (1999).

capitalism is in the use of employee voice mechanisms. These differences in part reflect different provision for employee voice in formal regulations at national or pan-national level; examples at national level include Germany's co-determination laws and at pan-national level, the EU directives on information and consultation. The impact of regulations also depends on social norms and political ideologies, with Germany's emphasis on co-determination in line with the wider institutions of consensus and non-market coordination. However, there may also be differences within countries on the importance that organizations place on systems that promote voice over exit (Freeman and Medoff 1984).

Reward and the employment relationship

Reward patterns are the outcome of institutions for pay setting; such institutions in most societies involve formal pay and grading systems, although the degree of formality and their constitution at national, sectoral, organizational, or occupational level will vary among, and indeed within, societies. These grading structures and their mode of operation tend to be strongly influenced by social norms with respect to the principles upon which pay is awarded; pay structures may be differentiated by qualification of the employee (e.g. separate pay scales for graduates), status (separate pay structures for blue- and white-collar workers), performance (individuals or group grading or bonuses), seniority (pay increments by years of service), age (age-related scales), family position (supplements for children or spouses), timing and length of working hours (different pay and benefits of part-timers) etc. Systems of reward are linked to social welfare systems (for example, the link between pay and pensions), to social and family systems (for example the embedding of gender discrimination in pay systems), and to production systems and employment security (for example, so-called 'deferred reward' systems can be more readily used in job for life systems and to reward staff with firm-specific skills).

Pay and reward systems may also influence the utilization of particular types of labour; for example an incentive for taking on non-standard employees in the past was that they tended to be excluded from elements of reward including pensions and other fringe benefits. Such discrimination within the same employing organization is now not allowed within the EU but is legal in the US. However, this does not necessarily lead to an increase in part-time workers as many employees are reluctant to take on part-time work if it does not provide access to important health insurance benfits. Thus, the take-up of opportunities for cost reduction is conditioned in turn by social norms and more specifically by the availability of a labour supply that accepts exclusion from social protection and other employment rights.

There are pressures for change in internal pay structures related to the use of alternative forms of employment and different sources of labour supply. These pressures are towards more individualized pay, less seniority pay, and less time-based pay (replaced by more results-based pay and fewer unsocial hours payments

(Rubery et al. 2005)) but scope still remains for divergence in norms and principles and in the range of pay across societies. There are also pressures to 'equalize' costs and risks associated with standard and non-standard employment within the EU. These include not only upward harmonization of employment protection and social security rules for non-standard workers but also reductions in the income security enjoyed by those on standard contracts (Supiot 2001), for example, through greater emphasis on performance-conditional pay and towards lower guaranteed pension entitlements. Nevertheless, significant differences in risk and entitlements remain between internalized standard employees and non-standard employees related to both formal and informal practices that distinguish between employment forms.

PRESSURES FOR CHANGE IN THE FORM OF THE EMPLOYMENT RELATIONSHIP

Pressures for change in the employment relationship raise two main issues for institutional analysis. First, are these pressures leading to a greater convergence in employment forms and if so, what are the prospects for the survival of distinct forms of employment organization, and therefore for the survival of divergent varieties of capitalism? This is the question addressed in the first part of this section. In the second section we consider the survival of the notion of a standard internalized employment relationship in the context of the growth of non-standard forms of employment.

Changes in the employment relationship and the implications for varieties of capitalism

The institutional form of the employment relationship is both multi-faceted and embedded in a range of social and economic institutions at a micro- and macro-level. The complexity of this institutionalization of the employment relationship provides a firm foundation for the proposition that there has been, and continues to be, scope for the development of divergent paths for capitalism (Hall and Soskice 2001; Whitley 1999). However, close analysis of the development of the specific form of the employment relationship suggests that the complementarities between and the interlocking of national institutional arrangements should not be overstressed. Firstly, the origins of these different forms of employment relations appear to be found in specific conjunctural factors and not in planned developments of different forms of capitalism; for example, the job for life system in Japan that became the backbone of the Japanese production model came into existence, according to Weiss (1993), through the actions of the state that sought to safeguard Japanese military interests in the Second World War period and was not linked to strategies of employers to develop a particular form of Japanese production model.

Similarly, the lack of legal employment protection in the UK is not to be explained by a dominant free market model with no countervailing power against employer prerogative but by the preference for a collective laissez faire system among both trade unions and by employers over a formal, legally enforceable labour code (Sisson 1987; Deakin and Wilkinson 2005). This approach allowed unions, where they were strong at the workplace level, to exercise their maximum strength but at the expense of the establishment and enforcement of a common minimum set of employment conditions and protection. Employee voice mechanisms in Germany were brought in as part of the post-Second World War settlement and not because they would sustain the high trust relations needed for diversified quality manufacturing (Roe 2003).

Secondly, although the emergence of interlocking institutional arrangements may provide a constraint on change, there is a danger in overstressing stability due to ever present conflicts and contradictions that may generate pressures to unpick or rework the institutional framework. The notion that within a variety of capitalism there may be not only a dominant but also dormant or deviant modes has been recently explored by Crouch and Keune (2005) to explain the ease by which the UK moved from a Keynesian and voluntaristic mode of production to a monetarist neo-liberal mode under Thatcher. The exclusion of the powerful City from the previous prevailing consensus was identified as providing an important source of support for her transformation agenda. Moreover, even those agents of capital that did acquiesce in the Keynesian and voluntarist mode were also willing to challenge the accepted mode of regulation once they perceived a new opportunity to rebalance power between capital and labour.[5]

Four main reasons can be suggested for the increased scepticism in recent years over the viability of alternative modes of employment organization and the associated varieties of capitalism. The first relates to the dominance of the standard employment form, as identified in typologies and comparative analyses. Ever since the surge of interest in comparative research, following the development of the societal effect school (Maurice et al. 1986) and the parallel interest in varieties of capitalism (Hall and Soskice 2001), there have been references to the problems of making comparisons between countries without reference to varieties within countries between sectors and types of firms (Hollingsworth et al. 1994). The focus in most comparative work was on the dominant sector, large firm manufacturing (sometimes in fact the car industry), that was considered to be the driving force in the economy. The growth of services as the dominant force in most advanced economies means that this argument can no longer hold sway; manufacturing

---

[5] This possibility allows for agency on the part of employers that is not present in versions of varieties of capitalism that stress the complementarities of the arrangements and downplay the continuing tensions between competing interests (Lane 2000).

cannot be the only area of interest and there is therefore an increased need to recognize the diversity between sectors and types of organization. The issue is not just that there may be a need for more heterogeneous employment arrangements but also that those institutions that support productive employment arrangements in manufacturing could inhibit the development of strong services sectors.

For example, the debate in Germany questions whether the successful manufacturing mode is creating problems for the growth and development of a more flexible service economy. Within the service economy, it is unclear if there will be a trend towards more egalitarian, team-based and flexible systems or towards new forms of polarization between high skilled and low skilled, low discretion work. However, the outcome will depend on trends in industrial organization, whether towards complex forms of network organization, based on varieties of outsourcing arrangements, or towards a reintegration of production systems to facilitate internal flexibility and the development of internal resource-based comparative advantage. Divergent tendencies may well be found at both national and sectoral level.

The second factor in the debate is the increased permeability of national employment and business systems, through trade, production chains, and international ownership. These developments not only place systems in more direct and short-term competition with each other but also lead to the introduction of actors—for example, foreign-owned MNCs—who have neither been party to nor have any real interest in the forms of social compromise that have underpinned the joint development of employment and welfare systems. Furthermore, MNCs may also bring into the national environment ways of doing things and ways of viewing current practices that challenge existing arrangements and may result in a wider variety of modes of employment arrangements existing within a national boundary. This diversity of course remains constrained by the need to meet legal requirements and to fit to some degree with some customary expectations in the host country. The introduction of new practices may also spill over on to practices in domestic companies. Much of the research around the impact of Japanese transplants has also studied the impact of the Japanese owned transplants not only on the transplants themselves but also on locally owned firms; in both cases there is evidence of hybridization but the foreign owned plants tend to follow more closely the practices in the home country, while the domestic plants adopt new practices in a more ad hoc and opportunistic fashion (Doeringer et al. 1998). The overall trend appears to be towards hybridization and the presence of both home and host country effects. Again much of this work has concentrated on manufacturing and rather little is known about the impact of transplants on employment practices in services.

The third factor is the growth of pan-national regulatory and ideological influences that are shaping policy at national level and questioning therefore the survival of distinct employment arrangements within national boundaries. Notions of one best way of managing employment emanates not only from business schools but also from international think tanks such as the OECD whose influential Jobs Study in 1994 provided a legitimation for governments to start or to continue to pursue a process of flexibilization of employment security and a process of reducing wage and social protection. A more direct influence on European economies has come from the European Employment Strategy under which all European countries have in principle signed up to pursuing a common set of guidelines in the interests of modernizing both the employment and the welfare dimensions of their specific social model (Rubery et al. 2008). All member states have adopted to some degree the notions of activation, flexibility, make work pay, and even gender equality as principles around which they should refashion their employment and welfare arrangements. These agendas have direct relevance for various aspects of the employment relationship; for security, working time, reward, and for divisions between these in standard and non-standard employment.

The fourth factor to challenge the survival of traditional dominant modes of employment organization is the changing composition of the labour force. One trend is towards both a higher qualified and potentially more individualistically oriented labour force. Another is towards an increasingly internationally mobile segment of the workforce, both among the higher and the lower qualified. These trends may lead to a rethink of institutional modes of recruitment, management, and career development. For example, interest in international mobility could reduce commitments by the educated elite to nationally-specific employment arrangements such as the job for life system in Japan. Likewise, employee voice systems as developed in countries such as Germany primarily around the traditions of craft labour may need to be reshaped to meet the interests of more individualistic graduate employees. Further, the increased flows of migrants even from within the EU may be seen to provide alternative sources of skilled labour, reducing commitments to internal training systems such as the German dual training system.

Another major trend is towards a much higher rate of feminization of the labour force. This increase in female labour may raise issues of the survival of the standard employment relationship, particularly where this is strongly tied to full-time continuous employment (Vosko 2006). While there are a number of examples of societies that have moved to a dual full-time earner family system, it might be more appropriate for societies to rethink the standard employment model to allow more variations in hours of work for both men and women over the life cycle without the incurrence of major penalties in wages and career prospects. However, such developments require a renewed political will to reshape the institution of the employment relationship to meet changing gender roles and aspirations. Certainly, the growth of female employment has meant that the non-standard employee can in most societies no longer be regarded as a marginal employment form. As a consequence such policies that have been based on exclusion of certain types of employment from employment security or social protection may become less and less acceptable. Extended life expectancy and the challenges this poses for both the timing and the funding of retirement is another factor requiring a rethinking of standard employment arrangements.

Under these four sets of factors, there is a clear likelihood that we will see wider varieties of forms of employment within national boundaries and the possible disappearance of an overwhelmingly dominant form of employment organization. The development of services and the changing composition of the labour force have served to highlight a heterogeneity that was already present. However, the sectors that were previously marginalized are now moving to centre stage. There is still scope for variations in the degree of heterogeneity within countries; the stronger and more inclusive the national forms of regulation and complementary institutional arrangements, the less scope there is for variations at sector or organizational level. However, the agenda of the European Employment Strategy has been to encourage the weakening of dominant national employment modes and to promote harmonization of protection and rights across the whole range of employment forms. These tendencies do not necessarily point to a simple convergence of employment and welfare models within Europe. The paths being followed by European member states, even if guided in some sense by the principles of the European Employment Strategy, are quite diverse and are having quite different impacts on social and economic outcomes (Jepsen and Serrano Pascual 2006; Rubery et al. 2008). However, these divergences are related primarily to divergent welfare institutions, gender regimes and patterns of domestic labour, and differences in political agendas and policy priorities. The notion at the heart of the varieties of capitalism concept that distinctive employment arrangements may promote comparative advantage in the international economy has not been integrated into the European policy agenda (Rubery et al. 2008). Evidence of convergence is thus weak but the implications of the different paths for future comparative advantage are not yet researched or understood.

Prospects for the institution of the employment relationship

The survival of the notion of a standard employment relationship has been put in question by the growth of network forms of work organization. The knowledge economy, in which the knowledge vested in individuals takes on greater economic significance, could allow these individuals to use their enhanced market power to operate as semi-autonomous workers, possibly on a freelance or self-employment basis. At the extreme it is argued there could be a reversal of the subordinate relationship between employee and employer, with employees holding the power in a knowledge-intensive society (Miles and Snow 1996). These predictions have so far not been well supported by strong trends either towards self-employment or towards evidence of empowerment. Examples of new forms of network relationships that blur the distinctions between employer and employee as in Hollywood (Marsden 1999: 239–40) or Silicon Valley (Saxenian 1996; Barley and Kunda 2004) have not spread to a wide range of sectors or countries.

Moreover, comparative research on the new media industry, an archetypal new knowledge economy sector, has found that the collapse of organization-centred employment careers in favour of freelance work has occurred more in the US than in Sweden or Germany. Furthermore, although the downturn after the 'dot.com bust' around the turn of the century led to more open unemployment in Germany following lay-offs, the high risks absorbed by the workforce in the USA were more disguised as the freelance workers continued to compete for a shrinking supply of work (Christopherson 2004). Thus, while network relationships may under some conditions provide considerable power and autonomy to the workers—for example IT and new media workers in the dot.com boom—in economic downturns they face major economic risks, including lack of work or falling prices for work, and even in the good years will have to devote a large amount of time to securing the new contracts (Christopherson 2004). Issues such as access to welfare benefits and health insurance clearly constrain the development of freelance working arrangements, particularly in the US, even in contexts where workers have considerable power through the importance of their tacit knowledge (Barley and Kunda 2006).

However, while the decline of the internalized employment relationship, even for highly mobile knowledge work, has been exaggerated, some changes to the nature of the internalized employment relationship may be taking place. These changes involve a blurring of the division between contracts of service and con-tracts for service in important respects, as pay and performance for employees rely more on their initiative in generating new business for their employers (Supiot 2001; Collins 2001).

A related development is the consequent tendency for business-to-business con-tracting to impact upon the employer–employee relationship (Marchington et al. 2005). The triangular relationships between employer, employee, and client result in employees often being subject as much to the control of the client as the employer. Indeed, the terms of the business-to-business contract may in many aspects prede-termine the terms of the employment relationship— particularly where performance requirements and rewards are specified in the subcontract. The extent to which the internal employment relationship is influenced by such contracts depends in part on the regulatory framework and social norms. However, it is also the case that in societies such as France, where the historical norm has been for the employer and the state to absorb risks in return for employees' subordination (Supiot 2001), the intrusion of commercial relations into the employment relationship may imply a more significant break with past precedent than in the US or the UK, where the absorption of employee risk has always been less complete.

This discussion of differences in the institutionalization of the employment relationship leads to a second debate and that is the extent to which protections associated with the standard employment relationship should be extended to en-compass non-standard forms. A strategy of extension allows for a widening of social protection and employment security provisions, but at the same time runs the risk of allowing for a weakening of the set of employment and social protections associated with the standard employment relationship. This issue has been at the heart of trade unions' reluctance in many countries to accept part-time work and temporary work as appropriate employment forms. However, erosion of the substantive content and function of an institution can happen through competition between the different forms and there is now widespread acceptance by social partners across Europe that part-time and temporary work should be included within a widened approach to social and employment protection, even though the result may be to reduce the level of protection afforded to full-time or permanent employees.

EU directives have extended protection to workers, not just employees, that is to include those who may be treated as self-employed but who in practice are working as subordinates to an employing organization. The International Labour Organization has also recently passed a recommendation on the employment relationship that recommends the extension of protection to those in disguised employment relationships but upheld the principle that the regulation 'should not interfere with genuine commercial and independent contracting arrangements.' This clause might lead to the continued exclusion of freelance and self-employed workers from employment protection.

However, there are problems in extending the definition of an employment relationship to include all forms of irregular and ambiguous employment statuses. A more inclusive policy could lead to an erosion of some of the key protections that characterize the institutional form, such as the requirement for the employer to provide work and guarantee income on a regular basis. In providing some protection for marginalized non-standard employees, the impact of such a change could be to erode the original form of the institution through 'layering'—to use Streeck and Thelen's (2005) term describing the attachment of new elements to existing institutions, leading to a gradual change in their status and structure.

These questions bring us back to the intertwining of employment and welfare regulations. The variety of these arrangements mean that undoubtedly there will be different responses at national level to the common problems posed by the diversification of employment forms and the increasing unacceptability of a welfare system predicated on a male breadwinner model of family and employment organization. Furthermore, the extent of opportunities to move beyond the internalized employment relationship depends in part on its embeddedness within the welfare and production system. It is perhaps paradoxical that there may be a limit to the growth of self-employment in the US because of the importance of access to health benefits that derives from employee status. Similarly, the Japanese production model is so linked to internalized employment that the issue is more the opportunity to move between employers than the disappearance of the form itself.

Finally, in returning to the issue of the nature of institutional change that is a key theme of this volume, we would argue that the internalized employment relationship provides a good example of processes of incremental change in action. Many of these changes are cumulative and are likely to give rise over time not only to changes in the management of social risks but also to a redistribution of risks away from employers and the state and towards employees or the self-employed. However, this direction of change is not inevitable, not only because of the potential for a swing of the political pendulum to bring employment and social rights back on to the agenda, but also because there are costs to employers as well as benefits from a weakening of the employment relationship as an institution. There is the potential for employers to rediscover the benefits of internalized employment and identify both the costs and the management problems of targeted performance regimes and fragmented contractual arrangements.

REFERENCES

AMUEDO-DORANTES, C. (2001). 'From "Temp-to-Perm": Promoting Permanent Employment in Spain', *International Journal of Manpower* 22 (7): 625–47.

ARTHUR, M. and D. ROUSSEAU (eds.) (1996). *The Boundaryless Career: A New Employment Principle for a New Organizational Era*, (Oxford: Oxford University Press).

BARLEY, S. and G. KUNDA (2004). *Gurus, Hired Guns, and Warm Bodies: Itinerant Experts in a Knowlege Economy*, (Princeton, NJ: Princeton University Press).

————(2006). 'Contracting: A New Form of Professional Practice', *Academy of Management Perspectives* 20(1): 45–66.

BARRETT, M. and M. McINTOSH (1980). 'The "Family Wage": Some Problems for Socialists and Feminists', *Capital and Class* (11) 51–72.

BOSCH, G. (1992). *Retraining—Not Redundancy: Innovative Approaches To Industrial Restructuring in Germany and France*. Geneva: International Institute for Labour Studies.

BOYER R. (1979). 'Wage Formation in Historical Perspective: The French Experience', *Cambridge Journal of Economics* 3: 99–118.

————(1986). *La flexibilité du travail en Europe*, (Paris: La Découverte).

BROWN, C., M. REICH, Y. NAKATA, and L. ULMAN (1997). *Work and Pay in the United States and Japan*, (Oxford: Oxford University Press).

BROWN, W. (1973). *Piecework Bargaining*, (London: Heineman Education).

CAPPELLI, P., L. BASSI, H. KATZ, D. KNOKE, P. OSTERMAN, and M. USEEM (1997). *Change at Work*, (New York: Oxford University Press).

CHRISTOPHERSON, S. (2004). 'The Divergent Worlds of New Media: How Policy Shapes Work in the Creative Economy', *Review of Policy Research* 21(4): 543–58.

COASE, RONALD (1937). 'The Nature of the Firm', *Economica*, 4(16): 386–405.

COLLINS, H. 'Regulating Employment for Competitiveness' (2001). 30 *Industrial Law Journal* 17–47.

CROUCH, C. and M. KEUNE (2005). 'Changing Dominant Practice: Making use of Institutional Diversity in Hungary and the United Kingdom', in W. Streeck and K. Thelen, *Beyond Continuity*, (Oxford, Oxford University Press).

————D. FINEGOLD, and M. SAKO (eds.) (1999). *Are Skills the Answer? The Political Economy of Skill Creation in Advanced Industrial Economies*, (Oxford: Oxford University Press).

DEAKIN, S. and F. WILKINSON (2005). *The Law of the Labour Market*, (Oxford: Oxford University Press).

————P. LELE, and M. SIEMS (2007). 'The Evolution of Labour Law: Calibrating and Comparing Regulatory Regimes', *International Labour Review* 146 (3–4): 133–62.

DOBBIN, F., J. SUTTON, J. MEYER, and R. SCOTT (1993). 'Equal Opportunity Law and the Construction of Internal Labor Markets', *The American Journal of Sociology* 99(2): 396–427.

DOERINGER, P. and M. PIORE (1971). *Internal Labour Markets and Manpower Analysis*, (Lexington, MA., D. C. Heath).

——C. Evans-Klock, and D. Terkla (1998). 'Hybrids or Hodgepodges? Workplace Practices of Japanese and Domestic Startups in the United States', *Industrial and Labor Relations Review* 51(2): 171–86.

Drago, R., A. Pirretti, and R. Scutella, (2007). 'Work and Family Directions in the USA and Australia: A Policy Research Agenda', *Journal of Industrial Relations* 49(1): 49–66.

Dundon, T., A. Wilkinson, and M. Marchington (2004). 'The Meanings and Purpose of Employee Voice', *International Journal of Human Resource Management* 15(6): 1149–70.

Esping-Andersen, G., D. Gallie, A. Hemerijck, and J. Myles (2002). *Why We Need a New Welfare State*, (Oxford: Oxford University Press).

Freeman, R. and J. Medoff (1984). *What Do Unions Do?* (New York: Basic Books).

Friedman, A. (1977). *Industry and Labour*, (London: Macmillan).

Gangl, M. (2001). 'Education and Labour Market Entry across Europe: The Impact of Institutional Arrangements In Training Systems and Labour Markets'. Prepared as part of the TSER project: *Comparative Analysis of Transitions from Education to Work in Europe*, Mannheim, Germany: Centre for European Social Research (MZES). http://www.mzes.uni-mannheim.de/projekte/catewe/papers/PAPER5.pdf.

Hall, P. and D. Soskice (2001). *Varieties of Capitalism. The Institutional Foundations of Comparative Advantage*, (New York: Oxford University Press).

Herrigel, G. and J. Zeitlin (this volume).

Hicks, J. (1932). *The Theory of Wages*, (London: Macmillan).

Hollingsworth, J. R., P. Schmitter, and W. Streeck (1994). *Governing Capitalist Economies: Performance and Control of Economic Sectors*, (New York: Oxford University Press).

ILO (2004). *A Fair Globalization: Creating Opportunities For All*, World Commission on the Social Dimension of Globalization, Geneva: ILO. http://www.ilo.org/public/english/wcsdg/docs/report.pdf.

Jackson, G. (this volume).

Jacoby, S. M. (1984). 'The Development of Internal Labor Markets in American Manufacturing Firms', in P. Osterman (ed.), *Internal Labor Markets*, (Cambridge, MA: MIT Press).

Jepsen, M. and A. Serrano Pascual (2006). 'The concept of the ESM and supranational model building', in M. Jepsen and A. Serrano Pascual (eds.), *Unwrapping the European Social Model*, (Bristol: Policy Press).

Karamessini, M. (2008). 'Continuity and Change in the Southern European Social Model', *International Labour Review* 147(1): 43–70.

Kato, T. (2001). 'The End of Lifetime Employment in Japan?: Evidence from National Surveys and Field Research', *Journal of the Japanese and International Economies* 15: 489–514.

Kersley, B., C. Alpin. J. Forth, A. Bryson. H. Bewley, G. Dix, and S. Oxenbridge (2006). *Inside the Workplace: Findings from the 2004 Workplace Employment Relations Survey*, (London: Routledge).

Lane, C. (2000). 'Understanding the Globalisation Strategies of German and British Multinational Companies: Is a "Societal Effects" Approach Still Useful?', in M. Maurice and A. Sorge (eds.), *Embedding Organizations*, (Amsterdam, John Benjamins Publishing).

Madsen, P. K. (2004). 'The Danish Model of "Flexicurity": Experiences and Lessons', *Transfer*, 10(2): 187–207.

Marchington, M., D. Grimshaw, J. Rubery, and H. Willmott (eds.) (2005). *Fragmenting Work: Blurring Organisational Boundaries and Disordering Hierarchies*, (Oxford: Oxford University Press).

Marglin, S. (1974). 'What do Bosses do?', in A. Gorz (ed.), *The Division of Labour: The Labour Process and Class Struggle in Modern Capitalism*, (Sussex, UK: Harvester Press).

MARSDEN, D. (1986). *The End of Economic Man? Custom and Competition in Labour Markets*, (Brighton, UK: Wheatsheaf Books).

——(1999). A *Theory of Employment Systems*, (Oxford: Oxford University Press).

MAURICE M. and A. SORGE (eds.) (2000). *Embedding Organizations*, (Amsterdam, John Benjamins Publishing).

——F. SELLIER, and J.-J. SILVESTRE (1986). *The Social Foundations of Industrial Power*, (Cambridge, MA: MIT Press).

MILES, R. E. and C. S. SNOW (1996). 'Twenty-first Century Careers', in M. B. Arthur and D. M. Rousseau (eds.), *The Boundaryless Career: A New Employment Principle for a New Organizational Era*, (Oxford: Oxford University Press).

MUHL, C. (2001). 'The Employment-at-will Doctrine: Three Major Exceptions', *Monthly Labor Review* (Jan.), 3–11.

OECD (1994). *The Jobs Study*, (Paris: OECD).

OFFE, C. (1976). *Industry and Inequality*, (London, Edward Arnold).

OSTERMAN, P. (1994). 'Internal Labour Markets: Theory and Change', in C. Kerr and P. D. Staudohar (eds.), *Labour Economics and Industrial Relations: Markets and Institutions*, (Cambridge MA.: Harvard University Press).

PFAU-EFFINGER, B. (1998). 'Culture or Structure as Explanations for Differences in Part-time Work in Germany, Finland and the Netherlands', in J. O'Reilly and C. Fagan (1998), *Part-time Prospects: An International Comparison of Part-time Work in Europe, North America and the Pacific Rim*, (London: Routledge).

PIORE, M. and S. SAFFORD (2006). 'Changing Regimes of Workplace Governance, Shifting Axes of Social Mobilization, and the Challenge to Industrial Relations Theory', *Industrial Relations* 45(3): 299–325.

ROE, M (2003). *Political Determinants of Corporate Governance: Political Context, Corporate Impact*, (Oxford: Oxford University Press).

ROSE, M. (1985). 'Universalism, Culturalism and the Aix Group: Promise and Problems of a Societal Approach to Economic Institutions', *European Sociological Review*, 1(1): 65–83.

RUBERY, J. (1978). 'Structured Labour Markets, Worker Organization and Low Pay', *Cambridge Journal of Economics* 2(1): 17–37.

——(1998). 'Working Time in the UK', *Transfer* 4: 657–77.

——(2007). 'Segmentation Theory Thirty Years on', *Économies et Sociétés* 28(6): 941–64.

——and D. GRIMSHAW (2003). *The Organisation of Employment: An International Perspective*, (Basingstoke: Palgrave).

——G. BOSCH, and S. LEHNDORFF (2008). 'Surviving the EU? The Future for National Employment Models in Europe', *Industrial Relations Journal* 39(6): 488–509.

——K. WARD, D. GRIMSHAW, and H. BEYNON (2005). 'Working Time, Industrial Relations and the New Employment Relationship', *Time and Society* 14(1): 89–111.

SAXENIAN, A. (1996). 'Beyond Boundaries: Open Labor Markets and Learning in Silicon Valley', in M. Arthur and D. Rousseau (eds.), *The Boundaryless Career*, (New York: Oxford University Press).

SCHETTKAT, R. (2003). *Differences in US-German Time-Allocation: Why Do Americans Work Longer Hours than Germans?* IZA Discussion Paper No. 697 Forschungsinstitut zur Zukunft der Arbeit, Bonn.

SCHMIDT, V. (2002). *The Futures of European Capitalism*, (Oxford: Oxford University Press).

SIMON, H. (1991). 'Organisations and Markets', *Journal of Economic Perspectives* 5(2): 25–44.

SISSON, K. (1987). *The Management of Collective Bargaining: An International Comparison*, (Oxford: Basil Blackwell).

STREECK, W. and K. THELEN (2005). *Beyond Continuity*, (Oxford: Oxford University Press).

SUPIOT, A. (2001). *Beyond Employment: Changes at Work and the Future of Employment Law in Europe*, (Oxford: Oxford University Press).

THOMPSON, E. P. (1967). 'Time, Work-Discipline, and Industrial Capitalism', *Past and Present* 38: 56–97.

VOSKO, L. (2006). *Precarious Employment: Understanding Labour Market Insecurity in Canada*, (Montreal: McGill-Queen's Press).

WEISS, L. (1993). 'War, the State and the Origins of the Japanese Employment System', *Politics and Society* 21(3): 325–54.

WHITLEY, R. (1999). *Divergent Capitalisms*, (Oxford: Oxford University Press).

WILLIAMSON, O. (1975). *Markets and Hierarchies*, (New York: Free Press).

CHAPTER 18

INTER-FIRM RELATIONS IN GLOBAL MANUFACTURING: DISINTEGRATED PRODUCTION AND ITS GLOBALIZATION

GARY HERRIGEL

JONATHAN ZEITLIN

INTRODUCTION

This chapter surveys the state of international scholarly debate on inter-firm relations in global manufacturing. It focuses on the evolving strategies of customers and suppliers within the value chains of core manufacturing industries, such as motor vehicles and complex mechanical engineering products. The analysis is divided into three parts. The first part discusses the historical emergence of clustered, flexible, and/or vertically disintegrated production (hereafter: disintegrated production) since the 1980s. It contrasts disintegrated production with production within hierarchical, vertically integrated Fordist/Chandlerian firms, arguing that the former has undermined the latter over the past thirty years, both in scholarly discussion and to a large extent in the practical orientations of the actors themselves. Two related but distinct variants of disintegrated production are presented: the industrial district/local production system model (ID/LPS) and the lean production/collaborative supply chain model (LP/CSC).

The second part addresses the globalization of disintegrated production. It examines the strengths and weaknesses of the modularity/contract manufacturing approach to transnational supply chains, and then goes on to contrast these with alternative forms of internationalization by multinational customer and supplier firms. Just as disintegration of production was seen to undermine hierarchy within and between firms in the preceding section, here the global dispersal of production appears to be gradually undermining old hierarchies between developed and developing regions. Recomposable hierarchy, collaboration, and mutual exchange increasingly shape interactions between the two types of manufacturing regions.

The subjects of the first two parts can usefully be thought of as historically sequential: vertical disintegration and regionalization occurred prior to extensive globalization of production. Today, however, the analytical distinction between the two has become less sharp as different systems of decentralized producer relations increasingly interact and interpenetrate in ways that generate their own distinctive dynamic. This is particularly true when our focus shifts to small- and medium-sized firms (SMEs). The third part analyses interactions between production in developed and developing regions, together with the evolution of SME strategies in high-wage regions in response to the resulting challenges and opportunities. The concluding section considers the implications of these developments for power and inequality in global supply chains.

Manufacturing Disintegration: Permanent Volatility, The Crisis of Fordist/ Chandlerian Organization, Industrial Districts and Lean Production

Much of the recent literature on inter-firm relations and disintegrated production in manufacturing dates back to discussions that began in the 1980s about the crisis of the vertically integrated firm (Piore and Sabel 1984; Hirst and Zeitlin 1991; Harrison

1994; Storper 1997) At that time, both actors and observers perceived that the environment in core sectors of manufacturing in advanced industrial economies had become distinctly more volatile and uncertain. Many factors were advanced to account for this qualitative transformation: macroeconomic destabilization, shortening product cycles, accelerating technological change, the differentiation of consumer taste, the intensification of competition, and the globalization of product markets. There is no consensus on what separates symptom from cause in this transformation. But all arrows point in the same direction: towards the conclusion that producers confront a permanent and ineradicable challenge of increased environmental volatility and uncertainty.

These new environmental conditions have resulted in organizational and strategic consequences for producers. At the most abstract level, debate since the 1980s points to a shift between two opposed ideal types: from the vertically integrated 'Fordist' or 'Chandlerian' firm to decentralized, clustered, networked, lean, flexibly specialized, and/or recombinatory producers. The former characterizes the dominant model of organization and practice prior to the onset of new environmental conditions; the latter the organizational forms and practices that have proved most successful in the new environment. Pervasive environmental volatility and uncertainty rewards continuous innovation. Competition elevates production quality and cost reduction capability to the fore. Flexible and specialized (disintegrated) producers, engaged in ever-shifting collaborative and market exchanges, flourish under these conditions while hierarchical and vertically integrated producers flounder. Put in a more evolutionary idiom, competition from recombinant coalitions of independent specialists gradually drives out firms seeking to integrate those specialties within their own operations.

Disintegrated production emerged along two main pathways during this historical transition. First, vertically integrated producers disintegrated their operations, focusing on core competences and shifting production operations and component design processes out to suppliers (Sabel 1989; Helper 1991; Storper 1997). Second, disintegrated districts and clusters of specialized, cooperative small- and medium-sized producers, both old (the Third Italy; Baden Württemberg; Jutland) and new (Silicon Valley), became strikingly competitive in world markets (Saxenian 1994; Herrigel 1996; Kristensen 1992; Kenney 2000; Zeitlin 2007).

Before proceeding further with this analysis, however, a few methodological observations are in order. First, this 'transition' narrative cannot be taken as a reliable empirical guide to understanding historical developments (though it is remarkably prevalent as a meme in the literature). As we have sought to show elsewhere, practices, strategies, and organizational forms supposedly characteristic of the 'new' environment could be found well before that environment emerged. The same is true of elements of the 'older' practices and organizational forms in the present (Sabel and Zeitlin 1985, 1997, 2004; Herrigel 2010). The movement in the last thirty years is much clearer in the analytical literature than in practice. There is much empirical evidence showing that large manufacturing firms across a wide range of sectors have disintegrated since the 1970s (Abraham and Taylor 1996; Lorenzoni and Lipparini 1999; Essletzbichler 2003). There is even more evidence that conglomerate forms have broken themselves up during the same time period. (Davis et al. 1994; Zenger and Hesterly 1997). But there is also significant variation within sectors. For example, large Japanese and Korean consumer electronics companies are much more vertically integrated than their American or European counterparts (Berger 2005; Sturgeon 2007). Conglomerate forms continue to prosper in the developing world where financial systems are less developed, as for example in the case of the Indian Tata group (Acemoglu et al. 2007). Many regions of specialized producers continue to flourish, such as Silicon Valley, or a variety of Italian industrial districts. But other specialized regions such Prato, Route 128, or the Ruhr have struggled or declined (Grabher 1993b; Saxenian 1994; dei Ottati 2003). Moreover, none of these regions emerged out of whole cloth, and many have histories that go back well into the eighteenth or nineteenth centuries (Herrigel 1996; Sabel and Zeitlin 1997; Zeitlin 2007). Finally, even though there is nothing about any particular national institutional system that prevents the emergence of successful disintegrated or Fordist production, both polar organizational forms allow for significant variation, both by sector and by national economy (Chandler 1990; Herrigel 1996; Storper and Salais 1997).

Thus, the analytical types presented in this section are stylizations. They highlight the distinctive features of contemporary disintegrated inter-firm practices. But they are by no means fictitious or imaginary, since much ethnographic evidence suggests that they inform the dominant orientations of firms and other economic actors about the nature of the environment and the organizational forms regarded as normal or paradigmatic (for a fuller theoretical discussion, see Sabel and Zeitlin 1997: 29–33). But such orientations should not be confused with the actual array of practices 'on the ground'. The Fordist/Chandlerian firm and the contrasting model of disintegrated production should be understood as orientations guiding (but not determining) the actions of firms and other actors. Practice itself is much more diverse, because actors themselves are frequently aware both of the complex dependence of forms of economic organization on multiple background conditions, and the possibility of sudden, unanticipated shifts in those conditions. Hence, they often seek to avoid definitive choices between polar alternatives and/or to anticipate in their forms of economic organization the need for future reconstruction in the face of changed circumstances. Actual disintegrated production is thus dramatically heterogeneous, both institutionally and strategically. Moreover, all the various configurations of disintegrated firms must reproduce themselves over time. They encounter challenges, suffer from internal disputes and many are not able to reproduce their success. The contingency of success and the significance of appropriate governance structures for enduring reproduction should be a core focus of any analysis of disintegrated production (Zeitlin 2007).

With these caveats in mind, the aim of this section is, first, to present the basic *orienting* contrast between the Fordist/Chandlerian and disintegrated types of manufacturing organization. The primary focus will be on the shifting boundaries of

the division of labour in production: the organizational location of design, development, component manufacturing, and assembly. Having established this basic contrast,
we then go to outline the two most common variants of disintegrated production: the
industrial district/local production system (ID/LPS) model, and the lean production/
collaborative supply chain model (LP/CSC). As we will see in the third section of this
chapter, these two variants increasingly overlap in actual manufacturing practice. But
the two forms remain distinct ways of conceptualizing disintegrated flexibility in
production. It is thus useful to draw out the contrast between the two at the outset.

Fordist/Chandlerian vs. disintegrated manufacturing

The archetypical Fordist/Chandlerian firm was developed for mass production of
standardized final goods. Its organization revolved around a logic of hierarchy, role
specialization, and control: product development and design were strictly separated
from manufacturing, while within manufacturing itself conception was separated
from the execution of particular tasks. In order to achieve economies of scale, ensure
stability of supply, and maximize throughput, firms vertically integrated their operations. Automobile producers in the United States and Europe, for example, typically
produced 50–80 per cent of value added inside the firm (Kwon 2005). Resort to
outside suppliers generally involved purchase of lower value-added parts, specialized
equipment (e.g. capital goods such as machine tools), or capacity subcontracting
where the blueprints for specific articles were bid out on a short-term basis, when in-
house facilities for making these items were overstretched. Hierarchy pervaded the
chain of development and production. Roles throughout the division of labour were
rigidly circumscribed. Authority and leverage were used to control the flow of
knowledge and material resources through the production process.

These principles became vulnerable in the new volatile environment because they
created rigidity: hierarchy and role specialization undercut communication across
locations in the division of labour. A good illustration of how these core Fordist/
Chandlerian principles could become quite cumbersome in practice is the product
development process in manufacturing. Product life cycles in automobiles during the
three decades after the Second World War, to take a quintessential example, could be
as long as ten years or more. Isolated designers developed new models and 'threw
designs over the wall' to their comparably isolated manufacturing colleagues. Problems encountered with the designs, if discovered, delayed their roll out significantly
as manufacturing had to wait for the designers (or its own engineers) to come up
with something that could be produced.

The organization of manufacturing itself further exacerbated these delays. Authority ran through layers of management, while shop-floor worker input was de-
emphasized. Problems in the flow of production had to be identified from above,
and solutions introduced similarly. This occurred again, and again, throughout
virtually all the myriad linked component processes and manufacturing stages in
complex technologies. Such intra-firm arrangements made the redesign of products,

recomposition of manufacturing processes, and reallocation of jobs extremely cumbersome. Change was costly and took a very long time. Yet (roughly) by the beginning of the 1980s, redesign, recomposition, and reallocation were becoming constant and increasingly inescapable for producers. A mismatch existed between the orienting principles of the hierarchical, pillarized, vertically integrated organization and the volatile, unpredictable, and rapidly changing character of the competitive environment.

By contrast, beginning in the 1980s, observers noticed that smaller, more specialized and/or less bureaucratic organizations showed remarkable flexibility and capacity for innovation in this volatile environment. Observation of successful cases gradually began to generate an alternative set of orienting principles for manufacturing organization. The successful alternative groupings of producers reversed the Fordist/Chandlerian emphasis on the separation of design and manufacture and conception and execution. Less organizational hierarchy and less specialization in the division of labour forced design and manufacturing to collaborate in new product development (Clark and Fujimoto 1991; Clark and Wheelwright 1994). Teams or groups of employees with different functional skills emerged as core sub-organizational units (Schumann et al. 1994; Osterman 1999; Helper et al. 2000). They allowed designers and engineers to solicit the input of manufacturing managers and even generally skilled workers when changes in production were required. Such interaction created greater flexibility and helped shorten product development cycles. In many cases, extensive labour involvement in teams created a form of stakeholderism that fostered internal experimentation and risk taking (Sabel 2005a; Kristensen 2008b).

These producers were much less vertically integrated than their Fordist/Chandlerian counterparts. Firms or production units specialized on particular technologies and aspects of development and manufacture. They relied on the complementary inputs of other specialists to offer a complete product to their customers. Collaboration across production unit boundaries proved a competitive advantage. Producers benefited from the market and technological knowledge of neighbouring specialists. They also did not have to carry the costs in manpower and equipment required to produce such know-how (Sabel 1989; Storper 1997; Powell 2001). *Embeddedness* of specialists in myriad repeated exchanges with complementary partners spread the practice as well as the cost of innovation across the networks (Granovetter 1985; Grabher 1993a). This made it easier (and less costly) for firms to experiment and take risks on new products and technologies, thereby accelerating change in both areas. In addition, the continuous encounter with outside expertise created the possibility for genuinely new ways of thinking about one's own expertise. In this way, repeated interaction among specialists fostered innovation (Amin and Cohendet 2004; Döring and Schnellenbach 2006).

Governance was also distinctive in the new disintegrated arrangements. Whereas in the Fordist/Chandlerian system, hierarchy and market tended to exhaust the mechanisms governing inter-positional and inter-firm relations, disintegrated production tended to be governed by a wider array of intermediate forms. Some of these intermediate forms could be quite formal and institutionalized, as in joint ventures, product development projects, development consortia, or supplier upgrading alliances. But in other cases, non-market and non-hierarchical relations among firms were governed either by explicit rules or by informal understandings of trust and mutual purpose. Through a wide array of specific exoskeletal institutional arrangements, these latter governance structures fostered a balance between competition and cooperation among specialists and thereby allowed for (even encouraged) continuous organizational recomposition (Sabel 1989; Grabher and Powell 2004).

In sum, the alternative disintegrated networks of producers avoided the pillarization of narrow role definitions and strong functional boundaries characteristic of Fordist/Chandlerian firms. Sequencing gave way to concurrency in product development and production. Provisional, revisable roles replaced rigidly specialized ones and collectively shared knowledge replaced hierarchical control and fragmentation. Indeed, in this disintegrated context, governance by the polar mechanisms of hierarchy and market gave way to a variety of intermediate mechanisms.

There is widespread agreement in the literature that current conditions are more congenial to the alternative vertically disintegrated, flexible, and networked forms of organization than to old-style hierarchical Fordist/Chandlerian forms. This does not mean that firms have completely abandoned ambitions towards hierarchy, authority, or control. Such powers are relinquished reluctantly, and opportunities to obtain them rarely forgone. Nor have the price mechanism and arm's-length contracting disappeared. The argument is not that such relations or mechanisms no longer exist in the current environment, but rather that hierarchical, role specialized, and vertically integrated organizations are less able to negotiate volatile, uncertain industrial environments than those based on more horizontal, flexible, and decentralized arrangements. There is still considerable debate, as we shall see, about the role of authority, control, hierarchy, and market relations within the alternative more disintegrated inter-firm arrangements.

This distinction between the logic of orienting principles and the logic of practice accounts for much of the confusion in academic debates (visible particularly during the 1980s and early 90s) (Wood 1989; Amin and Robins 1990; Harrison 1994). It also accounts for the peculiar character of the aggregate quantitative literature that has attempted to measure vertical disintegration, collaboration, and the flattening of hierarchies, across entire industries or even the entire manufacturing sector. Typically, such studies find that the results, while pointing in the direction of disintegration, are mixed. Vertical disintegration has increased, but integration has not disappeared. Collaboration is diffusing, but arm's-length competition continues to exist (Fieten et al. 1997; Helper and Sako 1998). Case-study research tends to show the same thing (Berger 2005; Whitford 2006; Herrigel 2010). This should not be surprising. The extreme claims for either pole depended on specific environmental conditions that are not found uniformly in all realms of practice. Actors do not enact orientations blindly; rather they are malleable frameworks or points of reference that actors adapt and recompose as they seek to resolve successive problems in their factories and markets. Moreover, at least one view holds that producers pursuing collaborative

strategies in uncertain environments systematically enter over time into a heterogeneous array of relations (collaborative, arm's-length, in-house production, capacity
subcontracting, etc.), in an effort to avoid becoming entrapped in local, bilateral ties,
while scanning the horizon of potential partners for new opportunities for innovation and cost reduction (Helper et al. 2000; Herrigel 2010; Sabel 2005a).

Predictably, all of this complexity has produced a significant sceptical literature
(Lovering 1999; Martin and Sunley 2003; Wolfe and Gertler 2004). Even here,
however, it is important to recognize that a bar has been crossed since the 1980s.
Scepticism is no longer directed at the viability of disintegrated forms of inter-firm
organization in relation to the Fordist/Chandlerian firm. Instead sceptics focus on
the limits of the diffusion, or the specific conditionality, of the flexible disintegrated
forms. Do the alternative forms appear spontaneously and/or inevitably? Are all
variants of decentralized organization equally successful? Is it possible to create
successful inter-firm practices everywhere? Such questions animate debate and
make for a very robust research programme.

Varieties of disintegrated production

Next, however, we need to parse the alternative disintegrated principles of production a bit more carefully. Though as a generic matter, all forms of flexible disintegrated production share the above qualities, there are a wide range of variants of
flexible organization identified in the literature (Grabher and Powell 2004; Smith-
Doerr and Powell 2004). Within manufacturing, two distinct models of disintegration and flexibility emerged in the wake of the crisis of the Fordist/Chandlerian
firm. As with the principles of disintegrated production in general, each of the
alternative models of flexible production was rooted in empirical cases of competitive success in the face of volatility. The first is the industrial district/local
production system model (ID/LPS); the second is the lean production/collabora-
tive supply chain model (LP/CSC). Today, the two models increasingly interpenetrate, but they have distinct origins, both in academic discussion and empirical
experience.

The ID/LPS model received a great deal of initial attention in public debate (Brusco
1982; Piore and Sabel 1984; Pyke et al. 1990). This was surely related to the fact that it
very nearly inverts the Fordist/Chandlerian model. In place of giant, hierarchical,
integrated firms, industrial districts are geographically localized clusters of small- and
medium-sized producers, interrelated by complementary and ever recombining specialties. Actually existing industrial districts vary widely, and there is significant
conceptual debate about how to define them (Whitford 2001; Zeitlin 2007). At one
end of the spectrum, we find extremely specialized regions where clusters of interrelated firms produce a single type of product, e.g., pottery, bicycles, cutlery, woven
textiles, shoes, packaging machinery, etc. At the other end, the clusters are less
specialized on particular end products. In such systems, complementary specialists
generate a broad and changing array of finished goods and intermediate components,

such as industrial machinery, motor vehicles, semi-conductors, consumer electronics, software, or biotechnology products (Crouch et al. 2001; Crouch 2004).

Whether specialized or diversified in industrial composition, however, the distinctive features of the ID/LPS model, at least initially, were the fluidity of roles among producers and spatial agglomeration. Fluidity or malleability of producer roles within the value chain in ID/LPS regions made for a distinctive mixture of collaboration and competition. Producers played multiple roles (customer, supplier, collaborator, arm's-length price-taker, competitor, etc) in multiple contracts both at the same time and over time. This made it difficult to establish consistent relational hierarchies: assembler, developer, and coordinator roles were unstable, provisional, shifting, and often simply enacted jointly. The spatial element within successful disintegrated regional economies involved, at one level, intense and frequent face-to-face exchange and common cultural understandings among producers. At another level, more importantly, sharing a common geographic space facilitated the creation of a shared extra-firm infrastructure for the provision of collective goods: institutions for training, finance, technical assistance, interest representation, dispute resolution etc. Without such institutions (however constituted) to govern competition and cooperation, and facilitate continuous recomposition, successful collaboration within ID/LPS regions has generally proven fragile and short-lived (Storper 1997; Bellandi 2006, 2009; Zeitlin 2007).

The LP/CSC model traces its genealogy back to the Japanese automobile industry (Cusumano 1985; Nishiguchi 1994; Fujimoto 1999). There, producers did not follow the vertically integrated path of Fordist mass production (Womack et al. 1990). Instead, the division of labour in automobile production remained disintegrated with large final assemblers, such as Toyota, directing and collaborating with extended chains of suppliers in the development and manufacture of their final products. Lean production had many striking advantages over traditional hierarchical forms of manufacturing organization. Crucially, it pioneered the radical integration of design and manufacture, known as 'simultaneous engineering'. Multifunctional teams of customers and suppliers designed a product and developed the techniques for its manufacture simultaneously in iterated rounds of conceptualization and experimentation. This practice radically reduced product development times and shortened product cycles. It also became possible to modify products quickly and add variety (Chanaron et al. 1999; Helper et al. 2000).

In addition, LP/CSC pushed collaborative team organization throughout the entire supply chain (Kochan et al. 1997; Adler et al. 1999). By giving teams self-governing autonomy (their own budgets, production targets, scheduling responsibility) and by utilizing formal mechanisms for group self-monitoring (mandatory intra-group benchmarking, local quality control, systematic error detection), LP/CSC made it possible to simultaneously improve production quality and lower total production costs (Helper et al. 2000). In contrast to the Fordist/Chandlerian 'push' logic, where production was driven by market forecasts, materials and parts ordered well in advance, and finished product placed in inventory waiting to be sold, LP/CSC followed a 'pull' logic. Customer orders prompted downstream teams to mobilize their upstream counterparts, in effect pulling material through production to final assembly. By delegating responsibility for quality and work flow directly to downstream teams, lean producers radically minimized inventory, work-in-progress, waste, and redundancy throughout the production process (Hines et al. 2004).

The LP/CSC model shared many features with the ID/LPS model. Both relied on the continuous blurring of boundaries between design and manufacture and between conception and execution in production. Both were significantly disintegrated, with independent producers collaborating across firm boundaries to exploit complementarities and achieve flexibility. But LP/CSC was distinctive in a number of ways. Unlike ID/LPS, the logic of lean production focused on value chains within industries rather than spatial relations among agglomerations of producers. Although lean production networks were also regionally clustered to some extent, with just-in-time suppliers located close to assembly plants, the linkage logic was not primarily spatial. As a result, collaboration could extend beyond particular regions and continue to be governed by the logic of LP/CSC. Moreover, in classic Japanese LP/CSC inter-firm relations, roles were more stable, since suppliers occupied positions in 'tiers'. The fluidity and ambiguity of roles among firms characteristic of the ID/LPS was much less pronounced in the initial Japanese version of LP/CSC, though even in the latter suppliers could be 'promoted' to higher tiers (or demoted to lower ones) based on their relative performance in previous product cycles. Finally, LP/CSC was distinctive in that cross-boundary collaboration, both within and across firms and teams, focused not just on technology and product development, but also on cost reduction. Organizational recomposition through continuous improvement processes—benchmarking, kaizen, self-analysis in error detection, etc.—was a systematic feature of the LP/CSC model. In striking contrast to the flexibility generated by the informal mix of collaboration and competition driving the ID/LPS model, LP/CSC relied on formal procedures that forced producers to evaluate their own practices and forced them to reform in the interest of product innovation, quality improvement, error detection, and/or cost reduction (MacDuffie 1997; Sabel 2005a).

THE GLOBALIZATION OF DISINTEGRATED PRODUCTION: OFFSHORING, MULTINATIONALS, AND MULTIPLE LOGICS IN TRANSNATIONAL SUPPLY CHAINS

Soon after disintegrated production emerged in the advanced industrial economies, it began to globalize. The process began in the 1970s with lighter, simpler, labour-intensive products like garments, footwear, and some electronics, but by the late

1990s had engulfed a wider range of industries, including heavier, more technologically complex, capital-intensive sectors, such as: motor vehicles; aerospace; industrial, construction, and agricultural machinery; electrical equipment; steel; and pharmaceuticals (Feenstra 1998; Arndt and Kierzkowski 2001). Globalization both intensified and modified the process of disintegration in production. The internationalization of disintegrated production is animated by two dynamics. Though they are analytically distinct and have separate origins, these dynamics have become increasingly interconnected, with very significant consequences, as we shall see below.

One dynamic is the increasing cost pressure facing customers and suppliers in high-wage regions. Firms are constantly forced to reduce their costs, even as they maintain or even improve the quality and sophistication of their products. These contradictory pressures have driven the trend toward vertical disintegration in production, as firms focus on 'core competences' and rely on specialists for everything else. The same pressures are now driving production across borders. Both customer and supplier firms are increasingly establishing production operations (or finding suitable contractors) in lower wage environments to relieve cost pressure on their product palettes. In this way, production in low-wage environments for delivery to customers in high-wage regions can be understood as a kind of pressure-release valve (in German, a *Ventile*).

The other dynamic driving the offshoring of production is the pursuit of access to foreign markets. Lead firms move to developing countries (especially large ones like China, India, or Brazil) to serve the local market more easily—in particular by adapting designs to local needs and even developing unique products for those markets (Buckley and Ghauri 2004; Ghemawat 2007). Suppliers follow lead firms to these new production locations in order to retain their key customers. Lead firms want the reliability of veteran collaborators as they attempt to produce in offshore markets. They also want the flexibility that more global suppliers are believed to provide. Global suppliers, on this view, can draw on know-how and capacity from around the world; they can also use scale as a means of exerting leverage with their own suppliers to achieve lower costs.

Taken separately, these two dynamics generate considerable complexity in the division of labour between high- and low-wage regions. Their interaction not only generates even greater complexity, but also very surprising and even counter-intuitive results. Where globalization strategies are succeeding, production becomes more sophisticated in lower-wage environments and more secure in high-wage ones.

How this is possible will gradually become apparent as the analysis proceeds through three steps. First, we will look at the strong claims for the emergence of a new production paradigm and a new global division of labour advanced by proponents of the modularity/contract manufacturing approach to supply-chain restructuring. Their arguments for a radical break between design and manufacture and the emergence of a stable hierarchy between developed and developing regions will be shown to be sharply limited. Not only is this logic circumscribed even in those industries where actors self-consciously pursue modularity, but it also does not apply to many manufacturing sectors, which continue to be characterized by 'integral' rather than modular product architectures (Ulrich 1995). Second, we will examine the progress of offshoring within integral architecture sectors such as motor vehicles and other complex mechanical engineering products from the perspective of firms seeking to reduce their costs. A distinctive feature of this process is the continuing interpenetration of design and manufacture throughout the supply chain. The complex dynamic between developed and developing countries that has emerged from this dimension of the offshoring process, we argue, appears to be destabilizing what was once considered a stable hierarchy between developed and developing regions. Third, we show that this emergent complexity and uncertain hierarchy of relations between regions and players within the manufacturing supply chain is further exacerbated by the second driver of offshoring noted above: lead firms' efforts to enter new markets and the resultant imperative for suppliers to follow their customers. Each of these offshoring dynamics creates complex spatial and organizational allocations of competence and capacity; together they generate an intriguing multiplicity of firm strategies and resource allocation logics. The rest of this section focuses primarily on the strategies of large multinational lead firms and their suppliers. The third section considers the strategies high-wage SMEs and the regions that support them are pursuing to cope with these same pressures of globalization.

Separation of design and manufacture, cost-driven disintegration, and offshoring: the limits of modularity

Within the dialectic of innovation and cost reduction driving productive disintegration in production, it was a logical step for firms to look to offshore locations with lower labour costs as a way to achieve quick cost reductions. Much of the initial literature on transnational supply chains focused on the apparel and consumer electronics sectors, where firms seemed to have had dramatic success in leveraging offshore cost differences in production (Gereffi and Korzeniewicz 1994; Borrus et al. 2000; Bair 2005). Those studying the sectors claimed that a distinctive new dynamic was emerging around the possibilities for reorganizing the global division of labour in production. Indeed, several authors argued that the dynamics in these sectors pointed to the emergence of a new model for manufacturing as a whole, which we will call the modularity/contract manufacturing (M/CM) model (Sturgeon 2002; Garud et al. 2003; Langlois 2007).

Distinctive about the sectors in which the M/CM model was pioneered is that large lead firms drove disintegration in the division of labour while at the same time maintaining a rigid divide between design and manufacture. This eliminated the need for the collaborative and recombinatory relations characteristic of the disintegrated model described in the previous section. Relations between designing customers and manufacturing suppliers were based on a clear and extreme division of roles which, at the limit, could be governed through arm's-length market exchange. This, it was claimed, created the possibility for dramatic spatial separation of design and production. Design and value added, according to this view, tended to concentrate in high-wage environments, while manufacturing, as a low value-added activity, gravitated to locations where labour and other costs were also lower.[1]

The key to this strategy, particularly in electronics, was the creation of modular product architectures, based on standard technical interfaces between the overall design and its constituent components or subsystems (Baldwin and Clark 2000; Langlois 2003; Schilling 2003). By developing products with stable, codified interfaces between internal functional elements, lead firms could focus on design and hand off production of standardized components to independent suppliers. Those supplier firms (so-called 'contract manufacturers'), in turn, were responsible for organizing production on behalf of the lead firm, seeking out the cheapest locations and coordinating the flow of components around the world (including final assembly in some cases). Such contract manufacturers worked with multiple lead design firms at the same time, filling their capacity by producing high volumes of differently designed but standardized modules in locations where labour costs were extremely low. Sturgeon's ideal type of these 'modular production networks' was concentrated in what he called 'product-level electronics' (televisions, computers, cell phones, personal digital assistants, etc.). But similarly sharp divisions between design and manufacture could also be observed in other sectors as well, particularly apparel, footwear, and bicycles. There, in addition to modularity (bicycles), the manufacturing process was labour-intensive and the product simple enough (apparel) to allow for the separation between design and manufacture (Gavin and Morkel 2001; Sturgeon and Lester 2001; Gereffi 2005a).

The M/CM perspective (Humphrey and Schmitz 2002; Bair 2005; Gereffi et al. 2005) envisages an emerging global hierarchy in which lead firms in rich countries increasingly abandon manufacturing for the exclusive control of knowledge, design, and marketing. For their part, developing regions struggle to lure footloose contract manufacturers in order to 'upgrade' their infrastructures of physical and human capital, and gain access to know-how and value added that will one day permit them to generate their own contract manufacturing operations. The clear boundary between design knowledge (and brand value) on the one hand and manufacturing know-how and expertise on the other, establishes a fixed hierarchy among stages of the value chain, even as producers, regions, and economies are able to upgrade within it.

In this literature, Taiwan, Israel, and Ireland have emerged as leapfrog cases, political economies capable of springing over the barriers dividing developed and developing regions through adroit state intervention. But such barrier hopping does not change the underlying spatial logic of relative costs relating design to manufacturing. Once the Taiwanese, for example, hopped over the design barrier, on this view, they began shifting their own manufacturing to contract manufacturers in lower-cost regions in China (Breznitz 2007). Design and manufacture map on to a

---

[1] Though as we will see immediately, control over manufacturing operations in those regions very frequently stayed under the control of independent developed-country multinationals.

specific conception of what it means to be developed and not yet developed. In the M/CM perspective, such hierarchy is a natural and inescapable feature of capitalism. Countries advance their position along a know-how and value hierarchy until they reach a point where it is possible to abandon manufacturing entirely.

These hierarchical lead firm/contract manufacturer arrangements have become a significant feature of global production (Kenney and Florida 2004; Berger 2005; Gereffi 2005b). There has also been significant manufacturing job loss in high-wage regions, some of which can be traced to offshoring (Bronfenbrenner and Luce 2004; Marchant and Kumar 2005; Boulhol and Fontagne 2006; Mankiw and Swagel 2006). For all of that, however, M/CM does not seem to be becoming the dominant model for global disintegrated production as its early scholarly proponents claimed. Manufacturing and design remain mutually dependent among producers in both high- and low-wage contexts (Brusoni et al. 2001; Prencipe et al. 2003; Sabel and Zeitlin 2004).

Regarding modularity, firms appear to be acutely aware that the separation of design from manufacturing can lead to so-called 'modularity traps', where irreversible commitments to a specific product architecture and set of technical interface standards result in a loss of system-level knowledge and capacity to participate in the development of the next new architecture on the part of component specialists (Chesbrough 2003; Fixon and Park 2007; Baldwin 2007). Thus, even within electronics, only a relatively small percentage of products have a genuinely modular character: estimates of contract manufacturers' share of the global cost of goods sold in this sector range from 13–17 per cent (Sturgeon 2002; Berger 2005). In the rest of electronics, the characteristic inter-firm collaboration of the disintegrated model plays an important role and the customer/supplier division of labour between design and manufacture is more complex. Indeed, the turbulence and rapidity of change in product markets and technologies seems to have undercut producers' capacity in these supposedly modular sectors to achieve stable codification systems (Berggren and Bengtsson 2004; Ernst 2005; Voskamp 2005). Sturgeon himself now acknowledges that 'as contractors seek new sources of revenue by providing additional inputs to lead firm design and business processes, and new circuit-board assembly technologies appear on the scene . . . the hand-off of design specifications is becoming more complex and less standardized', thereby requiring 'closer collaboration in the realm of product design' between customers and suppliers (Gereffi et al. 2005: 95).

More importantly, there appear to be many sectors within manufacturing where the technical capacity of lead firms to design modular product architectures is extremely limited. This is true of many complex metalworking sectors, such as automobiles, construction machinery, agricultural equipment, and virtually the whole vast capital goods area of mechanical engineering (Herrigel 2004; Whitford and Zeitlin 2004; Whitford 2006). In such 'integral' architecture products (Ulrich 1995), technical subsystems interpenetrate and their interfaces cannot be easily standardized, either from model generation to model generation, or across a palette of common product offerings (MacDuffie 2007). Lead firms in these sectors typically do not seek to break products down into fixed modules defined by a one-to-one mapping between a function and the physical devices that embody it, but instead engage in a process of iterated co-design with component suppliers, in which complex wholes are provisionally parsed into parts whose subsequent development then suggests modifications of the initial overall design, which are then provisionally parsed again, and so on. At any given moment, suppliers may be engaged in manufacturing 'black box' parts defined by the interfaces of a particular product architecture, but the most capable (and best remunerated) are also expected to assist their customers in redefining those interfaces for cost reduction and performance improvement in the next design iteration (Sabel and Zeitlin 2004).

Integral product architectures are no barrier to vertical disintegration or globalization—indeed many of the archetypical cases of disintegrated production described in the first section were found in these sectors, in both IS/LPS and LP/CSC versions. But if manufacturers of such products want to exploit the cost advantages of offshore production locations, they must do this in ways that take account of the continued indispensability of inter-firm collaboration. This has led to a different offshoring dynamic and, ultimately, to a mutually dependent global division of labour between developed and developing regions.

Offshoring, collaboration, and the destabilization of spatial hierarchy

The offshoring process in integral-architecture manufacturing unfolded in a distinctive sequence. Initially, lead firms and their suppliers sought to purchase simple, standardized components from offshore producers. Developed country suppliers, when they were able to do so, shifted production of their mature components—parts that had already been designed and that went into aftermarket or replacement markets—to offshore locations. These were arm's-length purchases of low value-added components. Such practices resembled the old-style subcontracting of Fordist/Chandlerian firms, except that instead of procuring parts locally, firms now sought out producers in lower-wage countries. But in the more disintegrated context this kind of offshoring represented an urgent effort to relieve cost pressures. For a time, such practices suggested to some that the radical separation of design from production characteristic of the modular technologies might be applicable in these sectors as well (Sturgeon and Florida 2004).

Unremitting cost pressures on both customer and supplier firms coupled with the inescapability of architectural integrality in product development, however, soon overwhelmed such simple arm's-length *Ventile* strategies. More complex strategies to create offshore outlets for cost reduction, involving new and collaboratively developed products, began to emerge (Dicken 2003; Ghemawat and Ghadar 2006). The impetus came initially from powerful final assembler firms in the automobile and complex machinery industries, which insisted that their suppliers develop lower-cost offshore production capacity for new co-designed components (Berger

2004).[2] Larger supplier firms dutifully shifted new and existing production capacity to lower-wage environments in order to retain their customers' business. This did not necessarily involve closing production facilities in high-wage environments. Instead, it meant the creation of new and more sophisticated supplemental capacity offshore. Indeed, many suppliers gradually realized that having a sophisticated 'outlet' in a lower-wage region made it possible for them to blend home and offshore production to make lower overall bids on collaborative projects with their customers. Paradoxically, offshoring has thus enabled suppliers to solidify their market position 'at home and abroad' as producers of high value-added specialized products (Herrigel 2007).

This shift in the strategic character of offshoring has initiated a dynamic process of capacity and know-how reallocation that appears to be radically redefining the division of labour between high- and low-wage regions. What is emerging is neither the radical spatial separation of design and manufacture forecast by the M/CM school, nor a traditional comparative advantage model of high value-added manufacturing in high-wage locations and lower value-added manufacturing in lower-wage locations. Instead, emergent practice increasingly blends design and manufacture capabilities and high and low value-added processes across global production locations. Different wage levels play an important but not decisive role in this new logic of competence and capacity allocation (Berger 2005).

At one level, there is still hierarchy between regions in these sectors. Product design and initial production ramp up of a component or subsystem are performed in high-wage contexts, along with especially high value-added production runs that can be efficiently automated or that have lower volumes but more value content. Once the large series process is up and running (six months/one year for complex products such as ball bearing units), it is then transplanted to the low-wage location.

But at another level, this process of technology transfer has begun to undermine the very hierarchy it presupposes. The transplantation of production processes results in the diffusion of current manufacturing practice to low-wage facilities. Increasingly, the machinery park in the low-wage location converges with that in the high-wage location.[3]

A key additional point of slippage in this new division of labour is the location of development and design capacity. Again, such capacity is still mainly located in high-wage regions, with their concentration of engineering know-how and experience with the recursive integration of development and manufacture. But significant restructuring of these competences has occurred within supplier firms across existing high-wage manufacturing locations. This is easiest to see in the case of bigger

---

[2] Large final assemblers often encouraged their suppliers to set up operations in lower-cost regions because they were themselves doing so with their own component production. GM's Delphi and Ford's Visteon, for example, had extensive operations in Mexico and Central Europe well before the two parent companies spun off their component divisions into independent companies.
[3] Much of the following material is based on interviews conducted by the authors and their colleagues in the Global Components research project (www.globalcomponents.org) in the US, Germany, Central Europe, and China between 2006 and 2008.

multinational suppliers with broader product palettes and multiple divisions, such as the large automobile suppliers Magna, ZF, Kolbenschmidt-Pierburg, Mahle, Schaeffler, or Robert Bosch. Such firms are increasingly locating competence for the development of specific products in distinct plants in specific high-wage locations. For example, a German piston producer concentrates development capacity for different models aimed at different end users (diesel, passenger cars, commercial vehicles, etc.) in different locations (south Germany, north Germany, France).[4] Such newly specialized locations are called 'lead plants' or 'centres of competence'. Lead plants assume responsibility for developing and ramping up the new generation of product and production technology (ramp up) for their particular type of piston. They are also responsible for transferring the new product and equipment needed to manufacture it to all the low-wage production locations in which the multinational supplier operates (in the piston case, the Czech Republic, Mexico, Brazil, and China). They send know-how and provide ongoing consultation to these offshore plants to help them get up to speed on the new processes and products.

As an initial step, this division of labour places manufacturing capability in the low-wage region, while retaining development and production, in an integrated way, in more specialized high-wage locations. Significantly, however, this hierarchy is not fixed. There is a slippage, resulting from unavoidable functional spillovers of know-how and competences to new production locations. Transferring new products and processes involves, among other things, training offshore engineers in the lead plant's own special competences in order to enable the latter to optimize production in the offshore location. The existence of a competent and increasingly experienced corps of engineers in low-wage locations also makes the process of 'handing off' production more efficient and allows for its subsequent optimization. It is difficult for firms to maintain completely 'headless' or 'know-how-less' manufacturing-only facilities in offshore locations. Some development capacity is indispensable for the smooth operation of production.

Finally, in most cases, multiple lead plants in high-wage regions maintain relations with the same offshore production facility. Low-wage region production facilities, as a result, have become remarkably diversified, with an array of products that in high-wage locations is increasingly manufactured—at least initially—in separate locations. In the case of the German piston maker, the Brazilian, Czech, and Chinese facilities can produce nearly the entire product range manufactured in all the firm's European plants, while the Mexican facility, although less diversified than its Brazilian, Czech, and Chinese sisters, is still more diversified than any western European production site within the MNC. In this way, benefits of productive diversity historically characteristic of plants in high-wage regions—synergies among seemingly unrelated operations, possibilities for using manufacturing techniques developed in one process on a wholly different product, etc.—are now extended and concentrated in low-wage locations.

---

[4] This example is taken from global components research interviews. Interviews were conducted under the promise of strict confidentiality, so the firm must remain anonymous.

Opening new markets and following the customer: multiple logics, multiple regions, multiple plants, multiple hierarchies

The division of labour within multinational supplier firms between high-wage 'lead plants' with integrated development/production capacities and modern low-wage 'high-volume production' locations is one important trend shaping the globalization of disintegrated manufacturing. But it is not the only logic shaping the distribution of production and competences among plants, even within such multinational suppliers. In addition to the logic of cost reduction, the allocation of production capacity within multi-product and multi-plant firms is also driven by pursuit of proximity to customers.

Multinational corporations (MNCs) operating as lead manufacturing firms in complex integral-architecture sectors such as motor vehicles and mechanical engineering have gradually begun to expand operations into developing regions in an effort to compete more effectively for local market share. These strategic investments have been driven both by the relative saturation of developed country markets and by the rapid emergence of technologically sophisticated demand in developing economies such as Brazil, India, and China, as well as newly capitalist regions such as Central and Eastern Europe. Many lead firms in these sectors (e.g. Ford, Caterpillar, John Deere, Volkswagen, BMW, Hyundai, Toyota, PSA, Volvo) had entered such markets in the past following a product life-cycle model (Wells 1972): i.e. offering older or mature versions of products developed for and long produced in their home regions. But increasingly they and many other major producers recognize the need to develop products more specifically adapted to the particular needs and demands of emerging market users. This involves the creation of significant production capacity in developing regions, as well as the transfer of technological know-how to local subsidiaries there. Manufacturing MNCs also increasingly need to upgrade the skills and technical capacities of their personnel in developing country locations (Depner and Dewald 2004; Ivarsson and Alvstam 2005).

Lead firm MNCs cannot pursue these globalization strategies without the collaboration of their suppliers. The increasing disintegration of production makes the expertise of home country suppliers indispensable for the competitiveness of their customers. Such expertise, moreover, is not immediately available among indigenous suppliers in developing regions, even rapidly growing ones like India or China. Thus, multinational customer firms have encouraged their suppliers to globalize along with them (Depner and Bathelt 2003; Depner and Dewald 2004; Voelzkow 2007).

In this way, globalization literally involves the transfer of the collaborative logic of disintegrated production governing inter-firm exchanges in developed regions into developing country contexts. This creates a distinct logic of globalization for suppliers, quite different from the cost-reduction logic described in the previous section. This alternative logic drives multinational producers to enhance the activities of existing offshore operations and/or to add complementary capacity to them in an effort to satisfy the local demands of their customers. Lead firms, for example, find that they can expand capacities and competences in their existing offshore manufacturing operations to service offshore markets as well as to reduce costs in their own home market.[5]

The result is that multiple global divisions of labour are superimposed on the global allocation of work among plant locations within multinational customer and supplier firms. Low-wage production locations are allocated high-volume work across a broad spectrum of the mother firm's product palette, leading them to become highly diversified. Customer demands for local supply likewise tend to expand their production capabilities. In addition to high-volume work, these plants are increasingly able to produce in shorter series and accommodate special requests from their customers. The development capacity that such facilities acquire in order to facilitate the hand-off of manufacturing operations from high-wage regions, then becomes extremely valuable in adapting other products to local customer needs.

A similar logic is affecting the structure and capabilities of lead plants in high-wage regions. Each lead plant, at a minimum, has the capacity to develop and ramp up a specific product or range of products to high-volume manufacture (e.g. small pistons for passenger cars). Development and production is highly integrated in such plants, which can engage in experimental, prototype production as well as very small series, customized, and batch-type operations. They also run highly automated high-volume production lines, where the automation plays a significant role in the creation of product value. At the same time, in unsystematic ways, these lead plants retain a more diverse set of competences in order to accommodate local customer demands for the full palette of component types. Thus, for example, a lead plant for small pistons in France may retain some production capacity for larger pistons to accommodate demand from big local customers for the latter. Since the small-piston lead plant has no local development competence for large pistons, it effectively allocates control over some of its own local production capacity to another lead plant (the one with development competence for large pistons). The small-piston plant's non-core large-piston production is then supervised and serviced by the engineers and developers from the lead plant for large pistons. Thus, in order to accommodate the contradictory and unpredictable demands of new product development, fluctuating series size, and customer demands, lead plants in high-wage regions, despite extensive offshoring and concentration on core competences, are also becoming remarkably diversified.[6]

The image that emerges from this stylized description of the interaction of different logics of global production allocation (cost reduction and new market

---

[5] Thus the Audi engine plant in Győr, Hungary, originally established as a low-cost manufacturing location sending engines back to the home assembly facility in Ingolstadt and to sister company VW's assembly plant in Wolfsburg, Germany, has developed new foreign assembly operations to service other local plants (e.g. the Octavia and Taureg assembly works in Mlada Boleslav, Czech Republic, and Bratislava, Slovakia respectively).

[6] There are of course limits to such diversification: lead plants do not manufacture wholly different products from other divisions of a large firm; thus piston plants do not produce fuel-injection systems.

entry/follow the customer) is that of a delicate multi-regional balancing game. Efforts to concentrate technological competence in particular plants, the continuous pursuit of cost reduction, the desire to maximize production runs while accommodating increasing product variety, and the need to respond to often contradictory customer pressures (to produce offshore and produce locally) are all constantly in play and combined in different ways.

The result of these logics and their interaction is to erode rigid hierarchies between developed and developing regions. Competences may be formally concentrated, yet they inevitably spill over and bleed out from one location to another. Capacity is allocated and reallocated, separated and recombined. Hierarchy is not eliminated: there are still 'leaders' and 'followers' or 'supporters' within the intra- and inter-firm division of labour. But such hierarchies are now increasingly recomposable, with the same actors occupying different roles in different contexts ('lead plants' both lead and follow). As a result, the major difference between high- and low-wage locations is that the former have larger concentrations of development competence and deeper integration between design, engineering, and production in particular specialized areas. But both types of location exhibit growing integration between development and production, and both operate in support relations with other facilities with greater competence in particular areas. As development competence bleeds out into emergent market locations, high-wage locations are likely to receive know-how from low-wage locations about production areas outside their own core competences. Even now, high-wage plants regularly receive some capacity-balancing work from low-wage sister plants running at full capacity, which are unable completely to fulfil their own customers' orders. In this model, producers and firms do not become 'developed' by abandoning manufacturing. Rather, development involves the continuous capacity to integrate and reintegrate design and manufacturing within and across firm and unit boundaries in an environment characterized by chronic uncertainty and urgent pressures for innovation and cost reduction.

COPING WITH DISINTEGRATED PRODUCTION ON A GLOBAL SCALE: SMALL- AND MEDIUM-SIZED FIRMS AND HIGH-WAGE REGIONS

An important undercurrent in this discussion of multiple globalization logics is that, apart from the early enthusiasm for modularity/contract manufacture, none of these logics of the globalization of disintegrated production involve or foresee the elimination of manufacture within high-wage regions. The continued existence of valuable expertise and human capital, proximity to customers, needs for short-term flexibility in the global allocation of capacity within MNCs—all make manufacturing 'sticky' in the developed world (Markusen 1996). Regardless of where production and design occur, they retain many of the features of disintegrated production analysed in the first section of this chapter. MNC lead firms and large suppliers collaborate on design and manufacture around the world, but they also collaborate with more locally based small- and medium-sized suppliers in each of the regions in which they operate. Uncertainty and the imperatives of innovation and cost reduction exert a centrifugal disintegrating pressure on the division of labour in production both globally and locally. This section focuses on the strategies that SMEs in high-wage regions and the local institutions that govern their relations have adopted to cope with the pressures of globalization.

The activities of MNCs described in the previous section generate a particular kind of market environment for SMEs in high-wage regions. Innovation and cost-reduction capability are the coin of the realm in disintegrated production. Specialized SME suppliers can take advantage of productive disintegration when they are able to bring know-how in these areas to the table. SMEs must be able to contribute value in larger processes of inter-firm collaboration. They also must be highly flexible, quick-response producers, capable of meeting short lead times (between finalization of order and delivery of finished parts). Finally, where MNC lead firms and the lead plants of MNC suppliers are interweaving various products in various series sizes from various locations across their production facilities, SME suppliers to these firms must be able to produce a mixture of components in fluctuating volumes. These general market characteristics have given rise to three developments among high-wage SMEs and regional governance institutions that modify the model of disintegrated production outlined in the first section of this chapter.

Interpenetration of industrial district/local production system and lean production/collaborative supply chain models

With the growing exposure to global logics of competition, innovation, cost reduction, and capacity allocation, the principles of ID/LPS and LP/CSC have begun increasingly to interpenetrate. Most strikingly, the role fluidity and ambiguity characteristic of ID/LPS has begun to mix with the formal self-reflection and attention to both product innovation and cost reduction of LP/SCS (Sabel 2005a). The ability to perform a variety of roles has become an indispensible competitive competence within disintegrated production. Even in sectors where tiering still exists—e.g. automobiles and complex industrial machinery—producers within the supply chain increasingly occupy a variety of positions over time. Indeed, in entering into a relationship, neither the customer nor the supplier can have a clear idea of how the specific content of their tie will evolve. Will it be an intimate collaboration? Will collaboration fail and the customer ask for some other more arm's-length service?

Will other collaborators turn out to be necessary for the successful construction of a component system? Will the initial supplier lead the collaboration, or the new supplier do so, or will the customer direct it all? These things are increasingly difficult to predict *ex ante*. The character of a tie with even a single customer can vary substantially over time and a series of discrete contracts. As a result, both customers and suppliers must be prepared to play a variety of roles (Kristensen 2008*a*, 2008*b*; Kristensen et al. 2008; Herrigel 2010). This is a core practice in the ID/LPS model of disintegrated production, but marks a departure from the originally more hierarchical LP/CSC model.

At the same time, all collaborators, regardless of their role, find themselves under continuous pressure to reduce their costs and improve the quality and content of their products and services. For this, it is widely recognized that the formal mechanisms of self-observation (kaizen, five-why error detection analysis, benchmarking, etc.) associated with the LP/CSC model of disintegrated production have become indispensable (MacDuffie 1997; Hines et al. 2004; Sabel 2005*a*). Many large customer firms insist that their suppliers develop these capabilities (MacDuffie and Helper 1997; Sako 2004). Indeed, many large customer firms have developed extensive internal supplier development organizations to teach their suppliers how to deploy these mechanisms of self-analysis (SEA 2008). The dissemination of these lean practices has also become an important goal of public institutions in many industrial clusters (Whitford and Zeitlin 2004; Kristensen et al. 2008). Such formal mechanisms facilitate cooperation and help ensure that its trajectory will be cost effective. These key practices of the LP/CSC model have begun to diffuse broadly, even among SME specialists within industrial districts and regional clusters where they were never central (Fieten et al. 1997; Whitford 2006). Thus, for example, collective benchmarking and training in quality assurance standards and related techniques have been among the most widely demanded services in Italian industrial districts over the past decade (Sabel 2004*b*; Zeitlin 2007).

Cooperative globalization of SMEs

In the context of dramatic cost competition and the globalization of their customers, SME supplier firms and specialists from high-wage regions have begun to globalize. This process occurs in two main variants. The first involves regional clusters of specialists who collectively produce and assemble all components of a product. Italian industrial districts for shoemaking, ceramic tiles, or packaging machinery, which organize the offshore production of crucial processes or lower value-added products illustrate this trend (Camuffo 2003; Bellandi and Di Tommaso 2005; Cainelli et al. 2006). The other variant is internationalization of SME suppliers to MNC lead firms and suppliers in integral-architecture manufacturing sectors. Typically, in these cases groupings of firms form an alliance to follow their customers into foreign markets (Herrigel 2007). The reasons for both variants of SME globalization, however, are the same as those that have driven the globalization of larger firms:

cost-reduction pressures, and customer demands for proximity of key collaborators in new locations.

In many cases, SMEs from high-wage regions seek to relieve cost pressure in their home markets either by identifying suppliers in low-wage regions or by establishing their own production facilities in those places. Such moves follow the trajectory outlined above regarding MNC suppliers: initially firms outsource offshore the simplest operations, then they establish their own production in low-wage regions, often simply to accommodate customer demands that they develop such capacity.

Either way, such moves are difficult for SMEs and are frequently undertaken in cooperation with external partners. This is particularly the case when it comes to identifying appropriate suppliers or locations in low-wage environments. Often, SMEs use network ties with larger customer firms to identify attractive potential suppliers or joint-venture partners in low-wage regions. Sometimes, SMEs will hire foreign nationals who know the terrain in their home country and can therefore help in setting up the offshore operation and managing the inevitable problems of communication, logistics, and quality assurance. In other cases, a number of non-competitive SMEs in related lines of manufacturing may cooperate in such offshore ventures. The Global Components project found a case of nine very small family-owned American metalworking firms, each with a related but non-competing proprietary product, which pooled their resources to contract with a firm in Shanghai to identify, audit, certify, and monitor appropriate Chinese suppliers for them (Herrigel 2007). In the case of Italian industrial districts, these tasks may be performed by agents of large groups created by SMEs in the district or by public agencies representing the regions (Bellandi and Caloffi 2008). German SMEs frequently work with the offshore branch of the German Chamber of Industry and Commerce to identify appropriate offshore regions and suppliers (Depner and Bathelt 2003).

SMEs from high-wage regions are much more severely challenged when it comes to the second driver of offshoring: following the customer into low-wage markets. Here the SME often simply lacks the financial leverage to establish on its own the higher-volume production facilities in offshore locations that their mostly large MNC customers require. Nonetheless, SMEs feel compelled to globalize for fear that if they did not, they would lose key customers. In order to make such moves, SMEs therefore seek out partners. This can involve outright merger between firms. But in a surprising range of cases, cooperation has taken very interesting alternative forms.

Take the example of the strategy pursued by a small German family-owned manufacturer of industrial springs. The company has been a specialist spring producer for over 120 years. In 2005, the company 'became part of' a larger group of spring and stamped metal parts producers—all of whom were small- or medium-sized, specialist family-owned firms just like themselves. The participating specialists were not all from the same place, but all came from traditional regions in Germany of specialized SME production (Herrigel 1996). The original spring family owns a proportional interest in the group, which is a limited liability corporation (GmbH), not a joint-stock company (AG). The owner family participates with the other families in the development of overall group strategy. The formation of the group has resulted in an internal rationalization of production capacity and competence among member firms. Exchange of information and experience among group members is ongoing and systematic. The group tries to optimize the specialties of its members on an ongoing basis.

In effect, this process has resulted in the creation of a 'lead plant' system very similar to the one described above for larger MNC component suppliers, though in this case each lead plant is one of the original SME specialists. The lead plants service jointly established production locations in foreign regions—the Czech Republic, China, the USA, and Latin America. As with the large MNC suppliers described above, each of those foreign locations produces the complete range of product offered by the group. As a result, the foreign locations are far more diversified production facilities than the lead plants in the high-wage regions themselves. And there is continuous know-how spillover between the lead plants in Germany and the subsidiaries abroad. The new collaborative entity is essentially a globalized specialization cartel of SME spring producers and precision metal stampers. The alliance pools the resources and competences of its members in order to provide production and financing leverage to one another at the same time that they are able to exchange technical, customer, and market know-how. The aim of the group is to create open flows of information and know-how about technology, product application, customers, and markets in order to foster new product and new application development among all participating members.

Analogous groups have emerged in Italian industrial districts. They differ from their German counterparts in that the members of the group are regionally concentrated, and may comprise the gamut of specialists needed to produce the end product(s) manufactured in the district (shoes, apparel, ceramic tiles, etc). These groups leverage the offshoring of production in the district and coordinate the allocation of capacity on a global basis among local members and offshore suppliers. They also play a key role in orchestrating technological innovation, product development and design, and international marketing among participating firms. In comparison with the German cases, Italian groups often have an even looser property structure, though they may be organized by larger 'leader firms', which take equity stakes in key suppliers. Depending on the degree of formalization of ownership ties, these ensembles of firms are variously referred to in the Italian literature as 'district groups', 'pocket multinationals', or 'open networks', (Corò and Micelli 2006; Chiarvesio et al. 2006; Brioschi et al. 2002; Colli 2002; Lazerson and Lorenzoni 1999).

SME globalization is also occurring quite extensively in Scandinavia, particularly in Denmark. Indeed, over 50 per cent of the Danish workforce is employed in firms with at least one foreign subsidiary, and over 34 per cent of those workers are employed in firms with fewer than 650 employees (Kristensen et al. 2008). The range of possible variants of SME cooperation on a global scale is thus extremely great. This is a promising area for future research.

Regional policy for the globalization of disintegrated production

Globalization places great pressure on the regional governance structures that have historically been indispensable for the sustained competitiveness of disintegrated production clusters. Unlike the firms that they serve, the governance institutions and practices in regions where disintegrated production has been embedded cannot easily shift their operations offshore. They must focus on keeping the operations that remain in the high-wage regions competitive and capable of participating in the fluid roles and formal self-monitoring processes of global competition. This has not been an easy adjustment. Several very significant regional clusters of disintegrated production, such as Prato in Italy, or (arguably) the traditional American automobile complex in Michigan, Ohio, and Indiana, have been largely overwhelmed by these globalization processes. They were not able to establish regional governance practices that could facilitate dynamic disintegrated globalization (dei Ottati 2003; Honeck 1998). Globalization of production, finance, and marketing can create asymmetries of access to technology and information, thereby undermining existing mechanisms for containing opportunism and balancing competition and cooperation (Zeitlin 2007). Further, the globalization of disintegrated production generates demands for new public goods among regional and industry producers, which existing institutional infrastructures are unable fully to supply or even anticipate (Sabel 2005b; Bellandi 2006). Currently, there is enormous experimentation across Europe and North America around these issues. Failure exists, everywhere it threatens, but there are also intriguing examples of success (cf. also Crouch et al. 2001, 2004).

A central feature of many regional processes of governance adjustment has been the development of public or public–private collaborations for upgrading the manufacturing supply base (mentioned above). These kinds of extra-firm efforts aim at enhancing the core skills that SMEs require to participate in contemporary disintegrated production networks: the development of technical know-how, the ability to perform multiple roles, and the capacity to engage in continuous self-analysis for collaboration and cost reduction. A wide variety of institutional arrangements for this purpose already exist in different national and regional settings (Whitford and Zeitlin 2004; Herrigel 2010; Kristensen 2008b). Yet, efforts to create a proactive, supportive architecture for the globalization of SMEs from high-wage regions remain very incipient. Public and extra-firm efforts trail behind the informal efforts supporting globalization outlined above, such as large multinational lead firms giving their SME suppliers tips on reliable offshore interlocutors and production locations, or SMEs collaborating amongst themselves to accomplish similar tasks. One interesting, but limited, example of public support in this area is the role of the German International Chamber of Commerce in offshore regions. This agency does not identify specific commercial interlocutors for globalizing SMEs, but does provide them with extensive market information about offshore areas. Perhaps most importantly, it helps SMEs deal with foreign bureaucracies when they move offshore.

More elaborate and multidimensional examples of proactive regional support for disintegrated globalization are only now being discovered. Perhaps the best-attested case is Bellandi and Caloffi's (2008) account of recent initiatives in Italian regions, especially Tuscany. They focus on the identification of 'cluster to cluster' public goods—common trade protocols (ERPs), educational facilities, technical languages, and specific business services—between Italian industrial districts and what they call 'proto-industrial districts' in China.[7] At the Italian federal level, an intergovernmental body has been created, the *Comitato Governativo Italia-Cina* (Italy-China Committee), which has sponsored an array of trans-territorial projects between the two countries, and there have been several regional-level 'China Projects'. Bellandi and Caloffi describe one of these, between the tanning and leather district of Santa Croce sull'Arno in Tuscany and an array of shoemaking regions and specialized towns located between Shanghai and Guangdong in China. At home, the Santa Croce district was crucially supported by a leather tanning trade association, the *Associazione Conciatori* (ASCON), which 'carries out lobbying activities, represents their associates in several contexts, supports the realization of promotional activities, organizes training courses, promotes the creation of loan consortia, looks after the procurement of raw materials and provides other specialized services' (Bellandi and Caloffi 2008: 11). With the support of its members and the regional government, ASCON identified an array of complementarities between its members and Chinese producers—opportunities for the sale of Italian leather as well as for cooperation on key technologies (anti-pollution and water purification) that were crucial for the creation of transnational supply chains. Extra-firm institutions seeking proactively to exploit opportunities created by globalization thus successfully generated mutual benefits and synergies between the clusters of regional specialists.

Bellandi and Caloffi's examples of proactive support for regional globalization efforts are striking. They represent what Sabel has called the shift in industrial districts from 'worlds in a bottle to windows on the world' (Sabel 2004b). Yet, the identification of opportunities for high-wage regions created by globalization are still often overshadowed by expressions of anxiety and distress about potential threats. Increasingly, however, similar discussions to those in Italy are occurring in many manufacturing clusters dominated by competitive and dynamically adjusting SMEs. The Wisconsin Manufacturing Extension Partnership, for example, which has played a crucial role in coordinating supplier upgrading and cooperation with large MNC customers, has recently begun discussions about proactively supporting the globalization of regional SMEs (interview). Analogous cooperative efforts have been identified in Norway and Denmark. (Kristensen 2008b; Kristensen et al. 2008) This is a

---

[7] The authors note that there are also cluster building policies sponsored by the Italian Federal Government between Italy and Russia: 'Task Force Italy-Russia on Industrial Districts and SMEs' (Bellandi and Caloffi 2008).

core area for future research on the governance of inter-firm relations as the globalization of disintegrated production continues.

CONCLUSION

This chapter has provided an overview of the main issues regarding inter-firm relations and supply chain dynamics within what we have called disintegrated production. It has focused primarily on the changing character of relations among producers and between regions over the past thirty years. Disintegrated production emerged as a dominant alternative orientation to the hierarchical Fordist/Chandlerian model in manufacturing. Its key distinguishing feature is intense and ongoing collaboration between design and manufacture in the context of increasing fragmentation of the division of labour within and across firms. Production units have become smaller, and frequently transformed into separate legal entities. Their relations are continuously recomposed through collaboration and negotiation, rather than market signals or hierarchical directives. Relations among collaborating producers, furthermore, are often governed by an array of extra-firm practices and institutions designed to balance cooperation and competition and facilitate continuous recomposition of roles and capacities. These relations characterize practices within developed and developing contexts as well as those that bridge both milieux.

Perhaps the most controversial element within studies of disintegrated production concern the power relations governing the supply chain. Our own view is that the chronic uncertainty and resultant fluidity of relations in disintegrated production reduces structural power imbalances across the community of producers. In the old Fordist/Chandlerian subcontracting world, power relations were structurally stable: suppliers were a community of proximate producers dependent on one or a few local vertically integrated customers for work. Such large manufacturing customers, in turn, viewed themselves as a privileged prince capable of producing prosperity for their underling suppliers, but ever conscious of the need to do so with a firm and strict hand (Kwon 2004; Whitford and Enrietti 2005). In the new world, power remains a central dimension of customer–supplier relations—especially in cases where role definition is relatively clear *ex ante* and/or arm's-length ties are in play. But even in the latter cases, there is the crucial difference that neither the customer nor the supplier views their power advantage as stable or secure: leverage is contextually defined and constantly shifting in both local and foreign contexts as roles and strategies are redefined.

Where roles are ambiguous and ties are collaborative, power in the sense of asymmetric leverage is still more elusive. Iterative co-design of innovative products and joint definition of competences create mutual dependence that increases switching costs and stimulates commitment to joint problem solving and dispute resolution.[8] So, in an important sense, the new mixture of close collaboration and open networks in the disintegrated supply chain has reduced structural power imbalances within the community of producers.[9]

A similar argument can be made about mutual benefits from exchange within disintegrated production. Collaboration can provide the parties with mutual benefits. This need not benefit all parties equally; nor does the existence of mutual benefit imply the absence of power relations in the collaboration. Collaboration can occur despite power asymmetries, with benefits nonetheless accruing to all parties. Players enter into exchange relations because they see the possibility of gain. This is true of market exchanges and it is true of collaborative exchanges. Power and equity are orthogonal in this regard.

The one certainty about power and reward in disintegrated production is that it is unstable and inconsistent. This is true of relations in the workplace. It is true of inter-firm relations along the supply chain. And it is true of relations between developed and developing regions. Roles and relationships, both global and local, are in a constant state of recomposition. Actors, firms, and regions that have developed proactive strategies and supporting institutions for participating in this process of continuous reorganization are most likely to succeed in the current international environment.

REFERENCES

ABRAHAM, K. G. and S. K. TAYLOR (1996). 'Firms' Use of Outside Contractors: Theory and Evidence', *Journal of Labor Economics* 14: 394–424.

ACEMOGLU, D., S. JOHNSON, and T. MITTON (2007). 'Determinants of Vertical Integration: Financial Development and Contracting Costs', Cambridge, MA, MIT/NBER.

ADLER, P., M. FRUIN, and J. LIKER (eds.) (1999). *Remade in America: Transforming and Transplanting Japanese Management Systems*, (New York: Oxford University Press).

AMIN, A. and P. COHENDET (2004). *Architectures of Knowledge. Firms, Capabilities, and Communities*, (Oxford: Oxford University Press).

——and K. ROBINS (1990). 'Industrial Districts and Regional Development: Limits and Possibilities', in F. Pyke, G. Becattini, and W. Sengenberger (eds.), *Industrial Districts and Interfirm Cooperation in Italy*, (Geneva, International Institute for Labor Studies), 185–219.

ARNDT, S. W. and H. KIERZKOWSKI (eds.) (2001). *Fragmentation: New Production Patterns in the World Economy*, (Oxford: Oxford University Press).

BAIR, J. (2005). 'Global Capitalism and Commodity Chains: Looking Back, Going Forward', *Competition and Change* 9(2): 153–80.

---

[8] For an important recent synthesis, see Gilson et al. (2008).

[9] There are also governance problems that emerge within the new serially collaborative relations. For a discussion see Whitford and Zeitlin (2004); Sabel (2004a).

BALDWIN, C. Y. (2007). 'Frameworks for Thinking about Modularity, Industry Architecture, and Evolution'. Paper presented to Sloan Industry Studies Conference, Cambridge, MA, Apr. 27.

——and K. B. CLARK (2000). *Design Rules: The Power of Modularity*, (Cambridge, MA: MIT Press).

BELLANDI, M. (2006). 'A Perspective on Clusters, Localities, and Specific Public Goods', in C. Pitelis, R. Sugden, and J. R. Wilson (eds.), *Clusters and Globalisation: The Development of Urban and Regional Economies*, (Cheltenham: Edward Elgar), 96–113.

——(2009). 'The Governance of Cluster Progressive Reactions to International Competitive Challenges', in M. J. Aranguren, C. Iturrioz, and J. R. Wilson (eds.), *Networks, Governance and Economic Development: Bridging Disciplinary Frontiers*, (Cheltenham: Edward Elgar).

——and A. CALOFFI (2008). 'District Internationalization and Trans-Local Development', *Entrepreneurship and Regional Development* 20(6): 517–32.

——and M. R. DI TOMMASO (2005). 'The Case of Specialized Towns in Guangdong China', *European Planning Studies* 13(5): 707–29.

BERGER, R. (2004). 'The Odyssey of the Auto Industry. Suppliers' Changing Manufacturing Footprint'. Paper presented to SAE World Congress, Detroit.

BERGER, S. (2005). *How We Compete: What Companies around the World Are Doing to Make it in Today's Global Economy*, (New York: Currency/Doubleday).

BERGGREN, C. and L. BENGTSSON (2004). 'Rethinking Outsourcing in Manufacturing: A Tale of Two Telecom Firms', *European Management Journal* 22(2): 211–23.

BORRUS, M., D. ERNST, and S. HAGGARD (eds.) (2000). *International Production Networks in Asia*, (London: Routledge).

BOULHOL, H. and L. FONTAGNE (2006). 'Deindustrialization and the Fear of Relocations in Industry.' *CEPII Working Papers*. Paris, Centre d'etudes prospectives et d'informations internationales.

BREZNITZ, D. (2007). *Innovation and the State: Political Choice and Strategies for Growth in Israel, Taiwan, and Ireland*, (New Haven, CT: Yale University Press).

BRIOSCHI, F., M. S. BRIOSCHI, and G. CAINELLI (2002). 'From Industrial District to the District Group: An Insight into the Evolution of Local Capitalism in Italy', *Regional Studies* 36(9): 1037–52.

BRONFENBRENNER, K. and S. LUCE (2004). *The Changing Nature of Corporate Global Restructuring: The Impact of Production Shifts on Jobs in the US, China, and Around the Globe*, Washington, DC: US-China Economic and Security Review Commission.

BRUSCO, S. (1982). 'The Emilian Model: Productive Decentralisation and Social Integration', *Cambridge Journal of Economics* 6: 167–84.

BRUSONI, S., A. PRENCIPE, and K. PAVITT (2001). 'Knowledge Specialization, Organizational Coupling, and the Boundaries of the Firm: Why Do Firms Know More Than They Make?', *Administrative Science Quarterly* 46: 597–621.

BUCKLEY, P. J. and P. N. GHAURI (2004). 'Globalization, Economic Geography and the Strategy of Multinational Enterprises', *Journal of International Business Studies* 35(2): 81–98.

CAINELLI, G., D. IACOBUCCI, and E. MORGANTI (2006). 'Spatial Agglomeration and Business Groups: New Evidence from Italian Industrial Districts', *Regional Studies* 40(5): 507–18.

CAMUFFO, A. (2003). 'Transforming Industrial Districts: Large Firms and Small Business Networks in the Italian Eyewear Industry', *Industry and Innovation* 10(4): 377–401.

CHANARON, J.-J., Y. LUNG, T. FUJIMOTO, and D. RAFF (eds.) (1999). *Coping with Variety: Flexible Productive Systems for Product Variety in the Auto Industry*, (Aldershot: Ashgate).

CHANDLER, A. (1990). *Scale and Scope: The Dynamics of Industrial Capitalism*, (Cambridge MA: Harvard University Press).

CHESBROUGH, H. (2003). 'Towards a Dynamics of Modularity', in A. Prencipe, A. Davies, and M. Hobday (eds.), *The Business of Systems Integration*, (Oxford: Oxford University Press), 174–98.

CHIARVESIO, M., E. DI MARIA, and S. MICELLI (2006). 'Global Value Chains and Open Networks: The Case of Italian Industrial Districts'. Paper presented to the annual meeting of the Society for the Advancement of Socio-Economics, University of Trier, June 28–30.

CLARK, K. B. and T. FUJIMOTO (1991). *Product Development Performance: Strategy, Organization, and Management in the World Auto Industry*, (Boston: Harvard Business School Press).

——and S. C. WHEELWRIGHT (eds.) (1994). *The Product Development Challenge: Competing Through Speed, Quality, and Creativity*, (Boston: Harvard Business School Press).

COLLI, A. (2002). *Il quarto capitalismo: Un profilo italiano*, (Venice: Marsilio).

CORÒ, G. and S. MICELLI (2006). *I nuovi distretti produttivi: Innovazione, internazionalizzazione e competitità dei territori*, (Venice: Marsilio).

CROUCH, C., P. LE GALES, C. TRIGILIA, and H. VOEZKOW (eds.) (2001). *Local Production Systems in Europe*, (Oxford: Oxford University Press).

——(2004). *Changing Governance of Local Economies: Responses of European Local Production Systems*, (Oxford: Oxford University Press).

CUSUMANO, M. A. (1985). *The Japanese Automobile Industry: Technology and Management at Nissan and Toyota*, (Cambridge, MA: Harvard University Press).

DAVIS, G. F., K. A. DIEKMANN, and C. H. TINSLEY (1994). 'The Decline and Fall of the Conglomerate Firm in the 1980s: The Deinstitutionalization of an Organizational Form', *American Sociological Review* 59(4): 547–70.

DEPNER, H. and H. BATHELT (2003). 'Cluster Growth and Institutional Barriers: The Development of the Automobile Industry Cluster in Shanghai, P. R. China', *SPACES* 2003–09, (Marburg: Philipps-University of Marburg).

——and U. DEWALD (2004). 'Globale Netzwerke und lokale Partner: Deutsche Automobilzulieferer und der Wachstumsmarkt China', *SPACES* 2004–02, (Marburg: Philipps-University of Marburg).

DICKEN, P. (2003). 'Global Production Networks in Europe and East Asia: The Automobile Components Industries'. *GPN Working Paper*, ESRC Research Project: Making the Connections: Global Production Networks in Europe and East Asia.

DÖRING, T. and J. SCHNELLENBACH (2006). 'What Do We Know about Geographical Knowledge Spillovers and Regional Growth? A Survey of the Literature', *Regional Studies* 40(3): 375–95.

ERNST, D. (2005). 'Limits to Modularity: Reflections on Recent Developments in Chip Design', *Industry and Innovation* 12(3): 303–35.

ESSLETZBICHLER, J. (2003). 'From Mass Production to Flexible Specialization: The Sectoral and Geographical Extent of Contract Work in US Manufacturing, 1963–1997', *Regional Studies* 37(8): 753–71.

FEENSTRA, R. C. (1998). 'Integration of Trade and Disintegration of Production in the Global Economy', *The Journal of Economic Perspectives* 12(4): 31–50.

FIETEN, R., W. FRIEDRICH, and B. LAGEMAN (1997). 'Globalisierung der Märkte—Herausforderung und Optionen für kleine und mittlere Unternehmen insbesondere für Zulieferer', *Schriften zur Mittelstandsforschung*, (Stuttgart: Verlag Schäffer-Poeschel).

FIXON, S. K. and J.-K. PARK (2007). 'The Power of Integrality: Linkages between Product Architecture, Innovation, and Industry Structure'. *MIT Sloan Working Paper*, (Cambridge, MA, MIT Sloan School of Management).

FUJIMOTO, T. (1999). *The Evolution of a Manufacturing System at Toyota*, (Oxford: Oxford University Press).

GARUD, R., A. KUMARASWAMY, and R. N. LANGLOIS (eds.) (2003). *Managing in the Modular Age: Architectures, Networks, and Organizations*, (Oxford: Blackwell).

GAVIN, P. and A. MORKEL (2001). 'The Effect of Product Modulatity on Industry Structure: The Case of the World Bicycle Industry', *Industry and Innovation* 8(1): 31–47.

GEREFFI, G. (2005a). 'The Global Economy: Organization, Governance, Development', in N. Smelser and R. Swedberg (eds.), *The Handbook of Economic Sociology*, 2nd edn., 160–182.

——(2005b). 'The New Offshoring of Jobs and Global Development'. *ILO Social Policy Lectures*, (Geneva: International Labour Office).

——and G. KORZENIEWICZ (eds.) (1994). *Commodity Chains and Global Capitalism*. Studies in the Political Economy of the World System, (Westport, CT: Greenwood Press).

——J. HUMPHREY, and T. J. STURGEON (2005). 'The Governance of Global Value Chains', *Review of International Political Economy* 12(1): 78–104.

GHEMAWAT, P. (2007). *Redefining Global Strategy: Crossing Borders in a World Where Differences Still Matter*, (Boston: Harvard Business School Press).

——and F. GHADAR (2006). 'Global Integration ≠ Global Concentration', *Industrial and Corporate Change* 15(4): 595–623.

GILSON, R. J., C. F. SABEL, and R. E. SCOTT (2008). 'Contracting for Innovation: Vertical Disintegration and Interfirm Collaboration'. Unpublished paper, Columbia Law School.

GRABHER, G. (ed.) (1993a). *The Embedded Firm: On the Socioeconomics of Interfirm Relations*, (London, Routledge).

——(1993b). 'The Weakness of Strong Ties: The Lock-in of Regional Development in the Ruhr Area', in G. Grabher (ed.), *The Embedded Firm: On the Socioeconomics of Interfirm Relations*, (London: Routledge), 255–78.

——and W. W. POWELL (2004). 'Introduction', in G. Grabher and W. W. Powell (eds.), *Critical Studies of Economic Institutions: Networks*, (Cheltenham: Edward Elgar).

GRANOVETTER, M. (1985). 'Economic Action and Social Structure: The Problem of Embeddedness', *American Journal of Sociology* 91(3): 481–510.

HARRISON, B. (1994). *Lean and Mean: The Changing Landscape of Corporate Power in the Age of Flexibility*, (New York: Basic Books).

HELPER, S. (1991). 'How Much Has Really Changed Between US Automakers and Their Suppliers?', *Sloan Management Review*, 32(4): 15–28.

HELPER, S. and M. SAKO (1998). 'Determinants of Trust in Supplier Relations. Evidence from the Automotive Industry in Japan and the United States', *Journal of Economic Behaviour and Organization* 34: 387–417.

——J. P. MACDUFFIE, and C. F. SABEL (2000). 'Pragmatic Collaborations: Advancing Knowledge While Controlling Opportunism', *Industrial and Corporate Change* 9(3): 443–83.

HERRIGEL, G. (1996). *Industrial Constructions: The Sources of German Industrial Power*, (New York: Cambridge University Press).

——(2004). 'Emerging Strategies and Forms of Governance in High-Wage Component Manufacturing Regions', *Industry and Innovation* 11(1–2): 45–79.

——(2007). Interim Report on Global Components Project. Chicago, University of Chicago-Global Components Project: 12.

——(forthcoming 2010). *Manufacturing Possibilities: Creative Action and the Recomposition of Industry in the USA, Germany, and Japan since World War II*, (Oxford: Oxford University Press).

HINES, P., M. HOLWEG, and N. RICH (2004). 'Learning to Evolve: A Review of Contemporary Lean Thinking', *International Journal of Operations and Production Management* 24(10): 994–1011.

HIRST, P. and J. ZEITLIN (1991). 'Flexible Specialization versus Post-Fordism: Theory, Evidence and Policy Implications', *Economy and Society* 20(1): 1–55.

HONECK, J. P. (1998). *Industrial Policy in Older Industrial Regions: A Comparison of Ohio and the Basque Region*. Unpublished PhD thesis, University of Wisconsin-Madison.

HUMPHREY, J. and H. SCHMITZ (2002). 'How Does Insertion in Global Value Chains Affect Upgrading in Industrial Clusters?', *Regional Studies* 36(9): 1017–27.

IVARSSON, I. and C. G. ALVSTAM (2005). 'Technology Transfer from TNCs to Local Suppliers in Developing Countries: A Study of AB Volvo's Truck and Bus Plants in Brazil, China, India and Mexico', *World Development* 33(8): 1325–44.

KENNEY, M. (ed.) (2000). *Understanding Silicon Valley: The Anatomy of an Entrepreneurial Region*, (Stanford, CA: Stanford University Press).

——and R. FLORIDA (eds.) (2004). *Locating Global Advantage: Industry Dynamics in the International Economy*, (Stanford, CA: Stanford University Press).

KOCHAN, T. A., R. D. LANSBURY, and J. P. MACDUFFIE (eds.) (1997). *After Lean Production: Evolving Employment Practices in the World Auto Industry*, (Ithaca, NY: Cornell University Press).

KRISTENSEN, P. H. (1992). 'Industrial Districts in West Jutland, Denmark', in F. Pyke and W. Sengenberger (eds.), *Industrial Districts and Local Economic Regeneration*, (Geneva: International Institute for Labor Studies), 122–73.

——(2008a). 'Introduction, Nordic Countries in Transition: Towards Enabling Welfare States and Experimentalist Business Systems'. Unpublished paper, TRANSLEARN project, (Copenhagen: Copenhagen Business School).

——(2008b). 'Translearn Conclusive Chapter: From Varieties of Welfare Capitalism to a Comprehensive, Enabling Welfare State'. Unpublished paper, TRANSLEARN project, (Copenhagen: Copenhagen Business School).

——M. LOTZ, and R. ROCHA (2008). 'The Danish Case: Complementarities of Local and National Dynamics'. Unpublished paper, TRANSLEARN project, (Copenhagen: Copenhagen Business School).

KWON, H.-K. (2004). *Fairness and Division of Labor in Market Societies: Comparison of U.S. and German Automotive Industries*, (New York/Oxford: Berghahn Books).

——(2005). 'National Model under Globalization: The Japanese Model and Its Internationalization', *Politics and Society* 33(2): 234–52.

LANGLOIS, R. N. (2003). 'The Vanishing Hand: The Changing Dynamics of Industrial Capitalism', *Industrial and Corporate Change* 12(2): 351–85.

——(2007). *The Dynamics of Industrial Capitalism: Schumpeter, Chandler and the New Economy*, (Abingdon, UK: Routledge).

LAZERSON, M. H. and G. LORENZONI (1999). 'The Firms that Feed Industrial Districts: A Return to the Italian Source', *Industrial and Corporate Change* 8(2): 235–66.

LORENZONI, G. and A. LIPPARINI (1999). 'The Leveraging of Interfirm Relationships as a Distinctive Organizational Capability: A Longitudinal Study', *Strategic Management Journal* 20(4): 317–38.

LOVERING, J. (1999). '"Theory Led by Policy: The Inadequacies of the New Regionalism" (Illustrated from the Case of Wales)', *International Journal of Urban and Regional Research* 23: 379–96.

MacDuffie, J. P. (1997). 'The Road to "Root Cause": Shop-Floor Problem-Solving at Three Auto Assembly Plants', *Management Science* 43(4): 479–501.

——(2007). 'Modularity and the Geography of Innovation'. Paper presented to Sloan Industry Studies Conference. Cambridge, MA, Apr. 27.

——and S. Helper (1997). 'Creating Lean Suppliers: The Honda Way', *California Management Review* 39(4): 118–51.

Mankiw, N. G. and P. Swagel (2006). 'The Politics and Economics of Offshoring Outsourcing'. Unpublished paper, (Cambridge, MA: Harvard University Press).

Marchant, M. and S. Kumar (2005). 'An Overview of US Foreign Direct Investment and Outsourcing', *Review of Agricultural Economics* 27(3): 379–86.

Markusen, A. (1996). 'Sticky Places in Slippery Space: A Typology of Industrial Districts', *Economic Geography* 72(3): 293–313.

Martin, R. and P. Sunley (2003). 'Deconstructing Clusters: Chaotic Concept or Policy Panacea?', *Journal of Economic Geography* 3(2003): 5–35.

Nishiguchi, T. (1994). *Strategic Industrial Sourcing: The Japanese Advantage*, (New York: Oxford University Press).

Osterman, P. (1999). *Securing Prosperity. The American Labor Market: How It Has Changed and What to Do About it*, (Princeton, NJ: Princeton University Press).

Ottati, G. D. dei (2003). 'Exit, Voice and the Evolution of Industrial Districts: The Case of the Post-World War II Economic Development of Prato', *Cambridge Journal of Economics* 27: 501–22.

Piore, M. and C. F. Sabel (1984). *The Second Industrial Divide*, (New York: Basic Books).

Powell, W. W. (2001). 'The Capitalist Firm in the Twenty-First Century: Emerging Patterns in Western Enterprise', in P. DiMaggio (ed.), *The Twenty-First-Century Firm: Changing Economic Organization in International Perspective*, (Princeton, NJ: Princeton University Press), 33–68.

Prencipe, A., A. Davies, and M. Hobday (eds.) (2003). *The Business of Systems Integration*, (Oxford: Oxford University Press).

Pyke, F., G. Becattini, and W. Sengenberger (eds.) (1990). *Industrial Districts and Inter-Firm Cooperation in Italy*, (Geneva: International Institute for Labor Studies).

Sabel, C. F. (1989). 'Flexible Specialisation and the Re-emergence of Regional Economies', in P. Hirst and J. Zeitlin (eds.), *Reversing Industrial Decline? Industry Structure and Policy in Britain and Her Competitors*, (Oxford: Berg), 17–70.

——(1994). 'Learning by Monitoring: The Institutions of Economic Development', in N. Smelser and R. Swedberg (eds.), *The Handbook of Economic Sociology*, 1st edn., (Princeton, NJ: Princeton University Press), 137–65.

——(2004a). 'Pragmatic Collaborations in Practice: A Reply to Herrigel and Whitford', *Industry and Innovation* 11(1–2): 81–8.

——(2004b). 'Mondo in bottiglia o finestra sul mondo? Domande aperte sul distretto industriale nel spirito di Sebastiano Brusco', *Stato e Mercato* 1: 143–58.

——(2005a). 'A Real Time Revolution in Routines', in C. Heckscher and P. Adler (eds.), *The Firm as a Collaborative Community*, (Oxford: Oxford University Press), 105–56.

——(2005b). 'Globalisation, New Public Services, Local Democracy: What's the Connection?', in *Local Governance and the Drivers of Growth*, (Paris: OECD), 111–31.

——and J. Zeitlin (1985). 'Historical Alternatives to Mass Production: Politics, Markets and Technology in Nineteenth Century Industrialization', *Past and Present* 108: 133–76.

————(1997). 'Stories, Strategies, Structures: Rethinking Historical Alternatives to Mass Production', in C. F. Sabel and J. Zeitlin (eds.), *Worlds of Possibilities: Flexibility and Mass Production in Western Industrialization*, (Cambridge: Cambridge University Press), 1–33.

————(2004). 'Neither Modularity nor Relational Contracting: Inter-Firm Collaboration in the New Economy', *Enterprise and Society* 5(3): 388–403.

SAKO, M. (2004). 'Supplier Development at Honda, Nissan and Toyota: Comparative Case Studies of Organizational Capability Enhancement', *Industrial and Corporate Change* 13(2): 281–308.

SAXENIAN, A. (1994). *Regional Advantage: Culture and Competition in Silicon Valley and Route 128*, (Cambridge, MA: Harvard University Press).

SCHILLING, M. A. (2003). 'Toward a General Modular Systems Theory and its Application to Interfirm Product Modularity', in R. Garud et al., *Managing in the Modular Age: Architectures, Networks, and Organizations*, (Oxford: Blackwell) (2003), 172–216.

SCHUMANN, M., V. BAETHKE-KINSKY, M. KYHLMAN, C. KURZ, and U. NUEMANN (1994). *Trendreport Rationalisierung: Automobil Industrie, Werkzeugmaschinenbau, Chemische Industrie*, (Berlin: Edition Sigma).

SEA (2008). 'Supplier Excellence Alliance', from http://www.seaonline.org/.

SMELSER, N. and R. SWEDBERG (eds.) (2005). *The Handbook of Economic Sociology*, 2nd edn., (Princeton, NJ: Princeton University Press).

SMITH-DOERR, L. and W. W. POWELL (2005). 'Networks and Economic Life', in Smelser and Swedberg (2005), 379–402.

STORPER, M. (1997). *The Regional World: Territorial Development in a Global Economy*, (New York: The Guilford Press).

————and R. SALAIS (1997). *Worlds of Production: The Action Frameworks of the Economy*, (Cambridge MA: Harvard University Press).

STURGEON, T. J. (2002). 'Modular Production Networks: A New American Model of Industrial Organization', *Industrial and Corporate Change* 11(3): 451–96.

————(2007). 'How Globalization Drives Institutional Diversity: The Japanese Electronics Industry's Response to Value Chain Modularity', *Journal of East Asian Studies* 7(1): 1–34.

————and R. FLORIDA (2004). 'Globalization, Deverticalization, and Employment in the Motor Vehicle Industry', in M. Kenney and R. Florida (eds.), *Locating Global Advantage: Industry Dynamics in the International Economy*, (Stanford, CA: Stanford University Press), 52–81.

————and R. K. LESTER (2001). 'The New Global Supply-Base: New Challenges for Local Suppliers in East Asia'. *Industrial Performance Center Working Paper Series*, (Cambridge, MA: MIT Press).

ULRICH, K. (1995). 'The Role of Product Architecture in the Manufacturing Firm', *Research Policy* 24: 419–40.

VOELZKOW, H. (2007). *Jenseits nationaler Produktionsmodelle? Die Governance regionaler Wirtschaftscluster. International vergleichende Analysen*, (Marburg: Metropolis Verlag).

VOSKAMP, U. (2005). 'Grenzen der Modularität: Chancen für Hochlohnstandorte in globalen Produktions-und Innovationsnetzwerken', *SOFI-Mitteilungen* 33: 115–30.

WELLS, L. T. (ed.) (1972). *The Product Life Cycle and International Trade*, (Boston: Harvard Business School Division of Research).

WHITFORD, J. (2001). 'The Decline of a Model? Challenge and Response in the Italian Industrial Districts', *Economy and Society* 30(1): 38–65.

————(2006). *The New Old Economy: Networks, Institutions, and the Organizational Transformation of American Manufacturing*, (New York: Oxford University Press).

————and A. ENRIETTI (2005). 'Surviving the Fall of a King: The Regional Institutional Implications of Crisis at Fiat Auto', *International Journal of Urban and Regional Research* 29.

————and J. ZEITLIN (2004). 'Governing Decentralized Production: Institutions, Public Policy, and the Prospects for Inter-firm Collaboration in US Manufacturing', *Industry and Innovation* 11(1/2): 11–44.

WOLFE, D. A. and M. S. GERTLER (2004). 'Clusters from the Inside and Out: Local Dynamics and Global Linkages', *Urban Studies* 41(5/6): 1071–93.

WOMACK, J., D. T. JONES and D. ROOS (1990). *The Machine that Changed the World*, (New York: Rawson Associates).

WOOD, S., (ed.) (1989). *The Transformation of Work?: Skill, Flexibility, and the Labour Process*, (London: Unwin Hyman).

ZEITLIN, J. (2007). 'Industrial Districts and Regional Clusters', in G. Jones and J. Zeitlin (eds.), *The Oxford Handbook of Business History*, (Oxford: Oxford University Press), 219–43.

ZENGER, T. R. and W. S. HESTERLY (1997). 'The Disaggregation of Corporations: Selective Intervention, High-Powered Incentives, and Molecular Units', *Organization Science* 8(3): 209–22.

PART IV

··

CHALLENGES FOR COMPARATIVE INSTITUTIONAL ANALYSIS

··

CHAPTER 19

INSTITUTIONAL TRANSFORMATION IN EUROPEAN POST-COMMUNIST REGIMES

IVAN SZELENYI
KATARZYNA WILK

INTRODUCTION

What is happening to institutions during the post-communist transition in Eastern and Central Europe? There is a consensus in the literature that in both Central and Eastern Europe the initial transitional reforms aimed at building up market institutions. They did not attempt the more complex and potentially costly political task of reforming social institutions 'The sequence of reforms in transition economies are roughly in line with what the prediction of political economy theory suggesting that reforms expected to be more popular should start first' (Roland 2002: 42). However, as predicted by Aghion and Blanchard (1994), fast economic reforms have raised the demand for social policies, which would compensate the transitional losers; 'Not only is the economy changing, but so is the government's role in buffering people from market forces' (Lipsmeyer 2002: 661). In the early stages, governments either sustained or expanded their already extensive commitments (Fultz and Ruck 2001), in order to contain the social costs generated by the transition. A dramatic increase of unemployment, for example, was compensated for by large-scale early retirement provision; the costs were transmitted to the pension systems increasing the level of state expenditure, thus having a long-term negative impact on the sustainability of public finances and prospects for further reforms. Major social institutions including pension and healthcare systems and educational services, thus, continued to be structured along socialist principles for some time (Fultz and Ruck 2001; Deacon 2000).

These tensions reflect a broader issue in institutional analysis concerning the way in which institutional structures reinforce and complement each other. In communist regimes, a certain balance had emerged between the political system, the form of economic organization and the social institutions of redistribution. With the collapse of communism, however, these institutional linkages were broken apart and actors had to develop new strategies as they sought to rebuild institutional coherence. In this chapter, we argue that in the early stages of transition, it was the reorganization of the economy that dominated the process of institutional change. This reorganization was in turn closely aligned with the development of new state structures and political processes. At this stage, the social institutions of redistribution were little affected. The second phase of transition has, however, seen the emergence of efforts to reform the welfare system in ways which better fit the developing neo-liberal economies. These efforts have been differentially successful because the political and economic institutions established in the first phase of transition shape and constrain the sorts of institutional change in welfare systems, which is being pursued in the second phase. During the first decade of the transition, the economic system was by and large successfully transformed into a market system, but the great distributive systems, (as they have been known in Eastern and Central Europe) such as healthcare, the pension system, and tertiary education remained very much as they had been during the socialist era. However, by the late 1990s, this situation was changing and institutional reform moved into a second phase, focusing particularly on how to make these welfare institutions fit more closely to the new context.

For some forty years of socialism, the former socialist countries had been on a convergence trajectory. They had entered the socialist experiment at very different levels of economic development, with different institutional arrangements and major cultural-religious differences. While these differences did not disappear altogether they were substantially reduced. But as communism broke down the old fault-lines re-emerged, and the European socialist countries split between Central and Eastern Europe just as Jenö Szücs predicted ([1983]1988). Dawson noted that although societies of the former Soviet Union and Eastern Europe ' . . . all share a common legacy of communist rule and confront similar challenges in attempting a transition away from Soviet-style communism' (Dawson 1999: 15), they differ with respect to the commitment to and the accomplishment of building capitalist economies, democratic institutions, and reformed social institutions.

We start this chapter by conceptualizing these different trajectories in European socialist countries from socialism and then proceed to show how this has impacted on the two phases of transformation which have taken place.

The two trajectories of transformation

Arguably there was a fault line between Central and Eastern Europe, which preceded the socialist period. Following The Second World War, the European countries that entered the path of socialist transformation were at strikingly different levels of social and economic development and they had quite different socio-economic institutions. Czechoslovakia, Poland, the Baltic States, Hungary, and the western states of Yugoslavia (Slovenia and Croatia) were more westernized, industrialized, and somewhat wealthier than the non-Baltic states of the USSR and the European regions east them, like Yugoslavia, Albania, Bulgaria, and Romania. In this chapter we call the former group of countries Central Europe (often referred to in the literature somewhat awkwardly as East Central Europe) and label the latter ones as Eastern Europe. For forty years, between the late 1940s and 1989 the European societies, which called themselves socialist, were on a convergence trajectory (Berend, 1996). During the four decades of socialism, differences did not disappear completely but they were substantially reduced. The convergence of economic and social institutions was particularly impressive. The institutions of the redistributive economy were almost indistinguishable. A Soviet model of legal, educational, and cultural institutions was also imposed in all the countries (though to a slightly different degree). Hence Central and Eastern Europe were on the road to be merged into the rather homogeneous category of 'Soviet type societies'.

For a short while, after the collapse of communism and the discrediting of those associated with the communist parties, it appeared that there was no alternative to the transition to a 'free market economy'. Neo-liberalism became the dominant ideology in the whole region. Economic reform scenarios were similar. Balcerowicz advocated shock therapy in Poland. Gaidar promised capitalism in one hundred days in Russia. But this consensus did not last too long. By the mid-1990s rather different socio-economic institutions were emerging in these two regions of Europe.

The differences between the Central and East European ways of building capitalism became apparent in the ways in which property was converted from public into private ownership. How this crucial step in the transition should be undertaken was debated. There was strong support for some sort of people's capitalism, hence privatization by vouchers. Vouchers were supposed to be either equally distributed among citizens or allocated to employees according to their length of service or their accumulated contribution to the value of the enterprise. The major alternative to this was public and competitive auctioning of formerly collective property to the highest bidders. Various countries followed different policies at different points in time, but after experimenting with a range of privatization techniques, the two regions of Europe found themselves moving in distinctly different directions.

In Russia voucher privatization facilitated management buy-outs and helped to create a new domestic grand bourgeoisie. Many of them came from the ranks of former high officials and their clients and hence they were seen as the 'red barons', or a 'nomenklatura bourgeoisie'. Gigantic private wealth was created over a short period of time. This was not quite what neo-liberals such as Gaidar wanted or advocated, but it was the result of Yeltsin's compromises with political bosses. Arguably the new grand bourgeoisie was created via state action and was intimately linked to political power. Nevertheless, the new property relations were also somewhat insecure. This became especially obvious as Putin came to power, and he was faced with challenges to his power by some of the 'oligarchs'. Putin managed to reallocate some of the property from now disloyal clients to loyal ones (even renationalized some of the wealth previously privatized), as well as locking up or exiling some who had begun to aspire to political power. Putin treated the post-communist oligarchs as 'pomesh-chiks', or service nobility, owners who have their property in exchange for their services and loyalty to their political master. During the 1990s there was a similar trend in changes in property relations in a number of other countries, Bulgaria, Romania, and even in Slovakia under Mečiar (O'Dwyer, 2006: 48; Elster, Offe and Preuss, 1998: 202).

Such patron–client relations were not restricted to the world of political bosses and new proprietors. In Eastern Europe, relationships between state authorities and citizens, and management and workers were also clientelistic. Unemployment grew relatively slowly, though wage arrears were frequent. But firms occasionally offered services typical of the socialist era (housing, even household plots, in order to enable workers to grow their own food when their wages not were paid). Barter comple-mented in significant ways the market transaction, and in some areas of life it was more important than markets (Southworth, 2004a, b; Woodruff 1999).

Given the importance of clientelism, especially the reassignment of former state property as private property by political patrons to clients in exchange for their loyalty, this type of domination and set of economic arrangements may be labelled neo-patrimonial (Eisenstadt 1973; Garcelon 2005). Neo-patrimonialism in its most general sense implies the uses of public or state resources in order to secure the loyalty of the clients. Patrimonialism is a technology of domination, a system of governmentality. It secures loyalty rather than material benefits to the patron (though patrimonial rulers can be corrupt and can be engaged in activities of political capitalism). What—if anything—is new or novel in the patrimonialism of the twenty-first century as described here? Eisenstadt (1973) emphasized that neo-patrimonial domination represents a mix of patrimonialism and bureaucracy, or legal rational authority. The rulers even in the most modernized patrimonial states were personal masters. In neo-patrimonial regimes even when the person of the patron is important, as in the case of Russia's Putin, some formally rational system of succession is in place. Hence Putin did not seek an unconstitutional third term as president. He managed the election of one of his clients to this office and then renegotiated the distribution of power between president and prime minister, the position he was able to occupy without violating the law. Neo-patrimonialism in its ideal type also coexists with a system of managed democracy. Elections are held at regular intervals. Opposition parties participate in these elections, though the elections rarely offer surprises and are managed through a variety of means whereby the state apparatus is used covertly and overtly to maintain the conditions for the victory of the existing order.

Economic transformation in Eastern Europe proceeded along neo-patrimonial lines with state and economy closely intertwined under the dominance of strong political leadership supported by a loyal class of oligarchs who accrued huge wealth through their control of certain key state assets. Meanwhile other assets of the state such as heavy industry and the production of consumer goods, which were uncompetitive in the new open economy, were left to decline, causing massive unemployment and poverty. Whilst this was partially cushioned by the old distributive systems, the use of traditional mechanisms of tight police control and appeals to Russian nationalism were also deployed to manage the maintenance of the neo-patrimonial regime.

During the early 1990s the Central European countries also experimented with various techniques of privatization and voucher privatization. Though Vaclav Klaus, while prime minister of the Czech Republic during the early 1990s, was usually praised for his staunch liberalism, early on he was committed to encouraging domestic capital formation and was careful in opening up Czech capital markets to foreign investors. As a result the Czech Republic (and Poland as well) until the second half of the 1990s lagged substantially behind Hungary in per capita FDI (see Table 19.1). Even in Hungary, which took an early lead in auctioning off formerly state owned corporations in competitive biddings to foreign investors, some of the privatization was achieved via compensation vouchers (in particular in agriculture; see Harcsa et al. 1998) and like in Eastern Europe the beneficiaries of this kind of privatization method were former cadres or their clients. Nevertheless by the late 1990s in the Central European region the main technique of privatization of the corporate sector was competitive bidding at auctions, and as these economies took off after 1995 the most dynamic and export oriented sectors of their economies were owned or controlled by foreign investors (Eyal et al. 1998).

The Central European countries in order to attract and keep foreign capital so vital for their economic growth strategy had to implement neo-liberal economic policies. This involved radical deregulation of the economy, offering tax benefits to foreign investors, opening their markets to importers, and free market reform of the banking sector. Central Europe was on a neo-liberal trajectory to post-communist capitalism (Kochanowicz 2006). On a number of economic indicators and institutions (in terms of per capita FDI, the extent of privatization, degree of liberalization of markets for foreign goods, and elimination of export subsidies) the Central European countries were arguably more neo-liberal than countries like the UK under Thatcher or the US under Reagan.

The differences between the neo-patrimonial transformation of Eastern Europe and the more neo-liberal transition in Central Europe can be seen in Table 19.1.

Table 19.1: Indicators of transformation of economic institutions

		1989	1990	1991	1992	1993	1994	1995	1996	1997	1998
Belarus	Private sector	5	5	5	10	10	15	15	15	20	20
	Admin. prices	100	100	90	80	70	60	45	30	27	27
	Bank reform	1	1	1	1	1	1	2	1	1	1
	Foreign direct investment	Na	Na	Na	Na	18	11	15	105	350	201
Bulgaria	Private sector	10	10	20	25	35	40	50	55	60	65
	Admin. prices	100	70	24	16	26	43	46	52	14	16
	Bank reform	1	1	1	1.7	2	2	2	2	2.7	2.7
	Foreign direct investment	Na	4	56	42	40	105	98	138	507	537
Czech Republic	Private sector	5	10	15	30	45	65	70	75	75	75
	Admin. prices	Na	Na	28	18	18	18	17	17	13	13
	Bank reform	1	1	2	3	3	3	3	3	3	3
	Foreign direct investment	Na	Na	983	564	762	2,531	1,280	1,259	3,574	6,219
Hungary	Private sector	5	25	30	40	50	55	60	70	75	80
	Admin. prices	18	16	11	11	11	12	13	13	14	15
	Bank reform	1	1	2	2	3	3	3	3	3	4
	Foreign direct investment	187	311	1,459	1,471	2,328	1,097	4,772	3,335	3,715	3,070
Poland	Private sector	30	30	40	45	50	55	60	60	65	65
	Admin. prices	19	11	11	11	11	12	12	11	11	11
	Bank reform	1	2	2	2	3	3	3	3	3	3.3
	Foreign direct investment	Na	0	117	284	580	1,846	3,617	4,445	4,863	6,049

Romania	Private sector	15	15	25	25	35	40	45	55	60	60
	Admin. prices	100	85	47	29	20	18	18	18	9	9
	Bank reform	1	1	1	1	2	2	3	3	2.7	2.3
	Foreign direct investment	Na	-18	37	73	87	341	417	415	1,267	2,079
Russia	Private sector	5	5	5	25	40	50	55	60	70	70
	Admin. prices	100	100	100	47	47	40	13	13	13	13
	Bank reform	1	1	1	1	2	2	2	2.7	2.7	1.7
	Foreign direct investment	Na	Na	Na	Na	408	1,460	1,656	1,681	1,492	
Slovakia	Private sector	5	10	15	30	45	55	60	70	70	75
	Admin. prices	Na	Na	Na	Na	22	22	22	22	21	18
	Bank reform	1	1	2	2.7	2.7	2.7	2.7	2.7	2.7	2.7
	Foreign direct investment	10	24	82	100	106	236	194	199	84	373
Ukraine	Private sector	10	10	10	15	40	45	50	55	55	55
	Admin. prices	Na	Na	Na	Na	Na	Na	Na	Na	Na	Na
	Bank reform	1	1	1	1	2	2	2	2	2	Na
	Foreign direct investment	Na	Na	200	458	151	257	516	581	747	

Source: Data are from www.ebrd/economicstatistics.

Private sector = private sector share in GDP (in per cent); Admin. prices = share of administered prices in CPI (in per cent); Bank reform = EBRD index of banking sector reform (1 = none; 4 = full); FDI = foreign direct investment net in US$ million.

The Czech Republic, Hungary, and Poland privatized the public sector early, and opened investment markets early to foreign capital. The acceleration of privatization tended to coincide with an influx of FDI (though much less so in Poland than in the Czech Republic and Hungary). They also deregulated the economy (reduced price controls and reformed the banking sector). Privatization was somewhat (or greatly) delayed in Belarus, Bulgaria, Romania, Russia, and the Ukraine (the later four countries were one to three years behind the Central European ones in this respect) and more importantly when privatization took off, their markets were still largely inaccessible to foreign investors, enabling the nomenklatura bourgeoisie to take advantage of mass privatization.

In the period up to the late 1990s, the regimes labelled neo-patrimonial offered poor economic performances, while the neo-liberal countries, which also suffered substantial early set-backs, recovered early and began to perform well. But around 1998–2000 the fortunes changed. As post-communist regimes entered the second phase of institutional transformation neo-patrimonial systems took off, while neo-liberal systems with some exceptions slowed down.

On the whole, neo-patrimonial regimes did poorly in the 1990s. They managed to keep unemployment rates low, but most suffered from hyperinflation and while they seemed to recover briefly they fell back into a rather deep recession by the end of the first post-communist decade. Taking into account falling living standards, increases in the poverty rate, and popular dissatisfaction with the transition it is even more obvious how neo-patrimonial regimes fell behind neo-liberal countries. According the World Bank data (www.worldbank.org) in countries like Belarus, Bulgaria, Romania, Russia, and the Ukraine, the percentage of population below the poverty line ranged from 25 per cent to over 40 per cent while at the same time in the Czech Republic, Hungary, and Poland it was between 2 and 15 per cent.

By 1999–2000 there was a sharp turnaround in several respects. There was a shift in the economic institutional arrangements of some countries. Most importantly, countries regarded as neo-patrimonial during the 1990s, such as Bulgaria and Romania, opened up their markets. The same occurred in Slovakia, which was during the first decade of transition a mix between neo-patrimonialism and neo-liberalism. During the past ten years these three countries have caught up with the Czech Republic, Hungary, and Poland in annual per capita FDI inflow, or even surpassed them. In 2007 FDI inflow in Hungary was a mere US$ 1,400 million, while Slovakia received 2,660 million, Bulgaria 8,150 million, Romania 9,660 million. Since these countries were about the join the EU they were under pressure to conform to EU requirements in opening up their markets and reducing corruption (though plenty of corruption still remains in Bulgaria and Romania). Their political system also shifted more towards liberal democracy (arguably EU pressure played a role in Mečiar's 1998 electoral defeat). Most significantly Russian economic growth took off and during the last decade Russia joined the Wunderkindern of the world economy consistently producing 7–10 per cent annual growth rates, while government debts declined consistently.

Table 19.2: Economic performance of neo-liberal and neo-patrimonial regimes during the first phase of transition

		1989	1990	1991	1992	1993	1994	1995	1996	1997	1998
Belarus	Growth of GDP	8	-3	-1	-10	-8	-12	-10	3	11	8
	Unemployment	0	0	0	1	1	2	3	4	3	2
	Inflation	2	5	94	970	1,190	2,221	709	53	64	73
	Government debt	Na	Na	Na	Na	Na	Na	18	10	12	11
Bulgaria	Growth of GDP	1	-9	-12	-7	-2	2	3	-10	-6	4
	Unemployment	Na	2	10	15	16	19	14	13	15	16
	Inflation	6	26	334	82	73	96	62	123	1,082	22
	Government debt	Na	Na	185	166	172	183	115	319	105	80
Czech Republic	Growth of GDP	1	-1	-12	-1	0	2	6	4	-1	-1
	Unemployment	Na	1	4	3	4	4	4	4	4	6
	Inflation	1	10	52	11	21	10	10	9	8	11
	Government debt	Na	Na	Na	Na	19	18	14	12	12	13
Hungary	Growth of GDP	1	-4	-12	-3	-1	3	2	1	5	5
	Unemployment	1	1	8	9	12	11	10	10	9	8
	Inflation	17	29	35	23	23	19	28	24	18	14
	Government debt	Na	Na	75	79	90	86	84	72	64	62
Poland	Growth of GDP	0	-12	-7	3	4	5	7	6	7	5
	Unemployment	Na	7	12	14	16	16	15	13	10	10
	Inflation	251	586	70	43	35	32	29	20	15	12
	Government debt	Na	95	82	87	89	72	50	44	44	39

(continued)

Table 19.2: Continued

		1989	1990	1991	1992	1993	1994	1995	1996	1997	1998
Romania	Growth of GDP	−6	−6	−13	−9	2	4	7	4	−6	−5
	Unemployment	Na	Na	3	8	10	11	10	7	6	6
	Inflation	1	5	170	210	256	137	32	39	154	59
	Government debt	Na	Na	Na	Na	Na	Na	21	28	16	18
		1989	1990	1991	1992	1993	1994	1995	1996	1997	1998
Russia	Growth of GDP	2	−3	−5	−15	−9	−13	−4	−4	1	−5
	Unemployment	Na	Na	Na	5	6	8	9	9	11	12
	Inflation	Na	Na	Na	1,526	875	311	198	48	15	28
	Government debt	Na	Na	Na	Na	Na	48	46	49	57	82
Slovakia	Growth of GDP	1	0	−16	−7	−4	6	6	6	5	4
	Unemployment	Na	Na	10	10	14	14	13	11	12	13
	Inflation	2	11	61	10	23	13	10	6	6	7
	Government debt	Na	Na	Na	Na	28	25	22	32	34	35
Ukraine	Growth of GDP	4	−4	−11	−10	−14	−23	−12	−10	−3	−2
	Unemployment	Na	0	0	0	0	0	0	1	2	4
	Inflation	2	4	91	1,210	4,734	891	377	80	16	11
	Government debt	Na	Na	Na	Na	Na	Na	22	24	30	38

Data are from www.ebrd/economicstatistics. GDP = growth in real terms; Unemployment = end-year, percentage of labour force; Inflation = consumer prices, annual average, percentage change; Government debt = in percent of GDP.

Table 19.3: Economic performance of neo–liberal and neo–patrimonial regimes during the second phase of transition

		1999	2000	2001	2002	2003	2004	2005	2006	2007 estimate	2008 Forecast
Belarus	Growth of GDP	3	6	5	5	7	11	10	10	8	8
	Unemployment	2	2	2	3	3	2	2	1	1	Na
	Inflation	294	169	61	43	28	18	10	7	8	13
	Government debt	13	17	13	11	10	9	8	9	12	Na
Bulgaria	Growth of GDP	2	5	4	5	5	7	6	6	6	6
	Unemployment	17	16	20	17	14	12	10	9	6	Na
	Inflation	1	10	7	6	2	6	5	7	8	11
	Government debt	79	74	66	54	46	38	29	23	21	Na
Czech Republic	Growth of GDP	1	4	3	2	4	5	7	6	6	5
	Unemployment	9	9	8	7	8	8	8	7	Na	Na
	Inflation	2	4	5	2	0	3	2	3	3	4
	Government debt	13	18	26	29	30	31	30	31	32	Na
Hungary	Growth of GDP	4	5	4	4	4	5	4	4	1	2
	Unemployment	7	6	6	6	6	6	7	8	7	Na
	Inflation	10	10	9	5	5	7	4	4	8	6
	Government debt	61	54	51	54	58	59	62	66	66	Na
Poland	Growth of GDP	5	4	1	1	4	5	4	6	7	5
	Unemployment	15	17	19	20	20	18	17	12	8	Na
	Inflation	7	10	6	2	1	4	2	1	3	4
	Government debt	40	37	38	42	47	46	47	48	45	Na
Romania	Growth of GDP	-1	2	6	5	5	9	4	8	6	5
	Unemployment	7	7	7	8	7	6	6	5	Na	Na
	Inflation	46	46	35	23	15	12	10	7	5	7
	Government debt	24	23	23	24	22	19	16	12	13	Na

(*continued*)

Table 19.3: Continued

		1999	2000	2001	2002	2003	2004	2005	2006	2007	2008
Russia	Growth of GDP	6	10	5	5	7	7	6	7	8	7
	Unemployment	13	10	9	9	9	8	8	7	Na	Na
	Inflation	86	21	22	16	14	11	13	8	9	12
	Government debt	90	63	48	41	32	26	17	11	10	Na
Slovakia	Growth of GDP	2	2	3	5	5	5	7	9	10	7
	Unemployment	16	19	19	19	17	18	16	13	10	Na
	Inflation	11	12	7	3	9	8	3	5	3	3
	Government debt	47	50	49	43	42	41	34	30	29	Na
Ukraine	Growth of GDP	0	6	9	5	10	12	3	7	7	6
	Unemployment	4	4	4	4	4	4	3	3	Na	Na
	Inflation	23	28	12	1	5	9	14	9	13	25
	Government debt	51	46	37	34	29	26	20	17	13	Na

Data from www.ebrd/economicstatistics. Nevertheless if one looks at the two decades of transition neo-liberal policies still win out over neo-patrimonial ones. In terms of economic growth Poland is leading the pack, its real GDP in 2007 was 169% of the 1989 level. Slovakia is next with 154%, the Czech Republic and Hungary are close third and fourth (136% and 135% respectively). Bulgaria lags behind with 107% and Russia with barely over-passing the 1989 level at 102% (data from EBRD).

At the same time, the Czech Republic, Hungary, and Poland—Hungary certainly more so than the other countries—were struggling with the threat of a second recession. In comparison with the neo-patrimonial regimes and with earlier years economic growth slowed down and their government debt after years of decline began to increase again. The Czech Republic was hit with economic slow down first in 1997 and it remained low until 2004–2005. Poland hit rock bottom in 2001–2002. The Czech Republic and Poland did extremely well in terms of their GDP growth between 2004 and 2008, though their government debt remains quite high and the trend during the first decade of the twenty-first century is upward. In contrast, neo-patrimonial regimes have seen declining and low levels of debt. Hungary in terms of its economic growth has been on a downward trend since 2002, but this became especially serious from 2007–2008 with debt so large that the social-liberal government had to implement serious austerity measures and eventually seek IMF support, sending its popularity to record lows and boosting the Conservative opposition party—which was campaigning effectively against welfare cuts.

The 'Russian miracle' of course can be attributed to the rising prices of raw materials, especially oil and gas and it remains to be seen whether Russia is on a sustainable trajectory of fast growth. Some commentators argue that the collapse of the rouble during the late 1990s led to an import substitution boom, giving a big boost to domestic industrial production as well. As a result, capital flight declined and domestic investment increased (Cook 2007: 149). It is also noticeable, though, that it is not only the oligarchs who are benefiting from Russia's take-off; the poverty rate (Alam et al. 2005) and even GINI (which exploded during the first phase of transition) is declining. There appears to be some trickle down of the benefits of economic growth in the Russian Federation and that is hardly attributable to populist hand-outs by the state.

Changes of the great distributive systems during the first phase of transition

During the first phase of transition some weak attempts were made to reform the great distributive systems into a welfare state, which was compatible with the logics of a market economy though this typically affected the providers more than the customers (Mihályi 2007: 16–17). Providers had to learn new ways to navigate in the post-communist world,. The most important changes were the following (see Elster, Offe and Preuss, 1988: 206–7; Orenstein and Haas, 2005, especially p. 139).

1. Funding of pensions and healthcare services were now separated from the state budget (Orenstein, 2000). Pension and healthcare funds were created, which were separately funded from taxes paid by employers and employees (Cook, 2007: 62; Mihályi 2007: 46–7). Management of health care funds was usually decentralized.

2. Private medical practices were legalized, though with the exception of some specialties (for instance dentistry) few people used private medical practices, most relied on public health facilities.
3. Private pension insurance firms were allowed to operate legally (Orenstein, 2000: 219), though the overwhelming majority of pensioners remained in the state-run PAYG system (Wilk and Wtorek 2008).
4. Private universities were legalized and they were allowed to charge tuition fees, but the overwhelming majority of student still attended public universities with tuition-free tertiary education.
5. Universities gained substantial autonomy and, while in socialist times research was separated into the institutes of Academy of Sciences, weak attempts were made to create 'research universities' (though the network of research institutes of Academies of Sciences was retained). The universities regained their right to award research degrees—PhDs.
6. Some forms of social assistance became means-tested. (This was highly contested, for instance as part of the so called Bokros package of 1995–96, the Hungarian social-liberal government introduced a means-tested family allowance, which was in 1998 withdrawn by the newly elected right-wing Orban government).

Despite such reforms in the early stages of the transition—at least in Central Europe—social spending was not reduced. In fact it systematically increased (Sachs 2001; see also Rinegold 1999: 30). According to Sachs, social expenditures in Hungary for instance increased from 15.8 per cent of GDP in 1989 to 22.5 per cent in 1993; in Poland the increase was from 10.0 to 21.0 per cent. Sachs attributes this change to the fact that the electoral system was dominated in the new democracies by 'interest group politics'. He attributes undisciplined welfare spending to the successor communist parties regaining political power. However, this does not take into account the fact that the increases of welfare expenditures to a large extent covered the social costs of economic transformation. As a result of market transition about a third of all jobs were lost—a substantial proportion of those who lost their positions were simply transferred to the pension system via early retirement or disability pensions, or had to be supported by formerly non-existent unemployment benefits.

Recipients of these systems hardly noticed any change. Seeking medical care in a policlinic or being hospitalized was pretty much the same—underwhelming—experience ten years after the fall of communism, as it had been previously. Publicly funded pensions in the Czech Republic and Hungary were close to general living standards. In Poland pensioners' living standards were actually higher than those of the general population (European Commission 2006 'Sustainability' Report). Students entering the universities were trained in an almost identical system (with some changes in the curriculum, but not in the level of and nature of specialization) and given the changing character of the labour market they faced more serious difficulties upon graduation than ever.

Changes in Distributive Systems during the Second Phase of Transition

During the second phase of the reforms, however, substantial differences emerged between post-communist regimes in the transformation of their distributive systems. Neo-patrimonial regimes implemented radical neo-liberal reforms to the welfare system, while such reforms were often defeated or at least hotly contested in neo-liberal systems.

Though Russia benefited in a major way from the oil boom and has not been under much fiscal pressure to reform the institutions of the great distributive systems, nevertheless, already in 2000, German Gref, the minister for Economic Development formulated a radically neo-liberal welfare reform scenario. Though after political negotiations with the Duma, Gref's plan was not fully implemented, nevertheless new substantial reforms were passed and implemented in Russia by the middle of the first decade of the twenty-first century. As a consequence of these reforms:

1. Free basic medical services are available only to the means-tested poor.
2. The publicly guaranteed pension is only at subsistence level; pensioners now can choose to transfer some of their pension contributions to privately managed pension funds (Cook 2007: 172; 191).
3. Various in-kind benefits (public transport, housing, medicine, and utilities, etc.) were monetized (i.e. replaced with cash payments) and their value was substantially reduced.
4. Tuition is charged in institutions of tertiary education and funding of universities is now linked to student enrolments, 'money follows the students'.

It is debatable whether these reforms played any role in the success of the Russian economy (high growth rate and declining government debt). While implementing these reforms the Russian government increased social spending modestly (Cook 2007: 185), so arguably Russia's robust economy enabled the construction of a neo-liberal welfare state rather than welfare austerity measures causing the economic dynamism and fiscal stability. The truth is probably between these two propositions. The Russian reforms, which emphasized targeting, means testing, and co-payments helped the fiscal health of the Russian economy, which was on a growth trajectory anyway.

In sharp contrast, the Czech Republic, Hungary, and Poland (Slovakia is an interesting exception) struggled with increasing budget deficits and debts and were under pressure from the European Union to meet EU standards. However, they either failed to implement similar reforms or, if they passed neo-liberal welfare legislation, those were met with strong popular resistance and sabotaged by institutional inertia and political uncertainty as opposition parties usually promised to roll back such reforms, if they came to power. The Central European countries struggle with the following problems with their distributive systems:

1. Healthcare: provision is claimed to be inefficient (too many visits to doctors, too long stays in hospitals, in comparison with old EU countries; see Mihályi and Petru 2001: 212; Rinegold 1999: 36). Furthermore, the health fund is in constant and increasing deficit (Mihályi 2007: 88). Efforts have been made to introduce systems of individual payment and private insurance but these have proved ineffective.

2. Pensions: as far as budget deficit is concerned the publicly funded pension is the single most important item (Gomułka 2001: 123–6). The electoral power of pensioners constitutes a formidable block to change even where this is a major factor in the fiscal crisis of the state. All three countries intend to increase the retirement age (Fox 1997) and to increase the role of funded private insurance schemes but these institutional changes are all strongly opposed.

3. Tertiary education and research funding: efforts to increase funding for tertiary education through introducing fees has met with strong resistance by university instructors, students, and their parents (in Hungary in the March 2008 referendum, 82 per cent voted against university tuition fees). Efforts to reform the structure of the universities and the research system are also having limited success.

During Putin's presidency, neo-patrimonial Russia introduced a largely neo-liberal system of social provisions, while the neo-liberal Central European countries (with the exception of Slovakia), which have increasing government debt and deficits in publicly funded healthcare, pensions, and tertiary education, retained a fundamentally statist, paternalist system of social provisions with only some complementary market mechanisms (Cook 2007: 53; 239, Table 7).

Why and how did Russia become a leader in liberalization and why has Central Europe run into a brick wall when government attempted radical liberalization? We can examine two explanations: one has to do with the differences in the political system, the other with the quality of socialist welfare provisions.

Table 19.4: Neo-patrimonial and neo-liberal regimes: comparison of economic institutions and the great distributive systems during the second phase of transition

	Neo-patrimonial regimes	Neo-liberal regimes
Property rights and economic system	Neo-patrimonial	Neo-liberal
Great distributive systems	Neo-liberal	Paternalistic

Political determinants of transformation of the institutions of great distributive systems

Russia had attempted the liberalization of the great distributive systems already during the first phase of transition, but Gaidar's priority was price-liberalization, fiscal stabilization, and privatization, hence the transformation of economic institutions (Cook 2007: 60). The price was of this institutional transformation high so Gaidar did not press the reform of social institutions. In 1995, the Communist party and its left-wing allies became a major force in parliament. They blocked any liberalization of the social institutions and even eliminated some of the earlier reforms. The constellation of political power changed radically, however, with Putin's election in 1999, and especially with his re-election in 2004. Putin had now firm control over the Duma and though his liberalization of distributive systems was met with popular protest, given his system of managed democracy, he could ignore or even squash protests. Putin could break the bureaucratic resistance of the medical establishment (ibid., 175), ignore the protest of pensioners (ibid., 181), and overcome the opposition by 'red rectors' and university students (ibid., 174).

The political realities in most Central European countries were strikingly different. The Czech Republic, Hungary, and Poland have—since 1990—reasonably well-functioning parliamentary democracies. Parties face competitive elections every fourth year, where they might not be elected for a second term (actually changes in governments from election to election is almost the rule rather than the exception in Central Europe). This creates a major barrier to institutional reform of the welfare system, which affects so many of the electorate.

The legacy of socialism

Another potential explanation lies in the legacy of the socialist era. In Czechoslovakia, Hungary, or Poland patients could expect reasonable attention in polyclinics and hospitals. Pensions were paid on time and were indexed to inflation. Students might not have acquired many marketable skills at the university, but education was free and, given the system of credentialing, once they got a degree they had an almost guaranteed job with an income set according to their level of education. In Eastern Europe these systems never worked quite as well, and given the depth of the transitional crisis during the second half of the 1990s they virtually ceased to exist. In this part of the world there did not seem to appear any alternative to private and market-based provisions, while in Central Europe there was still a system, which did not function well, but did function and seemed to be worth defending. In János Kornai's formulation the Central European post-communist countries live with a "prematurely born welfare state" (Kornai [1992] 1995: 131), by which he means the government took on responsibilities to fund healthcare, pensions, and tertiary education/research beyond their means (Kornai 1997). Kornai acknowledges that under the socialist systems the provisions of such services were often of 'very poor' quality (Kornai [1992]1995: 132) as well as being unequally distributed. Access to housing, education, healthcare, etc. was more likely to be made available to party members and the nomenklatura than ordinary citizens. The nomenklatura would also receive better quality services where this was a possibility.

During socialist times, social provisions were funded from the state budget whose source revenues were appropriated from state-owned firms. While funds appropriated this way were inadequate to provide high quality services this system did not generate a fiscal crisis of the state, since the resources were obtainable (though the downturn of socialist economies during the 1980s started to pose some problems, but the system still worked). During the first phase of transition this fiscal base for social provisions was undermined while the need for welfare substantially increased. As Wagener (2002: 161) pointed out: 'if the communist welfare state was not living beyond its means, the post-communist welfare state certainly was'. As the formerly state-owned enterprises were privatized (and the most profitable ones were sold first) the new owners had to be promised tax-breaks, especially in neo-liberal economies when the major investors were foreign owners. They were often offered tax breaks in order to keep them from moving further east to less expensive regions. There are severe limits as to how fast personal incomes and taxes on those incomes can increase in order to fill the state-funding gap. If incomes increase too fast (as they were doing during the 2000–2007 period in Central Europe) then businesses are discouraged from investing in the region or even keeping their investments there. If taxes are too high, it encourages tax-avoidance of various forms. This leads to a 'fiscal crisis' of the state, which is confronted with shrinking revenues and, at least in Central Europe, a citizenry with modest expectations though beyond the means available to the governments to satisfy. Governments tried to keep funding these services through budget deficits, borrowing and inflation, but given the competitiveness of the global economy (Deacon 2000; Orenstein and Hass 2005) and the expectations of the European Union (Kovacs 2002; Schneider and Stepanek 2001; Wagener 2002) this proved to be unsustainable. Hence the project for neo-liberal reform of welfare systems keeps re-entering the political agenda, but it is blocked by the nature of the political process. Neo-liberal reform parties are losing elections to parties which promise to undo such reforms if elected. In this deadlock the educational and health establishment struggle to keep business as usual.

Hence the fiscal trap, which to a large extent was created by the neo-liberal transformation of economic institutions, can hardly be resolved, especially in democratic political systems, by austerity measures. During the second phase of transition, Central Europe faces hard challenges: it has to convert an outdated socialist distributive system into a modern capitalist welfare regime at a time when it finds itself in a fiscal trap with shrinking resources for social expenditures, and increasing pressures from the global economy and, in particular the EU, to balance budgets, reduce debt, and control inflation.

CONCLUSIONS

As the post-communist societies are in the second phase of transition there is a fundamental inconsistency in the logic of their economic and welfare institutions. More concretely in Central Europe neo-liberal economic institutions coexist with outdated, malfunctioning distributive institutions, which are fundamentally state socialist in nature. Since the neo-liberal economic system does not permit any longer the funding of this socialist distributive system, the scene is set for further political conflict over efforts to create a system where the institutions in the major subsystems cohere.

One outcome may be change towards a middle ground in which those who can afford it find private, market alternatives to publicly funded healthcare, pensions, and education. One may not even need means testing to have better targeted welfare provisions if higher quality services on the market place and in the private sector seduce away the better off from the publicly funded provisions. But one has to deal with the supply or funding side as well. Neo-liberal Central Europe suffers from chronic revenue shortages, most of it attributable to the fact that it followed too closely the neo-liberal cookbook. The level of employment is far too low: if there is any growth it is growth without employment. The region needs industrial policies that create jobs for the labour force which is available, and educational systems that train the future labour force for a high-tech economy. Wages are far too low and in order to have higher tax revenues, one needs higher incomes. One also needs more tax discipline, less informal economy, and fewer tax breaks to the rich and to foreign investors. The new owners of the formerly publicly owned firms have to take responsibility to contribute more to the funding of a modern welfare system, which prevents splitting society into two—the very rich minority and a poor majority. This is not neo-patrimonialism, this is liberal capitalism with a human face.

Alternatively, instead of reducing the neo-liberalism of the economy and shifting the socialist distributive systems towards a social democratic welfare state it is possible—and probably likely—that the rest of Central Europe will follow the Slovak example. At least in the short run—if democracy is somewhat 'managed'—one can operate with low incomes, low taxes on individuals and corporations, low government regulation, and deep cuts in benefits and in general privatization of public services.

Social sciences are not very good in predicting the future. It is hard enough to describe the present accurately. But we might not be taking too much of a risk in predicting that the current inconsistency between economic and welfare institutions in Central Europe cannot be maintained on the long run. In one way or another, institutional rearrangements will be necessary to resolve the contradictions of the second phase of transition from socialism to capitalism, and to develop new forms of complementarity between the economic, political, and welfare institutions in these societies. In this process, the objectives, power, and beliefs of key actors within the society and influencing it from outside (MNCs, international organizations, the geopolitics of powerful states and regional blocs) will be crucial to the outcome.

REFERENCES

AGHION, P. and BLANCHARD, O. (1994). On the Speed of Transition in Central Europe, NBER Macro Annuals.

ALAM, ASAD et al. (2005). *Growth, Poverty and Inequality*, (Washinton DC: The World Bank).

BEREND, IVÁN (1996). *Central Europe 1944–1993: Detour from Periphery to Periphery*, (Cambridge: Cambridge University Press).

COOK, LINDA (2007). *Post-Communist Welfare States: Reform Politics in Russia and Eastern Europe*, (Ithaca, NY: Cornell University Press).

DAWSON, JANE (1999). 'Egalitarian Responses in Postcommunist Russia', *International Studies Review*, 1(3): 13–40.

DEACON, BOB (2000). 'Eastern European Welfare States: The Impact of the Politics of Globalization', *Journal of European Social Policy* 10(2): 146–61.

EISENSTADT, SHMUEL N. (1973). *Traditional Patrimonialism and Modern Neopatrimonialism*, (Beverly Hills: Sage Publications).

ELSTER, JON, CLAUS OFFE, and ULRICH K. PREUSS (1998). *Institutional Design in Post-Communist Societies*, (Cambridge: Cambridge University Press).

EUROPEAN COMMISSION (2006a). *Adequate and Sustainable Pensions. Synthesis Report 2006*, Brussels: Directorate-General for Employment, Social Affairs and Equal Opportunity, Unit E4.

EYAL, GIL, IVAN SZELENYI, and ELEANOR TOWNSLEY (1998). *Making Capitalism without Capitalists*, (London: Verso).

FOX, LOUISE (1997). 'Pension Reform in the Post-Communist Transition Economies', in Joan M. Nelson (ed.), *Transforming Post-Communist Political Economies*, (Washington: National Academy Press).

FULTZ, ELAINE and MARKUS RUCK (2001). 'Pension Reform in Central and Eastern Europe: Emerging Issues and Patterns', *International Labour Review* 140(1): 19–44.

GARCELON, MARC (2005). *Revolutionary Passage: From Soviet to Post-Soviet Russia, 1985–2000*, (Philadelphia: Temple University Press).

GOMUŁKA, STANISLAW (2001). 'A Great Leap Forward? Pension Development and Reforms in the Czech Republic, Hungary, Poland and Romania', in Marek Dabrowski and Jacek Rostowkin (eds.), *The Eastern Enlargement of the EU*, (Boston: Kluwer Academic Publishers), 109–27.

HARCSA, ISTVÁN, IMRE KOVACH, and IVAN SZELÉNYI (1998). 'The Price of Privatization', in I. Szelényi (ed.), *Privatizing the Land*, (London: Routledge), 214–44.

KOCHANOWICZ, JACEK (2006). *Backwardness and Modernization: Poland and Eastern Europe in the 16th–20th Centuries*, (Aldershot: Ashgate Publishing).

KORNAI, JÁNOS (1992). *The Socialist System*, (Princeton, NJ: Princeton University Press).

——(1995). *Highway and Byways*, (Cambridge, MA: MIT Press).

——(1997). 'Paying the Bill of Goulash Communism: Hungarian Development and Macro-stabilization in a Political Economy Perspective', in Janos Kornai (ed.), *The Struggle and Hope: Essays on Stabilization and Reform in a Post-Socialist Economy*, (Northampton, MA: Edgar Elgar).

Kovács, János Mátyás (2002). 'Approaching the EU and Reaching the US? Rival Narratives on Transforming Welfare Regimes in East-Central Europe', in Peter Mair and Jan Zielonka (eds.), *The Enlarged European Union*, (London: Frank Cass), 175–204.

Lipsmeyer, Christine, S. (2002). 'Parties and Policy: Evaluating Economic and Partisan Influences on Welfare Policy Spending during the European Post-communist Transition', *British Journal of Political Science* 32: 641–61.

Mihályi, Péter (2007). 'Disintegration of Healthcare in Post-Communist Economies', in Péter Mihályi (ed.), *Health Insurance Reform in Hungary*, (Budapest: Europe Ltd), 29–50.

——(ed.) (2007). *Health Insurance Reform in Hungary*, (Budapest: Europe Ltd).

——and Ryszard Petru (2001). 'The Fiscal Impact of Health Care Reforms in Central Europe', in Marek Dabrowski, and Jacek Rostowski (eds.), *The Eastern Enlargement of the EU*, (Boston/Dordrecht/London: Kluwer Academic Publishers), 203–32.

O'Dwyer, Conor (2006). *Runaway State Building*, (Baltimore: Johns Hopkins University Press).

Orenstein, M. A. (2000). 'How Politics and Institutions Affect Pension Reform in Three Postcommunist Countries', *World Bank Policy Research Working Paper 2310*, (Washington, DC: The World Bank).

——(2001). *Out of the Red: Building Capitalism and Democracy in Postcommunist Europe*, (Ann Arbor: University of Michigan Press).

——and Marine R. Hass (2005). 'Globalization and the Future of the Welfare State in Communist East-Central European Countries', in Miguel Glatzer and Dietrich Rueschemeyer (eds.), *Globalization and the Future of the Welfare State*, (Pittsburgh, PA: University of Pittsburgh Press), 130–52.

Rinegold, Dana (1999). 'Social Policy in Post-communist Europe: Legacies and Transition', in Linda Cook, Mitchell Orenstein, and Marilyn Rueschemeyer (eds.), *Left Parties and Social Policy in Post-communist Europe*, (Boulder, CO: Westview Press), 11–46.

Sachs, Jeffrey (2001). 'Postcommunist Parties and the Politics of Entitlements', *Beyond Transition. The Newsletter about Reforming Economies*, The World Bank.

Schneider, Ondřej and Pavel Štepanek (2001). 'A Looming Financial Crisis in the Czech Republic?', in Marek Dabrowski and Jacek Rostowski (eds.), *The Eastern Enlargement of the EU*, (Boston: Kluwer Academic Publishers), 151–68.

Southworth, Caleb and Leontina Hormel (2004a). 'Why Work "Off the Books"? Community, Household, and Individual Determinants of Informal Economic Activity in Post-Soviet Russia', in Leo McCann (ed.), *Russian Transformations: Challenging the Global Narrative*, (London: Routledge), 148–72.

——(2004b). 'The Development of Post-Soviet Neo-Paternalism in Two Enterprises in Bashkortostan: How Familial-Type Management Moves Firms and Workers Away from Labor Markets', in Leo McCann (ed.), *Russian Transformations: Challenging the Global Narrative*, (London: Routledge), 191–208.

Szücs, Jenö, ([1983] 1988). 'Three Historical Regions of Europe', in John Keane (ed.), *Civil Society and the State*, (London: Verso), 291–332.

Wagener, Hans-Jürgen (2002). 'The Welfare State in Transitional Economies and Accession to the EU', in Peter Mair and Jan Zielonka (eds.), *The Enlarged European Union*, (London: Frank Cass), 152–74.

Wilk, Katarzyna and Jakub Wtorek (2008). 'Reforms of Pension Systems in the New Member States'. Bureau of European Policy Advisers, European Commission, Working Paper.

Woodruff, David (1999). *Money Unmade: Barter and the Fate of Russian Capitalism*, (Ithaca, NY: Cornell University Press).

CHAPTER 20

STATE FAILURE

JOHN A. HALL

INTRODUCTION

One of the most clearly established generalizations in comparative social science is that economic development rests on the back of services provided by the state. Adam Smith, Max Weber, Karl Polanyi, and Alexander Gershenkron all produced substantial bodies of work arguing this case, albeit they differed slightly in their emphasis on which service was the most important. The main task of this paper is in a sense to reverse the picture, by considering the conditions under which states do and do not provide the institutional basis upon which economic activity can be built. Emphasis is accordingly on failed states. Now to discuss failure implies an understanding of success. Therefore, this is where we must begin. A successful state is one that provides order, belonging, and affluence to a society which controls it. This definition builds on Max Weber's definition of the state as the monopolist of violence in the light of the achievements of post-war Western liberal democracies. The sociological factors involved in the creation of states of this sort can be specified immediately, albeit later discussion of the absence of these factors elsewhere will highlight their character. Almost everything follows from one simple consideration, namely that these states were created in a Darwinian world, which mandated fiscal extraction (Mann 1986; Bates 2001). In consequence, bureaucracies were created to penetrate and organize social life (Evans and Rauch 1999). The state capacity that resulted was far from negative: it involved the provision of legal services, and the fostering and protection of economic activity—this being crucial since traders were mobile and prone to move (and thereby to increase the power of one's enemies) if they were treated badly (Hall 1985). The endless interaction between competitive states and their societies had two dramatic consequences. First, distinctive national identities were created over time as diverse linguistic and ethnic groups merged into the culture of their states (Smith 1986). Second, social forces reacted to the demands of their states for taxation and for conscription. The fight to control the state did much to enhance national identity; over time it led to the democratization of political life (Mann 1993).

If the definition of success is clear, and much in use, the definition of failure, in contrast, is a terrible mess (I draw heavily in this paragraph on *The Economist* 2009. Cf. Rotberg 2003, 2004). To begin with, distinctions need to be drawn between weak, collapsing, and failed states—together with some understanding that the failed can regain the capacity to function. Very few states have collapsed completely, and even those that have, such as Somalia, contain areas in which settled expectations survive. Analysing degrees of state failure does not create analytic clarity. States fail in different ways. Zimbabwe is comparatively secure, but its polity and economy are now disastrous. In contrast, Iraq has recently been deeply insecure, despite relative affluence and some measure of welfare provision—which is not to say, a moment's reflection suggests, that it was entirely successful before the American invasion when ruled by Saddam's iron fist. Further, collapse can take place in very different ways. Many sub-Saharan African countries are but lines drawn on the map, possessing 'states' that scarcely deserve the name, often lacking much infrastructural reach and faced with a mass of competing ethnic groups. In contrast, Colombia has suffered because the revolutionary armed forces (FARC) have been able to finance an insurgency through drug trafficking and kidnapping. And further confusion results when confronting the fact that interest in state failure has sharpened because of al-Qaeda's attacks on New York. The trouble here is that many of the most miserable places, from North Korea to the Democratic Republic of the Congo, and from Haiti to Myanmar, do not provide homes to international terrorists. Further, many of the terrorists in Iraq and Afghanistan are national rather than international. What may matter most to al-Qaeda are social networks, some of them in the West, rather than state failure per se. Still further distinctions need to be drawn. For one thing, it is a mistake to suggest that Muslim countries are weak: Arab countries have this character, particularly in terms of low levels of literacy, unsustainably high levels of fertility, and political repressiveness, but this is not the case for Muslim countries outside the classical heartland of Islam (Stepan and Robertson 2003).[1] For another, there is little correlation between dysfunctional states and disease—with South Africa suffering heavily from HIV/AIDS and Indonesia and Vietnam from bird 'flu.

Given the absence of any single clear character to the states within this general world, it makes sense to begin with a general account of the difficulties that latecomers face when seeking to establish states. This is followed by a discussion of what can best be termed the understated and by analysis of a key problem, namely that of the relationship between democracy and development. The concluding

---

[1] Very varied comments can of course be made about different states. Pakistan for instance is not really a failed state, as most of the country is under the state's control. But just as the state does not control the frontier provinces, nor does the President control all of the state.

section broadens the agenda. The state specified at the start is decent, gaining substantial power because it is engaged in a politics of reciprocal consent with its society. Not all states have this character. For one thing, we should at least note that the regimes of much of West Africa are successful predators: they serve the few, through exporting capital, for all that they fail the many. For another, we should take care not to worship powerful states. Nazi Germany and Soviet Russia killed millions, and they collapsed in horror and ignominy. The point that will emerge from this is very important: one should not take for granted that copying the Western route to state formation is desirable.

Latecomer state formation

By the end of the nineteenth century, a division in the world polity between the advanced world of the West and the backward condition of the rest was entirely obvious. This structured world politics. Development became a necessity. Elites needed this to prevent their states being dismembered; just as importantly, failure meant the possibility of being toppled from below, by peoples well aware that their lives could improve. There was of course both hesitation and dispute as to exactly what elements should be copied from the West in order to assure development. Still, the most general conclusion was that modernity's great power container was the nation-state. Countries with prior national homogeneity and a state tradition, especially if they had never been colonized, were able to adapt to this new world with relative ease. Japan is the most striking example. But there are not many countries with these characteristics, particularly among the large number of new states formed in the wake of post-war European decolonization. There are four reasons why most found adaptation difficult (I follow Lange 2010, especially on the first two factors).

First, geographical conditions hampered state construction in large areas of the world. This is especially true of sub-Saharan Africa (Herbst 2000). The arid and tropical conditions of this region of the world sustained only small populations— often blessed, it should be noted, with the ability to move at will, so as to escape control. Much the same can be said about mountainous terrain: population density is again low, whilst the pastoralists of this world know how to fight as well as how to move (Fearon and Laitin 2003). Nepal, Pakistan, and Afghanistan have had difficulty in building states in these circumstances—as have countries in the Caucasus.

Second, economic resources can cause difficulties for state construction, albeit in directly opposed ways. On the one hand, several countries possess lootable resources, concentrated geographically and easy to trade outside the reach of the state. Blood diamonds is one such resource, drugs such as cocaine and opium another (Snyder and Bhavnani 2005). When non-state groups get their hands on these resources, they can challenge state power all too effectively. This was true in Sierra Leone in the 1990s, and it seems to be true in Afghanistan today—where drug monies allow insurgents to receive greater emoluments than do members of the regular armed forces. It is important, on the other hand, to remember that states require resources to gain salience. A poor society is unlikely to allow much state construction (Collier 2000). Just as importantly, states in this situation tend to buy allegiance by expanding state employment, often at the expense of the meritocratic norms essential to the establishment of powerful bureaucracies.

Third, latecomers face systematic difficulties when trying to create and thicken their state structures. What matters most is the impact of imperialism. There was of course systematic difference in the British case between the Dominions and the areas of direct rule on the one hand, and limited or indirect rule that applied much more extensively on the other. Metropoles sought to extract resources as cheaply as possible. Their administrative core was very small, with rule depending on patrimonialism and occasional coercion. (Corbridge et al. 2005). Incoherence and division characterized these puny Leviathans. Decolonization did not leave pillars on which to build, merely a vacuum (Lange 2009).

Finally, state construction was hampered by the national question. For one thing, colonial rulers had no interest in creating a common national identity: their racism meant total exclusion of the native populations—which were often suspicious of and hostile to state structures thereafter. For another, imperialists often systematically worsened the situation through dividing so as better to rule. What was particularly damaging was the way in which the imperialists constructed ethnic identities, so as then to gain the support of one group against another (Mamdani 2001). Divide and rule strategies were enhanced by importing specialized middlemen—in the British case, South Asians into East Africa and the Caribbean. At worst the legacy of such divisiveness led to horror, most obviously in recent years in the conflict, which still continues, between Hutus and Tutsis. Beyond this, however, is the deleterious effect that ethnic fractionalization has, in the eyes of most scholars, on economic performance—both through making it hard to reach common agreement and because a sustained sense of energetic cooperation and self-sacrifice is missing (Posner 2004a). Failure in this area, of course, then makes it harder, through a negative feedback loop, to find the necessary resources for state construction.

The understated

These factors play out most strikingly among the understated, that is, the world habitually taken to include Haiti, East Timor, Nepal, Somalia, Afghanistan, Sudan, and a whole slew of West African states. Many of these countries have been marked by conflict, and about half return to this condition within ten years of peace agreements. The international system has not been able to prevent these reversions. In the past twenty years, for example, $300 billion has been spent in Africa alone, yet the continent is still rife with weak and collapsed regimes—two million people a year are dying of AIDS, three thousand children die every day of malaria, and forty million receive no schooling at all (Ghani and Lockhart 2008: 22). The image that best conveys the reality of this world is of a leader in a capital city lacking the means to know what is happening in the rest of the country. In a sense readers in the advanced world should not be too surprised by this picture. This lack of infrastructural power characterized their states until rather late in the historical record, as basic exercises in fiscal sociology have demonstrated. But there is a difference. Infrastructural powers in the advanced world have in virtually every case advanced enormously over time, and they continue to do so as states become responsible for ever larger areas of public health and economic competitiveness. In contrast, many of the states mentioned above have been going backwards, losing infrastructural reach. Perhaps the classic instance is that of the Democratic Republic of the Congo, formerly Zaire, whose colonial transport infrastructure has now all but collapsed. Against this should be set the consideration already noted, namely that predatory regimes of this sort sometimes had sufficient capacity to find ingenious ways to export capital for leaders and their entourages. The Zaire of Mobuto stands as the exemplar.

The character of this type of state derives from the nature of the post-war international order. The norm of non-intervention within the internal affairs of other states became a cornerstone of the world polity. What emerged in consequence were quasi-states, that is, states whose existence depended more upon international recognition than upon their own functional capacities for ruling their territories (Jackson 1990). This norm was not imposed by the advanced world on late developing countries. On the contrary, the norm was adopted and maintained by the Organization of African States—which went so far as being prepared to condemn one of its own members, Julius Nyerere, for his part in bringing down the hideous regime of Idi Amin in Uganda. Such visceral attachment to the norm is fully comprehensible. Many African states have boundaries drawn up by colonial powers caring so little about pre-existing social groupings that their straight lines went through them. The absolute artificiality of boundaries places a premium on maintaining them. As every state is artificial, rectification or simplification would surely lead to generalized disaster.

The sinews of the state, everywhere and at all times, rest upon the ability to extract taxes from society. European states lived in such a competitive surround, as noted, that they were forced to dig into their societies: no one state could afford to sit still, thereby being bound to adopt any innovation, military, economic, and ideological, created by the leading edge of power so as to survive. The contrasting point about Africa—and, for rather different reasons, Latin America (Centeno 2002)—is that militarized state competition has been avoided, ruled out by adherence to the international norm of non-intervention (Herbst 2000). Fiscal extraction is accordingly low, with many states receiving a large portion of their monies from the outside in the form of aid. This limited interaction between states and societies has meant that citizenship politics have scarcely developed. Just as important is the consequence of this fact for national identity formation. Ethnic and linguistic diversity in Europe blended into a singular national culture over time, for sure, but also as the result of shared struggle in war. The diversity within African countries, often enhanced by the actions of imperialists, has not had to be diminished in a similar way. National identities have yet to be constructed.

If these background conditions gave Africa weak states, it is quite clear that the state capacity has weakened in many countries in the last two decades (Bates 2008). What matters most is a diminution in fiscal capacities, particularly in Africa. One reason for this is internal: single party rule very often led to the granting of monopoly powers that severely impaired economic development. But other reasons are external, notably the oil shock followed by the lessening of geopolitically motivated aid consequent on the ending of the Cold War. In these circumstances, states have become more militarized, with predation ever more likely to replace the rule of law.

This is not to deny that other factors are at work. Sheer poverty makes state building difficult. But a measure of caution and scepticism is in order here. The initial poverty of Vietnam did not prevent it developing, while the comparative wealth of Zimbabwe has not prevented its decline—with the different trajectories being best explained by the facilitating and predatory character of the states involved (Easterly 2008: 52). Equally, oil and diamonds do not in every case lead to state failure; here too it is weakening of the state that allows rebels to seize such resources. Just as clearly ethnic conflict leading to civil war is often the result of state's weakness, so is its inability to provide basic order in the face, on occasion, of mere teenagers armed with Kalashnikovs (Laitin 2008: ch. 1). This is not to deny the ravages that resulted from conflict in Sierra Leone and Rwanda, and those that continue today in the Democratic Republic of the Congo. But the causal pattern deserves highlighting: poverty, the curse of lootable resources, and ethnic conflict result from state failure, which condition they then much exacerbate.

Democracy and development

The depressing picture that has been derived from considering institutional weakness must be darkened still further by turning attention to the task that confronts latecomers, that of modernizing their societies. This is a careful formulation. What is at issue is the potential conflict between economic and political modernization. The point in question was made with characteristic force by Gellner (1967) when arguing bluntly that forced development was bound to rule out democracy. It is easy to see what he meant—which is not to say, as we shall see, that his claim should be accepted without criticism. Industrialization requires fundamental change. One way in which this is true is in terms of nation-building. Creating an educational system typically requires a decision as to which language should be used in society. In Algeria this meant Arabic, given that a war had just been fought against the French and the fact that Berber was at that time a low rather than a high culture. Such a decision of course requires social engineering, the suppression or loss of some identities and the creation of a new one. Exactly the same point must be made about industrialization. Peasants move from the country to the city, in part through attraction but often quite as much because of government policies determined to provide labour for the infant industries they seek to build. The changes involved are so total that democratic control is almost a contradiction in terms. Crucially, the first fruits of development must not be spent: primitive accumulation effectively involves seizing the surplus created by the incoming generation of factory workers for investment purposes. Development is painful, as is utterly obvious to anyone who has lived outside the advanced world. Countries seeking to make the transition to the modern era very often have pictures of their leaders, Moses of their countries, in every classroom—perfectly symbolizing the centralization of power that is involved.

A moment's digression on the workings of this factor will allow us, by means of contrast, to further understand failed states. It can be noted to begin with that the centralization of power can successfully force industrialization. Kohli (2004: part 1) has shown in detail how this was possible in South Korea. The state was initially strengthened by the Japanese. Unlike the British system of indirect rule, the Japanese sought to build state capacity, and they pushed through land reform with the utmost vigour. Thereafter, a strong state cooperated closely with leading industrialists so as to accumulate capital for infrastructural and economic development by repressing wages in the interests of clear developmental strategies. Two points need to be underlined about this 'coercive-capitalist' route. First, it was probably dependent on prior national homogeneity, with the national cohesion of South Korea being greatly enhanced by anti-communist feeling consequent on the division of the Korean peninsula.[2] Second, the raising of living standards did eventually provide a social base for political liberalization. So here is a case in which great social pain was followed by successful political decompression. The centralization of power created the economic development that then allowed democratization.

But the centralization of power has not always worked in this benign and beneficent way, thereby putting into question Gellner's excessively clear formulation. The 'authoritarian high modernism' identified by Scott (Scott 1998) has caused enormous suffering—and it has, still more importantly, often massively set back economic development. Russia was one of the world's great grain exporters in 1914: collectivization so ruined Russian agriculture, that it is now dependent on the outside world for its supply of food. Kohli is aware of this, and anyway nervous about recommending authoritarian rule, so suggests that the fact that development in both India and Brazil has been slowed by democratic pressure may be less a catastrophe than an advantage given the long-term benefits of the politics of checks and balances (Kohli 2004: parts 2 and 3). An important consideration can be added to this—political decompression is never easy to achieve. Highly centralized polities, especially of a socialist hue, tend to destroy civil society because of their fear that self-organization can be turned against the regime. In the Russian case, liberalization failed in large part because the reforming elite had no organized groups with whom they could make bargains (Bova 1991).[3] Further, sudden democratization can be dangerous, releasing pent-up pressures, which

---

[2] Kohli's excellent book neglects this—indeed he is oddly blind to the significance of the national factor.

[3] With hindsight, the claim made by Kirkpatrick (1979)—that state socialism, unlike authoritarian capitalism, could not be liberalized—seems justified, despite the opprobrium it caused at the time. This is not to suggest that the policy proposals contained in that article were valid.

make consolidating any political opening almost impossible (Snyder 2000). The Soviet Union collapsed in large part because nationalism stepped into the vacuum caused by state breakdown. The Chinese are well aware of this, as they are of the certain fact that socialist planning from above, bereft of any market forces, is but a dead end. They seek to reverse Gorbachov's policies by having *perestroika* before *glasnost*. The extent to which this will allow the creation of partners able to engage in some process of political decompression is one of the questions of the age. One serious treatment of the problem suggests that political decompression may yet prove to be elusive (Hutton 2007).

But let us leave to one side speculation about potential state failure in China. The most immediate point to be made about the sorts of states with which this chapter is concerned is that they completely lack the capacity to force development in the way suggested by Gellner. This is made clear by Kohli through an analysis of Nigeria, at present a weak state, albeit one that may yet fail (Kohli 2004: part 4). Diversity in Nigeria is deep and multiple between regions, ethnicities, and religions, so that the state never repressed wages to use the surplus for developmental purposes. The funds derived from oil were either taken by the elite or spent on immediate gratification, particularly at election times—albeit, those elections were 'managed' rather than the real expression of popular control. The Nigerian case is tragic precisely because oil monies were so to speak free-floating, making the creation of a stronger state able to force development at least an imaginable outcome. That possibility scarcely existed elsewhere. But it is very important to realize that the ideology involved, the belief that power should be centralized in order to foster development, was widely accepted. It provided justification for dictatorships that did little except to prey on their own societies. And this brings us to the final point. Moments of democratization have often led to anarchy rather than to the consolidation of order. Posner (2004*b*) makes the point particularly forcefully in relation to civil society. Democratic openings often allow for the emergence and self-organization of highly undesirable groups—as has been the case with drug lords in Afghanistan in the wake of the defeat of the Taliban. To see the introduction of civil society groupings as a cure confuses correlation with causation; a vibrant civil society less a source than a symbol of a functioning state (Posner 2004*b*: 252). The dilemma involved in this can be seen in the near schizophrenia of Bates's analysis of state failure in Africa (2008: 108–20, 136–7). The analytical passages of Bates's book making much of the dangers of democratization, of the emergence of undesirable groups, and of the likelihood that the situation will spill out of control, are followed by a despairing insistence that democratization must be undertaken on the grounds that some way must be found to control predatory regimes.

The other end of the telescope

The necessary and entirely justified interim conclusion to which we must come is that of the immense difficulties facing the weakest latecomer states. State power is needed, but very often the wrong type of state power—predatory rather than enabling—has been in evidence, doing more to prevent than to occasion development. This suggests the need for democracy, but sudden democratization can release dangerous forces. And one could go beyond this. Consider just one example, the Zimbabwe of Robert Mugabe. A sensitive analysis by Mamdani (2008) begins by asking the question that facile moral condemnation so often obscures: how is it that his regime has lasted so long? The most basic consideration is simply that the handover of power by Britain did nothing to deal with inequalities in land holding. Land redistribution was always likely to be popular, and it was politically needed given the presence of former guerilla fighters. The removal of groups brought in by the prior imperial power, Asians in Uganda as much as farmers in Zimbabwe, is comprehensible. There may be more, perhaps especially in South Africa.

There have been two notable policy responses in the West to the general picture that has been presented here. Herbst (2004) is utterly logical in following his analysis of the different paths of state formation in Europe and Africa with a brutal prescription—namely, that the norm of non-intervention should be abandoned, so that European style wars of consolidation, with all that implies for increases in solidarity, taxation, and citizenship, be countenanced and accepted in Africa. In complete contrast, liberal humanitarians shocked by what they see on their television screens call ever more insistently for more intervention from the advanced world. One significant thinker calls for military involvement so that local wars can be brought to an end, seeing in this a precondition of every other form of development (Collier 2000). A more limited position suggests that intervention can take the form of Western involvement in running weak or failed states, a form of power-sharing between the weak and the strong (Krasner 2005).

These are dangerous counsels. If we look at the situation of failed states from a different angle, in effect from the other end of the telescope, it will become apparent that they should not be accepted. Our starting point is simple, namely, that the definition of a decent state given at the start misses out history. Further, it describes the ideal rather than the real. Explaining what is involved will allow better understanding of the states with which this chapter is concerned. Appreciating the two areas of Western 'vice' will make certain 'virtues' of the rest stand out clearly. So the counsels offered will be rejected on descriptive as much as prescriptive grounds.

The first point to remember about the history of Europe in the twentieth century is that it was incredibly bloody, with perhaps seventy million people killed and murdered in the course of population transfers, ethnic cleansing, and the Holocaust. The competition between states that had brought economic and social progress before the middle of the nineteenth century thereafter led to disaster. One reason for the change was simply the greater destructiveness caused once industrial means were applied to warfare. But still more important was the way in which nationalism became linked to imperialism. The great powers came to feel that the possession of empires, giving them secure sources of supply and markets, was necessary for their survival. Linked to this was the belief that national homogeneity was necessary for societal success. The areas of East and Central Europe in which national awakening came before state consolidation (that is, the areas in which diverse ethnicities had not blended into a single national culture) were necessarily affected by this belief—but so too were relatively homogeneous countries such as Germany, keen to remove the Jews and determined to cleanse Slavs from eastern territories conquered in war. The combination of these factors made Europe the dark continent of the modern world. The sad fact is that liberal democracy in the West rests in part on the back of the ethnic cleansing that took place. This should make us chary about presuming, as is very often the case, that our model of development should be recommended for others. Herbst is at least honest in acknowledging what is involved, but one still shudders to think of the deaths that would be caused.

The second consideration should be as much at the centre of our attention. One needs to be very cautious in recommending intervention, even thought it may be necessary and desirable in extreme cases (Easterly 2008). Troops welcomed initially often come to be seen, now that the nationalist principle structures world politics, as occupiers. Further, there is a dreadful tendency for those who recommend intervention not to think through the consequences of their policies. What matters about increasing hostility to the forces of intervention is that it puts up costs dramatically. There is very often a 'disconnect' between the desire to help and the willingness to pay, whether in terms of money or lives. The institutions to sustain liberal interventionism are very weak. Intervention followed by retreat can be disastrous, as is the case with American involvement with the Muslim world in the last decade (Rashid 2008). Two points that are implicit here need highlighting. First, Western institutions are far from some state of perfection; to the contrary, the lack of serious thought about foreign policymaking, the inability to work out and to accept the consequences of state actions, is a key weakness. Second, states in the developing and underdeveloped world have sometimes been affected negatively because of the Western dominated structure of the world polity. This is obviously true of failed interventions, but it applies quite as much to neo-liberal restructuring policies, which often undermine attempts to develop state powers. And the present condition of the world economy mandates a further comment. The failure of Western institutions, and the impact of that failure on the social world considered in this chapter, has a further element, namely, the lack of order at the centre of capitalist society (Reinhart and Rogoff 2008). For all the difficulties faced in the advanced West, the greater suffering will take place amongst the weakest of the non-European world.

Scepticism as to the merits of the West can be followed by recognition and appreciation of some institutional virtues among the weak. One reason for rejecting absolute pessimism is simply that the actual incidence of civil war resulting from ethnic fractionalization is in fact rather small (Fearon and Laitin 2003). Posner (2004a, 2005) adds to this a powerful demonstration that a very large number of ethnic differences never become politicized at all. Persson's (2008) sustained comparison of fiscal extraction rates in Botswana, Zambia, and Uganda in relation to the national factor goes further, showing that high rates of fiscal extraction are possible, given the right policies. All of these states contain several ethnic groups. In Botswana, ethnicity never became politicized, thereby allowing assimilationist policies, which in turn allowed quite considerable rates of fiscal extraction. In Zambia, a large number of ethnic groups were recognized, leading to a situation of genuine 'multiculturalism' in which none has been able to permanently dominate political life. Fiscal extraction in this world is somewhat less than in Botswana, but it is still significant. The least favourable of the cases is Uganda, where two large groups stand in opposition, thereby leading to very low rates of taxation. The last of these countries has, of course, been the site of considerable violence.

The more general point is that the logic of diversity within Africa is such that the best route is not to seek to homogenize populations, as Gellner's argument suggested. Forcible homogenization has led and is always likely to lead to the politicization of ethnic differences at the least, and then perhaps to pre-emptive ethnic cleansing and war, thereby so dislocating societies as to make development all but impossible (Laitin 2008: ch. 5). The record of partitions, often recommended as a solution for ethnically diverse societies, has been particularly disastrous (O'Leary 2007). Crucially, state-building in the face of conscious ethnic difference has sometimes been possible. Consider institutional developments concerning language (Laitin 1992). A citizen might have a linguistic repertoire of the state language, which might be English, as well as those of his or her tribe and region. The formula which explains the interesting Indian case is that of three plus or minus one languages in one's repertoire—comprising the two central state languages of English and Hindi, a third language of one's provincial state, a fourth if one is a minority in that state, with no third language needed if one's state is Hindi-speaking. The general point here is simple. The fact that not every developing state seems set on repeating the European pattern of national development, that is, the creation of linguistically homogeneous nation-states, is to be welcomed. India stands as the outstanding example of a political union sufficiently liberal as to maintain the loyalty of many nations; several African states are not far behind—that is, not all have failed, with weaker ones still having institutional capacities that might yet be utilized. It may be that a measure of unity sufficient for the workings of a modern economy can be gained by the recognition of diversity. A model of the 'state-nation' rather than the 'nation-state' is accordingly practicable as well as desirable (Stepan 2008). Further, the link between nationalism and imperialism has been broken; as this is not a period of great geo-political conflict, there may be less call for unitary states. It may be possible to bind together multinational societies through federal and consociational means. Such means may even work in Iraq, allowing that country to hold together in a minimalist manner that would allow for order and prosperity—and American withdrawal (O'Leary 2009).

The recognition of seeds of improvement in the world of weak and failed states, together with awareness that beneficent change often takes time, is not to say that policy prescriptions for the advanced West superior to those already noted cannot be created. Perhaps the most important is negative, namely the need for the advanced world to get its own house in order, especially to improve its current management of the world political economy. Still, it is encouraging in this regard to note that there is now some awareness that states are necessary. The Washington Consensus has gone, and we are now on a different track altogether (Goldstone, Bates, et al. 2005). It is a liberal fallacy to imagine that every problem has a neat and easy solution. With failed states what matters is a whole slew of policies designed to allow basic Hobbesian order to be established, from help in creating bureaucracies and armies, to the opening of markets in the advanced world to allow prosperity to come to those whose best chance lies in specializing in agricultural exports. Crucially the fear that failed states might house international terrorists needs to be set in context. For one thing, there are not many truly international terrorists: most terrorists are national, seeking political change within their own countries. Of course, self-defence against a regime that does harbour such terrorists is justified. But against that must be set two facts. First, policies designed to root out such terrorists must not increase their number through incautious military adventurism, especially when there are high-tech ways in which the networks of such groups can be penetrated and controlled. Second, international terrorists have not, at least as yet, been very successful. Al-Qaeda is responsible for fewer deaths than those of 'the Troubles' in Northern Ireland. There is something to be said for living with an element of fear.

It is of course all too easy to see the other side of the coin. If there is some realization that Hobbesian concerns must be addressed, there is rather little knowledge as to the mechanisms by which state-building can occur, and be helped to occur, in the weakest of states. Research is desperately needed on every aspect of this question—on ethnic difference in general, on the causes for its politicization, and on mechanisms designed to contain it in post-conflict societies. There is still less clarity as to how to encourage states to move, so to speak, from Hobbes to Locke—that is, to move to the softer political rule of liberal democracy. And anyone tempted to think that life is easy might consider the following problem. The stability of the rich world has depended upon growth to appease human greed. The United States consumes more than 20 per cent of the world's mineral production. Can a world be designed in which similar living standards are provided for every human being on the planet? This institutional challenge for the future takes one's breath away.

REFERENCES

BATES, R. (2001). *Prosperity and Violence: The Political Economy of Development*, (New York: Norton).

——(2008). *When Things Fell Apart: State Failure in Late-Century Africa*, (Cambridge: Cambridge University Press).

BOVA, R. (1991). 'Political Dynamics of the Post-Communist Transition: A Comparative Perspective', *World Politics* 44: 113–38.

CENTENO, M. (2002). *Blood and Debt: War and the Nation-State in Latin America*, (University Park: Pennsylvania State University).

COLLIER, P. (2000). 'Economic Causes of Civil War and Their Implications for Policy', in C. Crocker and F. O. Hampson (eds.), *Managing Global Chaos*, (Washington: US Institute for Peace).

CORBRIDGE, S., G. WILLIAMS, M. SRIVASTAVA, and R. VERON (2005). *Seeing the State: Governance and Governmentality in India*, (Cambridge: Cambridge University Press).

EASTERLY, W. (2008). 'Foreign Aid Goes Military!', *New York Review of Books*, 4 Dec. 51–4.

Economist, The. (2009). 'Failed States: Fixing a Broken World', 21 Jan. 65–7.

EVANS, P. and J. RAUCH (1999). 'Bureaucracy and Growth: A Cross-National Analysis of the Effects of "Weberian" State Structures on Economic Growth', *American Sociological Review* 64: 748–65.

FEARON, J. D. and D. D. LAITIN (2003). 'Ethnicity, Insurgency and Civil War', *American Political Science Review* 97 (1): 75–90.

GELLNER, E. A. (1967). 'Democracy and Industrialization', *European Journal of Sociology* 8: 47–70.

GHANI, A. and C. LOCKHART (2008). *Fixing Failed States: A Framework for Rebuilding a Fractured World*, (Oxford: Oxford University Press).

GOLDSTONE, J., R. BATES, et al. (2005). *A Global Forecasting Model of Political Instability*, (McLean, VA: State Failure Task Force, SAIC).

HALL, J. A. (1985). *Powers and Liberties: The Causes and Consequences of the Rise of the West*, (Oxford: Blackwell).

HERBST, J. (2000). *States and Power in Africa: Comparative Lessons in Authority and Control*, (Princeton, NJ: Princeton University Press).

——(2004). 'Let Them Fail: State Failure in Theory and Practice: Implications for Policy', in R. Rotberg (ed.), *When States Fail: Causes and Consequences*, (Princeton, NJ: Princeton University Press).

HUTTON, W. (2007). *The Writing on the Wall: China and the West in the 21st Century*, (New York: Little Brown).

JACKSON, R. H. (1990). *Quasi-States: Sovereignty, International Relations and the Third World*, (Cambridge: Cambridge University Press).

KIRKPATRICK, J. (1979). 'Dictatorships and Double Standards', *Commentary*, Nov. 2009.

KOHLI, A. (2004). *State-Directed Development: Political Power and Industrialization in the Global Periphery*, (Cambridge: Cambridge University Press).

KRASNER, S. D. (2005). 'The Case for Shared Sovereignty', *Journal of Democracy* 16 (1): 69–83.

LAITIN, D. D. (1992). *Language Repertoires and State Construction in Africa*, (Cambridge: Cambridge University Press).

——(2008). *Nations, States, and Violence*, (Oxford: Oxford University Press).

LANGE, M. (2009). *Lineages of Despotism and Development: British Colonialism and State Power*, (Chicago: Chicago University Press).

——(2010). 'State Formation, Consolidation, and the Security Challenge: Why Developing Countries are Not Becoming Stronger and more Secure', in T. V. Paul: (ed.), *Weak States and South Asia's Insecurity Predicament*, (Stanford: Stanford University Press).

MAMDANI, M. (2001). *When Victims Become Killers*, (Princeton, NJ: Princeton University Press).

——(2008). 'Lessons of Zimbabawe', *London Review of Books*, 4 Dec. 17–21.

MANN, M. (1986). *The Sources of Social Power*. Volume One: *From the Beginning to 1760 AD*, (Cambridge: Cambridge University Press).

——(1993). *The Sources of Social Power*. Volume Two: *The Rise of Classes and Nation-States*, (Cambridge: Cambridge University Press).

O'LEARY, B. (2007). 'Analyzing Partition: Definition, Classification and Explanation', *Political Geography* 26 (8): 886–908.

——(2009). *Getting Out of Iraq with Integrity*, (Philadelphia: University of Pennsylvania Press).

PERSSON, A. (2008). *The Institutional Sources of Statehood: Assimilation, Multiculturalism and Taxation in Sub-Saharan Africa*, (Gothenburg: University of Gothenburg Press).

Posner, D. N. (2004a). 'Measuring Ethnic Fractionalization in Africa', *American Journal of Political Science* 48 (4): 849–63.

——(2004b). 'Civil Society and the Reconstruction of Failed States', in R. Rotberg (ed.), *When States Fail: Causes and Consequences*, (Princeton, NJ: Princeton University Press).

——2005. *Institutions and Ethnic Politics in Africa*, (Cambridge: Cambridge University Press).

Rashid, A. (2008). *Descent into Chaos: The United States and the Failure of Nation Building in Pakistan, Afghanistan and Central Asia*, (New York: Viking).

Reinhart, C. and K. Rogoff (2008). 'We Need an International Regulator', *Financial Times*. 19 Nov.

Rotberg, R. (ed.) (2003). *State Failure and State Weakness in a Time of Terror*, (Washington: Brookings Institution Press).

——(ed.) (2004). *When States Fail: Causes and Consequences*, (Princeton, NJ: Princeton University Press).

Scott, J. C. (1998). *Seeing Like a State: How Certain Schemes to Improve the Human Condition Have Failed*, (New Haven, CT: Yale University Press).

Smith, A. D. (1986). 'State-Making and Nation-Building', in J. A. Hall (ed.), *States in History*, (Oxford: Blackwell).

Snyder, J. (2000). *From Voting to Violence: Democratization and Nationalist Conflict*, (New York: W. W. Norton).

Snyder, R. and R. Bhavnani (2005). 'Diamonds, Blood and Taxes: A Revenue-Centred Framework for Explaining Political Order', *Journal of Conflict Resolution*, 49 (4): 563–97.

Stepan, A. (2008). 'Comparative Theory and Political Practice: Do We Need a "State-Nation" Model as well as a "Nation-State" Model?', *Government and Opposition* 43 (1): 1–25.

——and G. Robertson (2003). 'An "Arab" More Than a "Muslim" Electoral Gap', *Journal of Democracy* 14 (3): 140–6.

CHAPTER 21

FINANCIAL CAPITALISM RESURGENT: COMPARATIVE INSTITUTIONALISM AND THE CHALLENGES OF FINANCIALIZATION

EWALD ENGELEN

MARTIJN KONINGS

INTRODUCTION

Approximately seven decades after the dramatic end of the first wave of globalization (1870–1914), financial markets once again re-established themselves as the most important arenas of economic internationalization and growth. The underlying causes behind the resurgence of financial capitalism are manifold. First, states have liberalized restrictions on financial transactions in response to the demise of the international monetary system that was set up in the immediate aftermath of the Second World War, thereby ushering in the gradual development of a truly international market in Foreign Exchange (FX) contracts. Second, financial pressures have forced governments to retrench the welfare arrangements they had set up to compensate for the sufferings of their populations during the great European wars of the twentieth century. As a result, households across the Western world have seen their state-backed guarantees being eroded and have been forced to turn to the financial markets to secure access to goods that used to be provided publicly, i.e. housing, higher education, unemployment benefits, health care, and pension benefits.

Third, as a result of pension reforms (the gradual replacement of pay-as-you-go systems by pre-funded pension systems), international trade imbalances, and rising commodity prices (oil), there is a growing 'wall of money' scouring global financial markets for liquid and profitable investment opportunities. As a result, the price of capital has decreased, allowing a growing range of actors (including pension funds, private equity funds, hedge funds, and sovereign wealth funds) to multiply their returns on investments by using highly leveraged investment strategies. Especially pension funds, faced with a rising number of retirees and a shrinking number of contributors, have been forced to play the financial markets ever more frantically, driving an endless quest for new financial products.

Fourth, technological developments have been key to the growth and dispersal of modern financial products and markets. In wholesale as well as retail markets the introduction of new information and communication technologies (ICT) has spawned new products and services, new modes of distribution and new techniques of pricing and risk management. Whether in the guise of ATMs, ALM-models or option price theory, ICT has allowed the rapid and radical transformation of the world's financial markets. The virtualization of trade and the digitization of financial data have been the preconditions for the take-off of financial markets. Only when the trade in claims on (future) income streams was decoupled from its physical carrier could financial trade take flight as it has since the early 1990s.

Finally, the development of new theoretical paradigms within economics, and their spread across business schools worldwide, has contributed substantially to the construction of a standardized set of techniques that allow anonymous traders, seated behind batteries of desk top screens, to recognize each other's expertise in the blink of an eye. The rise of Finance as an economic subdiscipline, so magisterially described by Peter Bernstein (1993; 2007) and Donald MacKenzie (2006), has not only spawned a number of Nobel prize winners (Fisher Black, Myron Scholes, Robert Merton) but also a large number of practical mathematical formulae, models, and theorems (Black-Scholes theorem; Efficient Market theory; Capital Asset Pricing Model; Option Pricing Model), which have turned into the regular fare of traders worldwide. While there is some discussion about the extent to which these techniques actually dominate real-world trading (see Taleb 2007), there can be little doubt that these innovations, together with the new digital environment in which they thrive, have been a key driver of the breakneck speed of innovation that has characterized financial markets in the twenty-first century.

Since a large part of cross-border financial transactions takes place off the radar screens of national and supranational regulators, it is hard to gain an accurate overview of recent developments in financial markets. Hence, the figures presented below should be seen as indicative only. The world's largest financial market, the market in FX-contracts, has increased in terms of value of daily trade from $ 650 billion in 1989 to $ 1880 billion in 2004. Most of this growth is caused not by trade-related increases in the buying and selling of currencies (spot trade) but predominantly by a steady rise in the trade of swaps and forward contracts, i.e. in contracts that contain an element of delay, allowing buyers to hedge against (or speculate on) future exchange rate movements. Compared with the overall annual value of cross-border trade in goods and services of approximately $ 15 trillion in 2005, the overwhelming majority of FX-trade necessarily must serve other purposes than simply facilitating the sale of goods and services—idle speculation according to some, oil for the wheels of global finance according to others (Grahl and Lysandrou 2003).

Other financial markets have undergone similar developments. The formal bond market, for instance, increased almost fourfold in a period of fifteen years. Equity trade grew a stunning tenfold over the same period. In 2006 a total annual value of $ 51 trillion in stocks was sold worldwide, against a mere $ 5 trillion in 1990. The strong rise in value of equity trade stands in stark contrast to the much slower growth of total capitalization, suggesting that owners hold their stock for much shorter periods than they used to (WFE 2007). This reflects the rise of active investors such as hedge funds, which account for over 40 per cent of daily equity trade, as well as the transformation of 'patient' institutional investors (insurers, pension funds) into confident and very active market players.

The growth of these markets, however, is overshadowed by the phenomenal surge in global derivative trade. This category captures a growing number of old and new financial instruments, which have in common the property of being formal contracts containing mere rights (or obligations) to buy or sell underlying assets—ranging from FX-swaps, forward contracts, shares and bonds to securitized mortgages, student loans, credit card debts, debit cards, car loans, and royalty rights—at particular, predetermined moments in time. Although the oldest derivate markets originated from collective attempts to hedge the seasonal uncertainties related to agrarian products and commodities, most formal derivative markets date from the last decades of the twentieth century. Since the 1990s, derivative trade has really taken off. While the value of annual trade amounted to $ 2.5 trillion in 1990, sixteen years later this had increased to $ 70 trillion.

The informal derivative, or 'over the counter' (OTC) market, surpasses in size all of the markets discussed so far. This segment of the financial system comprises all derivative-like contracts between two or more financial agents, which are designed to fulfil the specific risk and return requirements of clients like pension funds, hedge funds, banks, and other sophisticated financial agents. It is therefore a true 'market' only in a very loose sense, and as a result its size is hard to determine. However, three-yearly samples collected by the Basle-based BIS suggest that the OTC-derivative markets have virtually exploded. While almost non-existent in the early 1970s, in 2006 (the latest available sample) the total annual value of the outstanding contracts amounted to a stunning $ 370 trillion (BIS 2008a; 2008b).

These are also the markets that have spawned the new 'synthetic' financial products, e.g. the asset-backed securities that were at the root of the credit crunch of 2007–8 and that the financial press usually refers to as the 'alphabet soup' (Morgan 2008). Although of fairly recent origin, the design, construction, and marketing of these products has turned into one of the main sources of fee income for (investment) banks. Using sophisticated mathematical techniques to aggregate comparable future income streams, determine their present and future market value, price their risks and slice them into different tranches, these products are sold as brand new, 'synthetic' securities on secondary markets to clients with highly particular portfolio demands.

Despite the speed and size of these developments and their substantial linkages with the wider economic world, it is striking that their analysis has not featured very prominently in the branch of comparative institutionalism that seems pre-eminently equipped to investigate these issues, namely comparative political economy or what is better known as the Varieties of Capitalism-literature (VoC) (Hall and Soskice 2001). A quick glance at the four dominant strands within the VoC-literature (see Jackson and Deeg 2008 for an overview), reveals that financial agents, financial markets, and financial products have only a nebulous existence in the representations of contemporary capitalism that this literature has produced. Banks and financial markets are conceptualized in their Gershenkronian guise of intermediaries between households and firms, serving the classic functions of aggregating, mobilizing, and allocating capital to profitable investment opportunities (Gershenkron 1962).

In our contribution we argue that 'financialization' (which refers both to a set of empirical developments and to a budding literature that tries to come to grips with these empirical developments (see Engelen 2008; Erturk et al. 2008)) contains a number of empirical challenges for comparative institutionalism that it can only hope to address if it strips itself of its 'materialism', i.e. its near exclusive focus on the production of goods that one, in the memorable phrase of *The Economist*, can drop on one's foot, that it has inherited from classical political economy (see Deane 1978; Redman 1997). The reconceptualizations this requires demand the building of bridges with the recent studies of finance in their many guises, in order to align the strengths of comparative research aimed at causal explanations with those of a more developed conception of agency, and a greater appreciation of the contingencies of context as well as a theoretical recognition of the complex linkages between financial markets, households, firms, and the state in contemporary capitalism.

We start our contribution with a section on the literature on financialization, briefly sketching the different approaches, objectives, methodologies, and data sources that can be traced in that literature. The next section presents quantitative data on the extent of financialization in five political economies (UK, US, Netherlands, France, and Germany), highlighting both similarities and differences. We subsequently identify three different trajectories of financialization and give some suggestions as to how comparative institutionalism might conceptualize these. The final section offers some thoughts on possible ways forward.

FINANCIALIZATION: THE LITERATURE

The concept of financialization is not new: its roots can be traced back to the early twentieth-century work of Marxists like Hilferding and interbellum liberal collectivists such as Tawney, Berle and Means, and Keynes (see Erturk et al. (2008) for a historical introduction). Moreover, neither the concept nor its theoretical connotations ever fully disappeared from the world of radical political economy. Marxists like Harvey (1982) and those working in the field of world-systems theory (Arrighi 1996) have always drawn on the idea to describe key aspects of the crisis tendencies of twentieth-century capitalism.

But the recent rediscovery of financialization has been very significant. Over the past decade a growing number of scholars have used the concept to describe new trends in contemporary capitalism.[1] What this suggests is that since the 1990s the study of financial globalization has generated enough empirical observations that did not comfortably fit into extant conceptual frameworks as to prompt scholars to look for a new master concept to capture and explain the dynamics of financial change. Many of these observations are related to those aspects of financial markets that are bound up with their specifically financial qualities and often fall outside the explanatory purview of more traditional approaches, which tend to reduce financial markets to their functional intermediary role in the macro-economic relationship between households and firms and are consequently less attuned to their sui generis characteristics. The concept seems to have caught on, as scholars from such diverse disciplines as economic sociology, critical accounting studies, business administration, and comparative political economy have taken it up. Its growing usage suggests

---

[1] A web search on the PICARTA site, which covers the electronic catalogues of 13 Dutch university libraries, shows that the earliest publications on 'financiali(z/s)ation' date from 2000. Since 2000, 32 papers and books on finaciali(z/s)ation have been added, with a rapid increase from 2007 onward (see www.picarta.nl, accessed 2 February 2009). The number of hits in www.scholar.google.com (accessed 2 February 2009) is much higher, reaching 752 for financialisation and well over 1800 for financialization, suggesting a fertile American research community, most of them dating from after 2003. Finally, the web of science database gives an overall number of 35 hits for financialization. The earliest hits date from 1999, setting in motion a small but continuously broadening trickle of publications, generating a sum total of 9 titles in 2007.

both that changes responsible for the empirical anomalies that motivated the formulation of financialization perspectives have been structural rather than ephemeral and that the purchase provided by this conceptual innovation has been quite significant.[2]

The variety of approaches and disciplinary perspectives is reflected in the fact that there is, as yet, no uniform definition of financialization. Different scholars, coming from different scholarly traditions and theoretical backgrounds, tend to privilege different aspects of financialization processes. Those authors whose background is primarily in the discipline of International Political Economy have tended to focus on the transnationalized organizational structures of financial markets, i.e. the ever-closer links among liquid financial markets across local and national boundaries, facilitated by the shift from traditional intermediation towards disintermediated investment and trading (Sinclair 2005; Porter 2005). They concentrate on the growing connections among what were once solidly nation-based financial markets but emphasize that this is not a situation whereby market processes are imposing their logic on citizens and governments, but rather involves highly complex reconfigurations of private and public financial authority, in particular a redistribution of power from workers, managers, and politicians to shareholders (van Apeldoorn and Horn 2007). To a large extent this has been a reaction to an earlier shift in the political-economic study of global finance, which (against neo-liberal conceptions of the death of the state) emphasized the continued centrality of the national state yet in so doing tended to pay less and less attention to the specificities of the changing nature of those market processes themselves (e.g. Helleiner 1994).

Scholars working in a tradition that is now often referred to as comparative political economy also take into account the transnational aspects of financial change, but tend to concentrate more on what are still viewed as financial systems with recognizable national or regional coordinates. Many of the contributions to this field of study have considerable affinity with, or even roots in, Marxist theory, like regulation theory (Aglietta 2000; Boyer 2000) or the social structures of accumulation approach (Duménil and Lévy 2004). Others do not draw on Marx but have a firm foothold in the history of radical political economy such as the post-Keynesians (Stockhammer 2008; Crotty 2005). Still other contributions have a more institutionalist bent, but as many varieties of the new institutionalism have been formulated

---

[2] Of the 54 hits given by the web of science, 26 come from the field of economics, 11 from the spatial sciences (geography, area studies, environmental sciences), 13 from political science and 11 from sociology. Given the nature of the object, finance, the predominance of economics is to be expected. However, the journals in which the economics papers appeared are anything but mainstream economics journals, let alone finance journals. The largest number of papers (8) is published in *Economy & Society*, which is actually a sociological journal that publishes mainly critical sociological reflections on economic topics. The second largest source of publications, with six titles, is the *Review of International Political Economy*, the leading journal in the field of International Political Economy, which is an offshoot of International Relations and hence at root a political science journal. The only truly economic journals that carried financialization papers, are the *Cambridge Journal of Economics* and the *Journal of Post-Keynesian Economics*. However, these are considered to be heterodox and are hence at the margin of the economic discipline.

through critiques of Marxist determinism, they have tended to import and implicitly reproduce many of its conceptualizations, above all the conception of finance as performing an intermediary function channelling a nation's savings into productive investment. Consistent with this conceptual orientation, scholars in this approach devote most of their attention to the changing patterns and forms of corporate governance (Vitols 2001; Jacoby 2005). To the extent that the growth of financial markets goes beyond the marketization and growing liquidity of markets for corporate debt and equity, they equate this with the dysfunctional autonomization of finance from its institutional environment and the growth of rentiers' income.

Economic sociologists, who tend to be more interested in the concrete functioning of particular markets and to be less concerned with assessing the macro-economic efficiency of macro-level institutional arrangements, have suspended questions regarding the systemic viability of financialization and have instead described the ways in which financialization processes have been accompanied—as both cause and effect—by changing financial practices, routines, and dispositions. The literature that has come to be known as 'social studies of finance' was initiated by scholars working in the interdisciplinary field of 'social studies of science', which is dedicated to uncovering how the 'objective' field of the exact sciences is socially structured and discursively produced. Their aim was to show something similar for financial markets, i.e. that the world of 'high finance', even as it was conquered by mathematical models, was highly social in nature. Their accounts of social life in financial markets have tended to stress the cultural framework, conventions, and relations through which financial innovation is 'performed' (MacKenzie 2006; Knorr-Cetina and Preda 2005; Beunza and Stark 2004; MacKenzie and Millo 2003).

Other literatures have pursued the 'social' dimension even further. While the 'social studies of finance' literature is characterized by a healthy scepticism regarding the financial world's account of itself, it nevertheless limits its gaze to the traditional world of high finance. But this has been only part of the story. Not only have financial markets always been social in nature, it was precisely the globalization era that witnessed an extraordinary deepening of their social dimensions. A conspicuous feature of the new financial world has been the penetration of relations of credit and debt into new areas of social life. The past decades have seen an extraordinary growth of the public's role as both investor and borrower. The literature that came from the field of critical management and accounting studies greatly advanced our understanding of how financialization has been embedded in the wider structure of social life (Froud et al. 2006; Erturk and Solari 2007). It did so in two ways. First, even if rentier income retained some of its negative moral connotations, it was no longer seen as the passive creaming off of others' productive labour: the financial machinations that generated ever rising returns on financial capital required a great deal of creative activity. In this way, financialization was described as entailing a shift in the balance of social power. Second, the new financial techniques were not only a foundation for elites' ability to employ financial strategies (like private equity funds and hedge funds) that were hardly related to the 'traditional' markets for corporate financial intermediation, but were also a driving force behind the dramatic expansion of asset-backed securities, mortgage, and consumer debt.

The ways in which new financial techniques and relations transformed everyday social life received even more attention in the branch of literature that is increasingly referred to as 'cultural (political) economy' (De Goede 2005; Langley 2008; Martin 2002; Aitken 2007). Drawing on Foucauldian theories, which emphasize the capillary operation of power and the ways society-wide disciplinary imperatives are constructed through the intertwining of micro-level discursive practices, these theories have analysed how financialization has entailed a transformation of cultural norms and values situated at the level of everyday life. Just like the critical business and management literature, the cultural economy analysis tends to display considerable affinity with the sociological literature on 'governmentality' (Barry et al. 1993), which has sought to explain the socio-cultural consequences of the introduction of performance-enhancing techniques (audits, performance indicators, accountability requirements) that are the outgrowth of neo-liberal globalization at the level of mundane dispositions and practices within public organizations (Power 1994).

In addition, the concept of financialization has found fruitful application in the highly interdisciplinary field of economic geography. To some extent, the work on financialization by economic geographers tends to fall into one or more of the categories set out in the above. For instance, Leyshon and Thrift's (2007) analysis of 'the capitalization of almost everything' (i.e. the transformation of an increasing number of assets into financial commodities that can be easily traded on liquid financial markets) is a good example of a 'cultural economy' approach to finance. But the discipline has also begun to carve out a more distinctively geographic perspective, which uses the notion of financialization to analyse the spatially rooted institutional specificities of corporate governance practices (Clark and Wójzik 2007), the impact of demographic developments on the provision of pensions and the growing role of capitalized pension funds (Clark 2000; Engelen 2003), as well as shifts in employment and reconfigurations of competitiveness across different financial centres (see special issue of *Growth and Change* 2007).

While financialization theorists disagree about the precise causal pathways involved and differ in their research focus, they tend to agree in viewing financialization as a generalized trend, to be found in most Western national political economies. It thus supports the modernist thesis of institutional convergence: in a context of the rise of financial markets, the creation of new financial products, and the appearance of new border-crossing financial agents, the relevance of national institutional differences is supposed to be declining. While the comparative literature on financialization may seem to be an exception to this trend, that is the case only in a very qualified sense: it questions the extent to which financialization trends have eroded the distinctive institutional make-up of European political economies, but this research orientation is embedded in a problematic organized around the erosion of institutional differences between national political economies. As a consequence, the growth of the financialization literature has entailed a move away from the 'methodological nationalism' and static comparisons of self-enclosed political economies (Glick Schiller and Wimmer 2003).

This has in many ways been a very welcome development, but it has, like all theoretical advances, also generated some new issues and problems. Given the origins of the financialization literature (i.e. the dissatisfaction with the sterile state versus markets framework that dominated debates on globalization), the strong focus on the norms and techniques driving the expansionary dynamics of financial markets is understandable, as is the tendency to focus primarily on Anglo-American economies (where, after all, financial change and innovation was most dramatic). Yet the current conjuncture is making it increasingly difficult to understand financial change without paying ample attention to the often quite distinctive institutional specificities at the very heart of financialization processes. As different nations (and regions) are formulating often different responses to the crisis that has beset global financial markets, we need more fine-grained conceptual devices that are more attuned to the ways in which financialization processes assume fundamentally different forms in different polities. This certainly involves making use of, but also going beyond, the existing presence of comparative institutionalism in financialization studies: to consider national institutional frameworks primarily as reacting to financialization trends is to downplay their active role in shaping and constituting these dynamics. As the various parts of the financial world have become interlinked in more ways than ever before, the convergence thesis is no longer a reliable or useful heuristic tool to frame our investigations of this world. The next section seeks to demonstrate this in more detail.

FINANCIALIZATION: THE EMPIRICS

While there is no consensus on the metric of financialization, we have opted for a three dimensional approach to capture as many as possible of the developments described by the financialization literature. We begin with comparative data on the depth of different financial markets in the UK, the US, the Netherlands, France, and Germany. This measure encompasses differences in national (both public and private) indebtedness as well as the depth of the equity market. We have chosen these countries because in the VoC-literature they serve as the most true-to-type instances of a 'liberal market economy' (LME) and a 'coordinated market economy' (CME) respectively. We have added the Netherlands for reasons of contrast, given its hybrid nature (see Engelen et al. 2010 for an empirical demonstration of Dutch hybridity). We then proceed with the inflow and outflow of capital as an indicator of financial openness as well as the extent of financial internationalization. We use these two measures as a broad indicator of factor mobility in the financial domain. Large financial markets relative to GDP and a high degree of openness to

[handwritten in margin: Foreign Direct Investment]

foreign direct investment (FDI) are markers of a LME, i.e. a political economy where the logic of factor mobility rules supreme. The opposite serves as a marker of a CME, i.e. a political economy that is notable for its high degree of factor protection, especially labour.

However, these are both relatively traditional financial indicators based on a conceptualization of financial markets that is strongly geared towards its supposedly intermediating functionality for what is called the 'productive' or 'real' economy. As such, these indicators fail to capture what is a striking hallmark of current financial markets, namely, their innovativeness, responsible for the production of financial products that are at two or three removes from real financial assets (e.g. derivatives, securitized assets, and futures). We use data from the European Securitization Forum on the value of securitized assets as a proxy for the degree of innovativeness of financial agents in different political economies to capture at least part of these new segments of the world's financial markets. We dispense with measures concerning the spatial distribution of 'new financial agents' like hedge funds and private equity funds as indicators of financial innovativeness, since in the virtualized markets these agents can tap into 'national' financial markets from wherever they are located. And in the case of hedge funds and private equity funds that is often in exotic offshore financial centres, like the Cayman Islands, the Virgin Islands, and the Seychelles, which can hardly be described as themselves founts of financial innovation.

Financial market depth

Since the re-emergence of capital mobility in the 1970s, financial markets in almost every OECD member state have grown tremendously. After the setback triggered by the bursting of the ICT bubble in 2001, the expansion of financial markets has accelerated again since 2003. Figure 21.1 corroborates the picture suggested by the VoC-literature in the sense that the depth of the financial markets in the UK and the US surpasses that of French and German markets. However, the Netherlands, which Hall and Soskice situate squarely in the CME camp, defies these expectations. If we leave aside 'offshore' financial centres such as Ireland and Luxembourg, the Netherlands domiciles the largest capital markets relative to GDP in the OECD, surpassing both the US and the UK (IMF 2006: 95).

However, it is important to go beyond mere aggregate quantitative indicators and to take into account the concrete institutional dimensions of the depth of financial markets. It is often pointed out that most investment in market-based systems is not undertaken directly but indirectly, i.e. through intermediaries such as investment funds and pension funds who pool assets, diversify risks, provide expertise, lower transaction costs, and practice due diligence. It is especially the latter that have contributed to financial growth. As Toporowski (2000) and Clark (2000) have argued, the investment needs of large institutional investors are the drivers of financialization. Hence there appears to be a strong correlation between funded

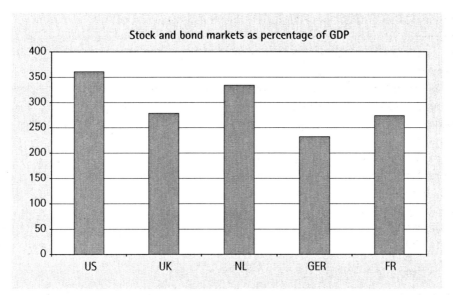

Figure 21.1: Stock and bond markets as percentage of GDP

Source: IMF Global Stability Report October 2008.

pension systems and deep financial markets on the one hand and a so-called pay-as-you-go system and a bank-based financial system on the other. In fact, the combination of large pension funds and deep and liquid financial markets has become a typical marker of the Anglo-American cluster, as is demonstrated by Figure 21.2 below.

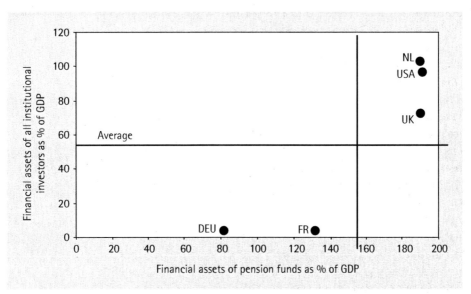

Figure 21.2: Correlation between pension fund reserves and the total assets of institutional investors relative to GDP in 2001

Source: OECD 2009. Institutional Investors Assets Database. Paris: OECD.

The US and the UK are situated solidly in the upper right corner: France and Germany in the lower-left quadrant. But the position of the Netherlands is telling: it clearly fits the Anglo-American pattern in which both total assets and the contribution of pension funds are extremely high. Here, the Netherlands and its corporatist neighbours clearly part institutional ways. Indeed, the Netherlands (together with puny Iceland and Switzerland) possesses the highest amount of pension savings relative to GDP worldwide, higher even than typical LMEs such as the US and the UK.

Financial openness

We take inward and outward foreign direct investment (FDI) as a proxy for financial openness. If financial internationalization means anything it should have become easier for domestic investors to invest in foreign capital markets and for foreign investors to invest in domestic capital markets, both because of the repeal of legal hindrances and the increasing transparency of foreign asset classes to domestic investors as a result of the virtualization of financial markets and the digitization of trading data. Hence, we should expect a sharp rise in cross-border transaction as measured by inward and outward FDI flows.

Figure 21.3 shows that to be the case. Across the board, we observe a rise in both inward and outward FDI relative to GDP from 1990 to 2005. However, the amount of FDI flows differs strongly among political economies, although in a pattern that is hard to reconcile with the VoC-narrative. While Germany and France demonstrate a relatively low level of openness and the UK a relatively large degree of openness, the US and the Netherlands disturb that pattern—the former due to its relative lack of openness, the latter both for its high absolute levels of inward and outward FDI as well as for the extreme speed with which these indicators have changed, illustrating the strong embeddedness of the Dutch political economy in global capital markets.

Another measure of financial openness is foreign ownership of publicly quoted shares. As Figure 21.4 demonstrates, there are huge differences with regard to the level of foreign investor penetration in national equity markets. While the overall level of foreign ownership of exchange traded equity has risen almost everywhere in Europe, in most cases growth has been fairly limited. Large European political economies like France and Germany have relatively stable shares of foreign ownership, ranging from 22 and 17 per cent respectively in 1990 to 39 and 21 per cent in 2005. Even in financialized economies like the UK the level of foreign ownership is fairly constant, amounting currently to only 35.2 per cent. Apart from the new accession countries, whose huge privatization programmes in the early 1990s attracted large numbers of foreign investors, it is small, open, and highly internationalized economies like Belgium, Ireland, and the Netherlands that truly stand out with shares of foreign ownership substantially exceeding the 50 per cent mark. From a level of 46 per cent in 1990, the share of foreign ownership in the Netherlands has now reached 69 per cent, making it one of the most internationalized market places in the world.

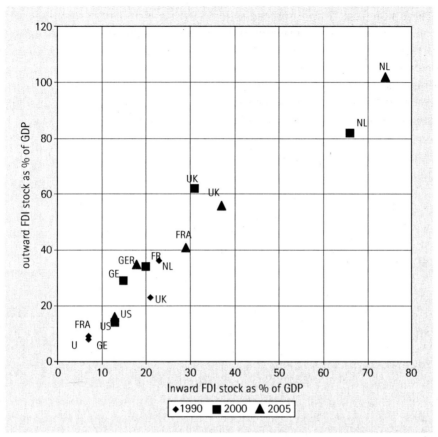

Figure 21.3: Inward and outward FDI stock relative to GDP in 1990, 2000, and 2005

Source: UNCTAD 2009. FDI Database Washington, UNCTAD.

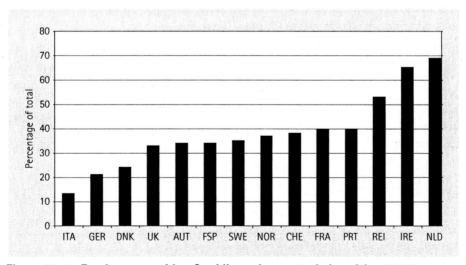

Figure 21.4: Foreign ownership of public exchange traded equities, 2005

Source: FESE 2007: 10.

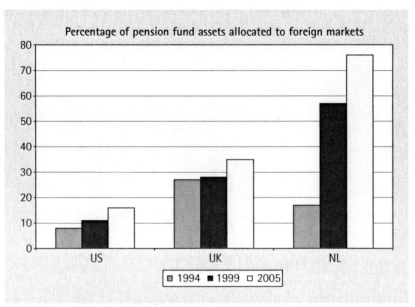

Figure 21.5: Percentage of pension fund assets allocated to foreign markets
Source: IMF Global Stability Report, April 2007: 71.

If foreign equity ownership illustrates the ease of capital inflow, the share of foreign equity in the portfolio of domestic institutional investors, especially pension funds, is a measure of the ease of capital outflow. Figure 21.5 presents comparative data on the share of foreign holdings in the portfolio of Dutch, American, and British pension funds.[3] The rapid growth of foreign holdings by Dutch pension funds is striking. Currently around 75 per cent of total Dutch pension fund assets is invested outside the Netherlands, while 58 per cent of it is managed by foreign, in particular Anglo-American, asset managers (Bureau Bosch 2007).

Financial innovation

As we sketched in the introduction, since the 1990s financial markets have undergone a radical transformation. Traders' creativity, promoted by new technologies and the knowledge of mathematicians and econometricians, has resulted in a veritable wave of financial innovation, especially in the OTC derivative markets. Since the three-yearly BIS data do not allow for a geographical breakdown, we have decided to use the available data on securitization as a proxy for financial innovativeness. Europe is a relative newcomer in the field of securitization and the American market for

---

[3] Since capitalized pension funds are virtually non-existent in France and Germany, we have restricted the data presented to these three economies.

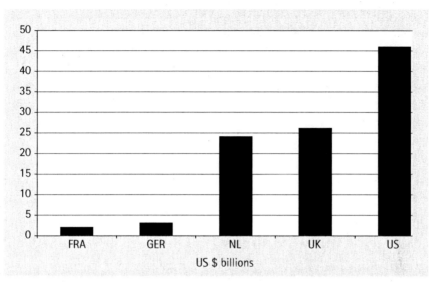

Figure 21.6: Securitization outstanding as a percentage of GDP, 2006

Source: European Securitization Data Report, Summer 2007.

securitized assets is almost eight times as large as the European one. The American market encompasses both commercial and residential property as well credit card debts, phone cards, student loans, and car loans (IFSL 2007). In Europe, the market is still dominated by mortgage-backed securities (MBS), primarily related to commercial property. However, the securitization of other forms of debt and especially residential mortgages is on the rise in most European economies. We expect the level of securitization to be related to the other measures of financialization presented in this section.

Figure 21.6 largely bears that out. When it comes to outstanding amounts of securitized assets, the UK and the US surpass by far the still fledgling securitization markets in France and Germany, corroborating the picture sketched of the two types of political economies in the VoC-literature. The outlier, once again, is the Netherlands. In terms of outstanding securitized assets the Netherlands is much closer to the systems of the UK and the US than to continental European countries. It is also worth observing that the amount of outstanding asset- and mortgage-backed securities in the Netherlands is increasing rapidly and, in contrast to the UK and the US, seems to be undented by the credit crunch of 2007–8.

Beyond intermediation?

To what extent do these indicators provide evidence for our hypothesis that finance has transcended its traditional intermediating functions? And how does this trend vary across different political economies? Unfortunately, there are no easy answers. We might get some further purchase on this issue from OECD data on the share of fee-based versus interest-based incomes of banks, often used as a proxy for the

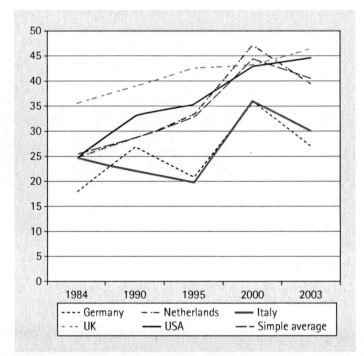

Figure 21.7: Share of banks' fee income as a percentage of their overall income

Source: OECD, Bank Profitability Database.

relative importance of 'traditional' versus 'financialized' banking. It is important to emphasize that, again, this is not more than a rough measure, since the category of fee-based income hides from view the transformations that have taken place in the types of fees earned by banks, and tracking these transformations requires data at the level of individual banks that have not been collected in any systematic fashion (see Erturk et al. 2009 for a first attempt).

Figure 21.7 gives data on the share of fee-based bank incomes for Germany, the UK, the US, and the Netherlands, showing a steady increase in the share of fee-based incomes in all four countries. The recent decline of fee-based incomes in Germany and the Netherlands is striking, which suggests a loss of fee earning opportunities to Anglo-American competitors.

Thus, it seems possible to conclude, with some caution, that the extent to which finance has moved beyond its traditional intermediating functions has been relatively well-documented for the US and the UK, both by the financialization literature and by a growing number of practitioners (e.g. Krippner 2001; Michie and Mollan 2008; Roberts 2008; Knee 2007; Augar 2005; Ellis 2008). The available indicators suggest only a limited extent of financialization in the case of France and Germany. The case of the Netherlands offers a third trajectory of financialization. Below we will sketch the outlines of the three pathways of financialization that our empirics suggest.

FINANCIALIZATION: DIFFERENT TRAJECTORIES

What our combination of comparative institutionalism and financialization studies suggests is a need to distinguish conceptually between different paths or trajectories of financialization—not just in the sense that universal processes of financialization are refracted differently in different institutional contexts, but rather as shaped by the contingent outcomes of actors' political struggles and compromises over how to negotiate the financial opportunities and pressures with which they are faced. On the basis of the empirical material presented above we distinguish between the following paths of financialization:

1. *consensual financialization* in the case of institutional configurations that possess a high degree of instititutional isomorphism and are based on the utilitarian logic of short-term profit maximization and high factor mobility;
2. *contested financialization* in the case of institutional configurations that possess a comparable degree of isomorphism, but are instead based on the deontological logic of loyalty, strong reciprocal commitments, and factor immobility;
3. *compartmentalized financialization* in the case of hybrid institutional configurations that lack institutional isomorphism but are instead loosely coupled institutional wholes that are nevertheless able to generate strong economic and financial performances.

Below, we discuss each of these pathways in turn.

Consensual financialization

Consensual financialization refers to a political economy where financial agents have been able to mould the institutional and regulatory environment in such a way that their wealth enhancing capabilities are produced and coordinated through exchange relations. This results in high scores on all indicators of financialization used above: high degrees of capital mobility, financial market openness, and financial innovativeness. The US and the UK are prime examples of this pathway, suggesting an 'elective affinity' between the LME-model of the VoC-literature, built around the importance of factor mobility for generating economic wealth, and this particular trajectory of financialization.

It is associated with a particular mode of political contestation. While populist backlashes were prevalent everywhere, especially in the immediate aftermath of the 2007–9 (and onwards?) credit crisis, their political reworking took on a particular form in the UK and the US. For what is striking about developments in both the US and the UK is that political initiatives aimed at the suppression of financial markets and the imposition of serious constraints on financial actors have generally failed to reach the legislative end stage. Instead, they have become bogged down in a slow and opaque legislative trajectory that is overlaid with conflicting aims and initiatives.

This has much to do with the ability of the financial sector to block attempts by legislators and regulators to impose measures that are seen as disruptive of its business. To a large extent this ability derives from the fact that while the electorate does not take kindly to the abuse of financial power, it has an abiding faith in the power of the marketplace to solve its own problems. Promises of self-regulation have therefore always been an effective response to attempts to impose a more restrictive regime (Robotti 2007; Engelen, Konings, and Fernandez 2008).

A similar observation can be derived from the state responses to the credit crisis. If Anglo-American finance picked up its pace of expansion relatively easily after the 2001 crisis, the subprime crisis clearly posed greater challenges to its capabilities and legitimacy. What is striking about the Anglo-American responses, however, is the differential treatment of 'Wall Street' and 'Main Street': the provision of tremendous amounts of funds to the world of high finance in the absence of significant direct assistance for ordinary people has not resulted in a substantial delegitimation of key financial institutions. While the electorate have loudly voiced their aversion to financial excesses, they have refrained from taking on the financial system as such, suggesting that they understand their own financial security as deeply bound up with the long-term soundness of the financial system at large (Engelen et al. 2010).

Contested financialization

Contested financialization tends to characterize political economies where financial agents have lacked the power to benefit from the opportunities that have been offered by the twin process of deregulation and technological change in financial markets—because of insufficient legitimacy or a lack of class coalitions. The latter has clearly been the case in Germany, the quintessential CME. Given its highly fragmented banking and equity markets, agents willing to pursue the opportunities offered by financial internationalization have found governments, the electorate as well as other fractions of the capitalist class in their way and have instead opted for an existence as transnational actors that have largely cut ties with their institutional and spatial domestic origins (e.g. Deutsche Bank and Deutsche Börse).

This is associated with a specific mode of contestation surrounding the distributive effects of financialization. What is striking about the German polity is its accessibility for those who resent the influx of foreign investors in the German economy. The dominant discursive frame in Germany is that of 'protecting' the German model against external onslaughts. Anglo-American activist investors are seen to have disrupted the trust-based foundation of the German production system. These new actors and the financial strategies they employ are perceived as foreign and exogenous, reflecting the still limited extent of financialization of the German economy and the German public's relative lack of familiarity with new financial actors, products, and services. Moreover, the perception that there is something worthwhile to protect reflects the newly gained self-confidence of the German political and economic elite because of improved macro-economic performance compared to the early 1990s (Engelen et al. 2008).

This configuration of economic and political forces has shaped Germany's particular response to the subprime crisis. Germany has been spared the disgrace of having to bail out its largest banks, while German firms appear to have been much less hit by the deleveraging of banks and the credit squeeze, prompting politicians to emphasize the superiority of Germany's three-pillared banking system. Nevertheless, through the channel of declining exports, the German economy too has taken severe hits from the credit crisis. In 2008 the German government embarked upon a Keynesian fiscal package to stimulate the domestic economy, but it did so grudgingly and in a context that stressed the pernicious influence of Anglo-American capitalism (Engelen et al. 2010).

Compartmentalized financialization

Compartmentalized financialization is typical for political economies that encompass institutional arrangements with contrasting logics, i.e. that combine corporatist labour market regimes and welfare states with deep financial markets, a high degree of financial openness, and a large financial sector. The Netherlands was used in this chapter as an example of this trajectory of financialization, but similar processes can be observed in countries like Switzerland, Austria, and the Scandinavian economies, suggesting a correlation between this mode of financialization and the characteristics of small open trading nations that have been described by Katzenstein (1985). The hallmark of this mode of financialization is that national financial agents such as banks, insurers, and pension funds take full advantage of the transnational opportunities that financialization has created, while simultaneously leaving the traditional integrity of the wider national economy largely untouched. One manifestation of this is the move of financial agents, either physically or virtually, to transnational nodes like the financial centre of London.

The Dutch case illustrates this compartmentalization well. Most of its pension savings are invested abroad and managed by Anglo-American asset managers. Most of the stocks listed at the Amsterdam exchange are owned by foreigners. The trade in synthetic products and other innovative financial instruments is increasingly conducted by the London desks of the largest Dutch banks or is even completely outsourced to foreign banks. The Amsterdam exchange has largely turned into a transnational trading platform whose primary market (for IPOs) is increasingly used by so-called 'Special Purpose Acquisition Companies' (SPACs), domiciled in offshore centres such as Guernsey, Jersey, and the Cayman Islands and managed by Anglo-American owners like Carlyle Capital and KKR. Similar forms of compartmentalization can be found in Switzerland and Sweden (Engelen and Grote 2009).

This translates, once more, into a highly specific mode of contestation. While there was considerable public uproar over a number of high-profile cases of foreign investor activism, this did not result in effective political action like in Germany. Rather, the political response was delegated to a committee of experts who reframed the issue not so much as the rise of activist investors but as a technical issue of corporate governance. In other words, a populist backlash was contained by political elites in a typical corporatist manner. The viability of such strategies is bound up with the Dutch-funded pension regime: because Dutch workers are dependent for their long-term welfare on the ability of pension funds to reap high returns on investment, Dutch workers in a very meaningful sense have themselves become shareholders. While politicians, unions, and managers do still wield the discourse of corporatism, the population's growing awareness of its dependence on capital returns means that they have generally failed to enact it (Engelen et al. 2008). The delicate balance that characterized this hybrid regime will no doubt be tested further as the current crisis develops forcing the Netherlands to face a quadruple whammy: a sharply declining contribution by financial activities to its GDP, a funded pension crisis that is affecting over 90 per cent of workers, a rapid fall in global consumption hitting its export-oriented economy particularly hard, and a rapidly rising public indebtedness as a result of the need to shore up Dutch banks to the tune of 6 to 10 per cent of GDP, one of the highest percentages worldwide (Engelen et al. 2010).

While this section has presented only a preliminary mapping that is in need of more robust testing, more detailed conceptualization, more fine-grained causal analyses, and further territorial extension, it does suggest that the cross-fertilization of comparative institutionalism and financialization studies would be a fruitful undertaking, providing us with greater insight into the agents, techniques, and institutional arrangements at work and the political constellations they produce. Below, we briefly sketch some of the implications for comparative institutionalism of such a collaborative approach.

CONCLUSION

This chapter began with the claim that the financialization of contemporary capitalism has not received sufficient attention from comparative institutionalism and the VoC-literature. We then presented an overview of financialization trends and argued for the existence of different trajectories or pathways of financialization. What the empirics suggest is that comparative instititionalism needs to move beyond its Gershenkronian roots and has to broaden its empirical 'catchment area' by taking the rise of finance more seriously. Comparative institutionalism needs to do more to come to terms with the structural transformation in contemporary capitalism, whereby finance has transcended its traditional intermediary role and has become a self-standing growth industry primarily geared to the production of liquidity. This change is reflected in the continuous role-shifting of investment banks. While these players used to earn their fees by providing intermediating and advisory services to firms who wanted to take over other firms or draw capital from public markets, increasingly they earn their fees by pursuing purely financial transactions (prime brokerage, constructing and marketing 'synthetic products', asset management, wealth management, treasury management, fiduciary management) and using the knowledge they gain in that process for proprietary business (Knee 2007).

This shift from intermediation to transaction functions implies that perspectives that view the functionality of the financial system as determined by the extent to which it mediates between households and firms and between savings and investments, are likely to become increasingly inadequate to the task of describing and explaining contemporary financial change (Konings 2008). The persistence of this normatively laden notion of functionality speaks to its roots in productivist visions of capitalism that ultimately go back to the assumptions of classical British political economy of the early nineteenth century (Deane 1978; Redman 1997). More specifically, the conceptualization of financial systems as conduits between society's savings and its productive investments can be said to represent a residual 'materialist' bias that has survived VoC's tendency to stake out its own theoretical terrain by criticizing the economic determinism and homogenizing assumptions of both Marxism and neo-classical economics. In so far as financial expansion is not connected to increases in productive investment, this tends to be equated with a dysfunctional uncoupling or disembedding of finance from the real economy, in a Polanyian sense (Blyth 2002; Block 2007). Thus, within the framework of the VoC-literature, financialization processes, like processes of disembedding, can, almost by definition, only be conceptualized in negative terms (see also Krippner 2001).

Indeed, the central distinction between bank-based systems and market-based systems can only be sustained on the notion that a financial system should be evaluated in terms of its ability to promote industrial growth and competitiveness. For from the point of view of industrial corporations' financing decisions, the distinction between bank credit and capital market financing largely holds. But as financial practitioners are well aware, the long-term stock and bond markets are only one part of a much more complex and variegated configuration of financial markets, much of which has traditionally remained under the radar of financial authorities (often with the latter's permission). And in the age of financialization and the incorporation of ever larger swathes of economic activity into expansionary financial dynamics, these configurations become crucial. They are better seen as constituting a highly complex structure of interacting funds, cross-cutting networks, and overlapping credit relations than as consisting of discrete realms of financial action.

Thus, contemporary capitalism is progressively undermining the viability of a dichotomous view of the economy, according to which clear-cut distinctions can be made between the 'real economy' and the 'financial sector'. The reality of financialization requires an extensive reworking of the way in which finance is currently conceptualized (see also Deeg in this volume). This chapter has argued that comparative institutionalists should consider turning to the growing financialization literature to that end. A cross-fertilization of themes found in the two literatures would certainly advance attempts to understand the patterns of change discussed in this paper.

REFERENCES

APELDOORN, B. VAN and L. HORN (2007). 'The Marketisation of European Corporate Control: A Critical Political Economy Perspective', *New Political Economy* 12(2).

AGLIETTA, M. (2000). 'Shareholder Value and Corporate Governance: Some Tricky Questions', *Economy and Society* 29(1): 146–59.

AITKEN, R. (2007). *Performing Capital*, (New York: Palgrave).

ARRIGHI, G. (1996). *The Long Twentieth Century: Money, Power, and the Origins of our Time*, (London: Verso).

AUGAR, P. (2005). *The Greed Merchants: How the Investment Banks Played the Free Market Game*, (London: Allen Lane).

BARRY, A., T. OSBORNE, and N. ROSE (1996). *Foucault and Political Reason: Liberalism, Neo-liberalism, and Rationalities of Government*, (Chicago: University of Chicago Press).

BERNSTEIN, P. (1993). *Capital Ideas: The Improbable Origins of Modern Wall Street*, (Hoboken, NJ: Wiley).

——(2007). *Capital Ideas Evolving*, (Hoboken, NJ: Wiley).

BEUNZA, D. and D. STARK (2004). 'Tools of the Trade: The Socio-Technology of Arbitrage in a Wall Street Trading Room', *Industrial and Corporate Change* 13 (2).

BIS (2008a). 'OTC Derivatives Market Activity in the Second Half of 2007', in www.bis.org, accessed 10 Sept. 2008.

——(2008b). 'Statistics on Exchange Traded Derivatives', in www.bis.org, accessed 10 Sept. 2008.

BLOCK, F. (2007). 'Understanding the Diverging Trajectories of the United States and Western Europe: A Neo-Polanyian Analysis', *Politics & Society*, 35(1): 3–33.

BLYTH, M. (2002). *Great Transformations: Economic Ideas and Institutional Change in the Twentieth Century*, (Cambridge: Cambridge University Press).

BOYER, R. (2000). 'Is a Finance-led Growth Regime a Viable Alternative to Fordism? A Preliminary Analysis', *Economy & Society* 29(1): 111–45.

BUREAU BOSCH (2007). 'Trends of the Dutch Investment Management Market' (Utrecht: Bureau Bosch), 10.

CLARK, G. (2000). *Pension Fund Capitalism*, (Oxford: Oxford University Press).

CLARK, G. L. and D. WÓJCIK (2007). *The Geography of Finance: Corporate Governance in the Global Marketplace*, (Oxford: Oxford University Press).

CROTTY, J. (2005). 'The Neoliberal Paradox: The Impact of Destructive Product Market Competition and "Modern" Financial Markets on Nonfinancial Corporation Performance in the Neoliberal Era', in G. Epstein (ed.), *Financialization and the World Economy*, (Cheltenham: Edward Elgar).

DEANE, P. (1978). *The Evolution of Economic Ideas*, (Cambridge: Cambridge University Press).

DUMÉNIL, G. and D. LÉVY (2004). *Capital Resurgent: Roots of the Neoliberal Revolution*, (Cambridge, MA: Harvard University Press).

ELLIS, C. (2008). *The Partnership: The Making of Goldman Sachs*, (Harmondsworth: Penguin Press).

ENGELEN, E. (2003). 'The Logic of Funding: European Pension Restructuring and the Dangers of Financialisation', *Environment & Planning* A, 35, 1357–72.

——(2008) 'The Case for Financialization', *Competition & Change* 12(2): 111–19.

——M. KONINGS, and R. FERNANDEZ (2008). 'The Rise of Activist Investors and Patterns of Political Responses: Lessons on Agency', *Socio-Economic Review* 6(4): 611–36.

——————(2010). 'Geographies of Financialization in Disarray: The Dutch Case in Comparative Perspective', *Economic Geography* 86 (1): forthcoming.

——and M. GROTE (2009). 'Stock Exchange Virtualisation and the Decline of Second Tier Financial Centres: The Cases of Amsterdam and Frankfurt', *Journal of Economic Geography* 9(5): 679–96.

ERTURK, I. and S. SOLARI (2007). 'Banks as Continuous Reinvention', *New Political Economy*, 12(3).

——J. FROUD, S. JOHAL, A. LEAVER, and K. WILLIAMS (eds.) (2008). *Financialization at Work: Key Texts and Analysis*, (London: Routledge).

——————————(2009). 'Rediscovering Banks as Utility' Memo for the Treasury Select Committee, Jan. 2009, 14.

FROUD, J., S. JOHAL, A. LEAVER, and K. WILLIAMS (2006). *Financialization and Strategy: Narratives and Numbers*, (New York: Palgrave).

GERSCHENKRON, A. (1962). *Economic Backwardness in Historical Perspective*, (Cambridge, MA: Harvard University Press).

GLICK SCHILLER, N. and A. WIMMER (2003). 'Methodological Nationalism, the Social Sciences, and the Study of Migration: An Essay in Historical Epistemology', *International Migration Review*, 37(3): 576–610.

GOEDE, M. DE (2005). *Virtue, Fortune and Faith: A Genealogy of Finance*, (Minneapolis: The University of Minnesota Press).

Grahl, J. and P. Lysandrou (2003). 'Sand in the Wheels or Spanner in the Works? The Tobin Tax and Global Finance', *Cambridge Journal of Economics* 27, 597–621.

Growth and Change (2007). *Special Issue on European Financial Geographies* 38(2).

HALL, P. and D. SOSKICE (2001). *Varieties of Capitalism: The Institutional Foundations of Comparative Advantage*, (Oxford: Oxford University Press).

HARVEY, D. (1982). *The Limits to Capital*, (Oxford: Blackwell).

HELLEINER, E. (1994). *The Reemergence of Global Finance*, (Ithaca, NY: Cornell University Press).

JACKSON, G. and R. DEEG (2008). 'From Comparing Capitalisms to the Politics of Institutional Change', *Review of International Political Economy*, 15(4): 680–709.

JACOBY, S. (2005). *The Embedded Corporation: Corporate Governance and Employment Relations in Japan and the United States*, (Princeton, NJ: Princeton University Press).

IFSL (2007). *Securitisation*, (London: IFSL).

IMF (2006). *Global Financial Stability Report*, Sept. 2006.

KNEE, J. (2007). *The Accidental Investment Banker: Inside the Decade that Transformed Wall Street*, (New York: John Wiley & Sons).

KNORR-CETINA, K. and A. PREDA (ed.) (2005). *The Sociology of Financial Markets*, (Oxford: Oxford University Press).

KONINGS, M. (2008). 'European Finance in the American Mirror: Financial Change and the Reconfiguration of Competitiveness', *Contemporary Politics*, 14(3), 2008, pp. 253–75.

KRIPPNER, G. R. (2001). 'The Elusive Market', Embeddedness and the Paradigm of Economic Sociology, *Theory and Society* 30(3): 775–810.

KYNASTON, D. (1997). *LIFFE: A Market and its Makers*, (Cambridge: Granta).

KYNASTON, D. (2005). 'The Financialization of the American Economy' *Socio-Economic Review*, 3(2): 173–208.

LANGLEY, P. (2008). *The Everyday Life of Global Finance: Saving and Borrowing in Anglo-America*, (Oxford: Oxford University Press).

LEYSHON, A. and N. THRIFT (2007). 'The Capitalization of Almost Everything: The Future of Finance and Capitalism', *Theory, Culture & Society*, 24 (7/8): 97–115.

MACKENZIE, D. (2006). *An Engine, Not A Camera: How Financial Models Shape Markets*, (Cambridge, MA: MIT Press).

——and Y. MILLO (2003). 'Negotiating a Market, Performing Theory: The Historical Sociology of a Financial Derivatives Exchange', *American Journal of Sociology* 109.

MARTIN, R. (2002). *Financialization of Daily Life*, (Philadelphia: Temple University Press).

MICHIE, R.C. and S.M. MOLLAN (2008). 'Networks and Clusters: The City of London as a Global Financial Center since 1870', paper presented at the workshop Financial Centers as Competing Clusters, Paris, 30 Jan.

MORGAN, G. (2008). 'Market Formation and Governance in International Financial Markets: The Case of OTC Derivatives', *Human Relations* 61(5): 637–60.

PORTER, T. (2005). 'Private Authority, Technical Authority, and the Globalization of Accounting Standards', *Business and Politics*, 7 (3).

POWER, M. (1994). *The Audit Society: Rituals of Verification*, (Oxford: Oxford University Press).

REDMAN, D. (1997). *The Rise of Political Economy as a Science: Methodology and the Classical Economists*, (Cambridge, MA: MIT Press).

ROBERTS, R. (2008) *A Guide to London's Global Financial Centre*. London: Profile Books.

ROBOTTI, P. (2007). 'Capture or Self-Capture? US Domestic Actions to Reach out to the World of Hedge Funds: Implications for International Negotiations,' paper presented at the workshop Corporate Governance and Labour in the Era of Financial Capitalism, Free University, Amsterdam, 2–3 Jul. 2007.

SINCLAIR, T. (2005). *The New Masters of Capital: American Bond Rating Agencies and the Politics of Creditworthiness*, (Ithaca, NY; London: Cornell University Press).

STOCKHAMMER, E. (2008). 'Some Stylized Facts on the Finance-dominated Accumulation Regime', *Competition & Change*, 12(2): 184–202.

TALEB, N. (2007). *The Black Swan: The Impact of the Highly Improbable*, (London: Penguin).

TOPOROWSKI, J. (2000). *The End of Finance: Capital Market Inflation, Financial Derivatives and Pension Fund Capitalism*, (London: Routledge).

VITOLS, S. (2001). 'Varieties of Corporate Governance: Comparing Germany and the UK', in P. Hall and D. Soskice (eds.), *Varieties of Capitalism: The Institutional Foundations of Comparative Advantage*, (Oxford: Oxford University Press).

WFE (2007). 'Annual Report 2007'. In www.world-exchanges.org, accessed 10 Sept. 2008.

CHAPTER 22

....

INSTITUTIONAL COMPETITIVENESS: HOW NATIONS CAME TO COMPETE

....

OVE K. PEDERSEN[1]

INTRODUCTION
....

This chapter will describe how policymakers and governments came to understand the role of institutions in shaping the growth trajectory of nations and later to act *as if* nations compete on the basis of their economic, political, and cultural institutions (Campbell and Pedersen 2007a; Pedersen 2006b). The chapter will cover the period from the 1970s onwards. In the immediate post-Second World War period mainstream economics limited its analysis of institutions to markets. Appropriated institutions '... were those that allowed for a functioning of markets as close as possible to that featured in general-equilibrium theory'[2] (Amable 2003: 26). The mission of the state was to correct the market in case of externalities and to convey public goods, i.e. national defence, law enforcement, etc. Institutions were

[1] Thanks for comments to Mark Blyth, John L. Campbell, Colin Crouch, Francesco Duina, Charlotte Epstein, Ian Marsh, Glenn Morgan, Ariyoshi Ogawa, Koji Ono, and Vivien A. Schmidt. Special thanks to John Campbell and Glenn Morgan and to the always intellectual energetic WIP seminar at the International Center for Business and Politics, Copenhagen Business School.
[2] See Eatwell (1987).

understood to be exogenous to markets as well as a static phenomenon with measurable characteristics and predictable outcomes. This understanding of institutions corresponded to the Keynesian practise of economic intervention during 'The Golden -Age of Capitalism' lasting from the immediate end of the Second World War till the beginning of the 1970s (Eichengreen 2007: 15–51). With the onslaught of the first post-war crisis in 1973 neo-classical economists began to advocate the free functioning of market mechanisms and initiated a critique of Keynesian demand-management policies calling for institutional reforms. Privatization of state companies and deregulation of labour markets became policy goals in concert with liberalization of financial institutions and the construction of markets. The dominance of neo-liberalism suggested that all governments needed to do was to set markets free through making such institutional reforms (Campbell and Pedersen 2001). Institutional reforms subsequently came to mark the whole period from the 1970s onward, and the concept of 'institutional reform' came to dominate the political debate. Today, for example, the completion of 'The Single Market' in the EU stands as a significant instance of such reform in this period. It was based on the neo-liberal idea that institutional reforms matter and that the free functioning of markets is well suited to provide allocative benefits (Egan 2001; Fligstein 2001; Duina 2006). It also stands as an example of how the concept of institutional reform was put to use in politics, and of how the general understanding of the role of institutions changed from an emphasis on institutions as exogenous to markets, to institutions being also endogenous to markets, and from institutions as static with predictable outcomes, to institutions being dynamic with unpredictable outcomes. Later in the 1990s, the neo-liberal view was contested when it did not seem to explain certain highly competitive economies like Denmark (Campbell and Pedersen 2007b) and did not appear to produce much in the way of positive results in Central and Eastern Europe, or in South America (Frieden 2006: 437–44).

In this chapter I will describe how the focus on institutions and institutional change developed from a pure academic dialogue into practices of institutional reforms. The purpose is threefold. First, to show how the concept of institutional reform ignited a policy interest in institutions as a political phenomenon and in institutional analysis as a policy tool; second, to show how this emphasis on institutional reform influenced the general understanding of international competition as part of a political project for initiating an institutional competition among nations; and third, to introduce the 'concept of institutional competitiveness' (CIC) as a particular but important way of framing the concept of international competitiveness. My basic claim will be that discourses of national and firm-level competitiveness and associated practices of institutional reform have become a 'political phenomenon' of interest and salience for policymakers and decision-takers. Knowledge of institutions is now applied to explain economic growth and to assess the potential relevance of institutional reforms. Institutional analysis has become 'a policy tool' for the implementation of political goals. It is this dual role of discourses and institutions I describe in the following. The whole debate on international competitiveness will be looked upon as an example of how institutions (as a political phenomenon) and institutional analysis (as a policy tool) have become part of a policy approach making it possible for governments, and international organizations to act *as if* nations compete. This is the first aim of the chapter. The second is to show how in this process the understanding of institutions has developed from a simple to a comprehensive, and from a static to a dynamic view—i.e. from institutions regarded as a context for markets, to markets as a set of institutions that can be built by means of politics.

Three caveats are necessary. First, it is not my intention to describe in detail the conflicts of interests and the accidents of history involved in advancing this discourse. Even if agents and actions have obviously been the driving force in this development I will not attempt to identify who did what in the sequence of others' actions. My ambition is only to identify some of the traces that a myriad of actions has left in the general understanding of the role of institutions. Second, neither is it my ambition to explain why the travel from academia to policy took place in the first place. Once again my ambitions are rather modest; I will point to how institutions and institutional analysis have become concepts used by actors in arguing for institutional reforms. Third, and finally, it is not my ambition to argue that nations 'can' compete or actually 'do' compete. The concept 'nations compete' is widely contested; some even call it 'a dangerous obsession' and debate whether nations or alternatively only companies can compete (Krugman 1996). The aim is to show that whatever the debates, which continue about whether nations can or cannot (do or do not) compete, there is by now an established discourse on institutional competitiveness and a set of institutions making it possible for policymakers and others to act *as if* nations actually do compete.[3]

The chapter will be organized as follows. First, I describe how the concept of international competitiveness is discussed. In order to describe how the concept has been redefined and advanced to become a discourse I include literature from economic theory and business analysis (Aiginger 2006*b*; Siggel 2006). It is in this context that the concept of institutional competitiveness (hereafter abbreviated to CIC) is introduced as a particular understanding of what makes national economies competitive. Second, I trace the institutionalization of the discussion into institutions and expert systems through two examples. One is the development of *The Post-Washington Consensus*; another is *The Open Method of Coordination* within the EU. The presentation is based on policy papers, reports, and other primary sources from international organizations and national governments. Third, I point to how institutionalization has moved into policy arenas and come to include a number of reforms transforming nation-states. I draw on primary and secondary literature in

---

[3] Wolfgang Streeck (2009) gives another reason for emphasizing the *as if* aspect. He rightly calls attention to the fact that '... the significance of national institutions for the market fortunes of firms is anything but certain or invariant in time and place' (p. 9). He is also one of the very first to emphasize that the view that 'nations compete' must be regarded as a paradigm that have to be challenged and criticized '... if the theory of political economy is to move forward' (p. 20; see also Cameron and Palan 2003).

presenting the concept of the 'Competition State' (Cerny 1990, 2007; Stopford et al. 1991; Jessop 1994*a*, 2003; Hirsch 1995; but also Rosecrance 1999; Bobbit 2003; Weiss 2003). Fourth, and finally, I emphasize how state–society relations have been changed. The concept of 'Competitive Arrangements' (Rhodes 1998; Molina and Rhodes 2002) is engaged with other related concepts. In the Conclusion the concept of institutional competitiveness (CIC) is defined and presented as a present understanding of international competitiveness among national governments and others.

The Rising Discourse on 'Nations Compete' and Institutional Competitiveness

The year 1993 was special for the new interest in international competitiveness. In February 1993, President Bill Clinton introduced his first economic programme and spoke of '. . . a global economy in which we must compete with people around the world'. In June of the same year, the President of the Commission of the European Communities, Jacques Delors, spoke in Copenhagen about the competitive race between Europe and the USA.[4] This was eight years after Peter J. Katzenstein had published *Small States in World Markets* (1985),[5] one of the first efforts to link institutions to the competitiveness of national economies; and almost three years after Michael E. Porter had published *The Competitive Advantage of Nations* (1990), one of the first books to talk about the competition of nations. It was also just one year before Paul Krugman, counterattacked by calling all the talk about the competitiveness of nations 'a dangerous obsession' (1994). Since then, the concept of international competitiveness has been one of the most contested in both academic and political dispute (Aiginger 2006*b*), while at the same time becoming part of the rhetoric of policymakers virtually ignoring Krugman's principled objections. Travelling between academia and politics, the concept has changed several times. In the following I describe how the concept has changed but also developed to become a discourse. By discourse I mean a world view in which individual as well as collective action (i.e. relations between nations) can be understood as dominated

---

[4] At the summit in Copenhagen the Commission was asked to submit a white paper on 'Global Competitiveness' before the European Council's meeting on 11 Dec. 1993, see 'White Paper on Growth, Competitiveness and Employment", Commission of the European Communities, http://aei.pitt.edu/1139/.

[5] From the very early 1980s comparative political economy together with organizational theory 'rediscovered' institutions and (re)introduced institutional analysis to social science disciplines. Among the most important contributors to bringing back in institutions one can mention Schmitter (1974); Schmitter and Streeck (1985); Aglietta (1976); also March and Olsen (1984 and 1989); for an overview see Campbell (2004).

by actors acting *as if* they are rational, and where the state of things (i.e. the competitiveness of nations) is understood to be changeable by deliberate acts.[6]

David Ricardo's famous trade model of comparative advantage (the *two* countries and *two* goods model) was an early attempt to construct such a world of action. Later his model was developed by Dornbusch, Fisher, and Samuelson (1977) to include *n* countries and *n* goods and by Heckscher and Ohlin (Leamer 1995) to emphasize variable capital endowments as the ultimate factor explaining comparative advantages. Today the international competitiveness of firms is evaluated using statistics on factor endowments like land, capital, natural resources, labour, and entrepreneurship and is based on the following assumptions:

- International competitiveness applies to firms;
- Comparative advantage (see review in Siggel 2006) pertains to economic microfoundations;
- Measurement of international competitiveness is based on a few indicators of competitiveness; and
- Competitiveness as well as comparative advantages is measured statically or objectively, i.e., *ex post* or as revealed competitiveness (see Balassa 1965 and the index of 'revealed comparative advantage').

Institutions—two lines of understanding

This was also the definition used by Paul Krugman (1994, 1996) when he criticized the concept of 'nations compete', and when he called Bill Clinton's belief that every nation is '... like a big corporation competing in the global marketplace' a dangerous obsession (ibid 1994). Yet over time the concept has evolved to include a greater number of endowments: Joseph Schumpeter for example emphasized the key role that entrepreneurship and the dynamic of ideas can play (Pack 2000); Paul Krugman drew attention to the advantages of large-scale operation (Krugman 1979); Robert Solow underlined the fundamental of increased know-how; Christopher Freeman (with Clark and Soete 1982) described the role of technical innovation (see Lipsey, et al., part I for overview), and the Swedish-Danish economist Bengt-Åke Lundvall among others has more recently emphasized the importance of 'knowledge' as an input factor for competitiveness (Lorenz and Lundvall 2006). But even if the concept has come to include additional examples of factor endowments, it is not before the 1980s and the dominance of neo-liberalism that a preoccupation with institutional reforms surged.

Equally it is not before the 1980s that this brought the attention of policy experts and policymakers to two lines of academic dispute, both engaged in explaining why

---

[6] As such a discourse is equivalent to a context for rationality—i.e. a world view in which action is believed to be rational, or understandable through its causal links and mechanisms; see Pedersen (1991); Campbell and Pedersen (2001: 1–23).

national economies and firms develop certain characteristics that enable them to compete successfully on global markets. The first is the theory of the firm linked to Oliver Williamson's theory of transaction costs.[7] The second is the line of research initiated by the publication of Andrew Shonfield's seminal book *Modern Capitalism* (1965) followed by Katzenstein's equally seminal *Small States in World Markets* (1985). The first starts from a micro-perspective and explains the existence of the firm by the fact that there are costs related to using the price mechanism and that these costs (like establishing contracts) must be made outside the market in a separate set of institutions. Based on this micro-oriented theory economists have studied the functioning of organizations (or firms) in overcoming problems related to information exchange, lack of cooperation, and shirking (Milgrom and Roberts 1992). The second starts from a macro-perspective and stresses that firms are embedded in labour market institutions and in financial systems; that they are dependent on governments' implementation capabilities, and in more general terms on forms of trust entrenched in social networks and local communities (Granovetter 2004). Both lines of research are regarded as influential in shaping the present interest in how institutional change and institutional analysis can be exploited to create comparative advantages. Furthermore, both have developed to become rich and diversified schools of thought in their own right. The micro-reading is part of the history of organization theory (Starbuck 2003); the macro-understanding is related to comparative political economy and to that part of institutional analysis (Aoki 2001) that is determined to answer how varieties of institutions can explain national competitiveness.[8]

Firms as embedded—the role of Porter

One way to make sense of this diversified evolution is to follow the influence of Michael Porter on the advance of the discourse on international competitiveness. The introduction of the CIC as a new reading of the concept of international competitiveness can be followed through the intellectual trajectory of Porter. In his first two books (1980, 1985) Porter was focused on internal firm strategy and the role of management in identifying market niches and it was only with the publication in 1990 of *The Competitive Advantage of Nations*[9] that he started to identify the national (and the institutional) dimension as important. However, it was not before 2000 (Porter 2000) that he began to use the term institution; and only by implication that the concept of institutional competitiveness can be affiliated with his writings. Hence, it is Porter's country-based empirical studies, policy reports, and general world wide activities (Porter 1998: pp. xvi–xx) that have contributed to put the idea

---

[7] Williamson (1985).

[8] Katzenstein (1985) is the influential work in this tradition, even so *Bringing the State Back In* co-edited by Evans, Rueschemeyer, and Skocpol (1985; see also Id. 2008) must be mentioned with Lindblom (1977) and Hirschman (1981, 1992).

[9] Published 1990, 2nd edn. (1998).

of national competitiveness on centre stage—and to make national governments as well as international organizations aware of institutions as important for the international competitiveness of nations. What is more, it is by his multiple activities at the intersection of academia and politics that his contribution eventually proved decisive in the development of the concept that nations compete. First of all he lifted the concept of comparative advantage from the micro-level, to the study of companies embedded in nations or geographic entities, even if he still emphasized the role of factor endowments in explaining comparative advantages (Porter 1998: 67 f.). He also changed focus from an aggregate and static economy-wide approach to emphasizing the dynamics of competition and the role of competitive strategies (Porter 1998: 131–75). By shifting the attention from the micro-level to the micro-and macro-level Porter took two steps of critical importance for a new way of framing the concept of competitiveness. First, he highlighted the importance of the locality in which a company was embedded and showed that the social, political, macroeconomic, and legal context had an influence on the competitiveness of firms (Porter 1998: 73–80). He made the institutional context—at the national, regional, and local level—an important condition in understanding the comparative advantages of business and also helped to point to public policies as important in promoting advantages or removing disadvantages (Ketels 2006). He thereby contributed to combining the mainstream micro-oriented study of *the comparative advantages of firms* with a more macro-oriented study of *the comparative advantages of nations* (Aiginger 2006a). Second, he laid emphasis on the significance of how the organization of competition within a country helps or hinders the creation of firms that are capable of competing as well as the capacity or readiness of a company to compete. He combined the static understanding of competitiveness as a question of revealed performance with a dynamic approach in which the potential of firms to adjust to exogenous changes was stressed. Even so he maintained that 'The only meaningful concept of competitiveness at the national level is national productivity' (Porter 1998: 6) and combined a static (*ex post*) with a dynamic (*ex ante*) approach, and thereby also combined two questions: (1) How is *competitiveness created*, i.e. what are the main sources of competitiveness, including the function of human resources and managerial skills, with (2) How is *competitiveness explained*, i.e. what is the function of the abundance of natural resources, the cheapness of labour, the use of technologies, economies of scale (Aiginger 2006b)? This combination of micro and macro, static and dynamic was forcefully supported by the now famous diamond model of 'The Determinants of National Advantage' (Porter 1998: 71–3, 173–5) in which Porter called attention to the macro- and micro-foundations of competitiveness and retained the enterprise (or clusters of firms) at the centre for the measuring and analysis of national competitiveness. Porter held that 'The basic unit of analysis for understanding is the industry' (Porter 1998: 33), which in itself was decisive because it put business in a context of a wide range of institutions and made the complementarity of company strategy and policy inputs important for enhancing, but also for explaining, the competitiveness of firms (Grilo and Koopman 2006: 82; Kohler 2006: 104–13). By the same token he introduced the relationship between *business and politics* as important (Ketels 2006: 124); and by emphasizing business as in an environment of politics (or business-as-the-core-of-politics), he also assisted in changing the concept that John Maynard Keynes in particular had introduced. In contrast to Keynes, who sought to formulate the means by which governments could stabilize and fine-tune markets (i.e. using policies to set *macroeconomic frameworks for free markets*), Porter emphasized the necessity for complementarity between politics and business (macro and micro) in creating comparative advantages. Doing so he pioneered a set of questions which subsequently gained influence among governments and international organizations.

I now describe this development in order to show how Porter's perception of competitiveness has been developed, and how correspondingly the definition and role of institutions has been changed. For this purpose I use Eckhard Siggel's review of the current theoretical history of the two concepts of competition and comparative advantages (Siggel 2006: 137–59). Like Siggel and others (see the special issue of *Journal of Industry, Competition and Trade*, volume 6, issue 2, 2006), I mix contributions from academia with contributions from international organizations as well as national policymakers, in order to emphasize three points: First, that at the present there is no accepted or mainstream definition of competitiveness, but that a large number of definitions have been proposed (Spence and Hazard 1988) including the concept of institutional competitiveness; second, that debates on the understandings are actually occurring in an epistemic community (Haas 1992) in which there is participation from academics, consultants, and policymakers (for a survey, see Cantwell 2005); and third, that classical and neo-classical trade theory tends to use the concept of comparative advantage, while international organizations as well as the business literature are more often inclined to use the concept of competitiveness. Based on an extensive reading of both academic and policy sources it can be concluded that the definition of competitiveness has evolved see Table 22.1:

- From emphasizing only micro-foundations for comparative advantages to mixing micro- and macro-foundations, as when monetary costs, and not only the costs of production factors, are included, and the real or the effective exchange rate is understood to be an important factor in measuring competitiveness (Lipschitz and McDonald 1991).
- From emphasizing only one dimension, and then primarily the real cost of production factors, to including many dimensions, as when technology as a condition, reflected, for example, by R & D expenditure is included (Fagerberg 1988), or when Porter in his diamond model includes production and demand conditions as well as company strategy and rivalry among firms and other determinants of comparative advantage.
- From a static understanding measured by the outcome of competition or market shares, for example, to a mix of static and dynamic indicators such as changes over time in GDP (gross domestic product) per capita, or in market shares, as when

Krugman used market share over time as an indicator of US competitiveness in manufacturing (Krugman and Hatsopoulos 1987).

- From a deterministic reading of competitiveness where the absolute level of productivity, the annual growth rate or the average income generated is taken as an objective indicator of (*ex post* or revealed) performance, to a more stochastic (*ex ante* or strategic) understanding, where the ability to create competitiveness through R & D investments, human resource developments, innovation, etc. is emphasized; and finally,

- From a positive (measured by objective indicators) towards a more normative (measured by political or subjective goals) understanding of competitiveness framed, for example, in terms of '... a country's ability to generate sustained economic well-being for its citizens...' (Kohler 2006: 87), or the ability of a country to create 'environmental quality', or to 'increase standards of living', or 'the ability to create welfare' (Aiginger 2006*b*: 163).

Institutions as linked—from embeddedness to complementarities

Even if this new way of framing the conception seems to have moved the understanding of international competition away from Ricardo's trade model, the classical model is actually untouched. Instead of being denounced the traditional trade model is being extended—by adding extra levels (meso- and macro), new dimensions (technology, the advantages of large-scale operation), further measurements (dynamic), and new positions (normative).

This extension from a simple to a more complex understanding is even more evident when we include the international organizations and their definition of competitiveness. Reviews of international organizations show that competitiveness is defined in various ways and that definitions have changed over time (see review done by the National Competitiveness Council 2004).[10] The most important

Table 22.1: The extension of the trade model

	From	To
Level	Micro	Micro–macro
Dimensions	One	Several
Measurements	Static	Static–dynamic
Indicators	Ex post	Ex Post–Ex ante
Position	Positive	Positive–Normative

---

[10] http://www.forfas.ie/ncc/reports/ncc_annual_01/approach.htm.

development though is the general acceptance that firms exist in a landscape of institutions, and that the complementarity between firms and a context of economic, legal, and institutional factors associated with the locality has an influence on the comparative advantages (or disadvantages) of companies. It has thus become possible to include additional and new dimensions and to open up for different approaches in measuring competitiveness. It has also become possible to see the importance of complementarities between politics and business. The context has changed from macroeconomic regulation (i.e. financial policy, labour market policies, or central wage agreements etc.) to linking micro to macro, business to politics, and to regard the context as including not only policy regulation but all relevant institutional factors (legal, economic, cultural, and political). At the same time, the number of relevant indicators has increased.[11]

If we compare the theoretical debate and the international organizations' definitions, it is clear that the gradual reframing of international competitiveness has introduced institutions and institutional analysis in several ways. First, it has become accepted that institutions set the framework for the comparative advantages of firms (Porter 2000); this is why it is now possible to reflect on institutions (i.e. institutional analysis) as a policy tool.[12] Second, the development from micro-foundations to micro- and-macro foundations has extended the number of players, institutional levels, and policy arenas of relevance to the study of comparative advantages; this is why the strategic interaction of economic and political players and the complementarity (or not) of business and politics as well as the interaction between institutions has become central to the explanation of comparative advantages (Crouch 2005: 46–73; Hall and Soskice 2001: 17; Amable 2003: 58–66; Kohler 2006). Third, this has made the question of institutional change a phenomenon of interest for policymakers; the capability to implement institutional reforms and to establish complementarities between institutions has become an important indicator of competitiveness. Fourth, a split has been established between those for whom the purpose of institutions is to make markets work better and more efficiently—here phrased as 'the exogenous understanding of institutions to markets'; and those for whom the purpose is to build markets and/or to make them work more fairly—here phrased as 'the endogenous understanding of markets to institutions' (Albert 1993). This finally, has established the basis for conflicts between policymakers and others basing their arguments on different national models for growth, i.e. between a liberal model associated with countries like the USA and United Kingdom; and a social model related to the EU and its member states (Pontusson 2005: 15–31). In all these ways, institutions have come to be central to the question of the competition of nations, and institutional analysis is introduced not only to explain, but also to promote, comparative advantages. Moreover, the understanding of the role of institutions has come to be looked

---

[11] For a more systematic review of scholarly contributions to the debate on competitiveness, see Siggel (2006: 144).

[12] And at the same time make concepts like 'the comparative institutional advantage' fully meaningful (Hall and Soskice 2001: 36–44).

upon as a differentiating marker for political attitudes in the ideological combat of ideas: if you believe in institutions as exogenous to markets you are a liberal or neo-liberal; if in contrast you believe in markets as endogenous (as well as exogenous) to institutions you are either a socio-liberal or a social democrat. The two under-standings have come to be templates for political cleavages among politicians and policymakers, but also for theoretical cleavages among scholars in politics, econom-ics, and sociology (Campbell and Pedersen 2001).

THE INSTITUTIONALIZATION OF THE DISCOURSE

I now change angle from the level of discourse to the level of the 'institutionalization' of discourse. The aim is to show how an expert system of measurement was institutionalized, constructing a social reality for governments and others establish-ing a potential to act *as if* nations compete. How this institutionalization is to be understood will become apparent when two elements in the process are described. The first treats how a number of expert systems are 'established' to measure the competitiveness of nations; the second considers how existing economic and political institutions are changed in order to 'develop' and to 'disseminate' the discourse.

The first kind of institutionalization is related to the construction of expert systems with the purpose of comparing the competitiveness of nations. 'This insti-tutionalization by the establishment of institutions' can be politically decided, as when the *European Council* in 1994 (by resolution of 22 November) decided to strengthen the 'competitiveness of Europe' and the Commission commenced to publish the *European Competitiveness Report* in 1995. It can also be privately pro-duced as when the *World Economic Forum* (Davos) in 1979 created the *Global Competitiveness Index* or when the *McKinsey Global* Institute was established in 1990 '. . . to assess the productivity performance and competitiveness of countries and sectors relative to global benchmarks'.[13] As of today, there are numerous international organizations, which systematically carry out international compari-sons of national competitiveness.[14] Also a number of national, public, and private

---

[13] http://www.mckinsey.com/mgi/rp/CSProductivity/

[14] The World Economic Forum (where Michael Porter played an important role) started in 1979 to publish the annual *Global Competitiveness Report*. The International Monetary Fund (IMF) did so with the *World Economic Outlook* in 1980 after having carried out multilateral monitoring since 1979. The Institute for Management Development (IMD) started 1989 to publish the *World Competitiveness Yearbook*. The Commission of the European Communities in 1995 began to publish *The European Competitiveness Report*. In 1992 the Commission established *The Observatory of European Small and Medium Sized Industries* to carry out a detailed screening of the Competitiveness of individual sectors of manufacturing industry in the EU. In 2002 the competitiveness Council was within the European Council. The OECD's *Global Forum on Competition* had its first meeting in 2001; since 2005 the Organization has published *Going for Growth*. The OECD started to publish *OECD Economic Outlook* in 1966 and number 82 was published in 2007.

organizations are contributing to the growing industry (for an overview see Bäck-lund and Werr 2001).

At the national level, the US government was the first to take an initiative. It happened in 1985, when President Ronald Reagan established the *President's Com-mission on Industrial Competitiveness.*[15] The *Competitiveness Policy Council* was subsequently established in 1988.[16] Ten years later, in 1998, the Irish government established the *National Competitiveness Council* (NCC), which has since published the *Annual Competitiveness Report.* In 2000 the NCC introduced the report *Compet-itiveness Challenge* to convey policy recommendations to the government and social partners.[17] Later, several other governments followed suit—Greece in 2003, Croatia in 2004, Bahrain in 2005, the Philippines in 2006, and Guyana and the Dominican Republic in 2007. In all instances advisory bodies or special government agencies were established to tackle competitiveness issues through international comparisons. Also private think tanks were established, above all in the USA, where the *Council on Competitiveness* was established in 1986;[18] but also in France where the semi-public think tank *Coe-Rexecode* in 2006 started the publication of an annual report on *La compétitivité française.*[19]

The second kind of institutionalization is related to institutional reforms with the purpose of developing and disseminating the discourse that nations compete. 'Insti-tutionalization by development' happens when already existing expert systems come to include mechanisms and routines for the accumulation of knowledge around a particular discourse through systematic data collection, forecasting based on model calculations, and a process of verification or falsification. 'Institutionalization by dissemination' occurs when expert systems are available to be disseminated and to be applied by national governments (Boli and Thomas 1999; Keck and Sikkink 1998; Meyer 2000).[20] Two examples of these processes will be examined. The first is 'The post-Washington Consensus', or how the IMF and the WB came to include an extended—or reformulated—understanding of institutions.[21] The second is The

[15] Which also gave Porter the inspiration to develop and extend the concept of competitiveness, and led him to write *The Competitive Advantage of Nations* (Porter 1998: p. xii).

[16] But later abolished in 1997.

[17] In so doing the Council has changed the definition of competitiveness several times; for example in the last two years (2005–7) alone, the well-known *Competitiveness Pyramid* developed by the Council has been redefined on important points.

[18] http://www.compete.org/about-us/

[19] See Coe-Rexecode (2007), *La compétitivité française en 2007,* Document de travail no. 3. In this report data from the IMF, WB, the Commission of the European Communities, and Ernst and Young is put to use.

[20] It is important to notice that by dissemination I DO NOT intend to claim that the concept that nations compete is actually diffused. I have no proof of such an effect, nor any need to claim it. The only point put forward is this: That a number of mechanisms for the development and the dissemination are established which I take as proof of the intention of WB and IMF to diffuse the concept and to develop it to become accepted and used by even more governments and international organizations.

[21] See the definition of the concept http://www.who.int/trade/glossary/story074/en/index.html. See also the justification for and introduction of the concept in Joseph E. Stiglitz, '*More Instruments and Broader Goals: Toward a Post-Washington Consensus*', The 1998 Wider Annual Lecture, Helsinki, Finland, Jan. 7, http://www.globalpolicy.org/socecon/bwi-wto/stig.htm; and Narcis Serra and Joseph E. Stiglitz (2008).

Open Method of Coordination (OMC), or how the EU established routines for learning from institutional reforms. Both will be used to exemplify three features. Firstly, that the discourse of CIC is becoming institutionalized in the EU and among international organizations. Secondly, that international organizations as well as national governments have come to put greater emphasize on the quality of institutions in establishing comparative advantages. Thirdly, that these expert systems create a potential for action but also a potential for discipline, i.e. for making it appropriate for governments and others to act *as if* nations compete.

From the Washington Consensus
to the post-Washington Consensus

From 2003, the IMF began to assume that the quality (and not only the mere existence) of institutions set the framework for comparative advantages. This renewed understanding of institutions was part of 'The post-Washington Consensus', in which the IMF and the WB had come to agree that the first 'Washington Consensus' was incomplete, and that countries needed to move beyond 'first generation' macroeconomic and trade reforms to a stronger focus on institutional reforms, including the elimination of red tape and corruption, and the strengthening and building of 'good institutions' (in areas like justice, finance, education, training, and innovation). 'The post-Washington Consensus' then was far more sensitive to the quality of institutions and to the importance of institutional variations (one size does not fit all!) as well as the dynamic aspect of institutions (institutions can be changed and experimented with) than the original (Stiglitz 2003: 186). It too was a result of a prolonged debate among government officials and economists on the role of institutions and of growing empirical evidence ' . . . that institutional quality holds the key to prevailing patterns of prosperity around the world' (Rodrik 2007: 184–5).

In the September 2004 issue of the annual *World Economic Outlook*, the IMF reviewed the established knowledge on institutions, including their impact and the role of institutional change and of 'good institutions' in establishing conditions for economic growth (WEO: chapter III). The review was based on Douglass North's definition of institutions as enabling and constraining the behaviour of actors and on econometric studies of institutions (North 1990, 2005). This in turn led the IMF to assess the role of institutions in a number of economies, including emerging, transitional, and developed economies. It also led the organization to establish a new set of expert systems (databases, indicators) in order to assess 'the quality of institutions' (see chapter III, appendix 3.1, 'Sample Composition, Data Sources, and Methods': 152–6). Likewise, it led both the IMF and the WB to emphasize the role of 'institutional quality' and to recommend 'good governance' reforms aimed at reducing corruption, improving the regulatory apparatus, strengthening corporate governance, etc. Finally it led the two to advocate using politics to compensate for the deficiencies of markets; i.e. by creating *compensating complementarities* (Crouch 2005, 47–59; see also Crouch this volume).[22] Together with the WB, the IMF thus integrated institutional analysis into their policy recommendations by posing questions that previously had been the preserve of neo-institutional theory in academia only and had had little influence on these bodies. Questions such as the following were asked: How important are institutions in explaining economic prosperity? How much does the institutional context explain the variation in the competitiveness of particular economies (ibid 125)? And what are the main factors explaining variations in the quality of institutions? The approach chosen by IMF and the WB became macro- and micro-oriented—institutions are looked upon as a context for individual decision-making in a situation of competition. It is also static as well as dynamic— the role of institutional reforms is measured by revealed comparative advantages. Finally, it is positive (competitiveness is measured by objective indicators like GDP per capita) as well as normative—the IMF is advocating the establishment of 'good institutions' or 'good governance'. Hence the IMF and the WB are taking part in the development of the discourse that nations compete by redefining what they mean by institutions but also by establishing new institutions, and new indicators. The IMF also began to expand the analytical apparatus on which the *World Economic Outlook* (World Economic Outlook, 2004: chapter III, appendix 3.1.) was based.

The Open Method of Coordination (OMC)

The same mix of levels, dimensions, and indicators is applied in the OMC, introduced in the European Union in 2000. However, where the OMC is designed to enable mutual learning,[23] and to so do by initiating stochastic and iterative processes for institutional change, the IMF and the WB tend to use only traditional mechanisms of coercive, mimetic, or normative diffusion. Because the OMC is designed to facilitate semi-voluntary forms of coordination (Scott and Trubek 2002) it is the most important example of the two in demonstrating how the discourse that nations compete has come to include institutional change (as a political phenomenon) and institutional analysis (as a policy tool). The two also differ in their understanding of institutions. Where the OMC perceives markets as both exogenous and endogenous to institutions and business as embedded in politics, IMF/WB takes institutions as a context for markets, and business as separated from politics.

The OMC can be traced to the Commission of the European Communities' White Paper on *Growth, Competitiveness and Employment* (1993), and represents a method for constructing what later became known as *Social Europe*. The white paper was

---

[22] Crouch defines compensating complementarities as 'Complementarity where components of a whole mutually compensate for each other's deficiencies in constituting the whole' (Crouch 2005: 50).
[23] The OMC was defined by the Portuguese EU Presidency in its conclusions from the European Council 2000 as 'mutual learning processes': http://ue.eu.int/ueDocs/cms_Data/docs/pressData/en/ec/00100-r1.eno.htm.

followed by the 'European Employment Strategy' (EES) branded as the 'Luxembourg process' (1997), and introduced in the *Treaty of Amsterdam* (1997). The OMC is based on the ambition of making the European Union into ' . . . the most competitive and dynamic knowledge-based economy in the world, capable of sustained economic growth, with more and better jobs and greater social cohesion' (European Council 2000). Apart from mixing the classic understanding of international competitiveness[24] with normative, dynamic, and stochastic aspects, the EES also opens the possibility for a more integrated use of politics in managing and changing markets (Radaelli 2003; Borrás and Jacobsson 2004). This happens in three ways:

(1) *Policies are used to change (or to build) markets.* From the start, the EES was designed to establish semi-voluntary forms of coordination between supranational and national authorities and between political institutions and social partners; all with the purpose to embed business in politics and to amplify normative goals (i.e. social cohesion or welfare). It was designed to ' . . . potentially reinforce established practices of social concentration and negotiated governance in reform of work and welfare at EU, national, and sub-national levels, from the European social dialogue through national social pacts to territorial employment pacts and local or plant-level collective agreements' (Zeitlin 2003: 5 f.). It included multiple levels of institutions; coordinated different policy arenas (labour market, social, education, and several other traditional policy fields); pointed to economic, political, and social players as relevant; and declared the well-being of the European citizens to be the overall goal of market building. Since the formulation of EES, the open method of coordination has been developed to cover EU policymaking in other policy areas such as pensions, health care, social inclusion, macro-economic management, education, and lifelong training to ' . . . become a virtual template for EU policy-making in other complex, politically-sensitive areas . . . ' (Zeitlin 2003: 5).[25]

(2) *Institutional analysis is introduced as a tool for institutional change.* Each year, the European Council adopts common European guidelines; member states report national employment policies to the Council; and the Council evaluates and reviews these 'National Reform Programmes' and gives recommendations back to member states. The use of benchmarking, evaluations, review processes and the absence of legal sanctions create significant room for institutional

---

[24] The Commission of the European Communities in the annual *European Competitiveness Reports* generally defines international competitiveness as: ' . . . to mean high and rising standards of living of a nation (or a group of nations) with the lowest possible level of involuntary unemployment, on a sustainable basis'.

[25] There has also been a comprehensive institutionalization and organization of procedures and processes for the development and extension of the EES (the European Employment Policy). These changes have taken place especially at the administrative level under the European Council and the Commission, where the *European Employment Committee* (EMCO) was established in 1997, and the *European Social Protection Committee* (SPC) and the *Advisory Committee on Vocational Training* (ACVT) was so in 2000. All three are comprised of officials from the national administrations, and in some cases even of representatives from social partners (Jacobsson and Vifell 2005).

experimentation.[26] The iterative process is deliberately used to promote common frames of reference, to disseminate good practice, to shape the interests of business and governments as well as social partners, and to promote mutual learning, i.e. to push firms as well as member states to reflect upon the institutional conditions for institutional change (Ferrara, Hemerijck, and Rhodes 2003). Thus reflections on institutions are turned into a tool for institutional change.

(3) *Recombination of institutions is used to construct comparative advantages.* In the mid-1990s the EES emerged from a situation with high levels of unemployment and low levels of ability to restructure labour markets (Trubek and Mosher 2003: 34–6; Goetschy 2003: 62 f.). Mass unemployment challenged national governments to coordinate a number of policies, and to cut across traditional boundaries between industrial relations and welfare policies. The EES in these circumstances was developed as a way for the Union to deal with challenges which the market and the member states were unable to face themselves (Kenner 1999). It was also developed to construct comparative advantages by complementing market and policies in new and experimental ways. In this manner, the recombination of institutions was granted a central position in the creation of comparative advantages; and the fact that business is understood to be embedded in politics is explored to *construct complementarities* (Crouch 2005: 52–4).[27]

This process of changing institutions highlights the role of reflection on institutions and of politics as a productive factor. Although the two examples highlight the fact that there are different ways in which institutions can be used to service economic prosperity, they both show that conflicts about how to define (and to breed) competitiveness are now institutionalized and turned into an iterative part of the policy formulation process.

THE IMPLEMENTATION OF THE DISCOURSE INTO REFORMS OF STATES

The IMF/WB and the OMC are two of many transnational networks established between national authorities and international organizations and show how the

---

[26] See description of OMC in Trubek and Mosher (2003: 40); and reference to evaluation of the OMC, High Level Group, chaired by Wim Kok, *Facing the Challenge. The Lisbon Strategy for Growth and Employment*; see also literature review, Zeitlin (2003).

[27] Crouch defines constructed complementarities as where innovative action by social actors is forging complementarities into a situation where the presence of one institution increases the returns of the other, without this construction of complementarities being either strategically planned or that the complementarity of institutions implies any kind of necessity of a relationship between the institutions (Crouch 2005: 52–4).

discourse that nations compete has become a resource for national governments in reforming the tasks or responsibilities of their states as *Competition States*.[28] For the purpose of simplicity it is necessary to distinguish between two forms of competition states.[29] The first is the *Regulatory State*; the second the *Active Welfare State*.

The term the 'regulatory state' is associated with the publication of *The Rise of the Regulatory State in Europe* by Giandomenico Majone in 1994. Since then, it has become commonplace to argue that the dominance of neo-liberalism has led to the emergence of the regulatory state, characterized by privatization of public services, the 'liberation' of markets through deregulation or reregulation, the establishment of quasi-autonomous regulatory authorities, and the building of complementarities between innovation, technology, and regulatory change in creating comparative advantages (Vogel 1996).[30] The term the 'active welfare state', on the other hand, is associated with the EU and the strategy for establishing a social model for Europe. Since the European Council in 2000 decided to 'Build an Active Welfare State', it has become common to state that the European social model has led to the emergence of the active welfare state, characterized by flexibilization of markets, decentralization of welfare states, and the creation of new social rights. While the regulatory state is looked upon as a context for business and de- or (re)regulation is used in order to create comparative advantages by 'setting markets free', it is different in the case of the active welfare state. Here markets are understood to be endogenous to politics and business, and politics to be related strategically by the creativity of firms, governments, and social partners in constructing complementarities between flexible markets and active welfare policies (Jessop 2007). Both definitions emphasize that state reforms are examples of how a discourse is being implemented through the recombination of institutions.[31]

---

[28] The concept is associated with Marxist state theory and the work of Cerny, Hirsch, and Jessop who see changes in nation-states as comprehensive including alterations in the tasks, the organization and the governance arrangements of states and markets (Cerny 1990, 2007; Hirsch 1995; Jessop 1994a, 2003). In what follows I describe only two aspects of transformations of nation-states: (1) changes in the tasks of states; and (2) in governmental arrangements, i.e. state–society relations. Other aspects can be added, for example changes in the organization of public administration by the use of New Public Management (Christensen and Lægreid 2001); changes in steering and managing of the public economy through the use of performance management (Kettl 2000; Hood 2007); and changes in political leadership by the use of 'joined up government', enhancing the strategic capability of the government through the establishment of strategy units close to the head of government.

[29] I do so, underlining that in reality states combine the two in attempts to co-evolve their tasks, policies, organization, and governmental arrangements with the discourse.

[30] The Enabling Welfare State is a concept very similar to the regulatory state in the sense that it describes the use of private enterprise and market-oriented approaches to the delivery of social provisions (Gilbert and Gilbert 1989). The notion gained currency in the UK during the 1990s under New Labour as an alternative to 'the providing welfare state'.

[31] The definition emphasizes that all 'capitalist states' do not necessarily take the form of a regulatory state or an active welfare state, and that only empirical investigations can decide which type of state is developed. It is also through empirical studies that it can be decided from where inspiration for reforms arises and by which mechanisms the reforms are formulated and implemented (Campbell and Pedersen 2007b). In the end we will have to expect a great number of rather different types of competition states.

It is in the *White Paper on Growth, Competitiveness and Employment* by the Commission of the European Communities (1993) and the following year in the *White Paper on a European Social Policy* by the Commission that the EU for the first time emphasizes the necessity of reforming welfare states. It is also here—for the first time—that it builds its arguments on the concept of 'global competitiveness'. But it is not before 2000, seven years later at a special meeting in Lisbon, that the European Council accepts the link between 'global competition' and state reforms, calling for the member states to 'Build an Active Welfare State' and to 'Modernise the European Social Model' (Sapir et al. 2003; Aiginger 2005).[32] Thus, it is through transnational relations and a co-evolutionary process of discourse and state reforms that the discourse is implemented[33] with the ambition of producing comparative advantages for national economies by reforming the welfare states. Doing so, the EU leaves it to member states to choose between two institutional factors in producing comparative advantages:

(1) *External flexibility.* In this strategy the institutional context for firms is at the centre of reforms; the object is to remove institutional rigidities and to create market flexibility (see Commission of the European Communities 2007 for description of country models, annex II; also OECD 2006a). In some cases flexibility of employment is combined with social security in attempts to create 'flexicurity'.[34] As early as 1997, the European Council was emphasizing the necessity of creating 'Flexibility with Security'.[35] However it was not before 2007 that The Commission of the European Communities selected flexicurity as a European strategy: *'Rather than job security, flexicurity focuses on*

---

[32] It is also on the basis of this that the European Council since has extended the OMC process to a great number of policy areas, making the Lisbon strategy the most important in guiding and developing comprehensive reforms in the missions, the organization, and the governance arrangements in the member states (Zeitlin 2005; Borrás and Jacobsson 2004). Among these, the use of *Broad Economic Guidelines* within the Economic and Monetary Union is of particularly importance. Since 2006, macroeconomic guidelines (EMU) have been synchronized with employment guidelines (EES), and both guidelines are now following the same triennial cycle making it possible for the national governments to coordinate their national employment reforms with macroeconomic issues. This extension of the use of the OMC has led to intense discussions among academics of whether or not there is a mutual learning based on OMC and whether this is leading to real changes in the organization of member states? Some give positive answers (Zeitlin 2005; Jacobsson 2004; Nedergaard 2006, 2007; Commission of the European Communities 2002b: 9–15, Zeitlin and Sabel 2007); others less so (Scharpf 2002; Alesina and Perotti 2004; Casey and Gold 2005; Kaiser and Prange 2005).

[33] Transnational connections are here defined as stable and enduring contacts and forms of participation between national and international, private and public players where one or more of the participants are not subject to any political control from their own government (Jacobsson et al. 2004: 27–48).

[34] This strategy for flexicurity was formulated for the first time by the Dutch Minister of Social Affairs and Employment, Ad Melkert, in a memorandum, *Flexibility and security,* Second Chamber 1995–6, No. 24 543: see http://www.eurofound.europa.eu/eiro/1997/06/feature/nl9706116f.htm. Implementation was done in some cases via special legislation (e.g. the Flexibility and Security Act in the Netherlands 1999; see Wilthagen and Tros 2004). In other cases it was done by a series of compromises between the government and social partners, which found expression in both legislation and general agreements (e.g. in Denmark from 1987 onwards; see Pedersen 2006a).

[35] This happened for the first time in connection with the adoption of the Luxembourg Process (Trubek and Mosher 2003: 42).

*"employment security". Employment security means staying in employment, within
the same enterprise or in a new enterprise. The philosophy behind flexicurity is that
workers are more prepared to make such moves if there is a good safety net'*
(Commission of the European Communities 2007: 7). Originally the flexicurity
strategy was developed in countries like the Netherlands, Sweden, and Denmark;
but over a period of more than twenty years it became a European strategy for
external flexibility (Jørgensen and Madsen 2007: 9–32).

(2) *Internal flexibility.* In this strategy human resource management is emphasized,
and individual employees are the object of policy measures to shape their attitudes
and aspirations.[36] The goal is '...to ensure the continual adaptability and
employability of workers' (Commission of the European Communities 2007: 12)
by making human beings more responsive to constantly changing requirements
and conditions through behavioural interventions.[37] Two aspects are included in
this strategy: one is creating institutions; the other is introducing a life span (or life
course) perspective. The emergence of institutions (entitlements, rules, and norms)
for internal flexibility can be found in Sweden and Denmark from the 1980s and
simultaneously or later in Norway, Finland, Austria, and the Netherlands. In all
cases a number of new social rights were introduced. This happened either by the
use of collective agreements, later on formalized by law-making, or by company-
specific agreements or in some cases even by agreements within specific sectors.[38]
The introduction of the life course perspective, on the other hand, is more difficult
to trace; but it is worth stressing that the life course perspective from 2007 became a
way to combine the static (Sweden, Denmark, the Netherlands) understanding of
flexicurity with the dynamic (Anglo-liberal) understanding of mobility. In the
definition of the Commission of the European Communities, '*Flexibility, on the
one hand, is about successful moves ('transitions') during one's life course: from school
to work, from one job to another, between unemployment and work, and from work to
retirement.... On the other hand, it is more than just the security to maintain one's
job: it is about equipping people with the skills that enable them to progress in their
working lives, and helping them find new employment. It is also about adequate
unemployment benefits to facilitate transitions. Finally, it encompasses training*

---

[36] A similar ambition to shape attitudes and aspirations by using 'soft law' mechanisms can be found
in the field of Corporate Social Responsibility (CSR). Here the Commission of the European
Communities had already in the '90s started to promote corporate self-regulation of business to take
responsibility for its social and environmental impact on society (Commission of the European
Communities 2001a, 2002a). Later CSR where being coordinated with the questions related to external
and internal flexibility (Commission of the European Communities 2006a, 2006b).

[37] See the review of knowledge on behavioural interventions in fields like welfare-to-work, health,
crime, and education, 'Personal Responsibility and Changing Behaviour: The State of Knowledge and its
implications for public policy', Prime Minister's Strategy Unit, Feb. 2004, http://74.125.77.132/search?
q=cache:PUA28rcOmIkJ:www.number10.gov.uk/files/pdf/pr.pdf+Personal+Responsibility+and
+Changing+Behaviour+PMSU+2004&hl=da&ct=clnk&cd=2&gl=dk

[38] These concern the right to transferable pension entitlements, (re)training, parental leave, various
leaves for education, and health assessments, etc., or the right to physical health training, individual
coaching, and other sorts of fringe benefits.

opportunities for all workers, especially the low skilled and older workers. (Commission of the European Communities 2007: 10).[39]

From the end of 2007, then, a search for the optimum life span contribution to the GDP is the official goal of the European Employment Strategy (EES). And it is precisely in this context that the concept of 'the active welfare state' has been introduced. The task of the welfare state is to 'make transitions pay' or to facilitate transitions in the life span of the individual, and to so do by helping workers to overcome transitions (e.g. from school to job, or from job to re-education by providing social services enabling families to work, or by making it possible for families and individuals to share the social risk of transitional labour markets with others;[40] but also by shaping the attitudes and incentives of citizens to social objectives like lifelong learning and a lifelong commitment to work.[41]

These two models of the competition state are at the heart of many national reform efforts, with some countries following the regulatory type of competition state like the USA and the United Kingdom and others like Sweden, Finland, Denmark, Belgium, and the Netherlands preferring (in general) the active welfare type of competition state. In the first case, countries reformed the institutional environment for firms (external flexibility); in the second case, countries combined external with internal flexibility in an effort to change the institutional context for firms together with the incentives and motivations of employees (through promoting internal flexibility).

The Implementation of the Discourse of Institutional Competitiveness into State–Society Relations

Both the regulatory and the active type of the competition state are examples of how the discourse has moved from a simple conversation among academics into political

---

[39] The mix of external and internal measures, and of a dynamic and static approach, makes it obvious to see flexicurity as an explicit attempt to manage the complementarities of three institutions—the labour law, the unemployment insurance regime, and labour market policies, and to coordinate the relation between three players—the firms, the employers, and the state (Boyer 2008: 18). But it can also be looked upon as a way of transferring social risks from the welfare state (or the family) to individuals or social groups (Schmid 2006), and to so do by entitling workers to choose and to manage their own transitions during the whole life cycle, i.e. 'to equip people for the markets' (Gazier 2007: 110); or in the words of the Commission of the European Communities '. . . to ensure the continual adaptability and employability of workers.' (Commission of the European Communities 2007: 12).

[40] New studies are pointing to the Scandinavian countries for positive examples of how welfare provisions can facilitate transitions in terms of life course (OECD 2005). Also Ireland, among other countries, is debating how to establish a 'developmental welfare state' (National Economic Social Council 2005: ch. 6 and 7) following these lines.

[41] See for an example, the Performance and Innovation Unit, PIU (2001). *In Demand: Adult Skills in the 21st Century: A Performance and Innovation Unit Report*, The Cabinet Office, London.

discussions with real-world effects. In this section I will look at how the building-up of external and internal flexibility co-evolved with the establishment of process flexibility, i.e. with flexibility in the governmental arrangements used to decide and implement state reforms. This implies changes in state–society arrangements. For the purpose of simplicity I once again distinguish between two types of arrangements. The first is *Partisan Arrangements*; the second is *Consensus Arrangements*. The first term covers cases like the United States and the United Kingdom, where private think tanks and advocacy groups have for a long time engaged in open competition trying to attract the attention of the public opinion, and where companies and private interests have been using lobbyism to influence politicians and political parties (Campbell and Pedersen 2010). The second term includes countries like Germany, Austria, the Netherlands, Denmark, Sweden, Finland, Belgium, and others where state institutions and private interest organizations in the post-war period were integrated into neo-corporatist wage and income policy-bargaining systems,[42] based on legislated, rule-governed, and mostly centralized power sharing arrangements (Katzenstein 1985; Schmitter 1974, 1982; Therborn 1998). In both cases distinct institutional arrangements were adapted and developed from the 1950s, and it was not before the 1990s that a shift away from partisanship in the first case and centralized negotiations in the second case took place. Instead, new arrangements were introduced with the ambition to create process flexibility, i.e. to establish routines for how to manage relations between the state and the social partners by 'learning by doing' or by experimentation with an incessant recombination of established institutions.

In most cases it was national governments that took the first initiatives, followed by years of harsh confrontations between governments and labour unions and trade organizations. This, for example, happened in England in the beginning of the 1980s, and in Denmark, Sweden, and the Netherlands from the mid-1980s and again later in Germany and France. But even if the general ambition was a belief in process flexibility, each country followed its own historical pathway—with important exceptions (see Rhodes 2003, for overview). Countries with a tradition of private think tanks and lobbyism adapted early. Already in the 1970s and 1980s a new generation of advocacy research units were developed to become influential from the 1980s onwards. These included conservative and neo-liberal think tanks like the conservative *Heritage Foundation*, and the neo-liberal *Cato Institute*, in the US, and the *Centre for Policy Studies* and the *Adam Smith Institute* in the UK. Private advocacy groups often resembled interest groups in so far as they pressured decision-makers to implement policies compatible with their ideological beliefs and those shared by their generous benefactors (Abelson 1998). Today, the partisan arrangements have gained ground (Gelner 1995) in both USA and the UK and a larger number of private think tanks and private consultancies apply more professionalized means to influence public

---

[42] While arrangements for the competitive market for ideas are looked upon as a context for politics and a way to influence policymakers from the outside, the corporatist type is understood to be endogenous to politics and business, and corporatist arrangements to be related to how firms, governments, and social partners are constructing complementarities.

opinion and government decisions. In terms of its larger number of advocacy research units, the increasingly partisan nature of their activities, and the intensely competitive nature of policy-relevant knowledge production and dissemination, competitive arrangements are dominating in the USA and UK and spreading from there to countries in Asia and South-East Asia, and even to the EU institutions and to formerly neo-corporatist countries like Sweden and France (Stone 2004).

On the other hand, countries with a tradition for neo-corporatist arrangements (Germany, Denmark, Belgium, Austria, and to some extent also the Netherlands) have adapted these, establishing a new generation of consensus arrangements. In other cases, like Sweden, central negotiating institutions have been abolished and bargaining has been transferred to cross-sectoral bipartite agreements. More important though are the cases in which countries with no previous traditions for institutionalized corporation have created new forms of consensus-seeking arrangements by linking incomes policies to broader social bargaining using national tripartite deals—e.g. Italy, Spain, Portugal, and Greece (Rhodes 2003: 132 f.). The full development thus is complex, but several general trends are visible. First, the US and the UK have developed partisan arrangements strengthening the competitive nature of knowledge production. Second, most EU member states have begun to see consensus-seeking arrangements as important mechanisms to produce comparative advantages. Third, in these countries, attempts are made to create comparative advantages by the coordination of incomes policies with broader employment and social policy measures by interlocking multiple agents (political, social, and economic), as well as manifold levels of agency (transnational, national, regional, local, and company level) and numerous policy arenas (employment, welfare, growth, income, industry, innovation, entrepreneurship) (Treu 1992). Accordingly, the new systems of governance are more complex, but also less static and more dynamic than traditional neo-pluralist and neo-corporatist arrangements. In some cases (Sweden, Italy, Spain, Portugal, and Greece) new directions away from historical pathways have been entered into. However, at present no fixed or stabilized arrangements can be found in either of the two cases—the partisan or the consensus types of competition arrangements. Instead a constant flux of arrangements seems to be the order of the day; new institutions are created and old ones abolished, in some cases even from policy case to policy case. All this has led to the creation of several types of agreements based on process flexibility.[43]

In this manner, partisan as well as consensus arrangements are an expression of the fact that the *management of governance* between state and society has become an important issue that has pushed most states to rethink established approaches and to re-examine their governance systems. Hence, what is characteristic is that the current era presents a picture of institutional experimentation and innovation, generally in the direction of process flexibility, i.e. towards the constant renegotiation of the agents to be included (or excluded), the policies to be interlocked (or unlocked), and the

---

[43] See for extensive descriptions (Molina and Rhodes 2002; Rhodes 2003; Traxler 2000; Traxler et al. 2001; Pedersen 2006a).

processes to be used to construct comparative advantages. In several countries a step towards creating meta-institutions to manage such processes has been established. In Finland, Sweden, and Denmark, for example, governments have created so-called *Globalisation Councils* (GCs) to negotiate national strategies for routine transformations in the organization of relations between social partners and governments.[44] In other countries like the USA and UK the discourse of 'joined up government' has emerged to suggest how strategy and policy units are established within government in order to enhance its capability to coordinate across departments and to influence public opinion in competition with private think tanks and the media.

Institutional Competitiveness— A Definition

In the last twenty-five years or so we have witnessed how an academic interest in institutions and institutional analysis has moved to become a discourse for international organizations and national governments alike. We have also witnessed how this discourse has become implemented with important consequences for what tasks states take upon themselves and for state–society relations. The discourse that nations compete has moved from academia to become a common understanding transforming transnational relations as well as states in its journey (Plehwe et al. 2006: 1–24). Hence, the most important point made so far is that the discourse that nations compete has become (almost or nearly?) generally accepted and that procedures (like those included in 'The post-Washington Consensus') and processes (like the OMC) are by now moving the process towards an even greater dissemination, and an even deeper development of the discourse and the institutions. Whether nations really compete is of course still contested, but even if nations do not compete, or even if the notion that nations compete is a 'dangerous obsession', there is by now an established set of institutions and of expert systems making it possible for policymakers and the like to act *as if* they do. Thus the notion is penetrating more deeply into the public discourse and reform plans of national policies. The same can be said with respect to negotiations within the EU, and with policy proposals formulated by the IMF, the WB, the OECD, and with proposals put forward by the great number of

---

[44] These councils differ from the already mentioned *National Competitiveness Councils* (NCPs). Where NCPs deal with the overall competitiveness of the national economy, GCs are concerned with meta-governance, i.e. how to manage ongoing changes in systems of governance. However, there are also some common features. The leadership structure of NCPs and GCs relies on strong support from the highest level of political authority, but also from designated private sector managers (CEOs and chairmen of national interest organizations).

private think tanks, consultancies, and expert groups now operating both internationally and transnationally. Indeed if one digs a little deeper, one finds an almost
universal restructuring of international economic relations and national models of
regulation all going in the same direction of enhancing the ability of nations to
compete and of international organizations to facilitate their competition.

Two current examples emphasize the point. A first example is reform of the
national education systems in the OECD's member countries. Many European
countries have implemented changes in their education and welfare legislation
with the object of strengthening the individual citizen's motivation to understand
work—or the lifelong commitment to employability—as *the* most important aspect
of being a citizen in a national (or local) community. The OECD's annual
Programme for International Student Assessment (PISA) survey plays an important
role here, not simply by making it clear that nations compete and that they so do on
the basis of the competences of their citizens, but also by making it obvious that it is
the work-related skills, which in themselves are a parameter of competition (OECD
PISA 2006). Following the inspiration provided by the PISA, debates on new forms
of education were ignited, and these have already led to the formulation of education
reforms and to changes in national legislation in several countries (Finland, France,
Germany, the UK, Denmark, Sweden, Norway, and the Netherlands). A second
example is the OECD's latest initiative on 'competitive cities' (OECD 2006*b*),
where the big cities' physical, social, educational, environmental, cultural, and
intellectual infrastructure is emphasized to explain why some cities are better suited
to attract foreign investment and highly educated manpower than others.

These examples however, must be enough to support the point that a routine has
been established for the dissemination and development of the concept that nations
compete. It is against this background that international competitiveness has come to
be defined by its institutional features. And on this background that I assert that over
more than twenty-five years, there has been a gradual development in the definition
and in the use of the concept of international competitiveness that places institutions
at the centre for business managers, policymakers, and international organizations
alike when they measure competitiveness and produce strategies to create comparative advantages. By institutional competitiveness (CIC) I formerly understood the
capacity of a country to achieve socio-economic success relative to comparable
countries as a result of its political and economic institutions (Campbell and
Pedersen 2007*a*, Pedersen 2006*b*). This definition can now be made more precise
by emphasizing three circumstances:

(1) Nations compete by reforming the institutional (legal, political, economic, and
    cultural) context for firms in an attempt to produce comparative advantages; e.g.
    by creating conditions for internal and external flexibility of working conditions;
(2) Nations compete by intervening in the attitudes, values, aspirations, and inter-
    ests of citizens and firms in attempts to use behavioural change as a means to
    create comparative advantages;

(3) Nations compete by deliberately constructing institutional complementarities, e.g. by coordinating a number of policy areas, societal players, and levels of government into governance systems equipped for mutual and ongoing learning and experimentation with institutional change.[45]

Analyses of institutions have become a policy tool, and reflections on how to promote comparative advantages and to so do by the management of institutional complementarities have become an everyday matter for national governments and international organizations. Knowledge of institutions has come to be understood as a tool—and even as a functional imperative—for governments in competing with other nations and for international organizations in facilitating this competition.

REFERENCES

ABELSON, DONALD E. (1998). 'Think Tanks in the United States', in Diane Stone, Andrew Denham, and Mark Garnett (eds.), *Think Tanks Across Nations: A Comparative Perspective*, (Manchester: Manchester University Press), 107–27.

AGLIETTA, MICHEL (1976). *Régulation et Crises du Capitalisme*, (Paris: Calmann-Lévy).

AIGINGER, KARL (2005). 'Towards a New European Model of the Reformed Welfare State: An Alternative to the United States Model', *Economic Commission for Europe, United Nations* No. 7, (New York and Geneva), 105–14.

——(2006a). 'Revisiting an Evasive Concept: Introduction to the Special Issue on Competitiveness', *Journal of Industry, Competition and Trade*, 6(2): 63–6.

——(2006b). 'Competitiveness: From a Dangerous Obsession to a Welfare Creating Ability with Positive Externalities', *Journal of Industry, Competition and Trade*, 6(2): 161–77.

ALBERT, MICHEL (1993). *Capitalism against Capitalism*, (London: Whurr).

ALESINA, A. F. and R. PEROTTI (2004). 'The European Union: A Politically Incorrect View', NBER Working Paper w10342, March. http://ssrn.com/abstract=515236

AMABLE, BRUNO (2003). *The Diversity of Modern Capitalism*, (Oxford: Oxford University Press).

AOKI, MASAHIKO (2001). *Towards a Comparative Institutional Analysis*, (Cambridge, MA.: MIT Press).

BÄCKLUND, JONAS and ANDREAS WERR (2001). 'The construction of global management consulting—a study of consultancies' web presentations'. *SSE/EFI Working Paper Series in Business Administration No 2001: 3 February 2001.* http://swoba.hhs.se/hastba/papers/hastba2001_003.pdf

BALASSA, BELA (1965). 'Trade Liberalization and "Revealed Comparative Advantage"', *Manchester School* 33 (May), 99–123.

BOBBIT, PHILIP (2003). *The Shield of Achilles: War, Peace, and the Course of History*, (New York: Anchor Books).

BOLI, JOHN and GEORGE M. THOMAS (1999). *Constructing World Culture*, (Palo Alto: Stanford University Press).

---

[45] See for an example *Cabinet Office, Strategy Unit*, 2007, 'Achieving Culture Change: A Policy Framework', http://www.cabinetoffice.gov.uk/strategy/work_areas/culture_change.aspx.

BORRÁS, SUSANA and KERSTIN JACOBSSON (2004). 'The Open Method of Co-ordination and New Governance Patterns in the EU', *Journal of European Public Policy* 11: 185–208.

BOYER, ROBERT (2008). 'La flexicurité danoise: quels enseignements pour la France?', in Philippe Askenazy and Daniel Cohen, *27 questions d'Economie Contemporaine*, (Paris: Economiques 1, Albine Michel), 175–208.

Cabinet Office, Strategy Unit (2007). 'Achieving Culture Change: A Policy Framework', for an example, http://www.cabinetoffice.gov.uk/strategy/work_areas/culture_change.aspx

CAMERON, ANGUS and RONEN P. PALAN (2003). *The Imagined Economies of Globalization*, (London: Sage).

CAMPBELL, JOHN L. (2004). *Institutional Change and Globalization* (Princeton, NJ: Princeton University Press).

——and OVE K. PEDERSEN (eds.) (2001). *The Rise of Neoliberalism and Institutional Analysis*, (Princeton, NJ: Princeton University Press).

————(2007a). 'Institutional Competitiveness in the Global Economy: Denmark, United States and the Varieties of Capitalism, *Regulation and Governance* 1(3): 230–46.

————(2007b). 'The Varieties of Capitalism and Hybrid Success: Denmark in the Global Economy', *Comparative Political Studies*, 40(3): 307–32.

————(forthcoming 2010). 'Knowledge Regimes and Comparative Political Economy', in Daniel Bèland and Robert H. Cox (eds.), *Ideas and Politics in Social Research*, (Oxford: Oxford University Press).

CANTWELL, J. (2005). 'Survey of Innovation and Competitiveness', in Jan Fagerberg, David C. Mowery, and Richard R. Nelson (eds.), *Oxford Handbook on Innovation*, (London: Oxford University Press), 543–67.

CASEY, B. H. and M. GOLD (2005). 'Peer Review of Labour Market Programmes in the European Union: What Can Countries Really Learn from One Another?', *Journal of European Public Policy* 12: 23–43.

CERNY, PHILIP G. (1990). *The Changing Architecture of Politics: Structure, Agency and the Future of the State*, (London and Newbury Park: Sage).

——(2007). 'Paradoxes of the Competition State: The Dynamics of Political Globalization', *Government and Opposition*, 32(2): 251–74.

CHRISTENSEN, TOM and PER LÆGREID (eds.) (2001). *New Public Management: The Transformation of Ideas and Practice*, (Aldershot: Ashgate).

CLINTON, BILL, Address to the Nation on the Economic Program, Feb. 15, 1993. http://findarticles.com/p/articles/mi_m2889/is_n7_v29/ai_14362491

COE-REXECODE (2007). *La compétitivité française en 2007*, Document de travail no. 3.

COMMISSION OF THE EUROPEAN COMMUNITIES (1993). *Growth, Competitiveness, Employment: The Challenges and Ways Forward into the 21st Century.* COM (93) 700 final, Dec., http://aei.pitt.edu/1139/01/growth_wp_COM_93_700_Parts_A_B.pdf

——(1994), *European Social Policy—A Way Forward for the Union.* A White Paper Com (94) 333 final. http://aei.pitt.edu/1118/01/social_policy_white_paper_COM_94_333_A.pdf

——(2001a). *Promoting a European Framework for Corporate Social Responsibility.* EU Doc. COM 366.

——(2002a). *Corporate Social Responsibility: A Business Contribution to Sustainable Development.* EU Doc. COM 347.

——(2002b). *Taking Stock of Five Years of the European Employment Strategy.* EU Doc. COM (2002) 416 final. http://www.socialdialogue.net/docs/cha_key/

——(2006a). *Implementing the Partnership for Growth and Jobs: Making Europe a Pole of Excellence on Corporate Social Responsibility.* EU Doc. COM 136. final.

——(2006b) *Promoting Decent Work for All: The EU Contribution to the Implementation of the Decent Work Agenda in the World*. EU Doc. COM 249.

——(2007). *Towards Common Principles of Flexicurity: More and Better Jobs through Flexibility and Security*. EU Doc. COM 359 Final http://ec.europa.eu/employment_social/ employment_ strategy/flexicurity%20media/flexicuritypublication_2007_en.pdf

COMPETITIVENESS ADVISORY GROUP (Ciampi Group) (1995). 'Enhancing European Competitiveness'. Second Report to the President of the Commission, the Prime Ministers and the Heads of State, Dec. Her citeret fra http://www.forfas.ie/ncc/reports/ncc/ann1.htm

COMPETITIVENESS POLICY COUNCIL, see http://en.wikipedia.org/wiki/Competitiveness_ Policy_Council

COUNCIL ON COMPETITIVENESS, Washington, http://www.compete.org/about-us/

CROUCH, COLIN (2005). *Capitalist Diversity and Change: Recombinant Governance and Institutional Entrepreneurs*, (Oxford: Oxford University Press).

DORNBUSCH, R., S. FISHER and PAUL SAMUELSON (1977). 'Comparative Advantage, Trade and Payments in a Ricardian model with a Continuum of Goods', *American Economic Review* 67(5): 823–39.

DUINA, FRANCESCO (2006). *The Social Construction of Free Trade: The European Union, NAFTA, and Mercosur*, (Princeton, NJ: Princeton University Press).

EATWELL, JOHN (1987). 'Walras's Theory of Capital', in John Eatwell, Murray Milgate, and Peter Newmann (eds.), *The New Palgrave: A Dictionary of Economics*, (London: Macmillan), 247–56.

EGAN, MICHELLE (2001). *Constructing a European Market*, (Oxford: Oxford University Press).

EICHENGREEN, BARRY (2007). *The European Economy Since 1945. Coordinated Capitalism and Beyond*, (Princeton: Princeton University Press).

EUROPEAN COUNCIL, EMCO; *The Employment Committee Indicators* http://orka2.sejm.gov.pl/ Koordynacja2.nsf/($All)/CCD98B57FEE48385C12573F6003A9020/$File/st06694-ad01.en08. pdf?OpenElement

——(2000). *Lisbon European Council 23 and 24 March 2000. Presidency Conclusions*, http:// www.europarl.europa.eu/summits/lis1_en.htm#b

EUROPEAN UNION, *Competitiveness of EU sectors*, http://ec.europa.eu/enterprise/enterprise_ policy/competitiveness/2_indics/indics_compet.htm

——*Competitiveness Report*, http://ec.europa.eu/enterprise/enterprise_policy/competitiveness/1_eucompetrep/eu_compet_reports.htm

——*Observatory of European SMEs*, http://ec.europa.eu/enterprise/enterprise_ policy/analysis/observatory_en.htm

EVANS, PETER, DIETRICH RUESCHEMEYER, and THEDA SKOCPOL (eds.) (1985). *Bringing the State Back In*, (Cambridge: Cambridge University Press).

FAGERBERG, J. (1988). 'International Competitiveness', *The Economic Journal* 391: 355–74.

FERRERA MAURIZIO, ANTON HEMERIJCK, and MARTIN RHODES (2003). 'Recasting European Welfare States', in Jack Hayward and Anand Menon (eds.), *Governing Europe*, (Oxford, Oxford University Press), 346–68.

FLIGSTEIN, NEIL (2001). *The Architecture of Markets: An Economic Sociology of Twenty-First-Century Capitalist Societies*, (Princeton, NJ: Princeton University Press).

FREEMAN, CHRISTOPHER, JOHN CLARK AND LUC SOETE (eds.) (1982). *Unemployment and Technical Innovation: A Study of Long Waves and Economic Development* (Chicago: University of Chicago Press).

FRIEDEN, JEFFRY A. (2006). *Global Capitalism: Its Fall and Rise in the Twentieth Century*, (New York: W. W. Norton & Company).

GAZIER, BERNARD (2007). 'Making Transitions Pay: The "Transnational Labour Markets" Approach to "Flexicurity"', in Henning Jørgensen and Per Kongshøj Madsen (eds.), *Flexicurity and Beyond: Finding a New Agenda for the European Social Model*, (Copenhagen: DJØF Publishing).

GELCNER, WINAND (1995). 'The Politics of Policy "Political Think Tanks" and Their Markets in the U.S. Institutional Environment', *Presidential Studies Quarterly* 25(3): 497.

GILBERT, NEIL and BARBARA GILBERT (1989). *The Enabling State: Modern Welfare Capitalism in America*, (Oxford: Oxford University Press).

GOETSCHY, JANINE (2003). 'The Employment Strategy, Multi-level Governance, and Policy Coordination: Past, Present and Future', in Jonathan Zeitlin and David M. Trubek (eds.), *Governing Work and Welfare in a New Economy: European and American Experiments*, (Oxford: Oxford University Press), 59–87.

GRANOVETTER, MARK (2004). 'Economic Action and Social Structure: The Problem of Embeddedness', in Frank Dobbin (ed.), *The New Economic Sociology: A Reader*, (Princeton, NJ: Princeton University Press), 245–73.

GRILO, ISABEL and GERT JAN KOOPMAN (2006). 'Productivity and Microeconomic Reforms: Strengthening EU Competitiveness', *Journal of Industry, Competition and Trade*. 6(2): 67–84.

HALL, PETER and DAVID SOSKICE (eds.) (2001). *The Varieties of Capitalism: The Institutional Foundations of Comparative Advantage*, (Oxford: New York: Oxford University Press).

HAAS, PETER M. (1992). 'Knowledge, Power, and International Policy Coordination', *International Organization* 46(1): 1–35.

HIRSCH, JOACHIM (1995). *Wettbewerbsstaat: Staat, Demokratie und Politik im globalen Kapitalismus*, (Amsterdam-Berlin: Edition ID-Archiv).

HIRSCHMAN, ALBERT O. (1981). *Essays in Trespassing: Economics to Politics and Beyond*, (Cambridge: Cambridge University Press).

——(1992). *Rival Views of Market Society: And Other Recent Essays*, (Cambridge, MA: Harvard University Press).

HOOD, CHRISTOPHER (2007). 'Public Service Management by Numbers: Why does it Vary? Where has it come from? What are the Gaps and Puzzles?', *Public Money and Management*, Apr., 95–237.

INTERNATIONAL MONETARY FUND, *World Economic Outlook*, (2007) http://www.imf.org/external/pubs/ft/weo/2007/01/index.htm

—— *World Economic Outlook, 2005*, Building Institutions, http://www.imf.org/external/pubs/ft/weo/2005/02/index.htm

INSTITUTE FOR MANAGEMENT DEVELOPMENT (IMD), *World Competitiveness Yearbook*, http://www.imd.ch/research/publications/wcy/index.cfm

JACOBSSON BENGT, PER LÆGREID, and OVE K. PEDERSEN (2004). *Europeanization and Transnational States: Comparing Nordic Central Governments*, (London: Routledge).

JACOBSSON, KERSTIN (2004). 'Between Deliberation and Discipline: Soft Governance in EU Employment Policy', in Ulrikke Mörth (ed.), *Soft Law in Governance and Regulation: An Interdisciplinary Analysis*, (Cheltenham: Edward Elgar).

——and ASA VIFELL (2005). 'New Governance Structures in Employment Policy Making? Taking Stock of the European Employment Strategy', in Ingo Linsenmann, Christoph O. Meyer, and Wolfgang Wessels (eds.), *Economic Government of the EU: A Balance Sheet of New Modes of Policy Coordination*, (London: Macmillan).

JESSOP, BOB (1994a). 'The Transition to post-Fordism and the Schumpeterian Workfare State', in Brian Loader and Roger Burrows (eds.), *Towards a Post-Fordist Welfare State?* (London: Routledge), 13–37.

——(1994b). 'Post-Fordism and the State', in Ash Amin (ed.), *Post-Fordism: A Reader*, (Oxford: Blackwell), 251–79.

——(2003). *The Future of the Capitalist State*, (Cambridge: Polity Press).

——(2007). *State Power*, (London. Polity Press).

Journal of Industry, Competition and Trade (2006). 6(2).

JØRGENSEN, HENNING and PER KONGSHØJ MADSEN (2007). 'Flexicurity and Beyond—Reflections on the Nature and Future of a Political Celebrity', in Henning Jørgensen and Per Kongshøj Madsen (eds.), *Flexicurity and Beyond: Finding a New Agenda for the European Social Model*, (Copenhagen: DJØF Publishing), 7–38.

KAISER, ROBERT and HEIKO PRANGE (2005). 'Missing the Lisbon Target? Multi-Level Innovation and EU Policy Coordination', *Journal of Public Policy* 25: 241–63.

KATZENSTEIN, PETER (1985). *Small States in World Markets: Industrial Policy in Europe*, (Ithaca, NY: Cornell University Press).

KECK, MARGARET and KATHRYN SIKKINK (1998). *Activists Beyond Borders: Advocacy Networks in International Politics*, (Ithaca, NY: Cornell University Press).

KENNER, JEFF (1999). 'The EC Employment Title and the "Third Way": Making Soft Law Work?', *The International Journal of Comparative Labour Law and Industrial Relations* 15(1): 33–60.

KETELS, CHRISTIAN H. M. (2006). 'Michael Porter's Competitiveness Framework—Recent Learning's and New Research Priorities', *Journal of Industry, Competition, and Trade* 6(2): 115–36.

KETTL, DONALD F. (2000). *The Global Public Management Revolution. A Report on the Transformation of Governance*, (Washington DC: Brookings).

KOHLER, WILHELM (2006). 'The "Lisbon Goal" of the EU: Rhetoric or Substance?', *Journal of Industry, Competition and Trade* 6(2): 85–113.

KRUGMAN, PAUL (1979). "*Increasing Returns, Monopolistic Competition, and International Trade*" *Journal of International Economics* 9: 469–479.

——(1994). 'Competitiveness: A Dangerous Obsession', *Foreign Affairs*. 73(2): 28–44.

——(1996). 'A Country is not a Company'. http://www.pkarchive.org/trade/company.html

——and GEORGE N. HATSOPOULOS (1987). 'The Problem of U.S. Competitiveness in Manufacturing', *New England Economic Review*, 18–29.

KOK, WIM (2004). *Facing the Challenge. The Lisbon Strategy for Growth and Employment* http://ec.europa.eu/growthandjobs/pdf/kok_report_en.pdf

LEAMER, EDWARD E. (1995). *The Heckscher-Ohlin Model in Theory and Practice. Princeton Studies in International Economics*, (Princeton, NJ: Princeton University Press).

LINDBLOM, CHARLES E. (1977). *Politics and Markets: The World's Political-Economic Systems*, (New York: Basic Books).

LIPSCHITZ, LESLIE and DONOGH MCDONALD (1991). 'Real Exchange Rates and Competitiveness: A Clarification of Concepts and some Measurements for Europe', *IMF Working Paper*, Mar.

LIPSEY, RICHARD G., KENNETH I. CARLAW, AND CLIFFORD T. BEKER (2005). *Economic Transformations. General Purpose Technologies and Long Term Economic Growth*, (Oxford: Oxford University Press).

LORENZ, EDWARD and BENGT-ÅKE LUNDVALL (eds.) (2006). *How Europe's Economies Learn*, (Oxford: Oxford University Press).

McKinsey Global Institute, http://www.mckinsey.com/mgi/rp/CSProductivity/

Majone, Giandomenico (1994). 'The rise of the regulatory state in Europe', *West European Politics* 17(3): 77–101.

March, James G. and Johan P. Olsen (1984). 'The New Institutionalism: Organizational Factors in Political Life'. *American Political Science Review* 78: 734–49.

———— (1989). *Rediscovering Institutions: The Organizational Basis of Politics*, (New York: The Free Press).

Melkert, Ad (1995). *Flexibility and security*, Second Chamber 1995-6, No. 24 543: see http://www.eurofound.europa.eu/eiro/1997/06/feature/nl9770616f.htm

Meyer, John (2000). 'Globalization and the Expansion and Standardization of Management', in Lars Engwall and Kerstin Sahlin-Andersson (eds.), *The Expansion of Management Knowledge: Carriers, Flows and Sources*, (Palo Alto: Stanford University Press), 33–44.

Milgrom, Paul and John Roberts (1992). *Economics, Organization and Management*, (Englewood Cliffs: Prentice Hall).

Molina, Oscar and Martin Rhodes (2002). 'Corporatism: The Past, Present, and Future of a Concept', *Annual Review of Political Science* 5: 305–31.

National Competitiveness Council, (2004). Dublin: Ireland, http://www.forfas.ie/ncc/reports/ncc_annual_01/approach.htm

National Economic Social Council (NESC) (2005). *The Developmental Welfare State*. No. 113, May. Dublin.

Nedergaard, Peter (2006). 'Which Countries Learn from Which: A Comparative Analysis of the Direction of Mutual Learning Processes with the Open Method of Coordination Committees of the European Union and among Nordic Countries', *Cooperation and Conflict* 41(4): 422–42.

——(2007). 'Maximizing Policy Learning in International Committees: An Analysis of the European Open Method of Coordination (OMC) Committees', *Scandinavian Political Studies* 30(4): 521–46.

North, Douglass C. (1990). *Institutions, Institutional Change and Economic Performance*, (Cambridge: Cambridge University Press).

——(2005). *Understanding the Process of Economic Change*, (Princeton, NJ: Princeton University Press).

OECD, *Economic Outlook*, http://www.oecd.org/document/18/0,3343,en_2649_34573_20347538_1_1_1_1,00.html

OECD, *Going for Growth*, http://www.oecd.org/dataoecd/16/29/39924903.pps

OECD (2005). *Extending Opportunities: How Active Social Policy Can Benefit Us All*. Issues/Migration/Health 3: 1–191.

OECD (2006a). *Economic Outlook, Boosting Jobs and Incomes, Policy Lessons from Reassessing the OECD Jobs Strategy*. http://www.oecd.org/document/38/0,2340,en_2649_201185_36261286_1_1_1_1,00.html

OECD (2006b). *Territorial Reviews. Competitive Cities in the Global Economy*. http://www.oecd.org/document/2/0,3343,en_2649_201185_37801602_1_1_1_1,00.html

Pack, Spencer J. (2000). "Entrepreneurs, Institutions and Economic Change: The Economic Thought of J.A. Schumpeter (1905–1925)" (review). *History of Political Economy*, 32(1): 175–173.

Pedersen, Ove K. (1991). 'Nine Questions to a Neo-institutional Theory in Political Science', *Scandinavian Political Studies* 14(2): 125–48.

——(2006a). 'Corporatism and Beyond: The Negotiated Economy', in John L. Campbell, John A. Hall, and Ove K. Pedersen (eds.), *National Identity and the Varieties of Capitalism: The Danish Experiment*, (Montreal: McGill & Queens University Press), 245–70.

——(2006*b*). 'Denmark: An Ongoing Experiment', in John L. Campbell, John A. Hall, and Ove K. Pedersen (eds.), *National Identity and the Varieties of Capitalism: The Danish Experiment*, (Montreal: McGill & Queens University Press), 453–70.

Performance and Innovation Unit, PIU (2001). *In Demand: Adult Skills in the 21st Century: A Performance and Innovation Unit Report*, The Cabinet Office, London.

PLEHWE, DIETER, BERNHARD WALPEN, and GISELA NEUNHÖFFER (eds.) (2006). *Neoliberal Hegemony: A Global Critique*, (London: Routledge).

PONTUSSON, JONAS (2005). *Inequality and Prosperity: Social Europe vs. Liberal America.* (Ithaca, NY: Cornell University Press).

PORTER, MICHAEL E. (1980). *Competitive Strategy: Techniques for Analyzing Industries and Competitors*, (New York: The Free Press).

——(1985). *Competitive Advantage: Creating and Sustaining Superior Performance*, (New York: The Free Press).

——(1998). *The Competitive Advantage of Nations*, 2nd edn., (London: Palgrave).

——(2000). 'Attitudes, Values, Beliefs, and the Microeconomics of Prosperity', in Lawrence E. Harrison and Samuel P. Huntington (eds.), *Culture Matters: How Values Shape Human Progress*, (New York: Basic Books), 14–28.

PRIME MINISTER'S STRATEGY UNIT (Feb.) (2004). 'Personal Responsibility and Changing Behaviour: The State of Knowledge and its Implications for Public Policy', http://74.125.77.132/search?q=cache:PUA28rcOmIkJ:www.number10.gov.uk/files/pdf/pr.pdf+Personal+Responsibility+and+Changing+Behaviour+PMSU+2004&hl=da&ct=clnk&cd=2&gl =dk

RADAELLI, CLAUDIO M. (2003). *The Open Method of Co-ordination: A New Governance Architecture for the European Union?* (Lund: Swedish Institute for European Policy Studies), 1, http://www.sieps.se/publ/rapporter/2003/2003_1_en.html

REGULATION AND GOVERNANCE (2007). *Special Issue on Globalization and Institutional Competitiveness* 1(3).

RHODES, MARTIN (1998). 'Globalization, Labour Markets and Welfare States: A Future of "Competitive Corporatism?"', in Martin Rhodes and Yves Meny (eds.), *The Future of European Welfare: A New Social Contract?*, (New York: St Martin's Press), 178–203.

——(2003). 'National "Pacts" and EU Governance in Social Policy and the Labor Market', in Jonathan Zeitlin and David M. Trubek (eds.), *Governing Work and Welfare in a New Economy: European and American Experiments*, (Oxford: Oxford University Press), 129–57.

RODRIK, DANI (2007). *One Economics Many Recipes: Globalization, Institutions, and Economic Growth*, (Princeton, NJ: Princeton University Press).

ROSECRANCE, RICHARD N. (1999). *The Rise of the Virtual State: Wealth and Power in the Coming Century*, (New York: Basic Books).

SAPIR, André et al. (2003). *An Agenda for a Growing Europe: Making the EU Economic System Deliver. Report of High-Level Study Group*, (Brussels: Commission of the European Communities), Jul. 2003. http://www.euractiv.com/ndbtext/innovation/sapirreport.pdf

SCHARPF, FRITZ (2002). 'The European Social Model: Coping with the Challenge of Diversity', *Journal of Common Market Studies* 40(4): 645–70.

SCHMID, GÜNTHER (2006). 'Social Risk Management through Transitional Labour Markets', *Socio-Economic Review* 4(1): 1–33.

SCHMITTER, PHILIPPE C. (1974). 'Still the Century of Corporatism?', *Review of Politics* 36: 85–131.

——(1982). 'Reflections on Where the Theory of Neo-Corporatism has Gone and Where the Praxis of Neo-corporatism May Be Going', in Gerhard Lehmbruch and Philippe C. Schmitter (eds.), *Patterns of Corporatist Policy Making*, (London: Sage), 259–79.

SCHMITTER, PHILIPPE C. and WOLFGANG STREECK (eds.) (1985). *Private Interest Governments: Beyond Market and State*, (London: Sage).

SCOTT, JOANNE and DAVID M. TRUBEK (2002). 'Mind the Gap: Law and New Approaches to Governance in the European Union', *European Law Journal* 8(1): 1–18.

SERRA, NARCIS and JOSEPH L. STIGLITZ (eds.) (2008). *The Washington Consensus Reconsidered: Towards a New Global Governance*, (Oxford: Oxford University Press).

SHONFIELD, ANDREW (1965). *Modern Capitalism: The Changing Balance of Public and Private Power*, (Oxford: Oxford University Press).

SIGGEL, ECKHARD (2006). 'International Competitiveness and Comparative Advantage: A Survey and a Proposal for Measurement', *Journal of Industry, Competition, and Trade* 6(2): 137–59.

SKOCPOL, THEDA (2008). 'Bringing the State Back In: Retrospect and Prospect'. The 2007 Johan Skytte Prize Lecture, *Scandinavian Political Studies* 31(2): 109–24.

SPENCE A. MICHAEL and HEATHER A. HAZARD (eds.) (1988). *International Competitiveness*, (Cambridge: Ballinger).

STARBUCK, WILLIAM H. (2003). 'The Origins of Organization Theory', in Haridimos Tsoukais and Christian Knudsen (eds.), *The Oxford Handbook of Organization Theory. Meta-Theoretical Perspectives*, (Oxford: Oxford University Press), 143–82.

STIGLITZ, JOSEPH E. (1998). 'More Instruments and Broader Goals: Toward a Post Washington Consensus'. The 1998 Wider Annual Lecture, Helsinki, Finland, Jan. 7, http://www.global-policy.org/socecon/bwi-wto/stig.htm

——(2003). *Globalization and its Discontents*, 2nd edn., (New York: W.W. Norton & Company).

STONE, DIANE (2004). 'Introduction: Think Tanks, Policy Advice and Governance', in Diane Stone and Andrew Denham (eds.), *Think Tank Traditions*, (Manchester: Manchester University Press), 1–18.

STOPFORD, JOHN M., SUSAN STRANGE, and JOHN S. HENLEY (1991). *Rival States, Rival Firms: Competition for World Market Shares*, (Cambridge: Cambridge Studies of International Relations).

STREECK, WOLFGANG (2009). *Re-Forming Capitalism: Institutional Change in the German Political Economy*, (Oxford: Oxford University Press).

THERBORN, GØSTA (1998). 'Does Corporatism Really Matter? The Economic Crisis and Issues of Political Theory', *Journal of Public Policy* 7(3): 259–84.

TRAXLER, FRANZ (2000) ' "National Pacts and Wage Regulation in Europe": A Comparative Analysis', in Giuseppe Fajertag and Philippe Pochet (eds.), *Social Pacts in Europe: New Dynamics*, (Brussels: European Trade Union Institute/Observatoire Social Européen), 401–17.

——SABINE BLASCHKE, and BERNARD KITTEL (eds.) (2001). *National Labour Relations in Internationalized Markets: A Comparative Study of Institutions, Change, and Performance*, (Oxford: Oxford University Press).

TREU, TIZIANO (1992). *Participation in Public Policy-Making: The Role of Trade Unions and Employers' Associations*, (Berlin: Aldine de Gruyter).

TRUBEK, DAVID M. and JAMES S. MOSHER (2003). 'New Governance, Employment Policy, and the European Social Model', in Jonathan Zeitlin and David M. Trubek (eds.), *Governing Work and Welfare in a New Economy: European and American Experiments*, (Oxford: Oxford University Press), 33–58.

VOGEL, STEVEN K. (1996). *Freer Markets, More Rules: Regulatory Reform in Advanced Industrial Countries*, (Ithaca, NY: Cornell University Press).

WEISS, LINDA (ed.) (2003). *States in the Global Economy: Bringing Domestic Institutions Back In*, (Cambridge: Cambridge University Press).

WILLIAMSON, OLIVER (1985). *The Economic Institutions of Capitalism: Firms, Markets, Relational Contracting,* (New York: Free Press).

WILLIAMSON, OLIVER (1985). *The Economic Institutions of Capitalism: Firms, Markets, Relational Contracting,* (New York: Free Press).

WILTHAGEN, TON and FRANK TROS (2004). 'The Concept of "Flexicurity": A New Approach to Regulating Employment and Labour Markets', *Transfer* 10(2): 166–87.

WORLD BANK, *Doing Business Database* (DB), http://rru.worldbank.org/DoingBusiness.

——*Investment Climate Survey* (IC), http://rru.worldbank.org/investmentclimate

WORLD ECONOMIC FORUM, *Global Competitiveness Report,* http://www.weforum.org/en/initiatives/gcp/Global%20Competitiveness%20Report/index.htm

WORLD ECONOMIC OUTLOOK, The International Monetary Fund, Sept. 2004, ch. III, 'Building Institutions', http://www.imf.org/external/pubs/ft/weo/2005/02/pdf/chapter3.pdf

ZEITLIN, JONATHAN (2003). 'Introduction: Governing Work and Welfare in a New Economy: European and American Experiments', in Jonathan Zeitlin and David M. Trubek (eds.), *Governing Work and Welfare in a New Economy: European and American Experiments,* (Oxford: Oxford University Press), 1–32.

——(2005). 'Conclusion. The Open Method of Coordination in Action: Theoretical Promise, Empirical Realities, Reform Strategy', in Jonathan Zeitlin, Philippe Pochet and Lars Magnusson (eds.), *The Open Method of Co-ordination in Action: The European Employment and Social Inclusion Strategies,* (Brussels: PIE Peter Lang).

——and CHARLES SABEL (2007). 'Learning from Difference. The New Architecture of Experimentalist Governance in Europe', *European Governance Papers (EUROGOV,* (Columbia University, Columbia Law School). http://scholar.google.dk/scholar?hl=da&rlz=1T4ADBR_enIT261IT261&q=author:%22Sabel%22+intitle:%22Learning+from+Difference:+The+New+Architecture+of+ . . . %22+&um=1&ie=UTF-8&oi=scholarr

....

INSTITUTIONS IN HISTORY: BRINGING CAPITALISM BACK IN

....

WOLFGANG STREECK

INTRODUCTION

....

> Political economy, in the widest sense, is the science of the laws governing
> the production and exchange of the material means of subsistence in
> human society . . . The conditions under which men produce and exchange
> vary from country to country, and within each country again from gener-
> ation to generation. Political economy, therefore, cannot be the same for
> all countries and for all historical epochs.
>
> (Friedrich Engels, [1878] (1947) *Anti-Dühring. Herr Eugen Dühring's
> Revolution in Science* (Progress Publishers), Part II, ch. 1)

Classical social science explored how the modern way of life grew out of the past, and
what this might imply for the future. Both early sociology and early economics
studied in one the 'functioning' and the 'transformation' of the emerging political-
economic institutions of capitalist society. In the writings of Marx, Durkheim, and
Weber—even of Adam Smith, and certainly of Schumpeter—static and dynamic

analyses were inseparable: the way modern institutions worked was explained in terms of their location in a historical process while the way that process would continue was assumed to be driven by institutions' present functions and dysfunctions.

The modern social sciences, in comparison, tend to be satisfied with a more static perspective. Empirical observations are organized into abstract concepts and property spaces that supposedly apply to all human societies at all times, without allowing for differences caused by historical or geographic location.[1] Clearly, the search for historically universal and invariant laws reflects the model of the physical sciences, which mostly feel comfortable assuming that they are dealing with an invariant, ahistorical nature. Another reason may be identification with that powerful disciplinary aggressor, modern economics—which, in mimicking eighteenth-century mechanics,[2] has long ceased to add indices of time and place to the supposedly universal principles it claims to discover.

A static approach also prevails in the comparative study of institutions, and sometimes even among those who consider themselves contributors to what is called 'historical institutionalism'. This is not difficult to understand. Comparative institutionalism as a theoretical concern in politics and political economy emerged out of a critical response to two dominant streams of social science in the 1960s: pluralist industrialism and orthodox Marxism (on the following see Streeck 2006). Both advertised themselves as theories of political-economic change, each of which offered its own grand historical narrative. Pluralist industrialism (Kerr et al. 1960)—or more generally, modernization theory—told of impending worldwide convergence somewhere between the political-economic models of the US and the then USSR, implying an end to ideological politics as known at the time, and its replacement with rational technocratic administration of the constraints and opportunities of industrial modernity. Orthodox Marxism, by contrast, predicted a gradual but irreversible decline of capitalism as a result of its own success, with an ever-growing organic composition of capital as the ultimate destiny and fate of the capitalist accumulation regime. Comparative politics and institutionalist political economy were rightly sceptical of both. Arguing against pluralist industrialism, they insisted on the continuing significance of politics as a collective agency and as a source of diversity in social organization. And in contrast to orthodox Marxism, they emphasized the capacity of the social institutions into which modern capitalism is organized—including the state—to modify and even suspend the alleged 'laws of motion' of the capitalist accumulation regime.

---

[1] I define a property space as a set of properties, or dimensions of measurement, conceived as variables with a finite range of possible values. It is populated by units, or cases, which are discrete combinations of variable or constant properties. The universe—or the units in it—changes when at least one property assumes a new value. Properties and units are related to other properties and units in partly unknown but in principle knowable ways, with change in an 'independent' property 'causing' proportionate change in a 'dependent' one. Theory is conceived as a template, which allows for the subsumption of any unit or measurement under a specified set of general, universal categories, properties, and relations.

[2] Adam Smith's favourite discipline as a university teacher was—Newtonian—astronomy.

In the process, however, comparative institutional analysis lost sight of the two main subjects of social science since its rise in the nineteenth century: the historical dynamics of the social world and the evolution of capitalism. In a healthy reaction against the implied teleological determinism of the leading macro-sociological paradigms of the 1950s and 1960s, what had begun as an investigation of the underlying social and economic forces driving the development of modern society turned into a 'comparative statics' of individual socio-economic institutions—mostly but not systematically located in contemporary capitalism. More often than not, comparative institutionalism turned into pseudo-universalistic 'variable sociology': if you have centralized collective bargaining and an independent central bank, you can expect an inflation rate lower or higher than that of countries whose institutional *ameublement* is different. The fact that most of the cases under examination were confined to a very small universe in time and space did not seem to matter. 'Historical' institutionalism meritoriously added policy legacies and institutional pasts to the set of variables that were routinely considered when trying to account for the structures and outcomes of political-economic institutions. Typically, however, it was not really history that was brought into play but—as in the study of 'path-dependency'—the costs of change as compared to its expected returns (Arthur 1994; Pierson 2004).

In this Epilogue to what has become an impressive attempt to codify the state of the art in comparative institutional analysis, I will take advantage of the liberty conceded to me by the editors and use my allotted space to explain what I believe will—or in any case, should—be the future frontiers of institutionalist political economy. In particular, I will make three points.

First, I will argue that progress in comparative institutional analysis will require a return from a static to a dynamic perspective. Developing such a perspective will be possible, I believe, if we use current work on institutional change, comparative or not, as a starting point, drawing on its core concepts for an approach in which change is no longer a special case but a universal condition of any social order. In effect, this will eradicate the distinction between institutional statics and institutional dynamics, conceived of as different states of the world requiring different conceptual frameworks.

Second, and related to this, I will address the challenge of placing individual institutions and their comparative analysis into a broader systemic context by locating them in a structured historical process. The question that will need to be discussed here is whether our theories and methods have the capacity to detect regularities in the continuous transformation of social institutions, or whether our justified suspicion of teleological accounts of history as unidirectional 'development', with the various implications that have been attached to them in the past, requires us to overlook the forest, if there be one, and recognize only single trees. Is institutional change just random fluctuation, or can it be a transition from one state of 'development' to another? In this context, I will revisit the old issue of historical direction and 'progress' that dominated nineteenth-century social science and continued to be present until the 1960s, when it was finally abandoned as intractable or politically incorrect or both.[3] The theoretical problem behind this is, of course, that of the apparently perennial tension between historical and systematic explanations in the social sciences, or between agency and contingency on the one hand and possible 'laws' of historical change on the other. The difficulties that we encounter here are so enormous that even Max Weber shied away from them—with the result that much of modern social science feels excused if it prefers to ignore them.

Third and finally, I will suggest that capturing the inevitably dynamic nature of social institutions—and of social order in general—will make it necessary to move beyond the universal and timeless concepts that much of social science still believes are required for scientific respectability to an analytical framework that is adapted to the historical specificities of concrete social formations.[4] In the case of the political economy of contemporary societies, the social formation in question is modern capitalism, just as it was in the nineteenth century when social science originated. In the same way that economic action is always 'embedded' in a society, I argue that institutional analysis of the contemporary political economy, comparative or not, should be situated within the context of a substantive theory of capitalism,[5] to be informed and enriched by it as well as contributing to its improvement. The general idea is that social science, perhaps unlike some of the natural sciences, benefits not from ever-advancing abstraction and generalization, but on the contrary, from fitting its theoretical template to the historical specificity of whatever society it is dealing with.

INSTITUTIONAL DYNAMICS

To clarify what I mean by a dynamic perspective on social institutions, I will begin—for reasons that will become apparent shortly—with the frequently made distinction, often just implicit, between 'real' and marginal institutional change. This distinction is of no small importance. Theoretical as well as political debates often become mired in the question of whether an observed or imagined change in the properties of a given institutional arrangement will cause it to be replaced by something new or, on the contrary, stabilize it: whether, in other words, the change is revolutionary or reformative in nature. To many, the only way to settle such disputes appears to be by definitional fiat, treating it as a matter of convention whether or not a given characteristic is central or peripheral to a specific institution or social order. For

---

[3] One could also suspect that as the Marxist vision of historical development finally fell into disrepute, the official American alternative seemed so unpalatable by the end of the 1960s that anything that looked like 'historical philosophy' was avoided.

[4] In other words, as will become more apparent below, I think that the quote from Friedrich Engels that introduces this paper is still of the highest methodological significance.

[5] For an extended argument to this effect, see Streeck (2009), in particular ch. 17.

example, one of the main themes in Tocqueville's late masterpiece on the *ancien régime* (Tocqueville 1983 [1856]) is whether it was the monarchy or administrative centralization that was the defining element of the institutional structure of pre-revolutionary France. Suggesting that it was the latter, Tocqueville concluded that in spite of all the bloodshed and the grandiose rhetoric, the rupture caused by the Revolution was far less significant than his contemporaries believed.

However, treating the continuity or discontinuity of a social order as a matter of definition is not always satisfactory, if only because definitions are ultimately arbitrary and everybody can feel free to stick to his own. The result tends to be fruitless debates of the sort of whether a glass is half full or half empty, the answer depending on one's point of view or on the mood of the day. An influential attempt to overcome this problem is Steven Krasner's suggestion (Krasner 1988) to distinguish between change and stability by assuming that social systems normally exist in a state of equilibrium, with change occurring only occasionally as a result of exogenous shocks. 'Real' change may then be recognized by the fact that it is rare and catastrophic, like defeat in war and subsequent conquest; whereas what others might consider incremental or gradual change serves in fact to defend and restore an existing order against environmental disturbances that are not strong enough to cause the system to break down. The upshot is that social institutions change by moving through a discontinuous or 'punctuated' sequence of temporarily stable equilibria, pushed on by a succession of short sharp shocks that are unpredictable from inside a system and force it to reconfigure itself from time to time for a new protracted period of stability.[6]

Krasner's model identifies 'real', i.e. transformative change with rapid systemic reorganization in response to an exogenous shock. In this way he makes it, at least in principle, empirically distinguishable from trivial, superficial, marginal, or restorative change, which may be recognized as such by the fact that it is gradual. The problem with this approach is that it runs counter to the intuition—based not least in everyday experience—that not only abrupt but also gradual change may have profound enough consequences to justify considering an institution or a social system to be fundamentally transformed. In historical institutionalism, the notion of 'gradual transformative change' was first advanced in the work of Kathleen Thelen (Thelen

---

[6] The concept of 'punctuated equilibrium', which Krasner uses to capture what he regards as the dynamics of institutional change, is taken from an important dissident stream in evolutionary biology (Gould and Lewontin 1979). I mention this because I will later also have recourse to evolutionary biology as a model for institutional analysis, and indeed partly to the same seminal article. In evolutionary biology, the notion of punctuated equilibrium is intended to account for the fact that the strict continuity, or gradualism, in the development of the life forms that the logic of Darwin's theory required is not fully borne out by the fossil record (e.g. the mystery of the 'Cambrian explosion'). Darwin insisted—and had to insist—that this could only have been because the fossil record is incomplete, for sound reasons of geology and natural history. By contrast, opponents of 'Darwinian fundamentalism' suggest that the fossil record may be less incomplete than Darwin thought and that there may have been long periods of relative stasis in natural history, interrupted by short moments of widespread and accelerated evolutionary change.

1999; 2002). With the concepts of 'conversion' and 'layering', Thelen offered two stylized, ideal-typical accounts of change processes, drawn from observation rather than from theory, which have in common that they take place slowly and incrementally and do not depend on exogenous shocks to get started.' Thelen's reconceptualization of institutional change opened up a perspective for modern institutional analysis on a type of change that is both continuous and fundamental, allowing for a much more dynamic concept of institutions than is possible in the long stability-short rupture model of punctuated equilibrium. It is important to note that conversion and layering were not meant to be an exhaustive typology. In joint work, we (Streeck and Thelen 2005) later added three more processes of gradual-cum-transformative institutional change: 'drift', 'displacement', and 'exhaustion', while leaving open the possibility that yet others may be found and stylized in comparable ways (see Thelen in this volume).

Rather than discussing the five types of incremental transformative change in detail, I will limit myself to noting that in all of them, the mechanism that makes for continuous revision of social institutions is their enactment. Institutions are norms that regulate social behaviour; they are realized and reproduced in practice through human agents applying them to their specific situations. Such enactment, as we have pointed out (Streeck and Thelen 2005), cannot be and never is mechanistic. The reason for this is that the conditions under which social rules are supposed to apply are inevitably unique and varying in time, due to the fact that the world is more complex than the principles we have devised to make it predictable. This forces actors to apply rules creatively, actualizing and modifying them in the process. Moreover, social actors are far from being norm-following machines; in fact they command a defining capacity to reinterpret or evade rules that are supposed to apply to them. Both creative modification and cunning circumvention are a permanent source of disturbance—and, from the perspective of the institution—of random variation from below, resulting in the reproduction of social institutions through their enactment being always and inevitably 'imperfect'. Time is crucial in this since in all five mechanisms of gradual transformation through imperfect reproduction, change accumulates only slowly, as a by-product of actors following rules 'in their own ways', either because they have to or because they want to.

Obviously, the Thelen and Streeck ideal types fall far short of settling the issue of how to distinguish real from trivial institutional change; but then again, they may ultimately render the distinction meaningless. While they clearly establish that gradual change may have deeply transformative effects, nowhere do they imply that 'all' gradual change is of this kind. Nor do they rule out the possibility that social systems may sometimes break down under the impact of exogenous shocks, bringing about the kind of rapid shift toward a radically new structure that is captured, even though unjustifiably privileged, by the punctuated equilibrium model. Further below, I will argue that the question of whether observed changes amount to fundamental systemic change cannot be decided in the abstract, but only in the context of a substantive theory of the historical social order in which they take place. Here I simply note that in hindsight, the most important contribution of the

Thelen and Streeck models seems to be that they introduce *time* into institutional analysis. In the punctuated equilibrium model, as in neo-classical economics, time is essentially irrelevant: How long the extended periods of stasis between the critical moments of punctuation last depends exclusively on contingent events that have nothing to do with how long they have already lasted; and the moments during which a system is reorganized are conceived as so infinitesimally short that they can ideally be considered as taking no time at all. In the Thelen and Streeck models, by contrast, institutions are, in principle, always in transition, with periods of stasis, if they occur at all, being so exceptional and short as to be negligible for theoretical purposes. In fact, conversion and layering (and later drift, displacement, and exhaustion) are defined as processes for which 'time is of the essence': they take place 'in time', and their effects accumulate 'with time'. 'Time matters' for them, but it matters 'all the time' and not just once in a while, since institutional change is basically conceived of as an unending process of 'learning' about the inevitably imperfect enactment of social rules in interaction with a complex and unpredictable environment.

Introducing time into institutional analysis—analysing 'institutions in time'— implies, among other things, that an important property of an institution may be its age. The longer an institution has been around, the more likely it is, everything else being equal, to have changed through layering or conversion, drift or displacement— certainly through exhaustion, and very likely through other, similar mechanisms. From here, it is not a long way to the notion that social institutions may be affected not just by the chronological time that has passed since their inception, but also by their location in historical time—i.e. in a more or less orderly succession of historically unique, contingent conditions and events. Taking this only a small step further and stretching the point somewhat, it appears that time passed may be something like a driver and even a 'cause' of institutional change. In fact, I suggest that it is precisely a conceptual framework like this, one in which time figures as a privileged explanatory factor, that distinguishes a dynamic from a static perspective on the social world in general and on institutional change in particular—a perspective that is complex enough to accommodate any combination gradual and disruptive change as well as to distinguish between trivial and non-trivial change on substantive rather than formal grounds.

Moving from a static approach to institutional theory to a dynamic one has deep ontological implications, which I can only touch upon here. The main point is that structures, or systems, must be reconceptualized as processes, and as irreversible ones if only because by occupying the time they take, they consume it once and for all, making it impossible for alternative processes to realize themselves in the same time-space.[7] How demanding it is to include time in an analytical framework, for the

---

[7] For an example see Streeck (2009), ch. 8. Irreversibility is the essence of historicity. Its meaning is illustrated by colloquial observations such as that you can turn eggs into scrambled eggs but not vice versa, or that you cannot put toothpaste back into the tube once it is out. A more respectable example is the second law of thermodynamics, or the law of increasing entropy, according to which differences in

social just as for any other world, is, or so it may seem to the uninitiated, illustrated by the difference between the three-dimensional Newtonian and the n-dimensional relativistic concept of space. The former is essentially time-invariant, regardless of all the motion going on inside it; the latter not only changes with time but is also, as the unfortunately unintelligible Einsteinian metaphor has it, 'bent' into it. Of course, the ultimate witness for a dynamic, processual perspective on the world is the ancient Greek philosopher, Heraclitus of Ephesus (540–475 BC) who, unfortunately, was not for nothing called 'the Obscure' already by his contemporaries. Even Plato, in the Kratylos dialogue, had to guess what Heraclitus had really meant to say: 'Heraclitus, I believe, says that all things go and nothing stays, and comparing existents to the flow of a river, he says you could not step twice into the same river.'[8]

Institutional analysis in Heraclitian fashion would assume that, as time passes, the social world continuously changes, not just ephemerally but fundamentally: constantly developing new properties and functioning according to ever-changing principles. The idea that one cannot step in the same river twice would have to be translated to mean that the historical process alters not just the 'properties' but the 'property space' of institutions and social orders, by turning variables into constants and constants into variables, redefining variable ranges, resetting parameters, introducing new kinds of units, and undoing or reversing causal links between properties as well as creating new ones. What happens changes the rules that govern what happens next, confronting actors at any given time with a world that is in part unexplored and will have changed further by the time it could, perhaps, be understood. Although this not only sounds metaphysical but in fact is, examples abound in the real world of politics and economics of events and developments that have irreversibly rewritten the rules of cause and effect, and redefined in an unforeseen way the realm of what is and is not possible: the combined liberalization and globalization of capitalism in the last two decades of the twentieth century; the privatization of council housing by the Thatcher government, which profoundly

---

temperature, density, and pressure in a closed system tend to even out over time, gradually and inevitably replacing order with disorder unless the process is halted from outside the system. The second law of thermodynamics is central to the work of the young Max Planck. Like the cosmological theory of an expanding universe, it may serve to show that biology is not the only natural science with an historical concept of the world.

[8] The shortest aphoristic formulation of Heraclitus' 'flow theory' consists of only two words: πάντα ρεί, everything flows. However, it comes not from Heraclitus himself but was attributed to him only several hundred years later. Interestingly, Heraclitus was also one of the first dialectical theorists. Fragment DK B10 posits: 'Connections: things whole and not whole, what is drawn together and what is drawn asunder, the harmonious and the discordant. The one is made up of all things, and all things issue from the one.' Goethe wrote two poems about Heraclitus, appropriately titled *Dauer im Wechsel* (Continuity in Change) and *Eins und Alles* (One and All). As always, he captures the core of the matter, and as always in irresistibly beautiful language. The second of the two poems brings together the two central Heraclitian themes, change and contradiction: '*Es soll sich regen, schaffend handeln,* | *Erst sich gestalten, dann verwandeln;* | *Nur scheinbar stehts Momente still.* | *Das Ewge regt sich fort in allen:* | *Denn alles muß in Nichts zerfallen,* | *Wenn es im Sein beharren will.*'

changed British electoral politics in favour of parties with a conservative programme; the introduction of social security in the United States, which created an active clientele strong enough to make social security politically sacrosanct (Campbell 2003); the self-destruction of Keynesian reflationary demand management as firms came rationally to expect ever-lower interest rates and ever-stronger fiscal stimulus; the slowly accumulating effects of solidaristic wage policies, increasing the pressure on firms to break away from multi-employer bargaining (Streeck 2009: ch. 2, *passim*); the gradual accumulation of public debt, reaching a point where the settlement of distributional conflicts by public dispensation of future resources becomes self-limiting or impossible; etc. (Streeck 2009: ch. 5).

Returning to my starting point, if the social world and its institutional order are, and ought to be, conceived of as inherently dynamic, it no longer makes much sense to distinguish between trivial and transformative institutional change. Instead, the question becomes whether our models of that world and the heuristics we apply in exploring it are capable of doing justice to its dynamic, historical-relativist nature, or whether they abstract from it for the sake of simplicity and convenience and organize it into a property space that is static or Newtonian. This question also applies to the study of institutional change, which we can imagine to be taking place within either a static or a historically dynamic set of parameters. Indeed, just as Newtonian mechanics can, even after the relativist revolution, still be usefully applied for limited purposes, a treatment of institutional change as fluctuation in a constant world—as it were: as 'static change'—may often be sufficient provided we restrict our theoretical ambitions. We should be aware, however, that findings generated in this way hold true only as long as one can afford to neglect their dynamic-historical context.

Summing up so far, static and dynamic concepts of institutional change may be compared as follows (Table 23.1). A static approach assumes that the 'laws governing the production and exchange of the material means of subsistence in human society' (Engels) apply at all times and everywhere. A dynamic approach, by contrast, recognizes time—and historical time in particular—as a force that is continuously reshaping institutions and the properties that define them. Where the institutional property space and the causal relationships existing within it are conceived of as constant and universal, individual institutions may change under the impact of changes in antecedent conditions, but there is nothing to prevent such conditions from returning to their former state and thereby reversing the change they have caused. Static change, in other words, knows no direction and is in principle always reversible. This is different with dynamic, historical change, whose location in an irreversible sequence is a defining characteristic. Furthermore, in a static perspective on change, institutions and social orders are as such considered stable, and change occurs only if it is forced on them from the outside; if the source of change is exogenous to the institution and its nature is contingent; the mode is that of Krasner's punctuated equilibrium; and the mechanism is unpredictable shocks strong enough to require structural adjustment. Dynamic change, by comparison, is mostly endogenous, as social orders are assumed to change on their own and from

Table 23.1: Two kinds of change

	Static change	Dynamic change
Property space	Constant universal	Historical periodic
Direction	Reversible fluctuating	Irreversible sequential
Source	Exogenous-contingent	Endogenous-dialectical Exogenous-contingent
Mode	Punctuated equilibrium	Incremental Crossing of thresholds
Mechanism	Short sharp shocks	Imperfect reproduction Time & age: layering, conversion, drift, exhaustion etc.

within under the impact of time: for example, as inherent contradictions mature. Like time, change proceeds incrementally, although there may be occasional fits and spurts where critical thresholds are crossed; and the central mechanism of institutional change, as pointed out, is the imperfect reproduction of institutions in the process of their enactment in time. Further on, I will return to some of these themes.

INSTITUTIONAL DEVELOPMENT

I have argued that a static conception of institutional change as reversible, fluctuating, and contingent cannot do justice to the historical nature of social structures—that is, to the fact that they are located in an irreversible sequence of events, and to the impact exerted on them by the passage of time. But how can we conceptualize the historically dynamic character of social arrangements? What pattern, if any, is governing the continuous transformation of the properties—actual as well as potential—of social arrangements over time? Does the historical process within which institutional change must be assumed to be taking place have a direction? The concept that inevitably comes to mind here is that of 'development'—a core concept, of course, of nineteenth- and twentieth-century social theory precisely because of its close association with historical philosophy and the notion of human progress. As previously noted, today's social science mostly prefers to be agnostic in this respect for a variety of reasons, and has instead taken refuge in an ahistorical, Newtonian image of its object world. If the theories this allows for are, however,

Table 23.2: The concept of development

	Development
Property space	Cumulative unfolding ('unwrapping') of embryonic pattern
Direction	Upward-growing
Source	Endogenous dynamic trumps exogenous contingencies
Mode	Continuous passing of successive thresholds and stages Maturation
Mechanism	Improved reproduction (learning)

found to miss essential aspects of that world, as I argue they do in the case of institutional change, it is impossible to avoid reopening the issue of whether and in what ways historical change may be governed by an underlying logic that in one way or other might be characterized as development. This is particularly true if we follow Engels's advice and specify the conceptual framework of historical-institutionalist analysis to fit the historical social formation of capitalism—a formation whose study has always been closely associated with the notion of a specific historical dynamic.

The concept of development is found in both the Latin and the Germanic languages, and interestingly, the basic meaning is always the same—in *développement* (French), *sviluppo* (Italian) and *desarrollo* (Spanish) as well as in *Entwicklung* (German) or *ontwikkling* (Dutch): the gradual release of something out of an 'envelope'— a hiding and confining condition, or a condition of being rolled or folded together. Development takes place where something that is already present *in nuce* comes out of a cover by which it was concealed and compressed, and starts gradually to unfold (Table 23.2).

In fact, it seems as though the notion of development is inseparable from that of growth: as something becomes unwrapped in the course of its development, it becomes bigger; and as it grows, it changes not only in size but also in structure, governed by rules of growth that were already present but not yet fully expressed in earlier, less developed stages. In fact, 'development' in modern, non-literal usage means orderly, regular, endogenous transformation in a process of growth controlled from within and proceeding according to a predetermined pattern, or *Bauplan*.[9] In this sense, development has mostly positive connotations—as in child development, human development, economic development, or social development—and tends to be identified with improvement and advancement. Its direction is imagined to be essentially forward and upward, with simultaneous growth and change driven from within (Table 23.2). In this mode, nineteenth-century theories of social development have posited an ultimately universal transition from 'lower' to 'higher' or from

---

[9] The German word, *Bauplan*, has come to be used in evolutionary biology to refer to the overall design of an organism. For more on evolution, see below.

'primitive' to 'advanced' societies—for example, in Durkheim's theorem of increasing 'dynamic density' causing functional differentiation (Durkheim 1964 [1893]); in Spencer's account of history as steady progress from status to contract (Spencer 2003 [1882]); or in Weber's grand narrative of a worldwide spread of occidental rationalism (Weber 2002 [1904/5]).[10] Similarly, after the Second World War, theories of 'modernization,' or 'industrialization,' assumed the presence of an irresistible endogenous force in contemporary societies, which moved them in a specifically 'Western' direction, at least once the seeds of 'development'—whatever they were believed to be—were sown and the necessary 'take-off' (Rostow 1990 [1960]) had set the process in motion. Soon it became common in United Nations parlance to distinguish between 'developed' und 'underdeveloped' countries, the latter soon to be renamed 'developing.' Conceptually, development involved the continuous crossing of thresholds and the passing into successive stages of a process of maturation in which societies learned to reproduce their social order in ways that made it continuously less traditional and more modern: i.e., more prosperous, equitable, efficient, democratic, and autonomous (Table 23.2).

What remains of the concept of development as a tool for understanding historical change if we leave behind post-war modernization theory and its obviously highly ideological connotations? I believe that today, the fundamental problem associated with any conceptualization of history as development is the inherent linearity and determinism of the implied process of transformative growth once it has started. Underlying this is a sense that development is governed by a pre-set, fixed endpoint toward which it is targeted—a future condition that is already present in embryonic, unfinished form in the current condition, which it strives to leave behind in order to realize itself. Development, in other words, is at its core a teleological concept: That which develops is pulled forward by a future state unfolding itself inside it and through it. Earlier stages contain later stages in unfinished, preliminary form, as in the growth of an organism from embryo to fully 'developed' adult. As the developing organism matures, it continuously passes thresholds, and while crises are possible the way they are resolved is also basically predetermined. The target, the *telos*, the *Ziel* is engraved into the process and is never in question: In fact, it is both the endpoint and the driver of the historical process through which it materializes.

History conceived of as development, then, is a frontloaded process governed by a pre-established final condition. This is why the notion of development has rightly—and, I believe, irredeemably—fallen into disrepute in the social sciences: It construes the social world in a deterministic fashion and leaves no space for agency and choice, conflict and contradiction, risk and uncertainty, and for the invention of the future as it unfolds. In many ways, developmentalism suffers from the same problem as did orthodox Marxism at the beginning of the twentieth century: If history is self-driven and progress is inevitable and self-sustained, why not just wait until it has completed

---

[10] I treat Marx's account of 'capitalist development' as a special case, for reasons that will be explained further on.

itself? If this seems unacceptable for reasons of practical experience and theoretical plausibility, the next question is whether rejecting teleological theories of historical change forces us to accept the nihilistic position that history is nothing but a chaotic sequence of reversible fluctuations. Is there something else beyond teleology other than accident and disorder?

A NOTE ON EVOLUTION

One way of addressing this question is by looking for a theoretical model of dynamic historical change in which the passage of time is a causal force; events and conditions are conceived as historically unique; and change, although driven by causes rather than pulled by effects, is illegibly patterned. The concept that suggests itself here is that of 'evolution'. Interestingly, the etymological origin of this word is very close to that of development. In Latin, *evolutio* means the unrolling of a scroll. Over time, the concept became linked to the notion of growth accompanied by the successive emergence of more complex structures, and in this sense, in fact, it did become partly synonymous with the concept of development. Remarkably, its first application to natural history is found in the writings of Charles Darwin's grandfather, Erasmus Darwin (1731–1802), although its modern usage was defined only by the grandson's epoch-making treatise on the origin of species (Darwin 2004 [1859]).

There have been innumerable attempts, both famous and infamous, to import Darwinian evolutionism into social science. To avoid a long albeit exciting discussion, I will simply suggest that there are several connotations to the concept of evolution as it is used today in evolutionary biology that are less than helpful, and in fact sometimes deeply misleading, when employed in the study of social order. Among the misapplications of biological-evolutionary theory to the social world are the following three in particular:

(1) *Socio-biological naturalism*, or *reductionism*, which suggests that social structures and social action are governed by biologically anchored, genetically hard-wired behavioural programmes inherited by humans through the long line of descent from their ancestors in the animal kingdom. Such programmes, all of them supposedly geared toward securing the survival of the species—or of a particular genetic strain within it—are imagined to function like a collective subconscious that is the deep cause of human behaviour and social arrangements, even where the latter are motivated by the actors involved in very different, non-biological, non-instinctive, normative terms.

(2) *Adaptive functionalism*, which posits that any trait exhibited by a species can and must be explained as a product of adaptation. Adaptation occurs through inter-generational selection, in the course of which a structure gradually changes to

become optimally capable of contributing to successful reproduction under conditions of a general 'struggle for existence'. Mainstream evolutionary biologists take this to mean that explanation of any structure requires the production of an 'adaptive story' which explains that structure as a superior solution to a problem faced in competition for reproductive opportunities. Especially when applied to the social world, the logic of this approach tends to give rise to a Panglossian functionalism,[11] which concludes that the mere fact that something exists means that it must be optimal for the fulfilment of some functional requirement, even if that requirement has yet to be detected. Theory, then, is the identification of the task for the performance of which a given thing represents an optimal solution. As far as the social sciences are concerned, it is in particular, but by no means only, efficiency and equilibrium theories that tend to exhibit a Panglossian logic.[12]

Nevertheless, even evolutionary biologists have noted that functionally backward explanations, or inductions, are highly dubious. The problem is not just that it is logically possible to invent an adaptive story about everything (Gould and Lewontin 1979). In addition, as Darwin already knew, the fitness of an organism can be assessed only in relation to its historical environment and the contingent challenges it happens to pose.[13] Assuming a priori that an observed structure must be perfect or ideal and from there interpolating the purpose that it perfectly and ideally serves may therefore be deeply misleading. In part, this is because in finding new solutions to newly arising problems, nature must work with the available organic material, which subjects evolution to what Gould and Lewontin (1979) call 'phyletic constraint' and makes the structures it creates less adapted to their purpose than they might ideally be if they could be designed 'from scratch'. For example, if a land-going animal returns to the sea, as did the ancestors of the whales, it cannot redevelop gills instead of lungs, even though gills would be

---

[11] Dr Pangloss is a character in a satirical novel by Voltaire, *Candide, ou l'Optimisme* (1759). His is a Leibnizian rational-deductive optimism, as expressed in his favorite dictum, 'All is for the best in the best of all possible worlds,' a philosophy that he continues to assert in the face of the most deplorable conditions and events. The logic he invokes—which Voltaire ridicules while Leibniz considered it a satisfactory solution to the problem of theodicy—is that the existing world is the *only* world that exists, and since only one world *can* exist it is the *only possible* world. If only one world is possible, however, then the world that exists must be the best world in the universe of N=1 possible worlds.

[12] For more on this see Streeck (2009), especially ch. 13.

[13] 'As natural selection acts by competition, it adapts the inhabitants of each country only in relation to the degree of perfection of their associates . . . Nor ought we to marvel if all the contrivances in nature, be not, as far as we can judge, absolutely perfect; and if some of them be abhorrent to our idea of fitness. . . . The wonder indeed is, on the theory of natural selection, that more cases of the want of absolute perfection have not been observed . . .' (Darwin 2004 [1859], 507 f.) See also the example of the bug Darwin discovered on an island which contained almost no flying insects. Apparently its ancestors had been those mutants of a former species that were not very good at flying. The better fliers were regularly driven into the sea by the strong winds, and they became extinct. Fittest for the 'struggle for existence' were those individuals that were least fit for flying.

much better adapted to its new-old environment. Furthermore, there is the possibility that an observed structure is 'not yet' optimally adapted as it is still in the process of gradually evolving toward optimality—a possibility that biologists may feel they can discount because of the geological time periods with which they are dealing. Social scientists, however, are concerned with comparatively very short time spans, during which it is not only possible, but in fact likely, that whatever structure they observe is still making its way toward optimality and equilibrium if at all, and in fact, due to fast-changing external conditions, may be best conceived as being in permanent transition.

(3) *Social Darwinism*, which is a prescriptive political ideology that stipulates that free markets and laissez-faire economic policies are optimal institutions for economic and social progress. They are believed to be that because they seem best to replicate the Darwinian 'struggle for existence', through which nature eliminates less 'fit' individuals from procreation and thereby continually improves and progressively optimizes the properties of organisms and species. Note that the key phrase of Social Darwinism, 'survival of the fittest', was not coined by Darwin but by the sociologist and philosopher Herbert Spencer,[14] who was certainly the most influential Social Darwinist. Darwin approved of the phrase when he read it and later adopted it, as it accorded with his deep-seated Malthusian convictions that had influenced his view of natural history early on. Today, of course, we understand that in human societies the institutions, including free markets, that determine the characteristics by which individuals are selected are not naturally given, but are a result of cultural and political choices. One implication is that the character traits that are 'fittest' for a competitive market may not be the only ones that a society may want to preserve in its members as they 'struggle for existence'—whatever that may mean in a social context.[15]

Outside of socio-biological reductionism, Panglossian adaptive functionalism, and Spencerian free market Social Darwinism, however, there are a number of elements in Darwinian evolutionary theory which appear highly suitable for import into a dynamic theory of institutional change (on the following see also Krasner 1988):

---

[14] See his *Principles of Biology* of 1864.

[15] A variant of Social Darwinism is the economistic, rational-choice version of neo-institutionalism. In rational-choice theory of institutional change, alternative institutional solutions to problems of economic efficiency are, as it were, experimentally generated by and within societies, where they then compete in a market for institutions in which the most efficient solution is selected and retained. This assumes, among other things, that institutions are created—or even rationally designed—to be efficient, and that there is something like a perfect market for institutions. One of the most obvious problems with this is how to explain the stubborn survival of 'inefficient' institutions. We suggest that evolutionary variation in social orders is not typically caused by design of competing institutions but by the imperfect, or innovative, enactment of extant ones. Moreover, we posit that institutional selection takes place not through competitive markets, but through processes of political and social control, including the reactions of rule-makers to the unruly behaviour of rule-takers (Streeck and Thelen 2005).

(1) The variation-cum-selective-retention model of natural history offers a concept of historical change that is distinctly non-teleological—i.e. not conditioned on the presence of a provident and all-powerful designer guiding change to a preconceived end. In Darwinism properly understood, variation is stochastic from the perspective of existing structures while retention is systematic without, however, being governed by a predetermined, intended result. As noted, unlike development, evolution is driven by causes, not by effects: It is back loaded rather than front loaded. A theory of institutional change constructed on the model of evolutionary theory, therefore, need not assume that the design of an institution is controlled by actors who know what they want and what they are doing, and have the capacity to do it.[16]

(2) In Darwinian evolution, change is both permanent and gradual, endogenously driven by stochastic imperfections in reproduction as well as exogenously conditioned either by random shocks such as natural disasters or by other, parallel processes of gradual change. The theory provides for unpredictable 'events' as well as for coherent 'sequences of events'. Evolutionary natural history accommodates contingency into order conceived as historical, suggesting the possibility in turn to think not only of nature but also of history as of an evolutionary process.

(3) The non-teleological continuity of evolutionary change—due to randomness of internal variation and exogeneity of selection—makes Darwin's world a genuinely Heraclitian world. Darwinian evolutionary theory can therefore serve as a model for a processual theory of social systems in which an explainable past and present meet with an open future for which human action and practice matter. A Darwinian historical-evolutionary perspective seems better to reflect the experience of human actors as historical actors in an historical world than do functionalist or rationalist sociological or economic theories.

(4) Darwinian evolutionism understands the causal contribution of the passage of time to structural change, just as it reserves a conceptual space for innovation through imperfect, deviant reproduction. In fact, evolutionary theory suggests that innovation is permanent and ongoing as there can be no perfect replication of any extant structure over time. This is in line with an Heraclitian concept of institutional change for which the perfect replication of a social institution in its enactment represents no more than a limiting case. Moreover, evolutionary theory appreciates the essentially anarchic or, which is the same, creative nature of innovation, conceiving of it as arising spontaneously and unpredictably from the perspective of the existing order and of established practice. Theoretical Darwinism also understands how processes of co-evolution may lead to complex non-linear interactions between the causal forces that shape historical structures and events which, again, cannot be predicted. Furthermore, co-evolution can serve as a model of separate lines of causation and sequences of events merging into a broad stream of systemic

---

[16] At the same time, there is no logical reason to preclude the possibility that the mechanism of selection may be one of collective-political decision-making.

change through mutual support or mutual subversion.[17] In these and other respects, Darwinian theory, when properly understood, is capable of restoring to the social sciences their good conscience in construing their object world as historically unique, a good conscience they seem to have lost in their encounter with modern economics and its godfather, eighteenth-century physics.

(5) As already mentioned, Darwinian evolutionism entails a conception of nature as a continuous historical process in which previous events circumscribe current and future ones. Evolution can only work with and transform material that it has itself produced in the past and inherited from that past. This material is not infinitely malleable—which is captured by the concept of phyletic constraint. New designs meeting new demands must be gradually developed out of old designs adapted to old demands. In evolutionary theory, structural change results from an encounter between underdetermined and unpredictable innovations and historically-grown determining conditions. Its ultimate direction depends upon which of the many continuously-arising combinations of old and new best meet the challenges and exploit the opportunities inherent in the internal and external environment. The affinity to notions of path dependency in the social sciences is obvious, especially to more sophisticated theories which provide for the possibility of significant change even on an established path, in addition or as an alternative to change from one path to another. Properly understood, evolutionary theory also militates against voluntaristic theories of action where the new arises out of nothing, as well as against static conceptions of the world as a constant analytical universe in which change can be undone at any time if the factors that have caused it disappear.

(6) Finally, also as indicated, Darwinian evolutionism in its pluralist version allows for less-than-optimal structures caused by, among other things, phyletic constraint, transitional disequilibrium, survival of historical adaptations that have become useless, and the purposeless reproduction of slack structures with no function at all. Functionalist explanations apply only to a limited range of phenomena. The message for the social sciences is that outside of adaptationist Darwinian dogmatism, for which organisms are by definition optimally rationalized reproduction machines, evolutionary theory is 'not' an efficiency theory, which makes it illegitimate for neo-classical economics to justify its foundational assumptions by anchoring them in evolutionary biology. Rather than providing a template for a functionalist efficiency-theoretical account of the world, evolutionary biology conceives of adaptation as embedded *in* and interacting *with* a historical context that cannot itself be explained as an outcome of rational construction aimed at maximizing efficiency. The implication is that evolutionary theory can be read as encouraging a historical approach to institutions and institutional change, which allows for historical as well as rational-functionalist explanations of observed conditions and makes it necessary precisely to theorize the limits of rationalization and functional explanations within evolving structures and processes.

---

[17] See Streeck (2009), ch. 7.

Darwinian evolutionism, that is to say, may serve as a model for a theory of institutional change in several ways. It provides an example of a non-teleological but nevertheless intelligible account of history in which the future is not predetermined, leaving space for human agency. It identifies imperfect reproduction as a source of continuous gradual change, and thereby defines a place where a (micro-) theory of action might be inserted into a dynamic (macro-) theory of social order. It elaborates a processual view of the natural world, which seems eminently transferrable to the social world; it introduces time as a central variable in a theory of nature, by implication suggesting its inclusion in theories of society as well; it demonstrates how path dependency may be accommodated in a non-teleological theory of change, recognizing the causal significance of past events for present and future ones; and when read correctly, it is fundamentally subversive of an efficiency-theoretical construction of historical structures and processes, making space for explicit recognition of the role of non-efficient or non-rational forces in the evolution of social order.

At least one central issue remains unresolved, however, which is the question of the direction of historical change or, for that matter, of development. The nineteenth century and Darwin himself as a matter of course considered evolution to be a more or less linear progression from 'lower' to 'higher' forms of life, its crowning peak being *homo sapiens*. 'Higher' forms of life were more composite organisms that combined an ever larger number of heterogeneous parts into a complex, organic, well-coordinated whole. Note that this was exactly the way Durkheim defined his 'higher', 'advanced' societies, based on organic as distinguished from mechanical solidarity. But just as the social sciences dissociated themselves from the notion of progress in the second half of the twentieth century, so, too, did evolutionary biology with the emergence of the neo-Darwinian synthesis. In fact, the way this happened was very similar, as the discovery of the genetic base of inheritance and mutation caused something like a micro-analytical turn in evolutionary theory comparable to the search in neo-classical economics for a universal, ahistoric theoretical 'micro-foundation'. In the new mainstream of evolutionary biology, it was the gene—now characteristically described as 'egoistic'—that became the agent of combat in the 'struggle for existence'. Organisms turned into vessels used by opportunistic genes to secure their survival at the expense of less well entrenched competitors (Dawkins 1989). Like actors in neo-classical economics, genes in modern evolutionary biology do not change; they know no progress; and their highest and only goal is survival, for the sake of which they may combine with other genes in composite structures, but only for strategic purposes.

The problem this raises is well known also to macro-sociologists deprived of the notion of development by the relativistic revolution: How can one explain the enormous build-up of complexity over the *longue durée* of history, natural as well as social, culminating in biological evolution in the human brain, and in social evolution in the rise of modern European, American, or global society? If survival in competition, of monadic genes or monadic actors, was all that the world is about, how is one to account for the growth of ever larger and ever more internally

differentiated structures, with proportionately growing needs for ever more sophisticated and ever more vulnerable mechanisms of coordination? The ultimate provo-
cation for late twentieth-century evolutionary biology is the observation that, if the
survival of egoistic genes was all that mattered in natural history, there would have
been no need whatsoever for life to 'advance' beyond the 'primitive' condition of
bacteria living on the ocean floor, where they have reproduced with unmatched
success in a basically unaltered form since the beginning of time. Why make the effort
and build ever more complex organisms that are also unendingly more at risk? What
is it that drives nature's, and society's, apparently endemic quest for continuously
rising levels of organized complexity? We may not be able to answer this question
unless we are willing to assume that deep within organic matter there is some sort of
desire not just for survival, but also for the autonomy, or freedom, or 'mastery' that
comes with complexity (Neuweiler 2008). Be this as it may, contemporary debates
among evolutionary biologists about whether or not there is something like self-
organized direction in evolution even in the absence of telos and design, encourage
us as social scientists no longer to suppress the analogous question in social theory:
What lies behind the historical 'progress' towards more complex and differentiated
societies and social-institutional orders, and why is there an apparent tendency for
segmental societies to become linked into composite ones over time, and for simple
social structures to become more complex?

CAPITALIST DEVELOPMENT

I will now proceed to argue that some of the historical specifications required for a
dynamic theory of contemporary institutions, or a theory of contemporary institutional
change, development, or evolution, may be contributed by a conceptualization of
capitalism as a system, or process, of social action. By capitalism as a system of social
action, or as an institutionalized social order, I mean a specific set of institutions
accommodating a specific, regularized actor disposition (*habitus*, character) and a
specific distribution of resources, or powers of agency. I do not claim that an account
of contemporary society as a process of capitalist institutional development will explain
everything, nor of course will it be capable of predicting the future. All it can aspire to,
I believe, is to serve as a heuristic indicating where to look first and what to look for
when trying to understand institutions and institutional change in the modern political
economy. In fact given the central role of human agency in history and society, anything
other than a heuristic providing observers and actors with a checklist to work through
when trying to come to terms with the social world may be impossible anyway.

In the following, I will suggest a list of what I think could be elements of an
institutionalist account of capitalism and capitalist development capable of founding
a historically grounded comparative analysis of contemporary political-economic

Table 23.3: Development and capitalist development

	Development	Capitalist development
Property space	Cumulative unfolding ('unwrapping') of embryonic pattern	Unfolding & expanding of market relations and extended reproduction
Direction	Upward-growing	Sideward-growing
Source	Endogenous dynamic trumps exogenous contingencies	Endogenous pressures for capital accumulation ('profit')
Mode	Continuous passing of successive thresholds and stages Maturation	Discontinuous sequence of subversion and restoration of order
Mechanism	Improved reproduction (learning)	Competitive innovation

institutions and their change. The critical reader will note that the list is still rather syncretistic and in dire need of systematic revision and completion.[18]

(1) Capitalist development may be conceived as a process of expansion of market relations as the privileged, normal mode of economic exchange and social intercourse (Table 23.3)—of competitive contracting at prices that fluctuate with changes in the relation between supply and demand. As capitalism develops, market exchange gradually takes the place of older forms of social relations, in particular ones based on obligations of reciprocity. The widening, or spatial spread, of markets coincides with their deepening, or intensification, as more and more social spheres and an increasing range of 'necessaries of life' (Adam Smith) become commodified—i.e. subsumed under a 'self-regulating' price mechanism driven by actors' self-interest, and made available in exchange for *'bare Zahlung'* (Karl Marx). The spread of market relations over ever new territorial spaces and social spheres, metaphorically characterized by Rosa Luxemburg (Luxemburg 1913) in her theory of imperialism as a process of *Landnahme* (land grabbing), continuously and irreversibly changes the property space of social orders and gives direction to their evolution, linking previously parochial, or particularistic, social relations into ever more encompassing, increasingly universal contexts (Marx and Engels' 'completion of the world market' by the 'bourgeoisie', as anticipated in the *Manifesto* of 1848).

(2) Capitalist *Landnahme*, the widening and deepening of market relations, is associated with a continuous restructuring of a society's apparatus of social regulation and coordination. (This is a notion well known to sociologists ever since Durkheim, in the *Division of Labor*, linked the transition from mechanic to organic solidarity

---

[18] I have introduced some of the following points at greater length in my book, *Re-Forming Capitalism* (Streeck 2009).

Table 23.4: Two types of political-economic institutions

Durkheimian	Williamsonian
Public order	Private ordering
Obligational	Voluntaristic
Exogenously imposed	Endogenously contracted
Authoritative organization	Voluntary coordination
Creation of obligations	Reduction of transaction costs
Third party enforcement	Self-enforcement
Government	Governance
Status	Contract

Source: Adapted from Streeck (2009: 155).

to increases in a society's size and density.) In the language of institutional analysis, the institutional change that comes with market expansion may be conceived in terms of a dialectical conflict between two types of institutions, obligatory and voluntaristic, or historically inherited and freely contracted (Table 23.4).

Elsewhere (Streeck 2009), I have called the two types Durkheimian and Williamsonian, respectively.[19] They correspond to two kinds of social order, one public and the other, private. Liberal progressivism, first and foremost Herbert Spencer, has described and still describes the expansion of markets as a long-term historical process replacing obligatory with contractual institutions—as an escape from traditionalism and as progress toward economic rationalization and political liberation. Durkheim, of course, argued that the regime of free contracts governing the division of labour could unfold only inside a society inherited, inevitably, from tradition: the 'order of freedom' must remain 'embedded', to use the key concept of contemporary economic sociology, in an 'order of obligation'. Unlike the various Robinsonian founding myths of modernity, society is, even under capitalism, not a 'product' of competitive contracting but its 'precondition'. A world constituted by contract alone—a Spencerian liberal utopia—is to Durkheim, in Polanyian language, no more than a 'frivolous experiment' that is doomed to fail.[20] In any case, the distinction between Durkheimian and Williamsonian institutions seems to offer an appropriate template for studying institutional change and the transformation of social order in societies driven by the dynamic of an expanding capitalist market.

(3) In a more substantive sense, social institutions under capitalism must circumscribe productive uncertainty with protective solidarity, as uncertainty must be

---

[19] In some of the institutionalist literature they appear as competing conceptualizations—rational choice vs. historical-sociological—of institutions in general.

[20] This is nicely summarized in Joseph Schumpeter's famous dictum, 'No social system can work which is based exclusively upon a network of free contracts between (legally) equal contracting parties and in which everyone is supposed to be guided by nothing except his own (short-run) utilitarian ends' (Schumpeter 1975 [1942], 417).

contained for the sake of both the functioning of the market and the stability of its surrounding society. As theorists from Marx to Polanyi have pointed out, self-regulating markets permanently destabilize social structures as they continuously and unpredictably reset relative prices. This is ultimately why they cannot replace social regulation but in fact must be subjected to it. Nevertheless, as markets expand they self-destructively eat into and threaten to replace non-market institutions, causing permanent tension at the borderline between the encircled market system trying to break out of its social containment, and the non-contractual institutions containing it. Even though markets cannot function without solidarity, they nevertheless undermine and consume it, calling forth as they advance pressures for a restoration of the non-utilitarian, obligational bases of social order.

(4) The distinction between Durkheimian and Williamsonian institutions yields a substantive concept of politics in capitalism as a struggle over the periodic reorganization of institutionalized social obligations in response to advancing contractual order, market expansion, and commodification. Societies with a market system residing inside them like a restless incubus must defend themselves against the market trying to break through and get out, a drive endemic in the logic of *Landnahme*, regardless of the fact that outside of a surrounding society market systems could not function. Politics under capitalism, then, is about the successive subversion and reorganization of public order, driven by the anomic and entropic tendencies emanating from self-regulating markets, and about the de- and reconstruction of normatively institutionalized limits on the egoistic-rational pursuit of interests.[21] A possible sequence of gradual market expansion, the liberalization and contractualization of institutions, and the periodic and inevitably provisional restoration of public order in 'political moments' (Streeck 2001) is shown in Figure 23.1.

(5) Studying institutional change as capitalist development provides institutional analysis with a substantive micro-foundation in a theory of social action that is far more complex and meaningful than, in particular, a theory of 'rational choice.' A firmer historical grounding of historical institutionalism, with capitalism 'brought back in', makes for a richer model of the actor in what has been called 'actor-centered institutionalism' (Mayntz and Scharpf 1995). In particular, the notion of capitalist development may be associated with the advance of a typically opportunistic, non-traditionalist, individualistic, rational-egoistic, and utility-maximizing actor disposition. 'Opportunism with guile' (Williamson 1987), as definitive of the *homo oeconomicus* of economic theory, represents the normalized ethos in the enactment of institutions in a historical context in which a competitive breach of solidarity is in principle socially licensed, and can never in any case be prevented or ruled out, and where restricting competition is

---

[21] This is at the core of what Marx called 'class struggle'.

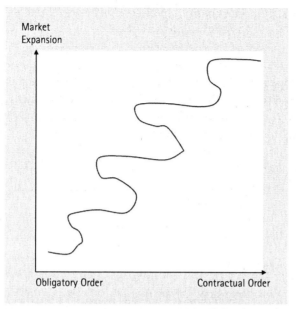

Figure 23.1: Political cycles in capitalism

fundamentally less legitimate than engaging in it (Streeck 2009: 242 ff.). Capitalist institutions must assume, and thereby encourage, a utility-maximizing disposition on the part of actors, given that any compact between potential competitors may at any time fall apart if only one market participant is no longer satisfied with an average customary rate of profit, threatening by breaking away the survival of the others unless they retort in kind.

(6) Actors in capitalism, therefore, given their characteristic non-traditionalist restlessness, appear *constitutively devious* from the perspective of the institutions that are supposed to govern them. The typical rule-taker in capitalism is a rule-bender: he reads rules entrepreneurially, i.e. 'in bad faith,' incessantly looking for ways of interpreting them in his favour. Typical capitalist actors are rational-utilitarian exploiters of gaps in rules, in a culture that fundamentally approves of innovation in rule following, if not in rule violation, and has few legitimate means to enforce informal traditional standards of good faith. Creative enactment or non-enactment of rules may, after all, be an important source of profit, and can routinely be justified as a necessary pre-emptive defence against elimination by competition. Interactions between rule-makers and rule-takers (Streeck and Thelen 2005) assume a specific flavour in capitalism that makes them specifically capitalist, with actors assumed and expected to be

fundamentally unruly: a permanent source of disorder from the perspective of social institutions, relentlessly whacking away at social rules, continuously forcing rulers to rewrite them, and undoing them again by creatively exploiting the inevitable gap between general rules and their local enactment.   (Streeck 2009: 241)

(7) This being so, while social order is always and inevitably imperfectly enacted, imperfect enactment under capitalism may be expected to be biased, and exhibit a specific substantive 'spin,' in the direction of liberalization and privatization, and indeed of 'disorganization' from the perspective of obligatory institutions. Creative reinterpretation of public order to replace it with private ordering may be construed as the micro-level dynamic at the base of the macro-level process of market expansion, giving historical definition to the general notion of unpredictable mutation in the production and reproduction of social structures. What is mutation for the evolution of life is the innovative individually-rational pursuit of advantage through competitive contracting for capitalist development. The resulting institutional dynamic is likely to be particularly visible at the border between market and society where social institutions condition and limit market exchange. Again competition seems to be the driving force as competitive contracting is assumed a priori to be legal whereas 'conspiracy against free trade' is a priori under suspicion of being illegal unless it is explicitly legalized; if it is, however, it is as any other rule exposed to competitive subversion. As pointed out, the power of competition to shape social relations derives from the fact that one individual is in principle enough to break up solidarity, whereas preventing competition requires collective action and, in principle, full cooperation among all potential competitors.

(8) Another mechanism that biases capitalist institutional change in the direction of market expansion and liberalization, as well as imparting a specific bias on political struggles over the reorganization of collective order, is the differential endowment of classes of social actors with resources, which is correlated with a differential distribution of behavioural dispositions. *Unruly opportunism* tends to come together with *resourcefulness*, or vice versa, jointly giving rise to 'continuous pressures on and within institutions that slowly and gradually subvert Durkheimian social obligations while expanding the realm of voluntary, utility-maximizing action and Williamsonian social arrangements' (Streeck 2009: 240). While imperfect reproduction of institutions is a general feature of all social orders, different groups have characteristically different incentives and capacities to circumvent institutionalized rules or challenge their received meanings. An example is large firms hiring lobbyists to influence or change legislation, or tax lawyers which are

just one category of specialists in creative reinterpretation of formal social obligations for the purpose of avoiding them in a legally unassailable way. Creativity in such a context typically involves studied absence of 'good faith,' in the sense of a determined rejection of shared informal understandings on the meaning of the norm in question, combined with . . . an 'undersocialized' attitude of skillful instrumentalism in relation to social rules in general.   (Streeck 2009: 240 f.)

Summing up, specification of contemporary institutional change as a process of capitalist development[22] opens up a prospect for a dynamic theory of social order free of teleological determinism and linear progressivism. Moreover, conducting institutional analysis, comparative or not, in the heuristic context of capitalist development helps avoid excessive abstractification and formalization depriving theory of substantive-historical content. In particular, analysing institutional change as capitalist development specifies the nature of the unfolding in time of the property space of institutional theory as a contested process of market expansion and advancing commodification, with competition and the pressures it creates for maximizing the return on invested capital as the driving force. Furthermore, by assigning a central place to conflict and discontinuity, the notion of capitalist development accommodates political action by situating it in an endemic tension between solidaristic traditionalism and self-interested innovation. It also draws attention to the endemic fragility of an institutional context that is continuously undermined by actors whose very capacity to act depends, paradoxically, on its continued existence. By grounding itself in a concept of capitalist development, contemporary political economy—the analysis of globalization and liberalization and of the crisis that followed both—would be usefully enriched by a historically concrete model of political-economic actors and of the relationship between actors and the institutions that embed them.

A BRIEF SUMMARY

A dynamic perspective on institutions and on the social world in general seems vastly preferable to a static one. A dynamic theory of society locates its objects in an irreversible flow of time, thereby recognizing their historical nature and uniqueness. Change appears both permanent and incremental, as the most important changes in human conditions are found to be related to or caused by the time it takes for them to take place.

Recognition of time as a constitutive element *in* and *of* social structures draws new attention to the notion of 'development' that was omnipresent in nineteenth-century social science but later came to be abandoned in favour of abstract analytical universalism and timeless generalization. Historical periods like the present one in which history seems to move faster than usual cast doubt on the applicability and usefulness of representations of the social world as a set of immutable causal mechanisms. Doing justice to the historicity of social facts without falling back on nineteenth-century ideas of historical determinism or linear progress may be made possible by a fresh reading of theories of 'evolution', which explain change by

---

[22] Characterized in Streeck and Thelen (2005) with reference to the 1990s as 'liberalization', and in Streeck (2009), following Polanyi (1957[1944]), as a conflict between the expansion of markets and political efforts at their social containment.

Table 23.5: Institutional change and capitalist development

	Static change	Dynamic change	Development	Capitalist development
Property space	Constant universal	Historical periodic	Cumulative unfolding ('unwrapping') of embryonic pattern	Unfolding & expanding of market relations and extended reproduction
Direction	Reversible fluctuating	Irreversible sequential	Upward-growing	Sideward-growing
Source	Exogenous-contingent	Endogenous-dialectical Exogenous-contingent	Endogenous dynamic trumps exogenous contingencies	Endogenous pressures for capital accumulation ('profit')
Mode	Punctuated equilibrium	Incremental Crossing of thresholds	Continuous passing of successive thresholds and stages Maturation	Discontinuous sequence of subversion and restoration of order
Mechanism	Short sharp shocks	Imperfect reproduction Time & age: layering, conversion, drift, exhaustion etc	Improved reproduction (learning)	Competitive innovation

interaction between spontaneous variation within an historically inherited repertoire of possibilities and a set of external conditions that are themselves in constant flux.

Modelling the dynamic of the contemporary social world and its political economy as a process of 'capitalist development' seems to be a promising way of specifying the forces and mechanisms driving institutional change today (Table 23.5). In particular, the notion of capitalist development identifies the expansion of market relations as the main source of change in extant forms of institutional coordination. It also suggests a specification of the relationship between actors and institutions that fills the empty spaces caused by over-generalized concepts of action, like rational choice, or by neglect of the need for a micro-foundation of macro-sociological theorizing. Most importantly, theories of capitalist development give historically concrete definition to the process of innovation effective, in principle, in all social structures, by spelling out a particular logic and accounting for the particular bias inherent in the imperfect, dynamic reproduction of a capitalist social order. And finally, the notion of capitalist development explicitly provides for tensions, conflicts, and contradictions in historical institutional change, specifying the nature of such conflicts as being over the extent to which society can insist on social obligations outside the voluntarism of a free pursuit of interests through competitive innovation and private contractual ordering.

REFERENCES

ARTHUR, BRIAN (1994). *Increasing Returns and Path Dependence in the Economy,* (Ann Arbor: University of Michigan Press).

CAMPBELL, ANDREA LOUISE (2003). *How Policies Make Citizens: Senior Citizen Activism and the American Welfare State,* (Princeton: Princeton University Press).

DARWIN, CHARLES (2004 [1859]). *The Origin of Species,* (London: CRW Publishing Limited).

DAWKINS, RICHARD (1989). *The Selfish Gene,* (Oxford: Oxford University Press).

DURKHEIM, EMILE (1964 [1893]). *The Division of Labor in Society,* (New York: The Free Press).

GOULD, STEPHEN JAY (1997). 'Darwinian Fundamentalism', *New York Review of Books* 44 (10).

——and R. C. LEWONTIN (1979). 'The Spandrels of San Marco and the Panglossian Paradigm: A Critique of the Adaptationist Programme'. *Proceedings of the Royal Society of London. Series B, Biological Sciences* 205(1161): 581–98.

KERR, CLARK, FREDERICK H. HARBISON, and CHARLES A. MYERS (1960). *Industrialism and Industrial Man: The Problems of Labor and Management in Economic Growth,* (Cambridge, MA: Harvard University Press).

KRASNER, STEPHEN D. (1988). 'Sovereignty: An Institutional Perspective', *Comparative Political Studies,* 21: 66–94.

LUXEMBURG, ROSA (1913). *Die Akkumulation des Kapitals: Ein Beitrag zur ökonomischen Erklärung des Imperialismus,* (Berlin: Buchhandlung Vorwärts Paul Singer GmbH).

MAYNTZ, RENATE and FRITZ W. SCHARPF (1995). 'Der Ansatz des akteurzentrierten Institutionalismus', in Renate Mayntz and Fritz W. Scharpf (eds.), *Gesellschaftliche Selbstregulierung und politische Steuerung,* (Frankfurt am Main: Campus), 39–72.

NEUWEILER, GERHARD (2008). *Und wir sind es doch—die Krone der Evolution,* (Berlin: Wagenbach).

PIERSON, PAUL (2004). *Politics in Time: History, Institutions, and Social Analysis,* (Princeton, NJ: Princeton University Press).

POLANYI, KARL (1957 [1944]). *The Great Transformation: The Political and Economic Origins of Our Time,* (Boston: Beacon Press).

ROSTOW, WALT W. (1990 [1960]). *The Stages of Economic Growth: A Non-Communist Manifesto,* (Cambridge: Cambridge University Press).

SCHUMPETER, JOSEPH A. (1975 [1942]). *Capitalism, Socialism, and Democracy,* (New York: Harper).

SPENCER, HERBERT (2003 [1882]). *The Principles of Sociology. In Three Volumes,* ed. Hg. von Jonathan H. Turner, (New Brunswick and London: Transaction Publishers).

STREECK, WOLFGANG (2001). 'Introduction: Explorations into the Origins of Nonliberal Capitalism in Germany and Japan', in Wolfgang Streeck and Kozo Yamamura (eds.), *The Origins of Nonliberal Capitalism: Germany and Japan,* (Ithaca; London: Cornell University Press), 1–38.

———(2006). 'The Study of Interest Groups: Before "The Century" and After', in Colin Crouch and Wolfgang Streeck (eds.), *The Diversity of Democracy: Corporatism, Social Order and Political Conflict*, (London: Edward Elgar), 3–45.

———(2009). *Re-Forming Capitalism: Institutional Change in the German Political Economy*, (Oxford: Oxford University Press).

———and KATHLEEN THELEN (2005). 'Introduction: Institutional Change in Advanced Political Economies', in Wolfgang Streeck and Kathleen Thelen (eds.), *Beyond Continuity: Institutional Change in Advanced Political Economies*, (Oxford: Oxford University Press), 1–39.

THELEN, KATHLEEN (1999). 'Historical Institutionalism in Comparative Politics', *Annual Review of Political Science* 2: 369–404.

———(2002). 'How Institutions Evolve: Insights from Comparative-Historical Analysis', in James Mahoney and Dietrich Rueschemeyer (eds.), *Comparative Historical Analysis in the Social Sciences*, (New York: Cambridge University Press), 208–40.

TOCQUEVILLE, ALEXIS DE (1983 [1856]). *The Old Regime and the French Revolution*, (New York: Anchor Books).

WEBER, MAX (2002 [1904/5]). 'Die protestantische Ethik und der "Geist" des Kapitalismus', in Dirk Kaesler (ed.), *Max Weber: Schriften 1894–1922*, (Stuttgart: Kröner), 150–226.

WILLIAMSON, OLIVER E. (1987). 'The Economic of Governance: Framework and Implications', in Richard N. Langlois (ed.), *Economics As a Process*, (Cambridge: Cambridge University Press).

INDEX